I0083927

E. Thompson Baird, CharlesC. Converse

Book of Hymns and Tunes

Comprising the Psalms and Hymns for the Worship of God

E. Thompson Baird, CharlesC. Converse

Book of Hymns and Tunes
Comprising the Psalms and Hymns for the Worship of God

ISBN/EAN: 9783337020798

Printed in Europe, USA, Canada, Australia, Japan

Cover: Foto ©Thomas Meinert / pixelio.de

More available books at **www.hansebooks.com**

elouze & Co., Franklin St.,
Stereotypers.

Randolph & Englis
Binders.

J. S. Heacock & Co., Tenth St.,
Printers.

PREFACE.

This Book of Hymns and Tunes has been prepared under the direction of the Presbyterian Committee of Publication, and by order of the General Assembly of the Presbyterian Church in the United States. A book of this kind was loudly called for; and it has been prepared on principles which, it is hoped, will make it acceptable to the church at large; since the whole matter was submitted to the General Assembly for its instructions, and the plan met with its unanimous approbation. In presenting it to the Christian public, it is only necessary to call attention to the following particulars:—

1. The object was to prepare a book to be used in congregational singing. No effort has been made to supply the wants of choirs for special occasions; but it was deemed best to leave it to choirs themselves, or other leaders of singing, to exercise their own judgment and taste in making selections for voluntaries, or for special occasions and purposes, from any source within their reach, subject only to the control of the spiritual officers of the church.

2. The tunes selected and introduced into the book are, for the most, part such as are familiar to our churches and congregations. New, that is, original tunes, have been introduced very sparingly: and then, only when there was a necessity for it, in order to supply a manifest want. Nearly all the tunes, all, indeed, but four, have been selected from other sources. Some of the newer or more unusual tunes have been inserted to gratify portions of the church where they have become favourites; and, also, a few tunes which have fallen into general disuse, but which are still used in various places, more on account of precious recollections or venerable associations, than because of musical merit, have also been inserted. In each of these instances, we have endeavoured to place on the opposite page a tune of a different character, adapted to the same hymns, in order to satisfy the wishes and the tastes of others. Some requests were received for the insertion of special favourites of one or the other of the above classes, after the work had advanced too far to admit of our doing so.

3. The hymns have been arranged wholly with reference to their adaptation to the tunes. The order of arrangement found in our present Hymn Book could not be preserved, without the too frequent repetition of the same tune, which would have made the book entirely too large and too expensive. The numbers of the Psalms and Hymns as found in the Hymn Book, have, however, been retained, so as to admit of the use of it in connection with this book of hymns and tunes.

4. The Indexes are full and complete. 1st, There is at the beginning of the book an Index of the Psalms and Hymns, arranged in the numerical order, the Hymns being divided off into general and special subjects, just as they are classified in the Hymn Book, thus presenting what might be called a table of contents. 2d, There is, at the end of the book, an Index of the first lines, arranged alphabetically. 3d, There is an alphabetical Index of the Tunes; 4th, A Metrical Index; 5th, An Index of Subjects.

5. About one-half of the music contained in this book is copy-righted, and those who wish to use the same music must apply to the proprietors of the copy-right for liberty to do so. The venerable composers, Drs. Lowell Mason and Thomas Hastings, during the time of the preparation of this book, passed from the service of song on earth to attune their voices in the holier worship of heaven. Each of them was kind enough to express their desire that we should use their tunes, and gave us liberty to do so, so far as the copy-rights were under their control. The other friends who favoured us in a similiar way, we desire to hold in thankful remembrance.

6. In order to use this book along with the Hymn Book, it is only necessary for the minister to announce, for example, "H. 1, on page 266." Those who have the Hymn Book will look for Hymn 1, and those who use this book will turn to page 266,

7. The Appendix was prepared under the direction of the Presbyterian Committee of Publication, by order of the General Assembly. The indexes for it are made separate and distinct, so as to prevent any confusion when this book is used in connection with the Hymn Book.

8. The gratitude of the Church is due to C. C. Converse, Esq., for his great labour in acting as Musical Editor, and for the use of tunes composed by him, or which were under his control, all of which service he has rendered us as a free-will offering. For his liberality and kindness, the General Assembly returned him a unanimous vote of thanks.

The work is now committed to the press in the hope that it will prove acceptable to the Church, and promote the service of song in our congregations. We pray that God's blessing will attend it, and make it a chosen instrument in sounding forth His glory.

RICHMOND, MARCH 1, 1874.

FIRST LINES OF PSALMS.

The Figures on the left designate the Numbers and Parts of the Psalms; those on the right the Pages.

FIRST LINES OF HYMNS.

The Figures on the left designate the Numbers of the Hymns; those on the right the Pages.

I. GOD.

1. BEING AND PERFECTIONS.

2. DECREES.

3. CREATION AND PROVIDENCE.

4. THE TRINITY.

II. THE SAVIOUR.

1. PERSON AND CHARACTER.

2. ADVENT.

3. EXAMPLE.

4. SUFFERINGS AND DEATH.

5. RESURRECTION AND ASCENSION.

6. INTERCESSION.

5. PRAISE TO CHRIST.

III. HOLY SPIRIT.

1. CHARACTER AND OFFICES.

IV. SALVATION NEEDED.

1. MAN'S RUINED CONDITION.

2. IMPORTANCE OF RELIGION.

3. VALUE OF THE SOUL.

V. SALVATION REVEALED.

1. THE SCRIPTURES.

2. HOPE.

3. LOVE.

4. JOY.

5. PEACE.

6. HOLY DESIRES.

7. SUBMISSION IN AFFLICTION.

XI. DUTIES.

1. RENUNCIATION OF THE WORLD.

2. SELF-DEDICATION.

3. CONFESSING CHRIST.

4. UNION WITH GOD'S PEOPLE.

5. PRAYER.

6. WATCHFULNESS.

7. SELF-DENIAL.

8. SELF-EXAMINATION.

9. ACTIVITY.

10. CONFLICTS.

11. PERSEVERANCE.

12. PRAISE.

XII. WORSHIP.

1. PRIVATE AND FAMILY.

2. SOCIAL AND PUBLIC.

XIII. PARTICULAR SEASONS.

1. THE LORD'S DAY.

2. THANKSGIVING.

3. HUMILIATION.

NEW YEAR.

5. SEASONS OF THE YEAR.

6. CHARITABLE OCCASIONS.

XIV. PARTICULAR CLASSES.

1. THE YOUNG.

2. SEAMEN.

3. SABBATH SCHOOLS.

XV. SACRAMENTS.

1. BAPTISM.

2. THE LORD'S SUPPER.

XVI. CHRIST'S KINGDOM.

1. GLORY AND SAFETY OF THE CHURCH.

2. DEDICATION OF A HOUSE OF WORSHIP.

3. OFFICE-BEARERS.

4. REVIVAL.

5. MISSIONS.

XVII. TIME AND ETERNITY.

1. PRESENT LIFE.

2. DEATH AND RESURRECTION.

3. THE JUDGMENT.

4. ETERNITY.

5. HEAVEN.

APPENDIX.

I. GOD AND THE TRINITY.

II. THE SAVIOUR.

III. THE HOLY SPIRIT.

IV. INVITATIONS.

V. PENITENCE AND FAITH.

VI. SUBMISSION.

VII. CHRISTIAN BENEFITS.

VIII. SOCIAL AND PUBLIC WORSHIP.

IX. THE SACRAMENTS.

X. CHRIST'S KINGDOM.

XI. TIME AND ETERNITY.

XII. MISCELLANEOUS.

Dr. L. Mason, 1830.

To God the Fa - ther, God the Son, And God the Spi - rit, Three in One,

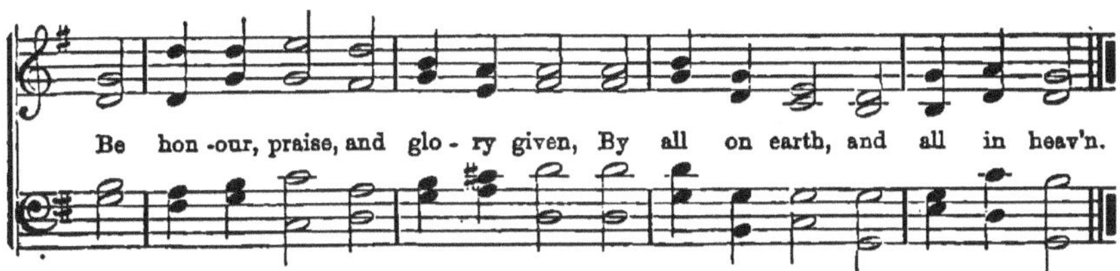
Be hon - our, praise, and glo - ry given, By all on earth, and all in heav'n.

Ps. 16

1 When God is nigh my faith is strong,
His arm is my almighty prop:
Be glad, my heart, rejoice, my tongue,
My dying flesh shall rest in hope.

2 Though in the dust I lay my head,
Yet, gracious God, Thou wilt not leave
My soul for ever with the dead,
Nor lose Thy children in the grave.

3 My flesh shall Thy first call obey,
Shake off the dust and rise on high;
Then shalt Thou lead the wondrous way,
Up to Thy throne above the sky.

4. There streams of endless pleasure flow;
And full discoveries of Thy grace—
Which we but tasted here below—
Spread heavenly joys thro' all the place.

Ps. 19 *Second Part.*

1 The heavens declare Thy glory, Lord;
In every star Thy wisdom shines;
But when our eyes behold Thy word,
We read Thy name in fairer lines.

2 The rolling sun, the changing light,
And nights and days Thy power confess;
But the blest volume Thou hast writ
Reveals Thy justice and Thy grace.

3 Sun, moon, and stars convey Thy praise
Round the whole earth, and never stand;
So when Thy truth began its race,
It touched and glanced on every land.

4 Nor shall Thy spreading gospel rest,
Till thro' the world Thy truth has run;
Till Christ has all the nations blest
That see the light, or feel the sun.

5 Great Sun of Righteousness, arise,
Bless the dark world with heavenly light;
Thy gospel makes the simple wise,
Thy laws are pure, Thy judgments right.

Ps. 84 *Second Part.*

1 Great God, attend while Zion sings
The joy that from Thy presence springs;
To spend one day with Thee on earth
Exceeds a thousand days of mirth.

2 Might I enjoy the meanest place
Within Thy house, O God of grace,
Not tents of ease, nor thrones of power,
Should tempt my feet to leave Thy door.

3 God is our sun, He makes our day;
God is our shield, He guards our way
From all th' assaults of hell and sin,
From foes without and foes within.

4 All needful grace will God bestow,
And crown that grace with glory too;
He gives us all things, and withholds
No real good from upright souls.

5 O God, our King, whose sovereign sway
The glorious hosts of heaven obey,
And devils at Thy presence flee;
Blest is the man that trusts in Thee.

English.
1. Lord, when Thou didst as - cend on high, Ten thou-sand an - gels filled the sky;
Those heav'n-ly guards a - round Thee wait, Like cha - riots that at - tend Thy state.

Ps. 68 *Second Part.*

2 Not Sinai's mountain could appear
More glorious when the Lord was there,
While He pronounced His holy law,
And struck the chosen tribes with awe.

3 How bright the triumph none can tell,
When the rebellious powers of hell,
That thousand souls had captive made,
Were all in chains, like captives, led.

4 Raised by His Father to the throne,
He sent His promised Spirit down,
With gifts and grace for sinful men,
That God might dwell on earth again.

H. 45 *Glory and Grace in the Person of Christ.*

1 Now to the Lord a noble song;
Awake, my soul, awake, my tongue;
Hosanna to the Eternal Name,
And all His boundless love proclaim.

2 See where it shines in Jesus' face,
The brightest image of His grace;
God, in the person of His Son,
Has all His mightiest works outdone.

3 The spacious earth and spreading flood
Proclaim the wise and powerful God;
And Thy rich glories from afar
Sparkle in every rolling star.

4 But in His looks a glory stands,
The noblest labour of Thine hands;
The pleasing lustre of His eyes
Outshines the wonders of the skies.

5 Grace! 'tis a sweet, a charming theme;
My thoughts rejoice at Jesus' name;
Ye angels, dwell upon the sound;
Ye heavens, reflect it to the ground.

6 O! may I live to reach the place,
Where He unveils His lovely face!
Where all His beauties you behold,
And sing His name to harps of gold.

H. 248 *Strength Equal to the Day.*

1 Afflicted saint, to Christ draw near,
Thy Saviour's gracious promise hear;
His faithful word declares to thee,
That "as thy day, thy strength shall be."

2 Thy faith is weak, thy foes are strong;
And if the conflict should be long,
Thy Lord will make the tempter flee;
For "as thy day, thy strength shall be."

3 Should persecution rage and flame,
Still trust in thy Redeemer's name;
In fiery trials thou shalt see,
That "as thy day, thy strength shall be."

4 When called by Him to bear the cross,
Reproach, affliction, pain, or loss,
Or deep distress and poverty,
Still "as thy day, thy strength shall be."

5 When death at length appears in view,
Christ's presence shall thy fears subdue;
He comes to set thy spirit free,
And "as thy day, thy strength shall be."

George Kingsley.

1. Great Shepherd of Thine Is - ra - el, Who didst between the cher - ubs dwell,
And lead the tribes, Thy chosen sheep, Safe thro' the de - sert and the deep.

Ps. 80 *Second Part.*

2 Thy church is in the desert now:
Shine from on high and guide us through;
Turn us to Thee, Thy love restore;
We shall be saved, and sigh no more.

3 Great God, whom heavenly hosts obey,
How long shall we lament and pray,
And wait in vain Thy kind return?
How long shall Thy fierce anger burn?

4 Instead of wine and cheerful bread,
Thy saints with their own tears are fed;
Turn us to Thee, Thy love restore,
We shall be saved, and sigh no more.

Ps. 82

1 Among th' assemblies of the great,
A greater Ruler takes His seat;
The God of heaven, as Judge, surveys
Those gods on earth, and all their ways.

2 Why will ye frame oppressive laws?
Or why support th' unrighteous cause?
When will ye once defend the poor,
That foes may vex the saints no more?

3 They know not, Lord, nor will they know;
Dark are the ways in which they go;
Their name of earthly gods is vain,
For they shall fall, and die like men.

4 Arise, O Lord, and let thy Son
Possess His universal throne,
And rule the nations with His rod;
He is our Judge, and He our God.

H. 54 *Christ a Saviour.*

1 Not to condemn the sons of men
Did Christ the Son of God appear;
No weapons in His hands are seen,
No flaming sword nor thunder there.

2 Such was the pity of our God,
He loved the race of men so well,
He sent His Son to bear our load
Of sins, and save our souls from hell.

3 Sinners, believe the Saviour's word,
Trust in His mighty name and live;
A thousand joys His lips afford,
His hands a thousand blessings give.

H. 295 *Jesus, Abide with Me.*

1 Sun of my soul, Thou Saviour dear,
It is not night if Thou be near;
Oh! may no earth-born cloud arise,
To hide Thee from Thy servant's eyes.

2 When soft the dews of kindly sleep,
My wearied eyelids gently steep,
Be my last thought—how sweet to rest
For ever on my Saviour's breast.

3 Abide with me from morn till eve,
For without Thee I cannot live;
Abide with me when night is nigh,
For without Thee I dare not die.

4 Be near to bless me when I wake,
Ere through the world my way I take;
Abide with me till, in Thy love,
I lose myself in heaven above.

LUTON. L.M.

G. Burder.

1. Je - ho-vah reigns, His throne is high, His robes are light and ma - jes - ty;
His glo-ry shines with beams so bright, No mor - tal can sus - tain the sight.

H. 7 *Glory and Condescension of God.*

2 His terrors keep the world in awe;
His justice guards His holy law;
His love reveals a smiling face,
His truth and promise seal the grace.

3 Thro' all His works His wisdom shines,
And baffles Satan's deep designs;
His power is sovereign to fulfil
The noblest counsels of His will.

4 And will this glorious Lord descend
To be my Father and my Friend?
Then let my song with angels join;
Heaven is secure, if God be mine.

Ps. 91 *Second Part.*

1 He that hath made his refuge God
Shall find a most secure abode;
Shall walk all day beneath His shade,
And there at night shall rest his head.

2 Then will I say, "My God, Thy power
Shall be my fortress and my tower;
I that am formed of feeble dust
Make Thine almighty arm my trust."

3 Thrice happy man! thy Maker's care
Shall keep thee from the fowler's snare;
From Satan's wiles, who still betrays
Unguarded souls, a thousand ways.

4 What though a thousand at thy side,
Around thy path ten thousand died,
Thy God His chosen people saves
Amongst the dead, amidst the graves.

5 The sword, the pestilence, or fire
Shall but fulfil their best desire;
From sins and sorrows set them free,
And bring Thy children, Lord, to Thee.

H. 390 *Self Examination.*

1 What strange preplexities arise,
What anxious fears and jealousies,
What crowds in doubtful light appear,
How few, alas, approved and clear!

2 And what am I? My soul, awake,
And an impartial survey take;
Does no dark sign, no ground of fear,
In practice or in heart appear?

3 What image does my spirit bear?
Is Jesus formed, and living there?
Say, do His lineaments divine,
In thought, and word, and action shine?

4 Searcher of hearts, O! search me still;
The secrets of my soul reveal;
My fears remove; let me appear
To God and my own conscience clear.

5 May I, consistent with Thy word,
Approach Thy table, O my Lord?
May I among Thy saints appear?
Shall I, a welcome guest, be there?

6 Have I the wedding-garment on?
Or do I, naked, stand alone?
O! quicken, clothe, and feed my soul;
Forgive my sins, and make me whole.

V. C. Taylor.

1. With bro - ken heart and con - trite sigh, A trem-bling sin - ner, Lord, I cry;
Thy pard'-ning grace is rich and free: O God, be mer - ci - ful to me!

H. 213 *Pleading for Mercy.*

2 I smite upon my troubled breast,
With deep and conscious guilt oppressed;
Christ and His cross my only plea:
O God, be merciful to me!

3 Far off I stand, with tearful eyes,
Nor dare uplift them to the skies;
But Thou dost all my anguish see:
O God, be merciful to me!

4 Nor alms, nor deeds that I have done,
Can for a single sin atone;
To Calvary alone I flee:
O God, be merciful to me!

5 And when, redeemed from sin and hell,
With all the ransomed throng I dwell,
My raptured song shall ever be:
God has been merciful to me!

H. 39 *Behold the Man.*

1 Behold the Man! how glorious He!
Before His foes He stands unawed;
And, without wrong or blasphemy,
He claims equality with God.

2 Behold the Man! by all condemned;
Assaulted by a host of foes;
His person and His claims contemned,
A Man of sufferings and of woes.

3 Behold the Man! He stands alone,
His foes are ready to devour;
Not one of all His friends will own
Their Master in this trying hour.

4 Behold the Man! He knew no sin,
Yet justice smites Him with her sword;
He bears the stroke that else had been
The sinner's portion from the Lord.

5 Behold the Man! so weak He seems,
His awful word inspires no fear;
But soon must he, who now blasphemes,
Before His judgment seat appear.

6 Behold the Man! though scorned below,
He bears the greatest name above;
The angels at His footstool bow,
And all His royal claims approve.

H. 484 *A Blessing Implored.*

1 Command Thy blessing from above,
O God! on all assembled here;
Behold us with a Father's love,
While we look up with filial fear.

2 Command Thy blessing, Jesus, Lord!
May we Thy true disciples be;
Speak to each heart the mighty word,
Say to the weakest, "Follow Me."

3 Command Thy blessing in this hour,
Spirit of Truth! and fill this place
With humbling and exalted power,
With quick'ning and confirming grace.

4 O Thou, our Maker, Saviour, Guide!
One true eternal God confessed;
May naught in life or death divide
The saints of Thy communion blest.

Dr. L. Mason, 1830.

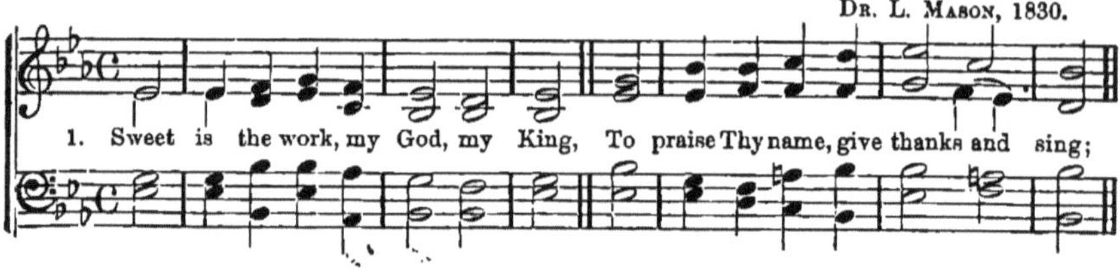
1. Sweet is the work, my God, my King, To praise Thy name, give thanks and sing;

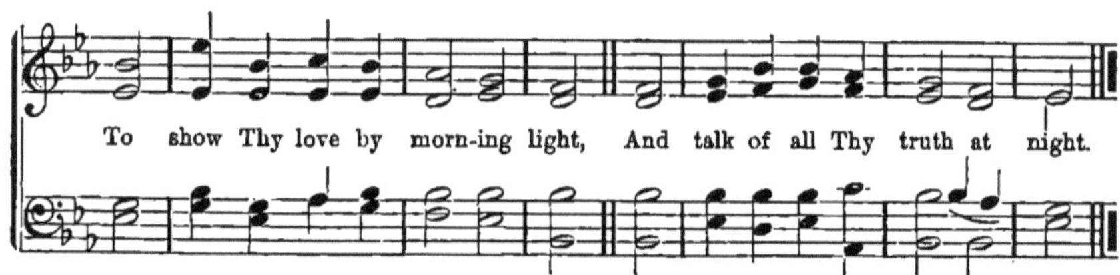
To show Thy love by morn-ing light, And talk of all Thy truth at night.

Ps. 92 *First Part.*

2 Sweet is the day of sacred rest;
No mortal care shall seize my breast;
O! may my heart in tune be found,
Like David's harp of solemn sound.

3 My heart shall triumph in my Lord,
And bless His works and bless His word;
Thy works of grace how bright they shine!
How deep Thy counsels! how divine!

4 Then I shall share a glorious part,
When grace hath well refined my heart,
And fresh supplies of joy are shed,
Like holy oil to cheer my head.

5 Sin, my worst enemy before,
Shall vex my eyes and ears no more;
My inward foes shall all be slain,
Nor Satan break my peace again.

6 Then shall I see, and hear, and know,
All I desired or wished below;
And every power find sweet employ
In that eternal world of joy.

Ps. 97

1 He reigns; the Lord, the Saviour reigns!
Praise Him in evangelic strains:
Let the whole earth in songs rejoice,
And distant islands join their voice.

2 Deep are His counsels and unknown,
But grace and truth support His throne;
Though gloomy clouds His ways sur-
Justice is their eternal ground. [round,

3 In robes of judgment, lo! He comes,
Shakes the wide earth and cleaves the
Before Him burns devouring fire, [tombs;
The mountains melt, the seas retire.

4 His enemies, with sore dismay,
Fly from the sight, and shun the day;
Then lift your heads, ye saints, on high,
And sing, for your redemption's nigh.

H. 549 *Memorial of our Absent Lord.*

1 Jesus is gone above the skies,
Where our weak senses reach Him not;
And carnal objects court our eyes,
To thrust our Saviour from our thought.

2 He knows what wandering hearts we
Apt to forget His glorious face; [have,
And to refresh our minds, He gave
These kind memorials of His grace.

3 The Lord of life this table spread,
With His own flesh and dying blood;
We on the rich provision feed,
We taste the wine, and bless our God.

4 Let sinful sweets be all forgot,
And earth grow less in our esteem;
Christ and His love fill every thought,
And faith and hope be fixed on Him.

5 While He is absent from our sight,
'Tis to prepare our souls a place;
That we may dwell in heavenly light,
And live for ever near His face.

WM. BEASTALL.

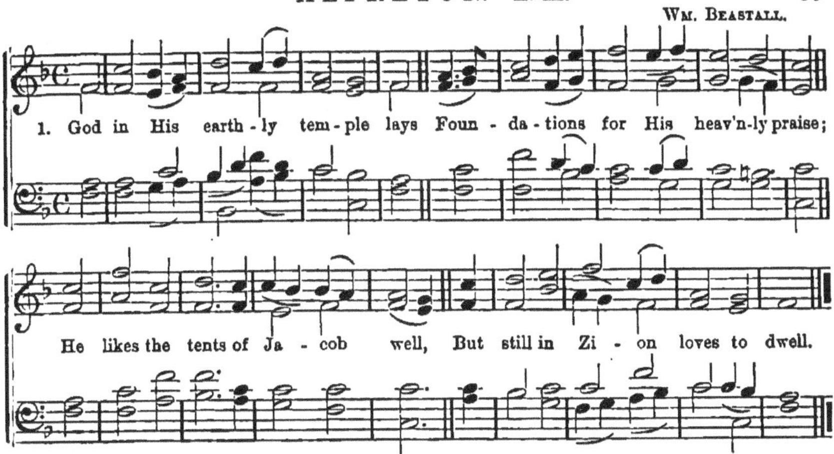
1. God in His earth - ly tem - ple lays Foun - da - tions for His heav'n-ly praise;
He likes the tents of Ja - cob well, But still in Zi - on loves to dwell.

Ps. 87

2 His mercy visits every house
That pay their night and morning vows;
But makes a more delightful stay
Where churches meet to praise and pray.

3 What glories were described of old!
What wonders are of Zion told!
Thou city of our God below,
Thy fame shall Tyre and Egypt know.

4 Egypt and Tyre, and Greek and Jew,
Shall there begin their lives anew;
Angels and men shall join to sing
The hill where living waters spring.

5 When God makes up His last account
Of natives in His holy mount,
'Twill be an honour to appear
As one new-born and nourished there.

Ps. 93 *First Part.*

1 JEHOVAH reigns: He dwells in light,
Girded with majesty and might;
The world, created by His hands,
Still on its first foundation stands.

2 But ere this spacious world was made,
Or had its first foundation laid,
Thy throne eternal ages stood,
Thyself the ever living God.

3 Like floods the angry nations rise,
And aim their rage against the skies;
Vain floods that aim their rage so high!
At Thy rebuke the billows die,

4 For ever shall Thy throne endure;
Thy promise stands for ever sure;
And everlasting holiness
Becomes the dwellings of Thy grace.

Ps. 95 *Second Part.*

1 COME, let our voices join to raise,
A sacred song of solemn praise;
God is a sovereign King; rehearse
His honour in exalted verse.

2 Come, let our souls address the Lord,
Who framed our nature with His word;
He is our Shepherd; we the sheep
His mercy chose, His pastures keep.

3 Come, let us hear His voice to-day,
The counsels of His love obey;
Nor let our hardened hearts renew
The sins and plagues that Israel knew.

4 Seize the kind promise while it waits,
And march to Zion's heavenly gates;
Believe, and take the promised rest;
Obey, and be for ever blest.

Ps. 117 *First Part.*

1 FROM all that dwell below the skies,
Let the Creator's praise arise;
Let the Redeemer's name be sung
Through every land, by every tongue.

2 Eternal are Thy mercies, Lord;
Eternal truth attends Thy word; [shore,
Thy praise shall sound from shore to
Till suns shall rise and set no more.

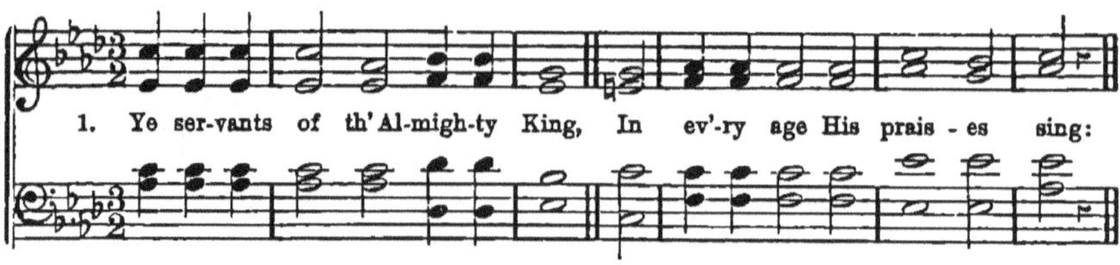
1. Ye ser-vants of th' Al-migh-ty King, In ev'-ry age His prais - es sing:

Where'-er the sun shall rise or set, The na - tions shall His praise re - peat.

Ps. 113

2 Above the earth, beyond the sky,
His throne of glory stands on high;
Nor time, nor place, His power restrain,
Nor bound His universal reign.

3 Which of the sons of Adam dare,
Or angels with their God compare?
His glories, how divinely bright,
Who dwells in uncreated light!

4 Behold His love! He stoops to view
What saints above and angels do;
And condescends yet more—to know
The mean affairs of men below.

5 From dust and cottages obscure,
His grace exalts the humble poor!
Gives them the honour of His sons,
And fits them for their heavenly thrones.

Ps. 88 *First Part.*

1 Shall man, O God of light and life,
For ever moulder in the grave?
Canst Thou forget Thy glorious work,
Thy promise, and Thy power to save?

2 Shall spring the faded world revive?
Shall waning moons their light return?
Again shall setting suns ascend,
And the lost day anew be born?

3 Shall life revisit dying worms,
And spread the joyful insect's wing?
And O! shall man awake no more,
To see Thy face, Thy name to sing?

4 Cease, cease, ye vain desponding fears;
When Christ, our Lord, from darkness sprung,
Death, the last foe, was captive led,
And heaven with praise and wonder rung

5 Faith sees the bright, eternal doors
Unfold, to make His children way;
They shall be clothed with endless life,
And shine in everlasting day.

Ps. 102 *First Part.*

1 Thou shalt arise, and mercy yet
Thou to Mount Zion shalt extend;
Her time for favour, which was set,
Behold, is now come to an end.

2 Thy saints take pleasure in her stones,
Her very dust to them is dear;
All heathen lands and kingly thrones
On earth Thy glorious name shall fear.

3 God in His glory shall appear,
When Zion He builds and repairs;
He shall regard, and lend His ear
Unto the needy's humble prayers.

4 The afflicted's prayer He will not scorn;
All times this shall be on record;
And generations yet unborn
Shall praise and magnify the Lord.

5 He from His holy place looked down,
The earth He viewed from heaven on high;
To hear the prisoner's mourning groan,
And free them that are doomed to die.

DR. CHARLES BURNEY, DIED 1814.

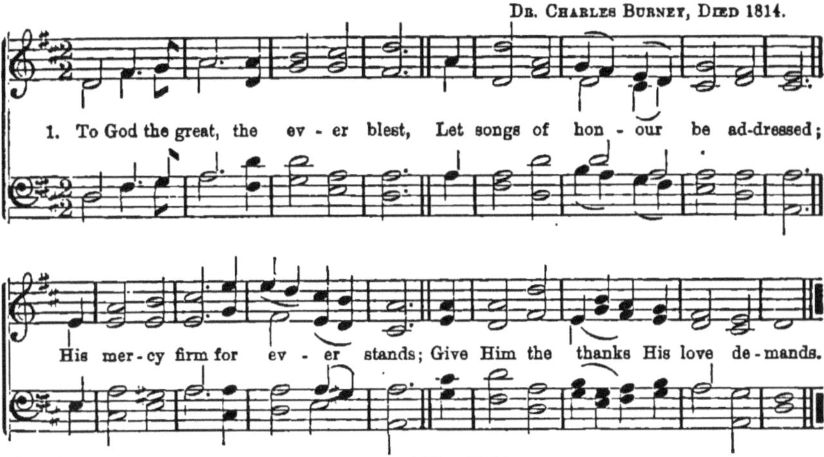
1. To God the great, the ev - er blest, Let songs of hon - our be ad-dressed;
His mer - cy firm for ev - er stands; Give Him the thanks His love de - mands.

Ps. 106

2 Who knows the wonders of Thy ways?
Who shall fulfil Thy boundless praise?
Blest are the souls that fear Thee still,
And pay their duty to Thy will.

3 Remember what Thy mercy did
For Jacob's race, Thy chosen seed;
And with the same salvation bless
The meanest suppliant of Thy grace.

4 O! may I see Thy tribes rejoice,
And aid their triumphs with my voice!
This is my glory, Lord, to be
Joined to Thy saints, and near to Thee.

Ps. 110 *First Part.*

1 Thus God, th' eternal Father, spake
To Christ the Son: "Ascend and sit
At My right hand, till I shall make
Thy foes submissive at Thy feet.

2 "From Zion shall Thy word proceed;
Thy word, the sceptre in Thy hand,
Shall make the hearts of rebels bleed,
And bow their wills to Thy command.

3 "That day will show Thy power is great,
When saints shall flock with willing minds,
And sinners crowd Thy temple gate,
Where holiness in beauty shines."

4 O blessed power! O glorious day!
What a large victory shall ensue!
And converts, who Thy grace obey,
Exceed the drops of morning dew.

Ps. 127

1 Except the Lord our labours bless,
In vain shall we desire success;
Except His guardian power restrain,
The watchman waketh but in vain.

2 'Tis useless toil our stores to keep—
Early to rise, and late to sleep—
Unless the Lord, who reigns on high,
His providential care supply.

3 Grant, Lord, that we may ever flee,
For guidance and for help to Thee;
Thy blessing ask, whate'er we do,
And in Thy strength our work pursue.

H. 32 *Address to the Trinity.*

1 Father of all, whose love profound,
A ransom for our souls hath found;
Before Thy throne we sinners bend;
To us Thy pardoning love extend.

2 Almighty Son, incarnate Word,
Our Prophet, Priest, Redeemer, Lord,
Before Thy throne we sinners bend;
To us Thy saving grace extend.

3 Eternal Spirit, by whose breath
The soul is raised from sin and death,
Before Thy throne we sinners bend;
To us Thy quickening power extend.

4 Jehovah! Father, Spirit, Son,
Mysterious Godhead, Three in One!
Before Thy throne we sinners bend;
Grace, pardon, life, to us extend.

Ignez Pleyel, Died 1830.

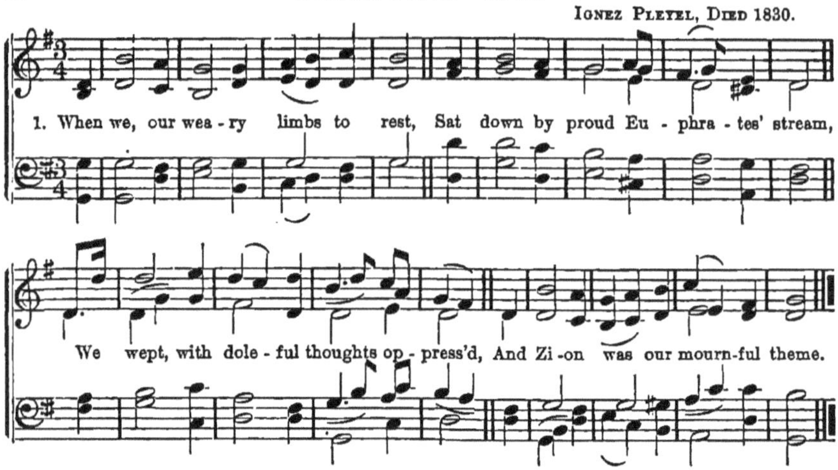
1. When we, our wea - ry limbs to rest, Sat down by proud Eu - phra - tes' stream,
We wept, with dole - ful thoughts op - press'd, And Zi - on was our mourn - ful theme.

Ps. 137

2 Our harps that, when with joy we sung,
Were wont their tuneful parts to bear,
With silent strings neglected hung
On willow trees that wither'd there.

3 O Salem, our once happy seat,
When I of thee forgetful prove,
Let then my trembling hand forget
The speaking strings with art to move.

4 If I to mention thee forbear,
Perpetual silence be my doom;
Or if my chiefest joy compare
With thee, Jerusalem, my home!

Ps. 141

1 My God, accept my early vows,
Like morning incense, in Thine house;
And let my nightly worship rise
Sweet as the evening sacrifice.

2 Watch o'er my lips, and guard them, Lord,
From every rash and heedless word;
Nor let my feet incline to tread
The guilty path where sinners lead.

3 O may the righteous, when I stray,
Smite and reprove my wandering way;
Their gentle words, like ointment shed,
Shall never bruise, but cheer my head.

4 When I behold them pressed with grief,
I'll cry to heaven for their relief;
And by my warm petitions prove
How much I prize their faithful love.

Ps. 143

1 My righteous Judge, my gracious God,
Hear when I spread my hands abroad,
And cry for succour from Thy throne:
O make Thy truth and mercy known.

2 For Thee I thirst, I pray, I mourn;
When will Thy smiling face return?
Shall all my joys on earth remove,
And God for ever hide His love?

3 Break off my fetters, Lord, and show
The path in which my feet should go;
If snares and foes beset the road,
I flee to hide me near my God.

4 Teach me to do Thy holy will,
And lead me to Thy heavenly hill;
Let the good Spirit of Thy love
Conduct me to Thy courts above.

H. 66 *Christ our Teacher.*

1 How sweetly flowed the gospel's sound
From lips of gentleness and grace,
When list'ning thousands gather'd round,
And joy and rev'rence filled the place.

2 From heav'n He came, of heav'n He spoke,
To heav'n He led His followers' way;
Dark clouds of gloomy night He broke,
Unveiling an immortal day.

3 "Come, wanderers, to my Father's home,
Come, all ye weary ones, and rest!"
Yes! sacred Teacher, we will come,
Obey Thee, love Thee, and be blest!

K. R., 1866.

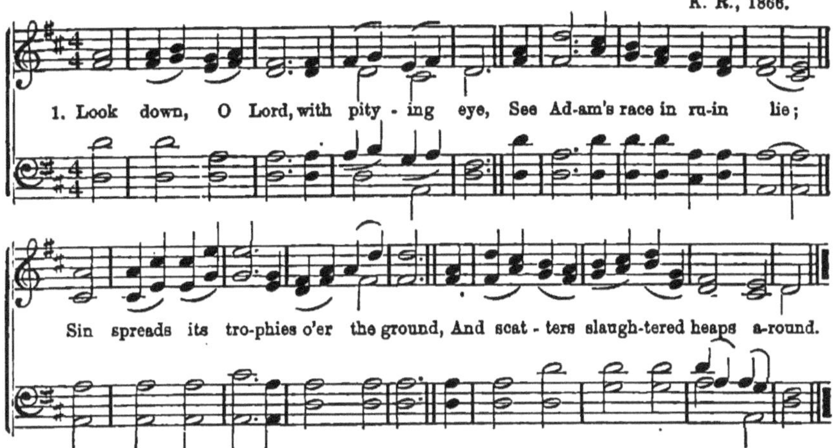
1. Look down, O Lord, with pity - ing eye, See Ad-am's race in ru-in lie;
Sin spreads its tro-phies o'er the ground, And scat - ters slaugh-tered heaps a-round.

H. 224 *Regeneration by the Spirit.*

2 And can these mouldering corpses live?
And can these perished bones revive?
That, mighty God, to Thee is known;
That wondrous work is all Thine own.

3 Thy ministers are sent in vain,
To prophesy upon the slain;
In vain they call, in vain they cry,
Till Thine almighty aid is nigh.

4 But if Thy Spirit deign to breathe,
Life spreads thro' all the realms of death,
Dry bones obey Thy powerful voice;
They move, they waken, they rejoice.

5 So, when Thy trumpet's awful sound
Shall shake the heavens and rend the ground,
Dead saints shall from their tombs arise,
And spring to life beyond the skies.

Ps. 145 *Third Part.*

1 O Lord, Thou art my God and King;
Thee will I magnify and praise:
I will Thee bless, and gladly sing
Unto Thy holy name always.

2 Each day I rise I will Thee bless,
And praise Thy name time without end.
Much to be praised, and great God is;
His greatness none can comprehend.

3 Race shall Thy works praise unto race,
The mighty acts show done by Thee.
I will speak of the glorious grace,
And honour of Thy majesty.

4 Thy wondrous works I will record;
By men the might shall be extolled,
Of all Thy dreadful acts, O Lord:
And I Thy greatness will unfold.

5 They utter shall abundantly
The memory of Thy goodness great;
And shall sing praises cheerfully,
Whilst they Thy righteousness relate.

Ps. 147

1 Praise ye the Lord; 'tis good to raise
Our hearts and voices in His praise:
His nature and His works invite
To make this duty our delight.

2 Great is our Lord, and great His might,
And all His glories infinite;
He crowns the meek, rewards the just,
And treads the wicked to the dust.

3 Sing to the Lord, exalt Him high,
Who spreads His clouds around the sky;
There He prepares the fruitful rain,
Nor lets the drops descend in vain.

4 He makes the grass the hills adorn,
And clothes the smiling fields with corn;
The beasts with food His hands supply,
And feed the ravens when they cry.

5 His saints are lovely in His sight;
He views His children with delight;
He sees their hope, He knows their fear,
And finds and loves His image there.

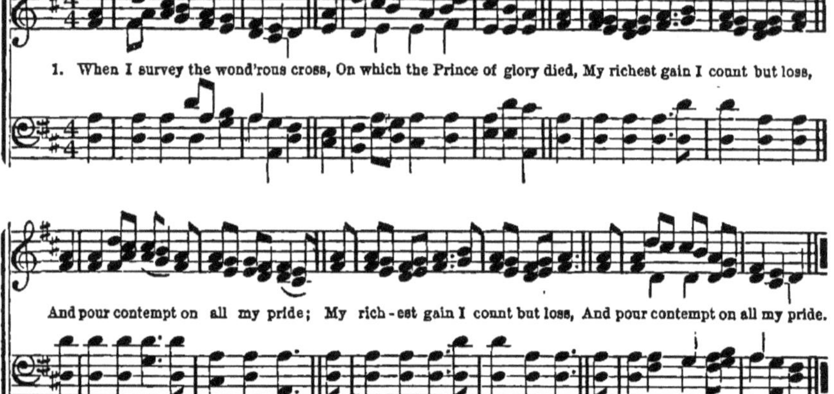
1. When I survey the wond'rous cross, On which the Prince of glory died, My richest gain I count but loss,
And pour contempt on all my pride; My rich-est gain I count but loss, And pour contempt on all my pride.

H. 352 *Crucifixion by the Cross.*

2 Forbid, it, Lord, that I should boast,
Save in the death of Christ, my God;
All the vain things that charm me most,
I sacrifice them to His blood.

3 See, from His head, His hands, His feet,
Sorrow and love flow mingled down;
Did e'er such love and sorrow meet,
Or thorns compose so rich a crown?

4 His dying crimson, like a robe,
Spreads o'er His body on the tree;
Then am I dead to all the globe,
And all the globe is dead to me.

5 Were the whole realm of nature mine,
That were a present far too small;
Love so amazing, so divine,
Demands my soul, my life, my all.

Ps. 136

1 Give to our God immortal praise;
Mercy and truth are all His ways;
Wonders of grace to God belong,
Repeat His mercies in your song.

2 He built the earth, He spread the sky,
And fixed the starry lights on high:
Wonders of grace to God belong,
Repeat His mercies in your song.

3 He fills the sun with morning light,
He bids the moon direct the night:
His mercies ever shall endure, [more.
When suns and moons shall shine no

4 He sent His Son with power to save
From guilt, and darkness, and the grave:
Wonders of grace to God belong,
Repeat His mercies in your song.

5 Thro' this vain world He guides our feet,
And leads us to His heavenly seat:
His mercies ever shall endure,
When this vain world shall be no more.

H. 51 *Christ the Priest, King and Judge.*

1 Now to the Lord that makes us know
The wonders of His dying love,
Be humble honours paid below,
And strains of nobler praise above.

2 'Twas He that cleansed our foulest sins,
And washed us in His richest blood;
'Tis He that makes us priests and kings,
And brings us rebels near to God.

3 To Jesus our atoning Priest,
To Jesus our exalted King,
Be everlasting power confessed,
And every tongue His glory sing.

4 Behold, on flying clouds He comes,
And every eye shall see Him move;
Tho' with our sins we pierced Him once,
Still He displays His pardoning love.

5 The unbelieving world shall wail,
While we rejoice to see the day;
Come, Lord, nor let Thy promise fail,
Nor let Thy chariots long delay.

Wm. Tansur, 1735.

1. Praise ye the Lord; all na - ture join In work and wor-ship so di-vine; Let heav'n and earth u-
nite, and raise High hal - le - lu - jahs to His praise—High hal-le - lu - jahs to His praise.

Ps. 150 *Second Part.*

2 While realms of joy, and worlds around,
Their hallelujahs high resound,
Let saints below and saints above,
Exulting sing redeeming love.

3 As instruments well tuned and strung,
We'll praise the Lord with heart and tongue;
While life remains we'll loud proclaim
High hallelujahs to His name.

4 Beyond the grave, in nobler strains,
When freed from sorrow, sin, and pains,
Eternally the church will raise
High hallelujahs to His praise.

H. 78 *Christ our Example.*

1 And is the gospel peace and love?
So let our conversation be;
The serpent blended with the dove,
Wisdom and meek simplicity.

2 Whene'er the angry passions rise,
And tempt our thoughts or tongues to strife,
On Jesus let us fix our eyes,
Bright pattern of the Christian life.

3 O! how benevolent and kind!
How mild, how ready to forgive;
Be His the temper of our mind,
And His the rule by which we live.

4 To do His heavenly Father's will,
Was His employment and delight;
Humility and holy zeal
Shone through His life divinely bright.

5 Dispensing good where'er He came,
The labours of His life were love:
If then we love our Saviour's name,
Let His divine example move.

6 But ah! how blind, how weak we are,
How frail, how apt to turn aside;
Lord, we depend upon Thy care,
And ask Thy Spirit for our guide.

H. 125 *Praise to the Lamb.*

1 Come, let us sing the song of songs—
The saints in heaven began the strain—
The homage which to Christ belongs:
"Worthy the Lamb, for He was slain."

2 Slain to redeem us by His blood,
To cleanse from every sinful stain,
And make us kings and priests to God—
"Worthy the Lamb, for He was slain."

3 To Him who suffered on the tree,
Our souls, at His soul's price, to gain,
Blessing, and praise, and glory be:
"Worthy the Lamb, for He was slain."

4 To Him enthroned by filial right,
All power in heaven and earth proclaim,
Honour, and majesty, and might:
"Worthy the Lamb, for He was slain."

5 Long as we live, and when we die,
And while in heaven with Him we reign,
This song our song of songs shall be,
"Worthy the Lamb, for He was slain."

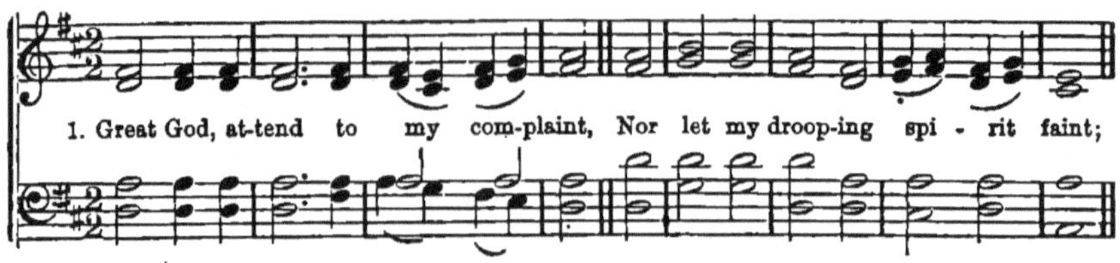
1. Great God, at-tend to my com-plaint, Nor let my droop-ing spi - rit faint;

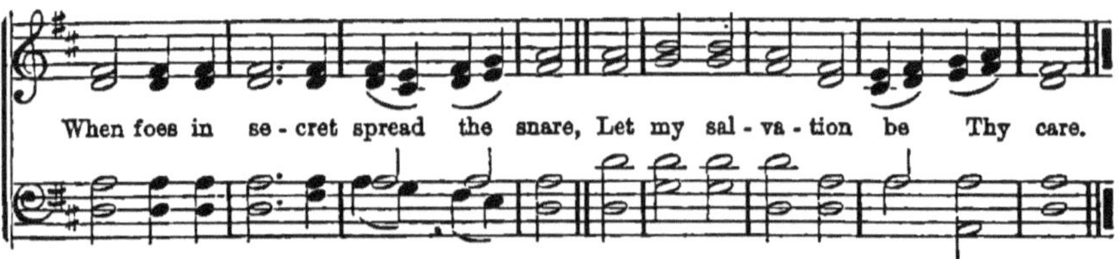
When foes in se - cret spread the snare, Let my sal - va - tion be Thy care.

Ps. 64

2 Shield me without, and guard within,
From treacherous foes and deadly sin;
May envy, lust, and pride depart,
And heavenly grace expand my heart.

3 Thy justice and Thy power display,
And scatter far Thy foes away;
While listening nations learn Thy word,
And saints triumphant bless the Lord.

4 Then shall Thy church exalt her voice,
And all that love Thy name rejoice;
By faith approach Thine awful throne,
And plead the merits of Thy Son.

Ps. 79

1 Behold, O God, what cruel foes
Thy peaceful heritage invade,
Thy holy temple stands defiled,
In dust Thy sacred walls are laid.

2 The insulting foes, with impious rage,
Reproach Thy children to their face:
"Where is your God of boasted power,
And where the promise of His grace?"

3 Deep from the prison's horrid gloom,
O hear the mourning captive sigh,
And let Thy sovereign power reprieve
The trembling souls condemned to die.

4 So shall Thy children, freed from death,
Eternal songs of honour raise,
And every future age shall tell
Thy sovereign power and pardoning grace.

Ps. 89 *Third Part.*

1 Remember, Lord, our mortal state,
How frail our life, how short its date!
Where is the man that draws his breath,
Safe from disease, secure from death?

2 Lord, while we see whole nations die,
Our flesh and strength repine and cry,
"Must death for ever rage and reign?
Or hast Thou made mankind in vain?

3 "Where is Thy promise to the just?
Are not Thy servants turned to dust?"
But faith forbids these mournful sighs,
And sees the sleeping dust arise.

4 That glorious hour, that dreadful day,
Wipes the reproach of saints away,
And clears the honour of Thy word:
Awake, our souls, and bless the Lord.

Ps. 140

1 O Thou Preserver of mankind,
Our hope, our shield, our strength, our God!
Thou hast an ear to prayer inclined;
Our cries have reached Thy dread abode.

2 Our cause Thy justice will maintain,
Avenge th' oppressed and guard the poor:
Ne'er shall Thy children ask in vain,
And our proud foes shall boast no more.

3 Their banded hosts shall fly, or fall;
A shaking leaf their thousands chase;
Our God shall hear our nation's call,
We shall be saved, and sing His praise.

Rev. Cæsar Malan, 1830.

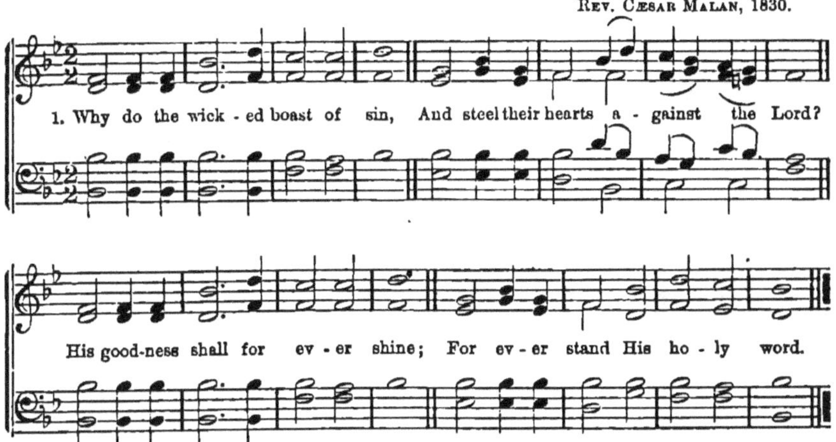
1. Why do the wick - ed boast of sin, And steel their hearts a - gainst the Lord?
His good-ness shall for ev - er shine; For ev - er stand His ho - ly word.

Ps. 52

2 But in Thy courts will I be seen,
Growing in faith and hope and love,
Like olives fair and fresh and green,
And ripening for the world above.

3 There will I learn Thy glory, Lord,
And songs for all Thy goodness raise;
There will I wait to hear Thy word,
While listening saints approve the praise.

H. 10 *God's Faithfulness.*

1 Praise, everlasting praise, be paid
To Him that earth's foundation laid!
Praise to the God whose strong decrees
Sway the creation as He please.

2 Praise to the goodness of the Lord,
Who rules His people by His word;
And there, as strong as His decrees,
He sets His kindest promises.

3 Firm are the words His prophets give,
Sweet words, on which His children live;
Each of them is the voice of God,
Who spoke, and spread the skies abroad.

4 Each of them powerful as that sound,
That bid the new-made world go round;
And stronger than the solid poles,
On which the wheel of nature rolls.

5 Whence then should doubts and fears [arise?
Why trickling sorrows drown our eyes?
Slowly, alas! our mind receives
The comforts that our Maker gives.

6 O! for a strong and lasting faith
To credit what th' Almighty saith!
T' embrace the message of His Son,
And call the joys of heaven our own.

H. 138 *Prayer for the Spirit's Influences.*

1 Come, gracious Spirit, heavenly Dove,
With light and comfort from above;
Be Thou our guardian, Thou our guide:
O'er every thought and step preside.

2 The light of truth to us display,
And make us know and choose Thy way;
Plant holy fear in every heart,
That we from God may not depart.

3 Lead us to holiness—the road
That we must take to dwell with God;
Lead us to Christ, the living way,
Nor let us from His precepts stray.

4 Lead us to God, our final rest,
In His enjoyment to be blest;
Lead us to heaven, the seat of bliss,
Where pleasure in perfection is.

H. 487 *Close of Worship.*

Dismiss us with Thy blessing, Lord,
Help us to feed upon Thy word;
All that has been amiss forgive,
And let Thy truth within us live.

2 Though we are guilty, Thou art good;
Wash all our works in Jesus' blood:
Give every fettered soul release,
And bid us all depart in peace.

THOMAS SHOEL, 1810.

1. Bu-ried in sha-dows of the night, We lie till Christ re-stores the light;
Wis-dom de-scends to heal the blind, And chase the dark-ness of the mind.

H. 52 *Christ our Wisdom and Righteousness.*

2 Our guilty souls are drowned in tears,
Till His atoning blood appears;
Then we awake from deep distress,
And sing "The Lord our righteousness."

3 Poor helpless worms in Thee possess
Grace, wisdom, power, and righteousness;
Thou art our mighty all, and we
Give our whole selves, O Lord, to Thee.

H. 99 *Sympathy of Christ.*

1 WHERE high the heavenly temple stands,
The house of God not made with hands,
A great High Priest our nature wears,
The Advocate of saints appears.

2 He who for men in mercy stood,
And poured on earth His precious blood,
Pursues in heaven His plan of grace,
The Saviour of the chosen race.

3 Though now ascended up on high,
He bends on earth a brother's eye;
Partaker of the human name,
He knows the frailty of our frame.

4 Our fellow-sufferer yet retains
A fellow-feeling of our pains;
And still remembers in the skies,
His tears, and agonies, and cries.

5 In every pang that rends the heart,
The Man of sorrows had a part;
He sympathizes in our grief,
And to the sufferer sends relief.

6 With boldness, therefore, at the throne,
Let us make all our sorrows known;
And ask the aids of heavenly power,
To help us in the evil hour.

H. 129 *The Spirit Eternal and Almighty.*

1 ETERNAL Spirit, we confess
And sing the wonders of Thy grace;
Thy power conveys our blessings down,
From God the Father, and the Son.

2 Enlightened by Thy heavenly ray,
Our shades and darkness turn to day;
Thine inward teachings make us know
Our danger, and our refuge too.

3 Thy power and glory work within,
And break the chains of reigning sin;
Do our imperious lusts subdue,
And form our wretched hearts anew.

4 The troubled conscience knows Thy voice,
Thy cheering words awake our joys;
Thy words allay the stormy wind,
And calm the surges of the mind.

H. 491 *Parting.*

1 COME, Christian brethren, ere we part,
Join every voice and every heart;
One solemn hymn to God we raise,
One final song of grateful praise.

2 Christians, we here may meet no more;
But there is yet a happier shore;
And there, released from toil and pain,
Dear brethren, we shall meet again.

Dr. Thos. Tallis, 1567.

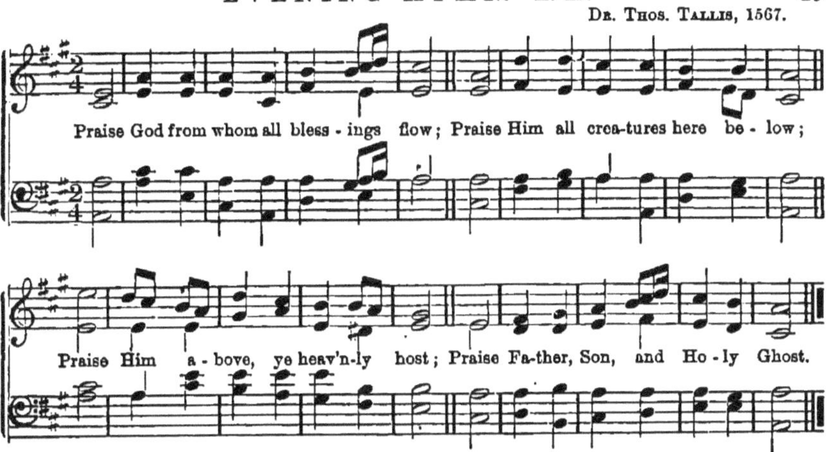
Praise God from whom all bless - ings flow; Praise Him all crea-tures here be - low;
Praise Him a - bove, ye heav'n-ly host; Praise Fa-ther, Son, and Ho - ly Ghost.

H. 454 *An Evening Hymn.*

1 Glory to Thee, my God, this night,
For all the blessings of the light;
Keep me, O keep me, King of kings,
Beneath Thine own almighty wings.

2 Forgive me, Lord, for Thy dear Son,
The ills that I this day have done;
That with the world, myself and Thee,
I, ere I sleep, at peace may be.

3 Teach me to live that I may dread
The grave as little as my bed;
Teach me to die, that so I may
Rise, glorious, at the awful day.

4 Oh! let my soul on Thee repose,
And may sweet sleep my eyelids close;
Sleep that shall me more vigorous make,
To serve my God, when I awake.

5 If in the night I sleepless lie,
My soul with heavenly thoughts supply;
Let no ill dreams disturb my rest,
No powers of darkness me molest.

6 Oh! when shall I, in endless day,
For ever chase dark sleep away;
And hymns divine with angels sing!
Glory to Thee, eternal King.

H. 438 *Morning Hymn.*

1 Awake, my soul, and with the sun,
Thy daily stage of duty run;
Shake off dull sloth, and joyful rise,
To pay thy morning sacrifice.

2 Lord, I my vows to Thee renew,
Scatter my sins as morning dew;
Guard my first springs of thought and will,
And with Thyself my spirit fill.

3 Direct, control, suggest this day,
All I design, or do, or say;
That all my powers, with all my might,
In Thy sole glory may unite.

4 All praise to Thee who safe hast kept
And hast refreshed me while I slept;
Grant, Lord, when I from death shall [wake,
I may of endless life partake.

Ps. 41

1 Blest is the man whose heart can move
And melt with pity to the poor,
Whose soul, by sympathizing love,
Feels what his fellow-saints endure.

2 His heart contrives for their relief
More good than his own hands can do:
He, in the time of general grief,
Shall find the Lord has mercy too.

3 His soul shall live secure on earth,
With secret blessings on his head,
When drought, and pestilence, and dearth,
Around him multiply their dead.

4 Or if he languish on his couch,
God will pronounce his sins forgiven,
Will save him with a healing touch,
Or take his willing soul to heaven.

MARTIN LUTHER.

1. The day of wrath, that dread-ful day, When heav'n and earth shall pass a-way! What pow'r shall be the
sin - ner's stay? How shall he meet that dread - ful day? How shall he meet that dread - ful day?

H. 661 *The Day of Wrath.*

2 When, shrivelling like a parched scroll,
The flaming heavens together roll;
When louder yet, and yet more dread,
Swells the high trump that wakes the dead.

3 O! on that day, that wrathful day,
When man to judgment wakes from clay,
Be Thou the trembling sinner's stay,
Tho' heaven and earth shall pass away.

H. 665 *Coming of the Lord.*

1 The Lord shall come! the earth shall quake,
The mountains to their centre shake,
And, withering from the vault of night,
The stars withdraw their feeble light.

2 The Lord shall come! but not the same
As once in lowly form He came;
A silent Lamb before His foes,
A weary man, and full of woes.

3 The Lord shall come! a dreadful form
With wreath of flame, and robe of storm,
On cherub wings, and wings of wind,
Anointed Judge of human kind.

4 Can this be He who wont to stray
A pilgrim on the world's highway,
By power oppressed, and mocked by pride,
The Nazarene, the Crucified?

5 While sinners in despair shall call,
"Rocks, hide us! mountains, on us fall!"
The saints, ascending from the tomb,
Shall sing for joy, "the Lord is come!"

H. 400 *Prayer answered by Crosses.*

1 I asked the Lord that I might grow
In faith, and love, and every grace;
Might more of His salvation know,
And seek more earnestly His face.

2 'Twas He who taught me thus to pray,
And He, I trust, has answered prayer;
But it has been in such a way,
As almost drove me to despair.

3 I hoped that in some favoured hour,
At once He'd answer my request;
And, by His love's constraining power,
Subdue my sins, and give me rest.

4 Instead of this, He made me feel
The hidden evils of my heart,
And let the angry powers of hell
Assault my soul in every part.

5 Yea, more; with His own hand He seemed
Intent to aggravate my woe;
Crossed all the fair designs I schemed,
Blasted my gourds, and laid me low.

6 "Lord, why is this?" I trembling cried,
"Wilt Thou pursue Thy worm to death?"
"'Tis in this way," the Lord replied,
"I answer prayer for grace and faith."

7 "These inward trials I employ
From self and pride to set thee free,
And break thy schemes of earthly joy,
That thou may'st seek thine all in Me."

WESTERN MELODY.

1. Blest Je - sus, when Thy cross I view, That mys-tery to th' an - ge - lic host,
I gaze with grief and rap - ture too, And all my soul's in won - der lost.

H. 114 *Praise for Redemption.*

2 What strange compassion filled Thy breast,
That brought Thee from Thy throne on high.
To woes that cannot be expressed,
To be despised, to groan and die!

3 Was it for man, rebellious man,
Sunk by his crimes below the grave,
Who, justly doomed to endless pain,
Found none to pity or to save?

4 For man didst Thou forsake the sky,
To bleed upon the accursed tree?
And didst Thou taste of death, to buy
Immortal life and bliss for me?

5 Had I a voice to praise Thy name,
Loud as the trump that wakes the dead,
Had I the raptured seraph's flame,
My debt of love could ne'er be paid.

6 Yet, Lord, a sinner's heart receive,
This burdened contrite heart of mine;
Thou know'st I've nought beside to give;
And let it be for ever Thine.

H. 128 *Praise to Christ.*

1 Thou only sovereign of my heart,
My Refuge, my almighty Friend;
And can my soul from Thee depart.
On whom alone my hopes depend?

2 Eternal life Thy words impart,
On Thee my fainting spirit lives;
Here sweeter comfort cheers my heart,
Than all the round of nature gives.

3 Let earth's alluring joys combine;
While Thou art near, in vain they call;
One smile, one blissful smile of Thine,
My dearest Lord, outweighs them all.

4 Thy name my inmost powers adore;
Thou art my life, my joy, my care;
Depart from Thee?—'tis death—'tis more!
'Tis endless ruin—deep despair!

5 Low at Thy feet my soul would lie;
Here safety dwells, and peace divine;
Still let me live beneath Thine eye,
For life, eternal life is Thine.

H. 579 *Wrestling for a Gracious Visitation.*

1 While filled with sadness and dismay
To see the work of God decline,
Methought I heard the Saviour say,
"Dismiss thy fear, the ark is Mine.

2 "Though for a time I hid My face,
Rely upon My love and power;
Still wrestle at the throne of grace,
And wait for a reviving hour.

3 "Take down thy long neglected harp,
I've seen thy tears, and heard thy prayers;
The winter season has been sharp,
But spring shall all its wastes repair."

4 Lord, I obey, my hopes revive;
Come, join with me, ye saints, and sing;
Our foes in vain against us strive,
For God will help and triumph bring.

Israel Holdrayd, 1753.

1 God, in the gos - pel of His Son, Makes His e - ter - nal coun-sels known;
Where love in all its glo - ry shines, And truth is drawn in fair - est lines.

H. 152 *Fulness of the Gospel.*

2 Here sinners of an humble frame,
May taste His grace and learn His name;
May read, in characters of blood,
The wisdom, power, and grace of God.

3 The prisoner here may break his chains;
The weary rest from all his pains;
The captive feel his bondage cease;
The mourner find the way of peace.

4 Here faith reveals to mortal eyes
A brighter world beyond the skies; [way
Here shines the light which guides our
From earth to realms of endless day.

5 O grant us grace, almighty Lord,
To read and mark Thy holy word;
Its truth with meekness to receive,
And by its holy precepts live.

H. 11 *God's Condescension to the Humble.*

1 Thus saith the high and lofty One,
"I sit upon My holy throne;
My name is God; I dwell on high;
Dwell in My own eternity.

2 "But I descend to worlds below;
On earth I have a mansion too;
The humble spirit and contrite
Is an abode of My delight.

3 "The humble souls My words revive,
I bid the mourning sinner live;
Heal all the broken hearts I find,
And ease the sorrows of the mind.

4 "When I contend against their sin,
I make them know how vile they've been;
But should My wrath for ever smoke,
Their souls would sink beneath My stroke."

5 O! may Thy pardoning grace be nigh,
Lest we should faint, despair, and die,
Thus shall our better thoughts approve
The methods of Thy chastening love.

H. 166 *Christ the Lamb Slain.*

1 Behold the sin-atoning Lamb,
With wonder, gratitude and love;
To take away our guilt and shame,
See Him descending from above!

2 Our sins and griefs on Him were laid;
He meekly bore the mighty load;
Our ransom-price He fully paid,
In groans and tears, in sweat and blood.

3 To save a guilty world He dies;
Sinners, behold the bleeding Lamb!
To Him lift up your longing eyes,
And hope for mercy in His name.

4 Pardon and peace through Him abound;
He can the richest blessings give;
Salvation in His name is found,
He bids the dying sinner live.

5 Jesus, My Lord, I look to Thee;
Where else can helpless sinners go?
Thy boundless love shall set me free
From all my wretchedness and woe.

SAMUEL STANLEY. 1810.

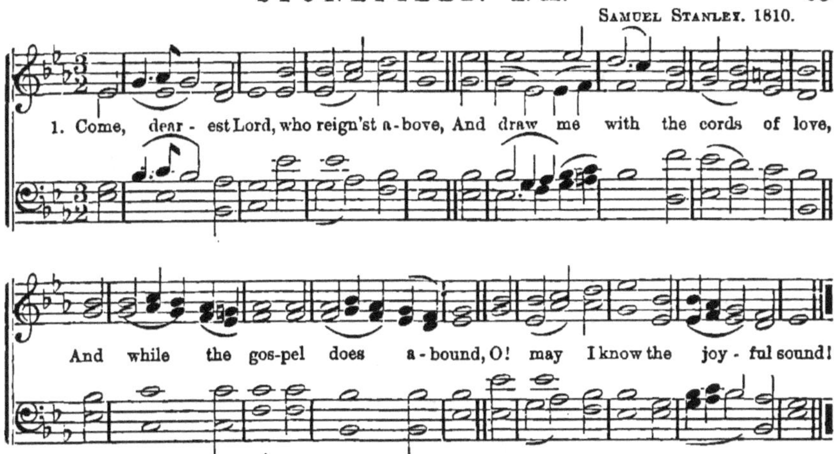
1. Come, dear - est Lord, who reign'st a - bove, And draw me with the cords of love,
And while the gos-pel does a - bound, O! may I know the joy - ful sound!

H. 153 *The Gospel's joyful Sound.*

2 Sweet are the tidings, free the grace,
It brings to our apostate race;
It spreads a heavenly light around;
O! may I know the joyful sound!

3 The gospel bids the sin-sick soul
Look up to Jesus and be whole;
In Him are peace and pardon found;
O! may I know the joyful sound!

4 It stems the tide of swelling grief;
Affords the needy sure relief;
Releases those by Satan bound;
O! may I know the joyful sound!

H. 156 *The Excellency of the Christian Religion.*

1 Let everlasting glories crown
Thy head, my Saviour, and my Lord;
Thy hands have brought salvation down,
And writ the blessings in Thy word.

2 In vain the trembling conscience seeks
Some solid ground to rest upon;
With long despair the spirit breaks,
Till we apply to Christ alone.

3 How well Thy blessed truths agree!
How wise and holy Thy commands!
Thy promises, how firm they be!
How firm our hope and comfort stands!

4 Should all the forms that men devise
Assault my faith with treacherous art,
I'll call them vanity and lies,
And bind the gospel to my heart.

H. 230 *Reliance on Christ's Righteousness.*

1 No more, my God, I boast no more
Of all the duties I have done;
I quit the hopes I held before,
To trust the merits of Thy Son.

2 Now for the love I bear His name,
What was my gain I count my loss;
My former pride I call my shame,
And nail my glory to His cross.

3 Yes, and I must and will esteem
All things but loss for Jesus' sake;
O! may my soul be found in Him,
And of His righteousness partake.

4 The best obedience of my hands
Dares not appear before Thy throne;
But faith can answer Thy demands,
By pleading what my Lord has done.

H. 226 *Joy in Heaven over Repenting Sinners.*

1 Who can describe the joys that rise,
Through all the courts of Paradise,
To see a prodigal return,
To see an heir of glory born?

2 With joy the Father doth approve
The fruit of His eternal love;
The Son with joy looks down and sees
The purchase of His agonies.

3 The Spirit takes delight to view
The holy soul He formed anew;
And saints and angels join to sing
The growing empire of their King.

1 'Tis by the faith of joys to come, We walk through des - erts dark as night,
Till we ar - rive at heav'n our home, Faith is our guide, and faith our light.

H. 261 *Christian Walking by Faith.*

2 The want of sight she well supplies;
She makes the pearly gates appear;
Far into distant worlds she pries,
And brings eternal glories near.

3 Cheerful we tread the desert through,
While faith inspires a heavenly ray,
Though lions roar and tempests blow,
And rocks and dangers fill the way.

4 So Abraham, by divine command,
Left his own house to walk with God;
His faith beheld the promised land,
And fired his zeal along the road.

H. 254 *The Voice of Jesus.*

1 When power divine, in mortal form,
Hushed with a word the raging storm,
In soothing accents Jesus said,—
"Lo! it is I! be not afraid."

2 Bless'd be the voice that breathes from heaven
To every heart in sunder riven,
When love, and joy, and hope are fled,—
"Lo! it is I; be not afraid."

3 And when the last dread hour is come,
While shuddering nature waits her doom,
This voice shall call the pious dead,—
"Lo! it is I; be not afraid."

H. 279 *The Father's House for Me!*

1 Thy Father's house! Thine own bright home!
And Thou hast there a place for me!
Though yet an exile here I roam,
That distant home by faith I see.

2 I see its domes resplendent glow,
Where beams of God's own glory fall,
And trees of life immortal grow,
Whose fruits o'erhang the sapphire wall.

3 I know that Thou, who on the tree
Didst deign our mortal guilt to bear,
Wilt bring Thine own to dwell with Thee,
And waitest to receive them there.

4 Thy love will there array my soul
In Thine own robe of spotless hue;
And I shall gaze, while ages roll,
On Thee, with raptures ever new.

5 Oh! welcome day, when Thou my feet
Shalt bring the shining threshold o'er,
A Father's warm embrace to meet,
And dwell at home for evermore.

H. 280 *Hope in God.*

1 The God of my salvation lives;
My nobler life He will sustain;
His word immortal vigour gives,
Nor shall my glorious hopes be vain.

2 Thy presence, Lord, can cheer my heart,
Though every earthly comfort die;
Thy smile can bid my pains depart,
And raise my sacred pleasures high.

3 Oh! let me hear Thy blissful voice,
Inspiring life and joy divine;
The barren desert shall rejoice;
'Tis paradise, if Thou art mine.

MENDON. L. M.

GERMAN AIR, ARRANGED BY MASON, 1832.

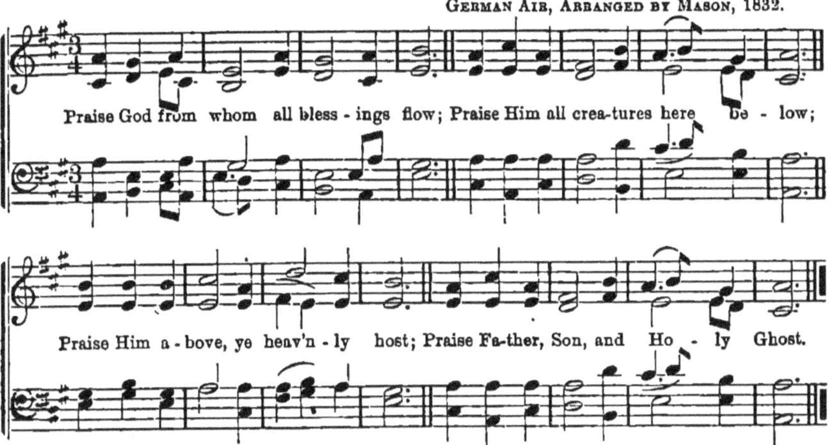
Praise God from whom all bless - ings flow; Praise Him all crea-tures here be - low;
Praise Him a - bove, ye heav'n - ly host; Praise Fa-ther, Son, and Ho - ly Ghost.

H. 343 *Renouncing the World.*

1 I SEND the joys of earth away;
Away ye tempters of the mind,
False as the smooth, deceitful sea,
And empty as the whistling wind.

2 Your streams were floating me along,
Down to the gulf of black despair;
And whilst I listened to your song,
Your streams had e'en conveyed me there.

3 Lord, I adore Thy matchless grace,
That warned me of that dark abyss,
That drew me from those treacherous seas,
And bade me seek superior bliss.

4 Now to the shining realms above,
I stretch my hands, and glance my eyes;
O for the pinions of a dove,
To bear me to the upper skies.

5 There, from the bosom of my God,
Oceans of endless pleasure roll;
There would I fix my last abode,
And drown the sorrows of my soul.

H. 256 *Jesus our Righteousness.*

1 JESUS, Thy blood and righteousness
My beauty are, my glorious dress;
'Midst flaming worlds, in these arrayed,
With joy shall I lift up my head.

2 When from the dust of earth I rise
To claim my mansion in the skies,
E'en then shall this be all my plea,
"Jesus hath lived and died for me."

3 Lord, I believe Thy precious blood,
Which at the mercy-seat of God
For ever doth for sinners plead,
For me, e'en for my soul, was shed.

4 This spotless robe the same appears,
When ruined nature sinks in years;
No age can change its glorious hue,
The robe of Christ is ever new.

5 Oh! let the dead now hear Thy voice,
Now bid Thy banished ones rejoice;
Their beauty this, their glorious dress,
Jesus, the Lord our Righteousness!

H. 611 *Latter-day Glory.*

1 THOUGH now the nations sit beneath
The darkness of o'erspreading death,
God will arise with light divine,
On Zion's holy towers shine.

2 That light shall glance on distant lands,
And heathen tribes, in joyful bands,
Come with exulting haste to prove
The power and greatness of His love.

3 Lord, may the triumphs of Thy grace
Abound, while righteousness and peace,
In mild and lovely forms, display
The glories of the latter day.

FOREST. L. M.

A. CHAPIN, 1823.

1. May He by whose kind care we meet, Send · His good Spi - rit from a - bove;
Make our com - u - ni - ca-tions sweet, And cause our hearts to burn with love.

H. 485 *Social Worship.*

2 FORGOTTEN be each earthly theme,
When Christians see each other thus;
We only wish to speak of Him,
Who lived, and died, and reigns, for us.

3 We'll talk of all He did and said,
And suffered for us here below;
The path He marked for us to tread,
And what He's doing for us now.

4 Thus as the moments pass away,
We'll love, and wonder, and adore;
And hasten on the glorious day,
When we shall meet to part no more.

H. 492 *Sabbath Morning.*

1 COME, dearest Lord, and bless this day,
Come, bear our thoughts from earth away;
Now, let our noblest passions rise,
With ardour to their native skies.

2 Come, Holy Spirit, all divine,
With rays of light upon us shine;
And let our waiting souls be blessed,
On this sweet day of sacred rest.

3 Then, when our Sabbaths here are o'er,
And we arrive on Canaan's shore,
With all the ransomed we shall spend
A Sabbath which shall never end.

H. 539 *Prayer for Baptized Children:*

1 GREAT Saviour who didst condescend
Young children in Thine arms to embrace,
Still prove Thyself the infants' Friend,
Baptize them with Thy cleansing grace.

2 Whilst in the slippery paths of youth,
Be Thou their Guardian and their Guide,
That they, directed by Thy truth,
May never from Thy precepts slide.

3 To love Thy word their hearts incline,
To understand it, light impart;
O Saviour, consecrate them Thine,
Take full possession of their heart.

H. 544 *Self-Dedication to God.*

1 LORD, I am Thine, entirely Thine,
Purchased and saved by blood divine;
With full consent Thine I would be,
And own Thy sovereign right in me.

2 Grant one poor sinner more a place
Among the children of Thy grace;
A wretched sinner lost to God,
But ransomed by Immanuel's blood.

3 Thine would I live, Thine would I die,
Be Thine through all eternity;
The vow is past beyond repeal;
Now will I set the solemn seal.

4 Here at that cross where flows the blood
That bought my guilty soul for God;
Thee, my new Master, now I call,
And consecrate to Thee my all.

5 Do Thou assist a feeble worm
The great engagement to perform;
Thy grace can full assistance lend,
And on that grace I dare depend.

JOSEPH HAYDN, DIED 1809.

1. New ev'-ry morn-ing is the love Our wak'-ning and up - ris - ing prove;
Through sleep and dark-ness safe - ly brought, Re-stored to life, and power, and thought.

H. 440 *God's Service in All Things.*

2 New mercies each returning day
Hover around us while we pray;
New perils past, new sins forgiven,
New thoughts of God, new hopes of heaven.

3 If on our daily course our mind
Be set to hallow all we find,
New treasures still, of countless price,
God will provide for sacrifice.

4 The trivial round, the common task,
Would furnish all we ought to ask;
Room to deny ourselves, a road
To bring us daily nearer God.

5 Only, O Lord, in Thy dear love,
Fit us for perfect rest above;
And help us, this and every day,
To live more nearly as we pray.

H. 450 *Retirement and Meditation.*

1 My God, permit me not to be
A stranger to myself and Thee;
Amidst a thousand thoughts I rove,
Forgetful of my highest love.

2 Why should my passions mix with earth,
And thus debase my heavenly birth?
Why should I cleave to things below,
And let my God, my Saviour, go?

3 Call me away from flesh and sense;
One sovereign word can draw me thence;
I would obey the voice divine,
And all inferior joys resign.

4 Be earth, with all her scenes, withdrawn;
Let noise and vanity be gone;
In secret silence of the mind,
My heaven, and there my God, I find.

H. 461 *Delight in Ordinances.*

1 Far from my thoughts, vain world, be-gone,
Let my religious hours alone;
Fain would my eyes my Saviour see;
I wait a visit, Lord, from Thee.

2 O warm my heart with holy fire,
And kindle there a pure desire;
Come, my dear Jesus, from above,
And feed my soul with heavenly love.

3 Blest Jesus, what delicious fare,
How sweet Thy entertainments are!
Never did angels taste above
Redeeming grace and dying love.

H. 465 *Prayer for Divine Instruction.*

1 Come, Jesus, heavenly Teacher, come,
Convey Thine own instructions home;
While men Thy sacred truth impart,
'Tis Thine alone to reach the heart.

2 Whene'er I read or hear Thy word,
Thine inward teachings, Lord, afford;
To me Thy holy will reveal,
Unfold the book, and loose the seal.

3 Call me, O! call me to Thy feet,
And there transported may I sit;
With joy Thy heavenly features trace,
And feast upon Thy richest grace.

Theo. Thorley.
1. The law com-mands and makes us know What du-ties to our God we owe·
But 'tis the gos - pel must re - veal Where lies our strength to do His will.

H. 159 *The Law and Gospel Contrasted.*

2 The law discovers guilt and sin,
And shows how vile our hearts have been;
Only the gospel can express
Forgiving love and cleansing grace.

3 What curses does the law denounce
Against the man that fails but once!
But in the gospel Christ appears,
Pardoning the guilt of numerous years.

4 My soul, no more attempt to draw
Thy life and comfort from the law;
Fly to the hope the gospel gives;
The man that trusts the promise, lives.

5 But power divine can do the deed,
And much to feel that power I need;
Thy Spirit can from dross refine,
And move and melt this heart of mine.

H. 202 *Repentance.*

1 O! for a glance of heavenly day,
To take this stubborn stone away;
And thaw, with beams of love divine,
This heart, this frozen heart of mine.

2 The rocks can rend; the earth can quake;
The sea can roar; the mountains shake;
Of feeling all things show some sign,
But this unfeeling heart of mine.

3 To hear the sorrows Thou hast felt,
Dear Lord, an adamant would melt;
But I can read each moving line,
And nothing move this heart of mine.

4 Thy judgments, too, unmoved I hear,
(Amazing thought!) which devils fear;
Goodness and wrath in vain combine,
To stir this stupid heart of mine.

H. 312 *The Pleasures of a Good Conscience.*

1 Lord, how secure and blest are they
Who feel the joys of pardoned sin;
Should storms of wrath shake earth and sea,
Their minds have heaven and peace within.

2 The day slides swiftly o'er their heads,
Made up of innocence and love;
And soft and silent as the shades,
Their nightly minutes gently move.

3 Quick as their thoughts their joys come on,
But fly not half so swift away;
Their souls are ever bright as noon,
And calm as summer evenings be:

4 How oft they look to th' heavenly hills
Where groves of living pleasure grow,
And longing hopes and cheerful smiles
Sit undisturbed upon their brow.

5 They scorn to seek our golden toys,
But spend the day and share the night
In numbering o'er the richer joys,
That heaven prepares for their delight.

6 While wretched we, like worms and moles,
Lie grovelling in the dust below;
Almighty grace, renew our souls,
And we'll aspire to glory too.

Hon. Nahum Mitchell, 1812.
1. Ah! wretched souls who strive in vain, Slaves to the world, and slaves to sin,
A no - bler toil may I sus - tain; A no - bler sat - is fac - tion win.

H. 350 *Devotion to Christ.*

2 May I resolve with all my heart,
With all my powers to serve the Lord;
Nor from His precepts e'er depart,
Whose service is a rich reward.

3 O! be His service all my joy!
Around let my example shine,
Till others love the blest employ,
And join in labours so divine.

4 Be this the purpose of my soul,
My solemn, my determined choice,
To yield to His supreme control,
And in His kind commands rejoice.

5 O! may I never faint nor tire,
Nor wandering leave His sacred ways;
Great God, accept my soul's desire,
And give me strength to live Thy [praise.

H. 367 *Prayer for the Divine Presence.*

1 O Thou to whose all-searching sight,
The darkness shineth as the light;
Search, prove my heart, it pants for Thee;
O! burst these bonds, and set it free.

2 If in this darksome wild I stray,
Be Thou my Light, be Thou my Way;
No foes, nor violence I fear,
Nor fraud, while Thou, my God, art near.

3 When rising floods my soul o'erflow,
When sinks my heart in waves of woe;
Jesus, Thy timely aid impart,
And raise my head, and cheer my heart.

4 Saviour, where'er Thy steps I see,
Dauntless, untired, I follow Thee;
Oh! let Thy hand support me still,
And lead me to Thy holy hill.

5 If rough and thorny be the way,
My strength proportion to my day;
Till toil, and grief, and pain shall cease,
Where all is calm, and joy, and peace.

H. 411 *Hope for the Suffering.*

1 Oh! deem not they are blest alone,
Whose lives a peaceful tenor keep;
For God, who pities man, has shown
A blessing for the eyes that weep.

2 The light of smiles shall fill again
The lids that overflow with tears;
And weary hours of woe and pain
Are promises of happier years.

3 There is a day of sunny rest
For every dark and troubled night;
And grief may bide an evening guest,
But joy shall come with early light.

4 Nor let the good man's trust depart,
Though life its common gifts deny;
Though with a pierced and broken heart,
And spurned of men, he goes to die.

5 For God has marked each sorrowing day,
And numbered every secret tear,
And heaven's long age of bliss shall pay
For all His children suffer here.

F. M. A. Venua, 1810.

1. Arm of the Lord, a - wake, a - wake, Put on thy strength, the na-tions shake, And let the
world, a-dor-ing, see Tri-umphs of mer-cy wrought by Thee—Triumphs of mercy wrought by Thee.

H. 593 *Payer for Zion's Increase.*

2 Say to the heathen, from Thy throne,
"I am Jehovah—God alone;"
Thy voice their idols shall confound,
And cast their altars to the ground.

3 No more let human blood be spilt,
Vain sacrifice for human guilt;
But to each conscience be applied
The blood that flowed from Jesus' side.

4 Almighty God, Thy grace proclaim,
In every land declare Thy name;
Let adverse powers before Thee fall,
And crown the Saviour—Lord of all.

H. 599 *Prayer for the Triumph of the Gospel.*

1 O Jesus, let Thy kingdom come;
Then sin and hell's terrific gloom
Shall, at Thy brightness, flee away,
The dawn of an eternal day.

2 Then shall the heathen, filled with awe,
Learn the blest knowledge of Thy law,
And Antichrist on every shore
Fall from his throne, to rise no more.

3 Then shall the Jew and Gentile meet,
In pure devotion, at Thy feet;
And earth shall yield Thee, as Thy due,
Her fulness, and her glory too.

4 O that from Zion now might shine
This heavenly light, this truth divine;
Till the whole universe shall be
But one great temple, Lord, for Thee.

H. 602 *Prayer for the Triumph of the Gospel.*

1 Sovereign of worlds, display Thy power,
Be this Thy Zion's favoured hour;
Bid the bright morning star arise,
And point the nations to the skies.

2 Set up Thy throne where Satan reigns,
On western wilds, and heathen plains;
Far let the gospel's sound be known,
And be the universe Thine own.

3 Speak, and the world shall hear Thy voice,
Speak, and the nations shall rejoice;
Scatter the shades of moral night,
With the blest beams of heavenly light.

H. 692 *Praise of Heaven.*

1 Hark! how the choral song of heaven
Swells full of peace and joy above;
Hark! how they strike their golden harps,
And raise the tuneful notes of love.

2 No anxious care, nor thrilling grief,
No deep despair, nor gloomy woe,
They feel, when high their lofty strains
In noblest, sweetest concord flow.

3 When shall we join the heavenly host,
Who sing Immanuel's praise on high,
And leave behind our doubts and fears,
To swell the chorus of the sky?

4 O! come thou rapture-bringing morn,
And usher in the joyful day;
We long to see thy rising sun
Drive all these clouds of grief away.

W. H. W. Darley.

1. Hap-py the church, thou sa-cred place, The seat of thy Cre-a-tor's grace; Thy ho-ly courts are
His a bode, Thou earth - ly pal-ace of our God—Thou earth-ly pal-ace of our God.

H. 563 *God the Defence of the Church.*

2 Thy walls are strength, and at thy gates
A guard of heavenly warriors waits;
Nor shall thy deep foundations move,
Fixed on His counsels and His love.

3 Thy foes in vain designs engage;
Against His throne in vain they rage;
Like rising waves, with angry roar,
That dash and die upon the shore.

4 Then let our souls in Zion dwell,
Nor fear the wrath of earth and hell;
His arms embrace this happy ground,
Like brazen bulwarks built around.

5 God is our shield, and God our sun;
Swift as the fleeting moments run,
On us He sheds new beams of grace,
And we reflect His brightest praise.

H. 570 *The Great Commission.*

1 "Go, preach My gospel," saith the Lord,
"Bid the whole earth My grace receive;
He shall be saved who trusts My word;
He shall be damned that won't believe.

2 "I'll make your great commission known,
And ye shall prove My gospel true,
By all the works that I have done,
By all the wonders ye shall do.

3 "Go heal the sick, go raise the dead;
Go cast out devils in My name;
Nor let My prophets be afraid, [pheme.
Though Greeks reproach, and Jews blas-

4 "Teach all the nations My commands;
I'm with you till the world shall end;
All power is trusted to My hands,
I can destroy, and can defend."

5 He spake, and light shone round His head;
On a bright cloud to heaven He rode;
They to the farthest nations spread
The grace of their ascended God.

H. 688 *Longing for Heaven.*

1 Now let our souls, on wings sublime,
Rise from the vanities of time;
Draw back the parting veil, and see
The glories of eternity.

2 Born by a new celestial birth,
Why should we grovel here on earth?
Why grasp at transitory toys,
So near to heaven's eternal joys?

3 Shall aught beguile us on the road,
When we are walking back to God?
For strangers into life we come,
And dying is but going home.

4 Welcome, sweet hour of full discharge,
That sets our longing souls at large:
Unbinds our chain, breaks up our cell,
And gives us with our God to dwell.

5 To dwell with God, to feel His love,
Is the full heaven enjoyed above;
And the sweet expectation now,
Is the young dawn of heaven below.

Samuel Holyoke, 1785.

1. Be - hold th'ex - pect - ed time draw near, The shades dis-perse, the dawn ap - pear;
Be - hold the wil - der-ness as - sume The beaut-eous tints of E - den's bloom.

H. 601 *Approaching Millennium.*

2 The untaught heathen waits to know,
The joy the gospel will bestow;
The exiled captive, to receive
The freedom Jesus has to give.

3 Come, let us with a grateful heart,
In the blest labour share a part;
Our prayers and offerings gladly bring,
To aid the triumphs of our King.

4 Invite the world to come and prove
A Saviour's condescending love;
And humbly fall before His feet,
Assured they shall acceptance meet.

H. 598 *Prayer for the General Effusion of the Spirit.*

1 O Spirit of the living God,
In all Thy plenitude of grace,
Where'er the foot of man hath trod,
Descend on our apostate race.

2 Be darkness, at Thy coming, light;
Confusion, order in Thy path; [might;
Souls without strength inspire with
Bid mercy triumph over wrath.

3 Baptize the nations; far and nigh,
The triumphs of the cross record;
The name of Jesus glorify,
Till every kindred call Him Lord.

4 God from eternity hath willed,
All flesh shall His salvation see;
So be the Father's love fulfilled, [Thee.
The Saviour's sufferings crowned thro'

H. 600 *Spread of the Gospel.*

1 Ascend Thy throne, almighty King,
And spread Thy glories all abroad;
Let Thine own arm salvation bring,
And be Thou known the gracious God.

2 Let millions bow before Thy seat,
Let humble mourners seek Thy face;
Bring daring rebels to Thy feet,
Subdued by Thy victorious grace.

3 O let the kingdoms of the world,
Become the kingdoms of the Lord;
Let saints and angels praise Thy name,
Be Thou through heaven and earth adored.

H. 577 *Prayer for Labourers.*

1 Lord of the harvest, bend Thine ear,
In Zion's heritage appear;
O send forth labourers filled with zeal,
Swift to obey their Master's will.

2 Our lifted eyes, O Lord, behold,
The ripening harvest tinged with gold;
Wide fields are opening to our view,
The work is great, the labourers few.

3 Led by Thine own almighty hand,
Let Zion's sons, in many a band,
Arise to bless the dying race,
As heralds of redeeming grace.

4 Lord of the harvest, bid them rise,
Trained by the influence of the skies,
In wisdom, knowledge, grace to shine.
Till every kingdom shall be Thine.

ENGLISH TUNE.

1. De-scend from heav'n, im-mor-tal Dove, Stoop down and take us on Thy wings,
And mount and bear us far a-bove The reach of these in-fe-rior things.

H. 680 *Longing for Heaven.*

2 Beyond, beyond this lower sky,
Up where eternal ages roll,
Where solid pleasures never die,
And fruits immortal feast the soul.

3 O for a sight, a pleasing sight,
Of our almighty Father's throne!
There sits our Saviour, crowned with light,
Clothed in a body like our own.

4 Adoring saints around Him stand,
And thrones and powers before Him fall;
The God shines gracious through the man,
And sheds sweet glories on them all.

5 O what amazing joys they feel,
While to their golden harps they sing,
And sit on every heavenly hill,
And spread the triumphs of their King.

6 When shall the day, dear Lord, appear,
That I shall mount to dwell above,
And stand and bow amongst them there,
And view Thy face, and sing, and love?

H. 676 *No Abiding City Here.*

1 We've no abiding city here;
We seek a land beyond our sight;
Zion its name—the Lord is there;
It shines with everlasting light.

2 Oh! sweet abode of peace and love,
Where pilgrims, freed from toil, are blest!
Had I the pinions of a dove,
I'd fly to Thee, and be at rest.

3 But hush, my soul, nor dare repine;
The time my God appoints is best;
While here, to do His will be mine,
And His to fix my time of rest.

H. 687 *Home in Heaven.*

1 As when the weary traveller gains
The height of some o'erlooking hill,
His heart revives, if 'cross the pains,
He eyes his home, though distant still.

2 While he surveys the much-loved spot,
He slights the space that lies between;
His past fatigues are now forgot,
Because his journey's end is seen.

3 Thus when the Christian pilgrim views,
By faith, his mansion in the skies,
The sight his fainting strength renews,
And wings his speed to reach the prize.

4 The thought of home his spirit cheers,
No more he grieves for troubles past;
Nor any future trial fears,
So he may safe arrive at last.

5 'Tis there, he says, I am to dwell,
With Jesus, in the realms of day;
Then I shall bid my cares farewell,
And He will wipe my tears away.

6 Jesus, on Thee our hope depends,
To lead us on to Thine abode;
Assured our home will make amends
For all our toil while on the road.

ENGLISH.

1. Stand up, my soul, shake off thy fears, And gird the gos - pel ar - mour on;
March to the gates of end - less joy, Where Je - sus, thy great Cap-tain's gone.

H. 394 *Christian Warfare.*

1 Stand up, my soul, shake off thy fears,
And gird the gospel armour on;
March to the gates of endless joy,
Where Jesus, thy great Captain's gone.

2 Hell and thy sins resist thy course,
But hell and sins are vanquished foes;
Thy Jesus nailed them to the cross,
And sung the triumph when He rose.

3 What though the prince of darkness rage,
And waste the fury of his spite,
Eternal chains confine him down
To fiery deeps and endless night.

4 What though thy inward lusts rebel?
'Tis but a struggling gasp for life:
The weapons of victorious grace,
Shall slay thy sins, and end the strife.

5 Then let my soul march boldly on,
Press forward to the heavenly gate;
There peace and joy eternal reign, [wait.
And glittering robes for conquerors

6 There shall I wear a starry crown,
And triumph in almighty grace;
While all the armies of the skies
Join in my glorious Leader's praise.

H. 75 *Christ our Pattern.*

1 When Jesus dwelt in mortal clay,
What were His works from day to day,
But miracles of power and grace,
That spread salvation through our race?

2 Teach us, O Lord, to keep in view
Thy pattern, and Thy steps pursue;
Let alms bestowed, let kindness done,
Be witnessed by each rolling sun.

3 The man who marks, from day to day,
In generous acts his radiant way,
Treads the same path his Saviour trod,
The path to glory and to God.

H. 294 *Love Essential to Religion.*

1 Had I the tongues of Greeks and Jews,
And nobler speech than angels use,
If love be absent, I am found
Like tinkling brass, an empty sound.

2 Were I inspired to preach, and tell
All that is done in heaven and hell;
Or could my faith the world remove,
Still I am nothing without love.

3 Should I distribute all my store,
To feed the bowels of the poor,
Or give my body to the flame,
To gain a martyr's glorious name:

4 If love to God, and love to men,
Be absent, all my hopes are vain;
Nor tongues, nor gifts, nor fiery zeal,
The work of love can e'er fulfil.

Doxology.

Praise God from whom all blessings flow;
Praise Him all creatures here below;
Praise Him above, ye heavenly host;
Praise Father, Son, and Holy Ghost.

RALPH HARRISON, 1786.

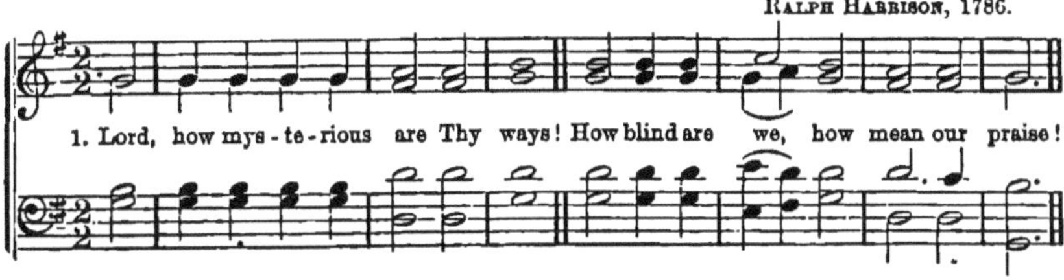
1. Lord, how mys-te-rious are Thy ways! How blind are we, how mean our praise!

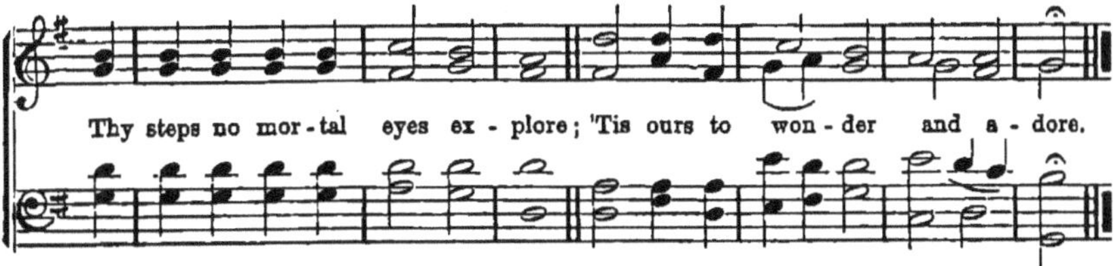
Thy steps no mor-tal eyes ex-plore; 'Tis ours to won-der and a-dore.

H. 27 *Mysteries of Providence.*

2 Thy purposes from creature sight
Are hid in shades of awful night;
Amid the lines, with curious eye,
Not angel minds presume to pry.

3 Great God! I do not ask to see
What in futurity shall be;
Let light and bliss attend my days,
And then my future hours be praise.

4 Are darkness and distress my share?
Give me to trust Thy guardian care;
Enough for me, if love divine [shine.
At length through every cloud shall

5 Yet this my soul desires to know,
Be this my only wish below,
That Christ is mine! this great request,
Grant, bounteous God, and I am blest.

H. 196 *To-Day.*

1 To-day, if ye will hear His voice,
Now is the time to make your choice;
Say, will you to Mount Zion go?
Say, will you have this Christ, or no?

2 Ye wand'ring souls, who find no rest,
Say, will you be for ever blest?
Will you be saved from sin and hell?
Will you with Christ in glory dwell?

3 Come now, dear youth, for ruin bound,
Obey the gospel's cheerful sound;
Come, go with us, and you shall prove
The joy of Christ's redeeming love.

4 Once more we ask you in His name,
For yet His love remains the same,
Say, will you to Mount Zion go?
Say, will you have this Christ, or no?

5 Leave all your sports and glittering toys,
Come, share with us eternal joys;
Or must we leave you bound to hell—
Then, dear young friends, a long farewell.

H. 425 *Praise to God.*

1 Thee we adore, eternal Lord!
We praise Thy name with one accord;
Thy saints, who here Thy goodness see,
Through all the world do worship Thee.

2 To Thee aloud all angels cry,
The heavens and all the powers on high;
Thee, holy, holy, holy, King,
Lord God of hosts, they ever sing.

3 Th' apostles join the glorious throng;
The prophets swell th' immortal song;
The martyrs' noble army raise
Eternal anthems to Thy praise.

4 From day to day, O Lord, do we
Highly exalt and honour Thee!
Thy name we worship and adore,
World without end, for evermore!

5 Vouchsafe, O Lord, we humbly pray,
To keep us safe from sin this day;
Have mercy, Lord! we trust in thee;
Oh! let us ne'er confounded be!

ANON.
Chorus.
1. O hap-py day, that fixed my choice On Thee, my Sa-viour and my God;
Well may this glow-ing heart re-joice, And tell its rap-tures all a-broad.
Hap-py day, hap-py day,
D. S. Hap-py day, hap-py day,
Fine.
D. S.
Here in Thy courts we'll glad-ly stay, And at Thy foot-stool humbly pray, That Thou wouldst take our sins a-way;
When Christ shall wash our sins a-way.

H. 354 *Union with the Church.*

1 O happy day, that fixed my choice
On Thee, my Saviour and my God;
Well may this glowing heart rejoice,
And tell its raptures all abroad.

CHO. Happy day, happy day,
Here in Thy courts we'll gladly stay,
And at Thy footstool humbly pray
That Thou wouldst take our sins away;
Happy day, happy day,
When Christ shall wash our sins away.

2 O happy bond, that seals my vows
To Him, who merits all my love!
Let cheerful anthems fill His house,
While to that sacred shrine I move.
Happy day, etc.

3 'Tis done!—the great transaction's done;
I am my Lord's, and He is mine!
He drew me, and I follow'd on,
Charmed to confess the voice divine.
Happy day, etc.

4 Now rest, my long-divided heart,
Fixed on this blissful centre, rest;
With ashes who would grudge to part,
When called on angel's bread to feast?
Happy day, etc.

5 High heaven, that heard the solemn vow,
That vow renew'd shall daily hear;
Till in life's latest hour I bow,
And bless in death a bond so dear.
Happy day, etc.

H. 50 *Christ the Way.*

1 JESUS, my all, to heaven is gone,
He whom I fix my hopes upon;
His track I see, and I'll pursue
The narrow way till Him I view.
Happy day, etc.

2 The way the holy prophets went,
The road that leads from banishment,
The King's highway of holiness,
I'll go, for all His paths are peace.
Happy day, etc.

3 This is the way I long have sought,
And mourned because I found it not;
My grief and burden long have been,
Because I could not cease from sin.
Happy day, etc.

4 The more I strove against its power,
I sinned and stumbled but the more,
Till late I heard my Saviour say,
"Come hither, soul, I am the way."
Happy day, etc.

5 Lo! glad I come, and Thou, blest Lamb,
Shalt take me to Thee as I am:
Nothing but sin I Thee can give,
Nothing but love shall I receive.
Happy day, etc.

6 Then will I tell to sinners round,
What a dear Saviour I have found;
I'll point to Thy redeeming blood,
And say—"Behold the way to God!"
Happy day, etc.

ROBERT SCHUMAN.

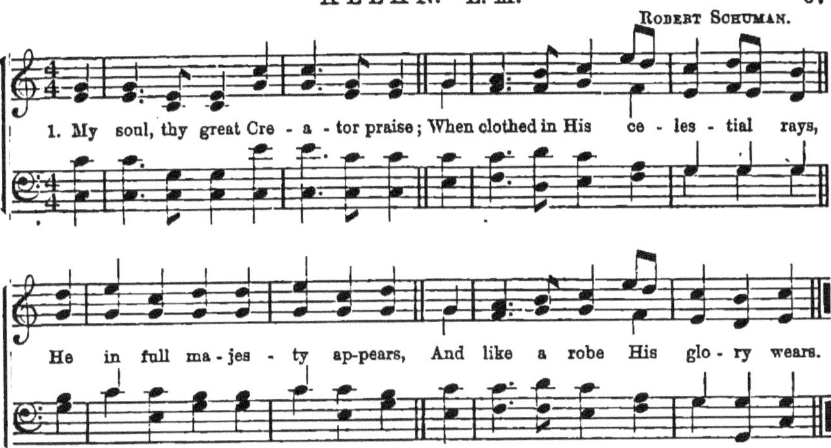
1. My soul, thy great Cre - a - tor praise; When clothed in His ce - les - tial rays,
He in full ma - jes - ty ap-pears, And like a robe His glo - ry wears.

Ps. 104

2 THE heavens are for His curtains spread;
Th' unfathomed deep He makes His bed;
Clouds are His chariot, when He flies
On winged storms across the skies.

3 Angels, whom His own breath inspires,
His ministers, are flaming fires;
And swift as thought their armies move,
To bear His vengeance or His love.

4 How strange Thy works! how great Thy
While every land Thy riches fill; [skill!
Thy wisdom round the world we see;
This spacious earth is full of Thee.

Ps. 85

1 SALVATION is for ever nigh
The souls that fear and trust the Lord;
And grace descending from on high,
Fresh hopes of glory shall afford.

2 Mercy and truth on earth are met,
Since Christ the Lord came down from
By His obedience, so complete, [heaven;
Justice is pleased, and peace is given.

3 Now truth and honour shall abound,
Religion dwell on earth again,
And heavenly influence bless the ground,
In our Redeemer's gentle reign.

4 His righteousness is gone before,
To give us free access to God;
Our wandering feet shall stray no more,
But mark His steps and keep the road,

Ps. 92 *Second Part.*

1 LORD, 'tis a pleasant thing to stand,
In gardens planted by Thy hand;
Let me within Thy courts be seen,
Like a young cedar, fresh and green.

2 There grow Thy saints in faith and love,
Blest with Thine influence from above;
Not Lebanon, with all its trees,
Yields such a comely sight as these.

3 The plants of grace shall ever live;
(Nature decays, but grace must thrive;)
Time, that doth all things else impair,
Still makes them flourish strong and fair.

4 Laden with fruits of age, they show
The Lord is holy, just and true;
None that attend His gates shall find
A God unfaithful or unkind.

H. 462 *Prayer for the Divine Presence.*

1 COME, gracious Lord, descend and dwell,
By faith and love in every breast;
Then shall we know, and taste, and feel,
The joys that cannot be expressed.

2 Come, fill our hearts with inward strength,
Make our enlarged souls possess,
And learn the height, and breadth, and
Of Thine immeasurable grace. [length,

3 Now to the God whose power can do
More than our thoughts or wishes know,
Be everlasting honours done; [Son.
By all the church, through Christ His

Felix Giardini, Died 1788.

To God the Fa - ther, God the Son, And God the Spi - rit, Three in One,
Be hon - our, praise, and glo - ry given, By all on earth, And all in heav'n.

H. 9 *God's Unbounded Love.*

1 Lord, what is man that he should prove
The object of Thy boundless love?
Say, why should he so largely share
Thy favour, and Thy tender care?

2 While these my lips draw vital breath,
Or till I close mine eyes in death,
I'll ne'er forget Thy wondrous love,
Nor thoughtless of Thy kindness prove.

3 Beneath Thy shadowing wings' defence,
I'll place my only confidence;
In every danger and distress,
To Thee will I my prayer address.

4 Should all my hopes on earth be lost,
In Thee I'll make my constant boast:
I'll spread the glories of Thy name,
And Thy unbounded love proclaim.

H. 552 *Not Ashamed of Christ.*

1 At Thy command, our dearest Lord,
Here we attend Thy dying feast;
Thy love has spread the sacred board,
To feed the faith of every guest.

2 Our faith adores Thy bleeding love,
And trusts for life in One that died;
We hope for heavenly crowns above,
From a Redeemer crucified.

3 Let the vain world pronounce it shame;
And cast contempt upon Thy cause;
We glory in our Saviour's name,
And make our triumphs in His cross.

4 With joy we tell the scoffing age,
He that was dead has left His tomb;
He lives above their utmost rage,
And we are waiting till He come.

H. 571 *At the Settlement of a Minister.*

1 Shepherd of Israel, Thou dost keep,
With constant care, Thy humble sheep;
By Thee, inferior pastors rise,
To feed our souls, and bless our eyes.

2 To all Thy churches such impart,
Resembling Thy own gracious heart;
Whose courage, watchfulness and love,
Men may attest, and God approve.

3 Fed by their active, tender care,
Healthful may all Thy sheep appear;
And by their fair example led,
The way to Zion's pasture tread.

4 Here hast Thou listened to our vows,
And scattered blessings on Thy house;
Thy saints are succoured, and no more
As sheep without a guide deplore.

5 Completely heal each former stroke,
And bless the shepherd and the flock;
Confirm the hopes Thy mercies raise,
And own this tribute of our praise.

6 When Thou, chief Shepherd, shalt appear,
When all the flock assembling here,
And small and great before Thee stand,
May they be found on Thy right hand.

W. Knapp, 1698–1768.

Praise God from whom all bless - ings flow; Praise Him, all crea-tures here be - low;
Praise Him a - bove, ye heav'n-ly host; Praise Fa - ther, Son, and Ho - ly Ghost.

H. 382 *Watchfulness in Prayer.*

1 Our Saviour's words are, "Watch and pray;"
Lord, make us willing to obey,
Able Thy counsel to fulfil;
From Thee must come both power and will.

2 The wisdom from above impart,
To keep our hand, our tongue, our heart,
In thought, word, deed—that so we may
Pray while we watch, watch while we pray.

3 Our strength be His omnipotence;
His truth our sole and sure defence;
His grace can help the feeblest saint,
To watch and pray, and never faint.

4 For He who hath commanded thus,
Oft watched and prayed on earth for us;
And still, with interceding love,
Watches and prays for us above.

H. 391 *Christian Consistency.*

1 So let our lips and lives express,
The holy gospel we profess;
So let our works and virtues shine,
To prove the doctrine all divine.

2 Thus shall we best proclaim abroad
The honours of our Saviour God,
When His salvation reigns within,
And grace subdues the power of sin.

3 Our flesh and sense must be denied,
Passion and envy, lust and pride;
While justice, temperance, truth and love,
Our inward piety approve.

4 Religion bears our spirits up,
While we expect that blessed hope,
The bright appearance of the Lord,
And faith stands leaning on His word.

H. 452 *Morning Hymn.*

1 O Christ! with each returning morn,
Thine image to our heart be borne;
And may we ever clearly see
Our God and Saviour, Lord, in Thee.

2 All hallowed be our walk this day;
May meekness form our early ray,
And faithful love our noontide light,
And hope our sunset, calm and bright.

3 May grace each idle thought control,
And sanctify our wayward soul;
May guile depart, and malice cease,
And all within be joy and peace.

4 Our daily course, O Jesus, bless;
Make plain the way of holiness;
From sudden falls our feet defend,
And cheer at last our journey's end.

H. 572 *The People's Prayer for their Pastor.*

1 With heavenly power, O Lord, defend
Him whom we now to Thee commend;
His person bless, his soul secure,
And make him to the end endure.

2 Gird him with all-sufficient grace;
Direct his feet in paths of peace;
Thy truth and faithfulness fulfil,
And help him to obey Thy will.

I. B. WOODBURY.

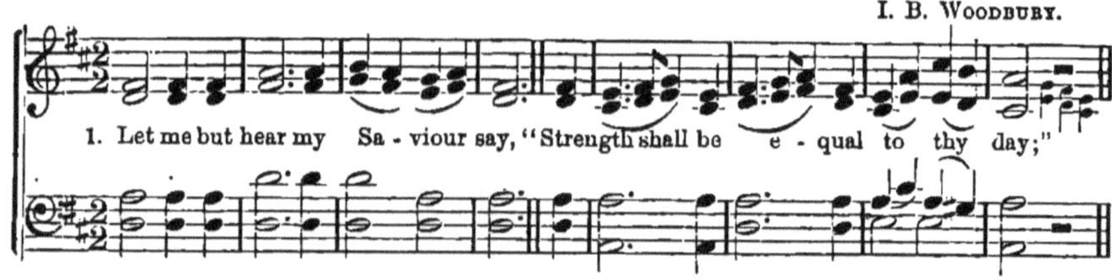
1. Let me but hear my Sa - viour say, "Strength shall be e - qual to thy day;"

Then I re - joice in deep dis - tress, Lean - ing on all - suf - fi - cient grace.

H. 59 *Christ our Strength.*

2 I GLORY in infirmity,
That Christ's own power may rest on me;
When I am weak, then am I strong,
Grace is my shield, and Christ my song.

3 I can do all things, or can bear
All sufferings, if my Lord be there;
Sweet pleasures mingle with the pains,
While His own hand my head sustains.

H. 65 *Christ's Meekness.*

1 How beauteous were the marks divine
That in Thy meekness seen to shine,
Did light Thy lonely pathway, trod
In wondrous love, O Son of God!

2 Oh! who like Thee so humbly bore
The scorn, the scoffs of men, before?
So meek, forgiving, Godlike, high,
So glorious in humility?

3 E'en death, which sets the prisoner free,
Was pang, and scorn, and scoff to Thee;
Yet love through all Thy torture glowed,
And mercy with Thy life-blood flowed.

4 Oh! in Thy light be mine to go,
Illuming all my way of woe!
And give me ever on the road
To trace Thy footsteps, Son of God.

H. 79 *Conformity to Christ.*

1 JESUS, my Saviour, let me be
More perfectly conformed to Thee;
Implant each grace, each sin dethrone,
And form my temper like Thine own.

2 My foe, when hungry, let me feed,
Share in his grief, supply his need;
The haughty frown may I not fear,
But with a lowly meekness bear.

3 To others let me always give,
What I from others would receive;
Good deeds for evil ones return,
Nor when provoked with anger burn.

4 This will proclaim how bright and fair
The precepts of the gospel are;
And God Himself, the God of love,
His own resemblance will approve.

H. 130 *The Spirit the Source of Life and Light.*

1 FATHER of mercies, God of love,
Send down Thy Spirit from above;
Let me His sacred influence feel,
To quicken, purify, and heal.

2 May He these stubborn lusts subdue,
And form my nature all anew;
To Thee my grovelling spirit raise,
Excite to humble prayer and praise.

3 He is the source of every grace,
Of light, and life, and holiness;
By Him alone may I be taught,
And all my works in Him be wrought.

4 O! let Thy Holy Spirit come,
And make my heart His constant home;
There His abundant grace display,
And lead me in a perfect way.

G. F. Handel, 1685–1759.

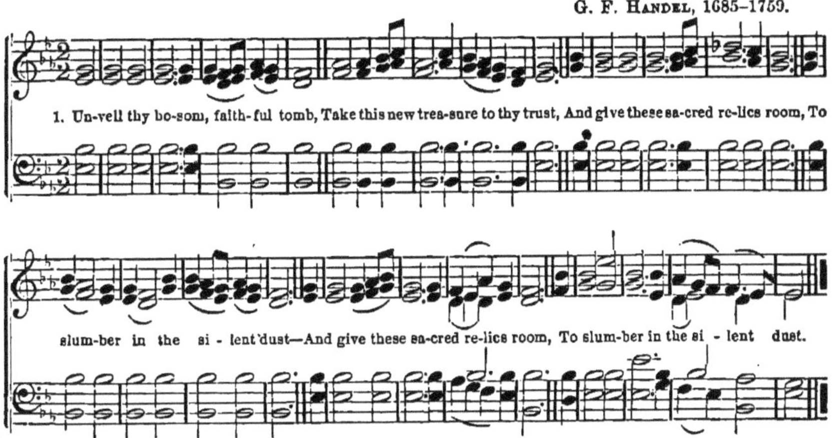
1. Un-veil thy bo-som, faith-ful tomb, Take this new trea-sure to thy trust, And give these sa-cred re-lics room, To
slum-ber in the si - lent dust—And give these sa-cred re-lics room, To slum-ber in the si - lent dust.

H. 645 *Death and Burial of a Christian.*

2 Nor pain, nor grief, nor anxious fear,
Invades thy bounds; no mortal woes
Can reach the peaceful sleeper here,
While angels watch his soft repose.

3 So Jesus slept; God's dying Son
Passed through the grave, and blessed the bed;
Rest here, blest saint, till from His throne
The morning break, and pierce the shade.

4 Break from His throne, illustrious morn,
Attend, O earth, His sovereign word;
Restore thy trust; a glorious form
Shall then arise to meet the Lord.

H. 637 *Death of the Saint and Sinner Contrasted.*

1 What scenes of horror and of dread
Await the sinner's dying bed!
Death's terrors all appear in sight,
Presages of eternal night.

2 His sins in dreadful order rise,
And fill his soul with sad surprise;
Mount Sinai's thunder stuns his ears,
And not one ray of hope appears.

3 Not so the heir of heavenly bliss:
His soul is filled with conscious peace;
A steady faith subdues his fear;
He sees the happy Canaan near.

4 His mind is tranquil and serene;
No terrors in his looks are seen;
His Saviour's smile dispels the gloom,
And smooths his passage to the tomb.

5 Lord, make my faith and love sincere,
My judgment sound, my conscience clear;
And when the toils of life are past,
May I be found in peace at last.

Ps. 22

1 Now let our mournful songs record
The dying sorrows of our Lord,
When He complained in tears and blood,
As one forsaken of His God.

2 The Jews behold Him thus forlorn,
And shake their heads and laugh in scorn:
"He rescued others from the grave,
Now let Him try Himself to save."

3 They wound His head, His hands, His feet,
Till streams of blood each other meet;
By lot His garments they divide,
And mock the pangs in which He died.

4 But God His Father heard His cry;
Raised from the dead He reigns on high;
The nations learn His righteousness,
And humble sinners taste His grace.

H. 180 *The Gospel Warning.*

1 Enter the ark, while patience waits,
Nor ever quit that sure retreat;
Then the wide flood that buries earth
Shall waft thee to a fairer seat.

2 Nor wreck nor ruin there is seen;
There not a wave of trouble rolls;
But the bright rainbow 'round the throne
Seals endless life to all their souls.

W. B. Bradbury, 1844.

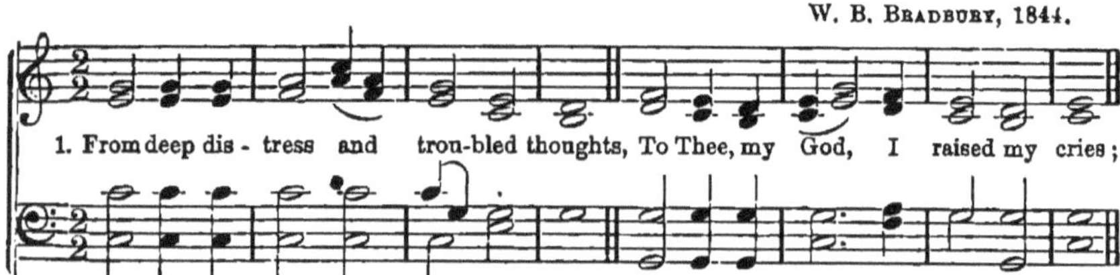
1. From deep dis - tress and trou-bled thoughts, To Thee, my God, I raised my cries;

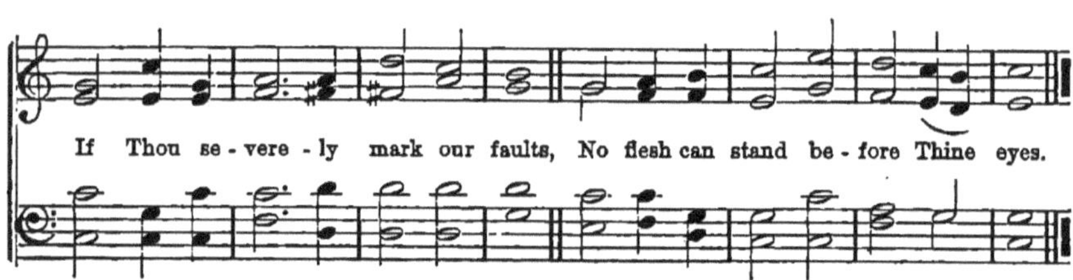
If Thou se - vere - ly mark our faults, No flesh can stand be - fore Thine eyes.

Ps. 130 *Second Part.*

2 But Thou hast built Thy throne of grace,
Free to dispense Thy pardons there,
That sinners may approach Thy face,
And hope, and love, as well as fear.

3 As the benighted pilgrims wait,
And long and wish for breaking day:
So waits my soul before Thy gate,
When will my God His face display?

4 My trust is fixed upon Thy word,
Nor shall I trust Thy word in vain;
Let mourning souls address the Lord,
And find relief from all their pain.

5 Great is His love, and large His grace,
Through the redemption of His Son;
He turns our feet from sinful ways, [done.
And pardons what our hands have

H. 333 *Submission under Dark Dispensations.*

1 Wait, O my soul, thy Maker's will;
Tumultuous passions, all be still;
Nor let a murmuring thought arise;
His ways are just, His counsels wise.

2 He in the thickest darkness dwells,
Performs His work, the cause conceals;
And though His footsteps are unknown,
Judgment and truth support His throne.

3 In heaven and earth, in air and seas,
He executes His wise decrees;
And by His saints it stands confessed,
That what He does is ever best.

4 Then, O my soul, submissive wait,
With reverence bow before His seat;
And midst the terrors of His rod,
Trust in a wise and gracious God.

H. 134 *The Striving of the Spirit.*

1 Say, sinner, hath a voice within
Oft whispered to thy secret soul;
Urged thee to leave the ways of sin,
And yield thy heart to God's control?

2 Hath something met thee in the path
Of worldliness and vanity,
And pointed to the coming wrath, [flee?
And warned thee from that wrath to

3 Sinner, it was a heavenly voice,
It was the Spirit's gracious call;
It bade thee make the better choice,
And haste to seek in Christ thine all.

4 Spurn not the call to life and light;
Regard in time the warning kind;
That call thou mayst not always slight,
And yet the gate of mercy find.

5 God's Spirit will not always strive
With hardened, self-destroying man;
Ye who persist His love to grieve,
May never hear His voice again.

6 Sinner, perhaps this very day
Thy last accepted time may be;
O! shouldst thou grieve Him now away,
Then hope may never beam on thee.

Wm. B. Bradbury, 1844.

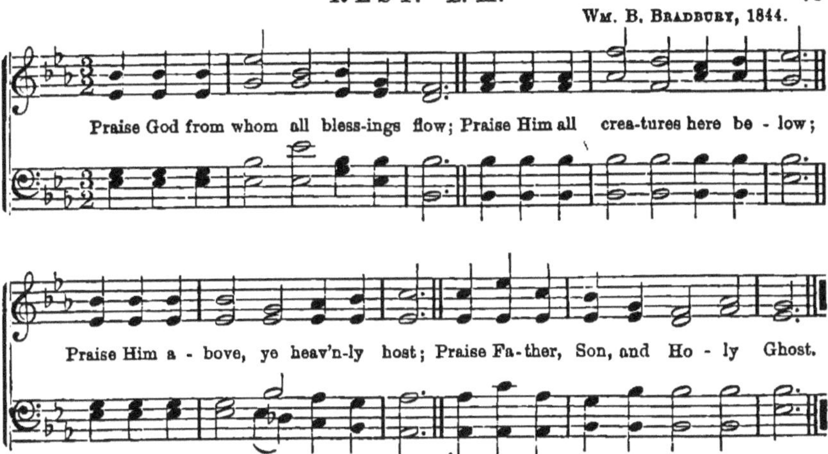
Praise God from whom all bless-ings flow; Praise Him all crea-tures here be - low;
Praise Him a - bove, ye heav'n-ly host; Praise Fa-ther, Son, and Ho - ly Ghost.

H. 650 *Asleep in Jesus.*

1 Asleep in Jesus! blessed sleep!
From which none ever wakes to weep!
A calm and undisturbed repose,
Unbroken by the last of foes!

2 Asleep in Jesus! oh! how sweet
To be for such a slumber meet;
With holy confidence to sing
That death hath lost its venomed sting!

3 Asleep in Jesus! peaceful rest!
Whose waking is supremely blest;
No fear—no woe, shall dim that hour,
That manifests the Saviour's power.

4 Asleep in Jesus! oh! for me
May such a blissful refuge be;
Securely shall my ashes lie,
Waiting the summons from on high.

5 Asleep in Jesus! time nor space
Debars this precious "hiding-place;"
On Indian plains, or Lapland snows,
Believers find the same repose.

6 Asleep in Jesus! far from Thee
Thy kindred and their graves may be;
But there is still a blessed sleep,
From which none ever wakes to weep.

H. 494 *Enjoyment of the Sabbath.*

1 Another six days' work is done,
Another Sabbath is begun;
Return, my soul, enjoy thy rest,
Improve the day thy God hath blessed.

2 O! that our thoughts and thanks may rise
As grateful incense to the skies;
And draw from heaven that sweet repose,
Which none but he that feels it knows.

3 This heavenly calm within the breast
Is the dear pledge of glorious rest,
Which for the Church of God remains,
The end of cares, the end of pains.

4 In holy duties let the day
In holy pleasures pass away;
How sweet a Sabbath thus to spend,
In hope of one that ne'er shall end.

H. 495 *The Eternal Sabbath.*

1 Thine earthly Sabbaths, Lord, we love,
But there's a nobler rest above;
To that our longing souls aspire
With ardent love and strong desire.

2 In Thy blest kingdom we shall be
From every mortal trouble free;
No groans shall mingle with the songs
Which warble from immortal tongues.

3 No rude alarms of raging foes,
No cares to break the long repose,
No midnight shade, no clouded sun,
But sacred, high, eternal noon.

4 O! long expected day, begin;
Dawn on this world of woe and sin:
Fain would we leave this weary road,
And sleep in death, and rest in God.

ROLLAND. L. M.

W. B. Bradbury, 1844.

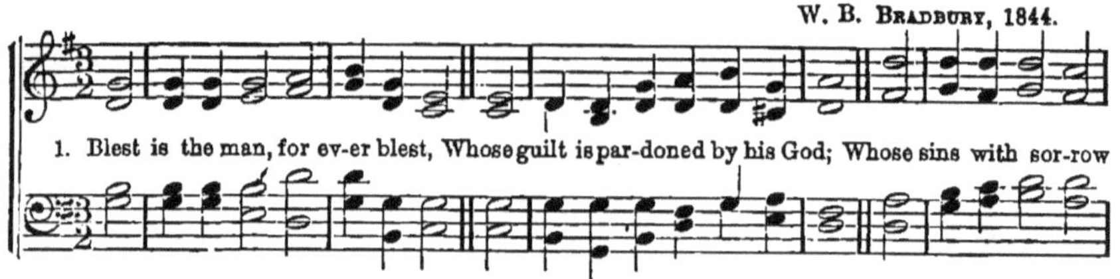
1. Blest is the man, for ev-er blest, Whose guilt is par-doned by his God; Whose sins with sor-row

are con-fessed, And cov-ered with his Sa-viour's blood—And cov-ered with his Sa-viour's blood.

Ps. 32 *Second Part.*

2 Before His judgment seat, the Lord
No more permits his crimes to rise;
He pleads no merit of reward,
And not on works, but grace, relies.

3 From guile his heart and lips are free;
His humble joy, his holy fear,
With deep repentance well agree,
And join to prove his faith sincere.

4 How glorious is that righteousness
That hides and cancels all his sins!
While a bright evidence of grace
Through all his life appears and shines.

H. 212 *Longing for Holiness.*

1 O that my load of sin were gone!
O that I could at last submit!
At Jesus's feet to lay me down—
To lay my soul at Jesus' feet.

2 Rest for my soul I long to find:
Saviour of all, if mine Thou art,
Give me Thy meek, Thy lowly mind,
And stamp Thine image on my heart.

3 Break off the yoke of inbred sin,
And fully set my spirit free;
I cannot rest till pure within,
Till I am wholly lost in Thee.

4 Fain would I learn of Thee, my God;
Thy light and easy burden prove—
The cross all stained with hallowed [blood—
The labour of Thy dying love.

5 I would—but Thou must give the pow'r;
My heart from every sin release;
Bring near, bring near the joyful hour,
And fill me with Thy perfect peace.

6 Come, Lord, the drooping sinner cheer,
Nor let Thy chariot-wheels delay;
Appear, in my poor heart appear;
My God, my Saviour, come away.

H. 351 *Determination.*

1 Awake our souls, away our fears,
Let every trembling thought be gone;
Awake, and run the heavenly race,
And put a cheerful courage on.

2 True, 'tis a strait and thorny road,
And mortal spirits tire and faint;
But they forget the mighty God,
Who feeds the strength of every saint.

3 The mighty God, whose matchless power
Is ever new and ever young,
And firm endures, while endless years
Their everlasting circles run.

4 From Thee, the overflowing spring,
Our souls shall drink a fresh supply;
While such as trust their native strength
Shall melt away, and droop, and die.

5 Swift as an eagle cuts the air,
We'll mount aloft to Thine abode;
On wings of love our souls shall fly,
Nor tire amidst the heavenly road.

FROM THE GERMAN, BY KARL REDEN, 1873.

1. Great God, we sing Thy might - y hand, By which sup - port - ed still we stand;
The open - ing year Thy mer - cy shows; Let mer - cy crown it till it close.

H. 510 *The New Year:*

1 GREAT God, we sing Thy mighty hand,
By which supported still we stand;
The opening year Thy mercy shows;
Let mercy crown it till it close.

2 By day, by night, at home, abroad,
Still we are guarded by our God;
By His incessant bounty fed,
By His unerring counsels led.

3 With grateful hearts the past we own;
The future, all to us unknown,
We to Thy guardian care commit,
And peaceful leave before Thy feet.

4 In scenes exalted or depressed,
Be Thou our joy and Thou our rest;
Thy goodness all our hopes shall raise,
Adored through all our changing days.

5 When death shall interrupt our songs,
And seal in silence mortal tongues,
Our helper, God, in whom we trust,
In better worlds our souls shall boast.

H. 533 *Children Worshipping.*

1 LORD, how delightful 'tis to see
A whole assembly worship Thee;
At once they sing, at once they pray;
They hear of heaven, and learn the way.

2 I have been there, and still would go,
'Tis like a little heaven below;
Not all that earth and sin can say
Shall tempt me to forget this day.

3 O write upon my mem'ry, Lord,
The text and doctrine of Thy word;
That I may break Thy laws no more,
But love Thee better than before.

4 With thoughts of Christ and things divine
Fill up this sinful heart of mine;
That, hoping pardon through His blood,
I may lie down and wake with God.

H. 546 *Christian Dedication.*

1 HERE at Thy cross, incarnate God,
I lay my soul beneath Thy love,
Beneath the droppings of Thy blood;
Jesus, nor shall it e'er remove.

2 Should worlds conspire to drive me thence,
Moveless and firm this heart should lie,
Resolved, for that's my last defence,
If I must perish, there to die.

3 But speak, my Lord, and calm my fear;
Am I not safe beneath Thy shade?
Thy vengeance will not strike me here,
Nor Satan dare my soul invade.

4 Yes, I'm secure beneath Thy blood,
And all my foes shall lose their aim;
Hosanna to my Saviour God,
And my best honours to His name.

Doxology:

To God the Father, God the Son,
And God the Spirit, Three in One,
Be honour, praise, and glory given,
By all on earth, and all in heaven.

FEDERAL STREET. L. M.

H. K. Oliver, 1832.

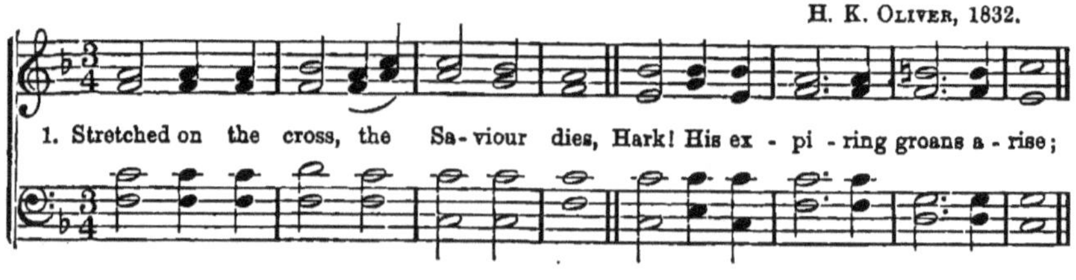
1. Stretched on the cross, the Sa-viour dies, Hark! His ex - pi - ring groans a - rise;

See, how the sa-cred crim - son tide, Flows from His hands, His feet, His side.

H. 85 *Sufferings of the Redeemer.*

1 Stretched on the cross, the Saviour dies,
Hark! His expiring groans arise;
See, how the sacred crimson tide
Flows from His hands, His feet, His side.

2 To suffer in the traitor's place,
To die for man—surprising grace!—
Yet pass rebellious angels by!
Oh! why for man, dear Saviour, why?

3 And didst Thou bleed, for sinners bleed?
And could the sun behold the deed?
No! he withdrew his sickening ray,
And darkness veiled the mourning day.

4 Can I survey this scene of woe,
Where mingling grief and wonder flow,
And yet my heart unmoved remain,
Insensible to love or pain?

5 Come, dearest Lord, Thy grace impart,
To warm this cold, this stupid heart;
Till all its powers and passions move,
In melting grief, and ardent love.

H. 581 *Prayer for Reviving Influences of the Spirit.*

1 Come, sacred Spirit, from above,
And fill the coldest heart with love;
Soften to flesh the flinty stone,
And let Thy God like power be known.

2 Speak Thou, and from the haughtiest eyes
Shall floods of pious sorrow rise;
While all their glowing souls are borne,
To seek that grace which now they scorn.

3 Oh! let a holy flock await,
Numerous, around Thy temple gate;
Each pressing on, with zeal, to be
A living sacrifice to Thee.

4 In answer to our fervent cries,
Give us to see Thy church arise;
Or, if that blessing seem too great,
Give us to mourn its low estate.

H. 628 *Fears of Death Removed.*

1 Why should we start and fear to die?
What timorous worms we mortals are!
Death is the gate of endless joy,
And yet we dread to enter there.

2 The pains, the groans, and dying strife,
Fright our approaching souls away;
Still we shrink back again to life,
Fond of our prison and our clay.

3 Oh! if my Lord would come and meet,
My soul would stretch her wings in haste,
Fly fearless through death's iron gate,
Nor feel the terrors as she passed.

4 Jesus can make a dying bed
Feel soft as downy pillows are,
While on His breast I lean my head,
And breathe my life out sweetly there.

Doxology.

To God the Father, God the Son,
And God the Spirit, Three in One,
Be honour, praise, and glory given,
By all on earth, and all in heaven.

WARD. L. M.

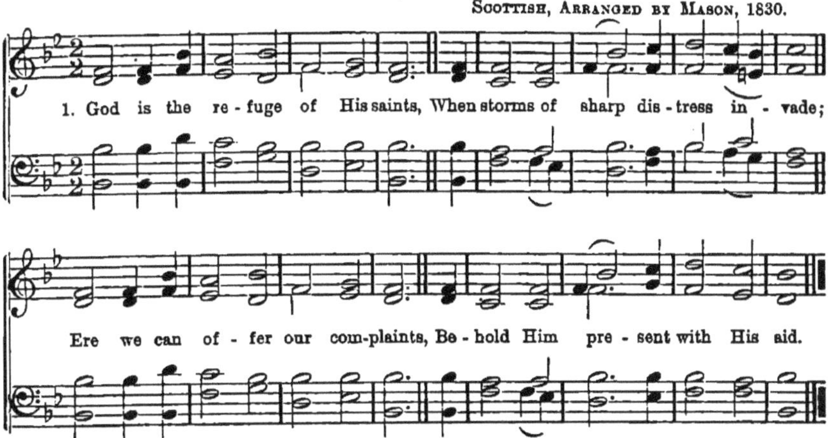
Scottish, Arranged by Mason, 1830.
1. God is the re - fuge of His saints, When storms of sharp dis - tress in - vade;
Ere we can of - fer our com-plaints, Be - hold Him pre - sent with His aid.

Ps. 46 *Second Part.*

2 Let mountains from their seats be hurled
Down to the deep, and buried there;
Convulsions shake the solid world,
Our faith shall never yield to fear.

3 Loud may the troubled ocean roar,
In sacred peace our souls abide,
While every nation, every shore,
Trembles, and dreads the swelling tide.

4 There is a stream, whose gentle flow
Supplies the city of our God!
Life, love, and joy still gliding through,
And watering our divine abode.

5 That sacred stream, Thine holy word,
Supports our faith, our fear controls;
Sweet peace Thy promises afford, [souls.
And gives new strength to fainting

6 Zion enjoys her Monarch's love,
Secure against a threatening hour;
Nor can her firm foundation move, [power.
Built on His truth, and armed with

H. 407 *Trials of the Christian.*

1 Thus far my God has led me on,
And made His truth and mercy known,
My hopes and fears alternate rise,
And comforts mingle with my sighs.

2 Through this wide wilderness I roam,
Far distant from my blissful home;
Lord, let Thy presence be my stay,
And guard me in this dangerous way.

3 Temptations everywhere annoy,
And sins and snares my peace destroy;
My earthly joys are from me torn,
And oft an absent God I mourn.

4 My soul with various tempests tossed,
Her hopes o'erturn'd, her projects cross'd,
Sees every day new straits attend,
And wonders where the scene will end.

5 Is this, dear Lord, that thorny road,
Which leads us to the mount of God?
Are these the toils Thy people know,
While in this wilderness below?

6 'Tis even so; Thy faithful love
Does all Thy children's graces prove;
'Tis thus our pride and self must fall,
That Jesus may be all in all.

H. 512 *The Seasons.*

1 Eternal Source of every joy,
Well may Thy praise our lips employ,
While in Thy temple we appear,
To hail Thee, Sovereign of the year.

2 Seasons, and months, and weeks and days,
Demand successive songs of praise;
And be the grateful homage paid,
With morning light and evening shade.

3 Here in Thy house let incense rise,
And circling Sabbaths bless our eyes,
Till to those lofty heights we soar,
Where days and years revolve no more,

JOHN HATTON, 1790.

1. Je-sus, the spring of joys di - vine, Whence all our hopes and com - forts flow;
Je - sus, no oth - er name but Thine Can save us from e - ter - nal woe.

H. 49 *Jesus the only Saviour.*

2 In vain would boasting reason find
The way to happiness and God;
Her weak directions leave the mind
Bewildered in a dubious road.

3 No other name will heaven approve;
Thou art the true, the living way,
Ordained by everlasting love,
To the bright realms of endless day.

4 Safe lead us through this world of night,
And bring us to the blissful plains,
The regions of unclouded light,
Where perfect joy for ever reigns.

Ps. 72 *Second Part.*

1 Jesus shall reign where'er the sun
Does his successive journeys run;
His kingdom stretch from shore to shore,
Till moons shall wax and wane no more.

2 For Him shall endless prayer be made,
And endless praises crown His head;
His name, like sweet perfume, shall rise
With every morning sacrifice.

3 People and realms of every tongue
Dwell on His love with sweetest song;
And infant voices shall proclaim
Their early blessings on His name.

4 Blessings abound where'er He reigns,
The joyful prisoner bursts his chains,
The weary find eternal rest,
And all the sons of want are blest.

5 Let every creature rise and bring
Peculiar honours to our King;
Angels descend with songs again,
And earth repeat the loud amen.

H. 503 *National Thanksgiving.*

1 God of the passing year, to Thee
Our hymn of gratitude we raise;
With swelling heart and bending knee,
We offer Thee our song of praise.

2 We bless Thy name, almighty God,
For all the kindness Thou hast shown
To this fair land our fathers trod,
This land we fondly call our own.

3 Here freedom spreads her banner wide,
And casts her soft and hallowed ray;
For Thou our country's arms didst guide,
And lead them on their conquering way.

4 We praise Thee, that the gospel light
Through all our land its radiance sheds;
Scatters the shades of error's night,
And heavenly blessings round us spreads.

5 When foes without, and foes within,
With threatening ills our land have pressed,
Thou hast our nation's bulwark been,
And, smiling, sent us peaceful rest.

6 O God, preserve us in Thy fear,
In troublous times our helper be;
Diffuse Thy truth's bright precepts here,
And may we worship only Thee.

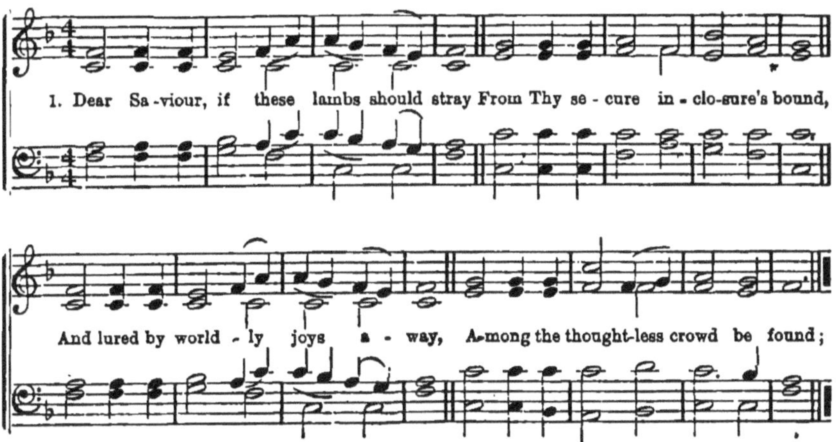
1. Dear Sa-viour, if these lambs should stray From Thy se-cure in-clo-sure's bound,
And lured by world-ly joys a-way, A-mong the thought-less crowd be found;

H. 524 *Prayer for the Children of the Church.*

2 Remember still that they are Thine,
That Thy dear sacred name they bear;
Think that the seal of love divine,
The sign of covenant grace, they wear.

3 In all their erring, sinful years,
Oh! let them ne'er forgotten be;
Remember all the prayers and tears
Which made them consecrate to Thee.

4 And when these lips no more can pray,
These eyes can weep for them no more,
Turn Thou their feet from folly's way,
The wanderers to Thy fold restore.

Ps. 114

1 When Israel, freed from Pharoah's hand,
Left the proud tyrant and his land,
The tribes with cheerful homage own
Their King, and Judah was His throne.

2 Across the deep their journey lay;
The deep divides to make them way;
Jordan beheld their march, and fled
With backward current to his head.

3 Let every mountain, every flood,
Retire and know th' approaching God,
The King of Israel; see Him here;
Tremble, Thou earth; adore and fear.

4 He thunders, and all nature mourns;
The rock to standing pools He turns;
Flint spring with fountains at His word,
And fires and seas confess the Lord.

Ps. 58

1 Judges, who rule the world by laws,
Will ye despise the righteous cause?
Dare ye condemn the righteous poor,
And let the rich escape secure?

2 Have ye forgot, or never knew,
That God will judge the judges too?
That ye invade the rights of God,
And send your bold decrees abroad.

3 Yet shall the vengeance of the Lord
Safety and joy to saints afford:
"Sure, there's a God that rules on high,
A God that hears His children cry."

Ps. 75

1 To Thee, most high and holy God,
To Thee our thankful hearts we raise;
Thy works declare Thy name abroad,
Thy wondrous works demand our praise.

2 To bondage doomed, Thy chosen sons
Beheld their foes triumphant rise;
And sore oppressed by earthly thrones,
They sought the Sovereign of the skies.

3 'Twas then, great God, with equal power,
Arose Thy vengeance and Thy grace,
To scourge their legions from the shore,
And save the remnant of Thy race.

4 Let haughty sinners sink their pride,
Nor lift so high their scornful head;
But lay their impious thoughts aside,
And own the empire God hath made.

OBERLIN. L. M.

FROM BOST, BY DR. HASTINGS, 1835.

1. While life pro - longs its pre - cious light, Mer-cy is found, and peace is giv'n;
But soon, ah soon! ap-proach-ing night Shall blot out ev'- ry hope of heav'n.

Ps. 88 *Second Part.*

2 While God invites, how blest the day!
How sweet the gospel's charming sound!
"Come, sinners, haste, O! haste away,
While yet a pardoning God He's found.

3 "Soon, borne on time's most rapid wing,
Shall death command you to the grave,
Before His bar your sprits bring,
And none be found to hear, or save.

4 "In that lone land of deep despair,
No Sabbath's heavenly light shall rise;
No God regard your bitter prayer,
Nor Saviour call you to the skies."

5 Silence, and solitude, and gloom,
In those forgetful realms appear,
Deep sorrows fill the dismal tomb,
And hope shall never enter there.

Ps. 121 *First Part.*

1 Up to the hills I lift mine eyes,
Th' eternal hills beyond the skies;
Thence all her help my soul derives;
There my almighty Refuge lives.

2 He lives! the everlasting God, [flood;
That built the world, that spread the
The heavens, with all their hosts He made,
And the dark regions of the dead.

3 He guides our feet, He guards our way;
His morning smiles adorn the day;
He spreads the evening veil, and keeps
The silent hours while Israel sleeps.

4 Israel, a name divinely blest,
May rise secure, securely rest;
Thy holy Guardian's wakeful eyes
Admit no slumber nor surprise.

5 Should earth and hell with malice burn,
Still thou shalt go, and still return,
Safe in the Lord; His heavenly care
Defends thy life from every snare.

H. 566 *Dedication Hymn.*

1 Lord! Thou hast said where two or three
Together come to worship Thee,
Thy presence, fraught with richest grace,
Shall ever fill and bless the place.

2 Then let us feel, as here we raise
A temple to Thy matchless praise,
The blest assurance of Thy love,
As it is felt in realms above.

3 Lord! here upon Thy sacred day,
Teach us devoutly how to pray,
Our weakness let Thy strength supply,
Nor to our darkness light deny.

4 Here teach our faltering tongues to sing
The glories of the Heavenly King,
And let our aspirations rise
To seek the Saviour in the skies.

5 And when at last, in life's decline,
This earthly temple we resign,
May we, O Lord! enjoy with Thee
The Sabbaths of eternity!

Mason, 1840.

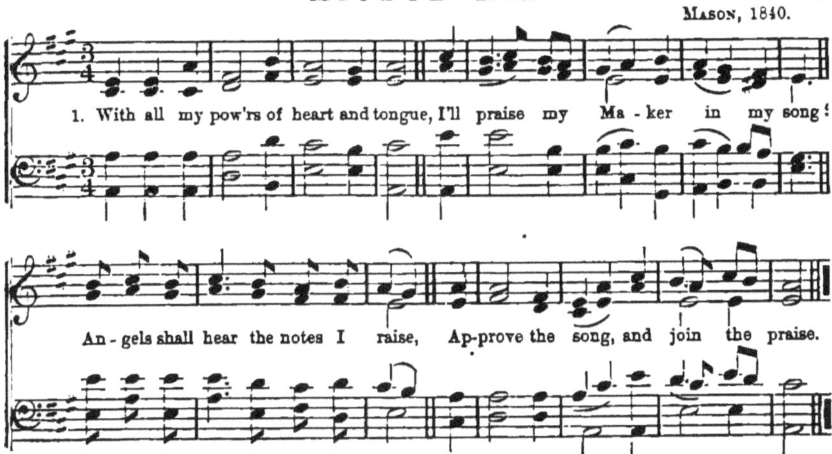
1. With all my pow'rs of heart and tongue, I'll praise my Ma - ker in my song!
An - gels shall hear the notes I raise, Ap-prove the song, and join the praise.

Ps. 138

2 Ill' sing Thy truth and mercy, Lord;
I'll sing the wonders of Thy word;
Not all the works and names below
So much Thy power and glory show.

3 To God I cried when troubles rose;
He heard me, and subdued my foes;
He did my rising fears control,
And strength diffused through all my soul.

4 The God of heaven maintains His state,
Frowns on the proud and scorns the great;
But from His throne descends to bless
The humble souls that trust His grace.

5 Amidst a thousand snares I stand,
Upheld and guarded by Thy hand;
Thy words my fainting soul revive,
And keep my dying faith alive.

6 Grace will complete what grace begins,
To save from sorrows and from sins;
The work that wisdom undertakes,
Eternal mercy ne'er forsakes.

Ps. 139 *First Part.*

1 Lord, Thou hast searched and seen me [through;
Thine eye commands with piercing view
My rising and my resting hours,
My heart and flesh, with all their powers.

2 My thoughts, before they are my own,
Are to my God distinctly known;
He knows the words I mean to speak,
Ere from my opening lips they break.

3 Within Thy circling power I stand,
On every side I find Thy hand;
Awake, asleep, at home, abroad,
I am surrounded still with God.

4 Amazing knowledge, vast and great!
What large extent! what lofty height!
My soul, with all the powers I boast,
Is in the boundless prospect lost.

5 O! may these thoughts possess my breast,
Where'er I rove, where'er I rest;
Nor let my weaker passions dare
Consent to sin, for God is there.

H. 506 *Prayer for Country.*

1 On Thee, O Lord, our God, we call;
Before Thy throne devoutly fall;
Oh! whither should the helpless fly?
To whom but Thee direct their cry?

2 Lord, we repent, we weep, we mourn,
To our forsaken God we turn;
Oh! spare our guilty country, spare
The Church Thine hand hath planted here!

3 We plead Thy grace, indulgent God!
We plead Thy Son's atoning blood;
We plead Thy gracious promises,
And are they unavailing pleas?

4 These pleas, presented at Thy throne,
Have brought ten thousand blessings [down
On guilty lands in helpless woe;
Let them prevail to save us, too.

QUITO. L. M.

Sir Wm. Horsley, 1774–1858.

1. Up to the fields where an-gels lie, And liv - ing wa-ters gent - ly roll, Fain would my
thoughts leap out and fly, But sin hangs hea-vy on my soul—But sin hangs hea - vy on my soul.

H. 345 *A sight of God Mortifies us to the World.*

2 Thy wondrous blood, dear dying Christ,
Can make this world of guilt remove;
And Thou canst bear me where Thou fliest,
On Thy kind wings, celestial Dove!

3 Oh! might I once mount up and see
The glory of the eternal skies,
What little things these worlds would be,
How despicable to my eyes!

4 Had I a glance of Thee, my God,
Kingdoms and men would vanish soon;
Vanish, as though I saw them not,
As a dim candle dies at noon.

5 Then they might fight, and rage and rave,
I should perceive the noise no more
Than we can hear a shaking leaf,
Whilst rattling thunders round us roar.

6 Great All in All, Eternal King,
Let me but view Thy lovely face,
And all my powers shall bow and sing
Thine endless grandeur and Thy grace.

H. 356 *Not Ashamed of Christ.*

1 Jesus, and shall it ever be,
A mortal man ashamed of Thee?
Ashamed of Thee, whom angels praise,
Whose glories shine thro' endless days!

2 Ashamed of Jesus! sooner far
Let evening blush to own a star;
He sheds the beams of light divine,
O'er this benighted soul of mine.

3 Ashamed of Jesus! just as soon
Let midnight be ashamed of noon;
'Tis midnight with my soul, till He,
Bright Morning Star, bid darkness flee.

4 Ashamed of Jesus! that dear Friend
On whom my hopes of heaven depend!
No, when I blush, be this my shame,
That I no more revere His name.

5 Ashamed of Jesus! Yes, I may,
When I've no guilt to wash away,
No tear to wipe, no good to crave,
No fears to quell, no soul to save.

6 Till then—nor is my boasting vain—
Till then, I boast a Saviour slain;
And oh! may this my glory be,
That Christ is not ashamed of me.

H. 366 *Prayer for Quickening Grace.*

1 O Sun of Righteousness divine,
On us with beams of mercy shine;
Chase the dark clouds of guilt away,
And turn our darkness into day.

2 While mourning o'er our guilt and shame,
And asking mercy in Thy name,
Dear Saviour, cleanse us with Thy blood,
And be our advocate with God.

3 Sustain, when sinking in distress,
And guide us through this wilderness;
Teach our low thoughts from earth to rise,
And lead us onward to the skies.

I. B. Woodbury.

1. Come in, thou bless-ed of the Lord, En - ter in Je - sus pre-cious name;
We wel-come thee with one ac - cord, And trust the Sa-viour does the same.

H. 363 *Welcome to the Church.*

2 Those joys which earth cannot afford,
We'll seek in fellowship to prove,
Joined in one spirit to our Lord,
Together bound by mutual love.

3 And while we pass this vale of tears,
We'll make our joys and sorrows known;
We'll share each other's hopes and fears,
And count a brother's cares our own.

4 Once more our welcome we repeat;
Receive assurance of our love;
Oh! may we all together meet
Around the throne of God above!

H. 369 *Hindrances to Prayer.*

1 What various hindrances we meet
In coming to a mercy-seat!
Yet who that knows the worth of prayer
But wishes to be often there?

2 Prayer makes the darkened cloud with-[draw,
Prayer climbs the ladder Jacob saw,
Gives exercise to faith and love,
Brings every blessing from above.

3 Restraining prayer, we cease to fight;
Prayer makes the Christian's armour [bright,
And Satan trembles when he sees
The weakest saint upon his knees.

4 Have you no words? Ah! think again.
Words flow apace when you complain,
And fill your fellow-creature's ear
With the sad tale of all your care.

5 Were half the breath thus vainly spent
To heaven in supplication sent,
Your cheerful song would oftener be,
"Hear what the Lord has done for me."

H. 373 *God Answers Prayer.*

1 Friend of the friendless and the faint,
Where shall I lodge my deep complaint?
Where, but with Thee, whose open door
Invites the helpless and the poor.

2 Did ever mourner plead with Thee,
And Thou refuse that mourner's plea?
Does not the word still fixed remain,
That none shall seek Thy face in vain?

3 That were a grief I could not bear,
Didst Thou not hear and answer prayer;
Thou, prayer-hearing, answering God,
Take from my heart this painful load.

H. 449 *Morning and Evening Hymn.*

1 My God, how endless is Thy love!
Thy gifts are every evening new;
And morning mercies from above,
Gently distil like early dew.

2 Thou spreadest the curtain of the night,
Great Guardian of my sleeping hours;
Thy sov'reign word restores the light,
And quickens all my drowsy powers,

3 I yield my powers to Thy command,
To Thee I consecrate my days;
Perpetual blessings from Thy hand
Demand perpetual songs of praise.

ERFURT. L. M.

Martin Luther, 1535.

1. There is one God, and on - ly one; No ri - vals can His es-sence share;
He is Je - ho - vah, He a - lone; And with the Lord none can com - pare.

H. 33 *The Trinity.*

1 There is one God, and only one,
No rivals can His essence share;
He is Jehovah, He alone,
And with the Lord none can compare.

2 Angels and men may strive to raise,
Harmonious, their adoring songs;
But who can fully speak His praise,
From human or angelic tongues!

3 Yet would I lift my trembling voice,
The eternal Three in One to sing;
And mingling faith, while I rejoice,
My humble, grateful tribute bring.

4 All glory to the eternal Three,
The sacred, undivided One:
To Father, Son, and Spirit be
Co-equal praise and honours done.

H. 372 *Constancy in Prayer.*

1 Prayer was appointed to convey
The blessings God designs to give,
Long as they live should Christians pray,
For only while they pray they live.

2 The Christian's heart his prayer indites,
He speaks as prompted from within;
The Spirit his petition writes,
And Christ receives and gives it in.

3 If pains afflict, or wrongs oppress,
If cares distract, or fears dismay;
If guilt deject, if sin distress,
The remedy's before thee—pray.

4 'Tis prayer supports the soul that's weak,
Though thought be broken, language lame;
Pray, if thou canst, or canst not speak,
But pray with faith in Jesus' name.

H. 585 *Prayer for Revival.*

1 Great Lord of all Thy churches, hear
Thy ministers' and people's prayer;
Perfumed by Thee, O may it rise,
Like fragrant incense to the skies.

2 May every pastor, from above
Be new inspired with zeal and love,
To watch Thy flock, Thy flock to feed,
And sow with care the precious seed.

3 Revive the churches with Thy grace,
Heal all our breaches, grant us peace;
Rouse us from sloth, our hearts inflame
With ardent zeal for Jesus' name.

4 May young and old Thy word receive,
Dead sinners hear Thy voice and live,
The wounded conscience healing find,
And joy refresh each drooping mind.

5 May aged saints, matured with grace,
Abound in fruits of holiness;
And when transplanted to the skies,
May younger in their stead arise.

6 Thus we our suppliant voices raise,
And weeping sow the seed of praise,
In humble hope that Thou wilt hear
Thy ministers' and people's prayer.

Mason.

To God the Fa-ther, God the Son, And God the Spi-rit, Three in One,

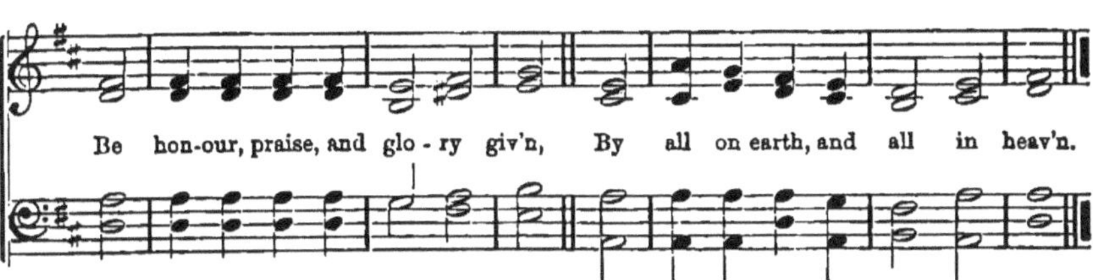
Be hon-our, praise, and glo-ry giv'n, By all on earth, and all in heav'n.

H. 181 *Come and See.*

1 Jesus, dear name, how sweet the sound!
Replete with balm for every wound!
His word declares His grace is free;
Come, needy sinner, come and see.

2 He left the shining courts on high,
Came to our world to bleed and die;
Jesus, the God, hung on the tree;
Come, careless sinner, come and see.

3 Our sins have pierced His bleeding heart;
Lo! death has done its dreadful part;
Yet His dear love still burns to thee;
Come, anxious sinner, come and see.

4 His blood can cleanse the foulest stain,
And make the filthy leper clean;
His blood at once availed for me;
Come, guilty sinner, come and see.

H. 239 *Security of the Believer.*

1 How oft have sin and Satan strove
To rend my soul from Thee, my God!
But everlasting is Thy love,
And Jesus seals it with His blood.

2 The oath and promise of the Lord
Join to confirm His wondrous grace;
Eternal power performs the word,
And fills all heaven with endless praise.

3 Amidst temptations sharp and long,
My soul to this dear refuge flies;
Hope is my anchor, firm and strong,
While tempests blow and billows rise.

4 The gospel bears my spirits up;
A faithful and unchanging God
Lays the foundation for my hope,
In oaths, and promises, and blood.

H. 302 *Brotherly Love.*

1 Now by the mercies of my God,
His sharp distress, His sore complaints,
By His last groans, His dying blood,
I charge my soul to love the saints.

2 Clamour, and wrath, and war begone;
Envy and spite for ever cease;
Let bitter words no more be known
Amongst the saints, the sons of peace.

3 The Spirit, like a peaceful dove, [strife;
Flies from the realms of noise and
Why should we vex and grieve His love,
Who seals our souls to heavenly life.

4 Tender and kind be all our thoughts,
Through all our lives let mercy run;
So God forgives our numerous faults,
For the dear sake of Christ His Son.

H. 519 *Importance of Early Religion.*

1 Now, in the heat of youthful blood,
Remember your Creator, God;
Behold, the months come hastening on,
When you shall say, "My joys are gone."

2 Eternal King, I fear Thy name;
Teach me to know how frail I am;
And when my soul must hence remove,
Give me a mansion in Thy love.

Mozart.
1. 'Tis fin-ished! so the Sa-viour cried, And meek-ly bowed His head and died;
'Tis fin-ished! yes, the race is run, The bat-tle fought, the vict'-ry won.

H. 80 *The Work Finished.*

1 'Tis finished! all that heaven decreed,
And all the ancient prophets said,
Is now fulfilled, as was designed,
In Me, the Saviour of mankind.

2 'Tis finished! heaven is reconciled,
And all the powers of darkness spoiled;
Peace, love, and happiness again
Return and dwell with sinful men,

3 'Tis finished! let the joyful sound
Be heard through all the nations round;
'Tis finished! let the echo fly [sky.
Thro' heaven and hell, thro' earth and

H. 106 *Christ Crucified, the Wisdom and Power of God.*

1 Nature with open volume stands,
To spread her Maker's praise abroad;
And every labour of His hands
Shows something worthy of a God.

2 But in the grace that rescued man
His brightest form of glory shines;
Here, on the cross, 'tis fairest drawn,
In precious blood and crimson lines.

3 O! the sweet wonders of that cross,
Where God the Saviour loved and died;
Her noblest life my spirit draws [side.
From His dear wounds and bleeding

4 I would for ever speak His name,
In sounds to mortal ears unknown;
With angels join to praise the Lamb,
And worship at His Father's throne.

Ps. 118 *Second Part.*

1 Lo! what a glorious corner-stone
The Jewish builders did refuse!
But God hath built His church thereon,
In spite of envy and the Jews.

2 Great God, the work is all divine,
The joy and wonder of our eyes;
This is the day that proves it Thine,
The day that saw our Saviour rise.

3 Sinners, rejoice, and saints, be glad;
Hosanna, let His name be blest;
A thousand honours on His head,
With peace, and light, and glory rest!

4 In God's own name He comes to bring
Salvation to our dying race;
Let the whole church address their King,
With hearts of joy, and songs of praise.

H. 140 *Invocation of the Spirit.*

1 Come, Holy Spirit, calm my mind,
And fit me to approach my God;
Remove each vain, each worldly thought,
And lead me to Thy blest abode.

2 Hast Thou imparted to my soul
A living spark of holy fire?
O! kindle now the sacred flame,
Make me to burn with pure desire.

3 A brighter hope and faith impart,
And let me now my Saviour see;
O! soothe and cheer my burdened heart,
And bid my Spirit rest in Thee.

ARRANGED BY J. P. HOLBROOK.

1. With tear-ful eyes I look a-round, Life seems a dark and storm-y sea; Yet, 'mid the gloom, I
hear a sound, A heav'n-ly whis-per, "Come to Me"—A heav'n-ly whis-per, "Come to Me."

H. 193 *Come to Jesus.*

2 It tells me of a place of rest,
It tells me where my soul may flee;
Oh! to the weary, faint, oppressed,
How sweet the bidding, "Come to me."

3 Oh! voice of mercy! voice of love!
In conflict, grief, and agony,
Support me, cheer me from above!
And gently whisper, "Come to me,"

4 I come; all else must fail and die;
Earth has no resting-place for me;
To Christ I lift my weeping eye:
Thou art my hope; I come to Thee.

H. 176 *Invitation to Wanderers.*

1 Return, O wanderer, return,
And seek an injured Father's face;
Those warm desires that in thee burn
Were kindled by reclaiming grace.

2 Return, O wanderer, return,
And seek a Father's melting heart;
His pitying eyes thy grief discern,
His hand shall heal thine inward smart.

3 Return, O wanderer, return,
Thy Saviour bids thy spirit live;
Go to His bleeding feet, and learn
How freely Jesus can forgive.

4 Return, O wanderer, return,
And wipe away the falling tear;
'Tis God who says, "No longer mourn,"
'Tis mercy's voice invites thee near.

H. 186 *Sinners urged to Religion.*

1 Why will ye waste on trifling cares,
That life which God's compassion spares;
While in the various range of thought,
The one thing needful is forgot?

2 Shall God invite you from above?
Shall Jesus urge His dying love?
Shall troubled conscience give you pain?
And all these pleas be urged in vain?

3 Not so your eyes will always view
Those objects which you now pursue;
Not so will heaven and hell appear,
When death's decisive hour is near.

4 Almighty God, Thy grace impart;
Fix deep conviction on each heart;
Nor let us waste, on trifling cares,
That life which Thy compassion spares.

H. 476 *Before Sermon.*

1 Thy presence, gracious God, afford;
Prepare us to receive Thy word;
Now let Thy voice engage our ear,
And faith be mixed with what we hear.

2 Distracting thoughts and cares remove,
And fix our hearts and hopes above;
With food divine may we be fed,
And satisfied with living bread.

3 To us Thy sacred word apply,
With sovereign power and energy;
And may we in true faith and fear
Reduce to practice what we hear.

From the German, by Dr. L. Mason, 1840.

1. Thy peo-ple, Lord, who trust Thy word, And wait the smil-ings of Thy face, As-sem-ble

round Thy mer-cy seat, And plead the pro-mise of Thy grace—And plead the pro-mise of Thy grace.

H. 604 *Prayer for the Success of Missions.*

2 We consecrate these hours to Thee,
Thy sovereign mercy to entreat;
And feel some animating hope,
We shall divine acceptance meet.

3 Hast Thou not sworn to give Thy Son
To be a light to Gentile lands;
To open the benighted eye, [bands?
And loose the wretched prisoner's

4 Hast Thou not said, from sea to sea
His vast dominions shall extend;
That every tongue shall call Him Lord,
And every knee before Him bend?

5 Now let the happy time appear,
The time to favour Zion come;
Send forth Thy heralds far and near,
To call Thy banished children home.

H. 620 *Life the Time to Serve God.*

1 There is a God who reigns above,
Lord of the heaven and earth and seas;
I fear His wrath, I ask His love,
And with my lips I sing His praise.

2 There is a law which He has made,
To teach us all that we must do;
My soul, be His commands obeyed,
For they are holy, just and true,

3 There is a gospel rich in grace, [draw;
Whence sinners all their comforts
Lord, I repent and seek Thy face,
For I have often broke Thy law.

4 There is an hour when I must die;
Nor do I know how soon 'twill come;
How many younger much than I, [doom!
Have passed by death to hear their

5 Let me improve the hours I have,
Before the day of grace is fled;
There's no repentance in the grave,
Nor pardon offered to the dead.

H. 667 *Nearness to Eternity.*

1 Eternity is just at hand;
And shall I waste my ebbing sand,
And careless view departing day,
And throw my inch of time away?

2 Eternity without a bound,
To guilty souls a dreadful sound!
But oh! if Christ and heaven be mine,
How sweet the accents! how divine!

3 Be this my chief, my only care,
My high pursuit, my ardent prayer,
An interest in the Saviour's blood,
My pardon sealed, and peace with God.

4 But should my highest hopes be vain,
The rising doubt, how sharp the pain!
My fears, O gracious God, remove;
Confirm my title to Thy love.

5 Search, Lord, O search my inmost heart,
And light, and hope, and joy impart;
From guilt and error set me free,
And guide me safe to heaven and Thee.

SOUTHERN MELODY.
1. Show pi - ty, Lord; O Lord, for - give; Let a re - pent - ing re - bel live;
Are not Thy mer - cies large and free? May not a sin - ner trust in Thee?

Ps. 51 *First Part.*

1 Show pity, Lord; O Lord, forgive;
Let a repenting rebel live;
Are not Thy mercies large and free?
May not a sinner trust in Thee?

2 My crimes are great, but don't surpass
The power and glory of Thy grace;
Great God, Thy nature hath no bound,
So let Thy pardoning love be found.

3 O! wash my soul from every sin,
And make my guilty conscience clean;
Here on my heart the burden lies,
And past offences pain mine eyes.

4 My lips with shame my sins confess,
Against Thy law, against Thy grace;
Lord, should Thy judgments grow severe,
I am condemned, but Thou art clear.

5 Should sudden vengeance seize my breath
I must pronounce Thee just in death;
And if my soul were sent to hell,
Thy righteous law approves it well.

6 Yet save a trembling sinner, Lord, [word,
Whose hope, still hovering round Thy
Would light on some sweet promise there,
Some sure support against despair.

H. 188 *Danger of Delay.*

1 Hasten, O sinner, to be wise,
And stay not for to-morrow's sun;
The longer wisdom you despise,
The harder is she to be won.

2 O! hasten mercy to implore,
And stay not for to-morrow's sun;
For fear thy season should be o'er,
Before this evening's course be run.

3 Hasten, O sinner, to return,
And stay not for to-morrow's sun;
For fear thy lamp should fail to burn,
Before the needful work is done.

4 Hasten, O sinner, to be blest,
And stay not for to-morrow's sun;
For fear the curse should thee arrest,
Before the morrow is begun.

H. 588 *Prayer for the Jews.*

1 Disowned of Heaven, by man oppressed,
Outcast from Zion's hallowed ground,
O! why should Israel's sons, once bless'd,
Still roam the scorning world around?

2 Lord, visit Thy forsaken race,
Back to Thy fold the wanderers bring;
Teach them to seek Thy slighted grace,
And hail in Christ their promised King.

3 The veil of darkness rend in twain, [light;
Which hides their Shiloh's glorious
The severed olive branch again
Firm to its parent stock unite.

4 Hail, glorious day, expected long, [pour,
When Jew and Greek one prayer shall
With eager feet one temple throng,
With grateful praise one God adore.

AMES. L. M.

Dr. Mason.

1. My dear Re-deem-er and my Lord, I read my du - ty in Thy word;

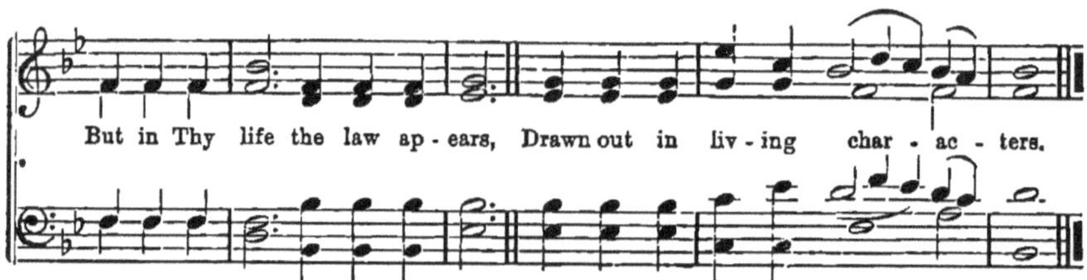
But in Thy life the law ap - ears, Drawn out in liv - ing char - ac - ters.

H. 77 *Christ our Pattern.*

2 Such was Thy truth, and such Thy zeal,
Such deference to Thy Father's will,
Such love, and meekness so divine,
I would transcribe and make them mine.

3 Cold mountains and the midnight air
Witnessed the fervour of Thy prayer;
The desert Thy temptations knew,
Thy conflict and Thy victory too.

4 Be Thou my pattern; make me bear
More of Thy gracious image here;
Then God the Judge shall own my name,
Among the followers of the Lamb.

H. 108 *Lamb of God to be Worshipped.*

1 What equal honours shall we bring
To Thee, O Lord our God, the Lamb,
When all the notes that angels sing
Are far inferior to Thy name!

2 Worthy is He that once was slain, [died,
The Prince of Peace, that groaned and
Worthy to rise, and live, and reign,
At His almighty Father's side.

3 Blessings for ever on the Lamb,
Who bore the curse for wretched men;
Let angels sound His sacred name,
And every creature say Amen.

H. 568 *On Opening a House of Worship.*

1 Here, in Thy name, eternal God,
We build this earthly house for Thee;
O! make it now Thy fixed abode,
And guard it long from error free.

2 Here, when Thy people seek Thy face,
And dying sinners pray to live, [place,
Hear Thou in heaven, Thy dwelling-
And when Thou hearest, Lord, forgive.

3 Here, when Thy messengers proclaim
The blessed gospel of Thy Son,
Still by the power of His great name,
Be mighty signs and wonders done.

4 When children's voices raise the song,
Hosanna to their heavenly King,
Let heaven, with earth, the strain prolong,
Hosanna let the angels sing.

5 But will, indeed, Jehovah deign
Here to abide, no transient guest?
Here will our great Redeemer reign,
And here the Holy Spirit rest?

6 Thy glory never hence depart;
Yet choose not, Lord, this house alone;
Thy kingdom come in every heart,
In every bosom fix Thy throne.

H. 582 *Prayer for Revival.*

1 O Sun of Righteousness, arise,
With gentle beams on Zion shine;
Dispel the darkness from our eyes,
And souls awake to life divine.

2 On all around let grace descend,
Like heavenly dew, or copious showers,
That we may call our God our friend,
That we may hail salvation ours.

George Oates.

1. O Lord, how ma-ny are my foes, In this weak state of flesh and blood!
My peace they dai-ly dis-com-pose; But my de-fence and hope is God.

Ps. 3

2 Tired with the burden of the day,
To Thee I raised an evening cry;
Thou heardst when I began to pray,
And Thine almighty help was nigh.

3 Supported by Thine heavenly aid,
I laid me down and slept secure:
Not death should make my heart afraid,
Though I should wake and rise no more.

4 But God sustained me all the night;
Salvation doth to God belong:
He raised my head to see the light, [song.
And makes His praise my morning

H. 155 *The Gospel is the power of God to Salvation.*

1 What shall the dying sinner do,
That seeks relief for all his woe?
Where shall the guilty conscience find
Ease for the torment of the mind?

2 How shall we get our crimes forgiven,
Or form our nature fit for heaven?
Can souls, all o'er defiled with sin, [clean?
Make their own powers and passions

3 In vain we search, in vain we try,
Till Jesus brings His gospel nigh;
'Tis there the power and glory dwell,
That save rebellious souls from hell.

4 This is the pillar of our hope,
That bears our fainting spirits up;
We read the grace, we trust the word,
And find salvation in the Lord.

H. 170 *Invitation to the Heavy Laden.*

1 Come hither, all ye weary souls,
Ye heavy-laden sinners, come;
I'll give you rest from all your toils,
And raise you to my heavenly home.

2 They shall find rest that learn of Me;
I'm of a meek and lowly mind;
But passion rages like a sea,
And pride is restless as the wind.

3 Blest is the man whose shoulders take
My yoke, and bear it with delight;
My yoke is easy to his neck,
My grace shall make the burden light.

4 Jesus, we come at Thy command,
With faith, and hope, and humble zeal;
Resign our spirits to Thy hand,
To mould and guide us at Thy will.

H. 652 *Warning of Death.*

1 Where are the living? On the ground,
Where prayer is heard and mercy found;
Where, in the compass of a span,
The mortal makes the immortal man.

2 Who are the living? They whose breath
Draws every moment nigh to death;
Of endless bliss or woe the heirs;
O what an awful lot is theirs!

3 Then, timely warned, let us begin
To follow Christ and flee from sin;
Daily grow up in Him our Head,
Lord of the living and the dead.

Dr. L. Mason, 1835.

1. When gath'r-ing clouds a - round I view, And days are dark and friends are few,
On Him I lean, who, not in vain, Ex-peri-enced ev' - ry hu-man pain;
He sees my wants, al - lays my fears, And counts and trea-sures up my tears.

H. 60 *Christ the Hope of the Disconsolate.*

2 If aught should tempt my soul to stray
From heavenly virtue's narrow way,
To fly the good I would pursue,
Or do the sin I would not do;
Still He who felt temptation's power,
Shall guard me in that dangerous hour.

3 When vexing thoughts within me rise,
And, sore dismayed, my spirit dies,
Yet He who once vouchsafed to bear
The sickening anguish of despair,
Shall sweetly soothe, shall gently dry,
The throbbing heart, the streaming eye.

4 When, sorrowing, o'er some stone I bend,
Which covers all that was a friend,
And from his voice, his hand, his smile,
Divides me for a little while,
Thou, Saviour, seest the tears I shed,
For Thou didst weep o'er Lazarus dead.

5 And O! when I have safely passed
Through every conflict but the last,
Still, still unchanging, watch beside
My painful bed, for Thou hast died;
Then point to realms of cloudless day,
And wipe the latest tear away.

Ps. 23 *Second Part.*

1 The Lord my pasture shall prepare,
And feed me with a shepherd's care;
His presence shall my wants supply,
And guard me with a watchful eye;
My noon-day walks He shall attend,
And all my midnight hours defend.

2 When on the sultry glebe I faint,
Or on the thirsty mountain pant;
To fertile vales and dewy meads,
My weary, wandering steps He leads,
Where peaceful rivers, soft and slow,
Amid the verdant landscape flow.

3 Though in the paths of death I tread,
With gloomy horrors overspread,
My steadfast heart shall fear no ill,
For Thou, O Lord, art with me still;
Thy friendly arm shall give me aid,
And guide me thro' the dreadful shade.

4 Though in a bare and rugged way,
Through devious, lonely wilds I stray,
Thy bounty shall my pains beguile,
The barren wilderness shall smile,
With sudden green and herbage crowned,
And streams shall murmur all around.

H. BOND.

1. I'll praise my Ma - ker with my breath, And when my voice is lost in death,
Praise shall em - ploy my no - bler pow'rs; My days of praise shall ne'er be past,
While life, and thought, and be - ing last, Or im - mor - tal - i - ty en - dures.

Ps. 146 *Second Part.*

1 I'LL praise my Maker with my breath,
And when my voice is lost in death,
Praise shall employ my nobler powers;
My days of praise shall ne'er be past,
While life, and thought, and being last,
Or immortality endures.

2 Why should I make a man my trust?
Princes must die and turn to dust;
Vain is the help of flesh and blood;
Their breath departs; their pomp and power
And thoughts all vanish in an hour;
Nor can they make their promise good.

3 Happy the man whose hopes rely
On Israel's God; He made the sky,
And earth, and seas, with all their train,
His truth for ever stands secure;
He saves th' oppressed, He feeds the poor,
And none shall find His promise vain.

4 The Lord hath eyes to give the blind;
The Lord supports the sinking mind;
He sends the labouring conscience peace,
He helps the stranger in distress,
The widow and the fatherless,
And grants the prisoner sweet release.

5 He loves His saints, He knows them well,
But turns the wicked down to hell;
Thy God, O Zion, ever reigns;
Let every tongue, let every age,
In this exalted work engage;
Praise Him in everlasting strains.

Doxology.

Now to the great and sacred Three,
The Father, Son, and Spirit, be
Eternal power and glory given,
Through all the worlds where God is known,
By all the angels near the throne,
And all the saints in earth and heaven.

AYRSHIRE. L. M. D.

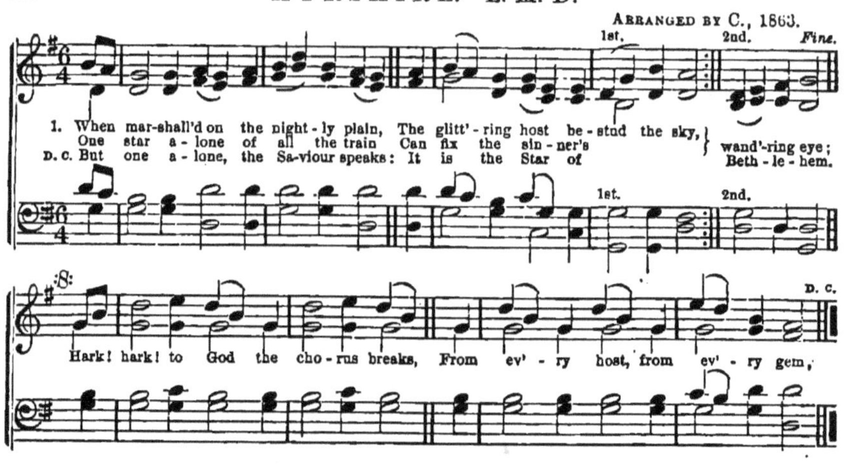
Arranged by C., 1863.
1st.
2nd.
Fine.
1. When mar-shall'd on the night-ly plain, The glitt'-ring host be-stud the sky,
One star a-lone of all the train Can fix the sin-ner's
wand'-ring eye;
D. C. But one a-lone, the Sa-viour speaks: It is the Star of
Beth-le-hem.
1st.
2nd.
D. C.
Hark! hark! to God the cho-rus breaks, From ev'-ry host, from ev'-ry gem,

H. 127 *The Star of Bethlehem.*

2 Once on the raging seas I rode,
The storm was loud, the night was dark;
The ocean yawned, and rudely blowed
The wind, that tossed my foundering [bark.
Deep horror then my vitals froze;
Death-struck, I ceased the tide to stem;
When suddenly a star arose!
It was the Star of Bethlehem.

3 It was my guide, my light, my all;
It bade my dark forebodings cease;
And thro' the storm and danger's thrall,
It led me to the port of peace.
Now, safely moored, my perils o'er,
I'll sing, first in night's diadem,
For ever and for evermore,
The Star—the Star of Bethlehem.

DRESDEN. L. M. D.

A. Williams' Collection, 1770.

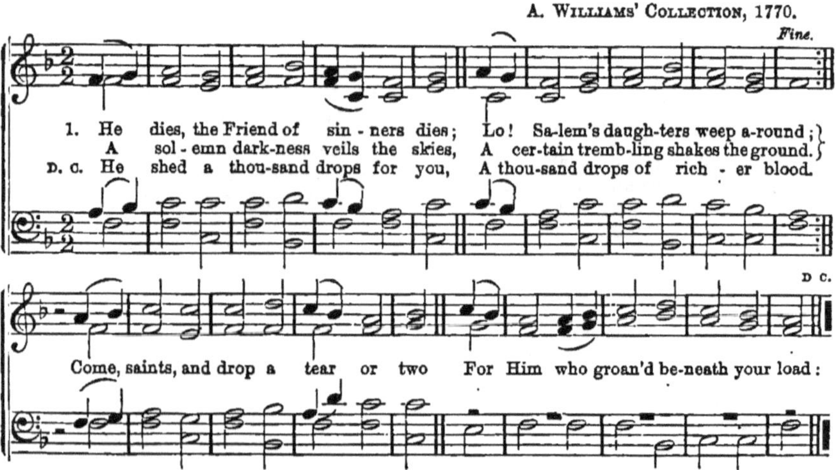
Fine.
1. He dies, the Friend of sin-ners dies; Lo! Sa-lem's daugh-ters weep a-round;
A sol-emn dark-ness veils the skies, A cer-tain tremb-ling shakes the ground.
D. C. He shed a thou-sand drops for you, A thou-sand drops of rich-er blood.
D. C.
Come, saints, and drop a tear or two For Him who groan'd be-neath your load:

1. Peace, trou-bled soul, whose plain-tive moan Hath taught each scene the note of woe;
Cease thy com-plaint, sup-press thy groan, And let thy tears for - get to flow;

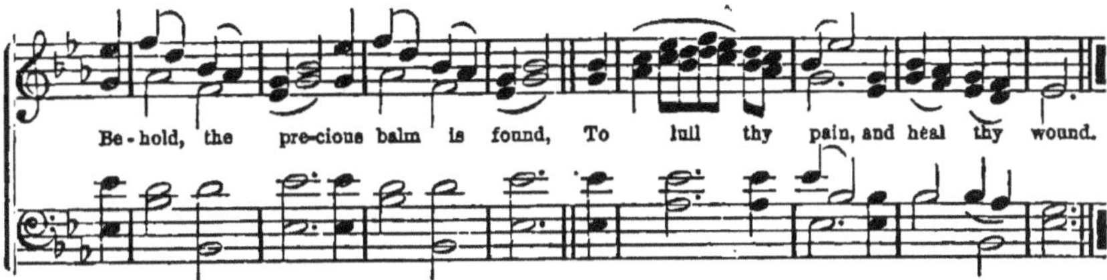
Be - hold, the pre-cious balm is found, To lull thy pain, and heal thy wound.

H. 414 *Peace in Believing.*

1 Peace, troubled soul, whose plaintive moan
  Hath taught each scene the note of woe;
Cease thy complaint, suppress thy groan,
  And let thy tears forget to flow;
Behold the precious balm is found,
To lull thy pain, and heal thy wound.

2 Come, freely come, by sin opprest,
  On Jesus cast thy weighty load;
In Him thy refuge find, thy rest,
  Safe in the mercy of thy God;
Thy God's thy Saviour, glorious word!
O hear, believe, and bless the Lord.

H. 110 *The Triumphs of Christ.*

[Tune, "Dresden."]

1 He dies, the Friend of sinners dies;
  Lo! Salem's daughters weep around;
A solemn darkness veils the skies,
  A sudden trembling shakes the ground.
Come, saints, and drop a tear or two,
  For Him who groaned beneath your load:
He shed a thousand drops for you,
  A thousand drops of richer blood.

2 Here's love and grief beyond degree,
  The Lord of glory dies for men;
But lo! what sudden joys we see,
  Jesus, the dead, revives again.
The risen God forsakes the tomb,
  Up to His Father's court He flies;
Cherubic legions guard Him home,
  And shout Him welcome to the skies.

3 Dry up your tears, ye saints, and tell
  How high your great Deliverer reigns;
Sing how He spoiled the hosts of hell,
  And led the monster death in chains.
Say, "Live for ever, wondrous King!
  Born to redeem, and strong to save."
Then ask the monster, "Where's thy sting,
  And where's thy victory, boasting grave?"

DR. THOS. HASTINGS, 1822.

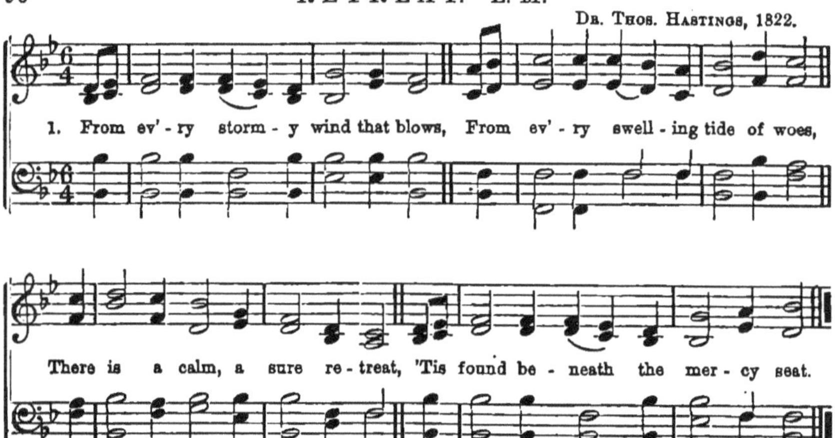
1. From ev'-ry storm-y wind that blows, From ev'-ry swell-ing tide of woes,
There is a calm, a sure re-treat, 'Tis found be-neath the mer-cy seat.

H. 475 *The Mercy Seat.*

2 There is a place where Jesus sheds
The oil of gladness on our heads;
A place than all besides more sweet,
It is the blood-bought mercy seat.

3 There is a scene where spirits blend,
Where friend holds fellowship with friend;
Though sundered far, by faith they meet
Around one common mercy seat.

4 Ah! whither could we flee for aid,
When tempted, desolate, dismayed?
Or how the hosts of hell defeat,
Had suffering saints no mercy seat?

5 There, there on eagle's wings we soar,
And sin and sense seem all no more;
And heaven comes down our souls to greet;
And glory crowns the mercy seat.

6 O let my hand forget her skill,
My tongue be silent, cold, and still,
This bounding heart forget to beat,
If I forget Thy mercy seat.

Ps. 11

1 My refuge is the God of love;
Why do my foes insult and cry,
"Fly, like a timorous trembling dove;
To distant woods or mountains, fly?"

2 The Lord in heaven has fixed His throne,
His eye surveys the world below;
To Him all mortal things are known,
His eyelids search our spirits through.

3 If He afflicts His saints so far,
To prove their love and try their grace,
What may the bold transgressors fear?
His soul abhors their wicked ways.

4 The righteous Lord loves righteous souls,
Whose thoughts and actions are sincere;
And with a gracious eye beholds
The men that His own image bear.

H. 133 *Grieved Spirit Besought.*

1 Stay, Thou insulted Spirit, stay;
Though I have done Thee such despite,
Cast not the sinner quite away,
Nor take Thine everlasting flight.

2 Though I have most unfaithful been
Of all who o'er Thy grace received,
Ten thousand times Thy goodness seen,
Ten thousand times Thy goodness griev'd.

3 Yet O! the chief of sinners spare,
In honour of my great High Priest;
Nor in Thy righteous anger swear,
I shall not see Thy people's rest.

4 If yet Thou canst my sins forgive,
E'en now, O Lord, relieve my woes;
Into Thy rest of love receive,
And bless me with a calm repose.

5 E'en now my weary soul release,
And raise me by Thy gracious hand;
Guide me into Thy perfect peace,
And bring me to the promised land.

Bost.

1. My Spi - rit looks to God a - lone; My rock and re- fuge is His throne;
In all my fears, in all my straits, My soul on His sal - va - tion waits.

Ps. 62 *Third Part.*

2 Trust Him, ye saints, in all your ways,
Pour out your hearts before His face;
When helpers fail, and foes invade,
God is our all-sufficient aid.

3 Once has His awful voice declared,
Once and again my ears have heard,
"All power is His eternal due;
He must be feared and trusted too."

4 For sovereign power reigns not alone,
Grace is a partner of the throne;
Thy grace and justice, mighty Lord,
Shall well divide our last reward.

Ps. 84 *First Part.*

1 How pleasant, how divinely fair,
O Lord of hosts, Thy dwellings are;
With long desire my spirit faints
To meet th' assemblies of Thy saints.

2 My flesh would rest in Thine abode;
My panting heart cries out for God;
My God, my King, why should I be
So far from all my joys and Thee?

3 Blest are the saints who sit on high,
Around Thy throne, above the sky;
Thy brightest glories shine above,
And all their work is praise and love.

4 Blest are the saints who find a place
Within the temple of Thy grace;
There they behold Thy gentle rays,
And seek Thy face, and learn Thy praise.

5 Blest are the men whose hearts are set
To find the way to Zion's gate;
God is their strength; and thro' the road
They lean upon their Helper, God.

6 Cheerful they walk with growing strength
Till all shall meet in heaven at length;
Till all before Thy face appear,
And join in nobler worship there.

H. 175 *The Voice of Mercy.*

1 I hear a voice that comes from far;
From Calvary it sounds abroad;
It soothes my soul, and calms my fear;
It speaks of pardon bought with blood.

2 And is it true, that many fly
The sound that bids my soul rejoice;
And rather choose in sin to die,
Than turn an ear to mercy's voice!

3 Alas for those! the day is near,
When mercy will be heard no more;
Then will they ask in vain to hear
The voice they would not hear before.

4 With such, I own, I once appeared,
But now I know how great their loss;
For sweeter sounds were never heard,
Than mercy utters from the cross.

5 But let me not forget to own,
That if I differ aught from those,
'Tis due to sovereign grace alone,
That oft selects its proudest foes.

HEBRON. L. M.

DR. L. MASON, 1830.

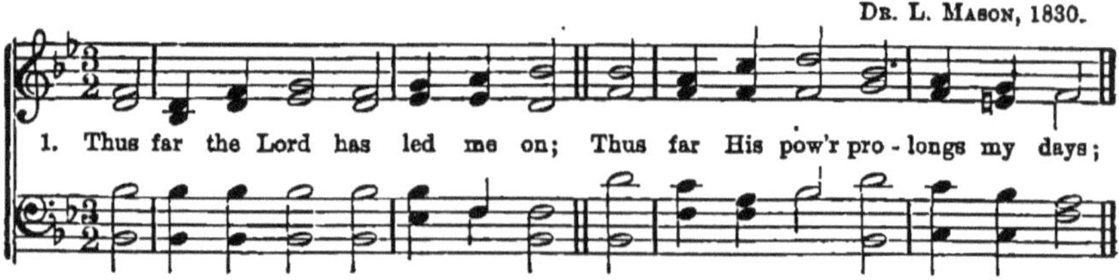
1. Thus far the Lord has led me on; Thus far His pow'r pro - longs my days;

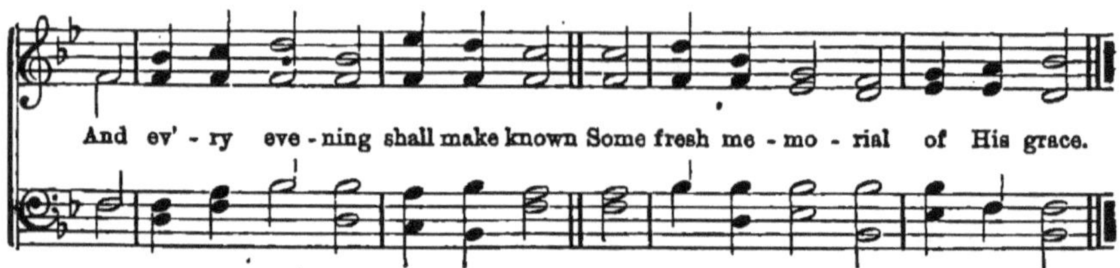
And ev' - ry eve - ning shall make known Some fresh me - mo - rial of His grace.

H. 434 *Evening Hymn.*

2 MUCH of my time has run to waste,
 And I, perhaps, am near my home;
But He forgives my follies past;
 He gives me strength for days to come.

3 I lay my body down to sleep,
 Peace is the pillow for my head;
While well appointed angels keep
 Their watchful stations round my bed.

4 Thus when the night of death shall come,
 My flesh shall rest beneath the ground,
And wait Thy voice to rouse the tomb,
 With sweet salvation in the sound.

H. 619 *Life the Time to Serve the Lord.*

1 LIFE is the time to serve the Lord,
The time to insure the great reward,
And while the lamp holds out to burn,
The vilest sinner may return.

2 Life is the hour that God has given
To escape from hell and fly to heaven;
The day of grace, and mortals may
Secure the blessings of the day.

3 The living know that they must die,
But all the dead forgotten lie;
Their memory and their sense are gone,
Alike unknowing and unknown.

4 Their hatred and their love are lost,
Their envy buried in the dust;
They have no share in all that's done
Beneath the circuit of the sun.

5 Then what my thoughts design to do,
My hands, with all your might pursue:
Since no device nor work is found,
Nor faith nor hope beneath the ground.

6 There are no acts of pardon past
In the cold grave to which we haste;
But darkness, death, and long despair
Reign in eternal silence there.

H. 187 *Expostulation with Sinners.*

1 PRISONERS of sin and Satan too,
The Saviour calls—He calls for you;
Ye who have sold yourselves for naught,
Jesus your liberty has bought.

2 The great Redeemer lived and died,
The Prince of Life was crucified;
He shed His own most precious blood
To ransom guilty souls for God.

3 He came to set the captive free;
He came to publish liberty;
To bind the broken-hearted up,
And give despairing sinners hope.

4 Prisoners of hope, why will you die?
Why from the only refuge fly?
Jesus, our hiding-place and tower,
Invites the guilty and the poor.

5 He came to comfort those that mourn;
He sweetly says to sinners, Turn!
Prisoners of hope, His voice attend,
Nor slight the calls of such a Friend.

ARRANGED BY DR. L. MASON, 1825.

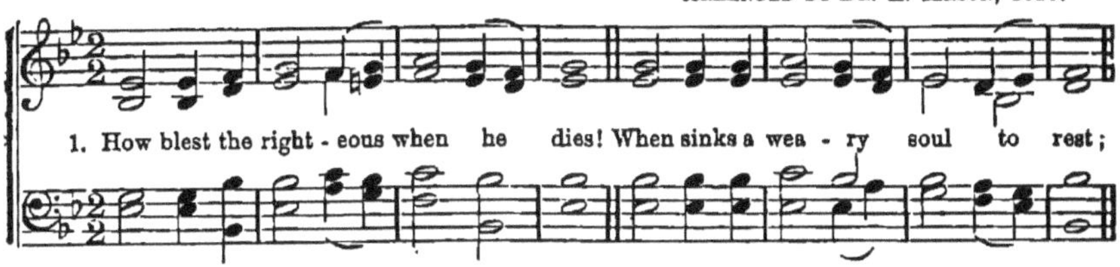
1. How blest the right - eous when he dies! When sinks a wea - ry soul to rest;

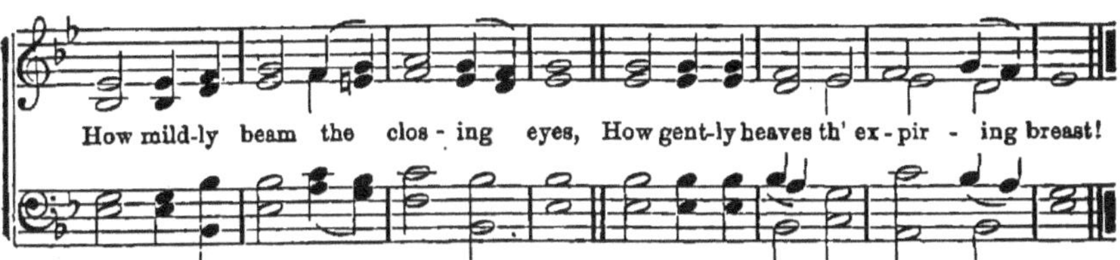
How mild-ly beam the clos - ing eyes, How gent-ly heaves th' ex - pir - ing breast!

H. 632 *Death of the Righteous.*

2 So fades a summer cloud away,
So sinks the gale when storms are o'er;
So gently shuts the eye of day,
So dies a wave along the shore.

3 A holy quiet reigns around,
A calm which life nor death destroys;
Nothing disturbs that peace profound,
Which his unfettered soul enjoys.

4 Farewell, conflicting hopes and fears,
Where lights and shades alternate dwell;
How bright th' unchanging morn appears;
Farewell, inconstant world, farewell.

5 Life's duty done, as sinks the clay,
Light from its load the spirit flies;
While heaven and earth combine to say,
"How blest the righteous when he dies?"

Ps. 73 *Second Part.*

1 Lord, what a thoughtless wretch was I,
To mourn, and murmur, and repine,
To see the wicked placed on high,
In pride and robes of honour shine.

2 But O, their end, their dreadful end!
Thy sanctuary taught me so:
On slippery rocks I see them stand,
And fiery billows roll below.

3 Now let them boast how tall they rise;
I'll never envy them again;
There they may stand with haughty eyes,
Till they plunge deep in endless pain.

4 Their fancied joys, how fast they flee,
Like dreams, as fleeting and as vain;
Their songs of softest harmony
Are but a prelude to their pain.

5 Now I esteem their mirth and wine,
Too dear to purchase with my blood;
Lord, 'tis enough that Thou art mine,
My life, my portion, and my God.

H. 191 *Christ Knocking at the Door.*

1 Behold a Stranger at the door!
He gently knocks, has knocked before,
Has waited long—is waiting still;
You treat no other friend so ill.

2 O lovely attitude! He stands
With melting heart and bleeding hands:
O matchless kindness! and He shows
This matchless kindness to His foes.

3 But will He prove a friend indeed?
He will; the very friend you need;
The Friend of sinners—yes, 'tis He,
With garments dyed on Calvary.

4 Rise, touched with gratitude divine;
Turn out His enemy and thine,
That soul-destroying monster, sin,
And let the heavenly stranger in.

5 Admit Him, ere His anger burn;
His feet, departed, ne'er return;
Admit Him, or the hour's at hand,
You'll at His door rejected stand.

GERMANY. L. M.

From Beethoven.

1. What sin-ners val-ue I re-sign; Lord, 'tis e-nough that Thou art mine:
I shall be-hold Thy bliss-ful face; And stand com-plete in right-eous-ness.

Ps. 17

1 What sinners value I resign;
Lord, 'tis enough that Thou art mine;
I shall behold Thy blissful face,
And stand complete in righteousness.

2 This life's a dream, an empty show;
But the bright world to which I go
Hath joys substantial and sincere;
When shall I wake and find me there?

3 O glorious hour! O blest abode!
I shall be near, and like my God;
And flesh and sin no more control
The sacred pleasures of the soul.

4 My flesh shall slumber in the ground
Till the last trumpet's joyful sound;
Then burst the chains with sweet surprise
And in my Saviour's image rise.

Ps. 57. *Second Part.*

1 My God, in whom are all the springs
Of boundless love and grace unknown,
Hide me beneath Thy spreading wings,
Till the dark cloud is overblown.

2 Up to the heavens I send my cry;
The Lord will my desires perform;
He sends His angels from the sky,
And saves me from the threat'ning storm.

3 Be Thou exalted, O my God,
Above the heavens where angels dwell;
Thy power on earth be known abroad,
And land to land Thy wonders tell.

4 My heart is fixed; my song shall raise
Immortal honours to Thy name;
Awake, my tongue, to sound His praise,
My tongue, the glory of my frame.

5 High o'er the earth His mercy reigns,
And reaches to the utmost sky;
His truth to endless years remains,
When lower worlds dissolve and die.

6 Be Thou exalted, O my God,
Above the heavens where angels dwell;
Thy power on earth be known abroad,
And land to land Thy wonders tell.

Ps. 72 *First Part.*

1 Great God, whose universal sway
The known and unknown worlds obey,
Now give the kingdom to Thy Son,
Extend His power, exalt His throne.

2 As rain on meadows newly mown,
So shall He send His influence down;
His grace on fainting souls distils,
Like heavenly dew on thirsty hills.

3 The heathen lands, that lie beneath
The shades of overspreading death,
Revive at His first dawning light,
And deserts blossom at the sight.

4 The saints shall flourish in His days,
Drest in the robes of joy and praise;
Peace, like a river, from His throne
Shall flow to nations yet unknown.

Samuel Holyoke.

1. Give to the Lord, ye sons of fame, Give to the Lord re - nown and pow'r; As-cribe due hon-ours

to His name, And His e - ter - nal might a - dore; And His e - ter - nal might a - dore.

Ps. 29

2 The Lord proclaims His power aloud,
  Through every ocean, every land;
His voice divides the watery cloud,
  And lightnings blaze at His command.

3 The Lord sits sovereign on the flood,
  The Thunderer reigns for ever King;
But makes His church His blest abode,
  Where we His awful glories sing.

4 In gentler language, there the Lord
  The counsel of His grace imparts;
Amidst the raging storm His word
  Speaks peace and courage to our hearts.

H. 259 *Faith in Christ.*

1 When sins and fears prevailing rise,
  And fainting hope almost expires,
Jesus, to Thee I lift mine eyes,
  To Thee I breathe my soul's desires.

2 Art Thou not mine, my living Lord?
  And can my hope, my comfort die,
Fixed on Thy everlasting word,
  That word which built the earth and sky?

3 If my immortal Saviour lives,
  Then my immortal life is sure;
His word a firm foundation gives,
  Here let me build and rest secure.

4 Here let my faith unshaken dwell,
  Immovable the promise stands;
Not all the powers of earth or hell,
  Can e'er dissolve the sacred bands.

5 Here, O my soul, thy trust repose;
  Since Jesus is for ever mine,
Not death itself, that last of foes,
  Shall break a union so divine.

H. 433 *Morning Hymn.*

1 God of the morning, at Thy voice
  The cheerful sun makes haste to rise,
And like a giant doth rejoice
  To run his journey through the skies.

2 From the fair chambers of the east
  The circuit of his race begins;
And, without weariness or rest,
  Round the whole earth he flies and shines.

3 Oh! like the sun, may I fulfil
  The appointed duties of the day,
With ready mind and active will,
  March on, and keep my heavenly way.

4 But I shall rove and lose the race,
  If God, my sun, should disappear,
And leave me in this world's wild maze,
  To follow every wandering star.

5 Lord, Thy commands are clean and pure,
  Enlightening our beclouded eyes;
Thy threatenings just, Thy promise sure,
  Thy gospel makes the simple wise.

6 Give me Thy counsel for my guide,
  And then receive me to Thy bliss;
All my desires and hopes beside
  Are faint and cold compared with this.

WESTERN MELODY.

1. A - wake, my soul, in joy - ful lays, And sing Thy great re-deem-er's praise;
He just - ly claims a song from Thee; His lov-ing kind - ness, O! how free—
His lov-ing kind-ness, lov - ing kind-ness— His lov-ing kind - ness, O! how free

H. 121 *Praise for Loving Kindness.*

2 He saw me ruined in the fall,
Yet loved me notwithstanding all;
He saved me from my lost estate;
His loving kindness, O! how great!

3 Though numerous hosts of mighty foes,
Though earth and hell my way oppose,
He safely leads my soul along;
His loving kindness, O! how strong!

4 When trouble, like a gloomy cloud,
Has gathered thick, and thundered loud,
He near my soul has always stood;
His loving kindness, O! how good!

5 Often I feel my sinful heart
Prone from my Saviour to depart;
But though I oft have Him forgot,
His loving kindness changes not.

6 Soon shall I pass the gloomy vale,
Soon all my mortal powers must fail;
O! may my last expiring breath,
His loving kindness sing in death.

7 Then, let me mount and soar away
To the bright world of endless day;
And sing, with rapture and surprise,
His loving kindness in the skies.

H. 97 *Christ's Intercession.*

[TUNE, "CHARLOTTE."]

1 O Thou, the contrite sinner's Friend,
Who loving, lov'st him to the end,
On this alone my hopes depend,
That Thou wilt plead for me.

2 When, weary in the Christian race,
Far off appears my resting place,
And, fainting, I mistrust Thy grace,
Then, Saviour, plead for me.

3 When Satan, by my sins made bold,
Strives from Thy cross to loose my hold,
Then with Thy pitying arms enfold,
And plead, O! plead for me.

4 And when my dying hour draws near,
Darkness with anguish, guilt and fear,
Then to my fainting sight appear,
Pleading in heaven for me.

CHARLOTTE. 8s, 8s & 6s.

Arranged by K. R., 1872.

1. Just as I am, with-out one plea, But that Thy blood was shed for me,
And that Thou bid'st me come to Thee, O Lamb of God, I come!

H. 218 *Just as I am.*

2 Just as I am, and waiting not,
To rid my soul of one dark blot, [spot,
To Thee, whose blood can cleanse each
O Lamb of God, I come.

3 Just as I am, though tossed about,
With many a conflict, many a doubt,
Fightings within, and fears without,
O Lamb of God, I come.

4 Just as I am, poor, wretched, blind—
Sight, riches, healing of the mind,
Yea, all I need in Thee to find,
O Lamb of God, I come.

5 Just as I am, Thou wilt receive,
Wilt welcome, pardon, cleanse, relieve,
Because Thy promise I believe,
O Lamb of God, I come.

6 Just as I am, for love unknown
Has broken every barrier down;
Now to be Thine, and Thine alone,
O Lamb of God, I come.

WALES. 8s, 4s & 8s.

Welch Air.

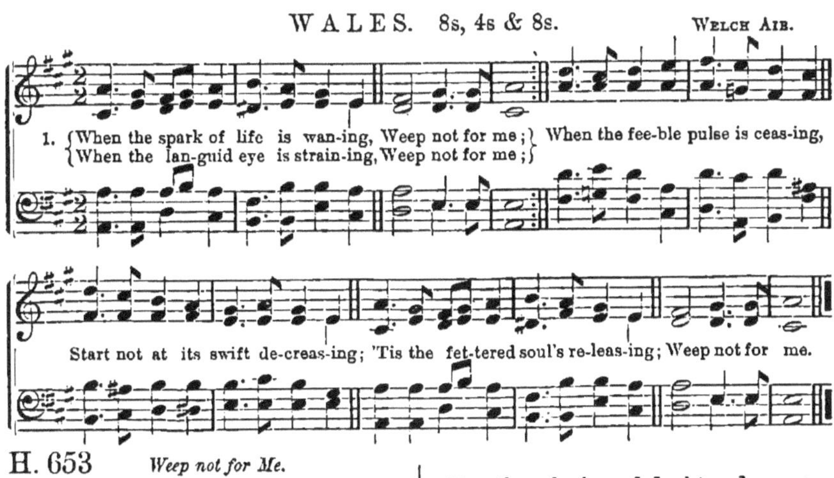
1. {When the spark of life is wan-ing, Weep not for me;} When the fee-ble pulse is ceas-ing,
{When the lan-guid eye is strain-ing, Weep not for me;}
Start not at its swift de-creas-ing; 'Tis the fet-tered soul's re-leas-ing; Weep not for me.

H. 653 *Weep not for Me.*

2 When the pangs of death assail me,
Weep not for me;
Christ is mine—He cannot fail me;
Weep not for me;
Yes, though sin and doubt endeavour
From His love my soul to sever,
Jesus is my strength for ever;
Weep not for me.

TIMOTHY SWAN, 1800.

1. Why do we mourn de - part - ing friends, Or shake at death's a - larms?
'Tis but the voice that Je - sus sends, To call them to His arms.

H. 630 *Death Disarmed.*

2 Are we not tending upward too,
As fast as time can move?
Nor should we wish our hours more slow
To keep us from our love.

3 The graves of all the saints He blest,
And softened every bed;
Where should the dying members rest,
But with their dying Head?

4 Thence He arose, ascending high,
And showed our feet the way;
Up to the Lord our flesh shall fly,
At the great rising day.

H. 479 *Before Sermon.*

1 Almighty God, eternal Lord,
Thy gracious power make known;
Touch, by the virtue of Thy word,
And melt the heart of stone.

2 Speak with the voice that wakes the dead,
And bid the sleeper rise;
And let his guilty conscience dread
The death that never dies.

H. 618 *Time is Short.*

1 "The time is short!" the season near,
When death will us remove,
To leave our friends, however dear,
And all we fondly love.

2 "The time is short!" sinners, beware,
Nor trifle time away;
The word of great salvation hear,
While it is called to-day.

3 "The time is short!" ye rebels, now
To Christ the Lord submit;
To mercy's golden sceptre bow,
And fall at Jesus' feet.

4 "The time is short!" ye saints rejoice,
The Lord will quickly come; [voice,
Soon shall you hear the Bridegroom's
To call you to your home.

5 "The time is short!" it swiftly flies,
The hour is just at hand
When we shall mount above the skies,
And reach the wished-for land.

6 "The time is short!" the moment near,
When we shall dwell above,
And be for ever happy there,
With Jesus, whom we love.

H. 626 *Happiness in Death.*

1 Hear what the voice from heaven pro-
For all the pious dead; [claims
Sweet is the savour of their names,
And soft their sleeping bed.

2 They die in Jesus, and are blessed;
How calm their slumbers are!
From suffering and from sin released,
And freed from every snare.

3 Far from this world of toil and strife,
They're present with the Lord;
The labours of their mortal life
End in a large reward.

Wm. Tansur, 1735.

1. Lord, in the morn - ing Thou shalt hear My voice as - cend - ing high;
To Thee will I di - rect my prayer, To Thee lift up mine eye:

Ps. 5

Second Part.

2 Up to the hills where Christ is gone
To plead for all His saints,
Presenting at His Father's throne
Our songs and our complaints.

3 Thou art a God before whose sight
The wicked shall not stand;
Sinners shall ne'er be Thy delight,
Nor dwell at Thy right hand.

4 But to Thy house will I resort,
To taste Thy mercies there;
I will frequent Thy holy court,
And worship in Thy fear.

5 O may Thy Spirit guide my feet
In ways of righteousness!
Make every path of duty straight
And plain before my face.

Ps. 7

1 My trust is in my heavenly Friend,
My hope in Thee, my God;
Rise, and my helpless life defend
From those that seek my blood.

2 If there be malice found in me,
I know Thy piercing eyes;
I should not dare appeal to Thee,
Nor ask my God to rise.

3 Arise, my God, lift up Thy hand,
Their pride and power control;
Awake to judgment, and command
Deliverance for my soul.

4 Let sinners and their wicked rage
Be humbled to the dust;
Shall not the God of truth engage
To vindicate the just?

H. 18

c *Electing Love.*

1 How vast the benefits divine,
Which we in Christ possess!
We're saved from guilt and every sin,
And called to holiness.

2 'Tis not for works which we have done,
Or shall hereafter do;
But He of His abounding love,
Salvation does bestow.

3 The glory, Lord, from first to last,
Is due to Thee alone;
Aught to ourselves we dare not take,
Or rob Thee of Thy crown.

4 Our glorious Surety undertook
Redemption's wondrous plan;
And grace was given us in Him,
Before the world began.

5 Safe in the arms of sovereign love
We ever shall remain;
Nor shall the rage of earth or hell
Make Thy wise counsels vain.

6 Not one of all the chosen race,
But shall to heaven attain;
Partake on earth the purposed grace,
And then with Jesus reign.

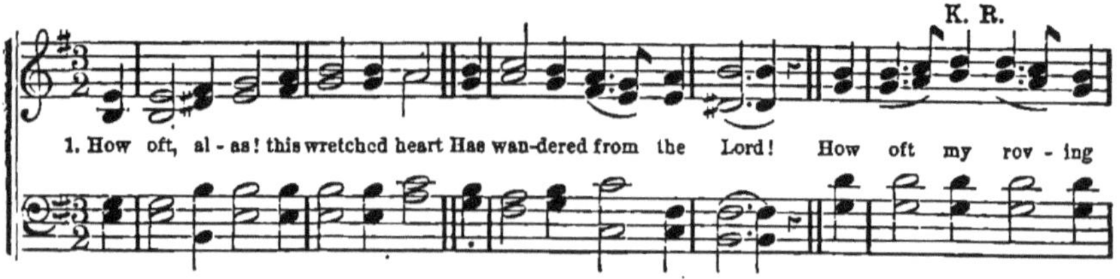
K. R.
1. How oft, al - as! this wretched heart Has wan-dered from the Lord! How oft my rov - ing

thoughts de - part, How oft my rov - ing thoughts de - part, For - get - ful of His word!

H. 210 *Backslider Returning.*

2 Yet sovereign mercy calls, "Return;"
Dear Lord, and may I come?
My vile ingratitude I mourn;
O! take the wanderer home.

3 And canst Thou, wilt Thou, yet forgive,
And bid my crimes remove?
And shall a pardoned rebel live
To speak Thy wondrous love?

4 Almighty grace, Thy healing power,
How glorious, how divine!
That can to life and bliss restore
So vile a heart as mine.

5 Thy pardoning love, so free, so sweet,
Dear Saviour, I adore;
O! keep me at Thy sacred feet,
And let me rove no more.

Ps. 38

1 Thy chastening wrath, O Lord, restrain,
Though I deserve it all;
Nor let on me the heavy storm
Of Thy displeasure fall.

2 My sins, which to a deluge swell,
My sinking head o'erflow,
And, for my feeble strength to bear,
Too vast a burden grow.

3 But, Lord, before Thy searching eyes,
All my desires appear;
The groanings of my burden'd soul
Have reached Thine open ear.

4 Forsake me not, O Lord, my God,
Nor far from me depart;
Make haste to my relief, O Thou
Who my salvation art.

Ps. 51 *Second Part.*

1 O God of mercy, hear my call,
My load of guilt remove;
Break down this separating wall
That bars me from Thy love.

2 Give me the presence of Thy grace;
Then my rejoicing tongue
Shall speak aloud Thy righteousness,
And make Thy praise my song.

3 No blood of goats nor heifers slain,
For sin could e'er atone;
The death of Christ shall still remain
Sufficient and alone.

4 A soul oppressed with sin's desert
My God will ne'er despise;
An humble groan, a broken heart
Is our best sacrifice.

Ps. 116 *Third Part.*

1 I love the Lord, because my voice
And prayers He did hear.
I, while I live, will call on Him
Who bowed to me His ear.

2 Of death the cords and sorrows did
About me compass round;
The pains of hell took hold on me:
I grief and trouble found.

3 Upon the name of God the Lord
Then did I call, and say,
Deliver Thou my soul, O Lord,
I do Thee humbly pray.

4 God merciful and righteous is,
Yea, gracious is our Lord.
God saves the meek: I was brought low;
He did me help afford.

5 O thou, my soul, do thou return
Unto thy quiet rest;
For largely, lo, the Lord to thee
His bounty hath expressed.

6 For my distressed soul from death
Delivered was by Thee;
Thou didst my mourning eyes from tears
My feet from falling free.

H. 87 *Christ's Agony in the Garden.*

1 Dark was the night, and cold the ground,
On which the Lord was laid;
His sweat as drops of blood ran down,
In agony He prayed.

2 "Father, remove this bitter cup,
If such Thy sacred will;
If not, content to drink it up,
Thy pleasure I fulfil."

3 Go to the garden, sinner, see
Those precious drops that flow;
The heavy load He bore for thee—
For thee He lies so low.

4 Then learn of Him the cross to bear,
Thy Father's will obey;
And when temptations press thee near,
Awake to watch and pray.

H. 88 *Crucifixion of Christ.*

1 Behold the Saviour of mankind
Nailed to the shameful tree!
How vast the love that Him inclined
To bleed and die for me.

2 Hark! how He groans, while nature [shakes,
And earth's strong pillars bend!
The temple's veil asunder breaks,
The solid marbles rend.

3 'Tis finished! now the ransom's paid,
"Receive my soul!" He cries;
See, how He bows His sacred head!
He bows His head and dies!

4 But soon He'll break death's iron chain,
And in full glory shine;
O Lamb of God! was ever pain,
Was ever love like Thine?

H. 198 *Conviction of Sin by the Law.*

1 Lord, how secure my conscience was,
And felt no inward dread;
I was alive without the law,
And thought my sins were dead.

2 My hopes of heaven were firm and bright,
But since the precept came,
With a convincing power and light,
I find how vile I am.

3 My guilt appeared but small before,
Till terribly I saw
How perfect, holy, just and pure,
Was Thine eternal law.

4 Then felt my soul the heavy load,
My sins revived again;
I had provoked a dreadful God,
And all my hopes were slain.

5 I'm like a helpless captive, sold
Under the power of sin;
I cannot do the good I would,
Nor keep my conscience clean.

6 My God, I cry with every breath,
For some kind power to save,
To break the yoke of sin and death,
And thus redeem the slave.

H. 200 *Sins Acknowledged.*

1 Great God, before Thy mercy seat
Abashed, in dust I fall;
My crimes of complicated guilt,
Aloud for judgment call.

2 I own my ways to be corrupt,
My duties stained with sin;
Make Thou my broken spirit whole,
My burdened conscience clean.

3 Lord, send Thy Spirit from above,
Implant a holy fear;
And through Thine all abounding grace,
Bring Thy salvation near.

4 On my distressed, benighted soul,
O! cause Thy face to shine;
Make me to hear Thy pardoning voice,
And tell me I am Thine.

YORK. C.M.

John Milton's Father.

To Fa - ther, Son, and Ho ly Ghost, The God whom we a - dore,

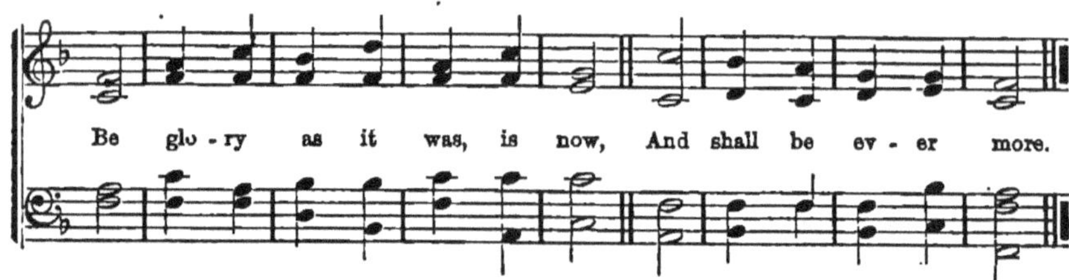
Be glo - ry as it was, is now, And shall be ev - er more.

H. 234 *Necessity of Sanctification.*

1 Nor eye has seen, nor ear has heard,
Nor sense nor reason known,
What joys the Father has prepared
For those that love the Son.

2 But the good Spirit of the Lord
Reveals a heaven to come;
The beams of glory in His word
Allure and guide us home.

3 Pure are the joys above the sky,
And all the region peace;
No wanton lips nor envious eye
Can see or taste the bliss.

4 Those holy gates for ever bar
Pollution, sin, and shame;
None shall obtain admittance there,
But followers of the Lamb.

5 He keeps the Father's book of life,
There all their names are found;
The hypocrite in vain shall strive
To tread the heavenly ground.

H. 236 *Confidence in the Promises.*

1 Our God, how firm His promise stands!
E'en when He hides His face;
He trusts in our Redeemer's hands
His glory and His grace.

2 Then why, my soul, these sad complaints,
Since Christ and we are one?
Thy God is faithful to His saints,
Is faithful to His Son.

3 Beneath His smiles my heart has lived,
And part of heaven possessed;
I praise His name for grace received,
And trust Him for the rest.

H. 245 *God the Believer's Happiness.*

1 My God, my portion, and my love,
My everlasting All,
I've none but Thee in heaven above,
Or on this earthly ball.

2 What empty things are all the skies,
And this inferior clod!
There's nothing here deserves my joys,
There's nothing like my God.

3 In vain the bright, the burning sun
Scatters his feeble light;
'Tis Thy sweet beams create my noon;
If Thou withdraw, 'tis night.

4 To Thee we owe our wealth and friends,
And health and safe abode:
Thanks to Thy name for meaner things;
But they are not my God.

5 Were I possessor of the earth,
And called the stars my own;
Without Thy graces and Thyself,
I were a wretch undone.

6 Let others stretch their arms like seas,
And grasp in all the shore;
Grant me the visits of Thy face,
And I desire no more.

DR. HASTINGS.

1. Faith adds new charms to earth - ly bliss, And saves me from its snares; Its aid in
ev'-ry du-ty brings, And sof-tens all my cares—And sof-tens all my cares.

H. 262 *Efficacy of Faith.*

2 EXTINGUISHES the thirst of sin,
  And lights the sacred fire
Of love to God, and heavenly things,
  And feeds the pure desire.

3 The wounded conscience knows its power,
  The healing balm to give;
That balm the saddest heart can cheer,
  And make the dying live.

4 Wide it unveils celestial worlds,
  Where deathless pleasures reign;
And bids me seek my portion there,
  Nor bids me seek in vain:

5 Shows me the precious promise sealed
  With the Redeemer's blood;
And helps my feeble hope to rest
  Upon a faithful God.

6 There, there unshaken would I rest,
  Till this vile body dies;
And then on faith's triumphant wings
  At once to glory rise.

H. 247 *Christian Confidence and Gratitude.*

1 How can I sink with such a prop
  As my eternal God,
Who bears the earth's huge pillars up,
  And spreads the heavens abroad?

2 How can I die while Jesus lives,
  Who rose and left the dead?
Pardon and grace my soul receives
  From my exalted Head.

3 All that I am, and all I have,
  Shall be for ever Thine;
Whate'er my duty bids me give,
  My cheerful hands resign.

H. 308 *The Believer's Joy in Life and Death.*

1 JOY is a fruit that will not grow
  In nature's barren soil;
All we can boast, till Christ we know,
  Is vanity and toil.

2 But where the Lord has planted grace,
  And made His glories known,
There fruits of heavenly joy and peace
  Are found, and there alone.

3 A bleeding Saviour seen by faith,
  A sense of pardoning love,
A hope that triumphs over death,
  Give joys like those above.

4 To take a glimpse within the veil;
  To know that God is mine;
Are springs of joy that never fail,
  Unspeakable, divine.

5 These are the joys which satisfy
  And sanctify the mind;
Which make the spirit mount on high,
  And leave the world behind.

6 No more, believers, mourn your lot;
  But since you are the Lord's,
Resign to them that know Him not,
  Such joys as earth affords.

Hugh Wilson.

1. In e - vil long I took de - light, Un - awed by shame or fear;
Till a new ob - ject struck my sight, And stopped my wild ca - reer.

H. 204 *Repentance at the Cross.*

2 I saw one hanging on a tree,
In agonies and blood,
Who fixed His languid eyes on me,
As near His cross I stood.

3 Sure, never to my latest breath,
Can I forget that look;
It seemed to charge me with His death,
Though not a word He spoke.

4 My conscience felt and owned the guilt,
And plunged me in despair;
I saw my sins His blood had spilt,
And helped to nail Him there.

5 Alas! I knew not what I did,
But now my tears are vain;
Where shall my trembling soul be hid?
For I the Lord have slain.

6 A second look He gave, which said,
"I freely all forgive;
This blood is for thy ransom paid;
I die that thou mayst live."

7 Thus, while His death my sin displays
In all its blackest hue,
Such is the mystery of grace,
It seals my pardon too.

8 With pleasing grief and mournful joy,
My spirit now is filled,
That I should such a life destroy,
Yet live by Him I killed.

H. 408 *Light in Darkness.*

1 O thou who driest the mourner's tear,
How dark this world would be,
If, pierced by sins and sorrows here,
We could not fly to Thee!

2 The friends who in our sunshine live,
When winter comes are flown;
And he who has but tears to give,
Must weep those tears alone.

3 But Thou wilt heal that broken heart,
Which, like the plants that throw
Their fragrance from the wounded part,
Breathes sweetness out of woe.

4 When joy no longer soothes or cheers,
And e'en the hope that threw
A moment's sparkle o'er our tears,
Is dimmed and vanished too;

5 O who could bear life's stormy doom,
Did not Thy wing of love
Come brightly wafting through the gloom
Our peace-branch from above?

6 Then sorrow, touched by Thee, grows
With more than rapture's ray; [bright
As darkness shows us worlds of light,
We never saw by day.

H. 463 *Invitation to Zion.*

1 Inquire, ye pilgrims, for the way
That leads to Zion's hill,
And thither set your steady face,
With a determined will.

2 Invite the strangers all around,
Your pious march to join;
And spread the sentiments you feel,
Of faith and love divine.

3 O come, and to His temple haste,
And seek His favour there;
Before His footstool humbly bow,
And pour your fervent prayer.

4 O come, and join your souls to God
In everlasting bands;
Accept the blessings He bestows,
With thankful hearts and hands.

H. 468 *Christ's Presence Invoked.*

1 Come, Thou Desire of all Thy saints,
Our humble strains attend;
While with our praises and complaints,
Low at Thy feet we bend.

2 Come, Lord, Thy love alone can raise
In us the heavenly flame;
Then shall our lips resound Thy praise,
Our hearts adore Thy name.

3 Dear Saviour, let Thy glory shine,
And fill Thy dwellings here,
Till life, and love, and joy divine,
And heaven on earth appear.

H. 472 *Prayer for Protection.*

1 O God of Bethel, by whose hand
Thy people still are fed;
Who through this weary pilgrimage
Hast all our fathers led;

2 Our vows, our prayers, we now present
Before Thy throne of grace:
God of our fathers, be the God
Of their succeeding race.

3 Through each perplexing path of life
Our wandering footsteps guide;
Give us each day our daily bread,
And raiment fit provide.

4 O! spread Thy covering wings around,
Till all our wanderings cease,
And at our Father's loved abode
Our souls arrive in peace.

5 Such blessings from Thy gracious hand
Our humble prayers implore;
And thou shalt be our chosen God,
And portion evermore.

H. 473 *Blessing on Public Worship.*

1 O Lord, our languid souls inspire,
For here, we trust Thou art:
Kindle a flame of heavenly fire,
In every waiting heart.

2 Dear Shepherd of Thy people, hear;
Thy presence now display;
As Thou hast given a place for prayer,
So give us hearts to pray.

3 Show us some token of Thy love,
Our fainting hope to raise;
And pour Thy blessing from above,
That we may render praise.

4 Within these walls let holy peace,
And love and concord dwell;
Here give the troubled conscience ease,
The wounded spirit heal.

5 The feeling heart, the melting eye,
The humbled mind bestow;
And shine upon us from on high,
To make our graces grow.

6 May we in faith receive Thy word,
In faith present our prayers;
And, in the presence of our Lord,
Unbosom all our cares.

7 And may the gospel's joyful sound,
Enforced by mighty grace,
Awaken many sinners round
To come and fill the place.

H. 478 *A Hymn Before Sermon.*

1 In Thy great name, O Lord, we come
To worship at Thy feet;
O pour Thy Holy Spirit down
On all that now shall meet.

2 We come to hear Jehovah speak,
To hear the Saviour's voice;
Thy face and favour, Lord, we seek;
Now make our hearts rejoice.

3 Teach us to pray and praise—to hear
And understand Thy word;
To feel Thy blissful presence near,
And trust our living Lord.

4 Let sinners now Thy goodness prove,
And saints rejoice in Thee:
Let rebels be subdued by love,
And to the Saviour flee.

Charles Zeuner, 1839.

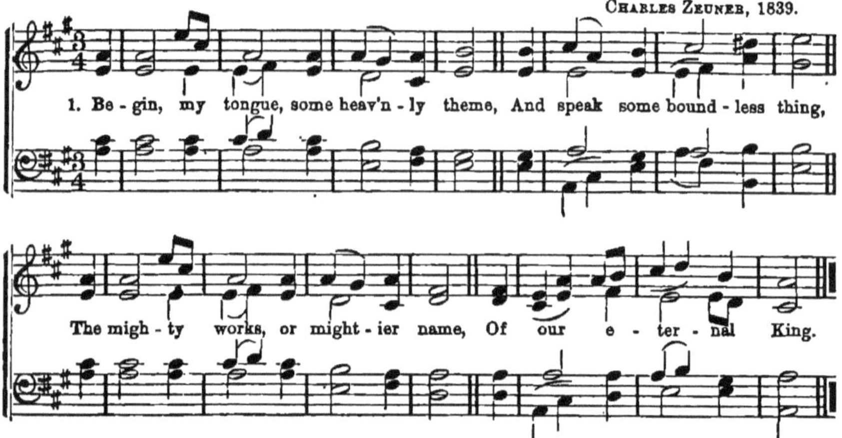
1. Be - gin, my tongue, some heav'n - ly theme, And speak some bound - less thing,
The migh - ty works, or might - ier name, Of our e - ter - nal King.

H. 8 *Faithfulness of God.*

2 Tell of His wondrous faithfulness,
And sound His powers abroad;
Sing the sweet promise of His grace,
And the performing God.

3 Proclaim "Salvation from the Lord,
For wretched dying men;"
His hand has writ the sacred word
With an immortal pen.

4 His very word of grace is strong
As that which built the skies;
The voice that rolls the stars along
Speaks all the promises.

5 O might I hear Thy heavenly tongue
But whisper, "Thou art mine!"
Those gentle words should raise my song
To notes almost divine.

6 How would my leaping heart rejoice,
And think my heaven secure!
I trust the all-creating voice,
And faith desires no more.

H. 348 *Renouncing the World.*

1 Let worldly minds the world pursue,
It has no charms for me;
Once I admired its follies too,
But grace has set me free.

2 Those follies now no longer please,
No more delight afford;
Far from my heart be joys like these,
Now I have known the Lord.

3 As by the light of op'ning day
The stars are all concealed,
So earthly pleasures fade away
When Jesus is revealed.

4 Creatures no more divide my choice,
I bid them all depart;
His name, and love, and gracious voice,
Shall fix my roving heart.

5 Now, Lord, I would be Thine alone,
And wholly live to Thee;
Yet worthless still myself I own,
Thy worth is all my plea.

H. 103 *The Redeeming Saviour.*

1 Behold the glories of the Lamb,
Amidst His Father's throne;
Prepare new honours for His name,
And songs before unknown.

2 Let elders worship at His feet,
The church adore around,
With vials full of odours sweet,
And harps of sweeter sound.

3 Now to the Lamb that once was slain,
Be endless blessings paid;
Salvation, glory, joy remain,
For ever on Thy head.

4 Thou hast redeemed our souls with blood,
Hast set the prisoners free,
Hast made us kings and priests to God,
And we shall reign with Thee.

1st.
2nd.
1. When I can read my ti - tle clear, ... To man-sions in the
D. C. And wipe my weep - ing . . . . eyes, And wipe my weep-ing
D. C.
skies— I bid fare - well to ev' - ry fear, And wipe my weep - ing eyes.
eyes. I bid, etc.,
D. C.

H. 672 *Joyful Anticipations of Heaven.*

2 Should earth against my soul engage,
And hellish darts be hurled,
Then I can smile at Satan's rage,
And face a frowning world.

3 Let cares like a wild deluge come,
And storms of sorrow fall;
May I but safely reach my home,
My God, my heaven, my all.

4 There shall I bathe my weary soul,
In seas of heavenly rest,
And not a wave of trouble roll
Across my peaceful breast.

H. 359 *Confessing Christ.*

1 Didst Thou, dear Jesus, suffer shame,
And bear the cross for me?
And shall I fear to own Thy name,
Or Thy disciple be?

2 Forbid it, Lord, that I should dread
To suffer shame or loss;
O! let me in Thy footsteps tread,
And glory in Thy cross.

3 Inspire my soul with life divine,
And holy courage bold;
Let knowledge, faith, and meekness shine,
Nor love nor zeal grow cold.

4 Say to my soul, "Why dost thou fear
The face of feeble clay?
Behold thy Saviour ever near,
Will guard thee in the way"

5 O! how my soul would rise and run,
At this reviving word;
Nor any painful sufferings shun
To follow Thee, my Lord.

6 Let sinful men reproach, defame,
And call me what they will,
If I may glorify Thy name,
And be Thy servant still.

H. 28 *Darkness of Providence.*

1 Thy way, O God! is in the sea,
Thy paths I cannot trace;
Nor comprehend the mystery
Of Thy unbounded grace.

2 Here the dark veils of flesh and sense
My captive soul surround;
Mysterious deeps of Providence
My wondering thoughts confound.

3 As through a glass, I dimly see
The wonders of Thy love;
How little do I know of Thee,
Or of the joys above!

4 'Tis but in part I know Thy will;
I bless Thee for the sight;
When will Thy love the rest reveal,
In glory's clearer light?

5 With rapture shall I then survey
Thy providence and grace;
And spend an everlasting day
In wonder, love and praise.

Dr. J. Lucas.

Let God the Fa-ther, and the Son, And Spi-rit be a-dored, Where there are
works to make Him known, Or saints to love the Lord—Or saints to love the Lord.

Ps. 54

1 Behold us, Lord, and let our cry
Before Thy throne ascend;
Cast Thou on us a pitying eye,
And still our lives defend.

2 For impious foes insult us round;
Oppressive, proud and vain;
They cast Thy temples to the ground,
And all our rights profane.

3 Yet Thy forgiving grace we trust,
And in Thy power rejoice;
Thine arm shall bring our foes to dust,
Thy praise inspire our voice.

4 Be Thou with those whose friendly hand
Upheld us in distress,
Extend Thy truth through every land,
And still Thy people bless.

H. 336 *Prayer for Submission.*

1 O Lord, my best desires fulfil,
And help me to resign
Life, health, and comfort to Thy will,
And make Thy pleasure mine.

2 Why should I shrink at Thy command,
Whose love forbids my fears?
Or tremble at the gracious hand,
That wipes away my tears?

3 No, rather let me freely yield,
What most I prize to Thee,
Who never hast a good withheld,
Or wilt withhold from me.

4 Wisdom and mercy guide my way,
Shall I resist them both?
A poor blind creature of a day,
And crushed before the moth!

5 But ah! my inward spirit cries,
Still bind me to Thy sway;
Else the next cloud that veils my skies
Drives all these thoughts away.

H. 338 *It is Well.*

1 It shall be well, let sinners know,
With those who love the Lord;
His saints have always found it so,
When resting on His word.

2 Peace, then, ye chastened sons of God,
Why let your sorrows swell?
Wisdom directs your Father's rod,
His word says, It is well.

3 Though you may trials sharp endure,
From sin, or death, or hell;
Your heavenly Father's love is sure,
And therefore, It is well.

4 Soon will your sorrows all be o'er,
And you shall sweetly tell,
On Canaan's calm and pleasant shore,
That all at last is well.

H. 383 *Watchfulness and Prayer.*

1 Alas! what hourly dangers rise,
What snares beset my way;
To heaven I fain would lift my eyes,
And hourly watch and pray.

2 How oft my mournful thoughts complain,
And melt in flowing tears!
Striving against my foes in vain,
I sink amid my fears.

3 O gracious God, in whom I live,
My feeble efforts aid;
Help me to watch, and pray, and strive,
Nor let me be dismayed.

4 Do Thou increase my faith and hope,
When fears and foes prevail;
And bear my fainting spirit up,
Or soon my strength will fail.

5 O keep me to Thy heavenly way,
And bid the tempter flee;
And never, never let me stray
From happiness and Thee.

H. 520 *Prayer for Youth.*

1 Bestow, dear Lord, upon our youth,
The gift of saving grace;
And let the seed of sacred truth
Fall in a fruitful place.

2 Grace is a plant, where'er it grows,
Of pure and heavenly root;
But fairest in the youngest shows,
And yields the sweetest fruit.

3 Ye careless ones, O hear betimes
The voice of sovereign love;
Your youth is stained with many crimes,
But mercy reigns above.

4 True, you are young, but there's a stone
Within the youngest breast;
Or half the crimes which you have done
Would rob you of your rest.

5 For you the public prayer is made,
O join the public prayer;
For you the secret tear is shed,
O shed yourselves a tear.

6 We pray that you may early prove
The Spirit's power to teach;
You cannot be too young to love
That Jesus whom we preach.

H. 614 *Brevity and Uncertainty of Life.*

1 Thee we adore, eternal Name,
And humbly own to Thee,
How feeble is our mortal frame;
What dying worms are we!

2 The year rolls round, and steals away
The breath that first it gave;
Whate'er we do, where'er we be,
We're travelling to the grave.

3 Great God, on what a slender thread
Hang everlasting things!
The eternal states of all the dead
Upon life's feeble strings.

4 Infinite joy or endless woe
Attends on every breath;
And yet how unconcerned we go
Upon the brink of death!

5 Waken, O Lord, our drowsy sense,
To walk this dangerous road;
And if our souls are hurried hence,
May they be found with God.

H. 636 *Triumph over Death.*

1 O for an overcoming faith
To cheer my dying hours,
To triumph o'er the monster, Death,
And all his frightful powers!

2 Joyful, with all the strength I have,
My quivering lips should sing,
"Where is thy boasted victory, grave,
And where the monster's sting?"

3 If sin be pardoned, I'm secure;
Death has no sting beside;
The law gives sin its damning power;
But Christ, my ransom, died.

4 Now to the God of victory
Immortal thanks be paid,
Who makes us conquerors while we die,
Through Christ our living Head.

H. 639 *Faith in Dying.*

1 O for the eye of faith divine,
To pierce beyond the grave;
To see that Friend, and call Him mine,
Whose arm is strong to save.

2 Lord, I commit my soul to Thee,
Accept the sacred trust;
Receive this nobler part of me,
And watch my sleeping dust.

3 Till that illustrious morning come,
When all Thy saints shall rise,
And, clothed in full, immortal bloom,
Attend Thee to the skies.

A. Williams' Collection, 1770.

1. Re - li - gion is the chief con - cern Of mor - tals here be - low; May
I its great im - por - tance learn, Its sov'-reign vir - tue know.

H. 145 *Excellence of Religion.*

2 More needful this than glittering wealth,
Or aught the world bestows;
Nor reputation, food nor health,
Can give us such repose.

3 Religion should our thoughts engage,
Amidst our youthful bloom;
'Twill fit us for declining age,
And for the awful tomb.

4 O! may my heart, by grace renewed,
Be my Redeemer's throne;
And be my stubborn will subdued,
His government to own.

5 Let deep repentance, faith, and love,
Be joined with godly fear;
And all my conversation prove
My heart to be sincere.

Ps. 15 *First Part.*

1 Who shall inhabit in Thy hill,
O God of holiness?
Whom will the Lord admit to dwell
So near His throne of grace?

2 The man that walks in pious ways,
And works with righteous hands;
That trusts his Maker's promised grace,
And follows His commands;

3 He speaks the meaning of his heart,
Nor slanders with his tongue;
Will scarce believe an ill report,
Nor do his neighbour wrong:

4 His hands disdain a golden bribe,
And never wrong the poor;
This man shall dwell with God on earth,
And find his heaven secure.

Ps. 56

1 In God, most holy, just, and true,
I have reposed my trust;
Nor will I fear what man can do,
The offspring of the dust.

2 Thy solemn vows are on me, Lord,
Thou shalt receive my praise:
I'll sing how faithful is Thy word,
How righteous all Thy ways.

3 Thou hast secured my soul from death;
O! set Thy prisoner free,
That heart and hand, and life and breath,
May be employed for Thee.

H. 144 *Deceitfulness of Sin.*

1 Sin has a thousand treacherous arts
To practise on the mind;
With flattering looks she tempts our hearts,
But leaves a sting behind.

2 With names of virtue she deceives
The aged and the young;
And while the heedless wretch believes,
She makes his fetters strong.

3 She pleads for all the joys she brings,
And gives a fair pretence;
But cheats the soul of heavenly things,
And chains it down to sense.

WM. TANSUR, 1735.

1 God, my sup - port - er and my hope, My help for - ev - er near,
Thine arm of mer - cy held me up, When sink - ing in des - pair.

Ps. 73 *First Part.*

2 Thy counsels, Lord, shall guide my feet,
Through life's dark wilderness;
Thine hand conduct me near Thy seat,
To dwell before Thy face.

3 Were I in heaven without my God,
'Twould be no joy to me;
And whilst this earth is my abode,
I long for none but Thee.

4 What if the springs of life were broke,
And flesh and heart should faint,
God is my soul's eternal rock,
The strength of every saint.

5 Behold! the sinners that remove
Far from Thy presence, die;
Not all the idol-gods they love
Can save them when they cry.

6 But to draw near to Thee, my God,
Shall be my sweet employ;
My tongue shall sound Thy works abroad,
And tell the world my joy.

Ps. 53

1 Are all the foes of Zion fools,
Who thus destroy her saints?
Do they not know her Saviour rules,
And pities her complaints?

2 They shall be seized with sad surprise;
For God's avenging arm
Shall crush the hand that dares arise
To do His children harm.

3 In vain the sons of Satan boast
Of armies in array;
When God on high dismays their host
They fall an easy prey.

4 O! for a word from Zion's King,
Her captives to restore!
The joyful saints Thy praise shall sing,
And Israel weep no more.

Ps. 71 *First Part.*

1 O Lord, my hope and confidence
Is placed in Thee alone;
Then let Thy servant never be
Put to confusion.

2 For even from my youth, O God,
By Thee I have been taught;
And hitherto I have declared
The wonders Thou hast wrought.

3 And now, Lord, leave me not, when I
Old and gray-headed grow;
Till to this age Thy strength and power
To all to come I show.

4 And Thy most perfect righteousness,
O Lord, is very high.
Who hast so great things done: O God,
Who is like unto Thee?

5 Thou Lord, who great adversities
And sore to me didst show,
Shalt quicken, and bring me again
From depths of earth below.

DANIEL READ, 1785.

Let God the Fa - ther, and the Son, And Spi - rit be a - dored,
Where there are works to make Him known, Or saints to love the Lord.

H. 25 *Gratitude for Providential Care.*

1 O THOU, my light, my life, my joy,
My glory, and my all;
Unsent by Thee, no good can come,
Nor evil can befall.

2 Such are Thy schemes of providence,
And methods of Thy grace,
That I may safely trust in Thee,
Through all the wilderness.

3 'Tis Thine outstretched and pow'rful arm
Upholds me in the way;
And Thy rich bounty well supplies
The wants of every day.

4 For such compassions, O my God!
Ten thousand thanks are due;
For such compassions, I esteem
Ten thousand thanks too few.

Ps. 28 *Second Part.*

1 LORD, I will Thee extol, for Thou
Hast lifted me on high,
And over me Thou to rejoice
Mad'st not mine enemy.

2 O Thou, who art the Lord my God,
I in distress to Thee,
With loud cries lifted up my voice,
And Thou hast healed me.

3 O Lord, my soul Thou hast brought up,
And rescued from the grave;
That I to pit should not go down,
Alive Thou didst me save.

4 O ye that are His holy ones,
Sing praise unto the Lord;
And give unto Him thanks, when ye
His holiness record.

5 But for a moment lasts His wrath;
Life in His favour lies;
Weeping may for a night endure,
At morn doth joy arise.

H. 36 *God Reconciled in Christ.*

1 DEAREST of all the names above,
My Jesus and my God,
Who can resist Thy heavenly love,
Or trifle with Thy blood?

2 'Tis by the merits of Thy death
The Father smiles again;
'Tis by Thine interceding breath
The Spirit dwells with men.

3 Till God in human flesh I see,
My thoughts no comfort find;
The holy, just, and sacred Three
Are terrors to my mind.

4 But if Immanuel's face appear,
My hope, my joy begins;
His name forbids my slavish fear,
His grace removes my sins.

5 While Jews on their own law rely,
And Greeks of wisdom boast,
I love the incarnate mystery,
And there I fix my trust.

G. Kirby, 1592.

How long wilt Thou for - get me, Lord, Must I for ev - er mourn?

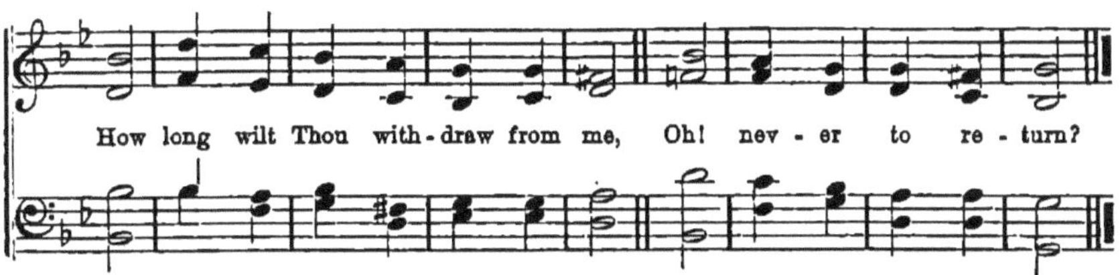
How long wilt Thou with - draw from me, Oh! nev - er to re - turn?

Ps. 13

2 O hear, and to my longing eyes
Restore Thy wonted light;
Dawn on my spirit, lest I sleep
In death's most gloomy night.

3 Since I have always placed my trust
Beneath Thy mercy's wing,
Thy saving health will come; and then
My heart with joy shall spring.

4 Then shall my song, with praise inspired,
To Thee, my God, ascend;
Who to Thy servant in distress,
Such bounty didst extend.

Ps. 27 *First Part.*

1 O Lord, give ear unto my voice,
When I do cry to Thee;
Upon me also mercy have,
And do Thou answer me.

2 When Thou didst say, Seek ye my face,
Then unto Thee reply
Thus did my heart, Above all things
Thy face, Lord, seek will I.

3 Far from me hide not Thou Thy face;
Put not away from Thee
Thy servant in Thy wrath: Thou hast
An helper been to me.

4 O God of my salvation,
Leave me not, nor forsake;
Tho' me my parents both should leave,
The Lord will me up take.

5 O Lord, instruct me in Thy way,
To me a leader be,
In a plain path, because of those
That hatred bear to me.

H. 576 *On the Death of Ministers.*

1 Why should our tears in sorrow flow,
When God recalls His own;
And bids them leave a world of woe,
For an immortal crown.

2 Is not e'en death a gain to those
Whose life to God was given?
Gladly to earth their eyes they close,
To open them in heaven.

3 Their toils are past, their work is done,
And they are fully blessed;
They fought the fight, the victory won,
And entered into rest.

4 The flock must feel the shepherd's loss,
And miss his tender care;
But they who bear with joy the cross,
The crown shall soonest wear.

5 And is not He who called them home
Still to His church most nigh;
To bid yet other labourers come,
And all her need supply?

6 Then let our sorrows cease to flow!
God has recalled His own;
But let our hearts, in every woe,
Still say, "Thy will be done."

G. Rossini, 1792-1868.

1. To God I cried with mourn-ful voice, I sought His gra-cious ear,
In the sad hour when trou - ble rose, And filled my heart with fear.

Ps. 77

2 Sad were my days, and dark my nights,
My soul refused relief;
I thought on God the just and wise;
But thoughts increased my grief.

3 Will He for ever cast me off?
His promise ever fail?
Has He forgot His tender love?
Shall anger still prevail?

4 I'll think again of all Thy ways,
And talk Thy wonders o'er,
Thy wonders of recovering grace,
When flesh could hope no more.

5 Grace dwells with justice on the throne;
And men that love Thy word
Have in Thy sanctuary known
The counsels of the Lord.

H. 275 *Power of Faith.*

1 When musing sorrow weeps the past
And mourns the present pain,
'Tis sweet to think of peace at last,
And feel that death is gain.

2 'Tis not that murmuring thoughts arise,
And dread a Father's will;
'Tis not that meek submission flies,
And would not suffer still:

3 It is that heaven-born faith surveys
The path that leads to light,
And longs her eagle plumes to raise,
And lose herself in sight.

4 Oh! let me wing my hallowed flight
From earth-born woe and care,
And soar above these clouds of night,
My Saviour's bliss to share!

H. 282 *Joy of Hope.*

1 How happy every child of grace
Who knows his sins forgiven!
This earth, he cries, is not my place;
I seek my place in heaven.

2 A country far from mortal sight,
Yet oh! by faith I see
The land of rest, the saint's delight—
The heaven prepared for me.

3 A stranger in the world below,
I calmly sojourn here;
Nor can its happiness or woe
Provoke my hope or fear;

4 Its evils in a moment end;
Its joys as soon are past;
But oh! the bliss to which I tend
Eternally shall last.

H. 629 *Death made Desirable.*

1 Jesus! the vision of Thy face
Hath overpowering charms!
Scarce shall I feel death's cold embrace,
If Christ be in my arms.

2 Then, while ye hear my heart-strings [break,
How sweet my minutes roll!
A mortal paleness on my cheek,
And glory in my soul.

Dr. Wm. Arnold, 1791.

1. Come, let us to the Lord our God, With con - trite hearts re - turn;
Our God is gra-cious, nor will leave The des - o - late to mourn.

H. 215 *Return to God:*

2 His voice commands the tempest forth,
And stills the stormy wave;
And though His arm be strong to smite,
'Tis also strong to save.

3 Long hath the night of sorrow reigned;
The dawn shall bring us light;
God shall appear, and we shall rise
With gladness in His sight.

4 Our hearts, if God we seek to know,
Shall know Him, and rejoice;
His coming like the morn shall be,
Like morning songs His voice.

5 As dew upon the tender herb,
Diffusing fragrance round;
As showers that usher in the spring,
And cheer the thirsty ground;

6 So shall His presence bless our souls,
And shed a joyful light;
That hallowed morn shall chase away
The sorrows of the night.

Ps. 90 *Second Part.*

1 Life like a vain amusement flies,
A fable or a song;
By swift degrees our nature dies,
Nor can our joys be long.

2 'Tis but a few whose days amount
To threescore years and ten;
And all beyond that short account,
Is sorrow, toil, and pain.

3 Almighty God, reveal Thy love,
And not Thy wrath alone;
O! let our sweet experience prove
The mercies of Thy throne.

4 Our souls would learn the heavenly art
T' improve the hours we have,
That we may act the wiser part,
And live beyond the grave.

H. 684 *Heaven traced through Sorrow.*

1 Lord, what a wretched land is this,
That yields us no supply,
No cheering fruits, no wholesome trees,
Nor streams of living joy.

2 Our journey is a thorny maze,
But we march upward still;
Forget these troubles of the ways,
And reach at Zion's hill.

3 See the kind angels, at the gates,
Inviting us to come;
There Jesus, the Forerunner, waits,
To welcome travellers home.

4 There, on a green and flowery mount,
Our weary souls shall sit,
And, with transporting joys, recount
The labours of our feet.

5 Eternal glory to the King,
Who brought us safely through;
Our tongues shall never cease to sing,
And endless praise renew,

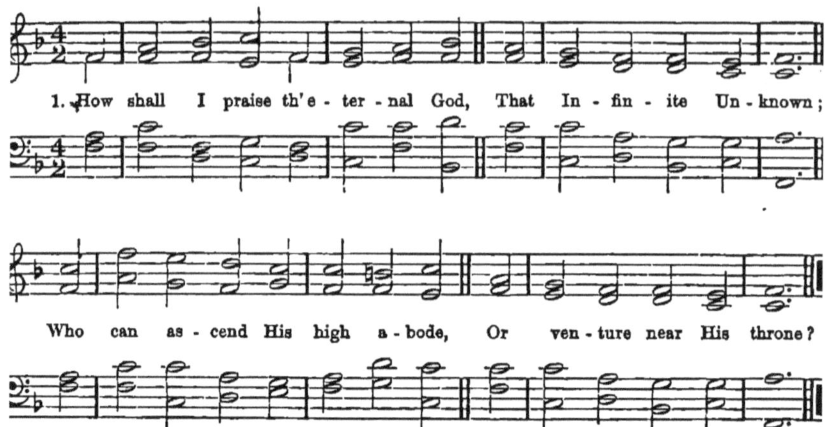
1. How shall I praise th'e - ter - nal God, That In - fin - ite Un - known;
Who can as - cend His high a - bode, Or ven - ture near His throne?

. 2 *The Divine Perfections.*

Those watchful eyes, that never sleep,
Survey the world around;
His wisdom is a boundless deep,
Where all our thoughts are drowned.

He knows no shadow of a change,
Nor alters His decrees;
Firm as a rock His truth remains,
To guard His promises.

.. 4 *Infinity of God.*

Great God! how infinite art Thou!
What worthless worms are we!
Let the whole race of creatures bow,
And pay their praise to Thee.

Thy throne eternal ages stood,
Ere seas or stars were made;
Thou art the ever living God,
Were all the nations dead.

Eternity, with all its years,
Stands present in Thy view;
To Thee there's nothing old appears;
Great God! there's nothing new.

Our lives through various scenes are
And vexed with trifling cares, [drawn,
While Thine eternal thought moves on
Thine undisturbed affairs.

Great God! how infinite art Thou!
What worthless worms are we!
Let the whole race of creatures bow,
And pay their praise to Thee.

H. 3 *God's Sovereignty.*

1 Keep silence, all created things,
And wait your Maker's nod;
My soul stands trembling while she sings
The honours of her God.

2 Life, death, and hell, and worlds unknown
Hang on His firm decree;
He sits on no precarious throne,
Nor borrows leave to be.

3 His providence unfolds His book,
And makes His counsels shine;
Each opening leaf, and every stroke,
Fulfil some deep design.

4 In Thy fair book of life and grace,
Oh! may I find my name
Recorded in some humble place,
Beneath my Lord the Lamb.

Ps. 101

1 To Thee, my righteous King and Lord,
My grateful soul I'll raise;
From day to day Thy works record,
And ever sing Thy praise.

2 Thy wondrous acts, Thy power and might,
My constant theme shall be;
That song shall be my soul's delight,
Which breathes in praise to Thee.

3 From all Thy works, O Lord, shall spring
The sound of joy and praise;
Thy saints shall of Thy glory sing,
And show the world Thy ways.

Ps. 124

1 Had not the God of truth and love.
When hosts against us rose,
Displayed His vengeance from above,
And crushed the conquering foes;

2 Their armies, like a raging flood,
Had swept the guardless land;
Destroyed on earth His blest abode,
And whelmed our feeble band.

3 But safe beneath His spreading shield
His sons securely rest;
Defy the dangers of the field,
And bare the fearless breast.

4 And now our souls shall bless the Lord,
Who broke the deadly snare;
Who saved us from the murdering sword,
And made our lives His care.

5 Our help is in Jehovah's name,
Who formed the heavens above;
He that supports their wondrous frame
Can guard His church by love.

Ps. 125 *First Part.*

1 Unshaken as the sacred hill,
And firm as mountains stand,
Firm as a rock the soul shall rest,
That trusts th' Almighty hand.

2 Not walls nor hills could guard so well
Old Salem's happy ground,
As those eternal arms of love,
That every saint surround.

3 Deal gently, Lord, with souls sincere,
And lead them safely on
To the bright gates of paradise,
Where Christ their Lord is gone.

Ps. 128

1 O Happy man, whose soul is filled
With zeal and reverend awe;
His lips to God their honours yield,
His life adorns the law.

2 A careful providence shall stand,
And ever guard thy head;
Shall on the labours of thy hand
Its kindly blessings shed.

3 Thy wife shall be a fruitful vine;
Thy children, 'round thy board,
Each like a plant of honour shine,
And learn to fear the Lord.

4 The Lord shall thy best hopes fulfil,
For months and years to come;
The Lord, who dwells on Zion's hill,
Shall send thee blessings home.

5 This is the man whose happy eyes
Shall see his house increase;
Shall see the sinking church arise,
Then leave the world in peace.

Ps. 132

1 Arise, O King of grace, arise,
And enter to Thy rest;
Lo! Thy church waits with longing eyes,
Thus to be owned and blest.

2 Enter, with all Thy glorious train,
Thy Spirit and Thy word;
All that the ark did once contain,
Could no such grace afford.

3 Here, mighty God, accept our vows;
Here let Thy praise be spread;
Bless the provisions of Thy house,
And fill Thy poor with bread.

4 Here let the Son of David reign,
Let God's Anointed shine;
Justice and truth His court maintain,
With love and power divine.

5 Here let Him hold a lasting throne;
And, as His kingdom grows,
Fresh honours shall adorn His crown,
And shame confound His foes.

H. 427 *Perpetual Praise.*

1 Yes, I will bless Thee, O my God,
Through all my mortal days;
And to eternity prolong
Thy vast, Thy boundless praise.

2 Nor shall my tongue alone proclaim
The honours of my God;
My life, with all its active powers,
Shall spread Thy praise abroad.

3 Not death itself shall stop my song,
Though death will close my eyes;
My thoughts shall then to nobler heights,
And sweeter raptures rise.

4 There shall my lips in endless praise,
Their grateful tribute pay;
The theme demands an angel's tongue,
And an eternal day.

ANON.

1. O send Thy light forth and Thy truth; Let them be guides to me,

And bring me to Thine ho - ly hill, Even where Thy dwell - ings be.

Ps. 43 *First Part.*

2 THEN will I to God's altar go,
To God, my chiefest joy;
Yea, God, my God, Thy name to praise
My harp I will employ.

3 Why art thou then cast down, my soul?
What should discourage thee?
And why with vexing thoughts art thou
Disquieted in me?

4 Still trust in God; for Him to praise
Good cause I yet shall have;
He of my countenance is the health,
My God that doth me save.

Ps. 43 *Second Part.*

1 JUDGE me, O God, and plead my cause,
Against a sinful race;
From vile oppression and deceit
Secure me by Thy grace.

2 On Thee my steadfast hope depends,
And am I left to mourn;
To sink in sorrow, and in vain
Implore Thy kind return?

3 O! send Thy light to guide my feet,
And bid Thy truth appear;
Conduct me to Thy holy hill,
To taste Thy mercies there.

4 Then to Thine altar, O my God,
My joyful feet shall rise;
And my triumphant songs shall praise
The God that rules the skies.

5 Sink not, my soul, beneath thy fear,
Nor yield to dark despair;
For I shall live to praise the Lord,
And bless His guardian care.

Ps. 48 *Part Third.*

1 GREAT is the Lord, and greatly He
Is to be praised still,
Within the city of our God,
Upon His holy hill.

2 Mount Zion stands most beautiful,
The joy of all the land;
The city of the mighty King
On her north side doth stand.

3 Walk about Zion, and go round;
The high tow'rs thereof tell:
Consider ye her palaces,
And mark her bulwarks well:

4 That ye may tell posterity,
For this God doth abide
Our God for evermore; He will
Ev'n unto death us guide.

H. 501 *Sabbath Blessings.*

1 BLEST day! thine hours too soon will cease,
Yet, while they gently roll,
Breathe, heavenly Spirit, source of peace,
A Sabbath o'er my soul.

2 When will my pilgrimage be done,
The world's long week be o'er,
That Sabbath dawn which needs no sun,
That day which fades no more?

ARRANGED BY REV. WM. H. HAVERGAL, 1849.

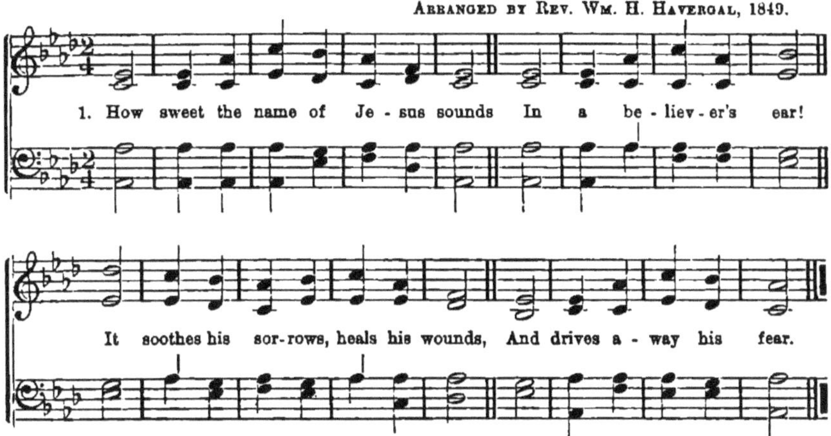
1. How sweet the name of Je - sus sounds In a be - liev - er's ear!
It soothes his sor - rows, heals his wounds, And drives a - way his fear.

H. 290 *Love to Christ.*

2 It makes the wounded spirit whole,
And calms the troubled breast;
'Tis manna to the hungry soul,
And to the weary, rest.

3 Dear Name, the rock on which I build,
My shield and hiding-place;
My never-failing treasury, filled
With boundless stores of grace?

4 Jesus, my Shepherd, Husband, Friend,
My Prophet, Priest, and King;
My Lord, my Life, my Way, my End,
Accept the praise I bring.

5 Weak is the effort of my heart,
And cold my warmest thought;
But when I see Thee as Thou art,
I'll praise Thee as I ought.

6 Till then I would Thy love proclaim
With every fleeting breath;
And may the music of Thy name
Refresh my soul in death.

H. 323 *Calmness from God.*

1 Calm, me, my God, and keep me calm;
Let Thy outstretched wing,
Be like the shade of Elim's palm,
Beside her desert spring.

2 Yes, keep me calm, though loud and rude
The sounds my ear that greet;
Calm in the closet's solitude;
Calm in the busy street.

3 Calm in the hour of buoyant health,
And in the hour of pain,
Calm in my poverty or wealth,
And in my loss or gain.

4 Calm in the sufferance of wrong,
Like Him who bore my shame,
Calm 'mid the threatening, taunting throng,
Who hate Thy holy name.

5 Calm me, my God, and keep me calm,
Soft resting on Thy breast;
Soothe me with holy hymn and psalm,
And bid my spirit rest.

H. 299 *Love to Christ's Disciples.*

1 Lord, Thou on earth didst love Thine own;
Didst love them to the end;
Oh! still from Thy celestial throne,
Let gifts of love descend.

2 As Thou for us didst stoop so low,
Warmed by love's holy flame,
So let our deeds of kindness flow
To all who bear Thy name.

3 One blessed fellowship in love
Thy living church should stand,
Till, faultless, she at last above
Shall shine at Thy right hand.

4 Oh! glorious day when she, the bride,
With her dear Lord appears;
When, robed in beauty at His side,
She shall forget her tears.

BELIEF. C. M.

ANON., WITH CHORUS BY K. R., 1873.

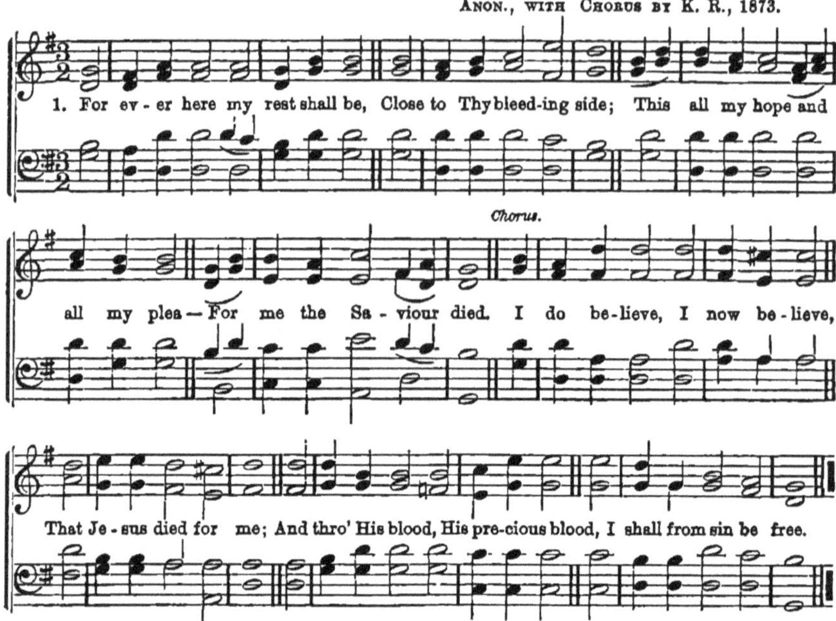

1. For ev - er here my rest shall be, Close to Thy bleed-ing side; This all my hope and
all my plea — For me the Sa - viour died. I do be-lieve, I now be-lieve,
Chorus.
That Je - sus died for me; And thro' His blood, His pre-cious blood, I shall from sin be free.

H. 220 *I do Believe.*

2 My dying Saviour and my God,
Fountain for guilt and sin,
Sprinkle me ever with Thy blood,
And cleanse and keep me clean.
I do believe, etc.

3 Wash me, and make me thus Thine own;
Wash me, and mine Thou art;
Wash me, but not my feet alone —
My hands, my head, my heart.
I do believe, etc.

H. 243 *Communion with Christ.*

1 Jesus, my Saviour, bind me fast,
In cords of heavenly love;
Then sweetly draw me to Thy breast,
Nor let me thence remove.
I do believe, etc.

2 Draw me from all created good,
From self, the world and sin;
To the dear fountain of Thy blood,
And make me pure within.
I do believe, etc.

3 O lead me to Thy mercy seat,
Attract me nearer still;
Draw me, like Mary, to Thy feet,
To sit and learn Thy will.
I do believe, etc.

4 O draw me by Thy providence,
Thy Spirit and Thy word,
From all the things of time and sense,
To Thee, my gracious Lord.
I do believe, etc.

H. 335 *Submission under Affliction.*

1 My times of sorrow and of joy,
Great God, are in Thy hand;
All my enjoyments come from Thee,
And go at Thy command.
I do believe, etc.

2 O Lord, shouldst Thou withhold them all,
Yet would I not repine;
Before they were by me possessed,
They were entirely Thine.
I do believe, etc.

3 Nor would I drop a murmuring word,
If all the world were gone;
But seek substantial happiness,
In Thee, and Thee alone.
I do believe, etc.

KARL REDEN, 1866.

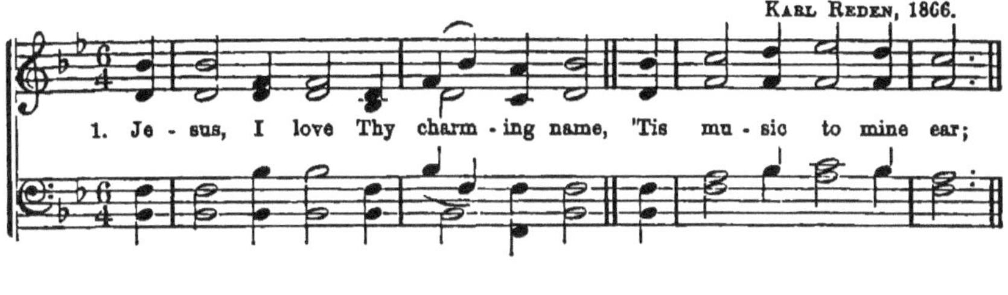
1. Je - sus, I love Thy charm - ing name, 'Tis mu - sic to mine ear;

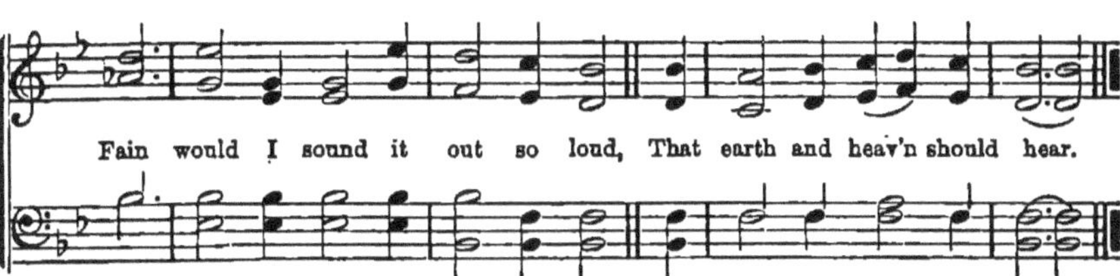
Fain would I sound it out so loud, That earth and heav'n should hear.

H. 297 *Christ the Object of Love.*

2 YES, Thou art precious to my soul,
My joy, my hope, my trust;
Jewels to Thee are gaudy toys,
And gold is sordid dust.

3 All my capacious powers can wish,
In Thee most richly meet;
Nor to mine eyes is light so dear,
Nor friendship half so sweet.

4 Thy grace still dwells upon my heart,
And sheds its fragrance there;
The noblest balm of all its wounds,
The cordial of its care.

5 I'll speak the honours of Thy name,
With my last labouring breath;
Then speechless clasp Thee in mine arms,
The antidote of death.

Ps. 90 *First Part.*

1 OUR God, our help in ages past,
Our hope for years to come,
Our shelter from the stormy blast,
And our eternal home.

2 Before the hills in order stood,
Or earth received her frame,
From everlasting Thou art God,
To endless years the same.

3 A thousand ages in Thy sight
Are like an evening gone;
Short as the watch that ends the night
Before the rising dawn.

4 Time, like an ever-rolling stream,
Bears all its sons away;
They fly, forgotten, as a dream
Dies at the opening day.

5 Our God, our help in ages past,
Our hope for years to come,
Be Thou our guard while troubles last,
And our eternal home.

H. 296 *Christians Drawn with Cords of Love.*

1 MY God, what gentle cords are Thine,
How soft, and yet how strong!
While power, and truth, and love combine
To draw our souls along.

2 Thou saw'st us crushed beneath the yoke
Of Satan and of sin;
Thy hand the iron bondage broke,
Our worthless hearts to win.

3 The guilt of twice ten thousand sins
One offering takes away;
And grace, when first the war begins,
Secures the crowning day.

4 Comfort, through all this vale of tears,
In rich profusion flows;
And glory of unnumbered years
Eternity bestows.

5 Drawn by such cords, we onward move,
Till round Thy throne we meet;
And captives in the chain of love,
Embrace our Conqueror's feet.

DUNLAP. C. M.

A. CHAPIN, 1823.

To Fa-ther, Son, and Ho-ly Ghost, The God whom we a-dore,
Be glo-ry as it was, is now, And shall be ev-er more.

Ps. 1 *Second Part.*

1 Blest is the man who shuns the place
Where sinners love to meet;
Who fears to tread their wicked ways,
And hates the scoffer's seat;

2 But in the statutes of the Lord
Has placed his chief delight;
By day he reads or hears the word,
And meditates by night.

3 He, like a plant of generous kind
By living waters set,
Safe from the storms and blasting wind,
Enjoys a peaceful state.

4 Green as the leaf, and ever fair
Shall his profession shine;
While fruits of holiness appear
Like clusters on the vine.

5 Not so the impious and unjust;
What vain designs they form!
Their hopes are blown away like dust,
Or chaff before the storm.

6 Sinners in judgment shall not stand
Among the sons of grace,
When Christ the Judge, at His right hand,
Appoints His saints a place.

H. 683 *Hope of Heaven.*

1 Blessed be the everlasting God,
The Father of our Lord;
Be His abounding mercy praised,
His majesty adored.

2 When from the dead He raised His Son,
And called Him to the sky,
He gave our souls a lively hope,
That they should never die.

3 What though our inbred sins require
Our flesh to see the dust;
Yet as the Lord our Saviour rose,
So all His followers must.

4 There's an inheritance divine,
Reserved against that day;
'Tis uncorrupted, undefiled,
And cannot fade away.

5 Saints by the power of God are kept,
Till that salvation come;
We walk by faith as strangers here,
Till Christ shall call us home.

H. 123 *Triumph in Christ.*

1 In every trouble, sharp and strong,
My soul to Jesus flies;
My anchor-hold is firm in Him,
When swelling billows rise.

2 His comforts bear my spirits up,
I trust a faithful God;
The sure foundation of my hope
Is in a Saviour's blood.

3 Loud hallelujahs sing, my soul,
To thy Redeemer's name;
In joy, in sorrow, life and death,
His love is still the same.

A. CHAPIN, 1823.

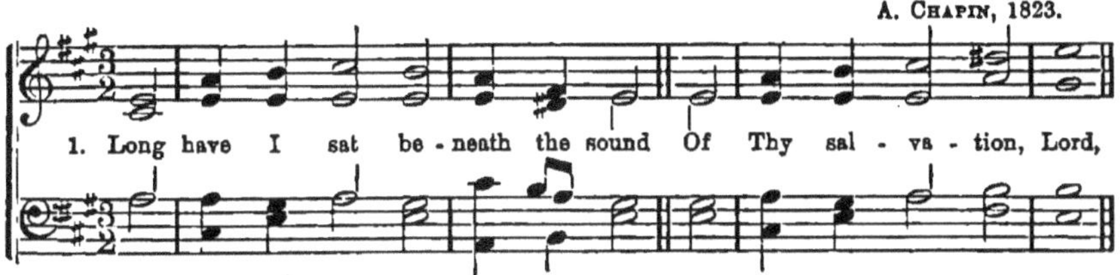
1. Long have I sat be - neath the sound Of Thy sal - va - tion, Lord,

But still how weak my faith is found, And know-ledge of Thy word!

H. 469 *Unfruitfulness Lamented.*

2 OFT I frequent Thy holy place,
And hear almost in vain;
How small a portion of Thy grace
Can my false heart retain!

3 How cold and feeble is my love!
How negligent my fear!
How low my hope of joys above!
How few affections there!

4 Great God, Thy sovereign power impart,
To give Thy word success;
Write Thy salvation in my heart,
And make me learn Thy grace.

5 Show my forgetful feet the way
That leads to joys on high;
There knowledge grows without decay,
And love shall never die.

H. 550 *Covenant Sealed with Christ's Blood.*

1 THE promise of my Father's love,
Shall stand for ever good,
He said, and gave His soul to death,
And sealed the grace with blood.

2 To this dear covenant of Thy word,
I set my worthless name;
I seal the engagement to my Lord,
And make my humble claim.

3 Thy light, and strength, and pardoning [grace,
And glory shall be mine;
My life and soul, my heart and flesh,
And all my powers are Thine.

4 I call that legacy my own,
Which Jesus did bequeath;
'Twas purchased with a dying groan,
And ratified in death.

5 Sweet is the memory of His name,
Who blessed us in His will,
And to His testament of love,
Made His own blood the seal.

H. 575 *On the Death of a Pastor:*

1 Now let our mourning hearts revive,
And all our tears be dry; [grief,
Why should those eyes be drowned in
Which view a Saviour nigh?

2 Though earthly shepherds dwell in dust,
The aged and the young,
The watchful eye in darkness closed,
And mute the instructive tongue;

3 The eternal Shepherd still survives,
New comfort to impart;
His eye still guides us, and His voice
Still animates our heart.

4 "Lo, I am with you," saith the Lord,
"My church shall safe abide;
For I will ne'er forsake My own,
Whose souls in Me confide."

5 Through every scene of life and death,
This promise is our trust;
And this shall be our children's song,
When we are cold in dust.

Glazer.

1. Plung'd in a gulf of dark de-spair, We wretched sin-ners lay,

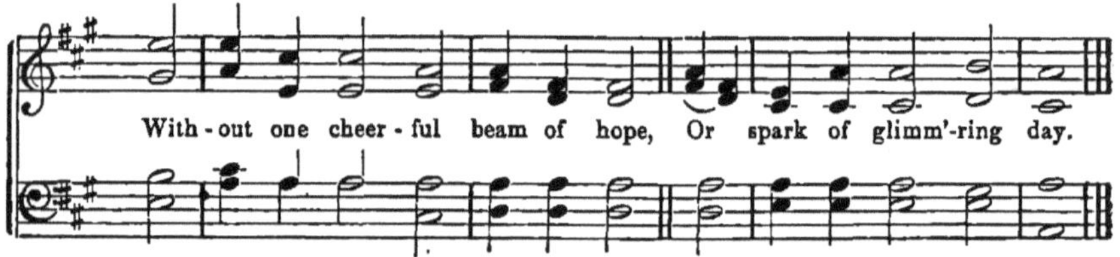
With-out one cheer-ful beam of hope, Or spark of glimm'ring day.

H. 162 *Wonders of Redemption:*

2 With pitying eye the Prince of grace
Beheld our helpless grief;
He saw, and, O amazing love!
He ran to our relief.

3 Down from the shining seats above,
With joyful haste He fled,
Entered the grave in mortal flesh,
And dwelt among the dead.

4 He spoiled the powers of darkness thus,
And brake our iron chains;
Jesus has freed our captive souls
From everlasting pains.

5 O! for this love let rocks and hills
Their lasting silence break;
And all harmonious human tongues
The Saviour's praises speak.

H. 174 *Gospel Invitation.*

1 The Saviour calls, let every ear
Attend the heavenly sound;
Ye doubting souls, dismiss your fear,
Hope smiles reviving round.

2 For every thirsty, longing heart,
Here streams of bounty flow,
And life, and health, and bliss impart,
To banish mortal woe.

3 Here springs of sacred pleasure rise,
To ease your every pain;
Immortal fountain! full supplies!
Nor shall we thirst in vain.

4 Ye sinners, come, 'tis mercy's voice,
The gracious call obey;
Mercy invites to heavenly joys,
And can you yet delay?

5 Dear Saviour, draw reluctant hearts;
To Thee let sinners fly,
And take the bliss Thy love imparts,
And drink and never die.

H. 410 *Mourning over Spiritual Declension.*

1 Why is my heart so far from Thee,
My God, my chief delight?
Why are my thoughts no more by day
With Thee—no more by night?

2 Why should my foolish passions rove?
Where can such sweetness be,
As I have tasted in Thy love,
As I have found in Thee?

3 When my forgetful soul renews
The savour of Thy grace,
My heart presumes I cannot lose
The relish all my days.

4 But ere one fleeting hour is past,
The flattering world employs
Some sensual bait to seize my taste,
And to pollute my joys.

5 Wretch that I am, to wander thus
In chase of false delight!
Let me be fastened to Thy cross,
Rather than lose Thy sight.

Part.
r hath
dear,
Lord to such
n fear.

we are dust,
well knows;
are like the grass,
he grows;

l doth pass,
ne;
ere once it was
e known.

do Him fear
r ends;
n's children still
extends:

covenant,
lway
nts just and true,
em obey.

Salvation.

yful sound;
ır ears;
r every wound,
fears.

d in sin,
r we lay;
ce divine,
day.

ho fly
n around;
of the sky
the sound.

Hymn.

t my evening song
rise;
of my tongue
skies.

gers of the day,
ll my guard;
y wants away,
prepared.

from above
around;
urns of love
ound!

4 What have I done for Him who died
To save my wretched soul?
How are my follies multiplied,
Fast as my minutes roll.

5 Lord, with this guilty heart of mine,
To Thy dear cross I flee,
And to Thy grace my soul resign,
To be renewed by Thee.

6 Sprinkled afresh with pardoning blood,
I'll lay me down to rest,
As in the embraces of my God,
Or on my Saviour's breast.

H. 456 *Evening Prayer and Praise.*

1 Indulgent Father, by whose care
I've passed another day,
Let me this night Thy mercy share;
Oh! teach me how to pray.

2 Show me my sins, and how to mourn
My guilt before Thy face;
Direct me, Lord, to Christ alone,
And save me by Thy grace.

3 Let each returning night declare
The tokens of Thy love;
And every hour Thy grace prepare
My soul for joys above.

4 And when on earth I close mine eyes,
To sleep in death's embrace,
Let me to heaven and glory rise,
To see Thy smiling face.

H. 466 *Divine Presence in Worship.*

1 Now, gracious Lord, Thine arm reveal,
And make Thy glory known;
Now let us all Thy presence feel,
And soften hearts of stone.

2 Help us to venture near Thy throne,
And plead a Saviour's name;
For all that we can call our own,
Is vanity and shame.

3 Send down Thy Spirit from above,
That saints may love Thee more;
That sinners now may learn to love,
Who never loved before.

4 And when before Thee we appear,
In our eternal home,
May growing numbers worship here,
And praise Thee in our room.

SAMUEL R. BROWN.

1. Praise waits for Thee in Zi - on, Lord: To Thee vows paid shall be;
O Thou that hear - er art of prayer, All flesh shall come to Thee.

Ps. 65 *Third Part.*

2 Iniquities, I must confess,
Prevail against me do;
But as for our transgressions,
Them purge away shalt Thou.

3 Blest is the man whom Thou dost choose,
And mak'st approach to Thee,
That he within Thy courts, O Lord,
May still a dweller be.

4 We surely shall be satisfied,
With Thy abundant grace,
And with the goodness of Thy house,
Even of Thy holy place.

5 O God of our salvation,
Thou, in Thy righteousness,
By fearful works unto our prayers,
Thine answer dost express:

6 Therefore the ends of all the earth,
And those afar that be
Upon the sea, their confidence,
O Lord, will place in Thee.

H. 673 *Rest in Heaven.*

1 O land of rest, for thee I sigh;
When will the moment come,
That I shall lay my armour by,
And dwell in peace at home?

2 No tranquil joys on earth I know,
No peaceful sheltering dome;
This world's a wilderness of woe,
This world is not my home.

3 To Jesus Christ I flee for rest;
He bids me cease to roam,
And lean for succour on His breast,
And He'll conduct me home,

4 Weary of wandering round and round,
This vale of sin and gloom,
I long to quit th' unhallowed ground,
And dwell with Christ at home.

H. 674 *The Unseen and Blessed World.*

1 Far from these narrow scenes of night,
Unbounded glories rise,
And realms of joy and pure delight,
Unknown to mortal eyes.

2 Fair distant land! could mortal eyes
But half its charms explore,
How would our spirits long to rise,
And dwell on earth no more.

3 No cloud those blissful regions know—
Realms ever bright and fair;
For sin, the source of mortal woe,
Can never enter there.

4 Oh! may the heavenly prospect fire
Our hearts with ardent love,
Till wings of faith and strong desire
Bear every thought above.

5 Prepare us, Lord! by grace divine,
For Thy bright courts on high;
Then bid our spirits rise and join,
The chorus of the sky.

ABRIDGE. C. M.

Isaac Smith, 1770.

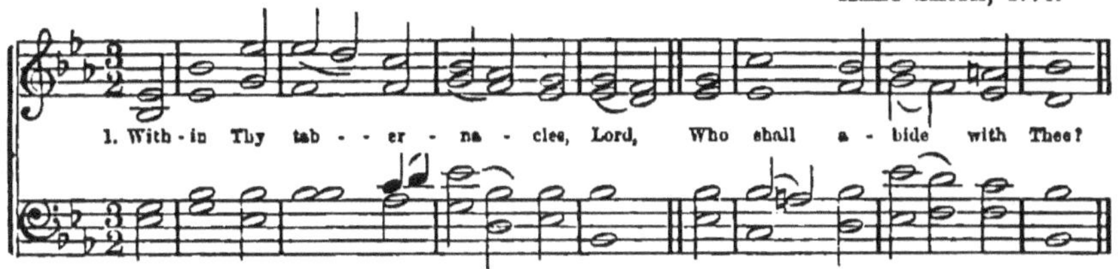
1. With-in Thy tab - - er - na - cles, Lord, Who shall a - bide with Thee?

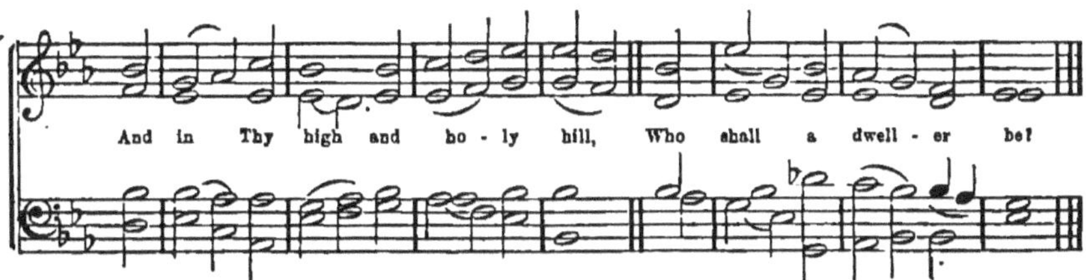
And in Thy high and ho - ly hill, Who shall a dwell - er be?

Ps. 15 *Third Part.*

2 The man that walketh uprightly,
 And worketh righteousness,
And as he thinketh in his heart,
 So doth he truth express:

3 Who doth not slander with his tongue,
 Nor to his friend doth hurt;
Nor yet against his neighbour doth
 Take up an ill report.

4 In whose eyes vile men are despised;
 But those that God do fear
He honoureth; and changeth not,
 Though to his hurt he swear.

H. 19 *The Book of God's Decrees.*

1 Let the whole race of creatures lie,
 Abased before their God;
Whate'er His sovereign voice has formed,
 He governs with a nod.

2 Ten thousand ages ere the skies
 Were into motion brought;
All the long years and worlds to come,
 Stood present to His thought.

3 There's not a sparrow, or a worm,
 But's found in His decrees;
He raises monarchs to their throne,
 And sinks them as He please.

4 If light attend the course I run,
 'Tis He provides those rays;
And 'tis His hand that hides my sun,
 If darkness cloud my days.

5 Yet I would not be much concerned,
 Nor vainly long to see,
In volumes of His deep decrees,
 What months are writ for me.

6 When He reveals the book of life,
 O! may I read my name
Amongst the chosen of His love,
 The followers of the Lamb.

Ps. 23 *First Part.*

1 The Lord's my Shepherd, I'll not want,
 He makes me down to lie
In pastures green; He leadeth me
 The quiet waters by.

2 My soul He doth restore again,
 And me to walk doth make
Within the paths of righteousness,
 Even for His own name's sake.

3 Yea, though I walk in death's dark vale,
 Yet will I fear no ill;
For Thou art with me, and Thy rod
 And staff me comfort still.

4 My table Thou hast furnished,
 In presence of my foes;
My head Thou dost with oil anoint,
 And my cup overflows.

5 Goodness and mercy all my life,
 Shall surely follow me;
And in God's house for evermore
 My dwelling-place shall be.

OLIVER HOLDEN, 1793.

1. All hail the pow'r of Je - sus' name! Let an - gels pros-trate fall, Bring forth the roy-al di - a - dem.

And crown Him Lord of all—Bring forth the roy-al di - a - dem, And crown Him Lord of all.

H. 119 *Jesus Lord of All.*

2 YE chosen seed of Israel's race,
Ye ransomed from the fall;
Hail Him, who saves you by His grace,
And crown Him Lord of all.

3 Sinners, whose love can ne'er forget
The wormwood and the gall;
Go, spread your trophies at His feet,
And crown Him Lord of all.

4 Let every kindred, every tribe,
On this terrestrial ball,
To Him all majesty ascribe,
And crown Him Lord of all.

5 O! that with yonder sacred throng,
We at His feet may fall;
We'll join the everlasting song,
And crown Him Lord of all.

Ps. 27 *Second Part.*

1 THE Lord of glory is my light,
And my salvation too;
God is my strength; nor will I fear
What all my foes can do.

2 One privilege my heart desires:
O! grant me mine abode
Among the churches of Thy saints,
The temples of my God.

3 There shall I offer my requests,
And see Thy beauty still,
Shall hear Thy messages of love,
And there inquire Thy will.

4 When troubles rise and storms appear,
There may His children hide;
God is a strong pavilion, where
He makes my soul abide.

5 Now shall my head be lifted high
Above my foes around,
And songs of joy and victory
Within Thy temple sound.

Ps. 81

1 To God, our strength, your voice, aloud,
In strains of glory raise;
High to Jehovah, Jacob's God,
Exalt the notes of praise.

2 With psalms of honour and of joy,
Let all His temples ring;
Your various instruments employ,
And songs of triumph sing.

3 Now let the gospel trumpet blow,
On His appointed feast,
And teach His waiting church to know
The Sabbath's sacred rest.

4 This was the statute of the Lord,
To Israel's favoured race;
And yet His courts preserve His word,
And there we wait His grace.

Doxology.

To Father, Son, and Holy Ghost,
The God whom we adore,
Be glory, as it was, is now,
And shall be evermore.

Ps. 108

1 Awake, my soul, to sound His praise,
Awake my harp to sing;
Join all my powers the song to raise,
And morning incense bring.

2 Among the people of His care,
And through the nations round,
Glad songs of praise will I prepare,
And there His name resound.

3 Be Thou exalted, O my God,
Above the starry train;
Diffuse Thy heavenly grace abroad,
And teach the world Thy reign.

4 So shall Thy chosen sons rejoice,
And throng Thy courts above;
While sinners hear Thy pard'ning voice,
And taste redeeming love.

Ps. 122 *Third Part.*

1 I joyed when to the house of God,
Go up, they said to me.
Jerusalem, within thy gates
Our feet shall standing be.

2 To Israel's testimony, there
To God's name thanks to pay;
For thrones of judgment, even the thrones
Of David's house there stay.

3 Pray that Jerusalem may have
Peace and felicity;
Let them that love thee and thy peace,
Have still prosperity.

4 Therefore I wish that peace may still
Within thy walls remain,
And ever may thy palaces
Prosperity retain.

5 Now, for my friends' and brethren's sake,
Peace be in thee, I'll say;
And for the house of God our Lord,
I'll seek thy good alway.

Ps. 149

1 All ye that love the Lord, rejoice,
And let your songs be new;
Amidst the church with cheerful voice,
His later wonders show.

2 The Jews, the people of His grace,
Shall their Redeemer sing;
And Gentile nations join the praise,
While Zion owns her King.

3 The Lord takes pleasure in the just,
Whom sinners treat with scorn;
The meek, that lie despised in dust,
Salvation shall adorn.

4 Saints shall be joyful in their King,
E'en on a dying bed;
And like the souls in glory sing,
For God shall raise the dead.

5 Then His high praise shall fill their tongues,
Their hand shall wield the sword;
And vengeance shall attend their songs,
The vengeance of the Lord.

6 When Christ His judgment-seat ascends,
And bids the world appear,
Thrones are prepared for all His friends,
Who humbly loved Him here.

7 Then shall they rule with iron rod,
Nations that dared rebel,
And join the sentence of their God,
On tyrants doomed to hell.

8 The royal sinners, bound in chains,
New triumph shall afford;
Such honour for the saints remain;
Praise ye, and love the Lord.

H. 560 *Glory and Safety of the Church.*

1 How glorious is the sacred place,
Where we adoring stand;
Zion, the joy of all the earth,
The beauty of the land.

2 Bulwarks of mighty grace defend
The city where we dwell;
The walls of strong salvation made,
Defy the assaults of hell.

3 Lift up the everlasting gates,
The doors wide open fling;
Enter, ye nations that obey
The statutes of our King.

4 Here shall you taste unmingled joys.
And live in perfect peace;
You that have known Jehovah's name,
And ventured on His grace.

5 Trust in the Lord, for ever trust,
And banish all your fears;
Strength in the Lord Jehovah dwells,
Eternal as His years.

FOUNTAIN. C. M.

DR. LOWELL MASON, 1831.

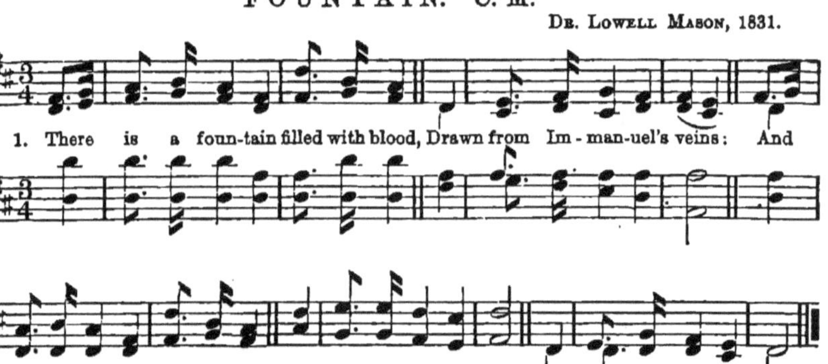
1. There is a foun-tain filled with blood, Drawn from Im-man-uel's veins; And
sin-ners plunged be-neath that flood, Lose all their guil-ty stains—Lose all their guil-ty stains.

H. 165 *Salvation by the Blood of the Lamb.*

2 THE dying thief rejoiced to see
That fountain in his day;
And there may I, though vile as he,
Wash all my sins away.

3 Dear dying Lamb, Thy precious blood
Shall never lose its power,
Till all the ransomed Church of God
Be saved to sin no more.

4 E'er since by faith I saw the stream
Thy flowing wounds supply,
Redeeming love has been my theme,
And shall be till I die.

5 Then, in a nobler, sweeter song,
I'll sing Thy power to save; [tongue
When this poor lisping, stammering
Lies silent in the grave.

H. 169 *Universal Invitation.*

1 LET every mortal ear attend,
And every heart rejoice;
The trumpet of the gospel sounds,
With an inviting voice.

2 Ho! ye that pant for living streams,
And pine away and die,
Here you may quench your raging thirst,
With springs that never dry.

3 Rivers of love and mercy here,
In a rich ocean join;
Salvation in abundance flows,
Like floods of milk and wine.

4 The happy gates of gospel grace
Stand open night and day;
Lord, we are come to seek supplies,
And drive our wants away.

H. 396 *The Christian Soldier.*

1 AM I a soldier of the cross,
A follower of the Lamb,
And shall I fear to own His cause,
Or blush to speak His name?

2 Must I be carried to the skies,
On flowery beds of ease,
While others fought to win the prize,
And sailed through bloody seas?

3 Are there no foes for me to face?
Must I not stem the flood?
Is this dark world a friend to grace,
To help me on to God?

4 Sure I must fight, if I would reign;
Increase my courage, Lord;
I'll bear the toil, endure the pain,
Supported by Thy word.

5 Thy saints, in all this glorious war,
Shall conquer though they die;
They see the triumph from afar,
With faith's discerning eye.

6 When that illustrious day shall rise,
And all Thine armies shine,
In robes of victory through the skies,
The glory shall be Thine.

1. A-maz-ing grace! how sweet the sound, That saved a wretch like me!
I once was lost, but now am found, Was blind, but now I see.
Was blind, but now I see— Was
blind, but now I see— I once was lost, but now am found, Was blind, but now I see.

H. 163 *Triumphant Grace.*

2 'Twas grace that taught my heart to fear,
And grace my fears relieved;
How precious did that grace appear,
The hour I first believed!

3 Through many dangers, toils and snares,
I have already come;
'Tis grace has brought me safe thus far,
And grace will lead me home.

4 The Lord has promised good to me,
His word my hope secures;
He will my shield and portion be,
As long as life endures.

5 And when this heart and flesh shall fail,
And mortal life shall cease,
I shall possess, within the veil,
A life of joy and peace.

6 The earth shall soon dissolve like snow,
The sun forbear to shine;
But God, who called me here below,
Will be for ever mine.

H. 337 *Consolations in Sickness.*

1 When languor and disease invade
This trembling house of clay,
'Tis sweet to look beyond my pains,
And long to fly away.

2 Sweet to look inward, and attend
The whispers of His love;
Sweet to look upward, to the place
Where Jesus pleads above.

3 Sweet to look back, and see my name
In life's fair book set down;
Sweet to look forward, and behold
Eternal joys my own.

4 Sweet to reflect how grace divine
My sins on Jesus laid;
Sweet to remember that His blood
My debt of suffering paid.

5 Sweet on His righteousness to stand,
Which saves from second death;
Sweet to experience, day by day,
His Spirit's quickening breath.

6 Sweet on His faithfulness to rest,
Whose love can never end;
Sweet on His covenant of grace
For all things to depend.

7 Sweet in the confidence of faith,
To trust His firm decrees;
Sweet to lie passive in His hands,
And know no will but His.

8 If such the sweetness of the streams,
What must the fountain be,
Where saints and angels draw their bliss
Immediately from Thee!

Doxology:

To Father, Son, and Holy Ghost,
The God whom we adore,
Be glory, as it was, is now,
And shall be evermore.

S. B. Pond, 1835.
ılt hear me when I pray; I am for ev - er Thine;
- fore Thee all the day, Nor would I dare to sin.

Part.

· weary head
ɪusiness free,
g on my bed
ırt and Thee.

acrifice ;
rk is done,
ı and hope relies
ılone.

ughts composed of
ȝ to sleep ; [peace,
keeps my days,
bers keep.

'art.

'ords, O Lord,
ɜigh ;
ny King, my God ;
l pray.

ırly hear my voice ;

and, looking up,
pect.

God that doth
ight ;
vell with Thee,
ı Thy sight.

Thou hat'st ;
rs be ;
eitful man
ɪee.

5 But I into Thy house will come,
In Thine abundant grace ;
And I will worship in Thy fear,
Toward Thy holy place.

Ps. 2

1 Why did the nations join to slay
The Lord's anointed Son ?
Why did they cast His laws away,
And tread His gospel down ?

2 The Lord that sits above the skies,
Derides their rage below ;
He speaks with vengeance in His eyes,
And strikes their spirits through.

3 "I call Him My eternal Son,
And raise Him from the dead ;
I make My holy hill his throne,
And wide His kingdom spread.

4 "Ask Me, My Son, and then enjoy
The utmost heathen lands ;
Thy rod of iron shall destroy
The rebel that withstands."

5 Be wise, ye rulers of the earth,
Obey the anointed Lord ;
Adore the King of heavenly birth,
And tremble at His word.

6 With humble love address His throne ;
For if He frown, ye die :
Those are secure, and those alone,
Who on his grace rely.

Melchoir Vulpius, 1616.

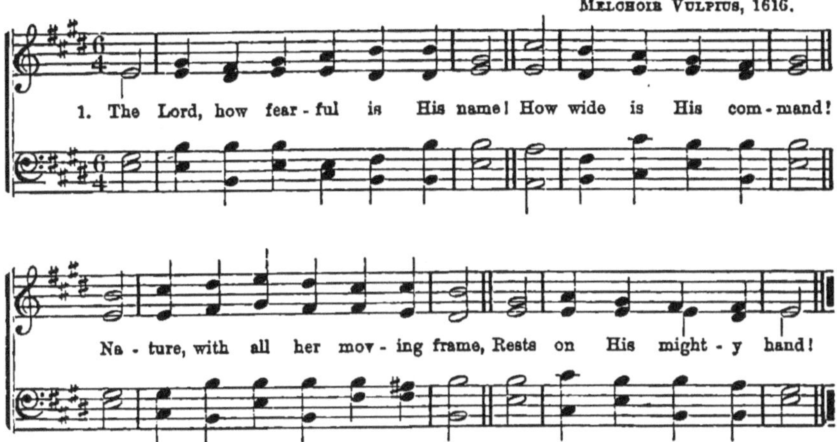
1. The Lord, how fear - ful is His name! How wide is His com - mand!
Na - ture, with all her mov - ing frame, Rests on His might - y hand!

H. 5 *Majesty and Dominion of God.*

2 Immortal glory forms His throne,
And light His awful robe;
While with a smile, or with a frown,
He manages the globe.

3 A word of His almighty breath
Can swell or sink the seas;
Build the vast empires of the earth,
Or break them, if He please!

4 Adoring angels round Him fall,
In all their shining forms;
His sovereign eye looks through them all,
And pities mortal worms.

Ps. 60

1 Lord, Thou hast scourged our guilty land,
Behold Thy people mourn;
Shall vengeance ever guide Thy hand;
Shall mercy ne'er return!

2 Beneath the terrors of Thine eye,
Earth's haughty towers decay;
Thy frowning mantle spreads the sky,
And mortals melt away.

3 Our Zion trembles at the stroke,
And dreads Thy lifted hand;
Oh! heal the people Thou hast broke,
And save the sinking land.

4 Exalt Thy banner in the field,
For those that fear Thy name;
From barbarous hosts our nation shield,
And put our foes to shame.

5 Attend our armies to the fight,
And be their guardian God;
In vain shall numerous powers unite
Against Thy lifted rod.

6 Our troops beneath Thy guiding hand,
Shall gain a glad renown;
'Tis God who makes the feeble stand,
And treads the mighty down.

Ps. 61 *First Part.*

1 O God, give ear unto my cry;
Unto my prayer attend.
From th' utmost corner of the land
My cry to Thee I'll send.

2 What time my heart is overwhelmed,
And in perplexity,
Do Thou me lead unto the rock
That higher is than I.

3 For Thou hast for my refuge been
A shelter by Thy power;
And for defence against my foes
Thou hast been a strong tower.

4 Within Thy tabernacle I
For ever will abide;
And under covert of Thy wings
With confidence me hide.

5 For Thou the vows that I did make,
O Lord, my God, didst hear;
Thou hast giv'n me the heritage
Of those Thy name that fear.

KINGSLEY'S "HARP OF DAVID."

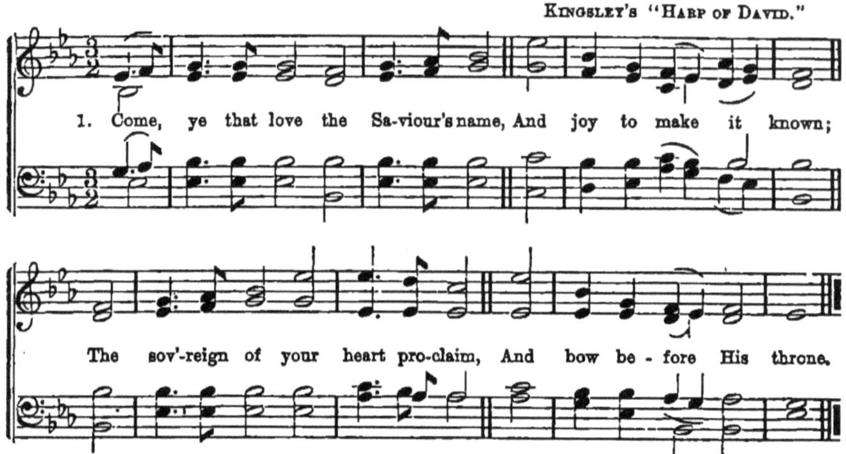
1. Come, ye that love the Sa-viour's name, And joy to make it known;
The sov'-reign of your heart pro-claim, And bow be - fore His throne.

H. 118 *Exhortation to Praise Christ.*

2 BEHOLD your King, your Saviour, crowned
With glories all divine;
And tell the wondering nations 'round,
How bright these glories shine.

3 Infinite power and boundless grace
In Him unite their rays;
Ye that have e'er beheld His face,
Can ye forbear His praise?

4 When in His earthly courts we view
The glories of our King,
We long to love as angels do,
And wish like them to sing.

5 And shall we long and wish in vain?
Lord, teach our songs to rise;
Thy love can animate the strain,
And bid it reach the skies.

6 O happy period! glorious day!
When heaven and earth shall raise,
With all their powers, the raptured lay,
To celebrate Thy praise.

Ps. 28 *First Part.*

1 ADORED for ever be the Lord;
His praise I will resound,
From whom the cries of my distress
A gracious answer found.

2 He is my strength and shield; my heart
Has trusted in His name;
And now relieved, my heart with joy
His praises shall proclaim.

3 The Lord, the everlasting God,
Is my defence and rock;
The saving health, the saving strength,
Of His anointed flock.

4 O save and bless Thy people, Lord,
Thy heritage preserve; [hearts,
Feed, strengthen, and support their
That we may never swerve.

Ps. 32 *Third Part.*

1 O BLESSED is the man to whom
Is freely pardoned
All the transgressions he hath done,
Whose sin is covered.

2 Blest is the man to whom the Lord
Imputeth not his sin,
And in whose spirit there's no guile,
Nor fraud is found therein.

3 I will confess unto the Lord
My trespasses, said I;
And of my sin Thou freely didst
Forgive th' iniquity.

4 For this shall every godly one
His prayer make unto Thee;
In such a time he shall Thee seek,
As found Thou mayest be.

5 Thou art my hiding-place, Thou shalt
From trouble keep me free;
Thou, with songs of deliverance,
About shalt compass me.

ELIZABETHTOWN. C. M.

George Kingsley, 1838.

1. God is our re - fuge and our strength, In straits a pre - sent aid;

There-fore, al - though the earth re - move, We will not be a - fraid;

Ps. 46 *First Part.*

2 Though hills amidst the seas be cast;
Though waters roaring make,
And troubled be; yea, though the hills
By swelling seas do shake.

3 A river is, whose streams do glad
The city of our God;
The holy place, wherein the Lord
Most high hath His abode.

4 God in the midst of her doth dwell;
Nothing shall her remove;
The Lord to her an helper will,
And that right early, prove.

5 The Lord of hosts upon our side
Doth constantly remain;
The God of Jacob's our refuge,
Us safely to maintain.

Ps. 39

1 Teach me the measure of my days,
Thou Maker of my frame;
I would survey life's narrow space,
And learn how frail I am.

2 A span is all that we can boast,
An inch or two of time;
Man is but vanity and dust
In all his flower and prime.

3 What should I wish or wait for, then,
From creatures, earth, and dust!
They make our expectations vain,
And disappoint our trust.

4 Now I forbid my carnal hope,
My fond desires recall;
I give my mortal interest up,
And make my God my all.

Ps. 72 *Third Part.*

1 O Lord, Thy judgments give the King,
His Son Thy righteousness.
With right He shall Thy people judge,
Thy poor with uprightness.

2 The just shall flourish in His days,
And prosper in His reign;
He shall, while doth the moon endure,
Abundant peace maintain.

3 His large and great dominion shall
From sea to sea extend;
It from the river shall reach forth
Unto earth's utmost end.

4 His name for ever shall endure;
Last like the sun it shall:
Men shall be blest in Him, and blest
All nations shall Him call.

5 Now blessed be the Lord our God,
The God of Israel,
For He alone doth wondrous works,
In glory that excel.

6 And blessed be His glorious name
To all eternity:
The whole earth let His glory fill
Amen, so let it be.

ENGLISH.
1. O Thou to whom all crea - tures bow, With - in this earth - ly frame,
Through all the world how great art Thou! How glo - rious is Thy name!

Ps. 8 *Second Part.*

2 When heaven, Thy beauteous work on
Employs my wondering sight; [high,
The moon that nightly rules the sky,
With stars of feebler light;

3 Lord, what is man, that Thou shouldst
To bear him in Thy mind! [deign
Or what his race, that Thou shouldst
To them so wondrous kind! [prove

4 O Thou to whom all creatures bow,
Within this earthly frame;
Through all the world, how great art
How glorious is Thy name! [Thou!

Ps. 14

1 The Lord from His celestial throne,
Looked down on things below,
To find the man that sought His grace,
Or did His justice know.

2 By nature all are gone astray,
Their practice all the same;
There's none that fears his Maker's hand,
There's none that loves His name.

3 Their tongues are used to speak deceit,
Their slanders never cease;
How swift to mischief are their feet,
Nor know the paths of peace!

4 O! that salvation might proceed
From Zion's sacred place,
Till Israel's captives all are freed,
And sing recovering grace.

H. 94 *Christ Enthroned.*

1 He who on earth as man was known,
And bore our sins and pains,
Now, seated on th' eternal throne,
The God of glory reigns.

2 While harps unnumbered sound His
In yonder world above, [praise,
His saints on earth admire His ways,
And glory in His love.

3 When troubles, like a burning sun,
Beat heavy on their head,
To this almighty Rock they run,
And find a pleasing shade.

4 How glorious He! how happy they,
In such a glorious Friend!
Whose love secures them all the way,
And crowns them at the end.

H. 541 *Children brought to Jesus.*

1 See Israel's gentle Shepherd stand,
With all-engaging charms;
Hark, how He calls the tender lambs,
And folds them in His arms!

2 "Permit them to approach," He cries,
"Nor scorn their humble name;
For 'twas to bless such souls as these,
The Lord of angels came."

3 We bring them, Lord, in thankful hands,
And yield them up to Thee;
Joyful that we ourselves are Thine—
Thine let our offspring be.

I. Tucker, 1800.

Let God the Fa-ther, and the Son, And Spi-rit be a-dored, Where there are works to
make Him known, Or saints to love the Lord— Or saints to love the Lord.

H. 55 *Efficacy of the Blood of Christ.*

1 Jesus, in Thee our eyes behold
A thousand glories more
Than the rich gems and polished gold
The sons of Aaron wore.

2 Once, in the circuit of a year,
With blood, but not his own,
Aaron within the veil appears,
Before the golden throne.

3 But Christ, by his own powerful blood,
Ascends above the skies;
And in the presence of our God,
Shows His own sacrifice.

4 Jesus, the King of glory, reigns
On Zion's heavenly hill;
Looks like a lamb that has been slain,
And wears His priesthood still.

5 He ever lives to intercede
Before His Father's face;
Give Him, my soul, thy cause to plead,
Nor doubt the Father's grace.

H. 58 *Christ the Shepherd.*

1 Father of peace, and God of love,
We own Thy power to save;
That power by which our Shepherd rose,
Victorious o'er the grave.

2 We triumph in that Shepherd's name,
Still watchful for our good,
Who brought the eternal covenant down,
And sealed it with His blood.

3 So may Thy Spirit seal my soul,
And mould it to Thy will;
That my fond heart no more may stray,
But keep Thy covenant still.

4 Still may we gain superior strength,
And press with vigour on,
Till full perfection crown our hopes,
And fix us near Thy throne.

H. 358 *Cleaving to Christ.*

1 To whom, my Saviour, shall I go,
If I depart from Thee:
My guide through all this vale of woe,
And more than all to me?

2 For I have felt Thy dying love,
Breathe gently through my heart,
To whisper hope of joys above;
And can we ever part?

3 Ah, no! with Thee I'll walk below,
My journey to the grave:
To whom, my Saviour, shall I go,
When only Thou canst save?

H. 537 *Children Dedicated.*

1 Now let the children of the saints
Be dedicate to God;
Pour out Thy Spirit on them, Lord,
And wash them in Thy blood.

2 Thus to the parents and their seed,
Shall Thy salvation come;
And numerous households meet at last,
In one eternal home.

BALERMA. C. M.

Arranged by R. Simpson.

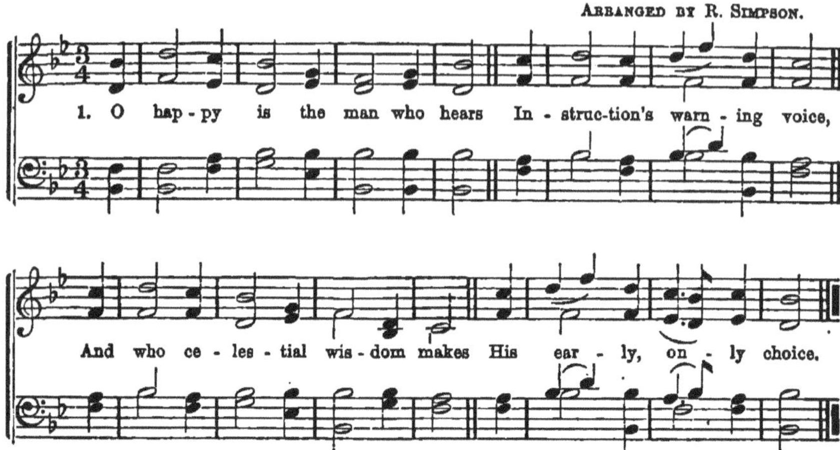
1. O hap - py is the man who hears In - struc-tion's warn - ing voice,
And who ce - les - tial wis - dom makes His ear - ly, on - ly choice.

H. 157 *Excellency of the Gospel.*

2 For she has treasures greater far
Than eastern climes unfold;
More precious are her bright rewards,
Than gems or stores of gold.

3 Her right hand offers to the just
Immortal, happy days;
Her left, imperishable wealth
And heavenly crowns displays.

4 And as her holy labours rise,
So her rewards increase;
Her ways are ways of pleasantness,
And all her paths are peace.

H. 148 *Christ's Glory unveiled in the Scriptures.*

1 Thou lovely Source of true delight,
Whom I unseen adore;
Unveil Thy beauties to my sight,
That I may love Thee more.

2 Thy glory o'er creation shines,
But in Thy sacred word,
I read in fairer, brighter lines,
My bleeding, dying Lord.

3 'Tis here, whene'er my comforts droop,
And sins and sorrows rise,
Thy love with cheerful beams of hope,
My fainting heart supplies.

4 Jesus, my Lord, my life, my light,
O! come with blissful ray;
Break radiant through the shades of night
And chase my fears away.

5 Then shall my soul with rapture trace
The wonders of Thy love;
But the full glories of Thy face
Are only known above.

H. 317 *Prayer for the Return of the Spirit.*

1 O for a closer walk with God,
A calm and heavenly frame;
A light to shine upon the road,
That leads me to the Lamb.

2 Where is the blessedness I knew,
When first I saw the Lord?
Where is the soul refreshing view
Of Jesus and His word?

3 What peaceful hours I once enjoyed,
How sweet their memory still!
But they have left an aching void,
The world can never fill.

4 Return, O holy Dove, return,
Sweet messenger of rest!
I hate the sins that made Thee mourn,
And drove Thee from my breast.

5 The dearest idol I have known,
Whate'er that idol be,
Help me to tear it from Thy throne,
And worship only Thee.

6 So shall my walk be close with God,
Calm and serene my frame;
So purer light shall mark the road,
That leads me to the Lamb.

H. 313 *Prayer for Increasing Holiness.*

1 O! for a heart to praise my God,
A heart from sin set free;
A heart that always feels Thy blood,
So freely shed for me:

2 A heart resigned, submissive, meek,
My great Redeemer's throne;
Where only Christ is heard to speak;
Where Jesus reigns alone;

3 A heart in every thought renewed,
And full of love divine;
Holy, and right, and pure, and good,
A copy, Lord, of Thine.

H. 314 *Prayer for Assurance.*

1 Why should the children of a King
Go mourning all their days?
Great Comforter, descend and bring
Some tokens of Thy grace.

2 Dost Thou not dwell in all the saints,
And seal the heirs of heaven?
When wilt Thou banish my complaints,
And show my sins forgiven?

3 Assure my conscience of her part
In the Redeemer's blood;
And bear Thy witness with my heart
That I am born of God.

4 Thou art the earnest of His love,
The pledge of joys to come;
And Thy soft wings, celestial Dove,
Will safe convey me home.

Ps. 37

1 My God, the steps of pious men
Are ordered by Thy will:
Though they should fall, they rise again;
Thy hand supports them still.

2 The heavenly heritage is theirs,
Their portion and their home;
He feeds them now, and makes them heirs
Of blessings long to come.

3 Wait on the Lord, ye sons of men,
Nor fear when tyrants frown;
Ye shall confess their pride was vain,
When justice casts them down.

4 The haughty sinner have I seen,
Not fearing man nor God,
Like a tall bay-tree, fair and green,
Spreading his arms abroad;

5 And lo! he vanished from the ground,
Destroyed by hands unseen:
Nor root, nor branch, nor leaf was found,
Where all that pride had been.

6 But mark the man of holy fear,
How blest is his decease!
He spends his days in duty here,
And leaves the world in peace.

Ps. 122 *First Part.*

1 How did my heart rejoice to hear
My friends devoutly say,
In Zion let us all appear
And keep the solemn day.

2 I love her gates, I love the road;
The church, adorned with grace,
Stands like a palace built for God
To show His milder face.

3 Up to her courts, with joys unknown,
The holy tribes repair;
The Son of David holds His throne,
And sits in judgment there.

4 He hears our praises and complaints;
And while His awful voice
Divides the sinners from the saints,
We tremble and rejoice.

5 Peace be within this sacred place,
And joy a constant guest;
With holy gifts and heavenly grace
Be her attendants blest.

6 My soul shall pray for Zion still,
While life or breath remains;
There my best friends, my kindred dwell;
There God, my Saviour, reigns.

Ps. 133 *Second Part.*

1 Behold, how good a thing it is,
And how becoming well,
Together such as brethren are
In unity to dwell!

2 Like precious ointment on the head,
That down the beard did flow,
Ev'n Aaron's beard, and to the skirts,
Did of his garments go.

3 As Hermon's dew, the dew that doth
On Zion hill descend;
For there the blessing God commands,
Life that shall never end.

English, Arranged by Mason, 1832.

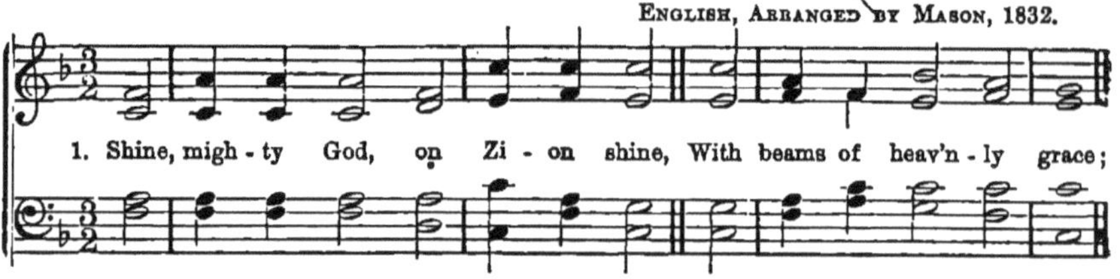
1. Shine, migh - ty God, on Zi - on shine, With beams of heav'n - ly grace;

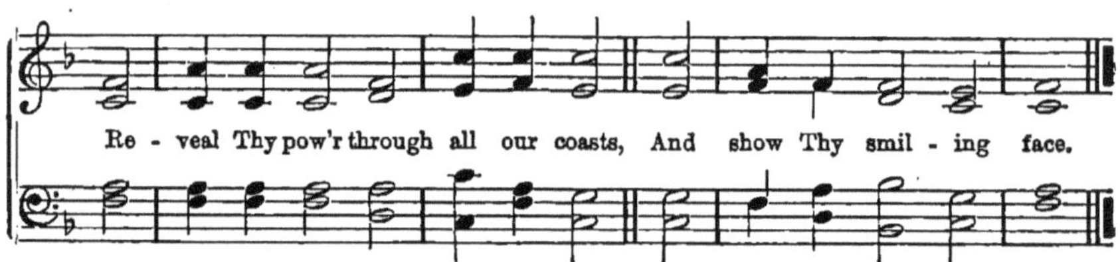
Re - veal Thy pow'r through all our coasts, And show Thy smil - ing face.

Ps. 67

2 When shall Thy name from shore to shore
Sound all the earth abroad;
And distant nations know and love
Their Saviour and their God?

3 Sing to the Lord, ye distant lands,
Sing loud with solemn voice;
Let every tongue exalt His praise,
And every heart rejoice.

4 He, the great Lord, the sovereign Judge,
That sits enthroned above,
In wisdom rules the worlds He made,
And bids them taste His love.

5 Earth shall obey His high command,
And yield a full increase;
Our God will crown His chosen land
With fruitfulness and peace.

Ps. 66 *Second Part.*

1 All lands to God, in joyful sounds,
Aloft your voices raise;
Sing forth the honour of His name,
And glorious make His praise.

2 All that fear God, come, hear, I'll tell
What He did for my soul;
I with my mouth unto Him cried,
My tongue did Him extol.

3 If in my heart I sin regard,
The Lord me will not hear;
But surely God me heard, and to
My prayer's voice did give ear.

4 O let the Lord our gracious God,
For ever blessed be;
Who turned not my prayer from Him,
Nor yet His grace from me.

Ps. 90 *Fifth Part.*

1 Lord, Thou hast been our dwelling [place
In generations all,
Before Thou ever hadst brought forth
The mountains great or small.

2 Ere ever Thou hadst formed the earth,
And all the world abroad;
Even Thou from everlasting art,
To everlasting God.

3 Thou dost unto destruction
Man that is mortal turn;
And unto them Thou say'st, Again,
Ye sons of men, return.

4 As with an overflowing flood,
Thou carriest them away;
They like a sleep are, like the grass
That grows at morn, are they.

5 At morn it flourishes and grows,
Cut down at even doth fade.
For by Thine anger we're consumed,
Thy wrath makes us afraid.

6 Our sins Thou and iniquities
Dost in Thy presence place,
And sett'st our secret faults before
The brightness of Thy face.

H. 334 *Christian Submission.*

1 O Lord, I would delight in Thee,
And on Thy care depend;
To Thee in every trouble flee,
My best, my only friend.

2 When all created streams are dried,
Thy fulness is the same;
May I with this be satisfied,
And glory in Thy name.

3 Why should the soul a drop bemoan,
Who has a fountain near,
A fountain which shall ever run,
With waters sweet and clear?

4 No good in creatures can be found,
But may be found in Thee;
I must have all things, and abound,
While God is God to me.

5 Oh! that I had a stronger faith
To look within the veil,
To credit what my Saviour saith,
Whose word can never fail.

6 He who has made my heaven secure,
Will here all good provide;
While Christ is rich can I be poor?
What can I want beside?

7 O Lord, I cast my care on Thee,
I triumph and adore;
Henceforth my great concern shall be,
To love and praise Thee more.

H. 426 *Call to Praise.*

1 Lift up to God the voice of praise,
Whose breath our souls inspired;
Loud and more loud the anthems raise,
With grateful ardour fired.

2 Lift up to God the voice of praise,
Whose goodness, passing thought,
Loads every moment, as it flies,
With benefits unsought!

3 Lift up to God the voice of praise,
From whom salvation flows,
Who sent His Son our souls to save
From everlasting woes.

4 Lift up to God the voice of praise,
For hope's transporting ray, [death,
Which lights through darkest shades of
To realms of endless day.

10A

H. 424 *Gratitude for Providential Care.*

1 Almighty Father, gracious Lord,
Kind Guardian of my days,
Thy mercies let my heart record,
In songs of grateful praise.

2 In life's first dawn my tender frame
Was Thy indulgent care,
Long ere I could pronounce Thy name,
Or breathe the infant prayer.

3 Around my path what dangers rose!
What snares spread all my road!
No power could guard me from my foes,
But my Preserver, God.

4 How many blessings round me shone,
Where'er I turned mine eye!
How many passed almost unknown,
Or unregarded, by!

5 Each rolling year new favours brought
From Thy exhaustless store;
But ah! in vain my labouring thought
Would count Thy mercies o'er.

6 While sweet reflection through my days
Thy bounteous hand would trace;
Still dearer blessings claim my praise,
The blessings of Thy grace.

7 Yes, I adore Thee, gracious Lord,
For favours more divine;
That I have known Thy sacred word,
Where all Thy glories shine.

8 Lord, when this mortal frame decays,
And every weakness dies,
Complete the wonders of Thy grace,
And raise me to the skies.

H. 547 *Praise for Redeeming Love.*

1 Jesus, with all Thy saints above,
My tongue would bear her part;
Would sound aloud Thy saving love,
And sing Thy bleeding heart.

2 Blest be the Lamb, my dearest Lord,
Who bought me with His blood,
And quenched His Father's flaming sword
In His own vital flood.

3 All glory to the dying Lamb,
And never ceasing praise,
While angels live to know His name,
Or saints to feel His grace.

Israel Holdroyd, 1753.

1. Ye tremb-ling souls, dis - miss your fears, Be mer - cy all your theme;
Mer - cy, which like a riv - er flows, In one per - pet - ual stream.

H. 251 *Fears dismissed.*

2 Fear not the powers of earth and hell,
God will those powers restrain;
His arm shall all their rage repel,
And make their efforts vain.

3 Fear not the want of outward good;
For His He will provide;
Grant them supplies of daily food,
And give them heaven beside.

4 Fear not that He will e'er forsake,
Or leave His work undone;
He's faithful to His promises,
And faithful to His Son.

5 Fear not the terrors of the grave,
Or death's tremendous sting;
He will from endless wrath preserve,
To endless glory bring.

H. 269 *Confidence in God.*

1 Whence do our mournful thoughts arise?
Where is our courage fled?
Have restless sin, and raging hell,
Struck all our comforts dead?

2 Have we forgot the almighty Name
That formed the earth and sea?
And can an all-creating Arm
Grow weary or decay?

3 Treasures of everlasting might
In our Jehovah dwell;
He gives the conquest to the weak,
And treads their foes to hell.

4 Mere mortal power shall fade and die,
And youthful vigour cease;
But we that wait upon the Lord
Shall feel our strength increase.

5 The saints shall mount on eagles' wings,
And taste the promised bliss,
Till their unwearied feet arrive
Where perfect pleasure is.

H. 693 *Freedom from sin and misery in heaven.*

1 Our sins, alas! how strong they be,
And like a raging sea!
They break our duty, Lord, to Thee,
And hurry us away.

2 The waves of trouble, how they rise!
How loud the tempests roar!
But death shall land our weary souls
Safe on the heavenly shore.

3 There, to fulfil His sweet commands,
Our speedy feet shall move;
No sin shall clog our winged zeal,
Or cool our burning love.

4 There shall we sit, and sing, and tell
The wonders of His grace,
Till heavenly raptures fire our hearts,
And smile in every face.

5 For ever His dear, sacred name
Shall dwell upon our tongue,
And Jesus and salvation be
The close of every song.

H. 238 *Safety of the Righteous.*

1 Firm as the earth Thy gospel stands,
My Lord, my hope, my trust;
If I am found in Jesus' hands,
My soul can ne'er be lost.

2 His honour is engaged to save
The meanest of His sheep;
All that His heavenly Father gave,
His hands securely keep.

3 Nor death nor hell shall e'er remove
His favourites from His breast;
In the dear bosom of His love,
They must for ever rest.

Ps. 10

1 Why doth the Lord depart so far,
And why conceal His face,
When great calamities appear,
And times of deep distress?

2 Arise, O God, lift up Thine hand,
Attend our humble cry;
No enemy shall dare to stand
When God ascends on high.

3 Why do the men of malice rage,
And say, with foolish pride,
"The God of heaven will ne'er engage
To fight on Zion's side?"

4 But Thou for ever art our Lord,
And mighty is Thy hand,
As when the heathen felt Thy sword,
And perished from Thy land.

5 Thou wilt prepare our hearts to pray,
And cause Thine ear to hear;
Accept the vows Thy children pay,
And free Thy saints from fear.

Ps. 62 *First Part.*

1 My soul, wait thou with patience
Upon thy God alone;
On Him dependeth all my hope
And expectation.

2 He only my salvation is,
And my strong rock is He;
He only is my sure defence;
I shall not moved be.

3 In God my glory placed is,
And my salvation sure;
In God the rock is of my strength,
My refuge most secure.

4 Ye people, place your confidence
In Him continually;
Before Him pour ye out your heart;
God is our refuge high.

Ps. 65 *First Part.*

1 Praise waits in Zion, Lord, for Thee,
There shall our vows be paid;
Thou hast an ear when sinners pray,
All flesh shall seek Thine aid.

2 Lord, our iniquities prevail,
But pardoning grace is Thine,
And Thou wilt grant us power and skill
To conquer every sin.

3 Blest are the men whom Thou wilt choose
To bring them near Thy face,
Give them a dwelling in Thy house,
To feast upon Thy grace.

4 In answering what Thy Church requests,
Thy truth and terror shine,
And works of dreadful righteousness
Fulfil Thy kind design.

5 Thus shall the wondering nations see
The Lord is good and just;
And distant islands fly to Thee,
And make Thy name their trust.

Ps. 66 *First Part.*

1 Now shall my solemn vows be paid
To that almighty Power,
That heard the long requests I made
In my distressful hour.

2 My lips and cheerful heart prepare
To make His mercies known;
Come ye that fear my God, and hear
The wonders He has done.

3 When on my head huge sorrows fell,
I sought His heavenly aid;
He saved my sinking soul from hell,
And death's eternal shade.

4 If sin lay covered in my heart
While prayer employed my tongue;
The Lord had shown me no regard,
Nor I His praises sung.

5 But God,—His name be ever blest—
Has set my spirit free;
Nor turned from Him my poor request,
Nor turned His heart from me.

THOMAS WILLIAMS' COLLECTION, 1768.

1. What is the thing of great - est price, The whole cre-a-tion round: That which was lost in
par - a - dise, That which in Christ was found-That which in Christ was found.

H. 146 *Value of the Soul.*

2 THE soul of man, Jehovah's breath,
That keeps two worlds at strife:
Hell moves beneath to work its death,
Heaven stoops to give it life.

3 God, to redeem it, did not spare
His well-beloved Son;
Jesus, to save it, deigned to bear
The sins of all in one.

4 And is this treasure borne below,
In earthen vessels frail?
Can none its utmost value know,
Till flesh and spirit fail?

5 Then let us gather round the cross,
That knowledge to obtain;
Not by the soul's eternal loss,
But everlasting gain.

H. 104 *Glory of Redemption.*

1 FATHER, how wide Thy glory shines!
How high Thy wonders rise! [signs,
Known through the earth by thousand
By thousands through the skies.

2 But when we view Thy strange design,
To save rebellious worms;
Where vengeance and compassion join
In their divinest forms;

3 Here the whole Deity is known,
Nor dares a creature guess,
Which of the glories brightest shone,
The justice or the grace.

4 Now the full glories of the Lamb
Adorn the heavenly plains;
Bright seraphs learn Immanuel's name,
And try their choicest strains.

5 O! may I bear some humble part,
In that immortal song!
Wonder and joy shall tune my heart,
And love command my tongue.

Ps. 69 *First Part.*

1 FATHER, I sing Thy wondrous grace,
I bless my Saviour's name;
He bought salvation for the poor,
And bore the sinner's shame.

2 His deep distress has raised us high,
His duty and His zeal
Fulfilled the law which mortals broke,
And finished all Thy will.

3 This shall His humble followers see,
And set their hearts at rest;
They by His death draw near to Thee,
And live for ever blest.

4 Let heaven and all that dwell on high,
To God their voices raise,
While lands and seas assist the sky,
And join t' advance His praise.

5 Zion is Thine, most holy God,
Thy Son shall bless her gates;
And glory, purchased by His blood,
For Thine own Israel waits.

Dr. Thomas Hastings, 1828.

1. Come, let us lift our joy - ful eyes Up to the courts a - bove,
And smile to see our Fa - ther there, Up - on a throne of love.

H. 242 *Access to God by Christ.*

2 Once 'twas a seat of dreadful wrath,
And shot devouring flame;
Our God appeared consuming fire,
And Vengeance was His name.

3 Rich were the drops of Jesus' blood
That calmed His frowning face,
That sprinkled o'er the burning throne,
And turned the wrath to grace.

4 Now we may bow before His feet,
And venture near the Lord;
No fiery cherub guards His seat,
Nor double flaming sword.

5 The peaceful gates of heavenly bliss,
Are opened by the Son;
High let us raise our notes of praise,
And reach the eternal throne.

6 To Thee ten thousand thanks we bring,
Great Advocate on high;
And glory to the almighty King,
That lays His fury by.

H. 203 *The Contrite Heart.*

1 The Lord will happiness divine
On contrite hearts bestow;
Then tell me, gracious God, is mine
A contrite heart, or no?

2 I hear, but seem to hear in vain,
Insensible as steel;
If aught is felt, 'tis only pain,
To find I cannot feel.

3 My best desires are faint and few,
I fain would strive for more;
But, when I cry "My strength renew,"
Seem weaker than before.

4 I see Thy saints with comfort filled,
When in Thy house of prayer;
But still in bondage I am held,
And find no comfort there.

5 O! make this heart rejoice or ache:
Decide this doubt for me;
And if it be not broken, break,
And heal it, if it be.

H. 287 *Brotherly Love.*

1 How sweet and heavenly is the sight,
When those who love the Lord
In one another's peace delight,
And so fulfil His word!

2 Oh! may we feel each brother's sigh,
And with him bear a part;
May sorrows flow from eye to eye,
And joy from heart to heart.

3 Let love, in one delightful stream,
Through every bosom flow;
Let union sweet, and dear esteem,
In every action glow.

4 Love is the golden chain that binds
The happy souls above;
And he's an heir of heaven who finds
His bosom glow with love.

GENEVA. C. M.

JOHN COLE, 1805.

1. Let Zi - on and her sons re - joice; Be - hold the pro-mised hour:
Let Zi - on and her sons re - joice;
Let Zi-on and her sons re-joice;
For God hath heard her mourn -ing voice, And comes t'ex - alt His pow'r.

Ps. 102 *Second Part.*

2 HER dust and ruins that remain
  Are precious in our eyes;
Those ruins shall be built again,
  And all that dust shall rise.

3 The Lord will raise Jerusalem,
  And stand in glory there;
Nations shall bow before His name,
  And kings attend with fear.

4 He sits a sovereign on His throne,
  With pity in His eyes;
He hears the dying prisoners' groan,
  And sees their sighs arise.

5 He frees the soul condemned to death;
  And, when His saints complain,
It sha'n't be said that praying breath
  Was ever spent in vain.

6 This shall be known when we are dead,
  And left on long record;
That ages yet unborn may read,
  And trust and praise the Lord.

H. 447 *Morning or Evening Hymn.*

1 HOSANNA with a cheerful sound,
  To God's upholding hand;
Ten thousand snares attend us round
  And yet secure we stand.

2 That was a most amazing Power,
  That raised us with a word;
And every day, and every hour,
  We lean upon the Lord.

3 The evening rests our weary head,
  And angels guard the room;
We wake, and we admire the bed,
  That was not made our tomb.

4 The rising morning can't assure
  That we shall end the day;
For death stands ready at the door,
  To take our lives away.

5 God is our Sun, whose daily light
  Our joy and safety brings;
Our feeble flesh lies safe at night,
  Beneath His spreading wings.

Ps. 111

1 GREAT is the Lord; His works of might
  Demand our noblest songs;
Let His assembled saints unite
  Their harmony of tongues.

2 Great is the mercy of the Lord,
  He gives His children food;
And, ever mindful of His word,
  He makes His promise good.

3 His Son, the great Redeemer, came
  To seal His covenant sure;
Holy and reverend is His name,
  His ways are just and pure.

4 They that would grow divinely wise,
  Must with His fear begin;
Our fairest proof of knowledge lies
  In hating every sin.

SAMUEL STANLEY, 1810.

1. Come, let us join our cheer-ful songs, With an-gels 'round the throne;
Ten thou-sand thou-sand are their tongues, But all their joys are one.

H. 107 *Lamb of God to be worshipped.*

2 "Worthy the Lamb that died," they cry,
"To be exalted thus."
"Worthy the Lamb," our lips reply,
"For He was slain for us."

3 Let all that dwell above the sky,
And air, and earth, and seas,
Conspire to lift Thy glories high,
And speak Thine endless praise.

4 The whole creation join in one,
To bless the sacred name
Of Him who sits upon the throne,
And to adore the Lamb.

H. 105 *Offices of Christ.*

1 We bless the Prophet of the Lord,
Who comes with truth and grace;
Jesus, Thy Spirit, and Thy word,
Shall lead us in Thy ways.

2 We reverence our High Priest above,
Who offered up His blood,
And lives to carry on His love,
By pleading with our God.

3 We honour our exalted King;
How sweet are His commands!
He guards our souls from hell and sin,
By His almighty hands.

4 Hosanna to His glorious name,
Who saves by different ways;
His mercies lay a sovereign claim
To our immortal praise.

H. 112 *Victory and Dominion of Christ.*

1 I sing my Saviour's wondrous death;
He conquered when He fell;
"'Tis finished," said His dying breath,
And shook the gates of hell.

2 His cross a sure foundation laid
For glory and renown,
When through the regions of the dead
He passed, to reach the crown.

3 Exalted at His Father's side,
Sits our victorious Lord;
To heaven and hell His hands divide
The vengeance or reward.

4 The saints from His propitious eye,
Await their several crowns;
And all the sons of darkness fly
The terror of His frowns.

H. 150 *The Bible Precious.*

1 How precious is the book divine,
By inspiration given!
Bright as a lamp its doctrines shine,
To guide our souls to heaven.

2 It sweetly cheers our drooping hearts,
In this dark vale of tears;
Life, light and joy it still imparts,
And quells our rising fears.

3 This lamp through all the tedious night
Of life, shall guide our way,
Till we behold the clearer light
Of an eternal night.

ANTIOCH. C. M.

From G. F. Handel, by Dr. Mason, 1836.

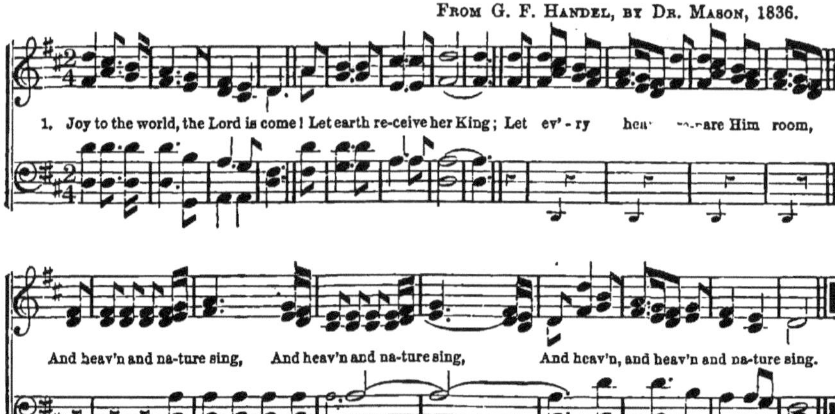
1. Joy to the world, the Lord is come! Let earth re-ceive her King; Let ev' - ry
Him room,
And heav'n and na-ture sing,
And heav'n and na-ture sing,
And heav'n, and heav'n and na-ture sing.

Ps. 98 *Second Part.*

2 Joy to the earth, the Saviour reigns,
Let men their songs employ; [plains
While fields and floods, rocks, hills and
Repeat the sounding joy.

3 No more let sins and sorrows grow,
Nor thorns infest the ground;
He comes to make His blessings flow,
Far as the curse is found.

4 He rules the world with truth and grace,
And makes the nations prove
The glories of His righteousness,
And wonders of His love.

Ps. 96 *Second Part.*

1 Sing to the Lord, ye distant lands,
Ye tribes of every tongue;
His new discovered grace demands
A new and nobler song.

2 Say to the nations, Jesus reigns,
God's own almighty Son;
His power the sinking world sustains,
And grace surrounds His throne.

3 Let heaven proclaim the joyful day,
Joy through the earth be seen;
Let cities shine in bright array,
And fields in cheerful green.

4 The joyous earth, the bending skies,
His glorious train display;
Ye mountains, sink, ye valleys, rise,
Prepare the Lord His way.

5 Behold, He comes, He comes to bless
The nations as their God;
To show the world His righteousness,
And send His truth abroad.

H. 70 *Advent of Christ.*

1 Hark the glad sound, the Saviour comes,
The Saviour promised long;
Let every heart prepare a throne,
And every voice a song.

2 On Him the Spirit, largely poured,
Exerts His sacred fire;
Wisdom, and might, and zeal, and love
His holy breast inspire.

3 He comes the prisoners to release,
In Satan's bondage held,
The gates of brass before Him burst,
The iron fetters yield.

4 He comes from thickest films of vice
To clear the inward sight;
And on the eyes obscured by sin
To pour celestial light.

5 He comes the broken heart to bind,
The bleeding soul to cure;
And with the treasures of His grace,
To enrich the humble poor.

6 Our glad hosannas, Prince of Peace,
Thy welcome shall proclaim,
And heaven's eternal arches ring
With Thy beloved name.

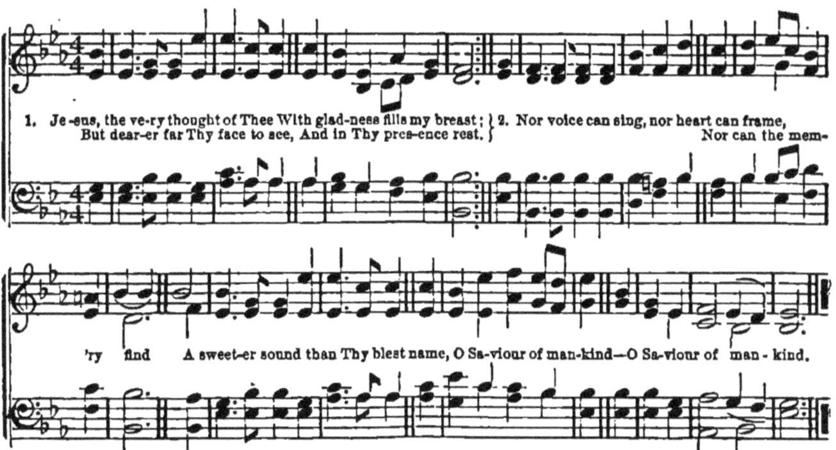
1. Je-sus, the ve-ry thought of Thee With glad-ness fills my breast;
But dear-er far Thy face to see, And in Thy pres-ence rest.
2. Nor voice can sing, nor heart can frame,
Nor can the mem-
'ry find A sweet-er sound than Thy blest name, O Sa-viour of man-kind—O Sa-viour of man - kind.

H. 305 *Joy in Christ.*

1 Jesus, the very thought of Thee
With gladness fills my breast;
But dearer far Thy face to see,
And in Thy presence rest.

2 Nor voice can sing, nor heart can frame,
Nor can the memory find
A sweeter sound than Thy blest name,
O Saviour of mankind!

3 O Hope of every contrite heart,
O Joy of all the meek,
To those who fall, how kind Thou art,
How good to those who seek!

4 And they who find Thee, find a bliss
Nor tongue nor pen can show;
The love of Jesus!—what it is,
None but His loved ones know.

H. 561 *Glory of Christ's Kingdom.*

1 Lo! what a glorious sight appears
To our believing eyes!
The earth and seas are passed away,
And the old rolling skies.

2 From the third heaven where God resides,
That holy, happy place,
The new Jerusalem comes down,
Adorned with shining grace.

3 Attending angels shout for joy,
And the bright armies sing;
"Mortals, behold the sacred seat
Of your descending King.

4 "The God of glory down to men
Removes His blessed abode;
Men, the dear objects of His grace,
And He the loving God.

5 "His own soft hand shall wipe the tears
From every weeping eye;
And pains, and groans, and griefs, and fears,
And death itself shall die."

6 How long, dear Saviour, O! how long
Shall this bright hour delay?
Fly swifter round, ye wheels of time,
And bring the welcome day.

H. 590 *Spread of the Gospel.*

1 Sing to the Lord in joyful strains;
Let earth His praise resound;
Ye who upon the ocean dwell,
And fill the isles around.

2 O city of the Lord, begin
The universal song;
And let the scattered villages
The cheerful notes prolong.

3 Let Kedar's wilderness afar
Lift up its lonely voice,
And let the tenants of the rock
With accents rude rejoice.

4 Till midst the streams of distant lands
The islands sound His praise;
And all combined with one accord,
Jehovah's glories raise.

ORTONVILLE. C. M.

Dr. Hastings, 1837.

1. The head that once was crown'd with thorns Is crown'd with glo-ry now; A roy-al di-a-
dem a-dorns The might-y Vic-tor's brow — The might-y Vic-tor's brow.

H. 124 *The Glory of Christ.*

2 The highest place that heaven affords
Is Thine, is Thine by right,
Thou King of kings, and Lord of lords,
And heaven's eternal light.

3 The joy of all who dwell above,
The joy of all below,
To whom Thou dost reveal Thy love,
And grant Thy name to know.

4 To whom the cross, with all its shame,
With all its grace, is given;
Their name, an everlasting name,
Their joy, the joy of heaven.

5 They suffer with Thee, Lord, below,
They reign with Thee above,
Their everlasting joy to know
The mystery of Thy love.

6 Thy cross, dear Lord, is life and health,
Though shame and death to Thee;
Thy people's hope, Thy people's wealth,
Their song eternally.

H. 63 *Glory of Christ.*

1 Majestic sweetness sits enthroned
Upon the Saviour's brow;
His head with radiant glories crowned,
His lips with grace o'erflow.

2 No mortal can with Him compare
Among the sons of men;
Fairer is He than all the fair,
Who fill the heavenly train.

3 He saw me plunged in deep distress,
And flew to my relief;
For me He bore the shameful cross,
And carried all my grief.

4 To Him I owe my life and breath,
And all the joys I have;
He makes me triumph over death,
And saves me from the grave.

5 To heaven, the place of His abode,
He brings my weary feet,
Shows me the glories of my God,
And makes my joys complete.

6 Since from His bounty I receive
Such proofs of love divine,
Had I a thousand hearts to give,
Lord, they should all be Thine,

Ps. 94

1 Lord, if Thy saints deserve rebuke,
Thou hast a gentle rod;
Thy providence, Thy sacred book,
Shall make them know their God.

2 Blest is the man Thy hands chastise,
And to his duty draw;
Thy scourges make Thy children wise,
When they forget Thy law.

3 But God will ne'er cast off His saints,
Nor His own promise break;
He pardons His inheritance,
For their Redeemer's sake.

Ps. 130 *Third Part.*

1 Lord, from the depths to Thee I cried,
My voice, Lord, do Thou hear;
Unto my supplication's voice
Give an attentive ear.

2 Lord, who shall stand, if Thou, O Lord,
Shouldst mark inquity?
But yet with Thee forgiveness is,
That feared Thou mayest be.

3 I wait for God, my soul doth wait,
My hope is in His word;
More than they that for morning watch,
My soul waits for the Lord;

4 I say, more than they that do watch
The morning light to see.
Let Israel hope in the Lord,
For with Him mercies be;

5 And plenteous redemption
Is ever found with Him;
And from all his iniquities
He Israel shall redeem.

H. 467 *Prayer for Sincerity in Worship.*

1 Lord, when we bend before Thy throne,
And our confessions pour,
O! may we feel the sins we own,
And hate what we deplore.

2 Our contrite spirits pitying see;
True penitence impart;
And let a healing ray from Thee
Beam hope on every heart.

3 Let faith each meek petition fill,
And waft it to the skies;
And teach our hearts, 'tis goodness still
That grants it or denies.

Ps. 139 *Fourth Part.*

1 O Lord, Thou hast me searched and [known,
Thou know'st my sitting down
And rising up; yea, all my thoughts
Afar to Thee are known.

2 For in my tongue before I speak,
Not any word can be,
But altogether, lo! O Lord,
It is well known to Thee.

3 Behind, before, Thou hast beset,
And laid on me Thine hand.
Such knowledge is too strange for me,
Too high to understand.

4 From Thy Spirit whither shall I go,
Or from Thy presence fly?
Ascend I heaven, lo! Thou art there;
There, if in hell I lie.

5 Take I the morning wings and dwell
In utmost parts of sea;
Even there, Lord, shall Thy hand me lead.
Thy right hand hold shall me.

6 If I do say that darkness shall
Me cover from Thy sight,
Then surely shall the very night
About me be as light.

H. 436 *Retirement.*

1 Far from the world, O Lord! I flee,
From strife and tumult far;
From scenes where Satan wages still
His most successful war.

2 The calm retreat, the silent shade,
With prayer and praise agree;
And seem, by Thy sweet bounty, made
For those who follow Thee.

3 There, if Thy Spirit touch the soul,
And grace her mean abode,
Oh! with what peace, and joy, and love,
She then communes with God.

4 There, like the nightingale, she pours
Her solitary lays;
Nor asks a witness of her song,
Nor thirsts for human praise.

5 Author and guardian of my life,
Sweet source of light divine,
And—all harmonious names in one—
Blest Saviour!—Thou art mine.

H. 442 *Evening Worship.*

1 O Lord, another day is flown,
And we, a little band,
Are met once more before Thy throne,
To bless Thy fostering hand.

2 And wilt Thou bend a listening ear,
To praises low as ours?
Thou wilt, for Thou dost deign to hear
The song that meekness pours.

3 And Jesus, Thou Thy smiles wilt deign
As we before Thee pray;
For Thou didst bless the infant train,
And we are less than they.

4 Oh! let Thy grace perform its part;
Let sin's dominion cease;
And shed abroad in every heart
Thine everlasting peace.

Wm. Mather, 1790.

1. Vain are the hopes the sons of men On their own works have built;
Their hearts by na - ture all un - clean, And all their ac-tions guilt.

H. 231 *Justification through Faith.*

2 Let Jew and Gentile stop their mouths,
Without a murmuring word,
And the whole race of Adam stand
Guilty before the Lord.

3 In vain we ask God's righteous law
To justify us now;
Since to convince and to condemn
Is all the law can do.

4 Jesus, how glorious is Thy grace!
When in Thy name we trust,
Our faith receives a righteousness
That makes the sinner just.

Ps. 80 *First Part.*

1 O God of hosts, we Thee beseech,
Return now unto Thine;
Look down from heaven in love, behold,
And visit this Thy vine.

2 This vineyard, which Thine own right [hand
Hath planted us among;
And that same branch which for Thyself
Thou hast made to be strong;

3 Burnt up it is with flaming fire,
It also is cut down;
They utterly are perished,
When e'er Thy face doth frown.

4 O let Thy hand be still upon
The man of Thy right hand,
The Son of man, whom for Thyself
Thou madest strong to stand.

5 So henceforth we will not go back,
Nor turn from Thee at all;
O do Thou quicken us, and we
Upon Thy name will call.

6 Turn us again, Lord God of hosts,
And upon us vouchsafe
To make Thy countenance to shine,
And so we shall be safe.

Ps. 89 *Fourth Part.*

1 Great fear in meeting of the saints
Is due unto the Lord;
And He of all about Him should
With reverence be adored.

2 O greatly blest the people are
The joyful sound that know;
In brightness of Thy face, O Lord,
They ever on shall go.

3 They in Thy name shall all the day
Rejoice exceedingly;
And in Thy righteousness shall they
Exalted be on high.

4 Because the glory of their strength
Doth only stand in Thee;
And in Thy favour shall our horn
And power exalted be.

5 For God is our defence; and He
To us doth safety bring;
The Holy One of Israel
Is our almighty King.

L. Von Beethoven, 1770–1827.

1. How shall the young se - cure their hearts, And guard their lives from sin?
Thy word the choic - est rules im - parts, To keep the con - science clean.

Ps. 119 *Fourth Part.*

2 When once it enters to the mind,
It spreads such light abroad,
The meanest souls instruction find,
And raise their thoughts to God.

3 'Tis like the sun, a heavenly light,
That guides us all the day;
And through the dangers of the night,
A lamp to lead our way.

4 The men that keep Thy law with care,
And meditate Thy word,
Grow wiser than their teachers are,
And better know the Lord.

5 Thy word is everlasting truth,
How pure is every page!
That holy book shall guide our youth,
And well support our age.

Ps. 119 *Fifth Part.*

1 O! how I love Thy holy law!
'Tis daily my delight;
And thence my meditations draw
Divine advice by night.

2 My waking eyes prevent the day
To meditate Thy word;
My soul with longing melts away
To hear Thy gospel, Lord.

3 Thy heavenly words my heart engage,
And well employ my tongue;
And in my tiresome pilgrimage
Yield me a heavenly song.

4 When nature sinks, and spirits droop,
Thy promises of grace
Are pillars to support my hope;
And there I write Thy praise.

Ps. 119 *Third Part.*

1 Thou art my portion, O my God;
Soon as I know Thy way,
My heart makes haste t' obey Thy word,
And suffers no delay.

2 I choose the path of heavenly truth,
And glory in my choice;
Not all the riches of the earth
Could make me so rejoice.

3 Now I am Thine, for ever Thine,
O save Thy servant, Lord;
Thou art my Shield, my Hiding-place,
My hope is in Thy word.

4 Thou hast inclined this heart of mine
Thy statutes to fulfil;
And thus till mortal life shall end
Would I perform Thy will.

H. 378 *The Mercy Seat.*

1 There is a heavenly mercy seat,
To calm the sinner's fears;
There is a Saviour, at whose feet
The mourner dries his tears.

2 When friends depart, and hopes are riven,
And gathering storms I see,
My soul is but the sooner driven,
Eternal Rock, to Thee.

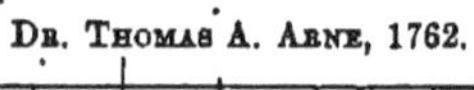
Dr. Thomas A. Arne, 1762.

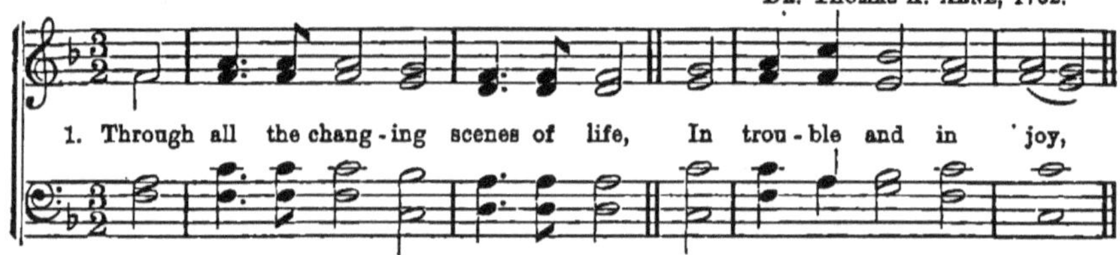
1. Through all the chang - ing scenes of life, In trou - ble and in joy,

The prais - es of my God shall still My heart and tongue em - ploy.

Ps. 34 *Second Part.*

2 My soul shall make her boast in Him,
And celebrate His fame;
Come magnify the Lord with me,
With me exalt His name.

3 The hosts of God encamp around
The dwellings of the just;
Deliverance He affords to all
Who on His succour trust.

4 O! make but trial of His love;
Experience will decide
How blest are they, and only they,
Who in His truth confide.

5 Fear Him, ye saints; and you will then
Have nothing else to fear;
Come, make His service your delight;
He'll make your wants His care.

Ps. 40

1 I waited patient for the Lord,
He bowed to hear me cry;
He saw me resting on His word,
And brought salvation nigh.

2 He raised me from a horrid pit,
Where mourning long I lay,
And from my bonds released my feet—
Deep bonds of miry clay.

3 Firm on a rock He made me stand,
And taught my cheerful tongue
To praise the wonders of His hand,
In a new thankful song.

4 I'll spread His works of grace abroad;
The saints with joy shall hear.
And sinners learn to make my God
Their only hope and fear.

5 How many are Thy thoughts of love!
Thy mercies, Lord, how great!
We have not words nor hours enough
Their numbers to repeat.

6 When I'm afflicted, poor and low,
And light and peace depart,
My God beholds my heavy woe,
And bears me on His heart.

H. 14 *Sincerity in Worship.*

1 God is a Spirit, just and wise,
He sees our inmost mind;
In vain to heaven we raise our cries,
And leave our souls behind.

2 Nothing but truth before His throne
With honour can appear;
The painted hypocrites are known
Through the disguise they wear.

3 Their lifted eyes salute the skies,
Their bending knees the ground;
But God abhors the sacrifice
Where not the heart is found.

4 Lord, search my thoughts, and try my
And make my soul sincere; [ways,
Then shall I stand before Thy face,
And find acceptance there.

Ps. 139 *Third Part.*

1 Lord, when I count Thy mercies o'er,
They strike me with surprise;
Not all the sands that spread the shore,
To equal numbers rise.

2 My flesh with fear and wonder stands,
The product of Thy skill;
And hourly blessings from Thy hands,
Thy thoughts of love reveal.

3 These on my heart by night I keep:
How kind, how dear to me!
O may the hour that ends my sleep,
Still find my thoughts with Thee.

Ps. 145 *First Part.*

1 Long as I live I'll bless Thy name,
My King, my God of love;
My work and joy shall be the same,
In the bright world above.

2 Great is the Lord, His power unknown,
And let His praise be great;
I'll sing the honours of Thy throne,
Thy works of grace repeat.

3 Thy grace shall dwell upon my tongue;
And, while my lips rejoice,
The men that hear my sacred song
Shall join their cheerful voice.

4 Fathers to sons shall teach Thy name,
And children learn Thy ways;
Ages to come Thy truth proclaim,
And nations sound Thy praise.

5 The world is managed by Thy hands,
Thy saints are ruled by love;
And Thine eternal kingdom stands,
Though rocks and hills remove.

Ps. 145 *Second Part.*

1 Sweet is the memory of Thy grace,
My God, my heavenly King;
Let age to age Thy righteousness
In sounds of glory sing.

2 God reigns on high, but ne'er confines
His goodness to the skies; [shines,
Through the whole earth His bounty
And every want supplies.

3 With longing eyes Thy creatures wait
On Thee for daily food;
Thy liberal hand provides their meat,
And fills their mouth with good.

4 How kind are Thy compassions, Lord!
How slow Thine anger moves!
But soon He sends His pardoning word,
To cheer the souls He loves.

5 Creatures with all their endless race
Thy power and praise proclaim;
But saints, that taste Thy richer grace,
Delight to bless Thy name.

Ps. 150 *First Part.*

1 In God's own house pronounce His praise,
His grace He there reveals;
To heaven your joy and wonder raise,
For there His glory dwells.

2 Let all your sacred passions move,
While you rehearse His deeds;
But the great work of saving love
Your highest praise exceeds.

3 All that have motion, life, and breath,
Proclaim your Maker blest;
Yet when my voice expires in death,
My soul shall praise Him best.

H. 513 *Collections for the Poor.*

1 Bright Source of everlasting love!
To Thee our souls we raise;
And to Thy sovereign bounty rear
A monument of praise.

2 Thy mercy gilds the path of life,
With every cheering ray;
Kindly restrains the rising tear,
Or wipes that tear away.

3 When sunk in guilt, our souls approached
The borders of despair, [claimed,
Thy grace, through Jesus' blood, pro-
A free salvation near.

4 What shall we render, bounteous Lord,
For all the grace we see?
Alas! the goodness we can yield,
Extendeth not to Thee.

5 To tents of woe, to beds of pain,
Our cheerful feet repair;
And, with the gifts Thy hand bestows,
Relieve the mourner's care.

6 The widow's heart shall sing for joy,
The orphan shall be fed;
The hungering soul we'll gladly point
To Christ, the living bread.

Isaac Tucker, 1800.

1. My drow - sy pow'rs, why sleep ye so? A - wake, my slug - gish soul?
Noth - ing has half thy work to do, Yet noth - ing's half so dull.

H. 393 *Slothfulness Lamented.*

2 The little ants, for one poor grain,
Labour, and toil, and strive;
Yet we, who have a heaven to obtain,
How negligent we live!

3 We, for whose sake all nature stands,
And stars their courses move;
We, for whose guard the angel bands
Come flying from above;

4 We, for whom God the Son came down,
And laboured for our good,
How careless to secure that crown
He purchased with His blood!

5 Lord, shall we lie so sluggish still,
And never act our parts?
Come, Holy Spirit, come, and fill
And wake and warm our hearts.

6 Then shall our active spirits move,
Upward our souls shall rise;
With hands of faith, and wings of love,
We'll fly and take the prize.

Ps. 21

1 Our land, O Lord, with songs of praise
Shall in Thy strength rejoice;
And, blest with Thy salvation, raise
To heaven their cheerful voice.

2 Thy sure defence, through nations round,
Has spread our wondrous name;
And our successful actions crowned
With dignity and fame.

3 Then let our land on God alone
For timely aid rely;
His mercy, which adorns His throne,
Shall all our wants supply.

4 Thus, Lord, Thy wondrous power declare,
And thus exalt Thy fame;
Whilst we glad songs of praise prepare
For Thine almighty name.

Ps. 118 *First Part.*

1 This is the day the Lord hath made,
He calls the hours His own;
Let heaven rejoice, let earth be glad,
And praise surround the throne.

2 To-day He rose and left the dead,
And Satan's empire fell;
To-day the saints His triumphs spread,
And all His wonders tell.

3 Hosanna to th' anointed King,
To David's holy Son;
Help us, O Lord, descend and bring
Salvation from Thy throne.

4 Blest is the Lord who comes to men,
With messages of grace;
Who comes in God His Father's name,
To save our sinful race.

5 Hosanna in the highest strains,
The church on earth can raise;
The highest heavens, in which He reigns,
Shall give Him nobler praise.

George Kingsley.

1. With my whole heart I'll raise my song; Thy won-ders I'll pro-claim;
Thou, Sov-reign Judge of right and wrong, Wilt put Thy foes to shame.

Ps. 9

2 I'll sing Thy majesty and grace;
My God prepares His throne
To judge the world in righteousness,
And make His justice known.

3 Then shall the Lord a refuge prove
For all the poor oppressed,
To save the people of His love,
And give the weary rest.

4 The men that know Thy name will trust
In Thy abundant grace;
For Thou wilt ne'er forsake the just,
Who humbly seek Thy face.

5 Sing praises to the righteous Lord,
Who dwells on Zion's hill,
Who executes His threatening word,
And doth His grace fulfil.

H. 21 *God Celebrated in His works of Creation.*

1 I sing the almighty power of God,
That made the mountains rise,
That spread the flowing seas abroad,
And built the lofty skies.

2 I sing the wisdom that ordained
The sun to rule the day;
The moon shines full at His command,
And all the stars obey.

3 I sing the goodness of the Lord,
That filled the earth with food;
He formed the creatures with His word,
And then pronounced them good.

4 Lord, how Thy wonders are displayed,
Where'er I turn mine eye!
If I survey the ground I tread,
Or gaze upon the sky.

5 There's not a plant or flower below,
But makes Thy glories known;
And clouds arise and tempests blow,
By order from Thy throne.

6 Creatures as numerous as they be,
Are subject to Thy care;
There's not a place where we can flee,
But God is present there.

H. 22 *Defence of Divine Providence.*

1 Let others boast how strong they be,
Nor death or danger fear;
But we'll confess, O Lord, to Thee,
What feeble things we are.

2 Fresh as the grass our bodies stand,
And flourish bright and gay;
A blasting wind sweeps o'er the land,
And fades the grass away.

3 Our life contains a thousand springs,
And dies if one be gone;
Strange! that a harp of thousand strings,
Should keep in tune so long.

4 But 'tis our God supports our frame,
The God that made us first;
Salvation to the almighty Name,
That reared us from the dust.

WOODSTOCK. C. M.

D. Dutton, Jr., 1829.

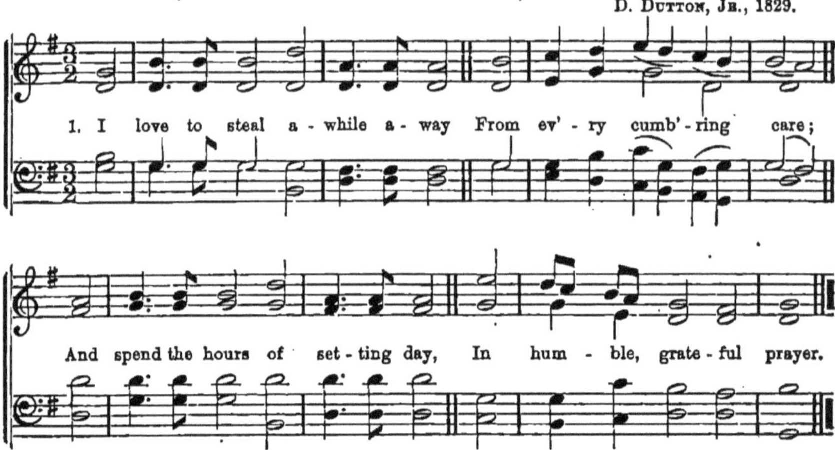
1. I love to steal a - while a - way From ev' - ry cumb' - ring care;
And spend the hours of set - ting day, In hum - ble, grate - ful prayer.

H. 451 *Twilight Meditation.*

2 I love in solitude to shed
The penitential tear,
And all His promises to plead,
Where none but God can hear.

3 I love to think on mercies past,
And future good implore,
And all my cares and sorrows cast
On Him whom I adore.

4 I love by faith to take a view
Of brighter scenes in heaven;
The prospect does my strength renew,
While here by tempests driven.

5 Thus, when life's toilsome day is o'er,
May its departing ray
Be calm as this impressive hour,
And lead to endless day.

Ps. 34 *First Part:*

1 The angel of the Lord encamps,
And round encompasseth
All those about that do Him fear,
And them delivereth.

2 O taste and see that God is good;
Who trusts in Him is blest,
Fear God, His saints; none that Him fear
Shall be with want oppressed.

3 The lions young may hungry be,
And they may lack their food;
But they that truly seek the Lord
Shall not lack any good.

4 O children, hither do ye come,
And unto me give ear;
I shall you teach to understand
How ye the Lord should fear.

5 What man is he that life desires,
To see good would live long?
Thy lips refrain from speaking guile,
And from ill words thy tongue.

H. 43 *Condescension of Christ.*

1 The Saviour! O what endless charms
Dwell in the blissful sound!
Its influence every fear disarms,
And spreads sweet comfort round.

2 Here pardon, life, and joys divine,
In rich effusion flow,
For guilty rebels lost in sin,
And doomed to endless woe.

3 The almighty Former of the skies
Stooped to our vile abode;
While angels viewed with wondering eyes,
And hailed the incarnate God.

4 O! the rich depths of love divine!
Of bliss a boundless store!
Dear Saviour, let me call Thee mine;
I cannot wish for more.

5 On Thee alone my hope relies,
Beneath Thy cross I fall;
My Lord, my Life, my Sacrifice,
My Saviour, and my All!

Ps. 119 *Eighth Part.*

1 Lord, I have made Thy word my choice,
My lasting heritage;
There shall my noblest powers rejoice,
My warmest thoughts engage.

2 I'll read the histories of Thy love,
And keep Thy laws in sight,
While through the promises I rove,
With ever fresh delight.

3 'Tis a broad land of wealth unknown,
Where springs of life arise;
Seeds of immortal bliss are sown,
And hidden glory lies.

4 The best relief that mourners have,
It makes our sorrows blest;
Our fairest hope beyond the grave,
And our eternal rest.

Ps. 119 *Tenth Part.*

1 Behold Thy waiting servant, Lord;
Devoted to Thy fear;
Remember and confirm Thy word,
For all my hopes are there.

2 Hast Thou not sent salvation down,
And promised quickening grace?
Doth not my heart address Thy throne?
And yet Thy love delays.

3 Mine eyes for Thy salvation fail;
O bear Thy servant up;
Nor let the scoffing lips prevail,
Who dare reproach my hope.

4 Didst Thou not raise my faith, O Lord?
Then let Thy truth appear:
Saints shall rejoice in my reward,
And trust as well as fear.

Ps. 119 *Thirteenth Part.*

1 With my whole heart I've sought Thy face,
O! let me never stray
From Thy commands, O God of grace,
Nor tread the sinner's way.

2 Thy word I've hid within my heart,
To keep my conscience clean,
To be an everlasting guard
From every rising sin.

3 I'm a companion of the saints,
Who fear and love the Lord;
My sorrows rise, my nature faints,
When men transgress Thy word.

4 My God, I long, I hope, I wait,
For Thy salvation still;
While Thy whole law is my delight,
And I obey Thy will.

H. 553 *Remembering Christ.*

1 According to Thy gracious word,
In meek humility,
This will I do, my dying Lord,
I will remember Thee.

2 Thy body, broken for my sake,
My bread from heaven shall be;
Thy testamental cup I take,
And thus remember Thee.

3 Gethsemane can I forget?
Or there Thy conflict see,
Thine agony and bloody sweat,
And not remember Thee?

4 When to the cross I turn mine eyes,
And rest on Calvary,
O Lamb of God, my sacrifice,
I must remember Thee.

5 Remember Thee and all Thy pains,
And all Thy love to me;
Yea, while a breath, a pulse remains,
Will I remember Thee.

6 And when these failing lips grow dumb,
And mind and memory flee,
When Thou shalt in Thy kingdom come,
Jesus, remember me.

H. 627 *Dying in God's Embrace.*

1 Death cannot make our souls afraid,
If God be with us there;
We may walk through its darkest shade,
And never yield to fear.

2 I could renounce my all below,
If my Creator bid;
And run, if I were called to go,
And die as Moses did.

3 Might I but climb to Pisgah's top,
And view the promised land,
My flesh itself would long to drop,
And pray for the command.

4 Clasped in my heavenly Father's arms,
I would forget my breath,
And lose my life among the charms
Of so divine a death.

Rev. Wm. Jones, 1780.

1. God moves in a mys - te - rious way, His won - ders to per - form;
He plants His foot - steps in the sea, And rides up - on the storm.

H. 26 *Mysteries of Providence.*

2 Deep in unfathomable mines
Of never failing skill,
He treasures up His bright designs,
And works His sovereign will.

3 Ye fearful saints, fresh courage take;
The clouds ye so much dread
Are big with mercy, and shall break
In blessings on your head.

4 Judge not the Lord by feeble sense,
But trust Him for His grace;
Behind a frowning providence,
He hides a smiling face.

5 His purposes will ripen fast,
Unfolding every hour;
The bud may have a bitter taste,
But sweet will be the flower.

6 Blind unbelief is sure to err,
And scan His work in vain;
God is His own interpreter,
And He will make it plain.

Ps. 68 *First Part.*

1 Thou hast, O Lord, most glorious,
Ascended up on high;
And in triumph victorious led
Captive captivity.

2 Thou hast received gifts for men,
From such as did rebel;
Yea, even for them, that God the Lord
In midst of them might dwell.

3 Bless'd be the Lord, who is to us
Of our salvation God;
Who daily with His benefits
Us plenteously doth load.

4 He of salvation is the God,
Who is our God most strong;
And unto God the Lord from death
The issues do belong.

Ps. 115

1 Lord, not to us, we claim no share,
But to Thy sacred name,
Give glory for Thy mercy's sake,
And truth's eternal fame.

2 O Israel, make the Lord your trust,
Who is your help and shield;
Priests, Levites, trust in Him alone,
Who only help can yield.

3 Let all who truly fear the Lord
On Him they fear rely;
Who them in danger can defend,
And all their wants supply.

4 They who in death and silence sleep,
To Him no praise afford;
But we will bless for evermore
Our ever-living Lord.

Doxology.

To Father, Son, and Holy Ghost,
The God whom we adore,
Be glory as it was, is now,
And shall be evermore.

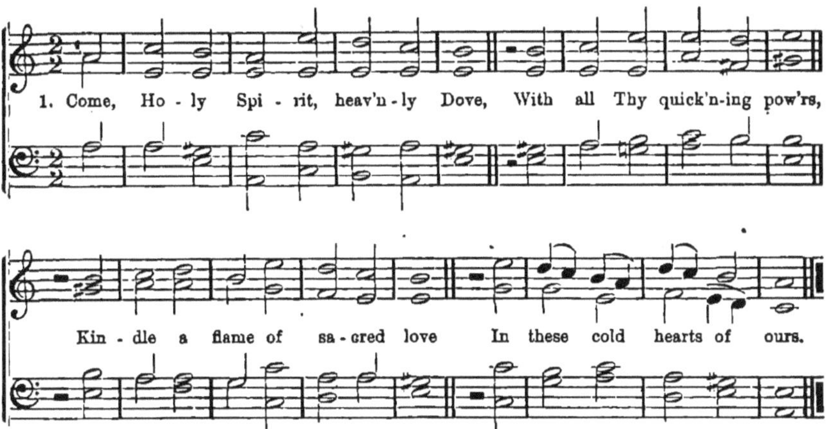
1. Come, Ho - ly Spi - rit, heav'n - ly Dove, With all Thy quick'n-ing pow'rs,
Kin - dle a flame of sa - cred love In these cold hearts of ours.

H. 137 *Prayer for the Descent of the Spirit.*

2 Look how we grovel here below,
Fond of these trifling toys;
Our souls can neither fly nor go,
To reach eternal joys.

3 In vain we tune our formal songs,
In vain we strive to rise;
Hosannas languish on our tongues,
And our devotion dies.

4 Dear Lord, and shall we ever live
At this poor dying rate;
Our love so faint, so cold to Thee,
And Thine to us so great?

5 Come, Holy Spirit, heavenly Dove,
With all Thy quickening powers,
Come, shed abroad a Saviour's love,
And that shall kindle ours.

H. 173 *Invitation to the Feast.*

1 Ye wretched, hungry, starving poor,
Behold a royal feast;
Where Mercy spreads her bounteous store,
For every humble guest.

2 See, Jesus stands with open arms,
He calls, He bids you come;
Guilt holds you back, and fear alarms;
But see, there yet is room.

3 Room in the Saviour's bleeding heart;
There love and pity meet;
Nor will He bid the soul depart,
That trembles at His feet.

4 O! come, and with His children taste,
The blessings of His love;
While hope attends the sweet repast,
Of nobler joys above.

5 There, with united heart and voice,
Before the eternal throne,
Ten thousand thousand souls rejoice,
In ecstasies unknown.

6 And yet ten thousand thousand more
Are welcome still to come;
Ye longing souls, the grace adore,
Approach, there yet is room.

H. 397 *Christian Activity.*

1 Awake, my soul, stretch every nerve,
And press with vigour on;
A heavenly race demands thy zeal,
And an immortal crown.

2 A cloud of witnesses around,
Hold thee in full survey;
Forget the steps already trod,
And onward urge thy way.

3 'Tis God's all-animating voice
That calls thee from on high;
'Tis His own hand presents the prize
To thine uplifted eye.

4 Then wake, my soul, stretch every nerve,
And press with vigour on;
A heavenly race demands thy zeal,
And an immortal crown.

W. Tansur's Collection, 1735.

1. How sweet and aw - ful is the place, With Christ with - in the doors,
While ev - er - last - ing love dis - plays The choic - est of her stores.

H. 551 *The Heavenly Feast.*

2 While all our hearts, in this our song,
Join to admire the feast,
Each of us cries with thankful tongue,
"Lord, why was I a guest?"

3 "Why was I made to hear Thy voice,
And enter while there's room;
When thousands make a wretched choice,
And rather starve than come?"

4 'Twas the same love that spread the feast
That sweetly forced us in;
Else we had still refused to taste,
And perished in our sin.

5 Pity the nations, O our God,
Constrain the earth to come;
Send Thy victorious word abroad,
And bring the strangers home.

6 We long to see Thy churches full,
That all the chosen race
May, with one voice, and heart, and soul,
Sing Thy redeeming grace.

Ps. 50

1 The Lord, the Judge, before His throne
Bids the whole earth draw nigh,
The nations near the rising sun,
And near the western sky.

2 No more shall bold blasphemers say,
"Judgment will ne'er begin;"
No more abuse His long delay
To insolence and sin.

3 Throned on a cloud our God shall come,
Bright flames prepare His way;
Thunder and darkness, fire and storm
Lead on the dreadful day.

4 Heaven from above His call shall hear,
Attending angels come,
And earth and hell shall know and fear
His justice and their doom.

5 "But gather all My saints," He cries,
"That made their peace with God
By the Redeemer's sacrifice,
And sealed it with His blood.

6 "Their faith and works, brought forth to light,
Shall make the world confess
My sentence of reward is right,
And heaven adore My grace."

H. 386 *Self-Denial.*

1 Strait is the way, the door is strait,
That leads to joys on high;
'Tis but a few that find the gate,
While crowds mistake and die.

2 Beloved self must be denied,
The mind and will renewed,
Passions suppressed and patience tried,
And vain desires subdued.

3 Flesh is a dangerous foe to grace,
Where it prevails and rules;
Flesh must be humbled, pride abased,
Lest they destroy our souls.

4 The love of gold be banished hence,
That vile idolatry;
And every member, every sense,
In sweet subjection lie.

5 The tongue, that most unruly power,
Requires a strong restraint;
We must be watchful every hour,
And pray, but never faint.

6 Lord, can a feeble, helpless worm
Fulfil a task so hard?
Thy grace must all my work perform,
And give a free reward.

H. 505 *Humiliation for National Sins.*

1 See, gracious God, before Thy throne,
Thy mourning people bend;
'Tis on Thy sovereign grace alone
Our humble hopes depend.

2 Tremendous judgments from Thy hand
Thy dreadful power display;
Yet mercy spares this guilty land,
And still we live to pray.

3 What numerous crimes increasing rise,
Through this apostate land!
What land so favoured of the skies,
Yet thoughtless of Thy hand?

4 How changed, alas! are truths divine,
For error, guilt and shame!
What impious numbers, bold in sin,
Disgrace the Christian name!

5 Regardless of Thy smile or frown,
Their pleasures they require;
And sink with gay indifference down
To everlasting fire.

6 O! turn us, turn us, mighty Lord,
By rich and sovereign grace;
Then shall our hearts obey Thy word,
And humbly seek Thy face.

7 Then should insulting foes invade,
We shall not sink in fear;
Secure of never-failing aid,
If God, our God is near.

H. 507 *Humiliation.*

1 Great King of nations, hear our prayer,
While at Thy feet we fall,
And humbly with united cry
To Thee for mercy call.

2 The guilt is ours, but grace is thine;
Oh! turn us not away;
But hear us from Thy lofty throne,
And help us when we pray.

3 With one consent we meekly bow
Beneath Thy chast'ning hand,
And, pouring forth confession meet,
Mourn with our mourning land.

4 With pitying eye behold our need,
As thus we lift our prayer;
"Correct us in Thy judgment, Lord,
But in Thy mercy spare."

H. 398 *Indwelling Sin Lamented.*

1 With tears of anguish I lament,
Here at Thy feet, my God,
My passion, pride, and discontent,
And vile ingratitude.

2 Sure there was ne'er a heart so base,
So false as mine has been;
So faithless to its promises,
So prone to every sin.

3 How long, dear Saviour, shall I feel
These struggles in my breast?
When wilt Thou bow my stubborn will
And give my conscience rest?

4 Break, sovereign grace, O break the
And set the captive free; [charm,
Reveal, almighty God, Thine arm,
And haste to rescue me.

H. 612 *Brevity of Life.*

1 Our days, alas! our mortal days
Are short and wretched too,
"Evil and few," the patriarch says,
And well the patriarch knew.

2 'Tis but at best a narrow bound
That heaven allows to men, [round
And pains and sins run through the
Of threescore years and ten.

3 Well, if ye must be sad and few,
Run on, my days, in haste;
Moments of sin, and months of woe,
Ye cannot fly too fast.

4 Let heavenly love prepare my soul,
And call her to the skies,
Where years of long salvation roll,
And glory never dies.

RETURN. C. M.

Dr. Thomas Hastings, 1831.

1. Re-turn, O wan-d'rer, to thy home, Thy Fa-ther calls for thee;
No long-er now an ex-ile roam, In guilt and mis-e-ry. Re-turn, re-turn!
Coda.

H. 182 *Return!*

2 Return, O wanderer, to thy home,
'Tis Jesus calls for thee;
The Spirit and the Bride say, Come!
Oh! now for refuge flee.
Return, return!

3 Return, O wanderer, to Thy home,
'Tis madness to delay;
There are no pardons in the tomb,
And brief is mercy's day.
Return, return!

Ps. 90 *Third Part.*

1 Return, O God of love, return;
Earth is a tiresome place;
How long shall we, Thy children, mourn
Our absence from Thy face.—*Chorus.*

2 Let heaven succeed our painful years;
Let sin and sorrow cease;
And in proportion to our tears,
So make our joys increase.

3 Thy wonders to Thy servant show,
Make Thine own works complete;
Then shall our souls Thy glory know,
And own Thy love was great.

4 Then shall we shine before Thy throne
In all Thy beauty, Lord;
And the poor service we have done
Meet a divine reward.

H. 171 *Sinners Invited and Entreated.*

1 Sinners, the voice of God regard;
'Tis mercy speaks to-day;
He calls you, by His sovereign word,
From sin's destructive way.—*Chorus.*

2 Like the rough sea that cannot rest,
You live devoid of peace;
A thousand stings within your breast
Deprive your souls of ease.

3 Your way is dark, and leads to hell;
Why will you persevere?
Can you in endless torments dwell
Shut up in black despair?

4 Why will you in the crooked ways,
Of sin and folly go?
In pain you travel all your days
To reap immortal woe.

5 But he that turns to God shall live,
Through His abounding grace:
His mercy will the guilt forgive
Of those that seek His face.

6 Bow to the sceptre of His word,
Renouncing every sin:
Submit to Him, your sovereign Lord,
And learn His will divine.

7 His love exceeds your highest thoughts;
He pardons like a God;
He will forgive your numerous faults,
Through a Redeemer's blood.

OLD AMERICAN TUNE.

1. Sov' - reign of life, I own Thy hand, In ev' - ry chast'n - ing stroke;
And while I smart be - neath Thy rod, Thy pres - ence I in - voke.

H. 332 *Submission and Hope of Heaven.*

1 Sovereign of life, I own Thy hand,
In every chastening stroke;
And while I smart beneath Thy rod,
Thy presence I invoke.

2 To Thee, in my distress, I cried,
And Thou hast bowed Thine ear;
Thy powerful word my life prolonged,
And brought salvation near.

3 Unfold, ye gates of righteousness,
That, with the pious throng,
I may record my solemn vows,
And tune my grateful song.

4 Praise to the Lord, whose gentle hand
Renews our labouring breath;
Praise to the Lord, who makes His saints
Triumphant e'en in death.

5 My God, in Thine appointed hour,
Those heavenly gates display,
Where pain and sin, and fear and death,
For ever flee away.

6 There, while the nations of the blest,
With raptures bow around,
My anthems to delivering grace
In sweeter strains shall sound.

H. 567 *On Opening a New Place of Worship.*

1 Dear Shepherd of Thy people, hear;
Thy presence now display;
As Thou hast given a place of prayer,
So give us hearts to pray.

2 Show us some token of Thy love,
Our fainting hope to raise;
And pour Thy blessings from above,
That we may render praise.

3 Within these walls let holy peace,
And love and concord dwell;
Here give the troubled conscience ease,
The wounded spirit heal.

4 And may the gospel's joyful sound,
Enforced by mighty grace,
Awaken many sinners round,
To come and fill the place.

H. 326 *Prayer for Resignation.*

1 Thou boundless Source of every good,
Our best desires fulfil:
Help us adore Thy wondrous grace,
And mark Thy sovereign will.

2 Teach us, in time of deep distress,
To own Thy hand, O God;
And in submissive silence learn,
The lessons of Thy rod.

3 In every changing scene of life,
Whate'er that scene may be,
Give us a meek and humble mind,
A mind at peace with Thee.

4 Then shall we close our eyes in death,
Free from distracting care;
For death is life, and labour rest,
If Thou art with us there.

GREGORIAN CHANT.

To Fa - ther, Son, and Ho - ly Ghost, The God whom we a - dore,

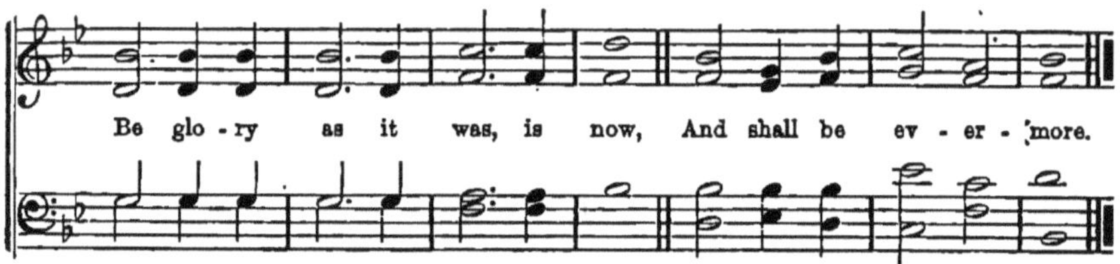
Be glo - ry as it was, is now, And shall be ev - er - more.

Ps. 112

1 HAPPY is he that fears the Lord,
And follows His commands,
Who lends the poor without reward,
Or gives with liberal hands.

2 As pity dwells within his breast
To all the sons of need;
So God shall answer his request
With blessings on his seed.

3 No evil tidings shall surprise
His well established mind;
His soul to God, his refuge, flies,
And leaves his fears behind.

4 In times of danger and distress
Some beams of light shall shine,
To show the world his righteousness,
And give him peace divine.

5 His works of piety and love
Remain before the Lord;
Honour on earth, and joys above,
Shall be his sure reward.

Ps. 119 *Twelfth Part.*

1 MY God, consider my distress,
Let mercy plead my cause;
Though I have sinned against Thy grace,
I can't forget Thy laws.

2 Forbid, forbid the sharp reproach,
Which I so justly fear;
Uphold my life, uphold my hopes,
Nor let my shame appear.

3 Be Thou a surety, Lord, for me,
Nor let the proud oppress;
But make Thy waiting servant see
The shinings of Thy face.

4 My eyes with expectation fail;
My heart within me cries,
"When will the Lord His truth fulfil,
And bid my comforts rise?"

5 Look down upon my sorrows, Lord,
And show Thy grace the same;
Thy tender mercies still afford
To those that love Thy name.

Ps. 120

1 THOU God of love, Thou ever blest,
Pity my suffering state;
When wilt Thou set my soul at rest,
From lips that love deceit?

2 Peace is the blessing that I seek,
How lovely are its charms!
I am for peace; but when I speak,
They all declare for arms.

3 New passions still their souls engage,
And keep their malice strong;
What shall be done to curb thy rage,
O thou devouring tongue!

4 Should burning arrows smite thee through,
Strict justice would approve;
But I would rather spare my foe,
And melt his heart with love.

H. 147 *The Excellence of the Scriptures.*

1 Laden with guilt, and full of fears,
I fly to Thee, my Lord;
And not a glimpse of hope appears,
But in Thy written word.

2 The volume of my Father's grace
Does all my grief assuage;
Here I behold my Saviour's face,
Almost in every page.

3 This is the field where hidden lies
The pearl of price unknown;
That merchant is divinely wise
Who makes the pearl his own.

4 Here consecrated water flows
To quench my thirst of sin;
Here the fair tree of knowledge grows,
Nor danger dwells therein.

5 O may Thy counsels, mighty God,
My roving feet command;
Nor I forsake the happy road
That leads to Thy right hand.

H. 217 *The Sinner's Recovery from Ruin.*

1 How sad our state by nature is!
Our sin, how deep it stains!
And Satan binds our captive minds
Fast in his slavish chains.

2 But there's a voice of sovereign grace
Sounds from the sacred word;
"Ho! ye despairing sinners, come,
And trust upon the Lord."

3 My soul obeys the almighty call,
And runs to this relief:
I would believe Thy promise, Lord,
Oh! help my unbelief.

4 To the dear fountain of Thy blood,
Incarnate God, I fly;
Here let me wash my spotted soul,
From crimes of deepest dye.

5 Stretch out Thine arm, victorious King,
My reigning sins subdue;
Drive the old dragon from his seat,
With all his hellish crew.

6 A guilty, weak, and helpless worm,
On Thy kind arms I fall;
Be Thou my strength and righteousness,
My Jesus and my all.

H. 222 *"Remember Me."*

1 Jesus! Thou art the sinner's Friend;
As such I look to Thee;
Now, in the fulness of Thy love,
O Lord, remember me.

2 Remember Thy pure word of grace,
Remember Calvary;
Remember all Thy dying groans,
And, then, Remember me.

3 Thou wondrous Advocate with God!
I yield myself to Thee;
While Thou art sitting on Thy throne,
Dear Lord! remember me.

4 Lord! I am guilty, I am vile,
But Thy salvation's free;
Then, in Thine all-abounding grace,
Dear Lord! remember me.

5 And, when I close my eyes in death,
When creature-helps all flee,
Then, Oh! my dear Redeemer-God!
I pray, remember me.

H. 278 *Communion with God.*

1 Father, I stretch my hands to Thee,
No other help I know;
If Thou withdraw Thyself from me,
Ah! whither shall I go?

2 What did Thine only Son endure,
Before I drew my breath!
What pain, what labour, to secure
My soul from endless death!

3 O Jesus, could I this believe,
I now should feel Thy power!
Now my poor soul Thou wouldst retrieve,
Nor let me wait one hour.

4 Author of faith, to Thee I lift
My weary, longing eyes;
Oh! let me now receive that gift,
My soul without it dies!

5 Surely Thou canst not let me die;
O speak, and I shall live;
And here I will unwearied lie,
Till Thou Thy Spirit give.

6 The worst of sinners would rejoice,
Could they but see Thy face;
Oh! let me hear Thy quickening voice,
And taste Thy pardoning grace.

German.
1. Je-ru-sa-lem, my hap-py home, Name ev-er dear to me! When shall my la - bours
have an end, In joy and peace and thee? In joy and peace and thee?

H. 668 *The New Jerusalem.*

1 Jerusalem, my happy home,
Name ever dear to me!
When shall my labours have an end,
In joy and peace and thee?

2 When shall these eyes thy heaven-built
And pearly gates behold? [walls,
Thy bulwarks, with salvation strong,
And streets of shining gold?

3 O! when, thou city of my God,
Shall I thy courts ascend,
Where congregations ne'er break up,
And Sabbaths have no end?

4 There happier bowers than Eden's bloom,
Nor sin nor sorrow know; [scenes.
Blest seats, through rude and stormy
I onward press to you.

5 Why should I shrink at pain and woe,
Or feel at death dismay?
I've Canaan's goodly land in view,
And realms of endless day.

6 Apostles, martyrs, prophets there
Around my Saviour stand;
And soon my friends in Christ below
Will join the glorious band.

7 Jerusalem, my happy home,
My soul still pants for thee;
Then shall my labours have an end,
When I thy joys shall see.

H. 669 *Mother Dear, Jerusalem.*

1 Oh! mother dear, Jerusalem,
When shall I come to thee?
When shall my sorrows have an end?
Thy joys when shall I see?

2 Oh! happy harbour of the saints!
Oh! sweet and pleasant soil!
In thee no sorrow may be found,
No grief, no care, no toil.

3 No dimly cloud o'ershadows thee,
No gloom, nor darksome night;
But every soul shines as the sun,
For God Himself gives light.

4 Thy gardens and thy gallant walks
Continually are green, [flowers
There grow such sweet and pleasant
As nowhere else are seen.

5 Quite through the streets, with silver
The flood of Life doth flow, [sound,
Upon whose banks, on every side,
The wood of Life doth grow.

6 There trees for evermore bear fruit,
And evermore do spring;
There evermore the angels sit,
And evermore do sing.

7 Oh! mother dear, Jerusalem,
When shall I come to thee?
When shall my sorrows have an end?
Thy joys when shall I see?

G. N. Allen.

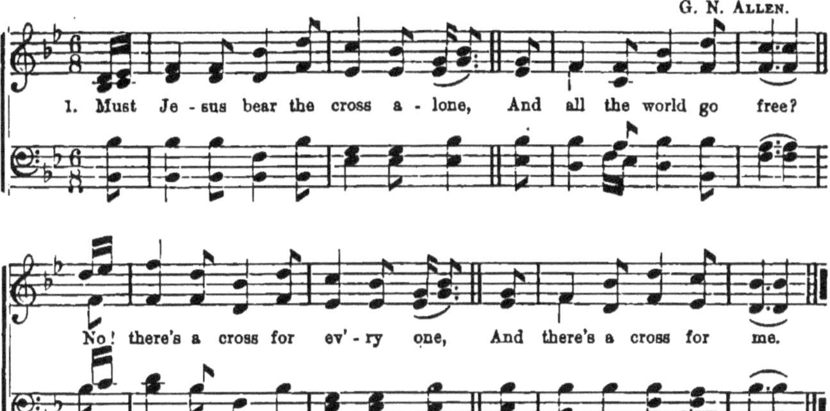
1. Must Je - sus bear the cross a - lone, And all the world go free?
No! there's a cross for ev' - ry one, And there's a cross for me.

H. 388 *Bearing the Cross.*

2 That consecrated cross I'll bear
Till death shall set me free;
And then go home, my crown to wear,
For there's a crown for me.

H. 227 *Joy over the Sinner that Repenteth.*

1 O! how divine, how sweet the joy,
When but one sinner turns,
And with an humble, broken heart,
His sins and errors mourns!

2 Pleased with the news the saints below
In songs their tongues employ;
Beyond the skies the tidings go,
And heaven is filled with joy.

3 Well pleased, the Father sees and hears
The conscious sinner's moan;
Jesus receives him in His arms,
And claims him for His own.

4 Nor angels can their joys contain,
But kindle with new fire;
"The sinner lost is found," they sing,
And strike the sounding lyre.

H. 418 *Voice of Jesus.*

1 When waves of sorrow round me swell,
My soul is not dismayed;
I hear a voice I know full well—
"'Tis I—be not afraid."

2 When black the threatening clouds appear,
And storms my path invade,
That voice shall calm each rising fear—
"'Tis I—be not afraid."

3 There is a gulf that must be crossed—
Saviour, be near to aid!
Whisper, when my frail bark is tossed,
"'Tis I—be not afraid."

4 There is a dark and fearful vale,
Death hides within its shade;
O say, when flesh and heart shall fail,
"'Tis I—be not afraid."

H. 379 *Call to Prayer.*

1 Approach, my soul, the mercy seat,
Where Jesus answers prayer;
There humbly fall before His feet,
For none can perish there.

2 Thy promise is my only plea,
With this I venture nigh;
Thou callest burdened souls to Thee,
And such, O Lord, am I.

3 Bowed down beneath a load of sin,
By Satan sorely pressed,
By war without, and fear within,
I come to Thee for rest.

4 Be Thou my shield and hiding-place,
That, sheltered near Thy side,
I may my fierce accuser face,
And tell him, "Thou hast died."

5 O, wondrous love! to bleed and die,
To bear the cross and shame,
That guilty sinners, such as I,
Might plead Thy gracious name.

WOODLAND. C.M.

N. D. Gould, 1832.

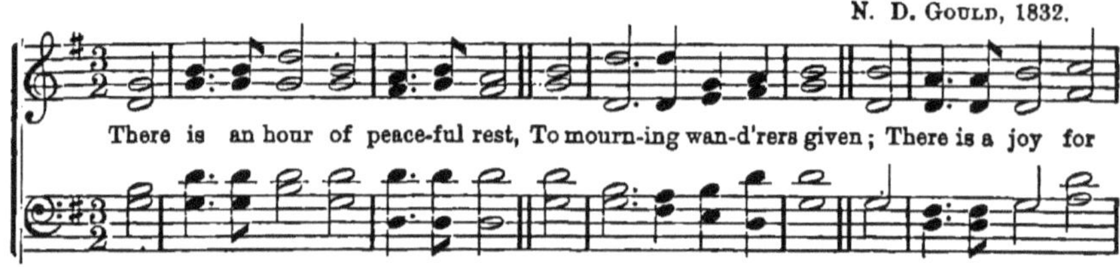
There is an hour of peace-ful rest, To mourn-ing wan-d'rers given; There is a joy for

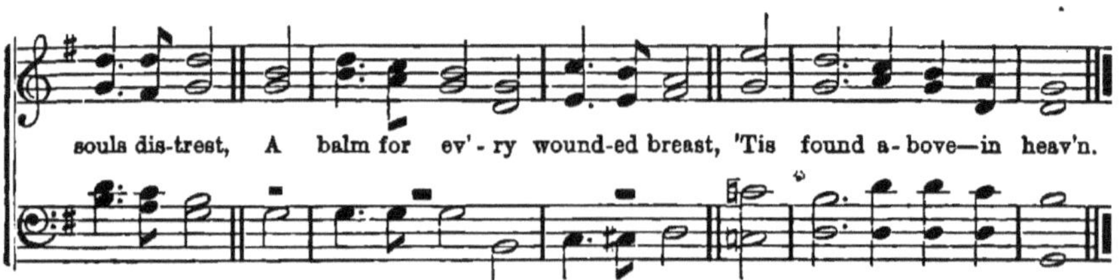
souls dis-trest, A balm for ev'-ry wound-ed breast, 'Tis found a-bove—in heav'n.

H. 696 *The Rest of Heaven.*

2 There is a home for weary souls,
By sin and sorrow driven;
When toss'd on life's tempestuous shoals,
Where storms arise, and ocean rolls,
And all is drear but heaven.

3 There, faith lifts up her cheerful eye,
To brighter prospects given;
And views the tempest passing by,
The evening shadows quickly fly,
And all serene in heaven.

4 There, fragrant flowers immortal bloom,
And joys supreme are given;
There, rays divine disperse the gloom—
Beyond the confines of the tomb
Appears the dawn of heaven.

H. 555 *Love of Jesus.*

1 With all His sufferings full in view,
And woes to us unknown,
Forth to His task the Saviour flew—
'Twas love that urged Him on.

2 Lord, we return Thee—what we can!
Our hearts shall sound abroad
Salvation to the dying man,
And to the rising God!

3 And while Thy bleeding glories here
Engage our wondering eyes;
We learn our lighter cross to bear,
And hasten to the skies.

H. 536 *Children included in the Covenant of Grace.*

1 How large the promise, how divine,
To Abraham and his seed!
"I'll be a God to thee and thine,
Supplying all their need."

2 The words of His extensive love,
From age to age endure;
The angel of the covenant proves
And seals the blessing sure.

3 Jesus the ancient faith confirms
To our great father given;
He takes young children to His arms,
And calls them heirs of heaven.

4 Our God! how faithful are His ways!
His love endures the same;
Nor from the promise of His grace,
Blots out the children's name.

Ps. 144 *First Part.*

1 For ever blessed be the Lord,
My Saviour and my Shield;
He sends His Spirit with His word,
To arm me for the field.

2 When sin and hell their force unite,
He makes my soul His care;
Instructs me in the heavenly fight,
And guards me through the war.

3 A Friend and Helper so divine
My fainting hope shall raise;
He makes the glorious victory mine,
And His shall be the praise.

H. 101 *Christ Interceding above.*

1 Now let our cheerful eyes survey
Our great High Priest above;
And celebrate His constant care,
And sympathetic love.

2 Though raised to a superior throne,
Where angels bow around,
And high o'er all the shining train,
'With matchless honours crowned;

3 The names of all His saints He bears,
Deep graven on His heart;
Nor shall the meanest Christian say,
That he hath lost his part.

4 Those characters shall fair abide
Our everlasting trust,
When gems, and monuments, and crowns,
Are mouldered down to dust.

5 So, gracious Saviour, on my breast
May Thy dear name be worn,
A sacred ornament and guard,
To endless ages borne.

Ps. 26 *First Part.*

1 Examine me, and do me prove;
Try heart and reins, O God;
For Thy love is before mine eyes,
Thy truth's paths I have trod.

2 With persons vain I have not sat,
Nor with dissemblers gone:
Th' assembly of ill men I hate;
To sit with such I shun.

3 Mine hands in innocence, O Lord,
I'll wash and purify:
So to Thine holy altar go,
And compass it will I:

4 That I, with voice of thanksgiving,
May publish and declare,
And tell of all Thy mighty works,
That great and wondrous are.

5 The habitation of Thy house,
Lord, I have loved well;
Yea, in that place I do delight
Where doth Thine honour dwell.

Ps. 119 *Ninth Part.*

1 Thy mercies fill the earth, O Lord,
How good Thy works appear!
Open my eyes to read Thy word,
And see Thy wonders there.

2 My heart was fashioned by Thy hand,
My service is Thy due;
O! make Thy servant understand
The duties he must do.

3 Since I'm a stranger here below,
Thy path, O! do not hide,
But mark the road my feet should go,
And be my constant guide.

4 When I have learned my Father's will,
I'll teach the world His ways;
My thankful lips, inspired with zeal,
Shall sing aloud His praise.

Ps. 121 *Third Part.*

1 I to the hills will lift mine eyes,
From whence doth come mine aid,
My safety cometh from the Lord
Who heav'n and earth hath made.

2 Thy foot He'll not let slide, nor will
He slumber that thee keeps,
Behold, He that keeps Israel,
He slumbers not, nor sleeps.

3 The Lord thee keeps; the Lord thy shade
On thy right hand doth stay;
The moon by night thee shall not smite,
Nor yet the sun by day.

4 The Lord shall keep thy soul; He shall
Preserve thee from all ill.
Henceforth thy going out and in
God keep for ever will.

Ps. 130 *First Part.*

1 I wait for Thy salvation, Lord,
With strong desires I wait;
My soul, invited by Thy word,
Stands watching at Thy gate.

2 Just as the guards that keep the night
Long for the morning skies,
Watch the first beams of breaking light,
And meet them with their eyes:

3 So waits my soul to see Thy grace;
And more intent than they,
Meets the first openings of Thy grace,
And finds a brighter day.

4 Then in the Lord let Israel trust,
Let Israel seek His face;
The Lord is good, as well as just,
And plenteous is His grace.

Wm. Gardiner.

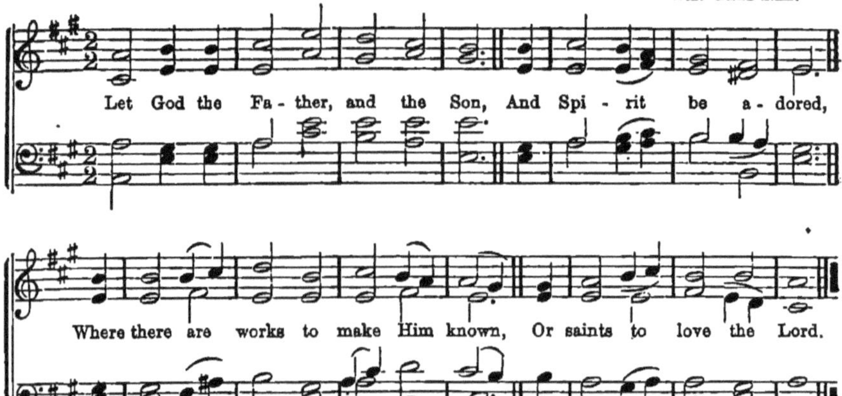
Let God the Fa - ther, and the Son, And Spi - rit be a - dored,
Where there are works to make Him known, Or saints to love the Lord.

Ps. 119 *First Part.*

1 Blest are the undefiled in heart,
Whose ways are right and clean;
Who never from Thy law depart,
But flee from every sin.

2 Blest are the men that keep Thy word,
And practise Thy commands;
With their whole heart they seek the Lord,
And serve Thee with their hands.

3 Great is their peace who love Thy law;
How firm their souls abide!
Nor can a bold temptation draw
Their steady feet aside.

4 Then shall my heart have inward joy,
And keep my face from shame,
When all Thy statutes I obey,
And honour all Thy name.

Ps. 119 *Second Part.*

1 To Thee, before the dawning light,
My gracious God, I pray;
I meditate Thy name by night,
And keep Thy law by day.

2 My spirit faints to see Thy grace;
Thy promise bears me up;
And while salvation long delays,
Thy word supports my hope.

3 Seven times a day I lift my hands,
And pay my thanks to Thee;
Thy righteous providence demands
Repeated praise from me.

4 When midnight darkness veils the skies,
I call Thy works to mind;
My thoughts in warm devotion rise,
And sweet acceptance find.

H. 216 *The Converted Thief.*

1 As on the cross the Saviour hung,
And wept, and bled, and died,
He poured salvation on a wretch,
That languished at His side.

2 His crimes, with inward grief and shame,
The penitent confessed;
Then turned his dying eyes to Christ,
And thus his prayer addressed:

3 "Jesus, Thou Son and Heir of heaven,
Thou spotless Lamb of God,
I see Thee bathed in sweat and tears,
And weltering in Thy blood.

4 "Yet quickly from these scenes of woe,
In triumph shalt Thou rise,
Burst through the gloomy shades of death,
And shine above the skies.

5 "Amid the glories of that world,
Dear Saviour, think on me,
And in the victories of Thy death
Let me a sharer be."

6 His prayer the dying Jesus hears,
And instantly replies;
"To-day thy parting soul shall be
With Me in paradise."

ARRANGED FROM GIPPERT.

1. Lord, I es-teem Thy judg-ments right, And all Thy sta-tutes just; Thence I main-tain a con-stant fight
With ev'-ry flatt'r-ing lust— Thence I main-tain a con-stant fight With ev'-ry flatt'r-ing lust.

Ps. 119 *Sixth Part.*

2 Thy precepts often I survey,
I keep Thy law in sight,
Through all the business of the day,
To form my actions right.

3 My heart in midnight silence cries,
"How sweet Thy comforts be!"
My thoughts in holy wonder rise,
And bring their thanks to Thee.

4 And when my spirit drinks her fill,
At some good word of Thine,
Not mighty men, that share the spoil,
Have joys compared to mine.

Ps. 119 *Seventh Part.*

1 Let all the heathen writers join
To form one perfect book;
Great God, if once compared with Thine,
How mean their writings look!

2 Not the most perfect rules they gave,
Could show one sin forgiven,
Nor lead a step beyond the grave;
But Thine conduct to heaven.

3 I've seen an end to what we call
Perfection here below;
How short the powers of nature fall,
And can no further go.

4 Yet men would fain be just with God,
By works their hands have wrought;
But Thy commands, exceeding broad,
Extend to every thought.

5 Our faith, and love, and every grace,
Fall far below Thy word;
But perfect truth and righteousness
Dwell only with the Lord.

Ps. 146 *First Part.*

1 Oh! happy is that man, and blest,
Whom Jacob's God doth aid;
Whose hope upon the Lord doth rest,
And on his God is stayed:

2 Who made the earth and heavens high,
Who made the swelling deep,
And all that is within the same;
Who truth doth ever keep:

3 Who righteous judgment executes
For those oppressed that be,
Who to the hungry giveth food;
God sets the prisoners free.

4 The Lord doth give the blind their sight,
The bowed-down doth raise;
The Lord doth dearly love all those
That walk in upright ways.

5 The stranger's shield, the widow's stay,
The orphan's help, is He;
But yet by Him the wicked's way
Turned upside down shall be.

6 The Lord shall reign for evermore;
Thy God, O Zion, He
Reigns to all generations:
Praise to the Lord give ye.

ENGLISH.

1. As pants the hart for cool-ing streams, When heat-ed in the chase; So longs my soul, O
God, for Thee, So longs my soul, O God, for Thee, And Thy re-fresh-ing grace.

Ps. 42

2 For Thee, my God, the living God,
My thirsty soul doth pine;
Oh! when shall I behold Thy face,
Thou Majesty divine?

3 Why restless, why cast down, my soul?
Trust God, and He'll employ
His aid for thee, and change these sighs
To thankful hymns of joy.

4 Why restless, why cast down, my soul?
Hope still; and thou shalt sing
The praise of Him who is thy God,
Thy health's eternal spring.

Ps. 45

1 I'll speak the honours of my King,
His form divinely fair;
None of the sons of mortal race
May with the Lord compare.

2 Sweet is Thy speech, and heavenly grace
Upon Thy lips is shed;
Thy God with blessings infinite
Hath crowned Thy sacred head.

3 Gird on Thy sword, victorious Prince,
Ride with majestic sway;
Thy terror shall strike through Thy foes,
And make the world obey.

4 Thy throne, O God, for ever stands;
Thy word of grace shall prove
A peaceful sceptre in Thy hands,
To rule Thy saints by love.

5 Justice and truth attend Thee still,
But mercy is Thy choice;
And God, Thy God, Thy soul shall fill
With most peculiar joys.

Ps. 116 *Second Part.*

1 What shall I render to my God
For all His kindness shown?
My feet shall visit Thine abode,
My songs address Thy throne.

2 Among the saints that fill Thy house,
My offerings shall be paid;
There shall my zeal perform the vows
My soul in anguish made.

3 How much is mercy Thy delight,
Thou ever blessed God!
How dear Thy servants in Thy sight!
How precious is their blood!

4 How happy all Thy servants are!
How great Thy grace to me!
My life, which Thou hast made Thy care,
Lord, I devote to Thee.

5 Now am I Thine, for ever Thine,
Nor shall my purpose move;
Thy hand has loosed my bonds of pain,
And bound me with Thy love.

6 Here in Thy courts I leave my vow,
And Thy rich grace record;
Witness, ye saints, who hear me now,
If I forsake the Lord.

Ps. 110 *Second Part.*

1 Jesus, our Lord, ascend Thy throne,
And near Thy Father sit;
In Zion shall Thy power be known,
And make Thy foes submit.

2 What wonders shall Thy gospel do?
Thy converts shall surpass
The numerous drops of morning dew,
And own Thy sovereign grace.

3 Jesus our Priest for ever lives
To plead for us above;
Jesus our King for ever gives
The blessings of His love.

4 God shall exalt His glorious head,
And His high throne maintain,
Shall strike the powers and princes dead
Who dare oppose His reign.

H. 277 *An Unseen Saviour.*

1 Jesus, these eyes have never seen
That radiant form of Thine;
The veil of sense hangs dark between
Thy blessed face and mine.

2 I see Thee not, I hear Thee not,
Yet art Thou oft with me;
And earth hath ne'er so dear a spot,
As where I meet with Thee.

3 Like some bright dream that comes unsought,
When slumbers o'er me roll,
Thine image ever fills my thought,
And charms my ravished soul.

4 Yet though I have not seen, and still
Must rest in faith alone;
I love Thee, dearest Lord, and will,
Unseen, but not unknown.

5 When death these mortal eyes shall seal,
And still this throbbing heart,
The rending veil shall Thee reveal,
All glorious as Thou art.

H. 286 *Love to Christ.*

1 Do not I love Thee, O my Lord?
Behold my heart, and see;
And turn each hateful idol out,
That dares to rival Thee.

2 Do not I love Thee from my soul?
Then let me nothing love;
Dead be my heart to every joy
Which Thou dost not approve.

3 Hast Thou a lamb in all Thy flock
I would disdain to feed?
Hast Thou a foe before whose face
I fear Thy cause to plead?

4 Thou knowest I love Thee, dearest Lord?
But Oh! I long to soar,
Far from the sphere of mortal joys,
That I may love Thee more.

H. 327 *God's Will Mine.*

1 One prayer I have, all prayers in one,
When I am wholly Thine:
Thy will, my God, Thy will be done,
And let that will be mine.

2 May I remember, that to Thee
Whate'er I have I owe;
And back in gratitude from me,
May all Thy bounties flow.

3 And though Thy wisdom takes away,
Shall I arraign Thy will?
No, let me bless Thy name, and say,
"The Lord is gracious still."

4 A pilgrim through the earth I roam,
Of nothing long possessed,
And all must fail when I go home,
For this is not my rest.

5 Write but my name upon the roll,
Of Thy redeemed above;
Then heart, and mind, and strength, and soul,
I'll love Thee for Thy love.

H. 362 *Uniting with the Church.*

1 Witness, ye men and angels, now;
Before the Lord we speak;
To Him we make our solemn vow,
A vow we dare not break:

2 That long as life itself shall last,
Ourselves to Christ we yield;
Nor from His cause will we depart,
Nor ever quit the field.

3 We trust not in our native strength,
But on His grace rely,
That, with returning wants, the Lord
Will all our need supply.

4 Lord, guide our doubtful feet aright,
And keep us in Thy ways;
And, while we turn our vows to prayers,
Turn Thou our prayers to praise.

1. Thou art the way; to Thee a - lone From sin and death we flee; And he who would the
Fa-ther seek, Must seek Him, Lord, in Thee, Must seek Him, Lord, in Thee, Must seek Him, Lord, in Thee.

H. 61 *Christ, the Way, Truth, and Life.*

1 Thou art the way; to Thee alone
From sin and death we flee;
And he who would the Father seek,
Must seek Him, Lord, in Thee.

2 Thou art the truth—Thy word alone
True wisdom can impart;
Thou only canst instruct the mind,
And purify the heart.

3 Thou art the life,—the rending tomb
Proclaims Thy conquering arm;
And those who put their trust in Thee,
Nor death nor hell shall harm.

4 Thou art the way, the truth, the life;
Grant us to know that way,
That truth to keep, that life to win,
Which lead to endless day.

H. 62 *Christ our Hiding-Place.*

1 Thou art my hiding-place, O Lord;
In Thee I put my trust,
Encouraged by Thy holy word,
A feeble child of dust.

2 I have no argument beside,
I urge no other plea;
And 'tis enough the Saviour died,
The Saviour died for me.

3 And when Thine awful voice commands
This body to decay,
And life, in its last ling'ring sands,
Is ebbing fast away,—

4 Then, though it be in accents weak,
My voice shall call on Thee,
And ask for strength in death to speak,
"My Saviour died for me."

H. 264 *Faith in Time of Declension.*

1 When any turn from Zion's way,
Alas! what numbers do!
Methinks I hear my Saviour say,
"Wilt thou forsake Me too?"

2 Ah! Lord, with such a heart as mine,
Unless Thou hold me fast,
I feel I must, I shall decline,
And prove like them at last.

3 Yet Thou alone hast power, I know,
To save a wretch like me;
To whom, or whither could I go,
If I should turn from Thee?

4 Beyond a doubt, I rest assured
Thou art the Christ of God;
Who hast eternal life secured,
By promise and by blood.

5 No voice but Thine can give me rest,
And bid my fears depart;
No love but Thine can make me blest,
And satisfy my heart.

6 What anguish has this question stirred,
"And wilt Thou also go?"
Dear Lord, relying on Thy word,
I humbly answer, "No!"

H. 316 *A Thankful Heart.*

1 Father, whate'er of earthly bliss,
Thy sovereign will denies,
Accepted at Thy throne of grace,
Let this petition rise:

2 Give me a calm, a thankful heart,
From every murmur free;
The blessings of Thy grace impart,
And make me live to Thee.

3 Let the sweet hope that Thou art mine,
My life and death attend;
Thy presence through my journey shine,
And crown my journey's end.

H. 404 *Looking to God in Trouble.*

1 Dear Refuge of my weary soul,
On Thee, when sorrows rise,
On Thee, when waves of trouble roll,
My fainting hope relies.

2 To Thee I tell each rising grief,
For Thou alone canst heal;
Thy word can bring a sweet relief
For every pain I feel.

3 But O! when gloomy doubts prevail,
I fear to call Thee mine;
The springs of comfort seem to fail,
And all my hopes decline.

4 Yet, gracious God, where shall I flee?
Thou art my only trust;
And still my soul would cleave to Thee,
Though prostrate in the dust.

5 Hast Thou not bid me seek Thy face?
And shall I seek in vain?
And can the ear of sovereign grace
Be deaf when I complain?

6 No, still the ear of sovereign grace
Attends the mourner's prayer;
O! may I ever find access,
To breathe my sorrows there.

7 Thy mercy-seat is open still,
Here let my soul retreat;
With humble hope attend Thy will,
And wait beneath Thy feet.

H. 406 *Spiritual Declension Lamented.*

1 Sweet was the time when first I felt
The Saviour's pardoning blood,
Applied to cleanse my soul from guilt,
And bring me home to God.

2 Soon as the morn the light revealed,
His praises tuned my tongue;
And when the evening shades prevailed,
His love was all my song.

3 In prayer my soul drew near the Lord,
And saw His glory shine;
And when I read His holy word,
I called each promise mine.

4 But now, when evening shade prevails,
My soul in darkness mourns;
And when the morn the light reveals,
No light to me returns.

5 Rise, Lord, and help me to prevail,
O! make my soul Thy care;
I know Thy mercy cannot fail,
Let me that mercy share.

Ps. 70

1 In haste, O God, attend my call,
Nor hear my cries in vain;
O let Thy speed prevent my fall,
And still my hope sustain.

2 Let all that love Thy name rejoice,
And glory in Thy word;
In Thy salvation raise their voice,
And magnify the Lord.

3 O Thou, my help in time of need,
Behold my sore dismay;
In pity hasten to my aid,
Nor let Thy grace delay.

Ps. 129

1 Up from my youth, may Israel say,
Have I been nursed in tears;
My griefs were constant as the day,
And tedious as the years.

2 Up from my youth I bore the rage,
Of all the sons of strife;
Oft they assailed my riper age,
But God preserved my life.

3 The Lord in anger, on His throne,
With an impartial eye,
Measured the mischiefs they had done,
Then let His arrows fly.

4 Thus shall the men that hate the saints
Be blasted from the sky;
Their glory fades, their courage faints,
And all their prospects die.

1. How love - ly is Thy dwell - ing place, O Lord of hosts, to me!
The ta - ber - na - cles of Thy grace, How plea - sant, Lord, they be!

Ps. 84 *Fourth Part.*

2 For in Thy courts one day excels
  A thousand; rather in
My God's house will I keep a door,
  Than dwell in tents of sin.

3 For God the Lord's a sun and shield;
  He'll grace and glory give;
And will withhold no good from them
  That uprightly do live.

4 O Thou that art the Lord of hosts,
  That man is truly blest,
Who, by assured confidence,
  On Thee alone doth rest.

Ps. 91 *First Part.*

1 He that doth in the secret place
  Of the Most High reside,
Under the shade of Him that is
  The Almighty shall abide.

2 I of the Lord my God will say,
  He is my refuge still,
He is my fortress, and my God,
  And in Him trust I will.

3 Thou shalt not need to be afraid
  For terrors of the night;
Nor for the arrow that doth fly
  By day, while it is light;

4 Nor for the pestilence, that walks
  In darkness secretly;
Nor for destruction, that doth waste
  At noon-day openly.

5 A thousand at thy side shall fall,
  On thy right hand shall lie
Ten thousand dead; yet unto thee
  It shall not once come nigh.

6 Only thou with thine eyes shalt look
  And a beholder be;
And thou therein the just reward
  Of wicked men shalt see.

Ps. 107

1 How are Thy servants blest, O Lord;
  How sure is their defence!
Eternal wisdom is their guide;
  Their help,—omnipotence.

2 When by the dreadful tempest borne
  High on the broken wave,
They know Thou art not slow to hear,
  Nor impotent to save.

3 The storm is laid, the winds retire,
  Obedient to Thy will;
The sea, that roars at Thy command,
  At Thy command is still.

4 In midst of dangers, fears, and deaths,
  Thy goodness we'll adore;
We'll praise Thee for Thy mercies past,
  And humbly hope for more.

5 Our life, while Thou preserv'st that life,
  Thy sacrifice shall be;
And death, when death shall be our lot,
  Shall join our souls to Thee.

WM. B. BRADBURY, 1840.

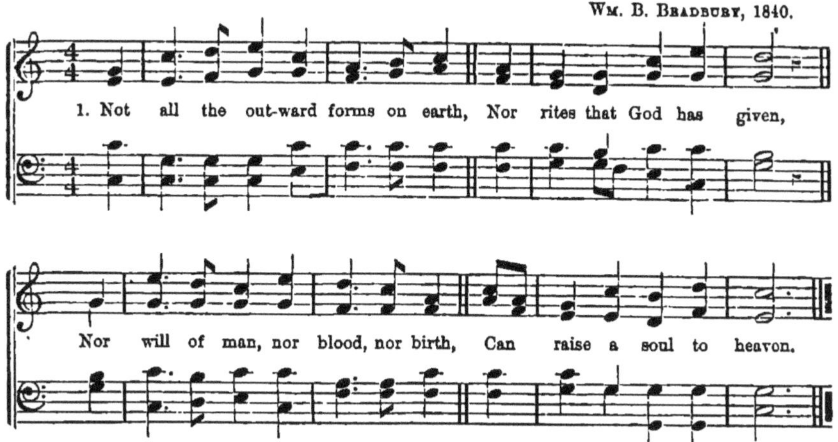
1. Not all the out-ward forms on earth, Nor rites that God has given,
Nor will of man, nor blood, nor birth, Can raise a soul to heaven.

H. 223 *Regeneration by the Spirit.*

2 THE sovereign will of God alone
Creates us heirs of grace:
Born in the image of His Son,
A new, peculiar race.

3 The Spirit, like some heavenly wind,
Blows on the sons of flesh;
New models all the carnal mind,
And forms the man afresh.

4 Our quickened souls awake and rise
From the long sleep of death;
On heavenly things we fix our eyes,
And praise employs our breath.

H. 249 *Blessedness of the Righteous.*

1 THERE is a safe and secret place
Beneath the wings divine,
Reserved for all the heirs of grace;
Oh! be that refuge mine!

2 The least and feeblest there may bide,
Uninjured and unawed;
While thousands fall on every side,
He rests secure in God.

3 He feeds in pastures large and fair,
Of love and truth divine;
O child of God, O glory's heir,
How rich a lot is thine!

4 A hand almighty to defend,
An ear for every call,
An honoured life, a peaceful end,
And heaven to crown it all.

H. 263 *Sustaining Faith.*

1 'TIS faith supports my feeble soul,
In times of deep distress;
When storms arise and billows roll,
Great God, I trust Thy grace.

2 Thy powerful arm still bears me up,
Whatever griefs befall;
Thou art my life, my joy, my hope,
And Thou my all in all.

3 Bereft of friends, beset with foes,
With dangers all around,
To Thee I all my fears disclose,
In Thee my help is found.

4 In every want, in every strait,
To Thee alone I fly;
When other comforters depart,
Thou art for ever nigh.

H. 583 *Prayer for Reviving.*

1 COME, Lord, and warm each languid heart,
Inspire each lifeless tongue;
And let the joys of heaven impart
Their influence to our song.

2 Come, Lord, Thy love alone can raise
In us the heavenly flame;
Then shall our lips resound Thy praise,
Our hearts adore Thy name.

3 Dear Saviour, let Thy glory shine,
And fill Thy dwellings here,
Till life, and love, and joy divine,
A heaven on earth appear.

C.
1. Mor - tals, a - wake, with an - gels join, And chant the sol - emn lay;
Joy, love, and gra - ti - tude com - bine To hail th' aus - pi - cious day.

H. 73 *Song of Angels at the Nativity of Christ.*

1 Mortals, awake, with angels join,
And chant the solemn lay;
Joy, love, and gratitude combine
To hail the auspicious day.

2 In heaven the rapturous song began,
And sweet seraphic fire
Through all the shining legions ran,
And strung and tuned the lyre.

3 Down through the portals of the sky
The impetuous torrent ran;
And angels flew with eager joy,
To bear the news to man.

4 Hark! the cherubic armies shout,
And glory leads the song:
Good will and peace are heard throughout
The harmonious, angel throng.

5 O! for a glance of heavenly love,
Our hearts and songs to raise;
Sweetly to bear our souls above,
And mingle with their lays.

6 With joy the chorus we'll repeat,
"Glory to God on high;
Good will and peace are now complete,
Jesus was born to die."

H. 233 *Spirit of Adoption.*

1 Sovereign of all the worlds on high,
Allow my humble claim;
Nor while poor worms would raise their heads,
Disdain a Father's name.

2 Our Father God! how sweet the sound!
How tender and how dear!
Not all the melody of heaven,
Could so delight the ear.

3 Come, sacred Spirit, seal Thy name
On my expanding heart;
And show, that in Jehovah's grace
I share a filial part.

4 Cheered by a signal so divine,
Unwavering I believe;
Thou knowest I, Abba, Father, cry,
Nor can Thy word deceive.

H. 439 *An Evening Song.*

1 Now from the altar of our hearts
Let flames of love arise;
Assist us, Lord, to offer up
Our evening sacrifice.

2 Minutes and mercies multiplied
Have made up all this day;
Minutes came quick, but mercies were
More swift and free than they.

3 New time, new favour, and new joys,
Do a new song require;
Till we shall praise Thee as we would,
Accept our heart's desire.

4 Lord of our days whose hand hath set
New time upon our score;
Thee may we praise for all our time,
When time shall be no more.

H. 83 *The Lamb of God.*

1 Sinners, behold the Lamb of God
Who takes away our guilt;
Look to the precious, priceless blood,
That Jews and Gentiles spilt.

2 From heaven He came to seek and save,
Leaving His blest abode;
To ransom us Himself He gave;
"Behold the Lamb of God."

3 He came to take the sinner's place,
And shed His precious blood;
Let Adam's guilty, ruined race,
"Behold the Lamb of God."

4 Sinners, to Jesus then draw near,
Invited by His word;
The chief of sinners need not fear;
"Behold the Lamb of God."

5 Backsliders, too, the Saviour calls,
And washes in His blood;
Arise, return from grievous falls;
"Behold the Lamb of God."

6 Spirit of grace, to us apply
Immanuel's precious blood;
That we may, with Thy saints on high,
"Behold the Lamb of God."

H. 497 *Lord's Day Evening.*

1 Frequent the day of God returns,
To shed its quickening beams;
And yet how slow devotion burns;
How languid are its flames!

2 Accept our faint attempts to love;
Our frailties, Lord, forgive;
We would be like Thy saints above,
And praise Thee while we live.

3 Increase, O Lord, our faith and hope,
And fit us to ascend,
Where the assembly ne'er breaks up,
The Sabbaths ne'er shall end.

4 Where we shall breathe in heavenly air,
With heavenly lustre shine;
Before the throne of God appear,
And feast on love divine.

H. 502 *"There Remaineth a Rest."*

1 Come, let us join with one accord
In hymns around the throne;
This is the day our rising Lord
Hath made, and called His own.

2 This is the day that God hath blessed,
The brightest of the seven,
Type of that everlasting rest
The saints enjoy in heaven.

3 Then let us in His name sing on,
And hasten to that day
When our Redeemer shall come down,
And shadows pass away.

4 Not one, but all our days below,
Let us in hymns employ?
And in our Lord rejoicing, go
To His eternal joy.

H. 515 *Christian Liberality.*

1 Rich are the joys that cannot die,
With God laid up in store;
Treasures beyond the changing sky,
Brighter than golden ore.

2 The seeds which piety and love
Have scattered here below,
In the fair, fertile fields above,
To ample harvests grow.

3 The mite my willing hands can give,
At Jesus' feet I lay;
Grace shall the humble gift receive,
Abounding grace repay.

Ps. 109

1 God of my mercy and my praise,
Thy glory is my song;
Though sinners speak against Thy grace
With a blaspheming tongue.

2 When in the form of mortal man,
Thy Son on earth was found;
With cruel slanders, false and vain,
They compassed Him around.

3 Their miseries His compassion move,
Their peace He still pursued;
They render hatred for His love,
And evil for His good.

4 Their malice raged without a cause,
Yet with His dying breath
He prayed for murderers on His cross,
And blessed His foes in death.

5 Lord, shall Thy bright example shine
In vain before my eyes?
Give me a soul akin to thine,
To love mine enemies.

6 The Lord shall on my side engage,
And in my Saviour's name
I shall defeat their pride and rage,
Who slander and condemn.

G. F. Handel, 1685-1759.

1. Once more, my soul, the ris - ing day Sa - lutes thy wak - ing eyes; Once more, my
voice, Thy tri - bute pay To Him that rules the skies— To Him that rules the skies.

H. 435 *Morning Hymn.*

2 Night unto night His name repeats,
The day renews the sound,
Wide as the heaven on which He sits,
To turn the seasons round.

3 'Tis He supports my mortal frame;
My tongue shall speak His praise;
My sins would rouse His wrath to flame,
And yet His wrath delays.

4 On a poor worm Thy power might tread,
And I could ne'er withstand;
Thy justice might have crushed me dead,
But mercy held Thy hand.

5 How many wretched souls are fled
Since the last setting sun;
And yet Thou lengthenest out my thread,
And yet my moments run.

6 Great God, let all my hours be Thine,
Whilst I enjoy the light;
Then shall my sun in smiles decline,
And bring a pleasant night.

H. 542 *Children Devoted to God.*

1 Thus saith the mercy of the Lord,
"I'll be a God to thee!
"I'll bless thy numerous race, and they
Shall be a seed for Me."

2 Abraham believed the promised grace,
And gave his son to God;
But water seals the blessing now,
That once was sealed with blood.

3 Thus later saints, eternal King,
Thine ancient truths embrace;
To Thee their infant offspring bring,
And humbly claim Thy grace.

H. 679 *Contemplation of Heaven:*

1 Raise thee, my soul, fly up and run
Through every heavenly street,
And say, there's nought below the sun
That's worthy of thy feet.

2 There, on a high majestic throne,
The almighty Father reigns,
And sheds His glorious goodness down
On all the blissful plains.

3 Bright like the sun, the Saviour sits,
And spreads eternal noon;
No evenings there, nor gloomy nights,
To want the feeble moon.

4 Amidst those ever shining skies,
Behold the sacred Dove,
While banished sin and sorrow flies
From all the realms of love.

5 The glorious tenants of the place
Stand bending round the throne;
And saints and seraphs sing and praise
The infinite Three-One.

6 Jesus! O when shall that blest day,
That joyful hour appear,
When I shall leave this house of clay,
To dwell amongst them there.

SHERBURNE. C. M.

DANIEL READ, 1785.

1. While shep-herds watch'd their flocks by night, All seat - ed on the ground, The
The an - gel of the Lord came down, and glo - - - - ry shone a-round, And
The an-gel of the Lord came down, And glo - - - ry
The an-gel of the Lord came down, And
an -gel of the Lord came down, And glo - - - - - - - - - - ry shone a-round, And
glo - - - ry shone a-round, - - - - - The an-gel of the Lord came down, And
shone a-round, And glo - - - - - - - - - ry shone a-round,- - The - - an-gel
glo - - - ry shone a-round, And glo - - - ry shone a-round, - - - - - The
glo - - - - - - - - ry - - shone a - round, - - - The an - gel of the
glo - - - - - - ry shone a-round, And glo - ry shone a - round,
of the Lord came down, And glo-ry shone a- - - - round.
an - gel of the Lord came down, And glo - - - ry -shone a - round. - -
Lord came down, And glo - - - - ry shone a - round. - - - - -

H. 68 *Nativity of Christ.*

2 "Fear not," said he, for mighty dread
Had seized their troubled mind;
"Glad tidings of great joy I bring
To you and all mankind.

3 "To you, in David's town, this day,
Is born of David's line,
The Saviour, who is Christ the Lord;
And this shall be the sign:

4 "The heavenly Babe you there shall [find,
To human view displayed,
All meanly wrapped in swaddling bands,
And in a manger laid."

5 Thus spake the seraph, and forthwith
Appeared a shining throng
Of angels praising God, who thus
Addressed their joyful song:

6 "All glory be to God on high,
And to the earth be peace;
Good will, henceforth, from heaven to [men,
Begin and never cease."

1. O! that I knew the se - cret place, Where I might find my God!
I'd spread my wants be - fore His face, And pour my woes a - broad.

H. 319 *In Distress Pleading with God.*

2 I'd tell Him how my sins arise,
What sorrows I sustain;
How grace decays, and comfort dies,
And leaves my heart in pain.

3 He knows what arguments I'd take
To wrestle with my God;
I'd plead for His own mercy's sake,
And for my Saviour's blood.

4 My God will pity my complaints,
And heal my broken bones;
He takes the meaning of His saints,
The language of their groans.

5 Arise, my soul, from deep distress,
And banish every fear;
He calls thee to His throne of grace,
To spread thy sorrows there.

H. 344 *Renunciation of the World.*

1 How vain are all things here below!
How false and yet how fair!
Each pleasure has its poison too,
And every sweet a snare.

2 The brightest things below the sky
Give but a flattering light;
We should suspect some danger nigh,
Where we possess delight.

3 Our dearest joys, and nearest friends,
The partners of our blood,
How they divide our wavering minds,
And leave but half for God!

4 The fondness of a creature's love,
How strong it strikes the sense!
Thither the warm affections move,
Nor can we call them thence.

4 Dear Saviour, let Thy beauties be
My soul's eternal food;
And grace command my heart away
From all created good.

H. 399 *Repentance for Backslidings.*

1 O thou, whose tender mercy hears
Contrition's humble sigh;
Whose hand indulgent wipes the tears
From sorrow's weeping eye.

2 See, low before Thy throne of grace,
A wretched wanderer mourn;
Hast Thou not bid me seek Thy face?
Hast Thou not said—return?

3 And shall my guilty fears prevail
To drive me from Thy feet?
O! let not this dear refuge fail,
This only safe retreat.

4 Absent from Thee, my Guide, my Light,
Without one cheering ray;
Thro' dangers, fears, and gloomy night,
How desolate my way!

4 O! shine on this benighted heart,
With beams of mercy shine!
And let Thy healing voice impart
A taste of joys divine.

H. 322 *Christ's Presence Desired.*

1 Oh! could I find, from day to day,
A nearness to my God!
Then should my hours glide sweet away
While leaning on His word.

2 Lord, I desire with Thee to live
Anew from day to day;
In joys the world can never give,
Nor ever take away.

3 Blest Jesus, come, and rule my heart,
And make me wholly Thine,
That I may never more depart,
Nor grieve Thy love divine.

4 Thus, till my last expiring breath,
Thy goodness I'll adore;
And when my frame dissolves in death,
My soul shall love Thee more.

H. 325 *"Thy will be Done."*

1 How sweet to be allowed to pray
To God, the Holy One,
With filial love and trust to say,
"O God, Thy will be done."

2 Here in these sacred words we find
A cure for every ill;
They calm and soothe the troubled mind,
And bid all care be still.

3 Oh! could my heart thus ever pray,
Thus imitate Thy Son!
Teach me, O God, with truth to say,
"Thy will, not mine, be done."

H. 417 *Remember Me.*

1 O thou, from whom all goodness flows,
I lift my heart to Thee;
In all my trials, conflicts, woes,
Dear Lord, Remember me.

2 When groaning, on my burdened heart
My sins lie heavily,
My pardon speak, new peace impart,
In love, remember me.

3 If on my face, for Thy dear name,
Shame and reproaches be;
I'll hail reproach, and welcome shame,
If Thou remember me.

4 The hour is near—consigned to death,
I own the just decree;
Saviour, with my last parting breath,
I'll cry—Remember me.

H. 616 *Man's Frailty and God's Goodness.*

1 Our life is ever on the wing,
And death is ever nigh;
The moment when our lives begin,
We all begin to die.

2 Yet, mighty God, our fleeting days
Thy lasting favours share;
Yet, with the bounties of Thy grace,
Thou load'st the rolling year.

3 'Tis sovereign mercy finds us food,
And we are clothed with love;
While grace stands pointing out the road
That leads our souls above.

4 His goodness runs an endless round;
All glory to the Lord!
His mercy never knows a bound;
And be His name adored.

5 Thus we begin the lasting song;
And when we close our eyes,
Let future ages praise prolong,
Till time and nature dies.

H. 631 *Preparation for Death.*

1 He is a God of sovereign love,
Who promised heaven to me,
And taught my thoughts to soar above,
Where happy spirits be.

2 Prepare me, Lord, for Thy right hand;
Then come the joyful day;
Come death, and some celestial band,
To bear my soul away.

H. 675 *The Peace and Repose of Heaven.*

1 There is an hour of hallowed peace
For those with cares oppressed,
When sighs and sorrowing tears shall cease,
And all be hushed to rest.

2 'Tis then the soul is freed from fears
And doubts, which here annoy;
Then they, who oft have sown in tears,
Shall reap again in joy.

3 There is a home of sweet repose,
Where storms assail no more:
The stream of endless pleasure flows,
On that celestial shore.

4 There, purity with love appears,
And bliss without alloy;
There, they who oft had sown in tears,
Shall reap again in joy.

GREGORY. C. M.

Arranged by Dr. L. Mason.

1. I'm not a-shamed to own my Lord, Nor to de-fend His cause,

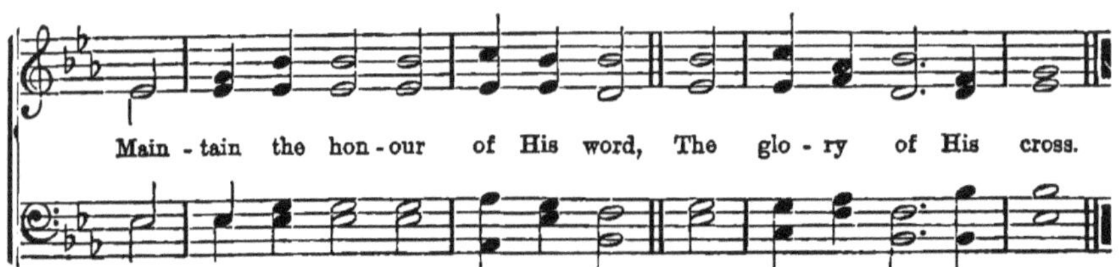
Main-tain the hon-our of His word, The glo-ry of His cross.

H. 355 *Not Ashamed of Christ.*

1 I'm not ashamed to own my Lord,
Nor to defend His cause,
Maintain the honour of His word,
The glory of His cross.

2 Jesus, my God, I know His name,
His name is all my trust;
Nor will He put my soul to shame,
Nor let my hope be lost.

3 Firm as His throne His promise stands,
And He can well secure,
What I've committed to His hands,
Till the decisive hour.

4 Then will He own my worthless name,
Before His Father's face,
And in the New Jerusalem,
Appoint my soul a place.

H. 643 *Funeral Hymn.*

1 Beneath our feet and o'er our head,
Is equal warning given;
Beneath us lie the countless dead,
Above us is the heaven.

2 Their names are graven on the stone,
Their bones are in the clay;
And ere another day is gone,
Ourselves may be as they.

3 Death rides on every passing breeze,
And lurks in every flower;
Each season has its own disease,
Its peril every hour.

4 Turn, mortal, turn, thy soul apply
To truths divinely given;
The bones which underneath thee lie,
Shall live for hell or heaven.

H. 647 *Death of a Young Child.*

1 Alas! how changed that lovely flower,
Which bloomed and cheered my heart;
Fair, fleeting comfort of an hour,
How soon we're called to part!

2 And shall my bleeding heart arraign
That God, whose ways are love?
Or vainly cherish anxious pain
For *her* who rests above?

3 No! let me rather humbly pay
Obedience to His will,
And with my inmost spirit say,
"The Lord is righteous still."

4 From adverse blasts and lowering storms,
Her favoured soul He bore;
And with yon bright, angelic forms,
She lives, to die no more,

5 Why should I vex my heart, or fast?
No more *she'll* visit me;
My soul will mount to *her* at last,
And there my child I'll see.

6 Prepare me, blessed Lord, to share
The bliss Thy people prove;
Who round Thy glorious throne appear,
And dwell in perfect love.

1. When in the light of faith di - vine We look on things be - low,

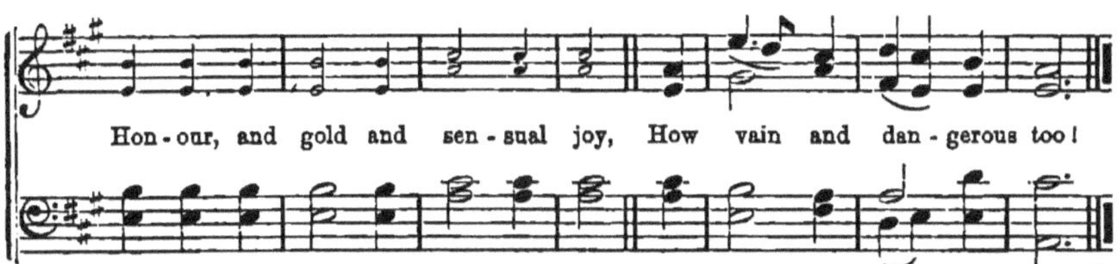
Hon - our, and gold and sen - sual joy, How vain and dan - gerous too!

H. 347 *The World's Three Chief Temptations.*

1 When in the light of faith divine
We look on things below,
Honour, and gold, and sensual joy,
How void and dangerous too!

2 Honour's a puff of noisy breath;
Yet men expose their blood,
And venture everlasting death,
To gain that airy good.

3 Whilst others starve the nobler mind,
And feed on shining dust,
They rob the serpent of his food,
To indulge a sordid lust.

4 The pleasures that allure our sense,
Are dangerous snares to souls;
There's but a drop of flattering sweet,
And dashed with bitter bowls.

5 God is my all-sufficient good,
My portion and my choice;
In Him my vast desires are filled,
And all my powers rejoice.

6 In vain the world accosts my ear,
And tempts my heart anew;
I cannot buy your bliss so dear,
Nor part with heaven for you.

H. 376 *Lord's Prayer.*

1 Our Father, God, who art in heaven,
All hallowed be Thy name!
Thy kingdom come; Thy will be done,
In earth and heaven the same!

2 Give us, this day, our daily bread;
And, as we those forgive
Who sin against us, so may we
Forgiving grace receive.

3 Into temptation lead us not;
From evil set us free,
And Thine the kingdom, Thine the power
And glory, ever be.

H. 471 *Exhortation to Praise.*

1 Come, happy souls, approach your God
With new melodious songs;
Come, render to almighty grace,
The tribute of your tongues.

2 So strange, so boundless was the love
That pitied dying men,
The Father sent His equal Son
To give them life again.

3 Thy hands, dear Jesus, were not armed
With a revenging rod,
No hard commission to perform,
The vengeance of a God.

4 But all was mercy, all was mild,
And wrath forsook the throne,
When Christ on the kind errand came,
And brought salvation down.

5 Here, sinners, you may heal your wounds,
And wipe your sorrows dry;
Trust in the mighty Saviour's name,
And you shall never die.

Anon.

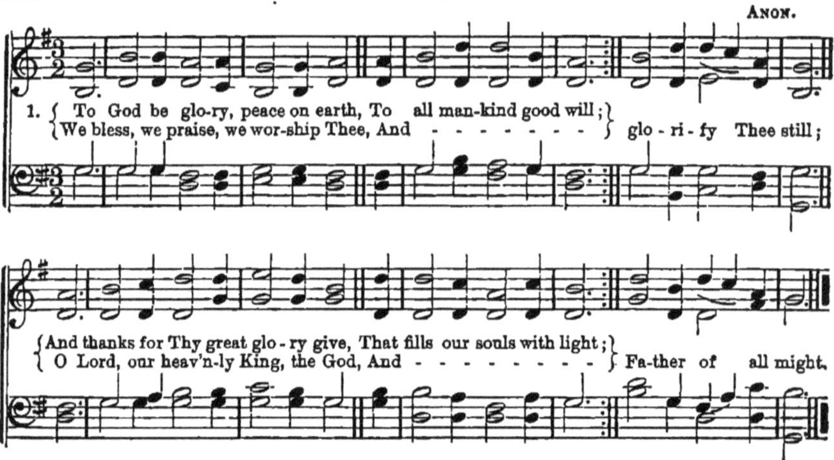
1. { To God be glo-ry, peace on earth, To all man-kind good will; }
{ We bless, we praise, we wor-ship Thee, And - - - - - - - - } glo - ri - fy Thee still;
{ And thanks for Thy great glo - ry give, That fills our souls with light; }
{ O Lord, our heav'n-ly King, the God, And - - - - - - - - - } Fa-ther of all might.

H. 126 *Praise to the Trinity.*

1 To God be glory, peace on earth,
To all mankind good will;
We bless, we praise, we worship Thee,
And glorify Thee still;
And thanks for Thy great glory give,
That fills our souls with light;
O Lord, our heavenly King, the God,
And Father of all might!

2 And Thou, begotten Son of God,
Before all time begun,
O Jesus Christ, Thou Lamb of God,
The Father's only Son;
Thou who the sins of all the world
Dost fully take away,
Have mercy, Saviour of mankind,
And hear us when we pray!

3 O Thou who art at God's right hand,
Upon the Father's throne,
Have mercy on us, Thou O Christ,
Who art the Holy One!
Thou, only, with the Holy Ghost,
Whom earth and heaven adore,
In glory of the Father art,
Most high for evermore!

H 201 *The Penitent.*

1 Prostrate, dear Jesus, at Thy feet,
A guilty rebel lies;
And upwards to Thy mercy seat,
Presumes to lift his eyes.

2 If tears of sorrow would suffice
To pay the debt I owe,
Tears should from both my weeping eyes
In ceaseless torrents flow.

3 But no such sacrifice I plead
To expiate my guilt;
No tears but those which Thou hast shed,
No blood, but Thou hast spilt.

4 Think of Thy sorrows, dearest Lord,
And all my sins forgive:
Justice will well approve the word
That bids the sinner live.

H. 448 *Children's Evening Hymn.*

1 Now condescend, almighty King,
To bless this little throng;
And kindly listen while we sing
Our pleasant evening song.
Brothers and sisters, hand-in-hand,
Our lips together move:
Oh! smile upon this little band;
Unite our hearts in love.

2 May we in safety sleep to-night,
From every danger free;
For, Lord, the darkness and the light
Are both alike to Thee.
And when the rising sun displays
His cheering beams abroad,
Then may our grateful morning lays
Declare the love of God.

I. B. Woodbury; from Hunten, 1842.

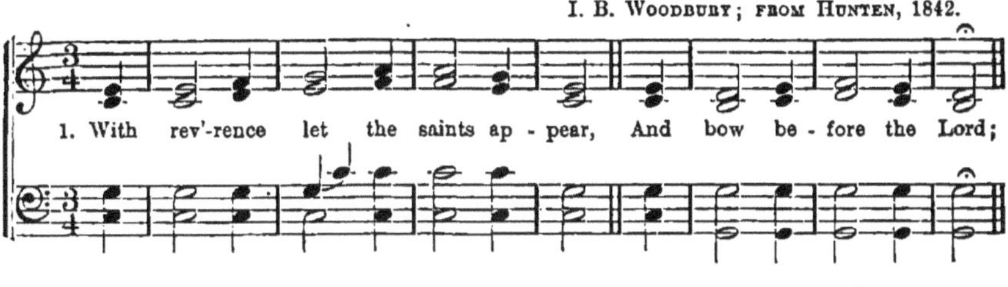
1. With rev'-rence let the saints ap - pear, And bow be - fore the Lord;

His high com - mands de - vout - ly hear, And trem - ble at His word.

Ps. 89 *First Part.*

2 How terrible Thy glories rise!
How bright Thine armies shine!
Where is the power with Thee that vies,
Or truth compared with Thine!

3 The northern pole and southern, rest
On Thy supporting hand;
Darkness and day, from east to west,
Move round at Thy command.

4 Thy words the raging winds control,
And rule the boisterous deep;
Thou mak'st the sleeping billows roll,
The rolling billows sleep.

5 Justice and judgment are Thy throne,
Yet wondrous is Thy grace;
While truth and mercy, joined in one,
Invite us near Thy face.

H. 368 *Prayer for the Divine Presence.*

1 Permit me, Lord, to seek Thy face,
Obedient to Thy call;
To seek the presence of Thy grace.
My Strength, my Life, my All.

2 All I can wish is Thine to give;
My God, I ask Thy love,
That greatest bliss I can receive,
That bliss of heaven above.

3 To heaven my restless heart aspires;
O for a quickening ray,
To wake and warm my faint desires,
And cheer the tiresome way.

4 The path to Thy divine abode,
Through a wild desert lies;
A thousand snares beset the road,
A thousand terrors rise.

5 Satan and sin unite their art,
To keep me from my Lord;
Dear Saviour, guard my trembling heart,
And guide me by Thy word.

6 My Guardian, my almighty Friend,
On Thee my soul would rest;
On Thee alone my hopes depend,
Be near, and I am blest.

H. 392 *Access to God.*

1 We find access at every hour
To God within the veil;
Hence we derive a quickening power,
And joys that never fail.

2 O happy souls, O glorious state
Of overflowing grace;
To dwell so near our Father's seat,
And see His lovely face.

3 Lord, I address Thy heavenly throne,
Call me a child of Thine;
Send down the Spirit of Thy Son,
To form my heart divine.

4 There shed Thy choicest love abroad,
And make my comforts strong;
Then shall I say, "My Father, God,"
With an unwavering tongue.

ENGLISH.

1. My God, the spring of all my joys, The life of my de-lights, The glo-ry of my

bright-est days—The glo - ry of my bright-est days, And com - fort of my nights.

H. 281 *Confident Hope.*

1 My God, the spring of all my joys,
The life of my delights,
The glory of my brightest days,
And comfort of my nights!

2 In darkest shades if He appear,
My dawning is begun;
He is my soul's bright morning star,
And He my rising sun.

3 The opening heavens around me shine
With beams of sacred bliss,
While Jesus shows His heart is mine,
And whispers, I am His.

4 My soul would leave this heavy clay,
At that transporting word,
Run up with joy the shining way,
To embrace my dearest Lord.

5 Fearless of hell and ghastly death,
I'd break through every foe;
The wings of love and arms of faith,
Should bear me conqueror through.

H. 377 *Seeking God.*

1 Author of good! to Thee we turn;
Thine ever-wakeful eye
Alone can all our wants discern,
Thy hand alone supply.

2 Oh! let Thy love within us dwell,
Thy fear our footsteps guide;
That love shall vainer loves expel,
That fear, all fears beside.

3 Not what we wish, but what we want,
Let mercy still supply;
The good we ask not, Father! grant;
The ill we ask, deny.

H. 509 *The New Year.*

1 God of our life, Thy various praise
Let mortal voices sound;
Thy hand revolves our fleeting days,
And brings the seasons round.

2 To Thee shall annual incense rise,
Our Father and our Friend;
While annual mercies from the skies
In genial showers descend.

3 In every scene of life, Thy care,
In every age we see;
And constant as Thy favours are,
So let our praises be.

4 Still may Thy love in every scene,
To every age appear;
And let the same compassion deign
To bless the opening year.

5 O! keep this foolish heart of mine
From anxious passions free,
Teach me each comfort to resign,
And trust my all to Thee.

6 If mercy smile, let mercy bring
My wandering soul to God;
And in affliction I shall sing,
If Thou wilt bless the rod.

H. 516 *Love to our Neighbour.*

1 Father of mercies, send Thy grace,
All-powerful from above,
To form, in our obedient souls,
The image of Thy love.

2 Oh! may our sympathizing breasts
That generous pleasure know,
Kindly to share in others' joy,
And weep for others' woe.

3 So Jesus looked on dying men,
When throned above the skies;
And mid th' embraces of Thy love,
He felt compassion rise.

4 On wings of love the Saviour flew,
To raise us from the ground;
And gave His own most precious blood,
A balm for every wound.

H. 562 *Glory and Safety of the Church.*

1 Daughter of Zion, from the dust
Exalt thy fallen head;
Again in thy Redeemer trust,
He calls thee from the dead.

2 Awake, awake, put on thy strength,
Thy beautiful array;
The day of freedom dawns at length,
The Lord's appointed day.

3 They come, they come; thine exiled
Where'er they rest or roam, [bands,
Have heard thy voice in distant lands,
And hasten to their home.

4 Thus, though the universe shall burn,
And God His works destroy,
With songs thy ransomed shall return,
And everlasting joy.

H. 594 *Prayer for the Spread of the Gospel.*

1 Great God, the nations of the earth
Are by creation Thine;
And in Thy works, by all beheld,
Thy radiant glories shine.

2 But, Lord, Thy greater love has sent
Thy gospel to mankind;
Unveiling what rich stores of grace
Are treasured in Thy mind.

3 Lord, when shall these glad tidings
The spacious earth around, [spread
Till every tribe, and every soul,
Shall hear the joyful sound?

4 Smile, Lord, on each sincere attempt
To spread the gospel's rays,
And build on sin's demolished throne
The temple of Thy praise.

H. 686 *The Christian Longing for Heaven.*

1 Father, I long, I faint to see
The place of Thine abode;
I'd leave Thine earthly courts, and flee
Up to Thy seat, my God.

2 I'd part with all the joys of sense,
To gaze upon Thy throne;
Pleasure springs fresh for ever thence,
Unspeakable, unknown.

3 There all the heavenly hosts are seen,
In shining ranks they move,
And drink immortal vigour in,
With wonder and with love.

4 The more Thy glories strike my eyes,
The humbler I shall lie;
Thus while I sink, my joys shall rise,
Immeasurably high.

H. 691 *Heaven Attained by Following Christ.*

1 Give me the wings of faith, to rise
Within the veil, and see
The saints above, how great their joys,
How bright their glories be.

2 Once they were mourning here below,
And wet their couch with tears;
They wrestled hard, as we do now,
With sins, and doubts, and fears.

3 I ask them, whence their victory came?
They, with united breath,
Ascribe their conquest to the Lamb,
Their triumph to His death.

4 They marked the footsteps that He trod,
His zeal inspired their breast;
And following their incarnate God,
Possessed the promised rest.

5 Our glorious Leader claims our praise
For His own pattern given;
While the long cloud of witnesses
Show the same path to heaven.

Dr. L. Mason.

1. Hap-py the heart where grac-es reign, Where love in-spires the breast; Love is the bright-est

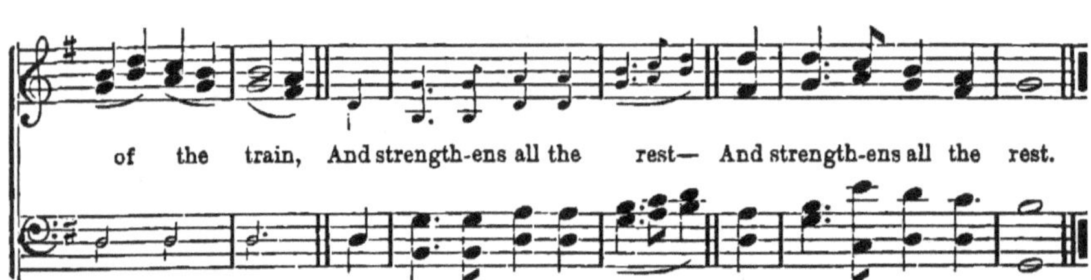
of the train, And strength-ens all the rest— And strength-ens all the rest.

H. 293 *Christian Love.*

2 Knowledge, alas! 'tis all in vain,
And all in vain our fear;
Our stubborn sins will fight and reign,
If love be absent there.

3 'Tis love that makes our cheerful feet
In swift obedience move;
The devils know and tremble too,
But devils cannot love.

4 This is the grace that lives and sings,
When faith and hope shall cease;
'Tis this shall strike our joyful strings,
In the sweet realms of bliss.

5 Before we quite forsake our clay,
Or leave this dark abode,
The wings of love bear us away,
To see our smiling God.

H. 306 *Rejoicing in Christ.*

1 O! for a thousand tongues to sing
My dear Redeemer's praise;
The glories of my God and King,
The triumphs of His grace.

2 My gracious Master, and my God,
Assist me to proclaim,
To spread through all the earth abroad,
The honours of Thy name.

3 Jesus, the name that claims our fears,
That bids our sorrows cease;
'Tis music in the sinner's ears;
'Tis life, and health, and peace.

4 He breaks the power of reigning sin,
He sets the prisoner free;
His blood can make the foulest clean,
His blood availed for me.

5 Let us obey; we then shall know,
Shall feel our sins forgiven;
Anticipate our heaven below,
And own that love is heaven.

H. 558 *"Fair as the Sun."*

1 Say, who is she that looks abroad,
Like the sweet blushing dawn,
When with her living light she paints
The dew-drops of the lawn?

2 Fair as the moon when in the skies,
Serene her throne she guides,
And o'er the twinkling stars supreme,
In full-orbed glory rides.

3 Clear as the sun, when from the East
Without a cloud he springs,
And scatters boundless light and heat
From his resplendent wings.

4 Tremendous as a host that moves,
Majestically slow,
With banners wide displayed, all armed,
All ardent for the foe.

5 This is the Church by heaven arrayed,
With strength and grace divine;
Thus shall she strike her foes with dread,
And thus her glories shine.

ANON.

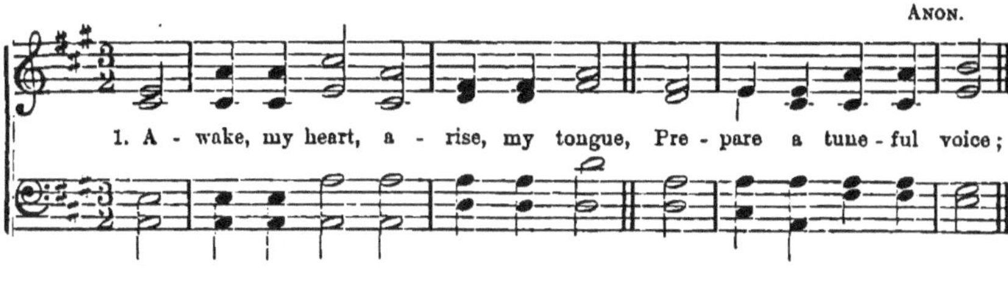
1. A - wake, my heart, a - rise, my tongue, Pre - pare a tune - ful voice;

In God, the life of all my joys, A - loud will I re - joice.

H. 120 *Gratitude for Redeeming Grace.*

2 'Tis He adorned my naked soul,
And made salvation mine;
Upon a poor polluted worm
He makes His graces shine.

3 And lest the shadow of a spot
Should on my soul be found,
He took the robe the Saviour wrought,
And cast it all around.

4 How far the heavenly robe excels
What earthly princes wear!
These ornaments, how bright they shine!
How white the garments are!

5 The Spirit wrought my faith and love,
And hope and every grace;
But Jesus spent His life to work
The robe of righteousness.

6 Strangely, my soul, art thou arrayed
By the great sacred Three;
In sweetest harmony of praise,
Let all Thy powers agree.

H. 272 *Prayer for Faith.*

1 Oh! for a faith that will not shrink,
Though pressed by every foe;
That will not tremble on the brink
Of any earthly woe.

2 That will not murmur nor complain,
Beneath the chastening rod;
But in the hour of grief or pain,
Can lean upon its God.

3 A faith that shines more bright and clear,
When tempests rage without;
That when in danger knows no fear,
In darkness feels no doubt:

4 That bears unmoved the world's dread
Nor heeds its scornful smile; [frown,
That sin's wild ocean cannot drown,
Nor its soft arts beguile.

5 A faith that keeps the narrow way,
By truth restrained and led,
And with a pure and heavenly ray,
Lights up a dying bed.

H. 283 *At Eve it shall be Light.*

1 We journey through a vale of tears,
By many a cloud o'er cast;
And worldly cares and worldly fears
Go with us to the last.

2 Not to the last: God's word hath said,—
Could we but read aright,—
Poor pilgrim, lift in hope thy head,
At eve it shall be light.

3 When tempest clouds are dark on high,
His bow of love and peace
Shines sweetly on the vaulted sky,
A pledge that storms shall cease.

4 Hold on thy way, with hope unchilled,
By faith and not by sight,
And thou shalt own His word fulfilled;
At eve it shall be light.

VARINA. C. M. D.

C. H. Rink, 1770–1846, by Root, 1849.

1. Blest are the souls who hear and know The gos-pel's joy-ful sound;
Peace shall at-tend the path they go, And light their steps sur-round.
2. Their joy shall bear their spi-rits up,
Through their Re-deem-er's name; His right-eous-ness ex-alts their hope, And fills their foes with shame.

Ps. 89 *Second Part.*

1 Blest are the souls who hear and know
The gospel's joyful sound;
Peace shall attend the path they go,
And light their steps surround.

2 Their joy shall bear their spirits up,
Through their Redeemer's name;
His righteousness exalts their hope,
And fills their foes with shame.

3 The Lord, our glory and defence,
Strength and salvation gives;
Israel, thy King for ever reigns,
Thy God for ever lives.

Ps. 12

1 Lord, when iniquities abound,
And blasphemies grow bold,
When faith is rarely to be found,
And love is waxing cold:

2 Is not Thy chariot hastening on?
Hast Thou not given the sign?
May we not trust and live upon
A promise so divine?

3 "Yes," saith the Lord, "now will I rise,
And make the oppressors flee;
I shall appear to their surprise,
And set my servants free."

4 Thy word, like silver seven times tried,
Through ages shall endure;
The men that in Thy truth confide
Shall find Thy promise sure.

H. 360 *Christian and Ministerial Fellowship.*

1 Joined in one Spirit to one Head,
Where He appoints we go;
And still in Jesus' footsteps tread,
And show His praise below.

2 Oh! may we ever walk in Him,
And nothing know beside;
Nothing desire, nothing esteem,
But Jesus crucified.

3 Closer and closer let us cleave
To His beloved embrace;
Expect His fulness to receive,
And grace to add to grace.

4 Partakers of the Saviour's grace,
The same in mind and heart,
Nor joy, nor grief, nor time, nor place,
Nor life, nor death can part.

H. 638 *Death and Glory.*

1 O could we die with those that die,
And place us in their stead;
Then would our spirits learn to fly,
And converse with the dead.

2 Then should we see the saints above,
In their own glorious forms;
And wonder why our souls should love
To dwell with mortal worms.

3 We should almost forsake our clay
Before the summons come,
And pray and wish our souls away
To their eternal home.

DR. T. HASTINGS, 1839.

1. God's law is per - fect, and con - verts The soul in sin that lies; God's tes - ti-
mo - ny is most sure, And makes the sim-ple wise—And makes the sim - ple wise.

Ps. 19 *Third Part.*

1 God's law is perfect, and converts
The soul in sin that lies;
God's testimony is most sure.
And makes the simple wise.

2 The statutes of the Lord are right,
And do rejoice the heart;
The Lord's command is pure, and doth
Light to the eyes impart.

3 Unspotted is the fear of God,
And doth endure for ever;
The judgments of the Lord are true,
And righteous altogether.

4 They more than gold, yea, much fine
To be desired are; [gold,
Than honey, honey from the comb,
That droppeth sweeter far.

5 Moreover, they Thy servant warn
How he his life should frame;
A great reward provided is
For them that keep the same.

6 The words which from my mouth proceed,
The thoughts sent from my heart,
Accept, O Lord, for Thou my strength
And my Redeemer art.

Ps. 63 *First Part.*

1 Early, my God, without delay,
I haste to seek Thy face;
My thirsty spirit faints away,
Without Thy cheering grace.

2 I've seen Thy glory and Thy power
Through all Thy temple shine;
My God, repeat that heavenly hour,
That vision so divine.

3 Not all the blessings of a feast
Can please my soul so well,
As when Thy richer grace I taste,
And in Thy presence dwell.

4 Not life itself, with all its joys,
Can my best passions move,
Or raise so high my cheerful voice,
As Thy forgiving love.

5 Thus till my last expiring day,
I'll bless my God and King;
Thus will I lift my hands to pray,
And tune my lips to sing.

H. 514 *Bible and Tract Distribution.*

1 Go to the heart with sin oppressed,
And dry the sorrowing tear;
Extract the thorn that wounds the breast,
The drooping spirit cheer.

2 Go, spread the page of truth divine
Before the sinner's eyes;
Go, tender him the word of life,
Descending from the skies.

3 Portray the joys that thrill through
When sinners turn to God; [heaven,
And humbly seek eternal life,
Through Christ's atoning blood.

JORDAN. C. M. D.

Wm. Billings, 1781.

1. {On Jor-dan's storm-y banks I stand, And cast a wish-ful eye,}
{To Ca-naan's fair and hap-py land, - - - - - - - - - - - - - -} Where
my pos-ses-sions lie. O the trans-port-ing, rap-turous scene, That ris-es

to my sight; Sweet fields ar-rayed in liv-ing green, And riv-ers of de-light.

H. 670 *Prospect of Heaven.*

3 There generous fruits, that never fail,
On trees immortal grow; [vales,
There rocks and hills, and brooks and
With milk and honey flow.

4 On all those wide extended plains
Shines one eternal day;
There God the Son for ever reigns,
And scatters night away.

5 No chilling winds nor poisonous breath
Can reach that healthful shore;
Sickness and sorrow, pain and death,
Are felt and feared no more.

H. 250 *Death is Gain.*

1 And let this feeble body fail,
And let it faint and die;
My soul shall quit this mournful vale,
And soar away on high;
Shall join the disembodied saints,
And find its long-sought rest,
The only bliss for which it pants,
On the Redeemer's breast.

2 Oh! what has Jesus done for me!
Before my ravished eyes
Rivers of love divine I see,
And trees of paradise;
I see a world of spirits bright,
Who taste the pleasures there;
They all are robed in spotless white,
And conquering palms they bear.

3 Oh! what are all my sufferings here,
If, Lord, Thou count me meet
With that enraptured host to appear,
And worship at Thy feet?
Give joy or grief, give ease or pain;
Take life or friends away;
But let me meet those friends again,
In that eternal day.

K. R., 1866.

1. I heard the voice of Je-sus say, Come un-to me and rest; Lay down, thou wea-ry
one, lay down Thy head up-on my breast. I came to Je-sus as I was, Weary, and worn, and sad, I found in Him a rest-ing-place, And He has made me glad.

H. 273 *The Voice of Jesus.*

2 I heard the voice of Jesus say,
Behold, I freely give
The living water; thirsty one,
Stoop down, and drink, and live.
I came to Jesus, and I drank
Of that life-giving stream;
My thirst was quenched, my soul revived,
And now I live in Him.

3 I heard the voice of Jesus say,
I am this dark world's light;
Look unto Me, thy morn shall rise,
And all thy day be bright.
I looked to Jesus, and I found
In Him my Star, my Sun;
And in that light of life I'll walk,
Till travelling days are done.

4 I heard the voice of Jesus say,
My Father's house above
Has many mansions; I've a place
Prepared for you in love.
I trust in Jesus: in that house,
According to His word,
Redeemed by grace, my soul shall live
For ever with the Lord.

H. 685 *Death Welcome in Prospect of Heaven.*

1 There is a land of pure delight,
Where saints immortal reign;
Infinite day excludes the night,
And pleasures banish pain.
2 There everlasting spring abides,
And never-withering flowers;
Death, like a narrow sea, divides
This heavenly land from ours.

3 Sweet fields, beyond the swelling flood,
Stand dressed in living green;
So to the Jews old Canaan stood,
While Jordan rolled between.
4 But timorous mortals start and shrink,
To cross this narrow sea;
And linger, shivering on the brink,
And fear to launch away.

5 O! could we make our doubts remove,
Those gloomy doubts that rise,
And see the Canaan that we love
With unbeclouded eyes;
6 Could we but climb where Moses stood,
And view the landscape o'er, [flood,
Not Jordan's stream, nor death's cold
Shall fright us from the shore.

ATHENS. C. M. D.

FELIX GIARDINI, 1760.

1. My Sa-viour, my al-might-y Friend, When I be-gin Thy praise, Where will the grow-ing num-bers end,
D. S. And since I knew Thy grac-es first,
The num-bers of Thy grace? 2. Thou art my ev-er - last-ing trust; Thy good-ness I a-dore;
I speak Thy glo-ries more.
Fine.
D. S.

Ps. 71 *Second Part.*

3 My feet shall travel all the length
Of the celestial road,
And march, with courage, in Thy strength,
To see my Father, God.

4 When I am filled with sore distress,
For some surprising sin,
I'll plead Thy perfect righteousness,
And mention none but Thine.

5 How will my lips rejoice to tell
The victories of my King;
My soul, redeemed from sin and hell,
Shall Thy salvation sing.

6 Awake, awake, my tuneful powers;
With this delightful song
I'll entertain the darkest hours,
Nor think the season long.

Ps. 116 *First Part.*

1 I LOVE the Lord; He heard my cries,
And pitied every groan;
Long as I live, when troubles rise,
I'll hasten to His throne.

2 I love the Lord; He bowed His ear,
And chased my griefs away;
O! let my heart no more despair,
While I have breath to pray.

3 My flesh declined, my spirits fell,
And I drew near the dead,
While inward pangs and fears of hell,
Perplexed my wakeful head.

4 "My God," I cried, "Thy servant save,
Thou ever good and just;
Thy power can rescue from the grave,
Thy power is all my trust."

5 The Lord beheld me sore distressed,
He bade my pains remove;
Return, my soul, to God, thy rest,
For thou hast known His love.

6 My God hath saved my soul from death,
And dried my falling tears;
Now to His praise I'll spend my breath,
And my remaining years.

H. 690 *Rejoicing in Prospect of Heaven.*

1 SING, ye redeemed of the Lord,
Your great Deliverer sing:
Pilgrims for Zion's city bound,
Be joyful in your King.

2 A Hand divine shall lead you on,
Through all the blissful road:
Till to the sacred mount you rise,
And see your smiling God.

3 The garlands of immortal joy,
Shall bloom on every head:
While sorrow, sighing, and distress,
Like shadows, all are fled.

4 March on in your Redeemer's strength,
Pursue His footsteps still;
And let the prospect cheer your eye,
While labouring up the hill.

Dr. Mason.

1. {With joy we med-i-tate the grace Of our High Priest a-bove;}
{His heart is made of ten-der-ness, - - - - - - - - - - } And all His soul is love.
2. Touched with a sym-pa-thy with-in, He knows our fee-ble frame; He
knows what sore temp-ta-tions mean, For He has felt the same—For He has felt the same.

H. 98 *Christ's Sympathy and Intercession.*

3 But spotless, innocent and pure,
The great Redeemer stood;
While Satan's fiery darts he bore,
And did resist to blood.

4 He in the days of feeble flesh,
Poured out His cries and tears;
And in His measure feels afresh
What every member bears.

5 He'll never quench the smoking flax,
But raise it to a flame;
The bruised reed He never breaks,
Nor scorns the meanest name.

6 Then let our humble faith address
His mercy and His power;
We shall obtain delivering grace,
In the distressing hour.

H. 102 *Christ's Intercession.*

1 Awake, sweet gratitude, and sing
The ascended Saviour's love;
Sing how He lives to carry on
His people's cause above.

2 With cries and tears He offered up
His humble suit below;
But with authority He asks,
Enthroned in glory now.

3 For all that come to God by Him,
Salvation He demands,
Points to their names upon His breast,
And spreads His wounded hands.

4 His sweet atoning sacrifice
Gives sanction to His claim:
"Father, I will that all My saints
Be with Me where I am.

5 "By their salvation recompense
The sorrows I endured;
Just to the merits of Thy Son,
And faithful to Thy word."

6 Eternal life, at His request,
To every saint is given:
Safety on earth, and, after death,
The plenitude of heaven.

Dr. Thos. Hastings.

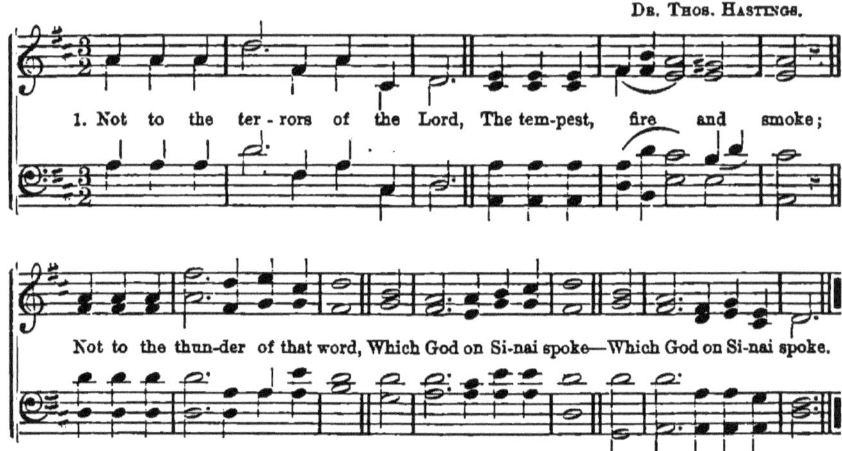
1. Not to the ter-rors of the Lord, The tem-pest, fire and smoke;
Not to the thun-der of that word, Which God on Si-nai spoke—Which God on Si-nai spoke.

H. 151 *The Gospel a Source of Blessedness.*

2 But we are come to Zion's hill,
The city of our God,
Where milder words declare His will,
And spread His love abroad.

3 Behold the innumerable host
Of angels clothed in light;
Behold the spirits of the just,
Whose faith is turned to sight.

4 Behold the blest assembly there,
Whose names are writ in heaven;
And God, the Judge of all, declares
Their vilest sins forgiven.

5 The saints on earth, and all the dead,
But one communion make;
All join in Christ their living Head,
And of His grace partake.

6 In such society as this
My weary soul would rest;
The man that dwells where Jesus is,
Must be for ever blest.

Ps. 18

1 The Lord descended from above,
And bowed the heavens most high;
And underneath His feet He cast
The darkness of the sky.

2 On cherub and on cherubim,
Full royally He rode;
And on the wings of mighty winds
Came flying all abroad.

3 He sat serene upon the floods,
Their fury to restrain;
And He, as Sovereign, Lord, and King,
For evermore shall reign.

4 The Lord will give His people strength
Whereby they shall increase;
And He will bless His chosen flock
With everlasting peace.

5 Give glory to His awful name,
And honour Him alone;
Give worship to His majesty
Upon His holy throne.

Ps. 49

1 Why doth the man of riches grow
To insolence and pride,
To see his wealth and honours flow
With every rising tide?

2 Why doth he treat the poor with scorn,
Made of the self-same clay.
And boast as though his flesh were born
Of better dust than they?

3 Not all his treasures can procure
His soul a short reprieve,
Redeem from death one guilty hour,
Or make his brother live.

4 Vain are his thoughts, his hopes are lost;
How soon his memory dies!
His name is buried in the dust,
Where his own body lies.

DR. L. MASON, 1840.

1. Sin, like a ven - om - ous dis - ease, In - fects our vi - tal blood;
The on - ly balm is sov'- reign grace, And the phy - si - cian God.

H. 142 *Total Depravity.*

1 Sin, like a venomous disease,
Infects our vital blood;
The only balm is sovereign grace,
And the physician God.

2 Our beauty and our strength are fled,
And we draw near to death;
But Christ, the Lord, recalls the dead,
With His almighty breath.

3 Madness by nature reigns within,
The passions burn and rage,
Till God's own Son, with skill divine,
The inward fire assuage.

H. 592 *Various Success of the Gospel.*

1 Christ and His cross is all our theme;
The mysteries that we speak
Are scandal in the Jew's esteem,
And folly to the Greek.

2 But souls enlightened from above,
With joy receive the word!
They see what wisdom, power and love,
Shine in their dying Lord.

3 The vital savour of his name
Restores their fainting breath;
But unbelief perverts the same
To guilt, despair, and death.

4 Till God diffuse His graces down,
Like showers of heavenly rain,
In vain Apollos sows the ground,
And Paul may plant in vain.

Ps. 44

1 Lord, we have heard Thy works of old,
Thy works of power and grace,
When to our ears our fathers told
The wonders of their days.

2 They saw the beauteous churches rise,
The spreading gospel run;
While light and glory from the skies
Through all their temples shone.

3 In God they boasted all the day,
And in a cheerful throng
Did thousands meet to praise and pray,
And grace was all their song.

4 But now our souls are seized with shame,
Confusion fills our face,
To hear the enemy blaspheme,
And fools reproach Thy grace.

5 Awake, arise, almighty Lord,
Why sleeps Thy wonted grace?
Why should we seem like men abhorred,
Or banished from Thy face?

6 Redeem us from perpetual shame,
Our Saviour and our God;
We plead the honours of Thy name,
The merits of Thy blood.

Doxology.

To Father, Son, and Holy Ghost,
The God whom we adore,
Be glory as it was, is now,
And shall be evermore.

I. B. Woodbury, 1842.

1. By cool Si - lo - am's sha - dy rill, How sweet the li - ly grows,
How sweet the breath be - neath the hill Of Sha - ron's dew - y rose.

H. 522 *Early Piety.*

1 By cool Siloam's shady rill
How sweet the lily grows;
How sweet the breath beneath the hill
Of Sharon's dewy rose.

2 And such the child whose early feet
The paths of peace have trod;
Whose secret heart, with influence sweet,
Is upward drawn to God.

3 By cool Siloam's shady rill
The lily must decay;
The rose that blooms beneath the hill
Must shortly fade away.

4 And soon, too soon, the wintry hour,
Of man's maturer age,
May shake the soul with sorrow's power,
And stormy passion's rage.

5 O Thou, whose infancy was found
With heavenly ray to shine,
Whose years, with changeless virtue
Were all alike divine; [crowned,

6 Dependent on Thy bounteous breath,
We seek Thy grace alone,
In childhood, manhood, and in death,
To keep us still Thy own.

H. 521 *Youth the Best Time to Serve the Lord.*

1 Amidst the cheerful bloom of youth,
With ardent zeal pursue
The ways of piety and truth,
With death and heaven in view.

2 Fair wisdom's paths with sweets are
And pleasures all refined; [strewed,
There joys divine are shed abroad,
That suit the immortal mind.

3 Youth is the most accepted time
To love and serve the Lord:
A flower presented in its prime,
Will much delight afford.

4 He'll crown with peace your rising years,
And make your fruit increase;
Will guide you through this vale of tears,
And bid your sorrows cease.

5 Give Him the morning of your days,
And be for ever blest;
'Tis none but those in wisdom's ways
Enjoy substantial rest.

Ps. 86 *First Part.*

1 Hear, Lord, my prayer; unto the voice
Of my request attend;
In troublous times I'll call on Thee;
For Thou wilt answer send.

2 Lord, there is none among the gods
That may with Thee compare;
And like the works which Thou hast done,
Not any work is there.

3 All nations whom Thou mad'st shall
And worship reverently [come
Before Thy face; and they, O Lord,
Thy name shall glorify.

4 Because Thou art exceeding great,
And works by Thee are done
Which are to be admired; and Thou
Art God Thyself alone.

5 Teach me Thy way, and in Thy truth,
O Lord, then walk will I;
Unite my heart, that I Thy name
May fear continually.

6 O Lord, my God, with all my heart
To Thee I will give praise;
And I the glory will ascribe
Unto Thy name always.

Ps. 119 *Sixteenth Part.*

1 My soul lies cleaving to the dust,
Lord, give me life divine;
From vain desires and every lust,
Turn off these eyes of mine.

2 When sore afflictions press me down,
I need Thy quickening powers;
Thy word, that I have rested on,
Shall help my heaviest hours.

3 Are not Thy mercies sovereign still,
And Thou a faithful God?
Wilt Thou not grant me warmer zeal,
To run the heavenly road?

4 Does not my heart Thy precepts love,
And long to see Thy face?
And yet how slow my spirits move,
Without enlivening grace!

5 Then shall I love Thy gospel more,
And ne'er forget Thy word,
When I have felt its quickening power
To draw me near the Lord.

Ps. 123

1 O Thou, whose grace and justice reign
Enthroned above the skies,
To Thee our hearts would tell their pain,
To Thee we lift our eyes.

2 As servants watch their master's hand,
And fear the angry stroke;
Or maids before their mistress stand,
And wait a peaceful look;

3 So, for our sins, we justly feel
Thy discipline, O God;
Yet wait the gracious moment still,
Till Thou remove the rod.

4 Those that in wealth and pleasure live,
Our daily groans deride;
And Thy delays of mercy give
Fresh courage to their pride.

5 Our foes insult us, but our hope
In Thy compassion lies;
This thought shall bear our spirits up,
That God will not despise.

Ps. 139 *Second Part.*

1 In all my vast concerns with Thee,
In vain my soul would try
To shun Thy presence, Lord, or flee
The notice of Thine eye.

2 Thy all-surrounding sight surveys
My rising and my rest,
My public walks, my private ways,
And secrets of my breast.

3 My thoughts lie open to the Lord,
Before they're formed within;
And ere my lips pronounce the word,
He knows the sense I mean.

4 O! wondrous knowledge, deep and high,
Where can a creature hide;
Within Thy circling arms I lie,
Enclosed on every side.

5 So let Thy grace surround me still,
And like a bulwark prove,
To guard my soul from every ill,
Secured by sovereign love.

H. 525 *Death of a Youth.*

1 When blooming youth is snatched away
By death's resistless hand,
Our hearts the mournful tribute pay,
Which pity must demand.

2 While pity prompts the rising sigh,
O may this truth, impressed
With awful power, "I too must die,"
Sink deep in every breast.

3 Let this vain world delude no more;
Behold the gaping tomb;
It bids us seize the present hour;
To-morrow death may come.

4 The voice of this alarming scene,
Let every heart obey;
Nor be the heavenly warning vain,
Which calls to watch and pray.

NORTHFIELD. C. M.

JER. INGALLS.

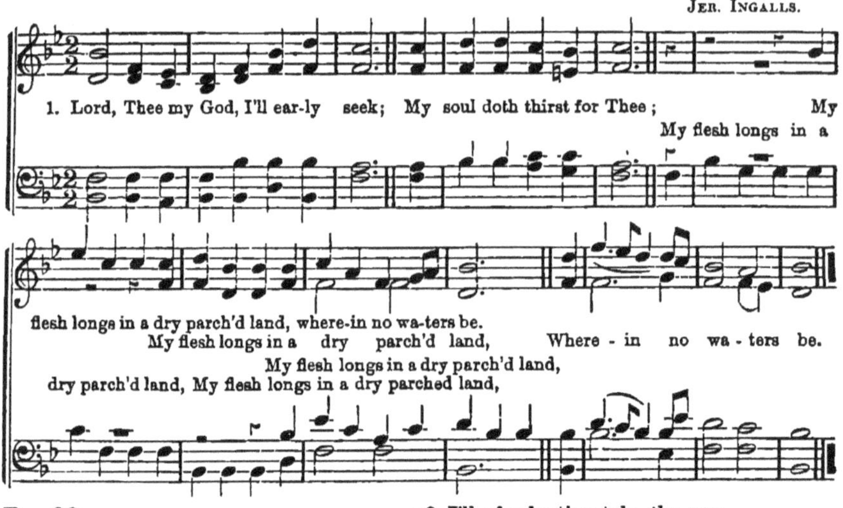
1. Lord, Thee my God, I'll ear-ly seek; My soul doth thirst for Thee; My
My flesh longs in a
flesh longs in a dry parch'd land, where-in no wa-ters be.
My flesh longs in a dry parch'd land, Where - in no wa - ters be.
My flesh longs in a dry parch'd land,
dry parch'd land, My flesh longs in a dry parched land,

Ps. 63 *Second Part.*

1 LORD, Thee my God, I'll early seek;
My soul doth thirst for Thee:
My flesh longs in a dry parched land,
Wherein no waters be:

2 That I Thy power may behold,
And brightness of Thy face,
As I have seen Thee heretofore
Within Thy holy place.

3 Since better is Thy love than life,
My lips Thee praise shall give;
I in Thy name will lift my hands,
And bless Thee while I live.

4 Even as with marrow and with fat
My soul shall filled be;
Then shall my mouth with joyful lips
Sing praises unto Thee:

5 When I do Thee upon my bed
Remember with delight,
And when on Thee I meditate
In watches of the night.

Ps. 116 *Fourth Part.*

1 I IN the land of those that live
Will walk the Lord before.
I did believe, therefore I spake;
I was afflicted sore.

2 I said, when I was in my haste,
That all men liars be.
What shall I render to the Lord
For all His gifts to me?

3 I'll of salvation take the cup,
On God's name will I call;
I'll pay my vows now to the Lord
Before His people all.

4 Dear in God's sight is His saint's death.
Thy servant, Lord, am I;
Thy servant sure, Thine handmaid's son;
My bands Thou didst untie.

5 Thank-offerings I to Thee will give,
And on God's name will call;
I'll pay my vows now to the Lord
Before His people all;

6 Within the courts of God's own house,
Within the midst of thee,
O city of Jerusalem;
Praise to the Lord give ye.

Ps. 131

1 Is there ambition in my heart?
Search, gracious God, and see;
Or do I act a haughty part?
Lord, I appeal to Thee.

2 I charge my thoughts, be humble still,
And all my carriage mild;
Content, my Father, with Thy will,
And peaceful as a child.

3 The patient soul, the lowly mind,
Shall have a large reward;
Let saints in sorrow lie resigned,
And trust a faithful Lord.

1. Be mer - ci - ful to me, O God; Thy mer - cy un - to me
2. Yea, in the sha - dow of Thy wings My ref - uge I will place,
Do Thou ex-tend; be - cause my soul Doth put her trust in Thee.
Un - til these sad ca - la - mi - ties Do whol - ly o - ver - pass.

Ps. 57 *First Part.*

1 Be merciful to me, O God;
Thy mercy unto me
Do Thou extend, because my soul
Doth put her trust in Thee.

2 Yea, in the shadow of Thy wings
My refuge I will place,
Until these sad calamities
Do wholly overpass.

3 My cry I will cause to ascend
Unto the Lord most high;
To God, who doth all things for me
Perform most perfectly.

4 From heaven He shall send down, and me
From his reproach defend
That would devour me: God His truth
And mercy forth shall send.

Ps. 65 *Second Part.*

1 'Tis by Thy strength the mountains stand,
God of eternal power;
The sea grows calm at Thy command,
And tempests cease to roar.

2 Thy morning light and evening shade
Successive comforts bring;
Thy plenteous fruits make harvest glad,
Thy flowers adorn the spring.

3 Seasons and times, and moons and hours,
Heaven, earth, and air are Thine;
When clouds distil in fruitful showers,
The Author is divine.

4 The thirsty ridges drink their fill,
And ranks of corn appear;
Thy ways abound with blessings still,
Thy goodness crowns the year.

Ps. 119 *Eleventh Part.*

1 O that the Lord would guide my ways
To keep His statutes still!
O that my God would grant me grace
To know and do His will.

2 O send Thy Spirit down to write
Thy law upon my heart;
Nor let my tongue indulge deceit,
Nor act the liar's part.

3 From vanity turn off my eyes;
Let no corrupt design,
Nor covetous desires arise
Within this soul of mine.

4 Order my footsteps by Thy word,
And make my heart sincere;
Let sin have no dominion, Lord,
But keep my conscience clear.

5 My soul hath gone too far astray,
My feet too often slip;
Yet, since I've not forgot Thy way
Restore Thy wandering sheep.

6 Make me to walk in Thy commands,
'Tis a delightful road;
Nor let my head, nor heart, nor hands
Offend against my God.

1. Come, let our hearts and voi - ces join, To praise the Sa-viour's name;

Whose truth and kind - ness are di - vine, Whose love's a con - stant flame.

H. 122 *Praise for the Love of Christ.*

2 When most we need His gracious hand,
This friend is always near;
With heaven and earth at His command,
He waits to answer prayer.

3 His love no end nor measure knows,
No change can turn its course;
Immutably the same it flows,
From one eternal source.

4 When frowns appear to veil His face,
And clouds surround His throne;
He hides the purpose of His grace,
To make it better known.

5 And when our dearest comforts fall,
Before His sovereign will,
He never takes away our all;
Himself He gives us still.

H. 131 *The Spirit Illuminating.*

1 The Spirit breathes upon the word,
And brings the truth to sight;
Precepts and promises afford
A sanctifying light.

2 A glory gilds the sacred page,
Majestic, like the sun;
It gives a light to every age,
It gives, but borrows none.

3 The hand that gave it still supplies
The gracious light and heat;
His truths upon the nations rise;
They rise, but never set.

4 Let everlasting thanks be Thine,
For such a bright display,
As makes a world of darkness shine
With beams of heavenly day.

5 My soul rejoices to pursue
The steps of Him I love,
Till glory breaks upon my view,
In brighter worlds above.

H. 573 *The Pastoral Office.*

1 Let Zion's watchmen all awake,
And take the alarm they give;
Now let them from the mouth of God
Their solemn charge receive.

2 'Tis not a cause of small import,
The pastor's care demands;
But what might fill an angel's heart,
And filled a Saviour's hands.

3 They watch for souls, for which the Lord
Did heavenly bliss forego;
For souls, which must for ever live
In raptures, or in woe.

4 All to the great tribunal haste,
The account to render there;
And shouldst Thou strictly mark our faults,
Lord, how should we appear?

5 May they that Jesus, whom they preach,
Their own Redeemer see;
And watch Thou daily o'er their souls,
That they may watch for Thee.

H. 481 *Before or after Sermon.*

1 Almighty God, Thy word is cast,
Like seed into the ground;
Now let the dew of heaven descend,
And righteous fruits abound.

2 Let not the foe of Christ and man
This holy seed remove;
But give it root in every heart,
To bring forth fruits of love.

3 Let not the world's deceitful cares
The rising plant destroy;
But let it yield a hundred-fold,
The fruits of peace and joy.

4 Oft as the precious seed is sown,
Thy quickening grace bestow,
That all, whose souls the truth receive,
Its saving power may know.

H. 517 *The Liberal Soul.*

1 Blest is the man whose softening heart
Feels all another's pain;
To whom the supplicating eye
Is never raised in vain.

2 He spreads his kind, supporting arms
To every child of grief;
His secret bounty largely flows,
And brings unasked relief.

3 To gentle offices of love
His feet are never slow:
He views, through mercy's melting eye,
A brother in a foe.

4 His breast expands with gen'rous warmth,
A stranger's woes to feel;
And bleeds in pity o'er the wound
He wants the power to heal.

H. 528 *Prayer for Seamen.*

1 We come, O Lord, before Thy throne,
And with united plea,
We meet and pray for those who roam
Far off upon the sea.

2 Oh! may the Holy Spirit bow
The sailor's heart to Thee,
Till tears of deep repentance flow
Like rain-drops on the sea.

3 Then may a Saviour's dying love
Pour peace into his breast,
And waft him to the port above,
Of everlasting rest.

H. 569 *Dedication Hymn.*

1 Thou whose unmeasured temple stands,
Built over earth and sea,
Accept the walls that human hands
Have raised, O God, to Thee.

2 And let the Comforter and Friend
Thy Holy Spirit, meet
With those who here in worship bend
Before Thy mercy seat.

3 May those who err be guided here
To find the better way,
And they who mourn and they who fear
Be strengthened as they pray.

H. 615 *Uncertainty of Life and its Comforts.*

1 'Tis God that lifts our comforts high,
Or sinks them in the grave;
He gives, and blessed be His name,
He takes but what He gave.

2 Peace, all our angry passions then,
Let each rebellious sigh
Be silent at His sovereign will,
And every murmur die.

3 If smiling mercy crown our lives,
Its praises shall be spread;
And we'll adore the justice too,
That strikes our comforts dead.

Ps. 8 *First Part.*

1 How excellent in all the earth,
Lord, our Lord, is Thy name!
Who hast Thy glory far advanced
Above the starry frame.

2 From infants' and from sucklings' mouth
Thou didest strength ordain,
For Thy foes' cause, that so Thou might'st
Th' avenging foe restrain.

3 When I look up unto the heav'ns,
Which Thine own fingers framed,
Unto the moon, and to the stars,
Which were by Thee ordained:

4 Then say I, What is man, that he
Remembered is by Thee?
Or what the son of man that Thou
So kind to him shouldst be?

5 For Thou a little lower hast
Him than the angels made;
With glory and with dignity
Thou crowned hast his head.

To Fa-ther, Son, and Ho - ly Ghost, The God whom we a - dore,
Be glo - ry as it was, is now, And shall be ev - er more.

Ps. 78 *First Part.*

1 The praises of the Lord our God,
And His almighty strength,
The wondrous works that He hath done,
We will show forth at length.

2 His testimony and His law
In Israel He did place,
And charged our fathers it to show
To their succeeding race;

3 That so the race which was to come
Might well them learn and know;
And sons unborn, who should arise,
Might to their sons them show:

4 That they might set their hope in God,
And suffer not to fall
His mighty works out of their mind,
But keep His precepts all.

Ps. 78 *Second Part.*

1 Let children hear the mighty deeds
Which God performed of old;
Which in our younger years we saw,
And which our fathers told.

2 He bids us make His glories known,
His works of power and grace;
And we'll convey His wonders down
Through every rising race.

3 Our lips shall tell them to our sons,
And they again to theirs,
That generations yet unborn
May teach them to their heirs.

4 Thus shall they learn, in God alone
Their hope securely stands,
That they may ne'er forget His works,
But practice His commands.

H. 260 *Living Faith.*

1 Mistaken souls, that dream of heaven,
And make their empty boast
Of inward joys, and sins forgiven,
While they are slaves to lust.

2 Vain are our fancies, airy flights,
If faith be cold and dead;
None but a living power unites
To Christ the living Head.

3 'Tis faith that changes all the heart;
'Tis faith that works by love,
That bids all sinful joys depart,
And lifts the thoughts above.

4 'Tis faith that conquers earth and hell,
By a celestial power;
This is the grace that shall prevail
In the decisive hour.

5 Faith must obey the Father's will,
As well as trust His grace;
A pardoning God is jealous still
For His own holiness.

6 When from the curse He sets us free,
He makes our nature clean;
Nor would He send His Son to be
The minister of sin.

1. After Thy loving kindness, Lord, Have mercy upon me;
For Thy compassions great, blot out All mine iniquity.

Ps. 51 *Third Part.*

2 Me cleanse from sin, and throughly wash
From mine iniquity;
For my transgressions I confess,
My sin I ever see.

3 'Gainst Thee, Thee only, have I sinned,
In Thy sight done this ill; [just,
That when Thou speak'st Thou may'st be
And clear in judging still.

4 Behold, I in iniquity
Was formed the womb within;
My mother also me conceived
In guiltiness and sin.

5 Behold, Thou in the inward parts
With truth delighted art;
And wisdom Thou shalt make me know
Within the hidden part.

6 Do Thou with hyssop sprinkle me,
I shall be cleansed so;
Yea, wash Thou me, and then I shall
Be whiter than the snow.

Ps. 76

1 In Judah God of old was known;
His name in Israel great;
In Salem stood His holy throne,
And Zion was His seat.

2 At Thy rebuke, O Jacob's God,
Both horse and chariot fell:
Who knows the terrors of Thy rod?
Thy vengeance who can tell?

3 What power can stand before Thy sight,
When once Thy wrath appears?
When heaven shines round with dreadful
The earth adores and fears. [light,

4 When God, in His own sovereign ways,
Comes down to save the oppressed,
The wrath of man shall work His praise,
And He'll restrain the rest.

H. 149 *Richness of the Scriptures.*

1 Father of mercies, in Thy word,
What endless glory shines!
For ever be Thy name adored,
For these celestial lines.

2 Here may the wretched sons of want
Exhaustless riches find;
Riches above what earth can grant,
And lasting as the mind.

3 Here the Redeemer's welcome voice
Spreads heavenly peace around;
And life and everlasting joys
Attend the blissful sound.

4 O! may these heavenly pages be
My ever dear delight;
And still new beauties may I see,
And still increasing light.

5 Divine Instructor, gracious Lord,
Be Thou for ever near!
Teach me to love Thy sacred word,
And view my Saviour there.

1. Thy good-ness, Lord, our souls con-fess; Thy good-ness we a-dore;

A spring, whose bless-ings nev-er fail— A sea with-out a shore.

H. 16 *God's Goodness.*

2 Sun, moon, and stars, Thy love declare
In every golden ray;
Love draws the curtain of the night,
And love brings back the day.

3 Thy bounty every season crowns,
With all the bliss it yields;
With joyful clusters loads the vines,
With strengthening grain, the fields.

4 But chiefly Thy compassion, Lord,
Is in the gospel seen;
There, like a sun, Thy mercy shines,
Without a cloud between.

5 There pardon, peace, and holy joy,
Through Jesus' name are given;
He on the cross was lifted high,
That we might reign in heaven.

H. 589 *The Latter Day Glory.*

1 Behold, the mountain of the Lord,
In latter days shall rise
Above the mountains and the hills,
And draw the wondering eyes.

2 To this the joyful nations round,
All tribes and tongues shall flow;
"Up to the hill of God," they say,
"And to His courts we'll go."

3 The beams that shine on Zion's hill
Shall lighten every land;
The King who reigns in Zion's towers
Shall all the world command.

4 No strife shall vex Messiah's reign,
Or mar the peaceful years; [swords,
To ploughshares men shall beat their
To pruning hooks their spears.

5 Come then, O come from every land,
To worship at His shrine;
And walking in the light of God,
With holy beauties shine.

H. 613 *Shortness of Human Life.*

1 How short and hasty is our life!
How vast our souls' affairs!
Yet senseless mortals vainly strive
To lavish out their years.

2 Our days run thoughtlessly along,
Without a moment's stay;
Just like a story or a song,
We pass our lives away.

3 God from on high invites us home,
But we march heedless on,
And ever hastening to the tomb,
Stoop downward as we run.

4 How we deserve the deepest hell,
Who slight the joys above!
What chains of vengeance should we feel,
Who break such cords of love!

5 Draw us, O God, with sovereign grace,
And lift our thoughts on high,
That we may end this mortal race,
And see salvation nigh.

H. 681 *Faith Contemplating Heaven.*

1 There is a house not made with hands,
Eternal and on high;
And here my spirit, waiting, stands,
Till God shall bid it fly.

2 Shortly this prison of my clay
Must be dissolved and fall;
Then, O my soul, with joy obey
Thy heavenly Father's call.

3 'Tis He, by His almighty grace,
That forms thee fit for heaven;
And, as an earnest of the place,
Has His own Spirit given.

4 We walk by faith of joys to come;
Faith lives upon His word;
But while the body is our home,
We're absent from the Lord.

5 'Tis pleasant to believe Thy grace,
But we had rather see;
We would be absent from the flesh,
And present, Lord, with Thee.

Ps. 1 *First Part.*

1 That man hath perfect blessedness
Who walketh not astray
In counsel of ungodly men,
Nor stands in sinners' way;

2 Nor sitteth in the scorner's chair;
But placeth his delight
Upon God's law, and meditates
On His law day and night.

3 He shall be like a tree that grows
Near planted by a river,
Which in his season yields his fruit,
And his leaf fadeth never;

4 And all he doth shall prosper well.
The wicked are not so;
But like they are unto the chaff,
Which wind drives to and fro.

5 In judgment therefore shall not stand
Such as ungodly are;
Nor in th' assembly of the just
Shall wicked men appear.

6 For why? the way of godly men
Unto the Lord is known;
Whereas the way of wicked men
Shall quite be overthrown.

Ps. 4 *First Part.*

1 Give ear unto me when I call,
God of my righteousness;
Have mercy, hear my prayer; Thou hast
Enlarged me in distress.

2 O who will show us any good?
Is that which many say;
But of Thy countenance the light,
Lord, lift on us alway.

3 Upon my heart, bestowed by Thee,
More gladness I have found,
Than they, ev'n then, when corn and wine
Did most with them abound.

4 I will both lay me down in peace,
And quiet sleep will take;
Because Thou only me to dwell
In safety, Lord, dost make.

Ps. 26 *Second Part.*

1 Judge me, O Lord, for I the paths
Of righteousness have trod;
I shall not fail, who all my trust
Repose on Thee, my God.

2 I'll wash my hands in innocence,
And round Thine altar go;
Pour the glad hymn of triumph thence,
And thence Thy wonders show.

3 My thanks I'll publish there, and tell
How Thy renown excels;
That seat affords me most delight,
In which Thy honour dwells.

Ps. 98 *First Part.*

1 O sing a new song to the Lord,
For wonders He hath done;
His right hand and His holy arm
Him victory hath won.

2 The Lord God His salvation
Hath caused to be known;
His justice in the heathen's sight
He openly hath shown.

3 He mindful of His grace and truth
To Israel's house hath been;
And the salvation of our God
All ends of the earth have seen.

4 Let all the earth unto the Lord
Send forth a joyful noise;
Lift up your voice aloud to Him,
Sing praises, and rejoice.

Dr. Wm. Croft, 1712.

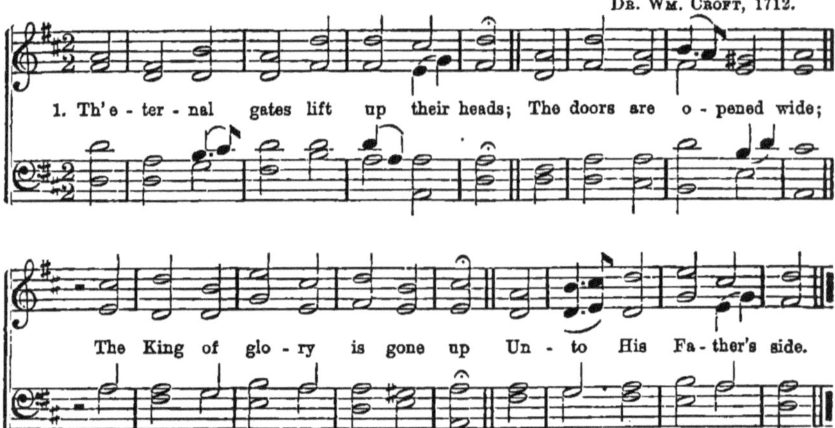
1. Th' e - ter - nal gates lift up their heads; The doors are o - pened wide;
The King of glo - ry is gone up Un - to His Fa - ther's side.

H. 93 *Christ's Ascension for us.*

2 For us Thou hast ascended, Lord,
Thou hast prepared a place,
That we may be where now Thou art,
And look upon Thy face.

3 And ever on Thine earthly path
A gleam of glory lies;
A light still breaks behind the cloud
That veils Thee from our eyes.

4 Lift up our thoughts, lift up our songs,
And let Thy grace be given,
That, while we linger here below,
Our hearts may be in heaven.

5 That, where Thou art at God's right hand,
Our hope, our love may be;
Dwell in us now, that we may dwell
For evermore in Thee.

Ps. 93 *Second Part.*

1 The Lord doth reign, and cloth'd is He
With majesty most bright;
His works do show Him cloth'd to be
And girt about with might;

2 The world is also 'stablished
That it cannot depart,
Thy throne is fixed of old, and Thou
From everlasting art.

3 The floods, O Lord, have lifted up,
They lifted up their voice;
The floods have lifted up their waves,
And made a mighty noise.

4 But yet the Lord, that is on high,
Is more of might by far
Than noise of many waters is,
Or great sea-billows are.

5 Thy testimonies every one
In faithfulness excel;
And holiness for ever, Lord,
Thine house becometh well.

Ps. 95 *Third Part.*

1 O come, let us sing to the Lord;
Come, let us every one
A joyful noise make to the Rock
Of our salvation.

2 Let us before His presence come
With praise and thankful voice;
Let us sing psalms to Him with grace,
And make a joyful noise.

3 For God, a great God, and great King
Above all gods, He is;
Depths of the earth are in His hand,
The strength of hills is His.

4 To Him the spacious sea belongs,
For He the same did make;
The dry land also from His hands
Its form at first did take.

5 O come, and let us worship Him,
Let us bow down withal,
And on our knees before the Lord
Our maker, let us fall.

H. 402 *"Strive to Enter."*

1 Oh! speed thee, Christian, on thy way,
And to thy armour cling;
With girded loins the call obey
That grace and mercy bring.

2 There is a battle to be fought,
An upward race to run,
A crown of glory to be sought,
A victory to be won.

3 Oh! faint not, Christian, for thy sighs
Are heard before His throne;
The race must come before the prize,
The cross before the crown.

H. 405 *Inconstancy Lamented.*

1 Eternal Source of light and grace,
We hail Thy sacred name;
Through every year's revolving round,
Thy goodness is the same.

2 On us, all worthless as we are,
It wondrous mercy pours;
Sure as the heavens' established course,
And plenteous as the showers.

3 Inconstant service we repay,
And treacherous vows renew,
False as the morning's fleeting cloud,
And transient as the dew.

4 In flowing tears our guilt we mourn,
And loud implore Thy grace,
To bear our feeble footsteps on,
In all Thy righteous ways.

5 Armed with this energy divine,
Our souls shall steadfast move;
And with increasing transports press
On to Thy courts above.

6 So by Thy power the morning sun
Pursues his radiant way;
Brightens each moment in his race,
And shines to perfect day.

H. 441 *Morning Hymn.*

1 God of my life, my morning song
To Thee I cheerful raise;
Thy acts of love 'tis good to sing,
And pleasant 'tis to praise.

2 Preserved by Thy almighty arm,
I passed the shades of night,
Serene and safe from every harm,
To see the morning light.

3 While numbers spent the night in sighs,
And restless pains and woes;
In gentle sleep I closed my eyes,
And rose from sweet repose.

4 When sleep, death's image o'er me spread,
And I unconscious lay,
Thy watchful care was round my bed,
To guard my feeble clay.

5 O! let the same almighty care
Through all this day attend;
From every danger, every snare,
My heedless steps defend.

6 Smile on my minutes as they roll,
And guide my future days;
And let Thy goodness fill my soul
With gratitude and praise.

Ps. 96 *First Part.*

1 O sing a new song to the Lord;
Sing all the earth to God;
To God sing, bless His name, show still
His saving health abroad.

2 For great's the Lord, and greatly He
Is to be magnified;
Yea, worthy to be feared is He
Above all gods beside.

3 For all the gods are idols dumb,
Which blinded nations fear;
But our God is the Lord, by whom
The heavens created were.

4 Great honour is before His face,
And majesty divine;
Strength is within His holy place,
And there doth beauty shine.

5 Do ye ascribe unto the Lord,
Of people every tribe,
Glory do ye unto the Lord,
And mighty power ascribe.

6 Give ye the glory to the Lord
That to His name is due;
Come ye into His courts, and bring
An offering with you.

Ps. 119 *Fifteenth Part.*

1 O! that Thy statutes every hour
Might dwell upon my mind!
Thence I derive a quickening power,
And daily peace I find.

2 To meditate Thy precepts, Lord,
Shall be my sweet employ;
My soul shall ne'er forget Thy word,
Thy word is all my joy.

3 How would I run in Thy commands,
If Thou my heart discharge
From sin and Satan's hateful chains,
And set my feet at large?

Dr. Lowell Mason.

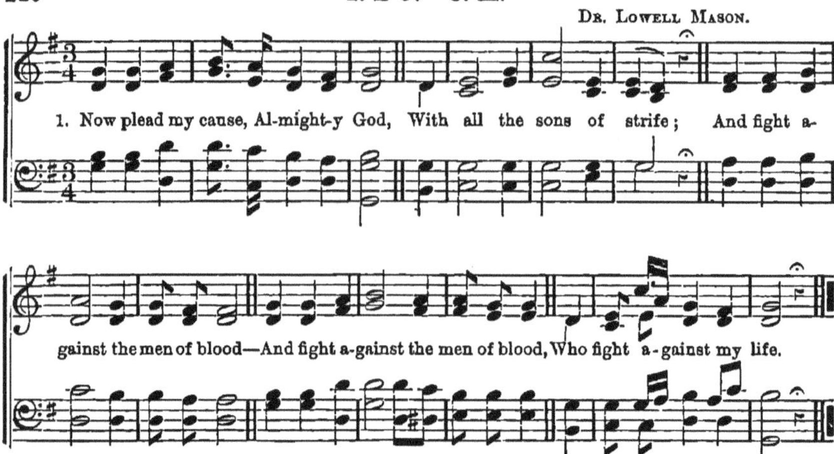
1. Now plead my cause, Al-might-y God, With all the sons of strife; And fight a-
gainst the men of blood—And fight a-gainst the men of blood, Who fight a-gainst my life.

Ps. 35

2 Draw out Thy spear and stop their way,
Lift their avenging rod;
But to my soul in mercy say,
"I am thy Saviour God."

3 They plant their snares to catch my feet,
And nets of mischief spread;
Plunge the destroyers in the pit,
That their own hands have made.

4 Then will I raise my tuneful voice,
To make Thy wonders known;
In their sålvation I'll rejoice,
And bless Thee for my own.

Ps. 36 *First Part.*

1 Thy mercy, Lord, is in the heavens;
Thy truth doth reach the clouds;
Thy justice is like mountains great;
Thy judgments deep as floods.

2 Lord, Thou preservest man and beast;
How precious is Thy grace!
Therefore in shadow of Thy wings,
Men's sons their trust shall place.

3 They with the fatness of Thy house
Shall be well satisfied;
From rivers of Thy pleasures Thou
Wilt drink to them provide.

4 Because of life the fountain pure
Remains alone with Thee;
And in that purest light of Thine
We clearly light shall see.

Ps. 36 *Second Part.*

1 Thy justice, Lord, maintains its throne,
Though mountains melt away;
Thy judgments are a world unknown,
A deep unfathomed sea.

2 Above these heavens' created rounds,
Thy mercies, Lord, extend;
Thy truth outlives the narrow bounds,
Where time and nature end.

3 From Thee, when creature-streams run [low,
And mortal comforts die,
Perpetual springs of life shall flow,
And raise our pleasures high.

4 Though all created light decay,
And death close up our eyes,
Thy presence makes eternal day,
Where clouds can never rise.

H. 341 *Submission in Trials.*

1 When I can trust my all with God,
In trial's fearful hour,
I bow resigned beneath His rod,
And bless His sparing power.

2 Oh! to be brought to Jesus' feet,
Though trials fix me there,
Is still a privilege most sweet;
For He will hear my prayer.

3 Then, blessed be the hand that gave,
Still blessed when it takes;
Blessed be He who smites to save,
Who heals the heart He breaks.

H. 268 *Faith's Struggle.*

1 Lord, I believe; Thy power I own;
Thy truth I would obey;
I wander comfortless and lone,
When from Thy paths I stray.
Lord, I believe; but gloomy fears,
Sometimes bedim my sight;
I look to Thee with prayers and tears,
And cry for strength and light.

2 Lord, I believe; yet Thou dost know,
My faith is cold and weak;
Pity my frailty, and bestow
The confidence I seek:
Yes, I believe; and only Thou,
Canst give my doubts relief;
Lord, to Thy truth my spirit bow,
Help Thou my unbelief.

H. 584 *Revival Prayed for.*

1 Blest Jesus, come Thou gently down,
And fill this hallowed place;
O! make Thy glorious goings known,
Diffuse around Thy grace.

2 Behold, and pity from above,
Our cold and languid frame;
O! shed abroad Thy quick'ning love,
And we'll adore Thy name.

3 All glorious Saviour, Source of grace,
To Thee we raise our cry;
Unveil the beauties of Thy face,
To every waiting eye.

4 Revive, O God, desponding saints,
Who languish, droop and sigh;
Refresh the soul that tires and faints,
Fill mourning hearts with joy.

H. 646 *On the Death of a Child.*

1 Life is a span, a fleeting hour,
How soon the vapour flies!
Man is a tender, transient flower,
That e'en in blooming dies.

2 Death spreads his withering, wintry
And beauty smiles no more; [arms,
Ah! where are now those rising charms,
Which pleased our eyes before!

3 That once loved form, now cold and dead,
Each mournful thought employs;
We weep, our earthly comforts fled,
And withered all our joys.

4 Hope looks beyond the bounds of time,
When what we now deplore
Shall rise in full, immortal prime,
And bloom to fade no more.

5 Cease, then, fond nature, cease thy tears;
The Saviour dwells on high:
There everlasting spring appears,
There joys shall never die.

H. 644 *The House Appointed for all Living.*

1 How still and peaceful is the grave,
Where, life's vain tumults past,
The appointed house, by heaven's decree,
Receives us all at last.

2 The wicked there from troubling cease,
Their passions rage no more;
And there the weary pilgrim rests
From all the toils he bore.

3 There servants, masters, poor and rich,
Partake the same repose;
And there, in peace, the ashes mix
Of those who once were foes.

4 All, levelled by the hand of death,
Lie sleeping in the tomb,
Till God in judgment call them forth,
To meet their final doom.

H. 655 *The Moment After Death.*

1 In vain the fancy strives to paint
The moment after death,—
The glories that surround a saint,
When yielding up his breath.

2 One gentle sigh the fetters breaks;
We scarce can say,—He's gone!
Before the willing spirit takes
Its mansion near the throne.

3 Faith strives, but all its efforts fail,
To trace the spirit's flight;
No eye can pierce within the veil
That hides the world of light.

4 We know—and 'tis enough to know—
Saints are completely blest;
Have done with sin, and care, and woe,
And with their Saviour rest.

5 On harps of gold they praise His name,
And see Him face to face;
Oh! let us catch the sacred flame,
And run the heavenly race.

DANIEL READ, 1785.

1. Al - as! and did my Sa - viour bleed, And did my Sov - reign die?
D. S. The Lamb of Cal - va - ry,
Would He de - vote that Sa - cred head - - - - - [OMIT.] - - - - - - -
- - - - [OMIT.] - - - - - The Lamb that was slain, and liv - eth a - gain,
Fine. CHORUS. D. S.
For such a worm as I. Oh, the Lamb! the bleed - ing Lamb!
To in - ter - cede for me.

H. 205 *Repentance at the Cross.*

2 Thy body slain, dear Jesus, Thine,
And bathed in its own blood,
While all exposed to wrath divine,
The glorious Sufferer stood.
Oh the Lamb! &c.

3 Was it for crimes that I had done
He groaned upon the tree?
Amazing pity! grace unknown!
And love beyond degree!
Oh the Lamb! &c.

4 Well might the sun in darkness hide,
And shut his glories in,
When God, the mighty Maker, died,
For man, the creature's sin.
Oh the Lamb! &c.

5 Thus might I hide my blushing face,
While His dear cross appears;
Dissolve my heart in thankfulness,
And melt my eyes to tears.
Oh the Lamb! &c.

6 But drops of grief can ne'er repay
The debt of love I owe;
Here, Lord, I give myself away;
'Tis all that I can do.
Oh the Lamb! &c.

H. 206 *Repentance at the Cross.*

1 'TWAS for my sins, my dearest Lord
Hung on the cursed tree,
And groaned away a dying life,
For thee, my soul, for thee.—*Chorus.*

2 O! how I hate those lusts of mine
That crucified my God;
Those sins that pierced and nailed His [flesh
Fast to the fatal wood.

3 Yes, my Redeemer, they shall die,
My heart has so decreed;
Nor will I spare the guilty things
That made my Saviour bleed.

4 Whilst with a melting broken heart,
My murdered Lord I view,
I'll raise revenge against my sins,
And slay the murderers too.

Dr. T. Hastings, 1810.

1. Prayer is the soul's sin - cere de - sire, Un - ut - tered or ex - pressed;
The mo - tion of a hid - den fire That trem - bles in the breast.

H. 364 *Nature of Prayer.*

2 Prayer is the burden of a sigh,
The falling of a tear;
The upward glancing of an eye,
When none but God is near.

3 Prayer is the simplest form of speech
That infant lips can try;
Prayer the sublimest strains that reach
The Majesty on high.

4 Prayer is the contrite sinner's voice
Returning from His ways,
While angels in their songs rejoice,
And say, "Behold, he prays."

5 Prayer is the Christian's vital breath,
The Christian's native air,
His watchword at the gate of death;
He enters heaven with prayer.

Ps. 144 *Second Part.*

1 Lord, what is man, poor feeble man,
Born of the earth at first!
His life a shadow, light and vain,
Still hastening to the dust.

2 O what is feeble dying man,
Or all his sinful race,
That God should make it His concern
To visit him with grace!

3 That God who darts His lightnings down,
Who shakes the worlds above!
What terrors wait His awful frown!
How wondrous is His love!

H. 649 *Death and Resurrection.*

1 Thro' sorrow's night and danger's path,
Amid the darkening gloom,
We, soldiers of an injured King,
Are marching to the tomb.

2 There, when the turmoil is no more,
And all our powers decay,
Our cold remains, in solitude,
Shall sleep the years away.

3 Our labours done, securely laid
In this our last retreat,
Unheeded, o'er our silent dust,
The storms of life shall beat.

4 Then love's soft light o'er every eye
Shall shed its mildest rays,
And the long silent dust shall burst:
With shouts of endless praise.

H. 682 *Assurance of Heaven.*

1 Death may dissolve my body now,
And bear my spirit home:
Why do my minutes move so slow,
Nor my salvation come?

2 With heavenly weapons I have fought
The battles of the Lord;
Finished my course, and kept the faith,
And wait the sure reward.

3 God has laid up in heaven for me
A crown which cannot fade;
The righteous Judge, at that great day,
Shall place it on my head.

4 Nor hath the King of grace decreed
This prize for me alone;
But all that love, and long to see
The appearance of His Son.

ZERAH. C. M.

DR. L. MASON, 1837.

1. Lift up your heads, e - ter - nal gates! Un - fold to en - ter - tain The King of glo - ry; see! He comes,
With His ce - les - tial train— The King of glo - ry; see! He comes, With His ce - les - tial train.

Ps. 24

2 Who is this King of glory—who?
  The Lord, for strength renowned;
In battle mighty; o'er his foes
  Eternal Victor crowned.

3 Lift up your heads, ye gates! unfold,
  In state to entertain
The King of glory; see! he comes,
  With all His shining train.

4 Who is the King of glory—who?
  The Lord of hosts renowned:
Of glory He alone is King,
  Who is with glory crowned.

Ps. 33

1 LET all the just to God with joy
  Their cheerful voices raise;
For well the righteous it becomes
  To sing glad songs of praise.

2 For faithful is the word of God;
  His works with truth abound;
He justice loves, and all the earth
  Is with His goodness crowned.

3 Whate'er the mighty Lord decrees
  Shall stand for ever sure;
The settled purpose of His heart
  To ages shall endure.

4 Our soul on God with patience waits;
  Our help and shield is He;
Then, Lord, still let our hearts rejoice,
  Because we trust in Thee.

5 The riches of Thy mercy, Lord,
  Do Thou to us extend;
Since we, for all we want or wish,
  On Thee alone depend.

Ps. 47

1 OH! for a shout of sacred joy,
  To God, the sovereign King!
Let every land their tongues employ,
  And hymns of triumph sing.

2 Jesus, our God, ascends on high;
  His heavenly guards around
Attend Him, rising through the sky,
  With trumpets' joyful sound.

3 While angels shout and praise their King,
  Let mortals learn their strains;
Let all the earth His honours sing;
  O'er all the earth He reigns.

4 Rehearse His praise with awe profound;
  Let knowledge guide the song;
Nor mock Him with a solemn sound
  Upon a thoughtless tongue.

5 In Israel stood His ancient throne,
  He loved that chosen race;
But now He calls the world His own,
  And heathens taste His grace.

6 The Gentile nations are the Lord's,
  There Abraham's God is known;
While powers and princes, shields and swords,
  Submit before His throne.

H. 72 *To us a Child is Born.*

1 To us a Child of hope is born,
To us a Son is given;
Him shall the tribes of earth obey,
Him all the hosts of heaven.

2 His name shall be the Prince of Peace,
For evermore adored,
The Wonderful, the Counsellor,
The great and mighty Lord.

3 His power, increasing, still shall spread,
His reign no end shall know;
Justice shall guard His throne above,
And peace abound below.

4 To us a Child of hope is born,
To us a Son is given,
The Wonderful, the Counsellor,
The mighty Lord of heaven.

H. 300 *Fellowship with the Saints.*

1 Come, let us join our friends above
That have obtained the prize;
And, on the eagle wings of love,
To joy celestial rise.

2 Let saints below His praises sing,
With those to glory gone;
For all the servants of our King,
In heaven and earth, are one.

3 One family, we dwell in Him,
One church, above, beneath;
Though now divided by the stream,
The narrow stream of death.

4 One army of the living God,
To His commands we bow;
Part of the host have crossed the flood,
And part are crossing now.

5 How many to their endless home,
This solemn moment, fly!
And we are to the margin come,
And soon expect to die.

6 Dear Saviour, be our constant guide,
Then, when the word is given,
Bid the cold waves of death divide,
And land us safe in heaven.

H. 301 *Christian Fellowship.*

1 Our souls, by love together knit,
Cemented, fixed in one;
One hope, one heart, one mind, one voice,
'Tis heaven on earth begun.

15

2 Our hearts have often burned within,
And glowed with sacred fire,
While Jesus spoke, and fed, and blessed,
And filled the enlarged desire.

3 The little cloud increases still,
The heavens are big with rain;
We haste to catch the teeming shower,
And all its moisture drain.

4 A rill, a stream, a torrent flows;
But pour a mighty flood;
O! sweep the nations, shake the earth,
Till all proclaim Thee God.

5 And when Thou mak'st Thy jewels up,
And sett'st Thy starry crown;
When all Thy sparkling gems shall shine,
Proclaimed by Thee Thine own;

6 May we, a little band of love,
We sinners, saved by grace,
From glory unto glory changed,
Behold Thee face to face.

H. 329 *No Tears in Heaven.*

1 What if our bark, o'er life's rough wave,
By adverse winds be driven,
And howling tempests round us rave,
There are no tears in heaven.

2 What though affliction be our lot,
Our hearts with anguish riven,
Still let it never be forgot,
There are no tears in heaven.

3 Our sweetest joys here vanish all,
And fade like hues at even;
Our fairest hopes like flowers fall;
There are no tears in heaven.

4 Thou, God, our joy and rest shalt be,
And sorrow far be driven;
And sin and death for ever flee;
There are no tears in heaven.

H. 331 *Submission under various Ills of Life.*

1 Through all the downward tracts of time,
God's watchful eye surveys;
Oh! who so wise to choose our lot,
And regulate our ways?

2 I cannot doubt His bounteous love,
Unmeasurably kind;
To His unerring, gracious will,
Be every wish resigned.

3 Good when He gives, supremely good,
Nor less, when He denies;
E'en crosses, from His sovereign hand,
Are blessings in disguise.

BRATTLE STREET. C. M. D.

IGNACE PLEYEL, 1757-1831.

1. Whilst Thee I seek, pro-tect-ing Power! Be my vain wish-es stilled; And may this con-se-
crat-ed hour With bet-ter hopes be filled. 2 Thy love the power of
D. S. That mer-cy I a-dore.
𝄋:
Fine.
thought be-stowed, To Thee my thoughts would soar; Thy mer-cy o'er my life has flowed,
D. S.

H. 24 *Goodness of Divine Providence.*

3 In each event of life, how clear
  Thy ruling hand I see;
Each blessing to my soul most dear,
  Because conferred by Thee.

4 In every joy that crowns my days,
  In every pain I bear,
My heart shall find delight in praise,
  Or seek relief in prayer.

5 When gladness wings the favoured hour,
  Thy love my thoughts shall fill;
Resigned, when storms of sorrow lower,
  My soul shall meet Thy will.

6 My lifted eye, without a tear,
  The gathering storm shall see,
My steadfast heart shall know no fear;
  That heart will rest on Thee.

H. 423 *Praise for Mercies.*

1 When all Thy mercies, O my God,
  My rising soul surveys,
Transported with the view, I'm lost
  In wonder, love and praise.

2 Unnumbered comforts to my soul
  Thy tender care bestowed,
Before my infant heart conceived
  From whom those comforts flowed.

3 When in the slippery paths of youth,
  With heedless steps I ran,
Thine arm, unseen, conveyed me safe,
  And led me up to man.

4 When worn by sickness, oft hast Thou
  With health renewed my face;
And when in sin and sorrow sunk,
  Revived my soul with grace.

5 Ten thousand thousand precious gifts
  My daily thanks employ;
Nor is the least a cheerful heart
  That tastes those gifts with joy.

6 Through every period of my life
  Thy goodness I'll pursue;
And after death, in distant worlds,
  The glorious theme renew.

7 Through all eternity to Thee
  A joyful song I'll raise;
But O! eternity's too short,
  To utter all Thy praise.

To Fa - ther, Son, and Ho - ly Ghost, The God whom we a - dore,
Be glo - ry as it was, is now, And shall be ev - er - more.

H. 642 *Funeral Hymn.*

1 Hark! from the tombs a doleful sound!
My ears attend the cry:
"Ye living men, come view the ground,
Where you must shortly lie.

2 "Princes, this clay must be your bed,
In spite of all your towers;
The tall, the wise, the reverend head
Must lie as low as ours."

3 Great God, is this our certain doom?
And are we still secure?
Still walking downward to the tomb,
And yet prepare no more!

4 Grant us the power of quickening grace,
To fit our souls to fly;
Then, when we drop this dying flesh,
We'll rise above the sky.

H. 657 *Judgment Anticipated.*

1 When rising from the bed of death,
O'erwhelmed with guilt and fear,
I see my Maker face to face,
O! how shall I appear?

2 If yet while pardon may be found,
And mercy may be sought,
My heart with inward horror shrinks,
And trembles at the thought.

3 When Thou, O Lord, shall stand dis- [closed,
In majesty severe,
And sit in judgment on my soul,
O! how shall I appear?

4 Yet never shall my soul despair
Her pardon to procure,
Who knows Thine only Son has died,
To make her pardon sure.

H. 664 *Consolation in Christ in View of the Judgment.*

1 That awful day will surely come,
Th' appointed hour makes haste,
When I must stand before my Judge,
And pass the solemn test.

2 Thou lovely Chief of all my joys,
Thou Sovereign of my heart,
How could I bear to hear Thy voice
Pronounce the word, "Depart!"

3 O! wretched state of deep despair,
To see my God remove,
And fix my doleful station, where
I must not taste His love.

4 Jesus, I throw my arms around,
And hang upon Thy breast;
Without a gracious smile from Thee,
My spirit cannot rest.

5 O! tell me that my worthless name
Is graven on Thy hands;
Show me some promise in Thy book,
Where my salvation stands.

6 Give me one kind, assuring word,
To sink my fears again;
And cheerfully my soul shall wait
Her threescore years and ten.

Mrs. Cuthbert.
1. Give thanks to God, in - voke His name, And tell the world His grace;
Sound through the earth His deeds of fame, That all may seek His face.

Ps. 105

2 His covenant, which He kept in mind
For numerous ages past,
To numerous ages yet behind
In equal force shall last.

3 He sware to Abraham and his seed,
And made the blessing sure;
Gentiles the ancient promise read,
And find His truth endure.

4 "Thy seed shall make all nations blest,"
Said the Almighty voice;
"And Canaan's land shall be their rest,
The type of heavenly joys."

Ps. 126

1 When God revealed His gracious name,
And changed my mournful state,
My rapture seemed a pleasing dream,
The grace appeared so great.

2 The world beheld the glorious change,
And did Thy hand confess;
My tongue broke out in unknown strains,
And sung surprising grace.

3 "Great is the work," my neighbours cried,
And owned the power divine;
"Great is the work," my heart replied,
And be the glory Thine.

4 The Lord can clear the darkest skies,
Can give us day for night;
Make drops of sacred sorrow rise
To rivers of delight.

5 Let those that sow in sadness wait
Till the fair harvest come;
They shall confess their sheaves are great,
And shout the blessings home.

Ps. 134

1 Ye that obey th' immortal King,
Attend His holy place;
Bow to the glories of His power,
And bless His wondrous grace.

2 Lift up your hands by morning light,
And send your souls on high;
Raise your admiring thoughts by night
Above the starry sky.

3 The God of Zion cheers our hearts,
With rays of quickening grace;
The God that spreads the heavens abroad,
And rules the swelling seas.

Ps. 135

1 Awake, ye saints, to praise your King,
Your sweetest passions raise;
Your pious pleasure, while you sing,
Increasing with the praise.

2 Great is the Lord, and works unknown
Are His divine employ;
But still His saints are near His throne,
His treasure and His joy.

3 Heaven, earth, and sea confess His hand;
He bids the vapours rise;
Lightning and storm at His command
Sweep through the sounding skies.

4 Ye nations, know the living God,
Serve Him with faith and fear;
He makes the churches His abode,
And claims your honours there.

Ps. 142

1 To God I made my sorrows known,
From God I sought relief:
In long complaints before His throne
I poured out all my grief.

2 My soul was overwhelmed with woes,
My heart began to break;
My God, who all my burdens knows,
Beholds the way I take.

3 On every side I cast mine eye,
And found my helpers gone,
While friends and strangers passed me
Neglected or unknown. [by

4 Then did I raise a louder cry,
And called Thy mercy near;
"Thou art my portion when I die,
Be Thou my refuge here."

5 Lord, I am brought exceeding low;
Now let Thine ear attend,
And make my foes, who vex me, know,
I've an almighty Friend.

6 From my sad prison set me free:
Then shall I praise Thy name;
And holy men shall join with me,
Thy kindness to proclaim.

H. 540 *Jesus receiving little Children.*

1 Behold, what condescending love,
Jesus on earth displays;
To babes and sucklings He extends
The riches of His grace.

2 He still the ancient promise keeps,
To our forefathers given;
Young children in His arms He takes,
And calls them heirs of heaven.

3 "Permit them to approach," He cries,
"Nor scorn their humble name;
For 'twas to bless such souls as these
The Lord of angels came."

4 We bring them, Lord, with thankful
And yield them up to Thee; [hearts,
Joyful that we ourselves are Thine,
Thine let our offspring be.

5 Thus to the parents and their seed,
Let Thy salvation come;
And numerous households meet at last,
In one eternal home.

H. 543 *Christ's Dying Love.*

1 How condescending and how kind
Was God's eternal Son!
Our misery reached His heavenly mind,
And pity brought Him down.

2 When justice, by our sins provoked,
Drew forth its dreadful sword,
He gave His soul up to the stroke,
Without a murmuring word.

3 He sunk beneath our heavy woes,
To raise us to His throne;
There's ne'er a gift His hand bestows
But cost His heart a groan.

4 This was compassion like a God,
That though the Saviour knew
The price of pardon was His blood,
His pity ne'er withdrew.

5 Now, though He reigns exalted high,
His love is still as great:
Well He remembers Calvary,
Nor lets His saints forget.

6 Here let our hearts begin to melt,
While we His death record,
And, with our joy for pardoned guilt,
Mourn that we pierced the Lord.

H. 557 *Gratitude unto Jesus.*

1 If human kindness meets return,
And owns the grateful tie;
If tender thoughts within us burn,
To feel a friend is nigh:

2 Oh! shall not warmer accents tell
The gratitude we owe
To Him who died, our fears to quell,
Our more than orphan's woe!

3 While yet His anguished soul surveyed
Those pangs He would not flee,
What love His latest words displayed,
"Meet and remember Me!"

4 Remember Thee! Thy death, Thy shame,
Our sinful hearts to share!
O memory, leave no other name
But His recorded there.

A. Williams' Collection, 1770.

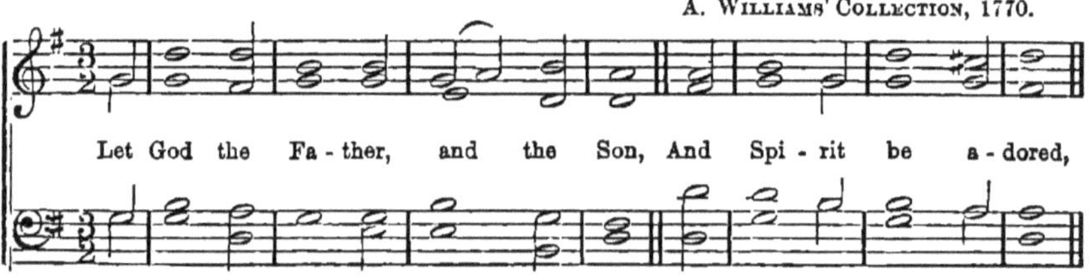
Let God the Fa - ther, and the Son, And Spi - rit be a - dored,

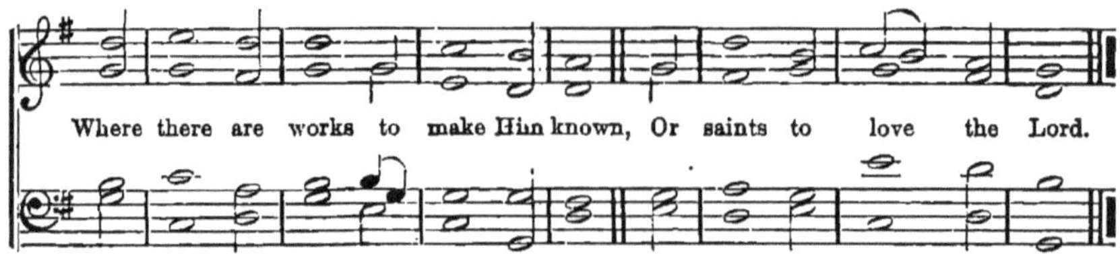
Where there are works to make Him known, Or saints to love the Lord.

H. 6 *The Goodness of God.*

1 God, in the high and holy place,
Looks down upon the spheres;
Yet in His providence and grace,
To every eye appears.

2 He bows the heavens; the mountains stand
A highway for our God:
He walks amid the desert land;
'Tis Eden where He trod.

3 In every stream His bounty flows,
Diffusing joy and wealth;
In every breeze His Spirit blows
The breath of life and health.

4 His blessings fall in plenteous showers,
Upon the lap of earth,
That teems with foliage, fruits, and flowers,
And rings with infant mirth.

5 If God hath made this world so fair,
Where sin and death abound;
How beautiful, beyond compare,
Will paradise be found!

Ps. 119 *Fourteenth Part.*

1 Consider all my sorrows, Lord,
And Thy deliverance send;
My soul for Thy salvation faints,
When will my troubles end?

2 Yet I have found 'tis good for me
To bear my Father's rod;
Afflictions make me learn Thy law,
And live upon my God.

3 This is the comfort I enjoy,
When new distress begins:
I read Thy word, I run Thy way,
And hate my former sins.

4 Had not Thy word been my delight,
When earthly joys were fled,
My soul, oppressed with sorrow's weight,
Had sunk amongst the dead.

5 I know Thy judgments, Lord, are right,
Though they may seem severe;
The sharpest sufferings I endure
Flow from Thy faithful care.

6 Before I knew Thy chastening rod,
My feet were apt to stray;
But now I learn to keep Thy word,
Nor wander from Thy way.

H. 328 *Asking Mercy in Affliction.*

1 O Thou whose mercy guides my way,
Though now it seems severe,
Forbid my unbelief to say
There is no mercy here.

2 Oh! grant me to desire the pain
That comes in kindness down,
More than the world's alluring gain
Succeeded by a frown.

3 Then, though Thou bend my spirit low,
Love only shall I see;
The very hand that strikes the blow,
Was wounded once for me.

Old American Tune.

1. Come, humble sinner, in whose breast A thousand thoughts revolve;
Come, with your guilt and fear oppress'd, And make this last resolve:
2. "I'll go to Je - sus, though my sin
High as a moun-tain rose; I know His courts, I'll en - ter in, What - ev - er may op - pose.

H. 208 *The Repenting Sinner returning.*

3 "Prostrate I'll lie before His throne,
And there my guilt confess;
I'll tell Him I'm a wretch undone
Without His sovereign grace.

4 "I'll to the gracious King approach,
Whose sceptre pardon gives;
Perhaps He may command my touch,
And then the suppliant lives.

5 "Perhaps He will admit my plea,
Perhaps will hear my prayer;
But if I perish, I will pray,
And perish only there.

6 "I can but perish if I go;
I am resolved to try;
For if I stay away, I know,
I must for ever die."

Ps. 119 *Seventeenth Part.*

1 O let my earnest prayer and cry
Come near before Thee, Lord;
Give understanding unto me,
According to Thy word.

2 Let my request before Thee come;
After Thy word me free.
My lips shall utter praise, when Thou
Hast taught Thy laws to me.

3 Let Thy strong hand make help to me;
Thy precepts are my choice;
I longed for Thy salvation, Lord,
And in Thy law rejoice.

4 O let my soul live, and it shall
Give praises unto Thee;
And let Thy judgments gracious
Be helpful unto me.

5 I, like a lost sheep, went astray;
Thy servant seek and find;
For Thy commands I suffered not
To slip out of my mind.

Ps. 74

1 How long, eternal God, how long,
Shall men of pride blaspheme?
Shall saints be made their endless song,
And bear immortal shame?

2 What strange deliverance hast thou shown,
In ages long before?
And now no other God we own,
No other God adore.

3 Thou didst divide the raging sea
By Thy resistless might,
To make Thy tribes a wondrous way,
And then secure their flight.

4 Is not the world of nature Thine,
The darkness and the day?
Didst Thou not bid the morning shine,
And mark the sun his way?

5 Think on the covenant Thou hast made,
And all Thy words of love;
Nor let the birds of prey invade
And vex the trembling dove.

BOYLSTON. S. M.

Dr. L. Ma[illegible]on, [illegible]32.

1. The pi - ty of the Lord, To those that fear
name,

Is such as ten - der pa - rents feel; He knows our fee - ble frame.

Ps. 103 *Third Part.*

2 He knows we are but dust,
  Scattered with every breath;
His anger, like a rising wind,
  Can send us swift to death.

3 Our days are as the grass,
  Or like the morning flower;
If one sharp blast sweep o'er the field,
  It withers in an hour.

4 But Thy compassions, Lord,
  To endless years endure;
And children's children ever find
  Thy words of promise sure.

Ps. 133 *First Part.*

1 Blest are the sons of peace,
  Whose hearts and hopes are one;
Whose kind designs to serve and please,
  Through all their actions run.

2 Blest is the pious house
  Where zeal and friendship meet;
Their songs of praise, their mingled vows,
  Make their communion sweet.

3 Thus, when on Aaron's head
  They poured the rich perfume,
The oil down to his raiment spread,
  And pleasure filled the room.

4 Thus, on the heavenly hills,
  The saints are blest above,
Where joy, like morning dew, distils,
  And all the air is love.

H. 30 *Sovereignty of God.*

1 Our times are in Thy hand;
  O God, we wish them there;
Our life, our friends, our souls we leave
  Entirely to Thy care.

2 Our times are in Thy hand,
  Whatever they may be,
Pleasing or painful, dark or bright,
  As best may seem to Thee.

3 Our times are in Thy hand,
  Why should we doubt or fear?
A Father's hand will never cause
  His child a needless tear.

4 Our times are in Thy hand,
  Jesus, the crucified;
The hand our many sins have pierced
  Is now our guard and guide.

H. 35 *Praise to the Trinity.*

1 To God the only wise,
  Who keeps us by His word,
Be glory now and evermore,
  Through Jesus Christ our Lord.

2 Hosanna to the Word,
  Who from the Father came;
Ascribe salvation to the Lord,
  And ever bless His name.

3 The grace of Christ our Lord,
  The Father's boundless love,
The Spirit's blest communion too,
  Be with us from above.

H. G. NAGELI, DIED 1836; ARRANGED BY DR. L. MASON, 1849.

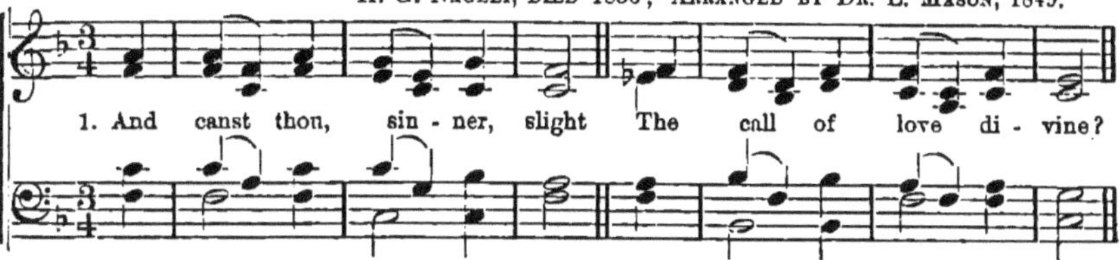
1. And canst thou, sin - ner, slight The call of love di - vine?

Shall God with ten - der - ness in - vite, And gain no thought of thine?

H. 132 *Grieving the Spirit.*

2 Wilt thou not cease to grieve
The Spirit from thy breast,
Till He thy wretched soul shall leave,
With all thy sins oppressed?

3 To-day a pardoning God
Will hear the suppliant pray;
To-day a Saviour's cleansing blood
Will wash Thy guilt away.

4 But grace so dearly bought,
If yet thou wilt despise,
Thy fearful doom with vengeance fraught,
Will fill thee with surprise.

H. 135 *The Comforter.*

1 Blest Comforter Divine,
Whose rays of heavenly love
Amid our gloom and darkness shine,
And point our souls above:

2 Thou who with "still small voice"
Dost stop the sinner's way,
And bid the mourning saint rejoice,
Though earthly joys decay.

3 Thou whose inspiring breath
Can make the cloud of care,
And e'en the gloomy vale of death,
A smile of glory wear;

4 Thou who dost fill the heart
With love to all our race,
Blest Comforter! to us impart
The blessings of Thy grace.

H. 654 *Certainty of Death.*

1 And am I born to die?
To lay this body down?
And must my trembling spirit fly
Into a world unknown?

2 How shall I leave my tomb?
With triumph or regret!
A fearful or a joyful doom,
A curse or blessing, meet?

Ps. 90 *Fourth Part.*

1 Lord, what a feeble piece
Is this our mortal frame!
Our life, how poor a trifle 'tis,
That scarce deserves the name!

2 Alas, the brittle clay
That built our body first!
And every month, and every day,
'Tis mouldering back to dust.

3 Our moments fly apace,
Our feeble powers decay;
Swift as a flood our hasty days
Are sweeping us away.

4 Yet, if our days must fly,
We'll keep their end in sight,
We'll spend them all in wisdom's way,
And let them speed their flight.

5 They'll waft us sooner o'er
This life's tempestuous sea;
Soon shall we reach the peaceful shore
Of blest eternity.

OLMUTZ. S. M.

From a Gregorian Chant

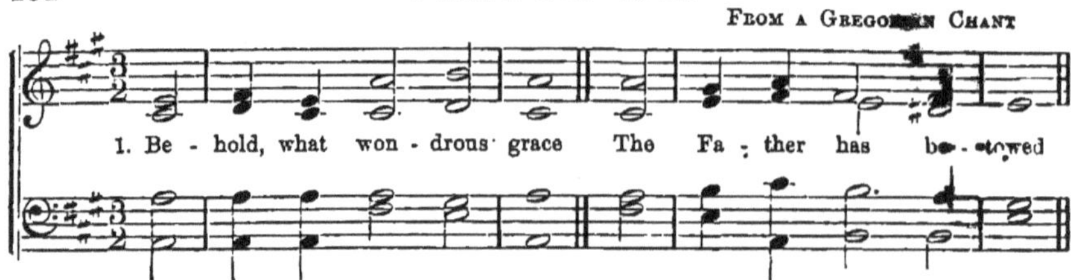
1. Be - hold, what won - drous grace The Fa - ther has be - stowed

On sin - ners of a mor - tal race, To call them sons of God.

H. 232 *Adoption.*

2 'Tis no surprising thing,
That we should be unknown;
The Jewish world knew not their King,
God's everlasting Son.

3 Nor doth it yet appear
How great we must be made;
But when we see our Saviour here,
We shall be like our Head.

4 A hope so much divine,
May trials well endure,
May purge our souls from sense and sin,
As Christ the Lord is pure.

5 If in my Father's Love
I share a filial part,
Send down Thy Spirit like a dove,
To rest upon my heart.

6 We would no longer lie
Like slaves beneath the throne;
My faith shall Abba, Father, cry,
And Thou the kindred own.

H. 252 *The Mourner Comforted.*

1 Your harps, ye trembling saints,
Down from the willows take;
Loud to the praise of love divine,
Bid every string awake.

2 Though in a foreign land,
We are not far from home,
And nearer to our house above,
We every moment come.

3 His grace will, to the end,
Stronger and brighter shine;
Nor present things, nor things to come,
Shall quench the love divine.

4 When we in darkness walk,
Nor feel the heavenly flame;
Then is the time to trust our God,
And rest upon His name.

5 Soon shall our doubts and fears
Subside at His control;
His loving-kindness shall break through
The midnight of the soul.

6 Blest is the man, O God,
That stays himself on Thee;
Who waits for Thy salvation, Lord,
Shall Thy salvation see.

Ps. 86 *Second Part.*

1 My God, my prayer attend;
Oh! bow Thine ear to me,
Without a hope, without a friend,
Without a help, but Thee.

2 Oh! guard my soul around,
Which loves and trusts Thy grace;
Nor let the powers of hell confound
The hopes on Thee I place.

3 Oh! bid my heart rejoice,
And every fear control;
Since at Thy feet, with suppliant voice,
To Thee I lift my soul.

DR. MASON, 1830.

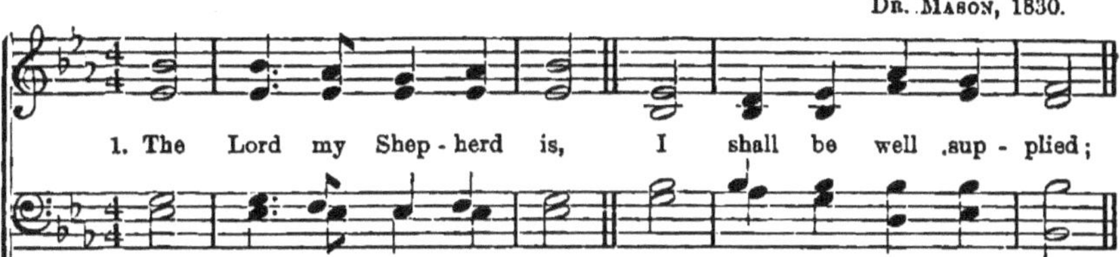
1. The Lord my Shep-herd is, I shall be well sup-plied;

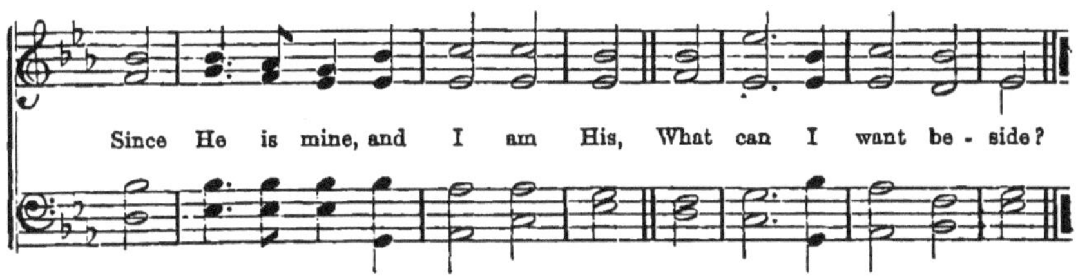
Since He is mine, and I am His, What can I want be-side?

Ps. 23 *Third Part.*

2 He leads me to the place
Where heavenly pasture grows,
Where living waters gently pass,
And full salvation flows.

3 If e'er I go astray,
He doth my soul reclaim,
And guides me in His own right way,
For His most holy name.

4 While He affords His aid,
I cannot yield to fear;
Tho' I should walk thro' death's dark shade,
My Shepherd's with me there.

5 Amid surrounding foes
Thou dost my table spread;
My cup with blessings overflows,
And joy exalts my head.

6 The bounties of Thy love
Shall crown my following days;
Nor from Thy house will I remove,
Nor cease to speak Thy praise.

Ps. 83

1 And will the God of grace
Perpetual silence keep?
The God of justice hold His peace,
And let His vengeance sleep?

2 Behold what cruel snares
The men of mischief spread;
The men that hate Thy saints and Thee,
Lift up their threatening head.

3 Convince their madness, Lord,
And make them seek Thy name,
Or else their impious rage confound,
And turn their pride to shame.

4 Then shall the nations know
Thy glorious, dreadful word;
Jehovah is Thy name alone,
And Thou the sovereign Lord.

H. 136 *The Scripture's Influence.*

1 Come, Holy Spirit, come;
Let Thy bright beams arise;
Dispel the darkness from our minds,
And open Thou our eyes.

2 Revive our drooping faith;
Our doubts and fears remove;
And kindle in our breasts the flame
Of never-dying love.

3 Convince us of our sin,
Then lead to Jesus' blood;
And to our wondering view reveal
The gracious love of God.

4 'Tis Thine to cleanse the heart,
To sanctify the soul,
To pour fresh life on every part,
And new create the whole.

5 Dwell, therefore, in our hearts;
Our minds from bondage free;
Then shall we know, and praise, and love
The Father, Son, and Thee.

From Handel, by Wm. Tansur, 1768.

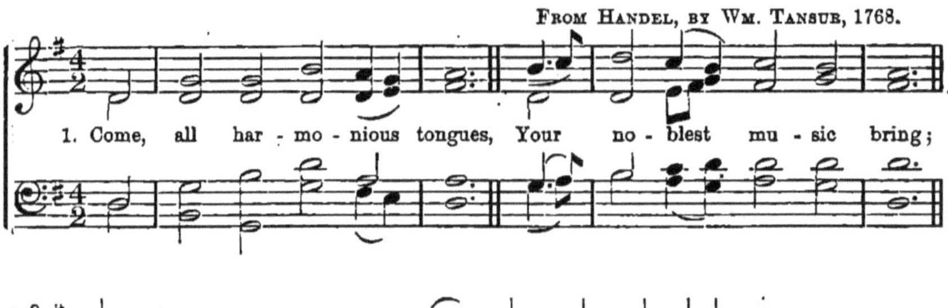
1. Come, all har - mo - nious tongues, Your no - blest mu - sic bring;

'Tis Christ the ev - er - last - ing God, And Christ the man, we sing.

H. 109 *Exaltation of Christ.*

2 Down to the shades of death,
He bowed His awful head;
Yet He arose to live and reign,
When death itself is dead.

3 No more the bloody spear,
The cross and nails no more;
For hell itself shakes at His name,
And all the heavens adore.

4 There the Redeemer sits,
High on the Father's throne;
The Father lays His vengeance by
And smiles upon His Son.

5 There His full glories shine
With uncreated rays,
And bless His saints and angels there,
To everlasting days.

Ps. 19 *First Part.*

1 Behold, the morning sun
Begins his glorious way;
His beams through all the nations run,
And life and light convey.

2 But where the gospel comes,
It spreads diviner light;
It calls dead sinners from their tombs,
And gives the blind their sight.

3 How perfect is Thy word!
And all Thy judgments just;
For ever sure Thy promise, Lord,
And men securely trust.

4 I hear Thy word with love,
And I would fain obey;
Send Thy good Spirit from above
To guide me lest I stray.

5 While with my heart and tongue
I spread Thy praise abroad;
Accept the worship and the song,
My Saviour and my God.

Ps. 25 *First Part.*

1 To Thee I lift my soul;
O Lord, I trust in Thee;
My God, let me not be ashamed,
Nor foes triumph o'er me.

2 Show me Thy ways, O Lord,
Thy paths, O teach Thou me;
And do Thou lead me in Thy truth,
Therein my teacher be.

3 For Thou art God that dost
To me salvation send,
And I upon Thee all the day
Expecting, do attend.

4 My sins and faults of youth
Do Thou, O Lord, forget;
After Thy mercy think on me,
And for Thy goodness great.

5 God good and upright is;
The way He'll sinners show;
The meek in judgment He will guide,
And make His path to know.

Lord Mornington, 1760.

1. My thirs - ty spi - rit faints To reach the land I love,
The bright in - he - ri - tance of saints, Je - ru - sa - lem a - bove.

H. 403 *Longing for Heaven.*

2 Yet clouds will intervene,
And all my prospect flies;
Like Noah's dove, I flit between
Rough seas and stormy skies.

3 Anon the clouds depart,
The winds and waters cease,
While sweetly o'er my gladdened heart
Expands the bow of peace.

H. 71 *Blessings of Christ's Advent.*

1 Raise your triumphant songs
To an immortal tune;
Let the wide earth resound the deeds
Celestial grace has done.

2 Sing how eternal Love
Its chief Beloved chose,
And bade Him raise our wretched race
From their abyss of woes.

3 His hand no thunder bears,
Nor terror clothes His brow;
No bolts to drive our guilty souls
To fiercer flames below.

4 'Twas mercy filled the throne,
And wrath stood silent by,
When Christ was sent with pardons down
To sinners doomed to die.

5 Now, sinners, dry your tears,
Let hopeless sorrow cease;
Bow to the sceptre of His love,
And take the offered peace.

6 Lord, we obey Thy call;
We lay an humble claim
To the salvation Thou hast brought,
And love and praise Thy name.

Ps. 48 *Second Part.*

1 Far as Thy name is known,
The world declares Thy praise;
Thy saints, O Lord, before Thy throne
Their songs of honour raise.

2 With joy Thy people stand
On Zion's chosen hill;
Proclaim the wonders of Thy hand,
And counsels of Thy will.

3 Let strangers walk around
The city where we dwell,
Compass and view Thy holy ground,
And mark the building well:

4 The orders of Thy house,
The worship of Thy court,
The cheerful songs, the solemn vows,
And make a fair report.

5 How decent and how wise!
How glorious to behold!
Beyond the pomp that charms the eyes,
And rites adorned with gold.

6 The God we worship now
Will guide us till we die;
Will be our God while here below,
And ours above the sky.

English Tune.

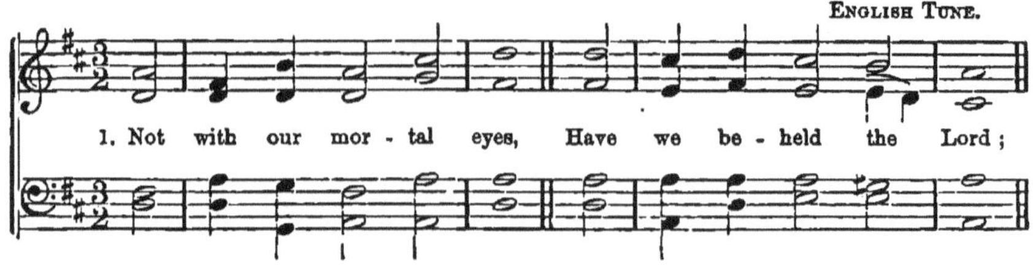
1. Not with our mor - tal eyes, Have we be - held the Lord;

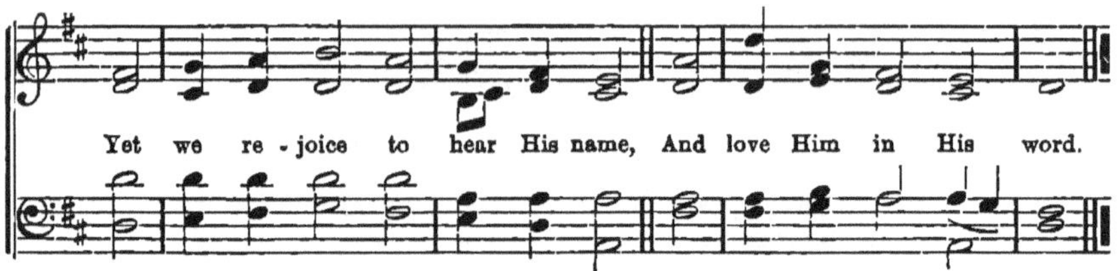
Yet we re - joice to hear His name, And love Him in His word.

H. 292 *Love to an Unseen Saviour:*

1 Not with our mortal eyes,
Have we beheld the Lord;
Yet we rejoice to hear His name,
And love Him in His word.

2 On earth we want the sight
Of our Redeemer's face;
Yet, Lord, our inmost thoughts delight
To dwell upon Thy grace.

3 And when we taste Thy love,
Our joys divinely grow,
Unspeakable, like those above,
And heaven begins below.

Ps. 30

1 Give to the winds thy fears;
Hope on, be not dismayed; [tears;
God hears thy sighs, and counts thy
God shall lift up thy head.

2 Through waves, and clouds, and storms,
He gently clears thy way;
Wait thou His time: the darkest night
Shall end in brightest day.

3 Far, far above thy thought
His counsel shall appear,
When fully He the work hath wrought,
That caused thy needless fear.

4 What though thou rulest not!
Yet heaven, and earth, and hell
Proclaim—God sitteth on the throne,
And ruleth all things well.

Ps. 48 *First Part.*

1 Great is the Lord our God,
And let His praise be great;
He makes His churches His abode,
His most delightful seat.

2 These temples of His grace,
How beautiful they stand!
The honours of our native place,
And bulwarks of our land.

3 In Zion God is known,
A refuge in distress;
How bright has His salvation shone!
How fair His heavenly grace!

4 When kings against her joined,
And saw the Lord was there,
In wild confusion of the mind
They fled with hasty fear.

5 When navies, tall and proud,
Attempt to spoil our peace,
He sends his tempests roaring loud,
And sinks them in the seas.

6 Oft have our fathers told
Our eyes have often seen,
How well our God secures the fold,
Where His own flocks have been.

7 In every new distress
We'll to His house repair;
Recall to mind His wondrous grace,
And seek deliverance there.

Dr. L. Mason, 1831.

1. My soul, be on thy guard, Ten thou - sand foes a - rise;
And hosts of sins are press - ing hard, To draw thee from the skies.

H. 384 *Watch and Pray.*

1 My soul, be on thy guard,
Ten thousand foes arise;
And hosts of sins are pressing hard,
To draw thee from the skies.

2 O watch, and fight, and pray,
The battle ne'er give o'er;
Renew it boldly every day,
And help divine implore.

3 Ne'er think the victory won,
Nor once at ease sit down;
Thy arduous work will not be done,
Till thou hast got the crown.

4 Fight on, my soul, till death
Shall bring thee to thy God;
He'll take thee, at thy parting breath,
Up to His blest abode.

H. 321 *Jesus my Strength and Hope.*

1 Jesus, my strength, my hope,
On Thee I cast my care;
With humble confidence look up,
And know Thou hear'st my prayer.

2 Give me on Thee to wait,
Till I can all things do,
On Thee, almighty to create,
Almighty to renew.

3 I want a godly fear,
A quick discerning eye,
That looks to Thee when sin is near,
And sees the tempter fly.

4 A spirit still prepared,
And armed with jealous care,
Forever standing on its guard,
And watching unto prayer.

5 I rest upon Thy word,
Thy promise is for me;
My succour and salvation, Lord,
Shall surely come from Thee.

6 But let me still abide,
Nor from my hope remove,
Till Thou my patient spirit guide
Into Thy perfect love.

H. 385 *A Charge to Keep.*

1 A charge to keep I have,
A God to glorify;
A never-dying soul to save,
And fit it for the sky.

2 From youth to hoary age,
My calling to fulfil;
O may it all my powers engage
To do my Master's will.

3 Arm me with jealous care,
As in Thy sight to live,
And O Thy servant, Lord, prepare
A strict account to give.

4 Help me to watch and pray,
And on Thyself rely;
Assured if I my trust betray,
I shall for ever die.

A Chapin, 1823.

1. O where shall rest be found, Rest for the wea - ry soul?
'Twere vain the o - cean depths to sound, Or pierce to eith - er pole.

H. 311 *Rest only found in God.*

1 Oh! where shall rest be found,
Rest for the weary soul?
'Twere vain the ocean depths to sound,
Or pierce to either pole.

2 The world can never give
The bliss for which we sigh;
'Tis not the whole of life to live,
Nor all of death to die.

3 Beyond this vale of tears
There is a life above,
Unmeasured by the flight of years;
And all that life is love.

4 There is a death whose pang
Outlasts the fleeting breath;
Oh! what eternal horrors hang
Around "the second death!"

5 Lord God of truth and grace,
Teach us that death to shun,
Lest we be banished from thy face,
And evermore undone.

6 Here would we end our quest;
Alone are found in Thee,
The life of perfect love, the rest
Of immortality.

H. 361 *The Believer's Safety in the Church.*

1 Oh! cease, my wandering soul,
On restless wing to roam;
All the wide world to either pole,
Has not for thee a home.

2 Behold the ark of God,
Behold the open door;
Hasten to gain that dear abode,
And rove, my soul, no more.

3 There, safe thou shalt abide,
There, sweet shall be Thy rest,
And every longing satisfied,
With full salvation blest.

Ps. 59

1 From foes that round us rise,
O God of heaven defend,
Who brave the vengeance of the skies,
And with Thy saints contend.

2 And will the God of grace,
Regardless of our pain,
Permit, secure, that impious race
To riot in their reign?

3 In vain their secret guile,
Or open force they prove;
His eye can pierce the deepest veil,
His hand their strength remove.

4 Yet save them, Lord, from death,
Subdue them by Thy word,
Confound their counsels with Thy breath,
But pardoning grace afford.

5 Then shall our grateful voice
Proclaim our guardian God:
The nations round the earth rejoice,
And sound Thy praise abroad.

GEORGE KINGSLEY, 1843.

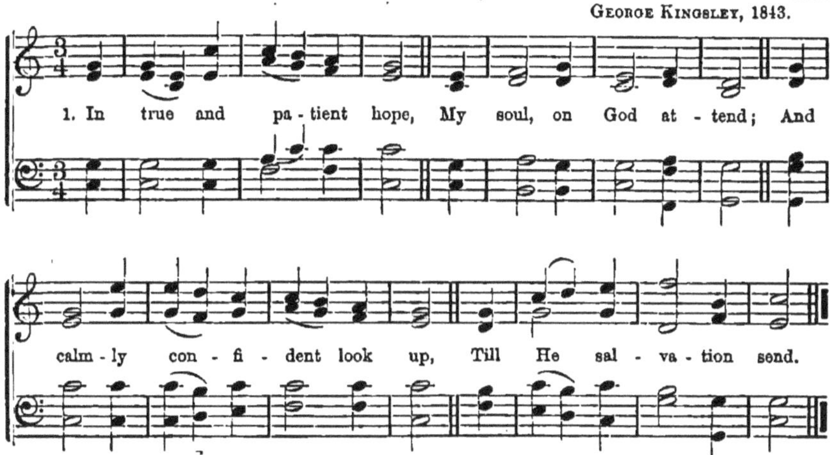
1. In true and pa - tient hope, My soul, on God at - tend; And
calm - ly con - fi - dent look up, Till He sal - va - tion send.

Ps. 62 *Second Part.*

2 I SHALL His goodness see,
While on His name I call;
He will defend and strengthen me,
And I shall never fall.

3 Jesus, to Thee I fly,
My refuge and my tower;
Upon Thy faithful love rely,
And find Thy saving power.

4 Trust in the Lord alone,
Who aids us from above;
In every strait surround His throne,
And hang upon His love.

H. 100 *Christ our Advocate.*

1 THE great Redeemer's gone,
To appear before our God,
To sprinkle o'er the flaming throne
With His atoning blood.

2 No fiery vengeance now,
No burning wrath comes down;
If justice calls for sinners' blood,
The Saviour shows His own.

3 Before His Father's eye
Our humble suit He moves;
The Father lays His thunder by,
And looks, and smiles, and loves.

4 Now may our joyful tongues
Our Maker's honour sing;
Jesus, the Priest, receives our songs,
And bears them to the King.

5 On earth Thy mercy reigns,
And triumphs all above;
But, Lord, how weak are mortal strains,
To speak immortal love!

6 How jarring and how low
Are all the notes we sing!
Blest Saviour, tune our songs anew,
And they shall please the King.

H. 443 *On Going to Rest.*

1 THE day is past and gone,
The evening shades appear;
O may we all remember well
The night of death draws near.

2 We lay our garments by,
Upon our beds to rest;
So death will soon disrobe us all
Of what is here possessed.

3 Lord, keep us safe this night,
Secure from all our fears;
May angels guard us while we sleep,
Till morning light appears.

4 And when we early rise,
And view the unwearied sun,
May we set out to win the prize,
And after glory run.

5 And when our days are past,
And we from time remove,
O may we in Thy bosom rest,
The bosom of Thy love.

AIN. S. M. D.

CORELLI.

Come, we that love the Lord, And let our joys be known; Join
in a song with sweet ac - cord, And thus sur - round the throne.
So
let our songs a - bound, And ev - ry tear be dried, We're
So let our songs a - bound, And ev - ry tear be
march - - - ing thro' Im - man - uel's ground, To fair - er worlds on high.
dried, We're march-ing thro', etc.

H. 470 *Reasons for Praise.*

2 The God that rules on high,
And thunders when He please,
That rides upon the stormy sky,
And manages the seas:

3 This awful God is ours,
Our Father and our Love;
He shall send down His heavenly powers
To carry us above.

4 There shall we see His face,
And never, never sin;
There, from the rivers of His grace,
Drink endless pleasures in.

5 The men of grace have found
Glory begun below:
Celestial fruits on earthly ground
From faith and hope may grow.

6 The hill of Zion yields
A thousand sacred sweets,
Before we reach the heavenly fields,
Or walk the golden streets.

7 Then let our songs abound,
And every tear be dry;
We're marching through Immanuel's ground,
To fairer worlds on high.

Daniel Read, 1785.

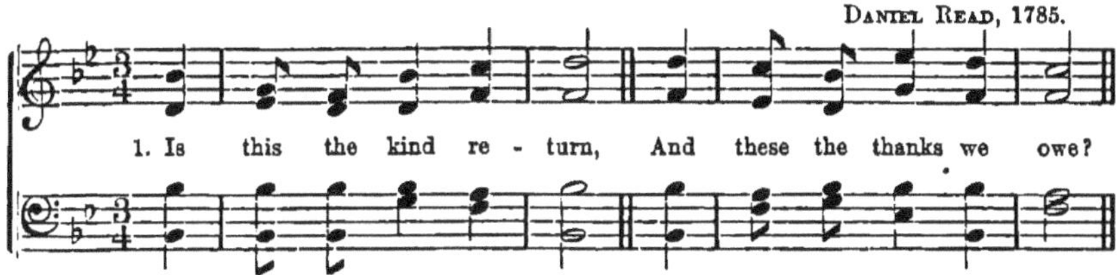
1. Is this the kind re - turn, And these the thanks we owe?

Thus to a - buse e - ter - nal love, Whence all our bless - ings flow!

H. 209 *Ingratitude Deplored.*

2 To what a stubborn frame
Has sin reduced our mind!
What strange rebellious wretches we,
And God as strangely kind!

3 On us He bids the sun
Shed his reviving rays;
For us the skies their circles run
To lengthen out our days.

4 The brutes obey their God,
And bow their necks to men;
But we, more base, more brutish things,
Reject His easy reign.

5 Turn, turn us, mighty God,
And mould our souls afresh; [stone,
Break, sovereign grace, these hearts of
And give us hearts of flesh.

6 Let past ingratitude
Provoke our weeping eyes,
And hourly as new mercies fall,
Let hourly thanks arise.

H. 241 *Union with Christ.*

1 Dear Saviour, we are Thine
By everlasting bands;
Our names, our hearts, we would resign,
And souls, into Thy hands.

2 Accepted for Thy sake,
And justified by faith,
We of Thy righteousness partake,
And find in Thee our life.

3 To Thee we still would cleave,
With ever growing zeal;
If millions tempt us Christ to leave,
O! let them ne'er prevail.

4 Thy Spirit shall unite
Our souls to Thee our head;
Shall form us to Thy image bright,
That we Thy paths may tread.

5 Death may our souls divide
From these abodes of clay;
But love shall keep us near Thy side,
Through all the gloomy way.

6 Since Christ and we are one,
Why should we doubt or fear?
Since He in Heaven has fixed His
He'll fix His members there. [throne,

H. 493 *The Sabbath a Delight.*

1 Welcome, sweet day of rest,
That saw the Lord arise;
Welcome to this reviving breast,
And these rejoicing eyes.

2 The King Himself comes near,
And feasts His saints to-day;
Here we may sit, and see Him here,
And love and praise and pray.

3 My willing soul would stay
In such a frame as this,
And sit and sing herself away
To everlasting bliss.

Isaac Smith, 1770.

1. See how the ris - ing sun Pur - sues his shin - ing way; And
wide pro-claims his Ma - ker's praise, With ev - 'ry bright'n-ing ray.

H. 445 *A Morning Hymn.*

2 Thus would my rising soul
Its heavenly Parent sing;
And to its great Original
The humble tribute bring.

3 Serene I laid me down
Beneath His guardian care;
I slept, and I awoke and found
My kind Preserver near.

4 My life I would anew
Devote, O Lord, to Thee;
And in Thy service I would spend
A long eternity.

Ps. 95 *First Part.*

1 Come, sound His praise abroad,
And hymns of glory sing;
Jehovah is the Sovereign God,
The universal King.

2 He formed the deeps unknown;
He gave the seas their bound;
The watery worlds are all His own,
And all the solid ground.

3 Come, worship at His throne,
Come, bow before the Lord;
We are His works, and not our own;
He formed us by His word.

4 To-day attend His voice,
Nor dare provoke His rod!
Come, like the people of His choice,
And own your gracious God.

5 But if your ears refuse
The message of His love;
And hearts grow hard and will not choose
The blessings from above;

6 The Lord, in vengeance drest,
Will lift His hand and swear,
"You that despise My promised rest
Shall have no portion there."

Ps. 125 *Second Part.*

1 Firm and unmoved are they
That rest their souls on God;
Firm as the mount where David dwelt,
Or where the ark abode.

2 As mountains stood to guard
The city's sacred ground,
So God and His almighty love
Embrace His saints around.

3 What though the Father's rod
Drop a chastising stroke;
Yet, lest it wound their souls too deep,
Its fury shall be broke.

4 Deal gently, Lord, with those
Whose faith and pious fear,
Whose hope and love, and every grace,
Proclaim their hearts sincere.

5 Nor shall the tyrant's rage
Too long oppress the saint;
The God of Israel will support
His children, lest they faint.

Thomas Clark, of England, 1804.

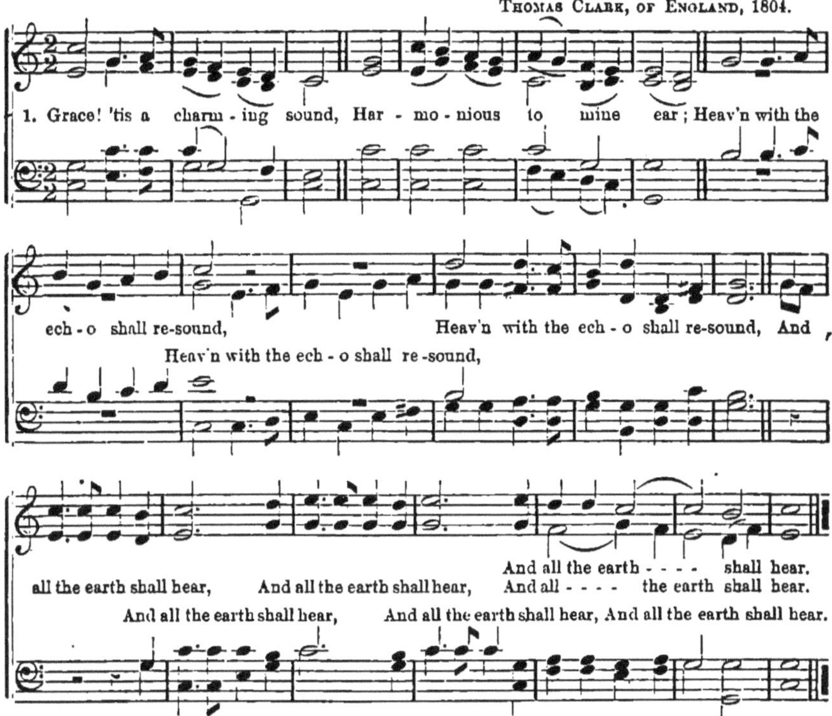
1. Grace! 'tis a charm - ing sound, Har - mo - nious to mine ear; Heav'n with the
ech - o shall re-sound, Heav'n with the ech - o shall re-sound, And
Heav'n with the ech - o shall re-sound,
all the earth shall hear, And all the earth shall hear, And all - - - - the earth shall hear.
And all the earth - - - - shall hear.
And all the earth shall hear, And all the earth shall hear, And all the earth shall hear.

H. 161 *Efficacy of Grace.*

1 Grace! 'tis a charming sound,
Harmonious to mine ear;
Heaven with the echo shall resound,
And all the earth shall hear.

2 Grace first contrived the way
To save the rebellious man;
And all the steps that grace display,
Which drew the wondrous plan.

3 Grace first inscribed my name
In God's eternal book;
'Twas grace that gave me to the Lamb,
Who all my sorrows took.

4 Grace led my roving feet
To tread the heavenly road;
And new supplies each hour I meet,
While pressing on to God.

5 Grace taught my soul to pray,
And made mine eyes o'erflow;
'Twas grace that kept me to this day,
And will not let me go.

6 Grace all the work shall crown,
Through everlasting days;
It lays in heaven the topmost stone,
And well deserves the praise.

H. 115 *Praise to the Redeemer.*

1 Awake, and sing the song
Of Moses and the Lamb;
Wake every heart, and every tongue,
To praise the Saviour's name.

2 Sing of His dying love,
Sing of His rising power;
Sing how He intercedes above
For those whose sins He bore.

3 Sing on your heavenly way,
Ye ransomed sinners, sing;
Sing on, rejoicing every day,
In Christ the eternal King.

4 Soon shall we hear Him say,
"Ye blessed children, come!"
Soon will He call us hence away,
And take His wanderers home.

SHAWMUT. S. M.

Dr. Mason, 1833.

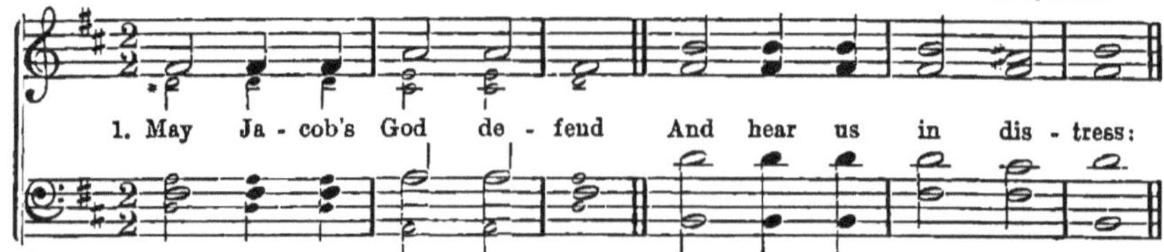
1. May Ja - cob's God de - fend And hear us in dis - tress:

Our suc - cour from His tem - ple send, Our cause from Zi - on bless!

* The small notes are for the Organ.

Ps. 20

2 May He accept our vow,
Our sacrifice receive,
Our heart's devout request allow,
Our holy wishes give!

3 O Lord! Thy saving grace,
We joyfully declare;
Our banner in Thy name we raise;
"The Lord fulfil our prayer!"

4 Now know we that the Lord
His chosen will defend;
From heaven will strength divine afford,
And will their prayer attend.

5 Some earthly succour trust,
But we in God's right hand;
Lo! while they fall, so vain their boast,
We rise and upright stand.

6 Still save us, Lord! and still
Thy servants deign to bless;
Hear, King of heaven, in times of ill,
The prayers that we address.

H. 29 *Submission to Providence.*

1 Thy way, not mine, O Lord,
However dark it be!
Lead me, O God, by Thine own hand,
Choose out the path for me.

2 I dare not choose my lot,
I would not, if I might;
Choose Thou for me, O Lord, my God,
So shall I walk aright.

3 The kingdom that I seek
Is Thine; so let the way
That leads to it, O Lord, be Thine,
Else I must surely stray.

4 Take Thou my cup, and it
With joy or sorrow fill,
As best to Thee, O Lord, may seem;
Choose Thou my good and ill.

5 Not mine, not mine the choice,
In things or great or small;
Be Thou, O Lord, my guide, my strength,
My wisdom, and my all.

H. 67 *Jesus, Lead Me!*

1 O Thou who wouldst not have
One wretched sinner die;
Who diedst Thyself, my soul to save
From endless misery!

2 Show me the way to shun
Thy dreadful wrath severe;
That when Thou comest on Thy throne,
I may with joy appear.

3 Thou art Thyself the way,
Thyself in me reveal;
So shall I spend my life's short day
Obedient to Thy will.

4 So shall I love my God,
Because He first loved me;
And praise Thee in Thy bright abode
To all eternity.

Dr. Thos. Hastings, 1835.

1. O! bless the Lord my soul; Let all with-in me join, And aid my tongue to

bless His name, Whose fa-vours are di - vine—Whose fa - vours are di - vine.

Ps. 103 *First Part.*

2 O! bless the Lord, my soul;
Nor let His mercies lie
Forgotten in unthankfulness,
And without praises die.

3 'Tis He forgives thy sins,
'Tis He relieves thy pains,
'Tis He that heals thy sicknesses,
And makes thee young again.

4 He crowns thy life with love,
When ransomed from the grave;
He that redeemed my soul from hell,
Hath sovereign power to save.

5 He fills the poor with good;
He gives the sufferers rest;
The Lord hath judgments for the proud,
And justice for th' oppressed.

6 His wondrous works and ways
He made by Moses known;
But sent the world His truth and grace
By His beloved Son.

Ps. 148 *Second Part.*

1 Let every creature join
To praise th' eternal God;
Ye heavenly hosts, the song begin,
And sound His name abroad.

2 Thou sun with golden beams,
And moon with paler rays,
Ye starry lights, ye twinkling flames,
Shine to your Maker's praise.

3 He built those worlds above,
And fixed their wondrous frame;
By His command they stand or move,
And ever speak His name.

4 Ye vapours, when ye rise,
Or fall in showers of snow,
Ye thunders, murmuring 'round the skies,
His power and glory show.

5 Wind, hail, and flaming fire,
Agree to praise the Lord;
When ye in dreadful storms conspire
To execute His word.

6 By all His works above,
His honours be expressed;
But saints that taste His saving love,
Should sing His praises best.

H. 538 *God's Blessing Invoked on Baptized Children.*

1 Great God, now condescend
To bless our rising race;
Soon may their willing spirits bend,
The subjects of Thy grace.

2 O what a pure delight
Their happiness to see!
Our warmest wishes all unite
To lead their souls to Thee.

3 Now bless, Thou God of love,
This ordinance divine;
Send Thy good Spirit from above,
And make these children Thine.

Dr. L. Mason.

1. Not all the blood of beasts On Jew - ish al - tars slain, Could give the

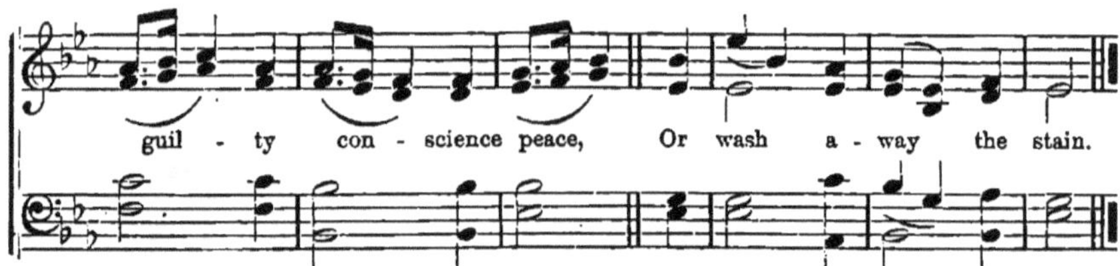
guil - ty con - science peace, Or wash a - way the stain.

H. 164 *Faith in the Sacrifice of Christ.*

2 But Christ, the heavenly Lamb,
Takes all our sins away;
A sacrifice of nobler name,
And richer blood than they.

3 My faith would lay her hand
On that dear head of Thine,
While like a penitent I stand,
And there confess my sin.

4 My soul looks back to see
The burdens Thou didst bear,
When hanging on the cursed tree,
And hopes her guilt was there.

5 Believing, we rejoice
To see the curse remove;
We bless the Lamb with cheerful voice,
And sing His bleeding love.

H. 240 *Grace.*

1 Man's wisdom is to seek
His strength in God alone;
And e'en an angel would be weak,
Who trusted in his own.

2 Retreat beneath His wings,
And in His grace confide;
This more exalts the King of kings,
Than all your works beside.

3 In Jesus is our store;
Grace issues from His throne;
Whoever says, "I want no more,"
Confesses he has none.

H. 271 *Faith Prevailing in Trouble.*

1 If, through unruffled seas,
Toward heaven we calmly sail,
With grateful hearts, O God, to Thee,
We'll own the prospering gale.

2 But should the surges rise,
And rest delay to come,
Blest be the sorrow—kind the storm,
Which drives us nearer home.

3 Teach us, in every state,
To make Thy will our own;
And when the joys of sense depart,
To live by faith alone.

Ps. 99 *First Part.*

1 The God Jehovah reigns,
Let all the nations fear;
Let sinners tremble at His throne,
And saints be humble there.

2 Jesus the Saviour reigns,
Let earth adore its Lord;
Bright cherubs His attendants stand,
Swift to fulfil His word.

3 In Zion stands His throne,
His honours are divine;
His church shall make His wonders known,
For there His glories shine.

4 How holy is His name!
How terrible His praise!
Justice, and truth, and judgment join
In all His works of grace.

Dr. Wm. Boyce, 1710-1779.

1. Ah! how shall fall - en man Be just be - fore his God?

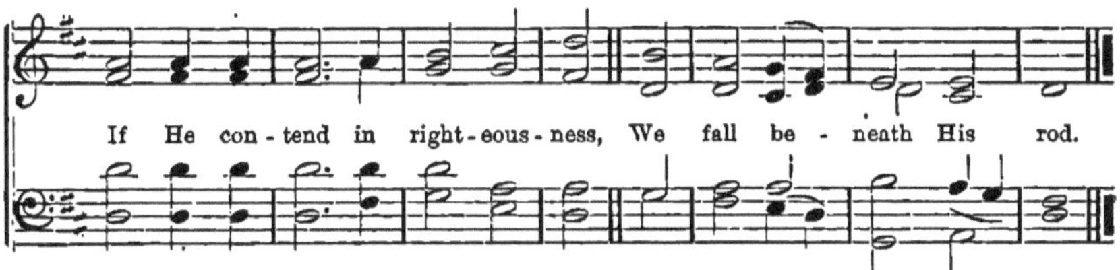
If He con - tend in right - eous - ness, We fall be - neath His rod.

H. 143 *Guilt and Helplessness of Man.*

2 If He our ways should mark
With strict inquiring eyes,
Could we for one of thousand faults,
A just excuse devise?

3 All-seeing, powerful God,
Who can with Thee contend?
Or who that tries the unequal strife,
Shall prosper in the end?

4 The mountains, in Thy wrath,
Their ancient seats forsake;
The trembling earth deserts her place,
Her rooted pillars shake.

5 Ah! how shall guilty man,
Contend with such a God?
None, none can meet Him and escape,
But through the Saviour's blood.

H. 197 *Oh! for True Repentance!*

1 Oh! that I could repent,
With every idol part,
And to Thy gracious eye present
An humble, contrite heart.

2 A heart with grief oppressed,
For having grieved my God;
A troubled heart that cannot rest,
Till sprinkled with Thy blood.

3 Jesus, on me bestow
The penitent desire;
With true sincerity of woe
My aching breast inspire.

4 With softening pity look,
And melt my hardness down;
Strike with Thy love's resistless stroke,
And break this heart of stone.

H. 416 *Soldiers of Christ.*

1 Soldiers of Christ, arise,
And put your armour on, [plies
Strong in the strength which God sup-
Through His eternal Son.

2 Strong in the Lord of Hosts,
And in His mighty power;
Who in the strength of Jesus trusts,
Is more than conqueror.

3 Stand then in His great might,
With all His strength endued;
But take to arm you for the fight,
The panoply of God:—

4 That having all things done,
And all your conflicts past,
Ye may o'ercome through Christ alone,
And stand entire at last.

5 From strength to strength go on,
Wrestle, and fight, and pray;
Tread all the powers of darkness down,
And win the well-fought day.

6 Still let the Spirit cry
In all His soldiers, "Come,"
Till Christ the Lord descend from high,
And take the conquerors home.

A. Chapin, 1823.

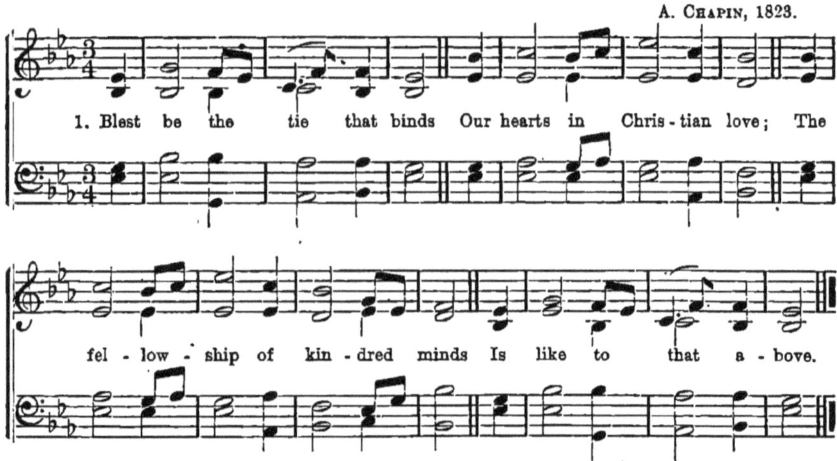
1. Blest be the tie that binds Our hearts in Christian love; The
fel - low - ship of kin - dred minds Is like to that a - bove.

H. 298 *Christian Fellowship.*

1 Blest be the tie that binds
Our hearts in Christian love;
The fellowship of kindred minds
Is like to that above.

2 Before our Father's throne
We pour our ardent prayers;
Our fears, our hopes, our aims are one,
Our comforts and our cares.

3 We share our mutual woes,
Our mutual burdens bear,
And often for each other flows
The sympathizing tear.

4 When we asunder part,
It gives us inward pain;
But we shall still be joined in heart,
And hope to meet again.

5 This glorious hope revives
Our courage by the way;
While each in expectation lives,
And longs to see the day.

6 From sorrow, toil, and pain,
And sin, we shall be free;
And perfect love and friendship reign,
Through all eternity.

Ps. 137 *Second Part.*

1 I love Thy kingdom, Lord,
The house of Thine abode;
The church our blest Redeemer saved
With His own precious blood.

2 I love Thy church, O God!
Her walls before Thee stand,
Dear as the apple of Thine eye,
And graven on Thy hand.

3 If e'er to bless Thy sons
My voice or hands deny,
These hands let useful skill forsake,
This voice in silence die.

4 If e'er my heart forget
Her welfare, or her woe,
Let every joy this heart forsake,
And every grief o'erflow.

5 For her my tears shall fall;
For her my prayers ascend;
To her my cares and toils be given,
Till toils and cares shall end.

6 Beyond my highest joy
I prize her heavenly ways,
Her sweet communion, solemn vows,
Her hymns of love and praise.

7 Jesus, Thou Friend divine,
Our Saviour and our King,
Thy hand from every snare and foe
Shall great deliverance bring.

8 Sure as Thy truth shall last,
To Zion shall be given
The brightest glories earth can yield,
And brighter bliss of heaven.

S. STANLEY, 1800.

1. O! bless - ed souls are they Whose sins are cov - ered o'er;
Di - vine - ly blessed, to whom the Lord Im - putes their guilt no more.

Ps. 32 *First Part.*

2 They mourn their follies past,
And keep their hearts with care:
Their lips and lives without deceit
Shall prove their faith sincere.

3 While I concealed my guilt,
I felt the painful wound,
Till I confessed my sins to Thee,
And ready pardon found.

4 Let sinners learn to pray,
Let saints keep near the throne;
Our help in times of deep distress
Is found in God alone.

Ps. 55

1 Let sinners take their course,
And choose the road to death;
But in the worship of my God
I'll spend my daily breath.

2 My thoughts address His throne,
When morning brings the light
I seek His blessing every noon,
And pay my vows at night.

3 Thou wilt regard my cries,
Oh! my eternal God!
While sinners perish in surprise,
Beneath Thine angry rod.

4 Because they dwell at ease,
And no sad changes feel,
They neither fear nor trust Thy name,
Nor learn to do Thy will.

5 But I, with all my cares,
Will lean upon the Lord;
I'll cast my burden on His arm,
And rest upon His word.

6 His arm shall well sustain
The children of his love;
The ground on which their safety stands,
No earthly power can move.

H. 267 *Appropriating Faith.*

1 Faith is a precious grace,
Where'er it is bestowed;
It boasts of a celestial birth,
And is the gift of God.

2 Jesus it owns as King,
And all-atoning Priest;
It claims no merit of its own,
But looks for all in Christ.

3 On Him it safely leans,
In times of deep distress;
Flies to the fountain of His blood,
And trusts His righteousness.

4 All through the wilderness,
It is our strength and stay;
Nor can we miss the heavenly road,
While it directs our way.

5 Lord, 'tis thy work alone,
And that divinely free;
Send down the Spirit of thy Son,
To work this faith in me.

STILLINGFLEET. S. M.

Swiss Air.

1. My God, my life, my love, To Thee, to Thee I call;

I can - not live if Thou re - move, for Thou art All in all.

H. 12 *God all, and in all.*

2 Not all the harps above
Can make a heavenly place,
If God His residence remove,
Or but conceal His face.

3 Nor earth, nor all the sky,
Can one delight afford;
No, not a drop of real joy,
Without Thy presence, Lord.

4 Thou art the sea of love,
Where all my pleasures roll;
The circle where my passions move,
And centre of my soul.

H. 31 *Address to the Trinity.*

1 O Lord our God, arise,
The cause of truth maintain;
And wide o'er all the peopled world
Extend her blessed reign.

2 Thou Prince of Life, arise,
Nor let Thy glory cease;
Far spread the conquests of Thy grace,
And bless the earth with peace.

3 Thou Holy Ghost, arise,
Expand Thy quickening wing,
And o'er a dark and ruined world,
Let light and order spring.

4 All on the earth, arise,
To God the Saviour sing;
From shore to shore, from earth to heav'n,
Let echoing anthems ring.

H. 158 *The Law and Gospel Contrasted.*

1 The law by Moses came,
But peace, and truth, and love
Were brought by Christ, a nobler name,
Descending from above.

2 Amidst the house of God,
Their different works were done;
Moses a faithful servant stood,
But Christ, a faithful Son.

3 Then to His new commands
Be strict obedience paid;
O'er all His Father's house He stands
The Sovereign and the Head.

Ps. 99 *Second Part.*

1 Exalt the Lord our God,
And worship at His feet;
His nature is all holiness,
And mercy is His seat.

2 When Israel was His church,
When Aaron was His priest,
When Moses cried, when Samuel prayed,
He gave His people rest.

3 Oft He forgave their sins,
Nor would destroy their race;
And oft He made His justice known,
When they abused His grace.

4 Exalt the Lord our God,
Whose grace is still the same;
Still He's a God of holiness,
And jealous for His name.

James Leach, 1789.

1. Je - sus, who knows full well The heart of ev - 'ry saint,

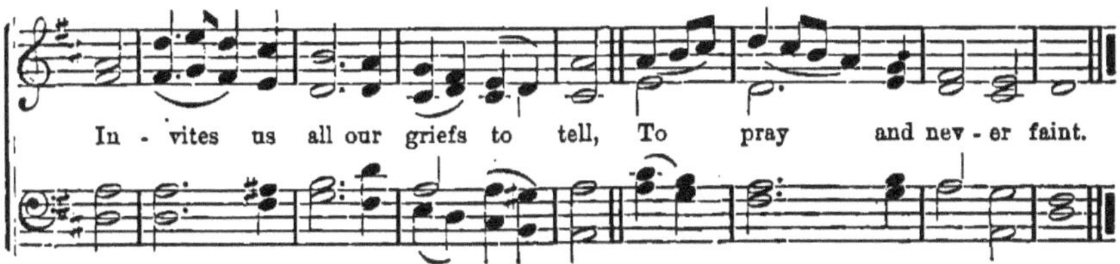
In - vites us all our griefs to tell, To pray and nev - er faint.

H. 371 *Importunate Prayer.*

2 He bows His gracious ear,
We never plead in vain;
Yet we must wait till He appear,
And pray, and pray again.

3 Though unbelief suggest,
Why should we longer wait?
He bids us never give Him rest,
But be importunate.

4 Jesus, the Lord, will hear
His chosen when they cry,
Yes, though He may a while forbear,
He'll help them from on high.

5 His nature, truth and love,
Engage Him on their side;
When they are grieved, His mercies move,
And can they be denied?

6 Then let us earnest be,
And never faint in prayer;
He loves our importunity,
And makes our cause His care.

H. 310 *All Things in Christ.*

1 Thou very-present Aid
In suffering and distress!
The mind which still on Thee is stayed,
Is kept in perfect peace.

2 The soul, by faith reclined
On the Redeemer's breast,
'Mid raging storms exults to find
An everlasting rest.

3 Sorrow and fear are gone,
Whene'er Thy face appears;
It stills the sighing orphan's moan,
And dries the widow's tears.

4 It hallows every cross,
It sweetly comforts me;
It makes me now forget my loss,
And lose myself in Thee.

5 Jesus, to whom I fly,
Will all my wishes fill;
What though created streams are dry,
I have the fountain still.

H. 474 *Christ in the Midst.*

1 Jesus, we look to Thee,
Thy promised presence claim;
Thou in the midst of us shall be,
Assembled in Thy name.

2 Thy name salvation is,
Which here we come to prove;
Thy name is life, and health, and peace,
And everlasting love.

3 Present we know Thou art,
But, oh! Thyself reveal;
Now, Lord, let every bounding heart
The mighty comfort feel.

4 Oh! may Thy quickening voice
The death of sin remove;
And bid our inmost souls rejoice,
In hope of perfect love.

DR. HASTINGS.

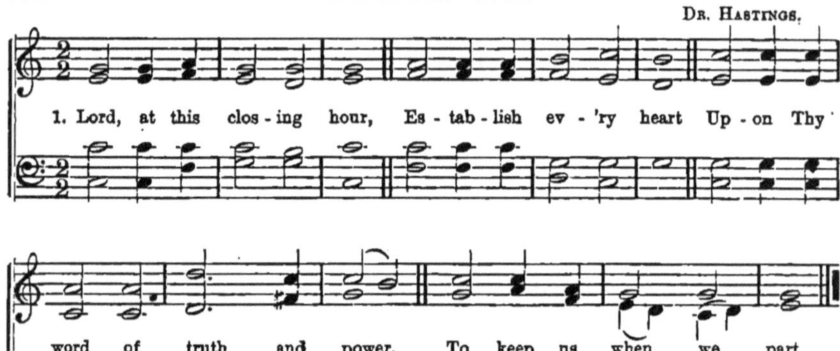
1. Lord, at this clos - ing hour, Es - tab - lish ev - 'ry heart Up - on Thy
word of truth and power, To keep us when we part.

H. 489 *Close of Worship.*

1 Lord, at this closing hour,
Establish every heart
Upon Thy word of truth and power,
To keep us when we part.

2 Peace to our brethren give,
Fill all our hearts with love;
In faith and patience may we live,
And seek our rest above.

3 Through changes, bright or drear,
We would Thy will pursue,
And toil to spread Thy kingdom here,
Till we its glory view.

4 To God, the Only Wise,
In every age adored,
Let glory from the church arise,
Through Jesus Christ our Lord.

H. 523 *Prayer of Youth.*

1 With humble heart and tongue,
Our God, to Thee we pray;
O make us learn while we are young,
How we may cleanse our way.

2 Make us, unguarded youth,
The objects of Thy care;
Help us to choose the way of truth,
And fly from every snare.

3 Our hearts, to folly prone,
Renew by power divine;
Unite them to Thyself alone,
And make us wholly Thine.

4 O let Thy word of grace
Our warmest thoughts employ;
Be this, through all our following days,
Our treasure and our joy.

5 To what Thy laws impart,
Be our whole soul inclined;
O let them dwell within our heart,
And sanctify our mind.

6 Make Thy young servants learn
By these to cleanse their way;
And may we here the path discern
That leads to endless day.

Ps. 61 *Second Part.*

1 When overwhelmed with grief,
My heart within me dies,
Helpless, and far from all relief,
To heaven I lift mine eyes.

2 Oh! lead me to the rock
That 's high above my head,
And make the covert of Thy wings
My shelter and my shade.

3 Within Thy presence, Lord,
For ever I'll abide;
Thou art the tower of my defence,
The refuge where I hide.

4 Thou givest me the lot
Of those that fear Thy name;
If endless life be their reward,
I shall possess the same.

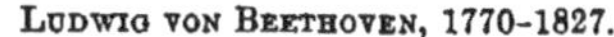
Ludwig von Beethoven, 1770-1827.

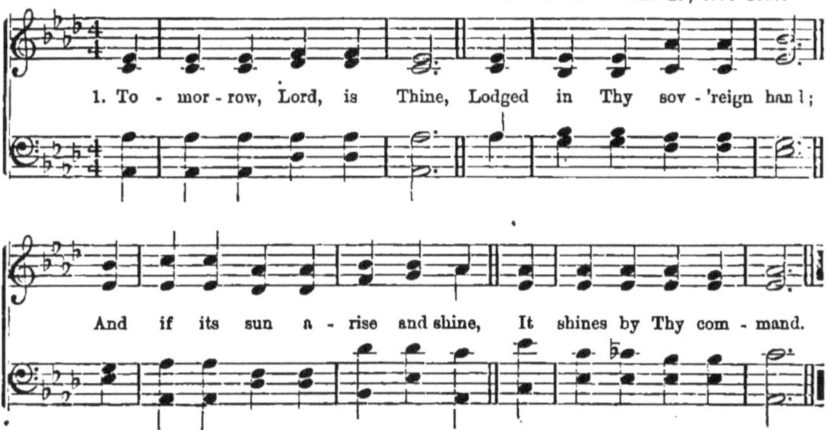
1. To - mor - row, Lord, is Thine, Lodged in Thy sov - 'reign han l;
And if its sun a - rise and shine, It shines by Thy com - mand.

H. 617 *Value of Present Time.*

2 The present moment flies,
And bears our life away;
O make Thy servants truly wise,
That they may live to-day.

3 Since on this winged hour
Eternity is hung,
Waken by Thy almighty power
The aged and the young.

4 One thing demands our care;
O be it still pursued,
Lest, slighted once, the season fair
Should never be renewed.

5 To Jesus may we fly,
Swift as the morning light,
Lest life's young golden beam should die
In sudden, endless night.

H. 633 *Peaceful Death.*

1 O! for the death of those
Who slumber in the Lord!
O be, like theirs, my last repose,
Like theirs my last reward!

2 Their bodies in the ground,
In silent hope may lie,
Till the last trumpet's joyful sound
Shall call them to the sky.

3 Their ransomed spirits soar,
On wings of faith and love,
To meet the Saviour they adore,
And reign with Him above.

4 With us their names shall live
Through long succeeding years,
Embalmed with all our hearts can give,
Our praises and our tears.

5 O for the death of those
Who slumber in the Lord!
O be, like theirs, my last repose,
Like theirs my last reward!

H. 648 *Joy in View of the Resurrection.*

1 And must this body die,
This mortal frame decay?
And must these active limbs of mine
Lie mouldering in the clay.

2 God my Redeemer lives,
And often from the skies
Looks down and watches all my dust,
Till He shall bid it rise.

3 Arrayed in glorious grace,
Shall these vile bodies shine,
And every shape and every face
Look heavenly and divine.

4 These lively hopes we owe
To Jesus' dying love;
We would adore His grace below,
And sing His power above.

5 Dear Lord, accept the praise
Of these, our humble songs,
Till tunes of nobler sound we raise
With our immortal tongues.

J. W. Belcher.

1. Sow in the morn thy seed, At eve hold not thy hand;
To doubt and fear give Thou no heed, Broad-cast it o'er the land.

H. 395 *"Sow beside all Waters."*

2 The good, the fruitful ground,
Expect not here nor there;
O'er hill and dale, by plots, 'tis found;
Go forth, then, everywhere.

3 Thou knowest not which may thrive,
The late or early sown;
Grace keeps the precious germs alive,
When and wherever strown.

4 Thou canst not toil in vain;
Cold, heat, and moist, and dry,
Shall foster and mature the grain,
For garners in the sky.

5 Thence, when the glorious end,
The day of God is come,
The angel reapers shall descend,
And heaven sing "Harvest home."

H. 659 *Preparation to meet God.*

1 Prepare me, gracious God,
To stand before Thy face;
Thy Spirit must the work perform,
For it is all of grace.

2 In Christ's obedience clothe,
And wash me in His blood;
So shall I lift my head with joy,
Among the sons of God.

3 Do Thou my sins subdue,
Thy sovereign love make known;
The spirit of my mind renew,
And save me in Thy Son.

4 Let me attest Thy power,
Let me Thy goodness prove,
Till my full soul can hold no more
Of everlasting love.

H. 695 *For ever with the Lord.*

1 "For ever with the Lord!"
Amen; so let it be;
Life from the dead is in that word,
'Tis immortality.

2 Here in the body pent,
Absent from Him I roam,
Yet nightly pitch my moving tent,
A day's march nearer home.

3 My Father's house on high,
Home of my soul, how near,
At times, to faith's far-seeing eye,
Thy golden gates appear.

4 "For ever with the Lord!"
Father, if 'tis Thy will,
The promise of that faithful word,
Even here to me fulfil.

5 So when my last breath
Shall rend the veil in twain,
By death I shall escape from death,
And life eternal gain.

6 Knowing as I am known,
How shall I love that word,
And oft repeat before the throne,
"For ever with the Lord."

KARL REDEN, 1866.

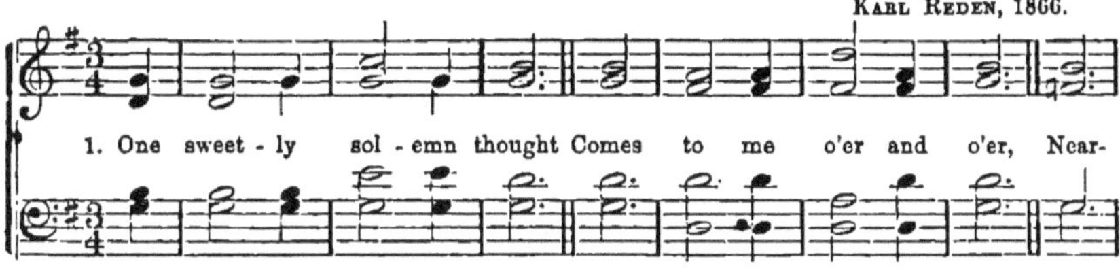
1. One sweet - ly sol - emn thought Comes to me o'er and o'er, Near-

er my part - ing hour am I Than e'er I was be - fore.

H. 624 *Nearing the end.*

2 NEARER my Father's house,
Where many mansions be;
Nearer the throne where Jesus reigns;
Nearer the crystal sea.

3 Nearer my going home,
Laying my burden down,
Leaving my cross of heavy grief,
Wearing my starry crown.

4 Nearer that hidden stream,
Winding through shades of night,
Rolling its cold dark waves between
Me and the world of light.

5 Jesus! to Thee I cling:
Strengthen my arm of faith;
Stay near me while my way-worn feet
Press through the stream of death.

H. 53 *Christ our Wisdom and Righteousness.*

1 How heavy is the night
That hangs upon our eyes,
Till Christ, with His reviving light,
Over our souls arise!

2 Our guilty spirits dread
To meet the wrath of heaven;
But, in His righteousness arrayed,
We see our sins forgiven.

3 Unholy and impure
Are all our thoughts and ways;
His hands infected nature cure,
With sanctifying grace.

4 The powers of hell agree
To hold our souls in vain;
He sets the sons of bondage free,
And breaks the accursed chain.

5 Lord, we adore Thy ways,
To bring us near to God;
Thy sovereign power, Thy healing grace,
And Thy atoning blood.

H. 84 *Sufferings of Christ.*

1 LIKE sheep we went astray,
And broke the fold of God;
Each wandering in a different way,
But all the downward road.

2 How dreadful was the hour
When God our wanderings laid,
And did at once His vengeance pour
Upon the Shepherd's head!

3 How glorious was the grace
When Christ sustained the stroke!
His life and blood the Shepherd pays,
A ransom for the flock.

4 His honour and His breath
Were taken both away;
Joined with the wicked in His death,
And made as vile as they.

5 But God shall raise His head
O'er all the sons of men,
And make Him see a numerous seed,
To recompense His pain.

6 "I'll give Him," saith the Lord,
"A portion with the strong;
He shall possess a large reward,
And hold His honours long."

DR. MAURICE GREEN, DIED 1755.

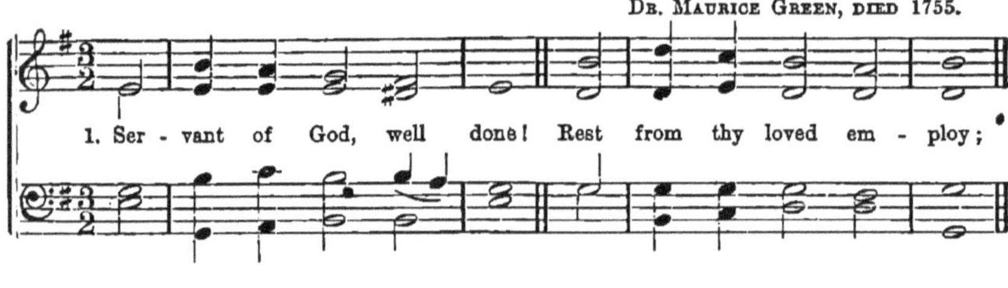
1. Ser - vant of God, well done! Rest from thy loved em - ploy;

The bat - tle fought, the vic - t'ry won, En - ter thy Mas - ter's joy.

H. 651 *The Soldier's Discharge.*

1 SERVANT of God, well done,
Rest from thy loved employ;
The battle fought, the victory won,
Enter thy Master's joy.

2 The voice at midnight came;
He started up to hear;
A mortal arrow pierced his frame;
He fell, but felt no fear.

3 At midnight came the cry,
"To meet thy God prepare!"
He woke, and caught his Captain's eye,
Then, strong in faith and prayer,

4 His spirit with a bound
Left its encumbering clay;
His tent, at sunrise, on the ground
A darkened ruin lay.

5 The pains of death are past;
Labour and sorrow cease;
And life's long warfare closed at last,
His soul is found in peace.

6 Soldier of Christ, well done!
Praise be thy new employ;
And while eternal ages run,
Rest in thy Saviour's joy.

H. 656 *The Sinner Warned.*

1 AND will the Judge descend?
And must the dead arise?
And not a single soul escape
His all-discerning eyes?

2 How will my heart endure
The terrors of that day,
When earth and heaven before His face
Astonished shrink away!

3 But ere the trumpet shakes
The mansions of the dead,
Hark, from the gospel's cheering sound,
What joyful tidings spread!

4 Ye sinners, seek His grace,
Whose wrath ye cannot bear!
Fly to the shelter of His cross,
And find salvation there.

5 So shall that curse remove,
By which the Saviour bled;
And the last awful day shall pour
His blessing on your head.

H. 666 *Coming of the Judge.*

1 I SAW, beyond the tomb,
The awful Judge appear!
Prepare to scan, with strict account,
The blessings wasted here.

2 Ye sinners, fear the Lord,
While yet 'tis called to-day;
Soon will the awful voice of death
Command your souls away.

3 Soon will the harvest close,
The summer soon be o'er;
And soon your injured, angry God,
Will hear your prayers no more.

THOMAS LINLEY, 1800.

1. Did Christ o'er sin - ners weep? And shall our cheeks be dry?

Let floods of pen - i - ten - tial grief Burst forth from ev - 'ry eye.

H. 86 *Suffering Saviour.*

2 The Son of God in tears
Angels with wonder see;
Be thou astonished, O my soul,
He shed those tears for thee.

3 He wept that we might weep;
Each sin demands a tear;
In heaven alone no sin is found,
And there's no weeping there.

H. 160 *The Law and Gospel joined in Scripture.*

1 The Lord declares His will,
And keeps the world in awe;
Amidst the smoke on Sinai's hill,
Breaks out His fiery law.

2 The Lord reveals His face,
And, smiling from above,
Sends down the gospel of His grace,
The epistles of His love.

3 We read the heavenly word,
We take the offered grace,
Obey the statutes of the Lord,
And trust His promises.

H. 168 *Invitation.*

1 The Lord on high proclaims
His Godhead from His throne;
"Mercy and justice are the names
By which I will be known.

2 "Ye dying souls, that sit
In darkness and distress,
Look from the borders of the pit
To My recovering grace."

3 Sinners shall hear the sound;
Their thankful tongues shall own,
"Our righteousness and strength is found
In Thee, the Lord, alone."

4 In Thee shall Israel trust,
And see their guilt forgiven;
God will pronounce the sinners just,
And take the saints to heaven.

H. 237 *Preserving Grace.*

1 To God the only wise,
Our Saviour and our King,
Let all the saints below the skies
Their humble praises bring.

2 'Tis His almighty love,
His counsel and His care,
Preserves us safe from sin and death,
And every hurtful snare.

3 He will present our souls,
Unblemished and complete,
Before the glory of His face,
With joys divinely great.

4 Then all the chosen seed
Shall meet around the throne;
Shall bless the conduct of His grace,
And make His wonders known.

5 To our Redeemer God,
Wisdom and power belongs,
Immortal crowns of majesty,
And everlasting songs.

THATCHER. S. M.

G. F. Handel, 1732.

1. The spi - rit, in our hearts, Is whis - p'ring, "Sin - ner, come;"

The bride, the church of Christ, pro - claims To all His chil-dren, "Come!"

H. 179 *The Gospel Call.*

1 The Spirit, in our hearts,
Is whispering, "Sinner, come;"
The bride, the church of Christ, pro-
To all His children, "Come!" [claims,

2 Let him that heareth say
To all about him, "Come;"
Let him that thirsts for righteousness,
To Christ, the Fountain, come!

3 Yes, whosoever will,
Oh! let him freely come,
And freely drink the stream of life;
'Tis Jesus bids him come.

4 Lo! Jesus, who invites,
Declares, "I quickly come;"
Lord, even so; we wait Thine hour;
O blest Redeemer, come!

H. 496 *Resurrection of Christ on the Sabbath.*

1 To-day the Saviour rose,
Our Jesus left the dead;
He conquered our malignant foes,
And Satan captive led.

2 He left His glorious throne,
To make our peace with God;
Blessings for ever on His name,
He bought us with His blood.

3 For us His life He paid,
For us the law fulfilled;
On Him our load of guilt was laid;
We by His stripes are healed.

4 Ye saints adore His name,
Who hath such mercy shown;
Ye sinners, love the bleeding Lamb,
And make His praises known.

H. 574 *Blessedness of the Gospel Ministry.*

1 How beauteous are their feet,
Who stand on Zion's hill,
Who bring salvation on their tongues,
And words of peace reveal!

2 How charming is their voice!
How sweet their tidings are!
"Zion, behold Thy Saviour King,
He reigns and triumphs here."

3 How happy are our ears
That hear this joyful sound,
Which kings and prophets waited for
And sought, but never found!

4 How blessed are our eyes,
That see this heavenly light!
Prophets and kings desired it long,
But died without the sight.

5 The watchmen join their voice,
And tuneful notes employ;
Jerusalem breaks forth in songs,
And deserts learn the joy.

6 The Lord makes bare His arm
Through all the earth abroad;
Let every nation now behold
Their Saviour, and their God.

JONATHAN C. WOODMAN, 1844.

1. I lift my soul to God, My trust is in His name;
Let not the foes that seek my blood Still tri-umph in my shame.

Ps. 25 *Second Part.*

1 I LIFT my soul to God,
My trust is in His name;
Let not the foes that seek my blood
Still triumph in my shame.

2 From the first dawning light
Till evening shades arise,
For Thy salvation, Lord, I wait,
With ever-longing eyes.

3 Remember all Thy grace,
And lead me in Thy truth;
Forgive the sins of riper days,
And follies of my youth.

4 The Lord is just and kind,
The meek shall learn His ways,
And every humble sinner find
The methods of His grace.

5 For His own goodness' sake
He saves my soul from shame;
He pardons, though my guilt be great,
Through my Redeemer's name.

Ps. 117 *Second Part.*

1 THY name, almighty Lord,
Shall sound through distant lands;
Great is Thy grace, and sure Thy word;
Thy truth for ever stands.

2 Far be Thine honour spread,
And long Thy praise endure,
Till morning light and evening shade
Shall be exchanged no more.

H. 415 *Brevity of the Conflict.*

1 A FEW more years shall roll
A few more seasons come,
And we shall be with those that rest,
Asleep within the tomb.

2 A few more struggles here,
A few more partings o'er,
A few more toils, a few more tears,
And we shall weep no more.

3 A few more storms shall beat
On this wild, rocky shore,
And we shall be where tempests cease,
And surges swell no more.

4 A few more Sabbaths here,
Shall cheer us on our way,
And we shall reach the endless rest,
Th' eternal Sabbath day.

5 'Tis but a little while,
And He shall come again,
Who died that we might live, who lives
That we with Him may reign.

6 Thou, O my Lord, prepare
My soul for that glad day;
Oh! wash me in Thy precious blood,
And take my sins away.

Doxology.

Give to the Father praise,
Give glory to the Son,
And to the Spirit of His grace,
Be equal honours done.

Karl Reden, 1866.

1. I was a wand'r- ing sheep, I did not love the fold; I did not love my
Shep-herd's voice, I would not be con - trolled; I was a way-ward child, I
did not love my home, I did not love my Fa-ther's voice, I loved a - far to roam.

H. 291 *The Wandering Sheep.*

1 I was a wandering sheep;
  I did not love the fold;
I did not love my Shepherd's voice,
  I would not be controlled;
I was a wayward child,
  I did not love my home,
I did not love my Father's voice,
  I loved afar to roam.

2 The Shepherd sought His sheep,
  The Father sought His child;
They followed me o'er vale and hill,
  O'er desert, waste, and wild:
They found me nigh to death,
  Famished, and faint, and lone;
They bound me with the bands of love,
  They saved the wandering one.

3 Jesus my Shepherd is;
  'Twas He that loved my soul,
'Twas He that washed me in His blood,
  'Twas He that made me whole;
'Twas He that sought the lost,
  That found the wandering sheep;
'Twas He that brought me to the fold;
  'Tis He that still doth keep.

4 No more a wandering sheep,
  I love to be controlled;
I love my tender Shepherd's voice,
  I love the peaceful fold:
No more a wayward child,
  I seek no more to roam;
I love my heavenly Father's voice;
  I love, I love His home.

Doxology.

1 We bless the Father's name,
  Who chose us in His love;
To God the Son we give the same,
  Our Advocate above.

2 The Spirit, too, we bless,
  And raise His honours high;
Who conquers by His sovereign grace,
  And brings us strangers nigh.

ENGLISH.

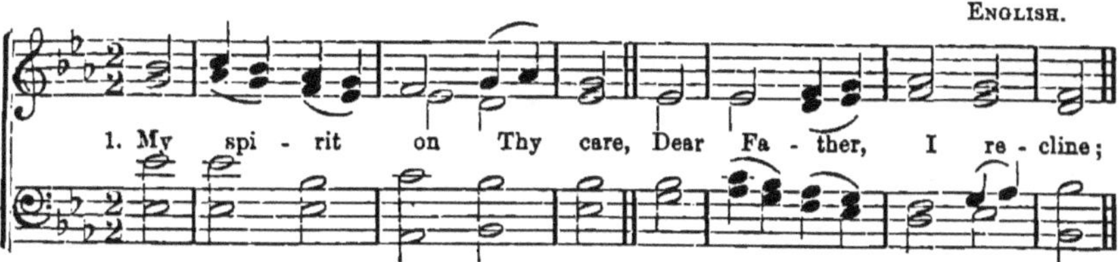
1. My spi - rit on Thy care, Dear Fa - ther, I re - cline;

Thou wilt not leave me to de - spair, For Thou art love di - vine.

Ps. 31

1 My spirit on Thy care,
  Dear Father, I recline;
Thou wilt not leave me to despair,
  For Thou art love divine.

2 In Thee I place my trust,
  On Thee I calmly rest;
I know Thee good, I know Thee just,
  And count Thy choice the best.

3 Whate'er events betide,
  Thy will they all perform;
Safe in Thy breast my head I hide,
  Nor fear the coming storm.

4 Let good or ill befall,
  It must be good for me;
Secure in having Thee in all,
  And having all in Thee.

Ps. 103 *Second Part.*

1 My soul, repeat His praise,
  Whose mercies are so great;
Whose anger is so slow to rise,
  So ready to abate.

2 God will not always chide;
  And when His strokes are felt,
His strokes are fewer than our crimes,
  And lighter than our guilt.

3 High as the heavens are raised
  Above the ground we tread,
So far the riches of His grace
  Our highest thoughts exceed.

4 His power subdues our sins;
  And His forgiving love,
Far as the east is from the west,
  Doth all our guilt remove.

H. 556 *Communion with Christ and with Saints.*

1 Jesus invites His saints
  To meet around His board;
Here pardoned rebels sit, and hold
  Communion with their Lord.

2 For food he gives His flesh;
  He bids us drink His blood;
Amazing favour, matchless grace
  Of our descending God.

3 This holy bread and wine
  Maintains our fainting breath,
By union with our living Lord,
  And interest in His death.

4 Our heavenly Father calls
  Christ and His members one:
We the young children of His love,
  And He the first-born Son.

5 We are but several parts
  Of the same broken bread;
One body hath its several limbs,
  But Jesus is the head.

6 Let all our powers be joined,
  His glorious name to raise;
Pleasure and love fill every mind,
  And every voice be praise.

DEPARTURE. S. H. M.

DR. HASTINGS, 1831.

1. Friend af-ter friend de-parts; Who has not lost a friend? There is no u-nion here of hearts,
That finds not here an end. Were this frail world our fi-nal rest, Liv-ing or dy-ing, none were blest.

H. 625 *Separations in Time.*

2 BEYOND the flight of time,
Beyond the reign of death,
There surely is some blessed clime
Where life is not a breath;
Nor life's affections, transient fire,
Whose sparks fly upward and expire.

3 There is a world above,
Where parting is unknown,
A long eternity of love,
Formed for the good alone;
And faith beholds the dying here,
Translated to that glorious sphere.

4 Thus star by star declines,
Till all are passed away,
As morning high and higher shines
To pure and perfect day;
Nor sink those stars in empty night,
But hide themselves in heav'n's own light.

DALSTON. S. P. M.

A. WILLIAMS, 1760.

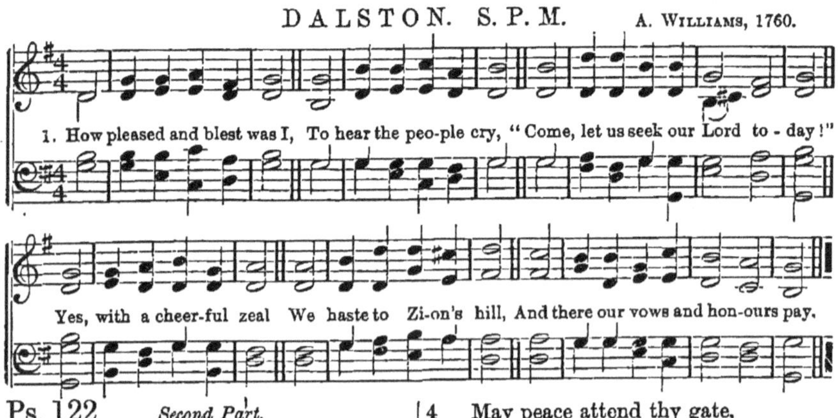
1. How pleased and blest was I, To hear the peo-ple cry, "Come, let us seek our Lord to-day!"
Yes, with a cheer-ful zeal We haste to Zi-on's hill, And there our vows and hon-ours pay.

Ps. 122 *Second Part.*

2 ZION, thrice happy place,
Adorned with wondrous grace,
And walls of strength embrace thee round:
In thee our tribes appear
To pray, and praise, and hear
The sacred gospel's joyful sound.

3 There David's greater Son
Has fixed His royal throne;
He sits for grace and judgment there:
He bids the saints be glad,
He makes the sinners sad,
And humble souls rejoice with fear.

4 May peace attend thy gate,
And joy within thee wait,
To bless the soul of every guest:
The man which seeks thy peace,
And wishes thine increase,
A thousand blessings on him rest!

5 My tongue repeats her vows;
Peace to this sacred house!
For here my friends and kindred dwell;
And since my glorious God
Makes thee His blest abode,
My soul shall ever love thee well.

DR. L. MASON, 1830.

1. Re - joice, the Lord is King; Your God and King a-dore; Mor-tals, give thanks and sing,

And tri-umph ev-er-more: Lift up the heart, lift up the voice, Re-joice a-loud, ye saints, rejoice.

H. 111 *Rejoicing in the Triumph of Christ.*

1 Rejoice, the Lord is King,
  Your God and King adore;
Mortals, give thanks and sing,
  And triumph evermore:
Lift up the heart, lift up the voice,
Rejoice aloud, ye saints, rejoice.

2 Rejoice, the Saviour reigns,
  The God of truth and love;
When He had purged our stains,
  He took His seat above:
Lift up the heart, lift up the voice,
Rejoice aloud, ye saints, rejoice.

3 His kingdom cannot fail,
  He rules o'er earth and heaven;
The keys of death and hell
  Are to our Jesus given;
Lift up the heart, lift up the voice,
Rejoice aloud, ye saints, rejoice.

4 He all His foes shall quell,
  Shall all our sins destroy;
And every bosom swell
  With pure seraphic joy:
Lift up the heart, lift up the voice,
Rejoice aloud, ye saints, rejoice.

5 Rejoice in glorious hope;
  Jesus the Judge shall come,
And take His servants up
  To their eternal home:
We soon shall hear the archangel's voice,
The trump of God shall sound, Rejoice.

H. 229 *God Reconciled.*

1 Arise, my soul, arise,
  Shake off thy guilty fears;
A bleeding sacrifice
  In my behalf appears:
Before the throne my Surety stands;
My name is written on His hands.

2 Five bleeding wounds He bears,
  Received on Calvary;
They pour effectual prayers,
  They strongly speak for me;
Forgive him, Oh! forgive, they cry,
Nor let that ransomed sinner die.

3 The Father hears Him pray,
  His dear Anointed One;
He cannot turn away
  The presence of His Son;
The Spirit answers to the blood,
And tells me I am born of God.

4 My God is reconciled,
  His pardoning voice I hear;
He owns me for a child,
  I can no longer fear;
With confidence I now draw nigh,
And Father, Abba Father, cry.

Doxology.

To God the Father's throne,
  Perpetual honours raise;
Glory to God the Son;
  To God the Spirit praise:
With all our powers, eternal King,
Thy name we sing, while faith adores.

LENOX. H. M.

J. Edson, 1782.

1. The Lord Je-ho-vah reigns, His throne is built on high; The gar-ments He as-sumes Are light and ma-jes-ty.
His glo-ries shine with beams so bright, No mor-tal eye can bear the sight—No mor-tal eye can bear the sight.

H. 1 *Divine Attributes.*

2 The thunders of His hand
Keep the wide world in awe;
His wrath and justice stand
To guard His holy law;
And where His love resolves to bless,
His truth confirms and seals the grace.

3 Through all His ancient works,
Surprising wisdom shines;
Confounds the powers of hell,
And breaks their cursed designs.
Strong is His arm, and shall fulfil
His great decrees, His sovereign will.

4 And can this mighty King
Of glory condescend,
And will He write His name,
My Father and my Friend?
I love His name, I love His word;
Join all my powers and praise the Lord.

H. 596 *The Gospel Jubilee.*

1 Blow ye the trumpet, blow;
The gladly solemn sound
Let all the nations know,
To earth's remotest bound;
The year of Jubilee is come;
Return, ye ransomed sinners, home.

2 Exalt the Son of God,
The sin-atoning Lamb;
Redemption in His blood
To all the world proclaim;
The year, etc.

3 Ye who have sold for nought
Your heritage above,
Come, take it back unbought,
The gift of Jesus' love:
The year, etc.

4 The gospel trumpet sounds,
Let all the nations hear,
And earth's remotest bounds
Before the throne appear;
The year, etc.

Ps. 148 *Third Part.*

1 The Lord of heav'n confess,
On high His glory raise.
Him let all angels bless;
Him all His armies praise.
Him glorify, sun, moon, and stars;
Ye higher spheres, and cloudy sky.

2 From God your beings are,
Him therefore famous make;
You all created were,
When He the word but spake.
And from that place where fix'd you be
By His decree, you cannot pass.

3 O let God's name be prais'd
Above both earth and sky:
For He His saints hath rais'd,
And set their horn on high;
Ev'n those that be of Israel's race,
Near to His grace, The Lord praise ye.

ARRANGED FROM THE GERMAN, BY DR. L. MASON, 1841.

1. Wel-come, de-light-ful morn, Thou day of sa-cred rest!
We hail thy kind re-turn; Lord, make these mo-ments blest.
From the low train of mor - tal toys,
We soar to reach im - mor - tal joys— We soar to reach im - mor-tal joys.

H. 499 *The Lord's Day Morning.*

2 Now may the King descend,
And fill His throne of grace;
Thy sceptre, Lord, extend,
While saints address Thy face;
Let sinners feel Thy quickening word,
And learn to know and fear the Lord.

3 Descend, celestial Dove,
With all Thy quickening powers;
Disclose a Saviour's love,
And bless these sacred hours;
Then shall our souls new life obtain,
Nor Sabbaths be bestowed in vain.

H. 365 *Invoking the Presence of Christ.*

1 COME, my Redeemer, come,
And deign to dwell with me;
Come, and Thy right assume,
And bid Thy rivals flee:
Come, my Redeemer, quickly come,
And make my heart Thy lasting home.

2 Exert Thy mighty power,
And banish all my sin;
In this auspicious hour,
Bring all Thy graces in:
Come, my Redeemer, quickly come,
And make my heart Thy lasting home.

3 Rule Thou in every thought
And passion of my soul,
Till all my powers are brought
Beneath Thy full control;
Come, my Redeemer, quickly come,
And make my heart Thy lasting home.

4 Then shall my days be Thine,
And all my heart be love,
And joy and peace be mine,
Such as are known above:
Come, my Redeemer, quickly come,
And make my heart Thy lasting home.

H. 500 *Captivity Captive.*

1 THE happy morn is come;
Triumphant o'er the grave,
The Saviour leaves the tomb,
Almighty now to save:
Captivity is captive led,
For Jesus liveth, who was dead.

2 Who now accuseth them
For whom the Surety died?
Or who shall those condemn
Whom God hath justified?
Captivity is captive led,
For Jesus liveth, who was dead.

3 The ransom Christ hath paid—
The glorious work is done;
On Him our help is laid,
By Him our victory won;
Captivity is captive led,
For Jesus liveth, who was dead.

4 All hail, triumphant Lord!
The resurrection, Thou!
All hail, incarnate Lord!
Before Thy throne we bow:
Captivity is captive led,
For Jesus liveth, who was dead.

Dr. Mason, 1832.

1. O Ho-ly, ho - ly Lord, Cre - a-tion's sov - 'reign King, Thy ma - jes - ty a - dored,
2. Great are Thy works of praise, O God of bound-less might! All just and true Thy ways,
Let all Thy crea-tures sing, Who wast, and art, and art to be, Nor time shall see Thy sway de-part.
Thou King of saints in light! Let all a-bove, and all be-low, Con-spire to show Thy pow'r and love.

H. 428 *Magnificat.*

3 Who shall not fear Thee, Lord,
  And magnify Thy name?
Thy judgments sent abroad
  Thy holiness proclaim:
Nations shall throng from every shore,
And Thee adore in holy song.

4 While all the powers on high
  Their swelling chorus raise,
We here on earth reply,
  And echo back Thy praise;
Thy glory own, first, last, and best,
God ever blest, and God alone!

H. 46 *Titles of Christ.*

1 Jesus, my great High-Priest,
  Offered His blood, and died;
My guilty conscience seeks
  No sacrifice beside.
His powerful blood did once atone,
And now it pleads before the throne.

2 To this dear Surety's hand
  Will I commit my cause;
He answers and fulfils
  His Father's broken laws.
Behold my soul at freedom set;
My Surety paid the dreadful debt.

3 My Advocate appears
  For my defence on high;
The Father bows His ears,
  And lays His thunder by.
Not all that hell or sin can say,
Shall turn His heart, His love away.

4 My great and glorious Lord,
  My Conquerer and my King,
Thy sceptre and Thy sword,
  Thy reigning grace I sing.
Thine is the power; behold, I sit
In willing bonds beneath Thy feet.

Ps. 121 *Second Part.*

1 Upward I lift mine eyes,
  From God is all mine aid;
The God that built the skies,
  And earth and nature made;
God is the tower to which I fly;
His grace is nigh in every hour.

2 My feet shall never slide,
  And fall in fatal snares,
Since God, my guard and guide,
  Defends me from my fears.
Those wakeful eyes that never sleep,
Shall Israel keep when dangers rise.

3 No burning heats by day,
  Nor blasts of evening air,
Shall take my health away,
  If God be with me there.
Thou art my sun, and Thou my shade,
To guard my head by night or noon.

4 Hast Thou not given Thy word
  To save my soul from death?
And I can trust my Lord
  To keep my mortal breath:
I'll go and come, nor fear to die,
Till from on high Thou call me home.

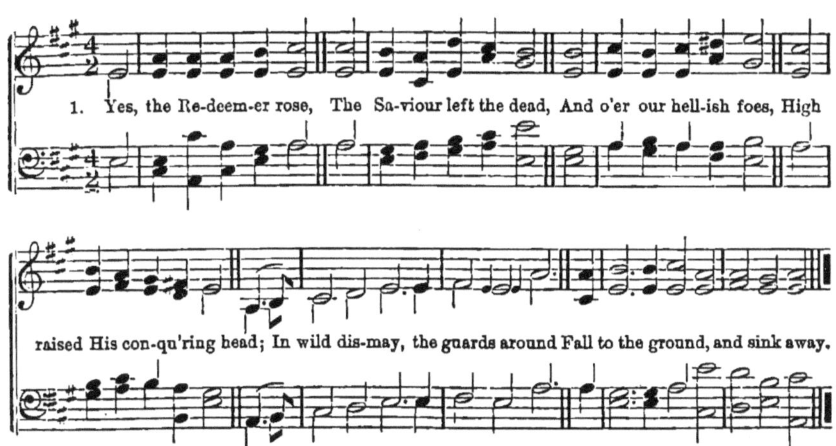
1. Yes, the Re-deem-er rose, The Sa-viour left the dead, And o'er our hell-ish foes, High
raised His con-qu'ring head; In wild dis-may, the guards around Fall to the ground, and sink away.

H. 90 *Resurrection of Christ.*

2 Lo! the angelic bands,
In full assembly meet,
To wait His high commands,
And worship at His feet;
Joyful they come, and wing their way,
From realms of day to Jesus' tomb.

3 Then back to heaven they fly,
The joyful news to bear;
Hark! as they soar on high,
What music fills the air!
Their anthems say, "Jesus, who bled,
Has left the dead; He rose to-day."

4 Ye mortals, catch the sound,
Redeemed by Him from hell;
And send the echo round
The globe on which you dwell;
Transported cry, "Jesus, who bled,
Hath left the dead, no more to die."

5 All hail, triumphant Lord,
Who savest us with Thy blood!
Wide be Thy name adored,
Thou rising, reigning God;
With Thee we rise, with Thee we reign,
And empires gain, beyond the skies.

Ps. 84 *Third Part.*

1 Lord of the worlds above,
How pleasant and how fair
The dwellings of Thy love,
Thine earthly temples are!
To Thine abode my heart aspires,
With warm desires, to see my God.

2 O happy souls that pray
Where God appoints to hear!
O happy men that pay
Their constant service there!
They praise Thee still, and happy they,
That love the way to Zion's hill.

3 They go from strength to strength,
Through this dark vale of tears,
Till each arrives at length,
Till each in heaven appears;
O glorious seat, when God our King
Shall thither bring our willing feet.

4 To spend one sacred day
Where God and saints abide,
Affords diviner joy
Than thousand days beside;
Where God resorts, I love it more
To keep the door, than shine in courts.

5 God is our sun and shield,
Our light and our defence;
With gifts His hands are filled;
We draw our blessings thence;
He shall bestow on Jacob's race
Peculiar grace and glory too.

6 The Lord His people loves;
His hand no good withholds
From those His heart approves,
From pure and pious souls.
Thrice happy he, O God of hosts,
Whose spirit trusts alone in Thee.

HADDAM. H. M.

FROM ENGLISH, BY DR. L. MASON, 1822.

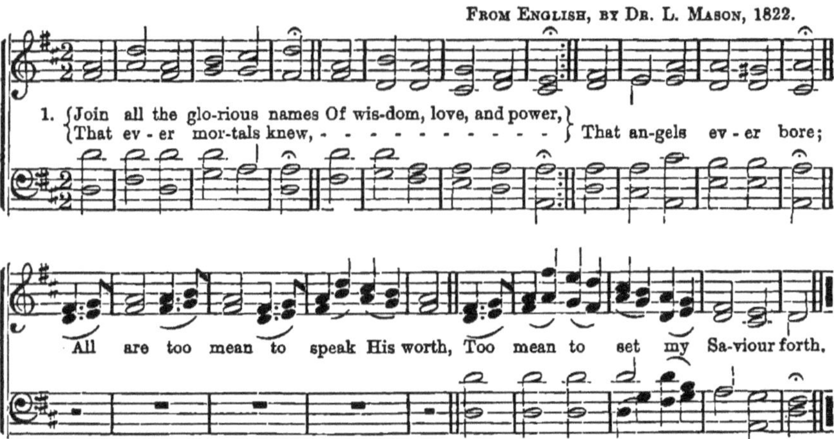
1. {Join all the glo-rious names Of wis-dom, love, and power,}
{That ev - er mor-tals knew, - - - - - - - - - - - -} That an-gels ev - er bore;
All are too mean to speak His worth, Too mean to set my Sa-viour forth.

H. 56 *Christ the Prophet and Shepherd.*

1 JOIN all the glorious names
Of wisdom, love, and power,
That ever mortals knew,
That ever angels bore:
All are too mean to speak His worth,
Too mean to set my Saviour forth.

2 But O! what gentle terms,
What condescending ways,
Doth our Redeemer use,
To teach His heavenly grace!
My eyes with joy and wonder see
What forms of love He bears for me.

3 Arrayed in mortal flesh,
He like an angel stands,
And holds the promises
And pardons in His hands;
Commissioned from His Father's throne,
To make His grace to mortals known.

4 Great Prophet of my God,
My tongue would bless Thy name;
By Thee the joyful news
Of our salvation came:
The joyful news of sins forgiven,
Of hell subdued, and peace with heaven.

5 Be Thou my Counsellor,
My Pattern and my Guide;
And through this desert land
Still keep me near Thy side;
Oh! let my feet ne'er run astray,
Nor rove, nor seek the crooked way.

6 I love my Shepherd's voice;
His watchful eyes shall keep
My wandering soul among
The thousands of His sheep:
He feeds His flock, He calls their names,
His bosom bears the tender lambs.

H. 586 *Rejoicing in a General Revival.*

1 O ZION, tune thy voice,
And lift thy hands on high;
Tell all the world thy joys,
And shout salvation nigh;
Cheerful in God, arise and shine,
While rays divine stream all abroad.

2 He gilds the mourning face
With beams that cannot fade;
His all-resplendent grace
He pours around thy head;
The nations round thy form shall view,
With lustre new divinely crowned.

3 In honour to His name,
Reflect that sacred light,
And loud that grace proclaim
Which makes thy darkness bright;
Pursue His praise, till sovereign love
In worlds above thy glory raise.

4 There on His holy hill
A brighter Sun shall rise,
And with His radiance fill
Those fairer, purer skies;
While round His throne ten thousand stars,
In nobler spheres His influence own.

1. Ye tribes of Adam, join With heav'n, and earth, and seas, And offer notes divine To your Creator's praise. Ye holy
Ye holy throng Of angels bright, In worlds of light Be - gin the song.
throng Of angels bright, In worlds of light, Be - gin the song.

Ps. 148 *First Part.*

1 Ye tribes of Adam, join,
With heaven, and earth, and seas,
And offer notes divine
To your Creator's praise.
Ye holy throng of angels bright,
In worlds of light, begin the song.

2 Thou sun with dazzling rays,
And moon that rules the night,
Shine to your Maker's praise,
With stars of twinkling light.
His power declare, ye floods on high,
And clouds that fly in empty air.

3 The shining worlds above
In glorious order stand,
Or in swift courses move,
By His supreme command.
He spake the word, and all their frame
From nothing came, to praise the Lord.

4 He moved their mighty wheels
In unknown ages past,
And each His word fulfils,
While time and nature lasts.
In different ways His works proclaim
His wondrous name, and speak His praise.

H. 44 *Condescension and Love of Christ.*

1 Come, every pious heart,
That loves the Saviour's name,
Your noblest powers exert,
To celebrate His fame:
Tell all above, and all below,
The debt of love to Him you owe.

2 Such was His zeal for God,
And such His love for you,
He freely undertook
What angels could not do:
His mighty deeds of love and grace,
All words exceed, and thoughts surpass.

3 He left His starry crown,
And laid His robes aside;
On wings of love came down,
And wept, and bled, and died;
What He endured, O! who can tell,
To save our souls from death and hell!

4 From the dark grave He rose,
The mansions of the dead;
And thence His mighty foes,
In glorious triumph led;
Up through the sky the Conqueror rode,
And reigns on high, the Saviour God.

5 Jesus, we ne'er can pay
The debt we owe Thy love,
Yet tell us how we may
Our gratitude approve;
Our hearts, our all, to Thee we give;
The gift, though small, Thou wilt receive.

Doxology.

To God the Father's throne,
Perpetual honours raise;
Glory to God the Son;
To God the Spirit praise:
With all our powers, eternal King,
Thy name we sing, while faith adores.

AUBURN. 7s.

MOZART.

1. Swell the an - them, raise the song; Prais - es to our God be - long;
Saints and an - gels join to sing Praise to heav'n's al - might - ty King.

H. 504 *Praise for National Blessings.*

2 Blessings from His liberal hand
Pour around this happy land;
Let our hearts, beneath His sway,
Hail the bright triumphant day.

3 Now to Thee our joys ascend,
Thou hast been our heavenly Friend;
Guarded by Thy mighty power,
Peace and freedom bless our shore.

4 Here, beneath a virtuous sway,
May we cheerfully obey;
Never feel a tyrant's rod,
Ever own and worship God.

5 Hark! the voice of nature sings
Praises to the King of kings;
Let us join the choral song,
And the heavenly notes prolong.

HOLLEY. 7s.

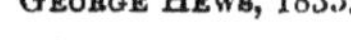

GEORGE HEWS, 1835.

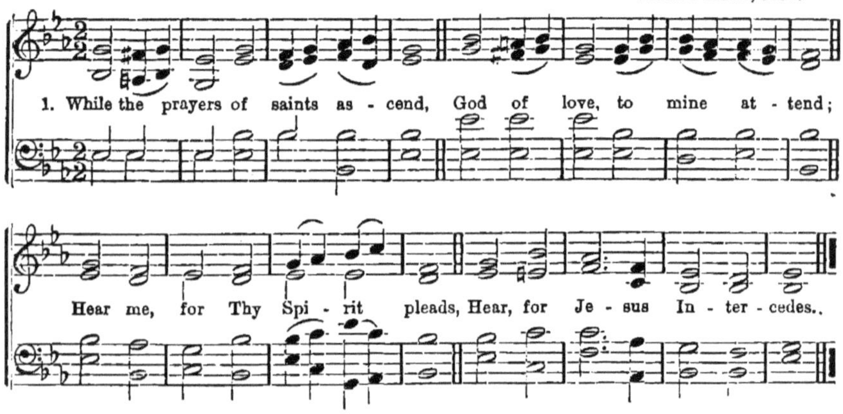
1. While the prayers of saints as - cend, God of love, to mine at - tend;
Hear me, for Thy Spi - rit pleads, Hear, for Je - sus In - ter - cedes.

H. 482 *Prayer for Divine Influence.*

2 While I hearken to Thy law,
Fill my soul with humble awe,
Till Thy gospel bring to me
Life and immortality.

3 From Thine house when I return,
May my heart within me burn,
And at evening let me say,
"I have walked with God to-day."

KARL REDEN. 1866.

1. Lord, we come be - fore Thee now, At Thy feet we hum - bly bow;
Oh! do not our suit dis - dain; Shall we seek Thee, Lord, in vain?

H. 477 *Before Sermon.*

1 LORD, we come before Thee now,
At Thy feet we humbly bow;
Oh! do not our suit disdain;
Shall we seek Thee, Lord, in vain?

2 Lord, on Thee our souls depend;
In compassion now descend;
Fill our hearts with Thy rich grace;
Tune our lips to sing Thy praise.

3 In Thine own appointed way,
Now we seek Thee, here we stay;
Lord, we know not how to go,
Till a blessing Thou bestow.

4 Send some message from Thy word,
That may joy and peace afford;
Let Thy Spirit now impart
Full salvation to each heart.

5 Comfort those who weep and mourn,
Let the time of joy return;
Those who are cast down lift up,
Make them strong in faith and hope.

6 Grant that all may seek and find
Thee a God supremely kind;
Heal the sick, the captive free;
Let us all rejoice in Thee.

H. 429 *God's Name Hallowed.*

1 HOLY, holy, holy, Lord,
In the highest heavens adored,
Author of all nature's frame,
Father! hallowed be Thy name.

2 Though estranged from Thee in heart,
Doubtless Thou our Father art;
From Thy hand our spirits came;
Father! hallowed be Thy name.

3 Nor by nature's tie alone
Thou art as our Father known;
Nearer now in Christ our claim,
Father! hallowed be Thy name.

4 Born anew, O may we feel
Filial love, the Spirit's seal,
Cleansed from guilt, redeemed from shame;
Father! hallowed be Thy name.

H. 431 *Praise in Affliction.*

1 LORD, should rising whirlwinds tear
From its stem the ripened ear;
Should the fig tree's blasted shoot
Drop her green untimely fruit:

2 Should the vine put forth no more,
Nor the olive yield her store;
Though the sickening flocks should fall,
And the herds desert the stall:

3 Should Thy chastening hand restrain
The early and the latter rain;
Blast each opening bud of joy,
And the rising year destroy:

4 Yet to Thee my soul should raise
Grateful vows and solemn praise;
And, when every blessing's flown,
Love Thee for Thyself alone.

I. Pleyel, 1757-1831.

1. Depth of mer - cy, can there be Mer - cy still re - served for me?
Canst Thou still Thy wrath for - bear, And the chief of sin - ners spare?

H. 211 *Cry for Penitence.*

2 We have long withstood Thy grace,
Long provoked Thee to Thy face,
Would not hear Thy gracious calls,
Grieved Thee by a thousand falls.

3 Jesus, answer from above,
Is not all Thy nature love?
Wilt Thou not our crimes forget?
Lo, we fall before Thy feet.

4 Lord, incline us to repent,
Help us now our fall lament,
Deeply our revolt deplore,
Weep, believe, and sin no more.

5 Lo! we come to Thee for peace,
True and gracious as Thou art;
Now our weary souls release,
Write forgiveness on our heart.

H. 219 *The Weary Come to Christ.*

1 Come, ye weary sinners, come,
All who feel your heavy load;
Jesus calls the wanderers home;
Hasten to your pardoning God.

2 Jesus, full of truth and love,
We Thy kindest call obey;
Faithful let Thy mercies prove,
Take our load of guilt away.

3 Weary of this war within,
Weary of the endless strife,
Weary of ourselves and sin,
Weary of a wretched life.

4 Burdened with a world of grief,
Burdened with our sinful load,
Burdened with this unbelief,
Burdened with the wrath of God.

H. 357 *Jesus the One Thing Needful.*

1 Jesus, let me cleave to Thee,
Thou my one thing needful be;
Let me choose the better part,
Let me give Thee all my heart.

2 Whom have I on earth below?
Thee, and only Thee I know;
Whom have I in heav'n but Thee?
Thou art all in all to me.

H. 258 *Peace in Jesus.*

1 Prince of Peace, control my will,
Bid this struggling heart be still;
Bid my fears and doubtings cease,
Hush my spirit into peace.

2 Thou hast bought me with Thy blood,
Opened wide the gate to God;
Peace I ask—but peace must be,
Lord, in being one with Thee.

3 May Thy will, not mine, be done,
May Thy will and mine be one;
Chase these doubtings from my heart,
Now Thy perfect peace impart.

4 Saviour, at Thy feet I fall,
Thou my life, my God, my all!
Let Thy happy servant be
One for evermore with Thee.

Rev. Cæsar Malan, 1830.

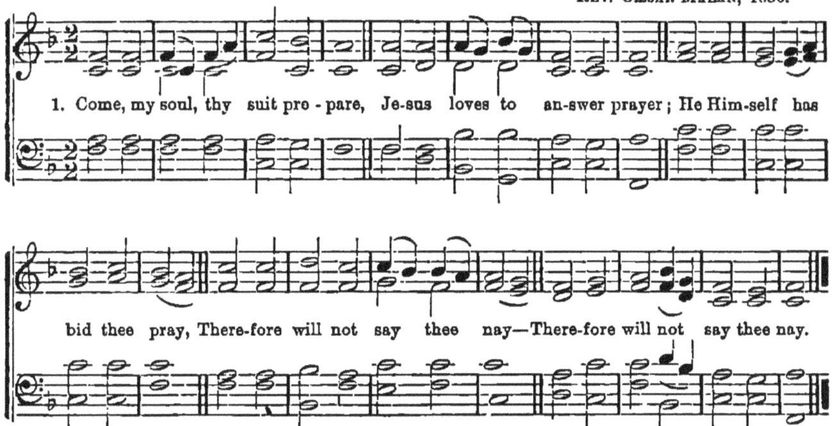
1. Come, my soul, thy suit pre - pare, Je-sus loves to an-swer prayer; He Him-self has
bid thee pray, There-fore will not say thee nay—There-fore will not say thee nay.

H. 375 *Encouragement to Prayer.*

2 Thou art coming to a King,
Large petitions with Thee bring;
For His grace and power are such,
None can ever ask too much.

3 With my burden I begin,
Lord, remove this load of sin;
Let Thy blood, for sinners spilt,
Set my conscience free from guilt.

4 Lord, I come to Thee for rest,
Take possession of my breast;
There Thy blood-bought right maintain,
And without a rival reign.

5 While I am a pilgrim here,
Let Thy love my spirit cheer;
As my Guide, my Guard, my Friend,
Lead me to my journey's end.

6 Show me what I have to do,
Every hour my strength renew;
Let me live a life of faith,
Let me die Thy people's death.

H. 389 *An Anxious Inquiry.*

1 'Tis a point I long to know,
Oft it causes anxious thought:
Do I love the Lord, or no?
Am I His, or am I not?

2 If I love, why am I thus?
Why this dull and lifeless frame?
Hardly, sure, can they be worse,
Who have never heard His name.

3 Could my heart so hard remain,
Prayer a task and burden prove,
Every trifle give me pain,
If I knew a Saviour's love?

4 When I turn my eyes within,
All is dark, and vain, and wild;
Filled with unbelief and sin,
Can I deem myself a child?

5 If I pray, or hear, or read,
Sin is mixed with all I do;
You who love the Lord indeed,
Tell me, is it thus with you?

6 Yet I mourn my stubborn will,
Find my sin a grief and thrall;
Should I grieve for what I feel,
If I did not love at all?

7 Could I joy His saints to meet,
Choose the ways I once abhorred,
Find at times the promise sweet,
If I did not love the Lord?

8 Lord, decide the doubtful case,
Thou who art Thy people's Sun:
Shine upon Thy work of grace,
If it be indeed begun.

9 Let me love Thee more and more,
If I love at all, I pray;
If I have not loved before,
Help me to begin to-day.

WILMOT. 7s.

C. M. Von Weber, 1786–1826.

1. Lo! the stone is rolled a - way, Death yields up his might - y prey;
Je - sus, ris - ing from the tomb, Scat - ters all its fear - ful gloom.

H. 95 *Praise to the risen Saviour.*

2 Praise Him, ye celestial choirs,
Praise, and sweep your golden lyres;
Praise him in the noblest songs,
From ten thousand thousand tongues.

3 Every note with rapture swell,
And the Saviour's triumph tell;
Where, O death, is now thy sting?
Where thy terrors, vanquished king?

4 Let Immanuel be adored,
Ransom, Mediator, Lord,
To creation's utmost bound,
Let the eternal praise resound.

H. 141 *Invocation to the Holy Ghost.*

1 Holy Ghost, with light divine,
Shine upon this heart of mine;
Chase the shades of night away,
Turn the darkness into day.

2 Holy Ghost, with power divine,
Cleanse this guilty heart of mine;
Long has sin, without control,
Held dominion o'er my soul.

3 Holy Ghost, with joy divine,
Cheer this saddened heart of mine;
Bid my many woes depart,
Heal my wounded, bleeding heart.

4 Holy Spirit, all divine,
Dwell within this heart of mine;
Cast down every idol throne,
Reign supreme, and reign alone.

H. 370 *Wrestling in Prayer.*

1 Lord, I cannot let Thee go,
Till a blessing Thou bestow;
Do not turn away Thy face,
Mine's an urgent, pressing case.

2 Dost Thou ask me who I am?
Ah! my Lord, Thou knowest my name,
Yet the question gives a plea,
To support my suit with Thee.

3 Thou didst once a wretch behold,
In rebellion blindly bold,
Scorn Thy grace, Thy power defy;
That poor rebel, Lord, was I.

4 Once, a sinner near despair
Sought Thy mercy-seat by prayer;
Mercy heard, and set him free;
Lord, that mercy came to me.

5 Many days have passed since then,
Many changes I have seen;
Yet have been upheld till now;
Who could hold me up but Thou?

6 Thou hast helped in every need;
This emboldens me to plead;
After so much mercy past,
Canst Thou let me sink at last?

7 No! I must maintain my hold;
'Tis Thy goodness makes me bold;
I can nc denial take,
When I plead for Jesus' sake.

REV. CÆSAR MALAN, 1830.

1. God with us! O glo-rious name! Let it shine in end-less fame;
God and man in Christ u-nite; O mys-te-rious depth and height!

H. 37 *Incarnation of the Son of God.*

2 God with us! the eternal Son
Took our soul, our flesh and bone;
Now, ye saints, His grace admire,
Swell the song with holy fire.

3 God with us! but tainted not
With the first transgressor's blot;
Yet did He our sins sustain,
Bear the guilt, the curse, the pain.

4 God with us! O wondrous grace!
Let us see Him face to face,
That we may Immanuel sing,
As we ought, our God and King.

H. 91 *Resurrection and Ascension of Christ.*

1 Hark! the herald angels say,
Christ the Lord is risen to-day;
Raise your joys and triumphs high,
Let the glorious tidings fly.

2 Love's redeeming work is done,
Fought the fight, the battle won;
Lo! the sun's eclipse is o'er,
Lo! he sets in blood no more.

3 Vain the stone, the watch, the seal;
Christ has burst the gates of hell:
Death in vain forbids Him rise,
Christ has opened paradise.

4 Lives again our glorious King;
Where, O death, is now thy sting?
Once He died our souls to save;
Where's thy victory, boasting grave?

5 What though once we perished all,
Partners of our parents' fall?
Second life we now receive,
And in Christ for ever live.

6 Hail! Thou dear almighty Lord,
Hail! Thou great incarnate Word,
Hail! Thou suffering Son of God,
Take the trophies of Thy blood.

H. 154 *The Gospel's Welcome.*

1 Now begin the heavenly theme,
Sing aloud in Jesus' name;
Ye who His salvation prove,
Triumph in redeeming love.

2 Ye who see the Father's grace
Beaming in the Saviour's face,
As to Canaan on ye move,
Praise and bless redeeming love.

3 Mourning souls, dry up your tears;
Banish all your guilty fears;
See your guilt and curse remove,
Cancelled by redeeming love.

4 Ye, alas! who long have been
Willing slaves to death and sin,
Now from bliss no longer rove,
Stop and taste redeeming love.

5 Welcome, all by sin oppressed,
Welcome to His sacred rest;
Nothing brought Him from above,
Nothing but redeeming love.

6 When His Spirit leads us home,
When we to His glory come,
We shall all the fulness prove
Of our Lord's redeeming love.

Von Wartensee, 1786.

1. Gent-ly, gent-ly, lay Thy rod On my sin-ful head, O God!
Stay Thy wrath, in mer-cy stay, Lest I sink be-neath its sway.

Ps. 6

1 Gently, gently lay Thy rod
On my sinful head, O God!
Stay Thy wrath, in mercy stay,
Lest I sink beneath its sway.

2 Heal me, for my flesh is weak;
Heal me, for Thy grace I seek;
This my only plea I make,—
Heal me for Thy mercy's sake.

3 Who, within the silent grave,
Shall proclaim Thy power to save?
Lord! my sinking soul reprieve;
Speak, and I shall rise and live.

4 Lo! He comes,—He heeds my plea;
Lo! He comes,—the shadows flee;
Glory round me dawns once more;
Rise, my spirit, and adore.

Ps. 15 *Second Part.*

1 Who, O Lord, when life is o'er,
Shall to heavenly mansions soar?
Who, an ever-welcome guest,
In Thy holy place shall rest?

2 He whose heart Thy love has warmed,
He whose will to Thine conformed,
Bids His life unsullied run;
He whose words and thoughts are one.

3 He who shuns the sinner's road,
Loving those who love their God;
Who, with hope and faith unfeigned,
Treads the path by Thee ordained.

4 He who trusts in Christ alone,
Not in aught himself hath done;
He, great God, shall be Thy care.
And Thy choicest blessings share.

H. 34 *The Trinity.*

1 Holy Father, hear our cry,
Holy Saviour, bend Thine ear,
Holy Spirit, come Thou nigh;
Father, Saviour, Spirit, hear.

2 Father, save us from our sin,
Saviour, we Thy mercy crave.
Gracious Spirit, make us clean;
Father, Son, and Spirit, save.

3 Father, let us taste Thy love,
Saviour, fill our souls with peace,
Spirit, come our hearts to move;
Father, Son, and Spirit, bless.

4 Father, Son, and Spirit, Thou
One Jehovah, shed abroad
All Thy grace within us now:
Be our Father and our God.

H. 183 *"Strive to enter in."*

1 Pilgrim, burdened with thy sin,
Haste to Zion's gate to-day;
There, till mercy let thee in,
Knock, and weep, and watch, and pray.

2 Knock, for mercy lends an ear;
Weep, she marks the sinner's sigh;
Watch, till heavenly light appear;
Pray, she hears the mourner's cry.

3 Mourning pilgrim, what for thee
In this world can now remain?
Seek that world from which shall flee
Sorrow, shame, and tears, and pain.

4 Sorrow shall for ever fly;
Shame shall never enter there;
Tears be wiped from every eye;
Pain in endless bliss expire.

Dr. L. Mason, 1825.

1. Hark! my soul, it is the Lord; 'Tis thy Sa-viour, hear His word;

Je - sus speaks, and speaks to thee: "Say, poor sin - ner, lov'st thou Me?"

H. 42 *Constancy of Christ's Love.*

2 "I delivered thee when bound,
And when wounded, healed thy wound;
Sought thee wandering, set thee right,
Turned thy darkness into light.

3 "Can a woman's tender care
Cease toward the child she bare?
Yes, she may forgetful be,
Yet will I remember thee.

4 "Mine is an unchanging love,
Higher than the heights above;
Deeper than the depths beneath,
Free and faithful, strong as death.

5 "Thou shalt see My glory soon,
When the work of grace is done;
Partner of My throne shalt be;
Say, poor sinner, lovest thou Me?"

6 Lord, it is my chief complaint,
That my love is weak and faint:
Yet I love Thee and adore,
O for grace to love Thee more

H. 185 *Sinners Admonished.*

1 Sinner, art thou still secure?
Wilt thou still refuse to pray?
Can thy heart or hand endure,
In the Lord's avenging day?

2 See, His mighty arm is bared,
Awful terrors clothe His brow;
For His judgments stand prepared;
Thou must either break or bow.

3 At His presence nature shakes,
Earth, affrighted, hastes to flee;
Solid mountains melt like wax,
What will then become of thee?

4 Who His coming may abide?
You that glory in your shame,
Will you find a place to hide,
When the world is wrapped in flame?

5 Lord, prepare us by Thy grace;
Soon we must resign our breath,
And our souls be called to pass
Through the iron gate of death.

H. 214 *Cry of Faith.*

1 Jesus, save my dying soul,
Make the broken spirit whole;
Humble in the dust I lie,—
Saviour, leave me not to die.

2 Jesus, full of every grace,
Now reveal Thy smiling face;
Grant the joys of sin forgiven,
Foretaste of the bliss of heaven.

3 All my guilt to Thee is known,
Thou art righteous, Thou alone;
All my help is from Thy cross,
All beside I count but loss.

4 Lord, in Thee I now believe,
Wilt Thou, wilt Thou not forgive?
Helpless at Thy feet I lie,
Saviour, leave me not to die.

Luigi Cherubini, 1760–1842.

1. Now the shades of night are gone; Now the morn - ing light is come;
Lord, may we be Thine to - day, Drive the shades of sin a - way.

H. 455 *Morning Hymn.*

2 Fill our souls with heavenly light,
Banish doubt, and clear our sight;
In thy service, Lord, to-day,
May we labour, watch, and pray.

3 Keep our haughty passions bound·
Save us from our foes around;
Going out and coming in,
Keep us safe from every sin.

4 When our work of life is past,
Oh! receive us then at last;
Night and sin will be no more,
When we reach the heavenly shore.

H. 464 *Delights of Public Worship.*

1 Lord of hosts, how lovely fair,
E'en on earth Thy temples are;
Here Thy waiting people see
Much of heaven, and much of Thee.

2 From Thy gracious presence flows
Bliss that softens all our woes;
While Thy Spirit's holy fire
Warms our hearts with pure desire.

3 Here we supplicate Thy throne,
Here Thou mak'st Thy glories known,
Here we learn Thy righteous ways,
Taste Thy love and sing Thy praise.

4 Thus with sacred songs of joy,
We our happy lives employ;
Love, and long to love Thee more,
Till from earth to heaven we soar.

H. 488 *Benediction.*

1 Now may He who from the dead
Brought the Shepherd of the sheep,
Jesus Christ, our King and Head,
All our souls in safety keep.

2 May He teach us to fulfil,
What is pleasing in His sight;
Make us perfect in His will,
And preserve us day and night.

3 To that great Redeemer's praise,
Who the covenant sealed with blood,
Let our hearts and voices raise,
Loud thanksgiving to our God.

H. 498 *Sabbath Evening.*

1 Softly fades the twilight ray
Of the holy Sabbath day;
Gently as life's setting sun,
When the Christian's course is run.

2 Peace is on the world abroad;
'Tis the holy peace of God;
Symbol of the peace within,
When the spirit rests from sin.

3 Still the Spirit lingers near,
Where the evening worshipper
Seeks communion with the skies,
Pressing onward to the prize.

4 Saviour, may our Sabbaths be
Days of peace and joy in Thee!
Till in heaven our souls repose,
Where the Sabbath ne'er shall close

T. B. Mason, 1836.

1. Gra - cious Spi - rit, love di - vine, Let Thy light with - in me shine;
All my guil - ty fears re - move, Fill me full of heav'n and love.

H. 139 *Prayer to the Spirit.*

1 Gracious Spirit, love divine,
Let Thy light within me shine;
All my guilty fears remove,
Fill me full of heaven and love.

2 Speak Thy pardoning grace to me,
Set the burdened sinner free;
Lead me to the Lamb of God,
Wash me in His precious blood.

3 Life and peace to me impart,
Seal salvation on my heart;
Breathe Thyself into my breast,
Earnest of immortal rest.

4 Let me never from Thee stray,
Keep me in the narrow way;
Fill my soul with joy divine,
Keep me, Lord, for ever Thine.

H. 453 *Evening Hymn.*

1 Softly now the light of day
Fades upon my sight away;
Free from care, from labour free,
Lord, I would commune with Thee.

2 Thou, whose all-pervading eye
Nought escapes without, within,
Pardon each infirmity,
Open fault, and secret sin.

3 Soon, for me, the light of day
Shall for ever pass away;
Then, from sin and sorrow free,
Take me, Lord, to dwell with Thee.

4 Thou who, sinless, yet hast known
All of man's infirmity;
Then, from Thine eternal throne,
Jesus, look with pitying eye.

H. 458 *Invocation.*

1 Father, let Thy smiling face,
Here within this holy place,
Sweetly shining on my heart,
Bid all sinful thoughts depart.

2 Jesus, Thou whose ceaseless love
Intercedes for us above,
Bend to me Thy listening ear,
Make my wayward heart sincere.

3 Comforter of all the saints,
Gently heal my soul's complaints;
May a foretaste now be given
Of the Sabbath day of heaven.

H. 554 *Sacramental Meditation.*

1 Jesus, Master, hear me now,
While I would renew my vow,
And record Thy dying love,
Hear, and help me from above.

2 Feed me, Saviour, with this bread,
Broken in Thy body's stead;
Cheer my spirit with this wine,
Streaming like that blood of Thine.

3 And as now I eat and drink,
Let me truly, sweetly think,
Thou didst hang upon the tree,
Broken, bleeding, there—for me.

J. Rahle, 1673.

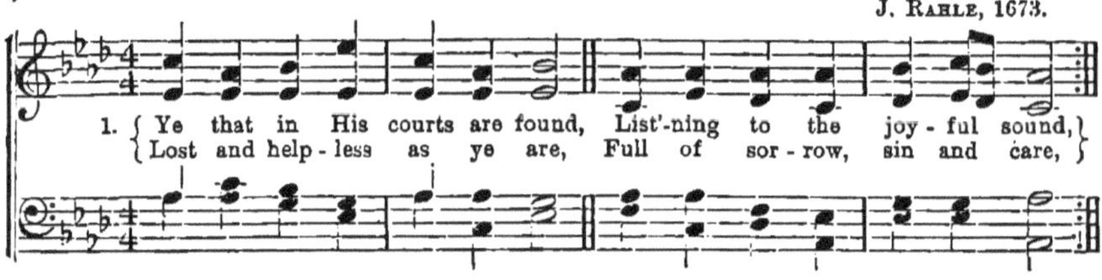
1. { Ye that in His courts are found, List'-ning to the joy - ful sound,
{ Lost and help - less as ye are, Full of sor - row, sin and care,

Glo - ri - fy the King of kings, Take the peace the gos - pel brings.

H. 167 *Sinners Exhorted.*

1 Ye that in His courts are found,
Listening to the joyful sound,
Lost and helpless as ye are,
Full of sorrow, sin and care,
Glorify the King of kings,
Take the peace the gospel brings.

2 Turn to Christ your longing eyes,
View His bleeding sacrifice;
See in Him your sins forgiven,
Pardon, holiness, and heaven;
Glorify the King of kings,
Take the peace the gospel brings.

H. 444 *Evening Hymn.*

1 Now from labour and from care,
Evening shades have set me free;
In the work of praise and prayer,
Lord I would converse with Thee;
Oh! behold me from above,
Fill me with a Saviour's love.

2 Sin and sorrow, guilt and woe,
Wither all my earthly joys;
Naught can charm me here below,
But my Saviour's loving voice:
Lord, forgive; Thy grace restore;
Make me Thine for evermore.

3 For the blessings of this day,
For the mercies of this hour,
For the gospel's cheering ray,
For the Spirit's quickening power,
Grateful notes to Thee I raise,
Oh! accept my song of praise.

H. 76 *Christ our Example in Suffering.*

1 Go to dark Gethsemane,
Ye who feel the tempter's power;
Your Redeemer's conflict see;
Watch with Him one bitter hour;
Turn not from His griefs away,
Learn of Jesus Christ to pray.

2 Follow to the judgment-hall,
View the Lord of life arraigned;
Oh! the wormwood and the gall!
Oh! the pangs His soul sustained!
Shun not suffering, shame, or loss;
Learn of Him to bear the cross.

3 Calvary's mournful mountain climb:
There, adoring at His feet,
Mark that miracle of time,
God's own sacrifice complete:
"It is finished!" hear Him cry;
Learn of Jesus Christ to die.

4 Early hasten to the tomb,
Where they laid His breathless clay;
All is solitude and gloom!
Who hath taken Him away?
Christ has risen! He meets our eyes;
Saviour, teach us so to rise.

H. 457 *Invocation.*

Great Jehovah!—Father, Son,
Holy Spirit—Three in one,
Let the blessing come from Thee,
Thine shall all the glory be!
Let the blessing come from Thee,
Thine shall all the glory be!

Dr. Thos. Hastings, 1830.

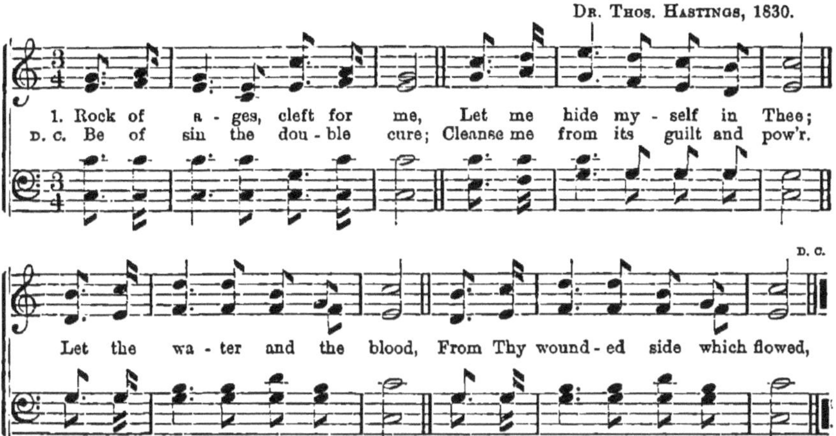
1. Rock of a - ges, cleft for me, Let me hide my - self in Thee;
D. C. Be of sin the dou - ble cure; Cleanse me from its guilt and pow'r.
Let the wa - ter and the blood, From Thy wound - ed side which flowed,
D. C.

H. 47 *Christ the Rock of Ages.*

2 Not the labour of my hands
Can fulfil the law's demands ;
Could my zeal no respite know,
Could my tears for ever flow,
All for sin could not atone,
Thou must save, and Thou alone.

3 Nothing in my hand I bring,
Simply to Thy cross I cling;
Naked, come to Thee for dress ;
Helpless, look to Thee for grace ;
Vile, I to the fountain fly,
Wash me, Saviour, or I die.

4 While I draw this fleeting breath,
When my heart-strings break in death,
When I soar to worlds unknown,
See Thee on Thy judgment-throne,
Rock of ages, cleft for me,
Let me hide myself in Thee.

H. 190 *Expostulation:*

1 Hearts of stone, relent, relent,
Break, by Jesus' cross subdued ;
See His body, mangled, rent,
Covered with His flowing blood !
Sinful soul, what hast thou done ?
Crucified the incarnate Son !

2 Yes, our sins have done the deed,
Driven the nails that fixed Him there ;
Crowned with thorns His sacred head,
Pierced Him with a soldier's spear ;
Made His soul a sacrifice :
For a sinful world He dies.

3 Will you let Him die in vain,
Still to death pursue the Lord ;
Open tear His wounds again,
Trample on His precious blood ?
No ! with all my sins I'll part :
Saviour, take my broken heart.

H. 257 *The Lamb of God.*

1 Jesus, Lamb of God, for me,
Thou, the Lord of life, didst die ;
Whither, whither, but to Thee,
Can a trembling sinner fly ?
Death's dark waters o'er me roll,
Save, O save my sinking soul !

2 Never bowed a martyred head,
Weighed with equal sorrow down ;
Never blood so rich was shed,
Never king wore such a crown !
To Thy cross and sacrifice
Faith now lifts her tearful eyes.

3 All my soul, by love subdued,
Melts in deep contrition there ;
By Thy mighty grace renewed,
New-born hope forbids despair ;
Lord, Thou canst my guilt forgive,
Thou hast bid me look and live.

4 While with broken heart I kneel,
Sinks the inward storm to rest ;
Life—immortal life !—I feel
Kindling in my throbbing breast ;
Thine, for ever Thine I am,
Glory to the bleeding Lamb !

Dr. L. Mason, 1840.

Fine.
1. { From the cross up - lift - ed high, Where the Sa - viour deigns to die, }
{ What me - lo - dious sounds I hear, Burst - ing on my rav - ished ear! }
D. C. Love's re - deem - ing work is done, Come and wel - come, sin - ner, come.
D. C.
Love's re-deem—
Come, and wel—
Love's re - deem - - - ing work is done, Come, and wel - - come, sin-ner, come.

H. 545 *Come, and Welcome.*

2 Sprinkled now with blood the throne,
Why beneath thy burdens groan?
On My pierced body laid,
Justice owns the ransom paid;
Bow the knee and kiss the Son,
Come, and welcome, sinner, come.
Bow the knee and kiss the Son,
Come, and welcome, sinner, come.

3 Spread for thee the festal board,
See with richest dainties stored;
To thy Father's bosom pressed,
Yet again a child confessed,
Never from His house to roam,
Come, and welcome, sinner, come.
Never from His house to roam,
Come, and welcome, sinner, come.

4 Soon the days of life shall end,
Lo! I come, your Saviour, Friend!
Safe your spirits to convey
To the realms of endless day:
Up to My eternal home,
Come, and welcome, sinner, come.
Up to My eternal home,
Come, and welcome, sinner, come.

H. 420 *Perseverance.*

1 Children of the heavenly King,
As ye journey, sweetly sing:
Sing your Saviour's worthy praise,
Glorious in His works and ways.

2 Ye are travelling home to God,
In the way the fathers trod;
They are happy now, and ye
Soon their happiness shall see.

3 O! ye mourning souls, be glad;
Christ our Advocate is made;
Us to save, our flesh assumes,
Brother to our soul becomes.

4 Shout, ye little flock, and blest,
Soon you'll enter into rest;
There your seat is now prepared,
There your kingdom and reward.

5 Fear not, brethren, joyful stand
On the borders of your land;
Jesus Christ, our Father's Son,
Bids us undismayed go on.

6 Lord, submissive make us go,
Gladly leaving all below;
Only Thou our Leader be,
And we still will follow Thee.

Doxology.

Praise the name of God most high,
Praise Him, all below the sky;
Praise Him, all ye heavenly host,
Father, Son, and Holy Ghost:
As through countless ages past,
Evermore His praise shall last.
As through countless ages past,
Evermore His praise shall last.

J. W. Belcher.

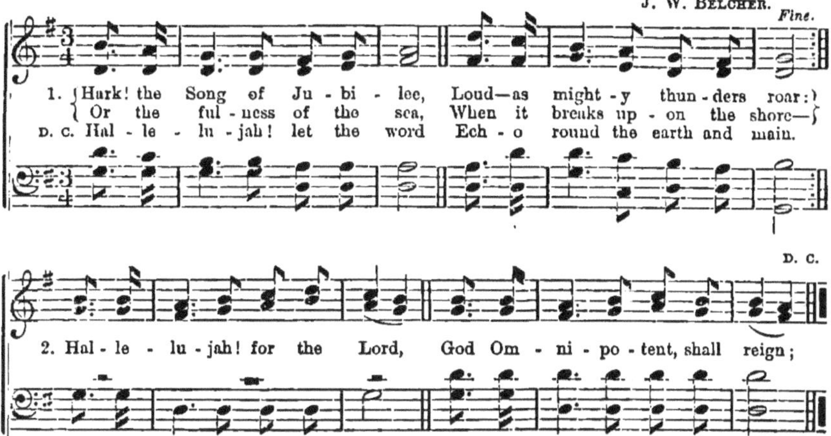
Fine.
1. Hark! the Song of Ju - bi - lee, Loud—as might - y thun - ders roar:
Or the ful - ness of the sea, When it breaks up - on the shore—
D. C. Hal - le - lu - jah! let the word Ech - o round the earth and main.
D. C.
2. Hal - le - lu - jah! for the Lord, God Om - ni - po - tent, shall reign;

H. 608 *The Song of Jubilee.*

1 Hark! the Song of Jubilee,
  Loud—as mighty thunders roar,
Or the fulness of the sea,
  When it breaks upon the shore:
2 Hallelujah! for the Lord,
  God Omnipotent, shall reign;
Hallelujah! let the word
  Echo round the earth and main.

3 Hallelujah! hark! the sound,
  From the centre to the skies,
Wakes, above, beneath, around,
  All creation's harmonies!
4 See Jehovah's banners furled,
  Sheathed His sword! He speaks—'tis done,
And the kingdoms of this world
  Are the kingdom of His Son.

5 He shall reign from pole to pole
  With illimitable sway;
He shall reign, when, like a scroll,
  Yonder heavens have passed away!
6 Then the end: beneath His rod,
  Man's last enemy shall fall;
Hallelujah! Christ in God,
  God in Christ, is All in All.

H. 694 *Praise of the Redeemed in Heaven.*

1 High, in yonder realms of light,
  Dwell the raptured saints above,
Far beyond our feeble sight,
  Happy in Immanuel's love.
Pilgrims in this vale of tears,
  Once they knew, like us below,
Gloomy doubts, distressing fears,
  Torturing pain, and heavy woe.

2 Oft the big unbidden tear,
  Stealing down the furrowed cheek,
Told, in eloquence sincere,
  Tales of woe they could not speak.
But these days of weeping o'er,
  Past this scene of toil and pain,
They shall feel distress no more,
  Never, never, weep again.

3 'Mid the chorus of the skies,
  'Mid the angelic lyres above,
Hark! their songs melodious rise,
  Songs of praise to Jesus' love.
Happy spirits, ye are fled,
  Where no grief can entrance find;
Lulled to rest the aching head,
  Soothed the anguish of the mind.

4 All is tranquil and serene,
  Calm and undisturbed repose;
There no cloud can intervene,
  There no angry tempest blows.
Every tear is wiped away,
  Sighs no more shall heave the breast;
Night is lost in endless day,
  Sorrow, in eternal rest.

ARRANGED FROM GERMAN, 1866.

1. 'Tis my hap - pi - ness be - low, Not to live with - out the cross; But the Sa-viour's
pow'r to know, Sanc - ti - fy - ing ev - 'ry loss. Tri - als must and will be - fall;
But with hum-ble faith to see Love in-scribed u.p-on them all, This is hap - pi - ness to me.

H. 330 *Welcome to the Cross.*

1 'Tis my happiness below,
  Not to live without the cross;
But the Saviour's power to know,
  Sanctifying every loss.
Trials must and will befall;
  But with humble faith to see
Love inscribed upon them all,
  This is happiness to me.

2 God, in Israel, sows the seeds
  Of affliction, pain and toil;
These spring up and choke the weeds
  Which would else o'erspread the soil.
Trials make the promise sweet,
  Trials give new life to prayer;
Trials bring me to His feet,
  Lay me low, and keep me there.

3 Did I meet no trials here,
  No chastisement by the way,
Might I not, with reason, fear
  I should prove a cast away?
Aliens may escape the rod,
  Sunk in earthly, vain delight;
But the true-born child of God,
  Must not, would not, if he might.

H. 677 *Whence came they?*

1 Who are these in bright array,—
  This innumerable throng
Round the Altar night and day,
  Hymning one triumphant song:
"Worthy is the Lamb once slain,
  Blessing, glory, honour, power,
Wisdom, riches to obtain,
  New dominion every hour?"

2 These through fiery trials trod,
  These from great affliction came;
Now before the throne of God,
  Sealed with His Almighty name,
Clad in raiment pure and white,
  Victor palms in every hand,
Through their dear Redeemer's might,
  More than conquerors they stand.

3 Hunger, thirst, disease unknown,
  On immortal fruits they feed;
Them the Lamb amid the throne
  Shall to living fountains lead:
Joy and gladness banish sighs,
  Perfect love dispels all fears,
And for ever from their eyes,
  God shall wipe away the tears.

PLEYEL, 1757-1831.

1. Lord of earth, Thy forming hand Well this beauteous frame hath planned; Woods that wave, and hills that tower,
O-cean roll-ing in His power; Yet a-mid this scene so fair, Should I cease Thy
smile to share, What were all its joys to me? Whom have I on earth but Thee?

H. 225 *Whom in Heaven or Earth but Thee.*

1 Lord of earth, Thy forming hand
Well this beauteous frame hath planned;
Woods that wave and hills that tower,
Ocean rolling in His power;
Yet amid this scene so fair,
Should I cease your smile to share,
What were all its joys to me?
Whom have I on earth but Thee?

2 Lord of heaven, beyond our sight
Shines a world of purer light;
Here, in love's unclouded reign,
Severed friends shall meet again
Oh! that world is passing fair!
Yet, if Thou wert absent there,
What were all its joys to me?
Whom have I in heaven but Thee?

3 Lord of earth and heaven, my breast
Seeks in Thee its only rest;
I was lost: Thy accents mild
Homeward lured Thy wandering child.
Oh! if once Thy smile divine
Ceased upon my soul to shine,
What were earth or heaven to me?
Whom have I in each but Thee?

H. 413 *Looking to Jesus.*

1 When, along life's thorny road,
Faints the soul beneath the load;
By its cares and sins oppressed,
Finds on earth no peace or rest:
When the wily tempter's near,
Filling us with doubts and fear,
Jesus, to Thy feet we flee;
Jesus, we will look to Thee.

2 Thou, our Saviour, from the throne
Listening to Thy people's moan:
Thou, the living Head, dost share
Every pang Thy members bear;
Full of tenderness Thou art,
Thou wilt heal the broken heart;
Full of power, Thine arms shall quell
All the rage and might of hell.

3 Mighty to redeem and save,
Thou hast overcome the grave:
Thou the bars of death hast riven,
Opened wide the gate of heaven;
Soon in glory Thou shalt come,
Taking Thy poor pilgrims home:
Jesus, then we all shall be
Ever, ever, Lord, with Thee!

S. B. Marsh, 1836.

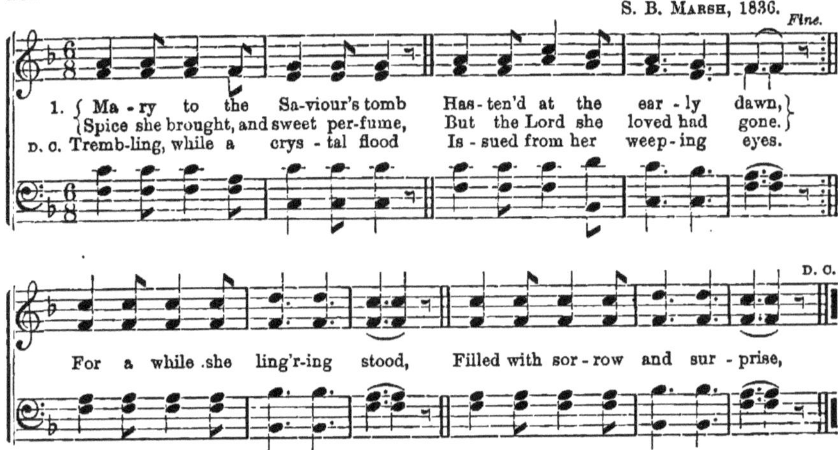
Fine.
1. { Ma - ry to the Sa-viour's tomb Has-ten'd at the ear - ly dawn, }
{ Spice she brought, and sweet per-fume, But the Lord she loved had gone. }
D. C. Tremb-ling, while a crys - tal flood Is - sued from her weep-ing eyes.
D. C.
For a while she ling'r-ing stood, Filled with sor - row and sur - prise,

H. 92 *Mary at the Tomb.*

1 Mary to the Saviour's tomb
  Hasten'd at the early dawn,
Spice she brought, and sweet perfume,
  But the Lord she loved had gone.
For awhile she lingering stood,
  Filled with sorrow and surprise,
Trembling, while a crystal flood
  Issued from her weeping eyes.

2 But her sorrows quickly fled
  When she heard His welcome voice;
Christ had risen from the dead,
  Now He bids her heart rejoice;
What a change His word can make,
  Turning darkness into day!
Ye who weep for Jesus' sake,
  He will wipe your tears away.

H. 324 *Leaning upon Jesus.*

1 Jesus, merciful and mild,
Lead me as a helpless child;
On no other arm than Thine
Would my weary soul recline:
Thou art ready to forgive,
Thou canst bid the sinner live;
Guide the wanderer, day by day,
In the straight and narrow way.

2 Thou canst fit me by Thy grace
For the heavenly dwelling place;
All Thy promises are sure,
Ever shall Thy love endure;
Then what more could I desire,
How to greater bliss aspire?
All I need in Thee I see;
Thou art all in all to me.

H. 349 *Surrendering to Christ.*

1 People of the living God,
  I have sought the world around,
Paths of sin and sorrow trod,
  Peace and comfort no where found:
Now to you my spirit turns,
  Turns a fugitive unblest;
Brethren, where your altar burns,
  O! receive me into rest.

2 Lonely I no longer roam,
  Like the cloud, the wind, the wave;
Where you dwell shall be my home,
  Where you die shall be my grave:
Mine the God whom you adore,
  Your Redeemer shall be mine;
Earth can fill my soul no more,
  Every idol I resign.

3 Tell me not of gain or loss,
  Ease, enjoyment, pomp and power;
Welcome poverty and cross,
  Shame, reproach, affliction's hour:
"Follow me;" I know Thy voice;
  Jesus, Lord, Thy steps I see;
Now I take Thy yoke by choice;
  Light Thy burden now to me.

MARTIN MADAN, 1776.

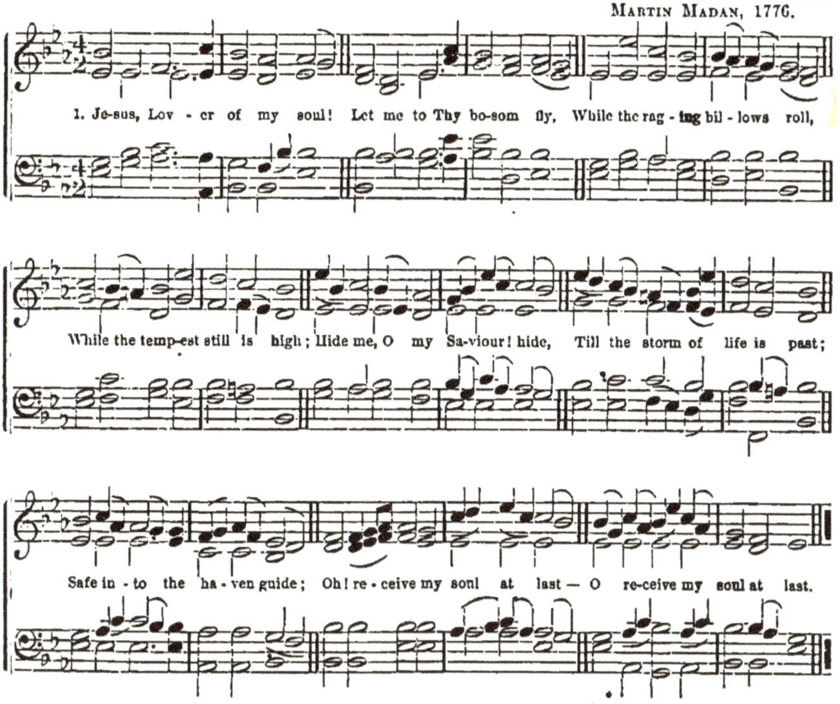
1. Je-sus, Lov - er of my soul! Let me to Thy bo-som fly, While the rag - ing bil - lows roll,
While the temp-est still is high; Hide me, O my Sa-viour! hide, Till the storm of life is past;
Safe in - to the ha - ven guide; Oh! re - ceive my soul at last — O re-ceive my soul at last.

H. 244 *Christians have all in Christ.*

2 OTHER refuge have I none;
  Hangs my helpless soul on Thee;
Leave, ah! leave me not alone,
  Still support and comfort me;
All my trust on Thee is staid,
  All my help from Thee I bring;
Cover my defenceless head
  With the shadow of Thy wing.

3 Thou, O Christ, art all I want;
  All in all in Thee I find;
Raise the fallen, cheer the faint,
  Heal the sick and lead the blind:
Just and holy is Thy name,
  I am all unrighteousness;
Vile and full of sin I am,
  Thou art full of truth and grace.

4 Plenteous grace with Thee is found,
  Grace to pardon all my sin;
Let the healing streams abound,
  Make and keep me pure within.
Thou of life the fountain art,
  Freely let me take of Thee;
Spring Thou up within my heart,
  Rise to all eternity.

H. 374 *God Everywhere.*

1 THEY who seek the throne of grace,
Find that throne in every place;
If we live a life of prayer,
God is present everywhere.

2 In our sickness or our health,
In our want or in our wealth,
If we look to God in prayer,
God is present everywhere.

3 When our earthly comforts fail,
When our foes and fears prevail,
'Tis the time for earnest prayer;
God is present everywhere.

4 Then, my soul, in every strait,
To thy Father come and wait;
He will answer every prayer;
God is present everywhere.

SAMUEL WEBBE, 1770.

1. While with cease-less course the sun Hast-ed thro' the form-er year, Ma-ny souls their race have run,
D. S. We a lit-tle long-er wait,
Fine.
D. S.
Nev-er more to meet us here; Fixed in their e-ter-nal state, They are done with all be-low;
But how lit-tle none can know.

H. 508 *The New Year.*

2 As the winged arrow flies
Speedily the mark to find;
As the lightning from the skies
Darts, and leaves no trace behind:
Swiftly thus our fleeting days
Bear us down life's rapid stream;
Upward, Lord, our spirits raise;
All below is but a dream.

3 Thanks for mercies past receive,
Pardon of our sins renew;
Teach us henceforth how to live,
With eternity in view.
Bless Thy word to young and old,
Fill us with a Saviour's love;
And when life's short tale is told,
May we dwell with Thee above.

H. 189 *Expostulation with Sinners.*

1 SINNERS, turn, why will ye die?
God your Maker asks you why;
God who did your being give,
Made you with Himself to live,
He the fatal cause demands,
Asks the work of His own hands;
Why, ye thankless creatures, why
Will ye cross His love and die?

2 Sinners, turn, why will ye die?
God your Saviour asks you why;
He who did your soul retrieve,
Died Himself that ye might live,
Will ye let Him die in vain,
Crucify your Lord again?
Why, ye rebel sinners, why
Will ye slight His grace and die?

3 Sinners, turn, why will ye die?
God the Spirit asks you why;
Many a time with you He strove,
Wooed you to embrace His love;
Will ye not His grace receive?
Will ye still refuse to live?
Why will ye for ever die,
O ye guilty sinners, why?

H. 307 *Rejoicing in the Light.*

1 BOUNDLESS glory, Lord, be Thine;
Thou hast made the darkness shine;
Thou hast sent a cheering ray;
Thou hast turned our night to day.

2 Darkness long involved us round,
Till we knew the joyful sound:
Then our darkness fled away,
Chased by truth's effulgent ray.

3 They are blest, and none beside,
They who in the truth abide;
Clear the light that marks their way,
Leading to eternal day.

4 Guide us, Saviour, through the road,
Till we reach the saints' abode;
Till we see Thee throned above,
As Thou art, the God of love.

DR. L. MASON, 1834.

1. Safe-ly thro' an-oth-er week, God has brought us on our way;
Let us now a bless-ing seek, [OMIT, ... Waiting in His courts to-day, Day of

all the week the best, Emblem of e-ter-nal rest—Day of all the week the best, Emblem of e-ter-nal rest.

H. 460 *Sabbath Worship.*

1 SAFELY through another week,
God has brought us on our way,
Let us now a blessing seek,
Waiting in His courts to-day;
Day of all the week the best,
Emblem of eternal rest.

2 While we seek supplies of grace,
Through the dear Redeemer's name,
Show Thy reconciling face,
Take away our sin and shame:
From our worldly cares set free,
May we rest this day in Thee.

3 Here we're come Thy name to praise;
Let us feel Thy presence near;
May Thy glory meet our eyes,
While we in Thy house appear:
Here afford us, Lord, a taste
Of our everlasting feast.

4 May the gospel's joyful sound
Conquer sinners, comfort saints;
Make the fruits of grace abound,
Bring relief for all complaints:
Such let all our Sabbaths prove,
Till we join the church above.

H. 380 *Litany.*

1 SAVIOUR, when in dust to Thee,
Low we bow th' adoring knee,—
When, repentant, to the skies
Scarce we lift our streaming eyes,
Oh! by all Thy pains and woe,
Suffered once for man below,
Bending from Thy throne on high,
Hear our supplicating cry.

2 By Thy birth and early years,
By Thy human griefs and fears,
By Thy fasting and distress
In the lonely wilderness,
By Thy vict'ry in the hour
Of the subtle tempter's power,—
Jesus, look with pitying eye,
Hear our deep, imploring cry.

3 By Thine hour of dark despair,
By Thine agony of prayer,
By the purple robe of scorn,
By Thy wounds, Thy crown of thorn,
By Thy cross, Thy pangs, and cries,
By Thy perfect sacrifice,—
Jesus, look with pitying eye,
Hear our sad, beseeching cry.

4 By Thy deep expiring groan,
By the sealed sepulchral stone,
By Thy triumph o'er the grave,
By Thy power from death to save,—
Mighty God, ascended Lord,
To Thy throne in heaven restored,—
Saviour, Prince, exalted high,
Hear our solemn litany.

WATCHMAN. 7s.

Dr. L. Mason, 1830.

1. Watch-man, tell us of the night, What its signs of prom-ise are. Trav'll-er, o'er yon moun-tain's height, See that glo - ry-beam-ing star. Watchman, does its beau-teous ray Aught of hope or joy fore-tell? Trav'll-er, yes, it brings the day, Promised day of Is - ra el.

Chorus to 1st and 2nd Verses.

Trav'll-er, yes, it brings the day, Promised day of Is-ra el.

Chorus to 3rd Verse.

Trav'll-er, lo! the Prince of peace! Lo! the Son of God is come, Lo! the Son of God is come.

H. 606 *Watchman, tell us of the Night.*

1 Watchman, tell us of the night,
What its signs of promise are;
Traveller, o'er yon mountain's height,
See that glory-beaming star;
Watchman, does its beauteous ray
Aught of hope or joy foretell?
Traveller, yes, it brings the day,
Promised day of Israel.

2 Watchman, tell us of the night—
Higher yet that star ascends;
Traveller, blessedness and light,
Peace and truth, its course portends;
Watchman, will its beams alone
Gild the spot that gave them birth?
Traveller, ages are its own,
See, it bursts o'er all the earth.

3 Watchman, tell us of the night,
For the morning seems to dawn;
Traveller, darkness takes its flight,
Doubt and terror are withdrawn;
Watchman, let thy wanderings cease;
Hie thee to thy quiet home:
Traveller, lo! the Prince of Peace,
Lo! the Son of God is come.

Arranged from German, 1872.

1. My days are glid-ing swift-ly by, And I a pil-grim stran-ger,
Would not de-tain them as they fly,— Those hours of toil and dan-ger.
CHORUS.
For now we stand on Jor-dan's strand,
Our friends are pass-ing o-ver; And, just be-fore, the shin-ing shore We may al-most dis-cov-er.

H. 623 *Shining Shore.*

2 Our absent King the watchword gave,
"Let every lamp be burning;"
We look afar, across the wave,
Our distant home discerning:
For now, etc.

3 Should coming days be dark and cold,
We will not yield to sorrow,
For hope will sing, with courage bold,
"There's glory on the morrow:"
For now, etc.

4 Let storms of woe in whirlwinds rise,
Each cord on earth to sever,
There, bright and joyous in the skies,
There is our home for ever:
For now, etc.

H. 303 *"A Little While."*

1 And is it so? "A little while,"
And then the life undying,
The light of God's unclouded smile,
The singing for the sighing?
"A little while!"—Oh! glorious word,
Sweet solace of our sorrow:
And then "for ever with the Lord,"
The everlasting morrow.

2 Then be it ours to journey on
In paths that He decrees us,
Where His own feet before have gone,
Our strength, our hope, our Jesus;
In lowly fellowship with Him
The cross appointed bearing;
For oh! a crown no grief can dim
One day we shall be wearing.

3 Oh! 'twill be passing sweet to gaze
On Him in all His glory;
And, lost in love and glad amaze,
To shout redemption's story;
Till angels bend to catch the strain
Our human lips are swelling,
And "Worthy is the Lamb once slain,"
Resounds thro' heaven's high dwelling.

H. 309 *Light Gilds the Clouds.*

1 This world is not my home, I know,
For sin and sorrow wound me;
But mercy tempers every blow,
And goodness smiles around me.

Cho.—Then let my lot be what it may,
Come gladness or come sorrow,
I'm nearer to my home to day,
And may be there to-morrow.

2 The tear may fall, the heart may bleed,
And all look dark and dreary;
But love divine supplies my need,
And cheers the spirit weary.

3 As falls the leaf when touched by frost,
So loved ones fall around me;
But 'tis by mercy's hand are loosed
The ties that fondly bound me.

4 With heart resigned, I bid adieu
To those who love, but leave me;
My home, my heavenly home's in view,
Where death shall ne'er bereave me.

5 My heavenly home, where Jesus reigns!
When I behold Thy glory,
I'll walk thy ever verdant plains,
And sing redemption's story.

BARTIMEUS. 8s & 7s.

Daniel Read, 1804.

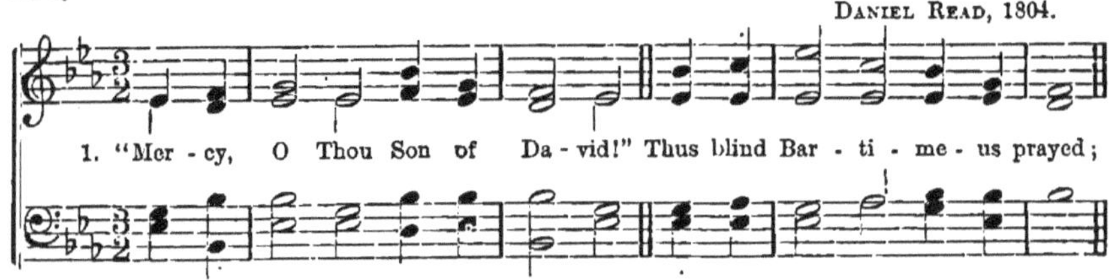
1. "Mer - cy, O Thou Son of Da - vid!" Thus blind Bar - ti - me - us prayed;

"Oth - ers by Thy word are sav - ed, Now to me af - ford thine aid."

H. 194 *Blind Bartimeus.*

1 "Mercy, O Thou son of David,"
Thus blind Bartimèus prayed;
"Others by Thy word are saved,
Now to me afford Thine aid."

2 Many for his crying chid him,
But he calls the louder still,
Till the gracious Saviour bid him
Come, and ask Me what you will.

3 Money was not what he wanted,
Though by begging used to live;
But he asked, and Jesus granted
Alms which none but He could give.

4 "Lord, remove this grievous blindness,
Let mine eyes behold the day!"
Straight he saw, and, won by kindness,
Followed Jesus in the way.

5 Oh! methinks I hear him praising,
Publishing to all around,
"Friends, is not my case amazing?
What a Saviour I have found!

6 "Oh! that all the blind but knew Him,
And would be advised by me,
Surely they would hasten to Him,
He would cause them all to see."

H. 207 *Repentance at the Cross.*

1 Jesus, full of all compassion,
Hear Thy humble suppliant's cry;
Let me know Thy great salvation:
See, I languish, faint, and die.

2 Guilty, but with heart relenting,
Overwhelmed with helpless grief,
Prostrate at Thy feet repenting,
Send, O! send me quick relief.

3 Whither should a wretch be flying,
But to Him who comfort gives?
Whither, from the dread of dying,
But to Him who ever lives?

4 While I view Thee, wounded, grieving,
Breathless, on the cursed tree,
Fain, I'd feel my heart believing,
That Thou sufferedst thus for me.

5 With Thy righteousness and Spirit,
I am more than angels blest;
Heir with Thee, all things inherit,
Peace, and joy, and endless rest.

6 Saved!—the deed shall spread new glory
Through the shining realms above;
Angels sing the pleasing story,
All enraptured with Thy love.

H. 490 *Close of Worship.*

1 Heavenly Father, grant Thy blessing,
On the teaching of this day;
That our hearts, Thy fear possessing,
May from sin be turned away.

2 Have we wandered? O forgive us;
Have we wished from truth to rove?
Turn, O turn us, and receive us,
And incline us Thee to love.

DORRNANCE. 8s & 7s.

I. B. WOODBURY.

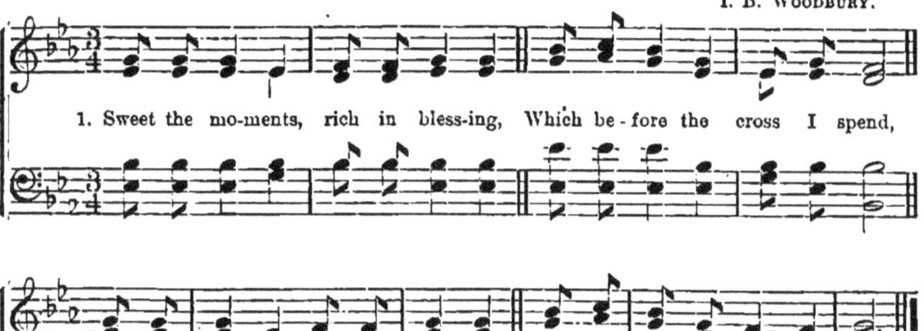
1. Sweet the mo-ments, rich in bless-ing, Which be - fore the cross I spend,

Life, and health, and peace pos - sess - ing, From the sin - ner's dy - ing Friend.

H. 353 *Sitting at the Foot of the Cross.*

1 SWEET the moments, rich in blessing,
Which before the cross I spend,
Life, and health, and peace possessing,
From the sinner's dying Friend.

2 Here I'll sit, for ever viewing
Mercy flow in streams of blood;
Precious drops, my soul bedewing,
Plead and claim my peace with God.

3 Truly blessed is this station,
Low before His cross to lie;
While I see divine compassion
Floating in His languid eye.

4 Here it is I find my heaven,
While upon the cross I gaze;
Love I much? I'm much forgiven,
I'm a miracle of grace.

5 Love and grief my heart dividing,
With my tears His feet I bathe;
Constant still in faith abiding,
Life deriving from His death.

H. 527 *At Sea.*

1 TOSSED upon the raging billow,
Sweet it is, O Lord, to know,
Thou didst press a sailor's pillow,
And canst feel a sailor's woe.

2 Never slumbering, never sleeping,
Though the night be dark and drear,
Thou the faithful watch art keeping,
"All, all's well," Thy constant cheer.

3 Thou canst calm the raging ocean,
All its noise and tumult still;
Hush the tempest's wild commotion
At the bidding of Thy will.

4 Thus my heart the hope will cherish,
While to Thee I lift my eyes;
Thou wilt save me ere I perish,
Thou wilt hear the sailor's cry.

H. 595 *The Heathen Crying for Help.*

1 HARK! what mean those lamentations,
Rolling sadly through the sky?
'Tis the cry of heathen nations,
"Come and help us, or we die!"

2 Hear the heathen's sad complaining,
Christians! hear their dying cry;
And, the love of Christ constraining,
Haste to help them, ere they die.

H. 634 *Dying Christian.*

1 WHY lament the Christian dying?
Why indulge in tears or gloom?
Calmly on the Lord relying,
He can greet the opening tomb.

2 Scenes seraphic, high and glorious,
Now forbid his longer stay;
See him rise o'er death victorious,
Angels beckon him away.

3 Hark! the golden harps are ringing,
Sounds unearthly fill his ear;
Millions now in heaven singing,
Greet his joyful entrance there.

MOZART.

1. Lord, dis - miss us with Thy bless - ing, Fill our hearts with joy and peace;

D. S.
Let us each, Thy love pos - sess-ing, Tri - umph in re - deem-ing grace;
D. S. O! re-fresh us, O! re - fresh us, Trav'l - ing through this wil - der-ness.

H. 486 *Close of Worship.*

2 Thanks we give and adoration,
For Thy gospel's joyful sound;
May the fruits of Thy salvation
In our hearts and lives abound;
May Thy presence
With us evermore be found.

3 So, whene'er the signal's given,
Us from earth to call away,
Borne on angels' wings to heaven,
Glad to leave our cumbrous clay,
May we, ready,
Rise and reign in endless day.

H. 609 *Missionary Farewell.*

1 Yes, my native land, I love thee!
All thy scenes, I love them well;
Home and friends that smile around me,
Can I bid you all farewell?
Can I leave you,
Far in heathen lands to dwell?

2 Scenes of sacred peace and pleasure,
Holy days and Sabbath bell,
Richest, brightest, sweetest treasure,
Can I, can I say "Farewell?"
Can I leave you,
Far in heathen lands to dwell?

3 Yes! I hasten from you gladly;
To the strangers let me tell
How He died—the blessed Saviour—
To redeem a world from hell;
Let me hasten,
Far in heathen lands to dwell.

4 Bear me on, thou restless ocean;
Let the winds my canvass swell:
Heaves my heart with warm emotion,
While I go far hence to dwell;
Glad I bid thee,
Native land, farewell, farewell!

H. 597 *Prayer for the Spread of the Gospel.*

1 O'er the gloomy hills of darkness,
Look, my soul, be still, and gaze;
All the promises do travail
With a glorious day of grace;
Blessed Jubilee,
Let thy glorious morning dawn.

2 Kingdoms wide, that sit in darkness,
Grant them, Lord, the glorious light;
And from eastern coasts to western,
May the morning chase the night;
And redemption,
Freely purchased, win the day.

3 Fly abroad, thou mighty gospel;
Win and conquer, never cease;
May thy lasting, wide dominions,
Multiply, and still increase;
Sway Thy sceptre,
Saviour, all the world around.

Dr. Hastings, 1830.

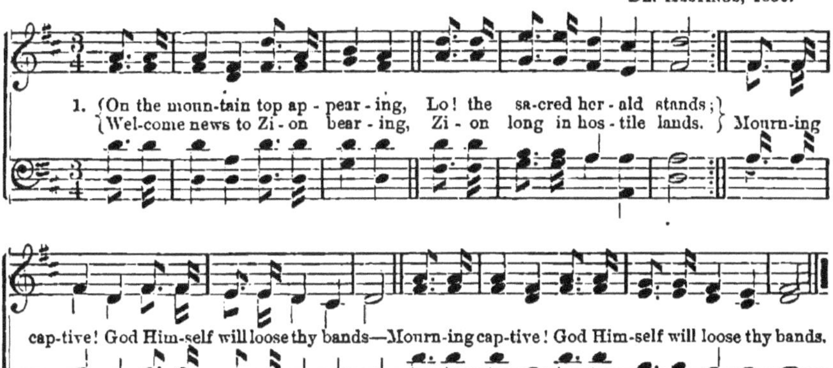
1. On the moun-tain top ap - pear - ing, Lo! the sa-cred her - ald stands;
Wel-come news to Zi - on bear - ing, Zi - on long in hos - tile lands. Mourn-ing
cap-tive! God Him-self will loose thy bands—Mourn-ing cap-tive! God Him-self will loose thy bands.

H. 578 *Joy to Zion.*

1 On the mountain top appearing,
Lo! the secred herald stands;
Welcome news to Zion bearing,
Zion long in hostile lands;
Mourning captive!
God Himself will loose thy bands.

2 Has thy night been long and mournful?
Have thy friends unfaithful proved?
Have thy foes been proud and scornful,
By thy sighs and tears unmoved?
Cease thy mourning,
Zion still is well beloved.

3 Lo! thy sun is risen in glory!
God Himself appears thy Friend;
All thy foes shall flee before thee;
Here their boasted triumphs end:
Great deliverance
Zion's King will surely send.

4 Peace and joy shall now attend thee,
All thy warfare now is past;
God, thy Saviour, will defend thee,
Victory is thine at last;
All thy conflicts
End in everlasting rest.

H. 532 *Story of the Lamb.*

1 Children, hear the melting story,
Of the Lamb that once was slain;
'Tis the Lord of life and glory;
Shall He plead with you in vain?
Oh! receive Him,
And salvation now obtain.

2 All your sins to Him confessing,
Who is ready to forgive,
Seek the Saviour's richest blessing;
On His precious name believe;
He is waiting,
Will you not His grace receive?

H. 559 *The God of Zion.*

1 Zion stands with hills surrounded,
Zion, kept by power divine;
All her foes shall be confounded,
Though the world in arms combine;
Happy Zion!
What a favoured lot is thine.

2 Every human tie may perish,
Friend to friend unfaithful prove,
Mothers cease their own to cherish,
Heaven and earth at last remove;
But no changes
Can attend Jehovah's love.

3 In the furnace God may prove thee,
Thence to bring thee forth more bright;
But can never cease to love thee,
Thou art precious in His sight;
God is with thee,
God, thine everlasting light.

Doxology.

Glory be to God the Father,
Glory to the eternal Son;
Sound aloud the Spirit's praises;
Join the elders round the throne;
Hallelujah,
Hail the glorious Three in One.

Dr. L. Mason, 1840.

1. { Glorious things of thee are spoken, Zion, city of our God;
He whose word cannot be broken, Form'd thee for His own abode: }
On the Rock of ages founded,
On the Rock, etc.
What can shake thy sure repose?
What can shake, etc.
With salvation's walls surrounded, Thou may'st smile at all thy foes.

H. 564 *Zion's Security.*

2 See the streams of living waters,
Springing from eternal love,
Well supply thy sons and daughters,
And all fear of want remove;
Who can faint while such a river
Ever flows their thirst to assuage;
Grace which, like the Lord, the giver,
Never fails from age to age.

3 Round each habitation hovering,
See the cloud and fire appear,
For a glory and a covering,
Showing that the Lord is near:
Thus deriving from their banner
Light by night, and shade by day;
Safe they feed upon the manna
Which He gives them when they pray.

H. 610 *Christ's Kingdom.*

1 Hark! ten thousand harps and voices
Sound the note of praise above;
Jesus reigns, and heav'n rejoices,
Jesus reigns, the God of love:
See, He sits on yonder throne,—
Jesus rules the world alone.

2 Saviour, hasten Thine appearing—
Bring, oh, bring the glorious day,
When, the awful summons hearing,
Heav'n and earth shall pass away;
Then with angel choirs, we'll sing
"Glory, glory to our King."

H. 663 *Christ Coming to Judgment.*

1 Lo! He comes, with clouds descending,
Once for favoured sinners slain;
Thousand thousand saints attending,
Swell the triumph of His train:
Hallelujah!
Jesus comes, and comes to reign.

2 Every eye shall now behold Him,
Robed in dreadful majesty;
Those who set at naught, and sold Him,
Pierced and nailed Him to the tree,
Deeply wailing,
Shall the true Messiah see.

3 Every island, sea and mountain,
Heaven and earth shall flee away;
All who hate Him must, confounded,
Hear the trump proclaim the day:
"Come to judgment!
Come to judgment! come away."

4 Now redemption, long expected,
See in solemn pomp appear:
All His saints by man rejected,
Now shall meet Him in the air.
Hallelujah!
See the day of God appear.

5 Mighty King, let all adore Thee,
High on Thine eternal throne;
Saviour, take the power and glory,
Claim the kingdom for Thine own!
O come quickly,
Hallelujah! come, Lord, come.

J. J. Rosseau, 1775.

1. { Sa-viour, vis-it Thy plan-ta-tion, Grant us, Lord, a gra-cious rain; }
{ All will come to de-so-la-tion, Un-less Thou re-turn a-gain. } Lord, re-vive us, Lord, re-vive us;
All our help must come from Thee—Lord, re-vive us, Lord, re-vive us, All our help must come from Thee.

H. 580 *Prayer for Revival.*

1 Saviour, visit Thy plantation,
Grant us, Lord, a gracious rain;
All will come to desolation,
Unless Thou return again:
Lord, revive us;
All our help must come from Thee.

2 Keep no longer at a distance,
Shine upon us from on high,
Lest, for want of Thine assistance,
Every plant should droop and die;
Lord, revive us;
All our help must come from Thee.

3 Let our mutual love be fervent,
Make us prevalent in prayers;
Let each one esteemed Thy servant
Shun the world's bewitching snares.
Lord, revive us;
All our help must come from Thee.

4 Break the tempter's fatal power;
Turn the stony heart to flesh;
And begin, from this good hour,
To revive Thy work afresh:
Lord, revive us;
All our help must come from Thee.

H. 318 *The Pilgrim.*

1 Gently, Lord, O! gently lead us,
Through this lonely vale of tears;
Through the changes Thou'st decreed us,
Till our last great change appears.
When temptation's darts assail us,
When in devious paths we stray,
Let Thy goodness never fail us,
Lead us in Thy perfect way.

2 In the hour of pain and anguish,
In the hour when death draws near,
Suffer not our hearts to languish,
Suffer not our souls to fear;
And when mortal life is ended,
Bid us in Thine arms to rest,
Till by angel bands attended,
We awake among the blest.

H. 15 *Praise to God.*

1 Praise to Thee, Thou great Creator,
Praise to Thee from every tongue:
Join, my soul, with every creature,
Join the universal song.
2 Father, source of all compassion,
Pure, unbounded grace is Thine:
Hail the God of our salvation!
Praise Him for His love divine.

3 For ten thousand blessings given,
For the hope of future joy,
Sound His praise thro' earth and heaven,
Sound Jehovah's praise on high.
4 Joyfully on earth adore Him,
Till in heaven our song we raise;
There, enraptured, fall before Him,
Lost in wonder, love, and praise.

HALLELUJAH. 8s & 7s.

WESTERN MELODY; ARRANGED 1873.

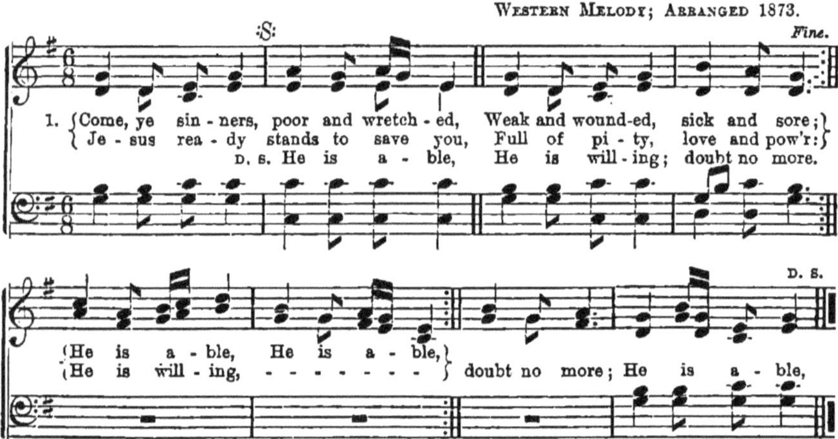
Fine.
1. {Come, ye sin-ners, poor and wretch-ed, Weak and wound-ed, sick and sore;}
{Je-sus rea-dy stands to save you, Full of pi-ty, love and pow'r:}
D. S. He is a-ble, He is will-ing; doubt no more.
D. S.
{He is a-ble, He is a-ble,}
{He is will-ing, - - - - - - - -} doubt no more; He is a-ble,

H. 177 *Come and Welcome.*

2 Ho! ye needy, come and welcome,
God's free bounty glorify;
True belief and true repentance,
Every grace that brings us nigh,
Without money,
Come to Jesus Christ and buy.

3 Let not conscience make you linger,
Nor of fitness fondly dream;
All the fitness He requireth
Is, to feel your need of Him;
This He gives you;
'Tis the Spirit's rising beam.

4 Come, ye weary, heavy-laden,
Lost and ruined by the fall;
If you tarry till you're better,
You will never come at all.
Not the righteous,
Sinners Jesus came to call.

5 Agonizing in the garden,
Lo! your Maker prostrate lies;
On the bloody tree behold Him;
Hear Him cry, before He dies,
"It is finished!"
Sinner, will not this suffice?

6 Lo! the incarnate God, ascended,
Pleads the merits of His blood;
Venture on Him, venture wholly,
Let no other trust intrude;
None but Jesus
Can do helpless sinners good.

7 Saints and angels joined in concert,
Sing the praises of the Lamb;
While the blissful seats of heaven
Sweetly echo with His name;
Hallelujah!
Sinners here may sing the same.

H. 117 *Grateful Recollections.*

[TUNE, "FOUNT."]

1 COME, Thou Fount of every blessing,
Tune my heart to sing Thy grace;
Streams of mercy, never ceasing,
Call for songs of loudest praise;
Teach me some melodious sonnet,
Sung by flaming tongues above;
Praise the mount—O fix me on it—
Mount of God's unchanging love.

2 Here I raise my Ebenezer,
Hither by Thy help I'm come;
And I hope, by Thy good pleasure,
Safely to arrive at home;
Jesus sought me when a stranger,
Wandering from the fold of God,
He, to rescue me from danger,
Interposed with precious blood.

3 Oh, to grace how great a debtor
Daily I'm constrained to be!
Let that grace, Lord, like a fetter,
Bind my wand'ring heart to Thee;
Prone to wander, Lord, I feel it,
Prone to leave the God I love,
Here's my heart, Lord, take and seal it—
Seal it from Thy courts above.

THOMPSON. 8s & 7s.

KARL REDEN.

1. Sa-viour, hast Thou fled for ev-er, From my temp-est-riv-en breast? Will Thy gra-cious Spi-rit nev-er
D. S. Hoping, on some sweet to-mor-row,
Come and cheer and make me blest? Long, dear Lord, in si-lent sor-row, I have sighed to taste Thy love;
Thou wouldst all my guilt re-move.
Fine.
D. S.

H. 409 *Light Shining in Darkness.*

2 PEACE, my soul, the Saviour hears thee,
He will chase thy fears away;
'Tis His gracious presence cheers thee,
Turning darkness into day.
Precious Saviour, have I found Thee?
Wilt Thou then my portion be?
Spread Thy sheltering arm around me,
Let me lean alone on Thee.

3 Through this world, so dark and dreary,
Be my constant friend and guide;
Hungry, thirsty, faint and weary,
Keep me ever near Thy side.
Blessed be His name for ever,
For His pardoning grace to me;
Sinners, doubt His promise never,
Jesus' love is full and free.

FOUNT. 8s & 7s.

ASAHEL NETTLETON, D. D., 1825.

Fine.
1. Come, Thou Fount of eve-ry bless-ing, Tune my heart to sing Thy grace;
Streams of mercy, never ceas-ing, Call for songs of loud-est praise;
D. C. Praise the mount—O fix me on it— Mount of God's un-chang-ing love.
Teach me some me-lodi-ous son-net, Sung by flaming tongues a-bove.
D. C

Doxology.

MAY the grace of Christ our Saviour,
And the Father's boundless love,
With the Holy Spirit's favour,
Rest upon us from above.

Thus may we abide in union
With each other and the Lord,
And possess, in sweet communion,
Joys which earth cannot afford.

Fine.
D. S.
1. Hark! the voice of love and mercy Sounds a - loud from Cal - va - ry; See, it rends the rocks a-
D. S. "It is fin - ished, It is
sun-der, Shakes the earth and veils the sky. "It is fin-ished, It is fin-ished!" Hear the dy - ing Sa-viour cry;
fin-ished!" Hear the dy-ing Sa-viour cry.

H. 81 *Atonement Accomplished.*

1 Hark! the voice of love and mercy
Sounds aloud from Calvary;
See, it rends the rocks asunder,
Shakes the earth and veils the sky.
"It is finished!"
Hear the dying Saviour cry.

2 It is finished! Oh! what pleasure
Do these precious words afford!
Heavenly blessings, without measure,
Flow to us from Christ the Lord:
It is finished!
Saints, the dying words record.

3 Finished—all the types and shadows
Of the ceremonial law;
Finished—all that God had promised;
Death and hell no more shall awe:
It is finished!
Saints, from hence your comfort draw.

4 Tune your harps anew, ye seraphs;
Join to sing the pleasing theme:
All on earth and all in heaven,
Join to praise Immanuel's name:
Hallelujah!
Glory to the bleeding Lamb!

H. 184 *Expostulation with Sinners.*

1 Sinners, will ye scorn the message
Sent in mercy from above?
Every sentence, O how tender!
Every line is full of love;
Listen to it:
Every line is full of love.

2 Hear the heralds of the gospel,
News from Zion's King proclaim
To each rebel sinner, "Pardon,
Free forgiveness in His name;"
How important!
Free forgiveness in His name.

3 Tempted souls, they bring you succour,
Fretful hearts, they quell your fears;
And with news of consolation,
Chase away the falling tears;
Tender heralds,
Chase away the falling tears.

4 False professors, grovelling worldlings,
Callous hearers of the word,
While the messengers address you.
Take the warnings they afford;
We entreat you,
Take the warnings they afford.

5 Who hath our report believed?
Who received the joyful word?
Who embraced the news of pardon
Offered to you by the Lord?
Can you slight it,
Offered to you by the Lord.

GERMAN, ARRANGED BY MASON, 1832.

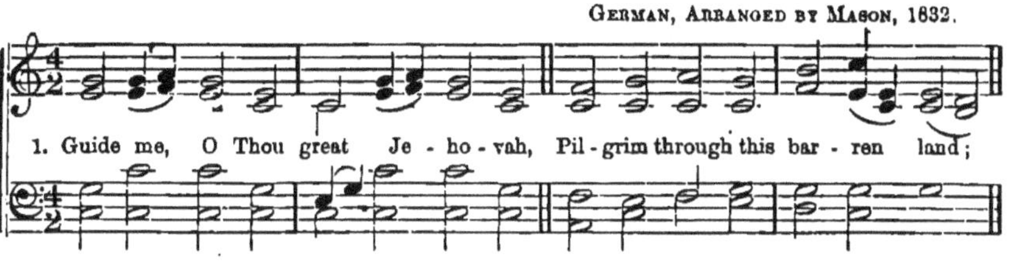
1. Guide me, O Thou great Je - ho - vah, Pil - grim through this bar - ren land;

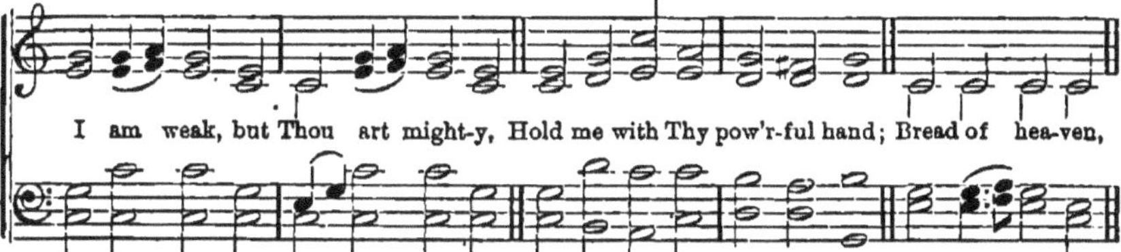
I am weak, but Thou art might-y, Hold me with Thy pow'r-ful hand; Bread of hea-ven,

Bread of hea-ven, Feed me till I want no more — Feed me till I want no more.

H. 57 *Christ our Guide.*

2 OPEN now the crystal fountain,
Whence the healing streams do flow;
Let the fiery, cloudy pillar
Lead me all my journey through;
Strong Deliverer,
Be Thou still my strength and shield.

3 When I tread the verge of Jordan,
Bid my anxious fears subside;
Death of death, and hell's destruction,
Land me safe on Canaan's side:
Songs of praises
I will ever give to Thee.

H. 480 *Before or After Sermon.*

1 COME, Thou soul-transforming Spirit,
Bless the sower and the seed;
Let each heart Thy grace inherit,
Raise the weak, the hungry feed;
From the Gospel
Now supply Thy people's need.

2 Oh! may all enjoy the blessing,
Which Thy word's designed to give;
Let us all Thy love possessing,
Joyfully the truth receive;
And for ever
To Thy praise and glory live.

H. 446 *Evening Song.* [TUNE—AUTUMN.

1 SAVIOUR, breathe an evening blessing,
Ere repose our spirits seal;
Sin and want we come confessing,
Thou canst save and Thou canst heal;
Though destruction walk around us,
Though the arrow near us fly,
Angel guards from Thee surround us,
We are safe if Thou art nigh.

2 Though the night be dark and dreary,
Darkness cannot hide from Thee;
Thou art He who, never weary,
Watchest where Thy people be.
Should swift death this night o'ertake us,
And our couch become our tomb,
May the morn in heaven awake us,
Clad in light and deathless bloom.

MIDDLETON. 8s & 7s.

SHIELDS.

Fine.
1. Hail! my ev - er bless - ed Je - sus; On - ly Thee I wish to sing;
To my soul Thy name is pre- cious, Thou my Pro - phet, Priest, and King.
D. C. Love I much? I'm much for - giv - en, I'm a mir - a - cle of grace.
D. C.
2. O! what mer - cy flows from hea - ven! O! what joy and hap - pi - ness!

H. 228 *Praise for Conversion.*

1 Hail! my ever blessed Jesus,
 Only Thee I wish to sing;
To my soul Thy name is precious,
 Thou my Prophet, Priest, and King.

2 O! what mercy flows from heaven!
 O! what joy and happiness!
Love I much? I'm much forgiven,
 I'm a miracle of grace.

3 Once with Adam's race in ruin,
 Unconcerned in sin I lay;
Swift destruction still pursuing,
 Till my Saviour passed that way.

4 Witness, all ye hosts of heaven,
 My Redeemer's tenderness;
Love I much? I'm much forgiven,
 I'm a miracle of grace.

5 Shout, ye bright angelic choir,
 Praise the Lamb enthroned above;
Whilst astonished I admire
 God's free grace and boundless love.

6 That blest moment I received Him,
 Filled my soul with joy and peace;
Love I much? I'm much forgiven,
 I'm a miracle of grace.

H. 315 *Prayer for the Graces of the Spirit.*

1 Love divine, all love excelling,
 Joy of heaven, to earth come down;
Fix in us Thy humble dwelling,
 All Thy faithful mercies crown.
Jesus, Thou art all compassion,
 Pure, unbounded love Thou art;
Visit us with Thy salvation,
 Enter every longing heart.

2 Breathe, O breathe Thy loving Spirit,
 Into every troubled breast;
Let us all in Thee inherit,
 Let us find Thy promised rest;
Take away the love of sinning,
 Alpha and Omega be,
End of faith, as its beginning,
 Set our hearts at liberty.

3 Come, almighty to deliver,
 Let us now Thy life receive,
Suddenly return, and never,
 Nevermore Thy temples leave.
Thee we would be always blessing,
 Serve Thee as Thine hosts above;
Pray, and praise Thee without ceasing,
 Glory in Thy precious love.

4 Finish then Thy new creation,
 Pure, unspotted may we be;
Let us see our whole salvation,
 Perfectly secured by Thee:
Changed from glory into glory,
 Till in heaven we take our place;
Till we cast our crowns before Thee,
 Lost in wonder, love, and praise.

ENGLISH.
1. {Sin-ners, we are sent to bid you To the gos - pel - feast to - day;}
{Will you slight the in - vi - ta - tion? Will you, can you, yet de - lay?}
Je - sus calls you, Je - sus calls you, Come, poor sin - ners, come a - way;
Je - sus calls you, Je - sus calls you, Come, poor sin - ners, come a - way.

H. 195 *Sinners Invited.*

1 Sinners, we are sent to bid you
To the gospel-feast to-day;
Will you slight the invitation?
Will you, can you, yet delay?
Jesus calls you;
Come, poor sinners, come away.

2 Come, O! come, all things are ready,
Bread to strengthen, wine to cheer;
If you spurn this blood-bought banquet,
Sinners, can your souls appear
Guests in heaven,
Scorning heaven's rich bounty here?

3 Come, O! come, leave father, mother;
To your Saviour's bosom fly:
Leave the worthless world behind you,
Seek for pardon, or you die:
"Pardon, Saviour!"
Hear the sinking sinner cry.

4 Even now the Holy Spirit
Moves upon some melting heart,
Pleads a bleeding Saviour's merit;
Sinner, will you say, "Depart?"
Wretched sinner,
Can you bid your God depart?

5 What are all earth's dearest pleasures,
Were they more than tongue could tell?
What are all its boasted treasures,
To a soul once sunk in hell?
Treasure! pleasure!
No such sounds are heard in hell.

6 Fly, O! fly ye to the mountain,
Linger not in all the plain;
Leave this Sodom of corruption,
Turn not, look not back again;
Fly to Jesus,
Linger not in all the plain.

H. 221 *Welcome to Christ.*

1 Welcome, welcome, dear Redeemer,
Welcome to this heart of mine;
Lord, I make a full surrender,
Ev'ry power and thought be Thine;
Thine entirely,
Through eternal ages Thine.

BREST. 8s, 7s & 4s.

Dr. Mason.

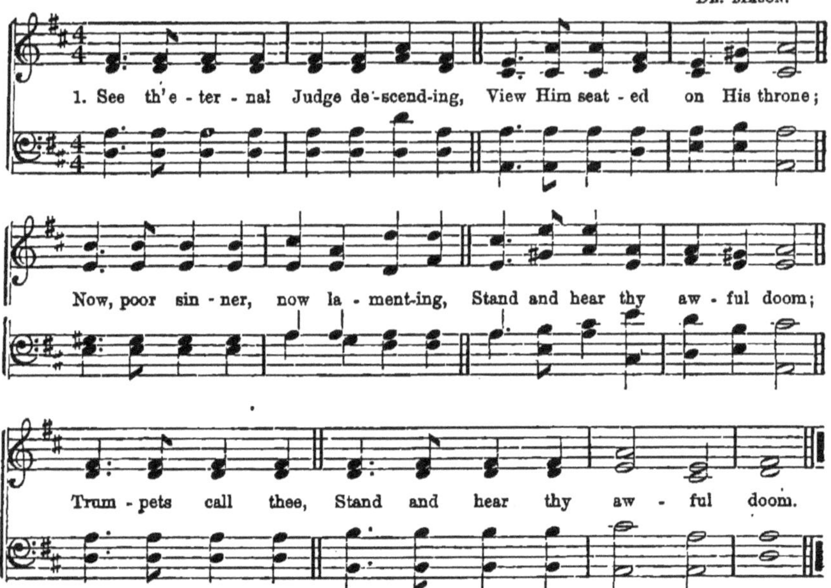
1. See th'e - ter - nal Judge de-scend-ing, View Him seat - ed on His throne;
Now, poor sin - ner, now la - ment-ing, Stand and hear thy aw - ful doom;
Trum - pets call thee, Stand and hear thy aw - ful doom.

H. 660 *Christ Descending to Judgment.*

1 See the eternal Judge descending,
View Him seated on His throne;
Now, poor sinner, now lamenting,
Stand and hear Thy awful doom;
Trumpets call thee,
Stand and hear thy awful doom.

2 Hear the cries he now is venting,
Filled with dread of fiercer pain,
While in anguish thus lamenting,
That he ne'er was born again;
Greatly mourning,
That he ne'er was born again.

3 "Yonder sits the slighted Saviour,
With the marks of dying love;
O that I had sought His favour,
When I felt His Spirit move;
Golden moments,
When I felt His Spirit move."

4 Now, despisers, look and wonder;
Hope and sinners here must part;
Louder than a peal of thunder,
Hear the dreadful sound, "Depart!"
Lost for ever,
Hear the dreadful sound, "Depart!"

H. 662 *The Day of Judgment.*

1 Day of judgment, day of wonders!
Hark! the trumpet's awful sound,
Louder than a thousand thunders,
Shakes the vast creation round!
How the summons
Will the sinner's heart confound!

2 At His call the dead awaken,
Rise to life from earth and sea;
All the powers of nature, shaken
By His looks, prepare to flee;
Careless sinner,
What will then become of thee?

3 See the Judge, our nature wearing,
Clothed in majesty divine;
You who long for His appearing,
Then shall say, This God is mine!
Gracious Saviour,
Own me in that day for Thine.

Doxology.

Glory be to God the Father,
Glory to the eternal Son;
Sound aloud the Spirit's praises;
Join the elders round the throne;
Hallelujah,
Hail the glorious Three in One.

JOHN CONKEY, 1851.

1. Hail, Thou once de - spis - ed Je - sus! Hail, Thou Gal - li - le - an King!
Thou didst suf - fer to re - lease us; Thou did'st free sal - va - tion bring.

H. 82 *Paschal Lamb.*

1 Hail, Thou once despised Jesus!
Hail, Thou Galilean King!
Thou didst suffer to release us;
Thou didst free salvation bring.

2 Hail, Thou agonizing Saviour,
Bearer of our sin and shame!
By Thy merits we find favour,
Life is given through Thy name.

3 Paschal Lamb, by God appointed,
All our sins on Thee were laid;
By almighty love anointed,
Thou hast full atonement made.

4 All Thy people are forgiven,
Through the virtue of Thy blood;
Opened is the gate of heaven;
Peace is made 'twixt man and God.

H. 113 *Christ exalted and interceding.*

1 Jesus hail, enthroned in glory,
There for ever to abide;
All the heavenly hosts adore Thee,
Seated at Thy Father's side.

2 There for sinners Thou art pleading,
There Thou dost our place prepare;
Ever for us interceding,
Till in glory we appear.

3 Worship, honour, power and blessing,
Thou art worthy to receive;
Loudest praises, without ceasing,
Meet it is for us to give.

H. 340 *Prayer for Submission.*

1 Step by step, my Father, lead me
Through this dark and dreary day;
Hour by hour, my Saviour, feed me,
Fainting, drooping, by the way.

2 One by one, my joys declining,
Bear, O! bear my spirit up;
May Thy grace prevent repining,
Fill Thou now my empty cup.

3 Day by day, my Father, measure
All my changes yet to be,
And may each in Thy good pleasure
Bring me nearer unto Thee.

H. 285 *Hope Encouraged.*

[Tune, "Brest."]

1 O my soul! what means this sadness?
Wherefore art thou thus cast down?
Let thy grief be turned to gladness,
Bid thy restless fear begone;
Look to Jesus,
And rejoice in His dear name.

2 Though ten thousand ills beset thee,
Though thy heart is stained with sin,
Jesus lives, He'll ne'er forget thee,
He will make thee pure within;
He is faithful
To perform His gracious word.

3 Though distresses now attend thee,
And thou tread'st the thorny road;
His right hand shall still defend thee,
Soon He'll bring thee home to God;
Thou shalt praise Him,—
Praise the great Redeemer's name.

DISCIPLE. 8s & 7s.

MOZART.

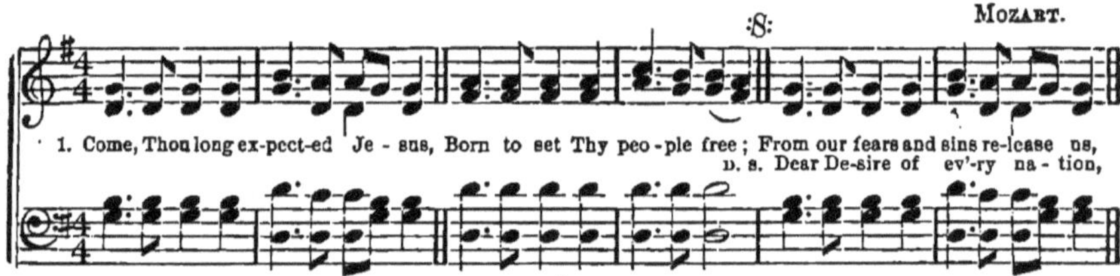
1. Come, Thou long ex-pect-ed Je - sus, Born to set Thy peo-ple free; From our fears and sins re-lease us,
D. S. Dear De-sire of ev'-ry na - tion,

Fine.
D. S.
Let us find our rest in Thee: Is-rael's Strength and Con-so-la-tion, Hope of all the saints Thou art;
Joy of ev' - ry long-ing heart.

H. 41 *Christ the Desire of all Nations.*

2 Born Thy people to deliver;
Born a child, and yet a King;
Born to reign in us for ever,
Now Thy precious kingdom bring:
By Thine own eternal Spirit,
Rule in all our hearts alone;
By Thine all-sufficient merit,
Raise us to Thy glorious throne.

H. 48 *Christ the Friend of Sinners.*

1 One there is, above all others
Well deserves the name of Friend;
His is love beyond a brother's,
Costly, free, and knows no end.

2 Which of all our friends, to save us,
Could or would have shed his blood?
But this Saviour died to have us
Reconciled in Him to God.

3 When He lived on earth abased,
Friend of sinners was His name;
Now, above all glory raised,
He rejoices in the same.

4 Oh! for grace our hearts to soften,
Teach us, Lord, at length to love:
We, alas! forget too often,
What a Friend we have above.

H. 346 *The World Renounced.*

1 Jesus, I my cross have taken,
All to leave and follow Thee;
Naked, poor, despised, forsaken,
Thou from hence my All shalt be:
Let the world neglect and leave me;
They have left my Saviour too;
Human hopes have oft deceived me;
Thou art faithful, Thou art true.

2 Perish, earthly fame and treasure,
Come, disaster, scorn, and pain:
In Thy service, pain is pleasure;
With Thy favour, loss is gain.
Oh! 'tis not in grief to harm me,
While Thy bleeding love I see;
Oh! 'tis not in joy to charm me,
When that love is hid from me.

H. 591 *"The Morning Cometh."*

1 "Lift your heads" with faith; the morrow
Dawneth brighter than to-day;
Angel hands will lift the shadows,
Chase the gathering gloom away.

Cho.—"Lift your heads," the day is breaking,
Soon the morning will appear;
See the earth from slumber waking;
"Lift your heads," the day draws [near.

2 Does the night seem long and weary,
Dangers threatening all the way?
Joy will soon return to bless thee,
Soon will dawn a brighter day.—*Cho.*

3 What though wars and dire commotions
Try your faith and cause dismay;
God, your Father, rules the nations;
He will send a brighter day.—*Cho.*

FROM THE GERMAN.

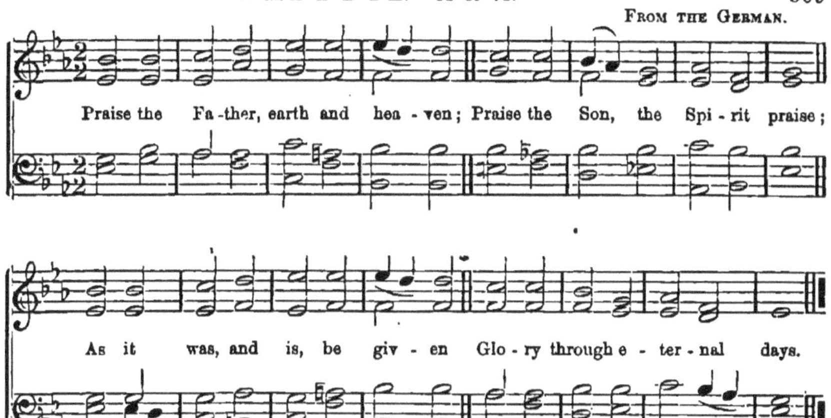
Praise the Fa-ther, earth and hea-ven; Praise the Son, the Spi-rit praise;
As it was, and is, be giv-en Glo-ry through e-ter-nal days.

H. 38 *The Deity and Glory of Christ.*

1 Lord of every land and nation,
Ancient of eternal days,
Sounded through the wide creation,
Be Thy just and awful praise.

2 For the grandeur of Thy nature,
Grand beyond a seraph's thought;
For created works of power,
Works with skill and kindness wrought.

3 For Thy providence, that governs
Through Thine empire's wide domain,
Wings an angel, guides a sparrow;
Blessed be Thy gentle reign.

4 But Thy rich, Thy free redemption,
Dark through brightness all along;
Thought is poor, and poor expression;
Who can sing that awful song?

5 Brightness of the Father's glory,
Shall Thy praise unuttered lie?
Fly, my tongue, such guilty silence;
Sing the Lord, who came to die.

6 Did the angels sing Thy coming?
Did the shepherds learn their lays?
Shame would cover me ungrateful,
Should my tongue refuse to praise.

7 From the highest throne in glory,
To the cross of deepest woe!
All to ransom guilty captives!
Flow, my praise, for ever flow.

8 Go, return, immortal Saviour,
Leave Thy footstool, take Thy throne;
Thence return, and reign for ever!
Be the kingdom all Thy own.

H. 74 *Song of the Angels.*

1 Hark! what mean those holy voices,
Sweetly sounding through the skies?
Lo! the angelic host rejoices,
Heavenly hallelujahs rise.

2 Listen to the wondrous story
Which they chant in hymns of joy;
Glory in the highest, glory!
Glory be to God most high!

3 Peace on earth, good will from heaven,
Reaching far as man is found;
Souls redeemed, and sins forgiven,
Loud our golden harps shall sound.

4 Christ is born, the great Anointed,
Heaven and earth His praises sing;
O! receive whom God appointed,
For your Prophet, Priest and King,

5 Hastens mortals to adore Him,
Learn His name, and taste His joy;
Till in heaven ye sing before Him,
Glory be to God most high!

6 Let us learn the wondrous story
Of our great Redeemer's birth,
Spread the brightness of His glory,
Till it covers all the earth.

K. R., 1872.

1. {Lord, I hear of showers of bless-ing Thou art scatt'r-ing full and free;}
{Showers the thirs-ty land re-fresh-ing— Let some dropp-ings fall on me.}
E-ven me, E-ven me, Let some dropp-ings fall on me.

H. 587 *Prayer for Blessing.*

2 Pass me not, O God our Father!
Sinful though my heart may be;
Thou might'st leave me, but the rather
Let Thy mercy light on me,—Even *me.*

3 Pass me not, O gracious Saviour!
Let me live and cling to Thee;
Oh! I'm longing for Thy favour—
While Thou'rt calling, oh! call me,

4 Pass me not, O mighty Spirit,
Thou canst make the blind to see;
Witnesser of Jesus' merit,
Speak some word of power to me.

5 Pass me not! Thy lost one bringing,
Bind, O bind my heart to Thee;
While the streams of life are springing,
Blessing others, O bless me.

PEREZ. 8s & 7s.

1. Praise the Lord! ye heav'ns adore Him; Praise Him angels in the height; Sun and moon rejoice before Him;
Sun - and moon rejoice before Him;
Praise Him, all ye stars of light! Hal-le-lu-jah, Amen, Amen, Amen, A-men.
Praise - - Him, all ye stars of light! Amen, Hal-le-lu-jah, Amen, A-men.

Ps. 148 *Fourth Part.*

2 Praise the Lord, for He hath spoken;
Worlds His mighty voice obeyed;
Laws which never can be broken,
For their guidance He hath made.

3 Praise the Lord for He is glorious;
Never shall His promise fail;
God hath made His saints victorious,
Sin and death shall not prevail.

4 Praise the God of our salvation,
Hosts on high His power proclaim;
Heaven, and earth, and all creation,
Praise and magnify His name!
Hallelujah, Amen.

SAMUEL WEBBE, 1740-1824.

1. Come, let us a - new our jour-ney pur - sue, Roll round with the year, And
nev - er stand still till the Mas - ter ap - pear. His a - dor - a - ble will Let us
glad - ly ful - fil, And our tal - ents im - prove By the pa-tience of hope, and the
la - bour of love—By the pa - tience of hope, and the la - bour of love.

H. 511 *New Year.*

1 Come, let us anew
Our journey pursue,
Roll round with the year,
And never stand still till the Master appear.
His adorable will
Let us gladly fulfil,
And our talents improve, [love.
By the patience of hope and the labour of

2 Our life is a dream;
Our time, as a stream,
Glides swiftly away,
And the fugitive moment refuses to stay:
The arrow is flown,
The moment is gone,
The millennial year
Rushes on to our view, and eternity's here.

3 Oh! that each in the day
Of Thy coming, may say,
"I have fought my way through,
I have finished the work Thou didst give me to do!"
Oh! that each from Thee, Lord,
May receive the glad word,
"Well and faithfully done; [throne."
Enter into My joy, and sit down on My

AMSTERDAM. 7s, 6s & 7s.

Dr. James Nabes, 1780.

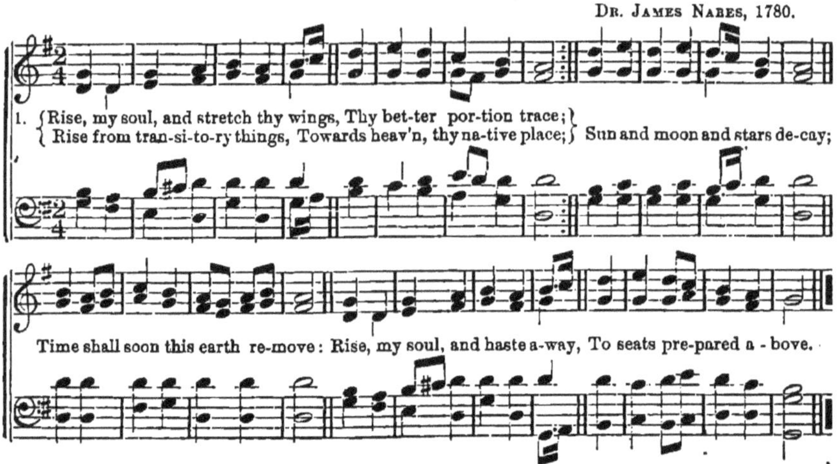
1. {Rise, my soul, and stretch thy wings, Thy bet-ter por-tion trace;}
{Rise from tran-si-to-ry things, Towards heav'n, thy na-tive place;} Sun and moon and stars de-cay;
Time shall soon this earth re-move: Rise, my soul, and haste a-way, To seats pre-pared a - bove.

H. 671 *Aspiring after Heaven.*

1 Rise, my soul, and stretch thy wings,
  Thy better portion trace;
Rise from transitory things,
  Towards heaven, thy native place;
Sun and moon and stars decay;
  Time shall soon this earth remove:
Rise, my soul, and haste away,
  To seats prepared above.

2 Rivers to the ocean run,
  Nor stay in all their course;
Fire ascending seeks the sun;
  Both speed them to their source:
So a soul that's born of God
  Pants to view His glorious face,
Upward tends to His abode,
  To rest in His embrace.

3 Cease, ye pilgrims, cease to mourn;
  Press onward to the prize;
Soon our Saviour will return,
  Triumphant in the skies.
Yet a season, and you know,
  Happy entrance will be given;
All our sorrows left below,
  And earth exchanged for heaven.

H. 342 *None but Jesus Crucified.*

1 Vain, delusive world, adieu!
  With all of creature good;
Only Jesus I pursue,
  Who bought me with His blood.
All thy pleasures I forego;
  All thy wealth, and all thy pride;
Only Jesus will I know,
  And Jesus crucified.

2 Him to know is life and peace,
  And pleasure without end;
This is all my happiness—
  On Jesus to depend;
Daily in His grace to grow,
  In His favour to abide;
Only Jesus will I know,
  And Jesus crucified.

H. 20 *God First Chose Me.*

[Tune, "Missionary Hymn."]

1 'Tis not that I did choose Thee,
  For, Lord, that could not be;
This heart would still refuse Thee;
  But Thou hast chosen me:
Thou from the sin that stained me,
  Hast cleansed and set me free;
Of old Thou hast ordained me,
  That I should live to Thee.

2 'Twas sovereign mercy called me,
  And taught my opening mind;
The world had else enthralled me,
  To heavenly glories blind;
My heart owns none before Thee;
  For Thy rich grace I thirst;
This knowing, if I love Thee,
  Thou must have loved me first.

MISSIONARY HYMN. 7s & 6s.

Dr. L. Mason, 1824.

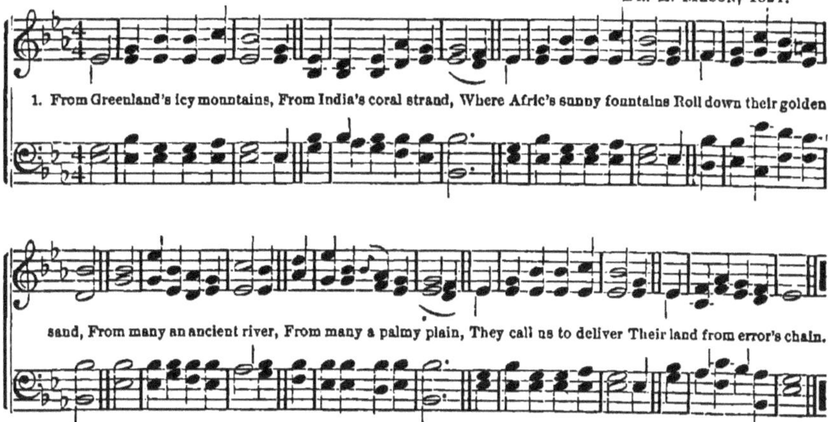
1. From Greenland's icy mountains, From India's coral strand, Where Afric's sunny fountains Roll down their golden
sand, From many an ancient river, From many a palmy plain, They call us to deliver Their land from error's chain.

H. 603 *Missionary Hymn.*

2 What though the spicy breezes
  Blow soft o'er Ceylon's isle,
Though every prospect pleases,
  And only man is vile;
In vain with lavish kindness
  The gifts of God are strown,
The heathen, in his blindness,
  Bows down to wood and stone.

3 Shall we, whose souls are lighted
  With wisdom from on high,
Shall we to men benighted
  The lamp of life deny?
Salvation! O salvation!
  The joyful sound proclaim,
Till earth's remotest nation
  Has learned Messiah's name.

4 Waft, waft, ye winds, His story,
  And you, ye waters, roll,
Till, like a sea of glory,
  It spreads from pole to pole;
Till o'er our ransomed nature
  The Lamb, for sinners slain,
Redeemer, King, Creator,
  In bliss returns to reign.

H. 246 *Divine Light Breaking into the Soul.*

1 Sometimes a light surprises
  The Christian while he sings;
It is the Lord who rises,
  With healing in His wings;
When comforts are declining,
  He grants the soul again
A season of clear shining,
  To cheer it after rain.

2 In holy contemplation,
  We sweetly then pursue
The theme of God's salvation,
  And find it ever new:
Set free from present sorrow,
  We cheerfully can say,
Let the unknown to-morrow
  Bring with it what it may.

3 It can bring with it nothing,
  But He will bear us through;
Who gives the lilies clothing,
  Will clothe His people too:
Beneath the spreading heavens,
  No creature but is fed;
And He who feeds the ravens,
  Will give His children bread.

4 Though vine nor fig-tree neither,
  Their wonted fruit should bear,
Though all the fields should wither,
  Nor flocks nor herds be there;
Yet God the same abiding,
  His praise shall tune my voice;
For while in Him confiding,
  I cannot but rejoice.

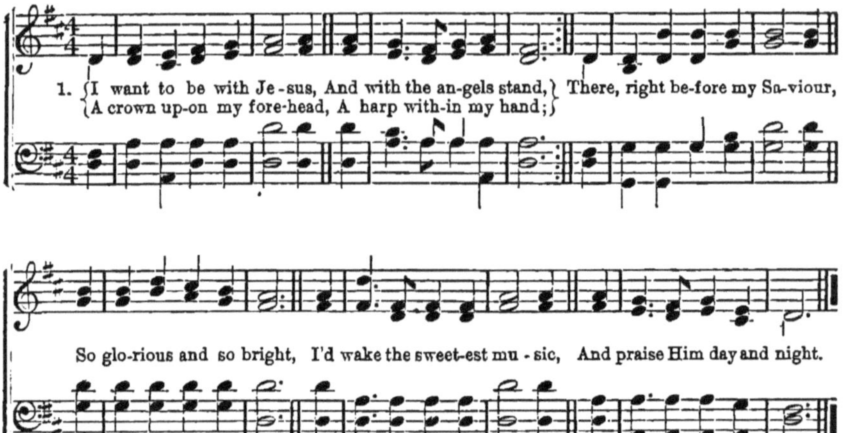
1. {I want to be with Je-sus, And with the an-gels stand,} There, right be-fore my Sa-viour,
{A crown up-on my fore-head, A harp with-in my hand;}
So glo-rious and so bright, I'd wake the sweet-est mu-sic, And praise Him day and night.

H. 531 *With Jesus.*

1 I WANT to be with Jesus,
And with the angels stand,
A crown upon my forehead,
A harp within my hand;
There, right before my Saviour,
So glorious and so bright,
I'd wake the sweetest music,
And praise Him day and night.

2 I never would be weary,
Nor ever shed a tear,
Nor ever know a sorrow,
Nor ever feel a fear;
But blessed, pure, and holy,
I'd dwell in Jesus' sight,
And with ten thousand thousands,
Praise Him both day and night.

3 I know I'm weak and sinful,
But Jesus will forgive;
For many little children
Have gone to heav'n to live.
Dear Saviour, when I languish,
And lay me down and die,
Oh! send a shining angel,
And bear me to the sky.

4 Oh! there I'll be with Jesus,
Among the angels stand,
A crown upon my forehead,
A harp within my hand;
And there, before Thee, Saviour,
So glorious and so bright,
I'll join the heavenly music,
And praise Thee day and night.

H. 276 *Faith in Jesus.*

1 I LAY my sins on Jesus,
The spotless Lamb of God;
He bears them all, and frees us
From the accursed load.
I bring my guilt to Jesus,
To wash my crimson stains
White in His blood most precious,
Till not a spot remains.

2 I lay my wants on Jesus;
All fulness dwells in Him;
He healeth my diseases,
He doth my soul redeem;
I lay my griefs on Jesus,
My burdens and my cares;
He from them all releases,
He all my sorrow shares.

4 I long to be like Jesus,
Meek, loving, lowly, mild;
I long to be like Jesus,
The Father's holy Child;
I long to be with Jesus
Amid the heavenly throng,
To sing with saints His praises,
And learn the angels' song.

Geo. J. Webb, 1837.

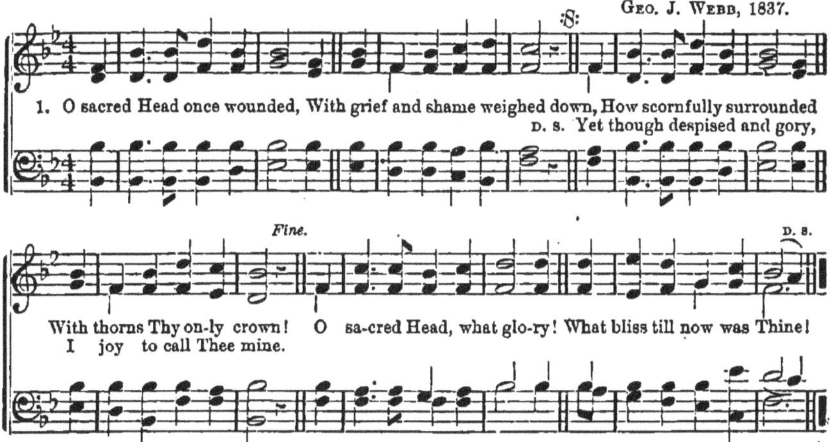
1. O sacred Head once wounded, With grief and shame weighed down, How scornfully surrounded
D. S. Yet though despised and gory,
Fine.
D. S.
With thorns Thy on-ly crown! O sa-cred Head, what glo-ry! What bliss till now was Thine!
I joy to call Thee mine.

H. 89 *Sacred Head.*

2 How art Thou pale with anguish,
With sore abuse and scorn;
How does that visage languish
That once was bright as morn!
What language shall I borrow,
To thank Thee, dearest Friend,
For this Thy dying sorrow,
Thy pity without end?

3 Oh! make me Thine for ever;
And should I fainting be,
Lord, let me never, never
Outlive my love to Thee.
Be near when I am dying;
Oh! show Thy cross to me;
And, for my succour flying,
Come, Lord, and set me free.

H. 412 *Cheer up the Fainting.*

1 O faint and feeble-hearted,
Why thus cast down with fear?
Fresh aid shall be imparted;
Thy God unseen is near.
2 His eye can never slumber,
He marks thy cruel foes;
Observes their strength, their number,
And all thy weakness knows.

3 Though heavy clouds of sorrow
Make dark thy path to-day,
There may shine forth to-morrow
Once more a cheering ray.

4 Though doubts and griefs assailing
Conceal heaven's fair abode;
Yet now faith's power prevailing
Should stay thy mind on God.

H. 607 *The Gospel Banner.*

1 Now be the gospel banner
In every land unfurled;
And be the shout, hosanna!
Re-echoed through the world:
Till every isle and nation,
Till every tribe and tongue
Receive the great salvation,
And join the happy throng.

2 What though the embattled legions
Of earth and hell combine?
His arm throughout their regions,
Shall soon resplendent shine;
Ride on, O Lord, victorious;
Immanuel, Prince of peace,
Thy triumph shall be glorious;
Thy empire still increase.

3 Yes, Thou shalt reign for ever,
O Jesus, King of kings;
Thy light, Thy love, Thy favour,
Each ransomed captive sings;
The isles for Thee are waiting,
The deserts learn Thy praise;
The hills and valleys greeting,
The song responsive raise.

Felix Giardini, 1760.

1. Come, Thou al - might - y King, Help us Thy name to sing, Help us to praise.
Fa - ther all glo - ri - ous,
O'er all vic - to - ri - ous,
Come, and reign o - ver us, An- cient of days.

H. 459 *Invocation of the Trinity.*

1 Come, Thou almighty King,
Help us Thy name to sing,
Help us to praise.
Father all glorious,
O'er all victorious,
Come and reign over us,
Ancient of days.

2 Jesus, our Lord, arise,
Scatter our enemies,
And make them fall;
Let Thine almighty aid,
Our sure defence be made;
Our souls on Thee be staid;
Lord, hear our call.

3 Come, Thou incarnate Word,
Gird on Thy mighty sword;
Our prayer attend.
Come, and Thy people bless,
And give Thy word success;
Spirit of holiness,
On us descend.

4 Come, Holy Comforter,
Thy sacred witness bear,
In this glad hour.
Thou, who almighty art,
Now rule in every heart,
And ne'er from us depart,
Spirit of power.

5 To the great One in Three,
The highest praises be,
Hence evermore.
His sovereign majesty,
May we in glory see,
And to eternity,
Love and adore.

H. 483 *Before Preaching.*

[Tune, "America."]

1 O holy Lord, our God,
By heavenly hosts adored,
Hear us, we pray;
To Thee the Cherubim,
Angels and Seraphim,
Unceasing praises hymn—
Their homage pay.

2 Here give Thy word success,
And this Thy servant bless,
His labours own;
And while the sinner's Friend
His life and words commend,
Thy Holy Spirit send,
And make him known.

3 May every passing year
More happy still appear
Than this glad day;
With numbers fill the place,
Adorn Thy saints with grace,
Thy truth may all embrace,
O Lord, we pray.

OLIVET. 6s, 6s & 4s.

Dr. L. Mason, 1831.

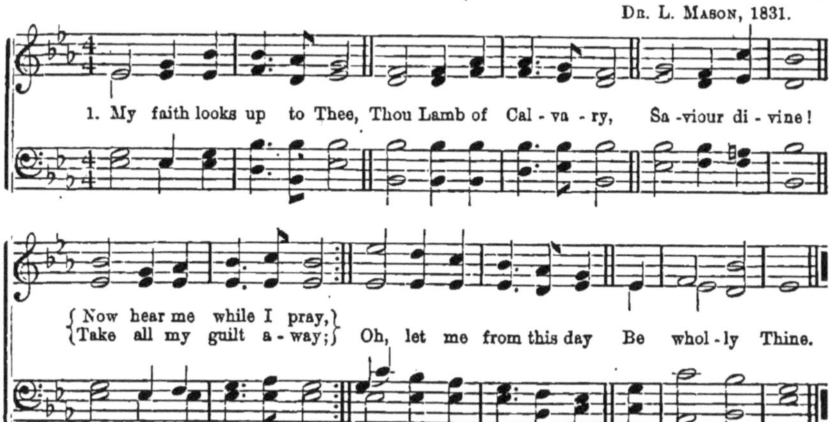
1. My faith looks up to Thee, Thou Lamb of Cal - va - ry, Sa -viour di - vine!
{Now hear me while I pray,}
{Take all my guilt a - way;} Oh, let me from this day Be whol - ly Thine.

H. 274 *Faith in Christ.*

1 My faith looks up to Thee,
Thou Lamb of Calvary,
Saviour divine!
Now hear me while I pray,
Take all my guilt away;
Oh let me, from this day,
Be wholly Thine.

2 May Thy rich grace impart
Strength to my fainting heart—
My zeal inspire.
As Thou hast died for me,
Oh may my love to Thee
Pure, warm, and changeless be—
A living fire.

3 While life's dark maze I tread,
And griefs around me spread,
Be Thou my guide;
Bid darkness turn to day,
Wipe sorrow's tear away,
Nor let me ever stray
From Thee aside.

4 When ends life's transient dream,
When death's cold sullen stream
Shall o'er me roll,
Blest Saviour, then in love
Fear and distress remove;
Oh, bear me safe above—
A ransomed soul.

AMERICA. 6s, 6s & 4s.

English; H. T. Carey, died 1783.

1. O ho - ly Lord, our God, By heav'n-ly hosts a-dored, Hear us, we pray; To Thee the

Che - ru-bim, An-gels and Se - ra-phim, Un - ceas - ing prais-es hymn—Their hom-age pay.

OAK. 6s, 4s & 6s.

Dr. L. Mason, 1834.

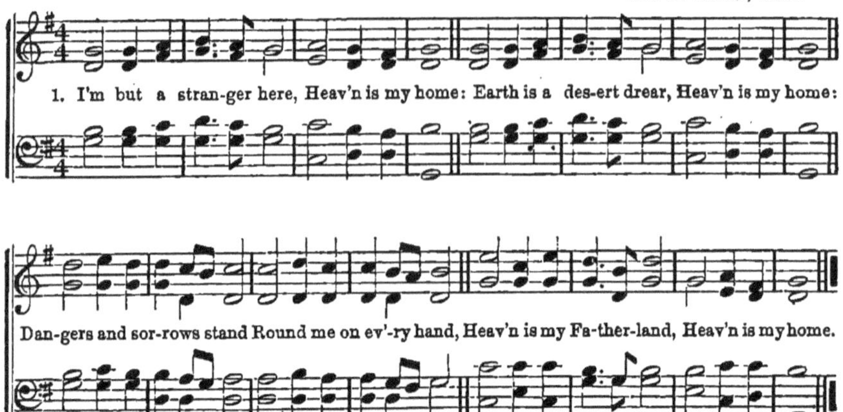
1. I'm but a stran-ger here, Heav'n is my home: Earth is a des-ert drear, Heav'n is my home:
Dan-gers and sor-rows stand Round me on ev'-ry hand, Heav'n is my Fa-ther-land, Heav'n is my home.

H. 697 *Heaven the Christian's Home.*

1 I'm but a stranger here,
   Heav'n is my home;
Earth is a desert drear,
   Heav'n is my home;
Dangers and sorrows stand
Round me on every hand,
Heav'n is my Father-land.
   Heav'n is my home.

2 What though the tempests rage,
   Heav'n is my home;
Short is my pilgrimage,
   Heav'n is my home;
And time's wild wintry blast
Soon will be over past,
I shall reach home at last,--
   Heav'n is my home.

3 Therefore I murmur not,
   Heav'n is my home;
Whate'er my earthly lot,
   Heav'n is my home;
And I shall surely stand
There at my Lord's right hand;
Heav'n is my Father-land,—
   Heav'n is my home.

4 There, at my Saviour's side,
   Heav'n is my home;
I shall be glorified,
   Heaven is my home;
There are the good and blest;
Those I love most and best;
There too I soon shall rest,
   Heav'n is my home.

H. 529 *Happy Land.*

[Tune, "Beulah."]

1 There is a happy land,
   Far, far away,
Where saints in glory stand,
   Bright, bright as day;
Oh! how they sweetly sing,
Worthy is our Saviour King;
Loud let His praises ring,
   Praise, praise for aye.

2 Come to that happy land,
   Come, come away;
Why will ye doubting stand,
   Why still delay?
Oh! we shall happy be,
When from sin and sorrow free,
Lord, we shall live with Thee,
   Blest, blest for aye.

3 Bright, in that happy land,
   Beams every eye;
Kept by a Father's hand,
   Love cannot die.
Oh! then to glory run,
Be a crown and kingdom won;
And bright above the sun,
   We reign for aye.

BETHANY. 6s, 4s & 6s.

Dr. L. Mason, 1859.

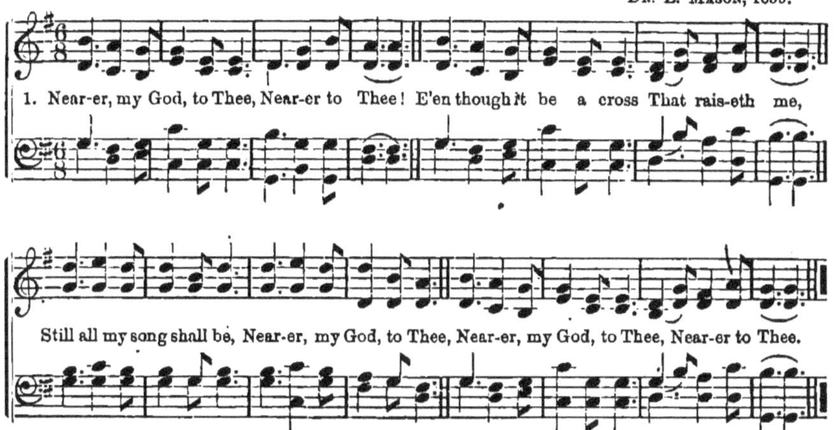
1. Near-er, my God, to Thee, Near-er to Thee! E'en though it be a cross That rais-eth me,
Still all my song shall be, Near-er, my God, to Thee, Near-er, my God, to Thee, Near-er to Thee.

H. 320 *Nearness to God*

2 Though like a wanderer,
Daylight all gone,
Darkness be over me,
My rest a stone,
Yet in my dreams I'd be
Nearer, my God, to Thee,
Nearer to Thee.

3 Then, with my waking thoughts
Bright with Thy praise,
Out of my stony griefs
Bethel I'll raise;
So by my woes to be
Nearer, my God, to Thee,
Nearer to Thee.

4 Or if, on joyful wing,
Cleaving the sky,
Sun, moon, and stars forgot,
Upward I fly,
Still all my song shall be,
Nearer, my God, to Thee,
Nearer to Thee.

BEULAH. 6s, 4s & 7s.

1. {There is a hap-py land, Far, far a-way,} Oh! how they sweet-ly sing,
{Where saints in glo-ry stand, Bright, bright as day;}
Wor-thy is our Sa-viour King, Loud let His prais-es ring, Praise, praise for aye.

Fine.
1. {Out on an o-cean all bound-less we ride, We're home-ward bound, home-ward bound;}
{Toss'd on the waves of a rough, rest-less tide, We're home-ward bound, home-ward bound;}
D. C. Pro-mise of which on us each He be-stowed, We're home-ward bound, home-ward bound;
D. C.
Far from the safe, qui-et har-bour we've rode, Seek-ing our Fa-ther's ce-les-tial a-bode,

H. 401 *Homeward Bound.*

1 Out on an ocean all boundless we ride,
We're homeward bound; [tide,
Toss'd on the waves of a rough, restless
We're homeward bound; [rode,
Far from the safe, quiet harbour we've
Seeking our Father's celestial abode,
Promise of which on us each He bestowed;
We're homeward bound.

2 Wildly the storm sweeps us on as it roars,
We're homeward bound; [shores,
Look, yonder lie the bright heavenly
We're homeward bound;
Steady, O pilot, stand firm at the wheel;
Steady, we soon shall outweather the gale;
Oh! how we fly 'neath the loud creaking
We're homeward bound. [sail;

3 Into the harbour of heaven we glide,
We're home at last;
Softly we drift on its bright silver tide,
We're home at last.
Glory to God! all our dangers are o'er;
We stand secure on the glorified shore;
Glory to God! we will shout evermore;
We're home at last.

H. 289 *Chief Object of a Believer's Love.*

Tune, "De Fleury."

1 How tedious and tasteless the hours,
When Jesus no longer I see;
Sweet prospects, sweet birds, and sweet flowers,
Have lost all their sweetness with me.
The midsummer sun shines but dim,
The fields strive in vain to look gay;
But when I am happy in Him,
December's as pleasant as May.

2 His name yields the richest perfume,
And sweeter than music His voice;
His presence disperses my gloom,
And makes all within me rejoice;
I should, were He always thus nigh,
Have nothing to wish or to fear;
No mortal so happy as I,
My summer would last all the year.

3 Content with beholding His face,
My all to His pleasure resigned,
No changes of season or place
Would make any change in my mind.
While blessed with a sense of His love,
A palace a toy would appear;
And prisons would palaces prove,
If Jesus would dwell with me there.

4 Dear Lord, if indeed I am Thine,
If Thou art my sun and my song,
Say, why do I languish and pine,
And why are my winters so long?
O! drive these dark clouds from my sky,
Thy soul-cheering presence restore;
Or take me unto Thee on high,
Where winter and clouds are no more.

K. R., 1866.

1. Ye an-gels who stand round the throne, And view my Im-man-u-el's face, In rap-tur-ous
songs make Him known; Tune, tune your soft harps to His praise. He formed you the spi-rits you are, So
hap-py, so no-ble, so good; While oth-ers sunk down in de-spair, Con-firmed by His pow-er, ye stood.

H. 678 *Longing after Heaven.*

2 Ye saints who stand nearer than they,
And cast your bright crowns at His feet,
His grace and His glory display,
And all His rich mercy repeat;
He snatched you from hell and the grave,
He ransomed from death and despair;
For you He was mighty to save,
Almighty to bring you safe there.

3 O! when will the period appear,
When I shall unite in your song?
I'm weary of lingering here,
And I to your Saviour belong,
I'm fettered and chained up in clay;
I struggle and pant to be free;
I long to be soaring away,
My God and my Saviour to see.

4 I want to put on my attire,
Washed white in the blood of the Lamb;
I want to be one of your choir,
And tune my sweet harp to His name.
I want—O! I want to be there,
Where sorrow and sin bid adieu,
Your joy and your friendship to share,
To wonder and worship with you.

DE FLEURY. 8s.

De Fleury.

Fine.
1. How tedious and tasteless the hours, When Jesus no longer I see; Sweet prospects, sweet birds, and sweet flowers,
D. C. But when I am hap-py in Him, December's as pleasant as May.
Have all lost their sweetness with me. The midsummer suns shines but dim; The fields strive in vain to look gay;
D. C.

RICHMOND. 11s & 12s.

KARL REDEN, 1874.

1. Soon—soon and for ev - er our u - nion shall be, Made per-fect, our glo-rious Re-deem-er, in Thee;
The sins and the sor-rows of time shall be o'er, Its pangs and its part-ings re-mem-bered no more.
When life can-not fail, and when death can-not sev-er, Then Chris-tians with Christ shall be—soon and for ev-er.

H. 284 *Soon and for ever.*

1 SOON—soon and for ever our union shall be
Made perfect, our glorious Redeemer, in Thee;
The sins and the sorrows of time shall be o'er,
Its pangs and its partings remembered no more,
When life cannot fail, and when death cannot sever,
Then Christians with Christ shall be—soon and for ever

2 Yes, soon and for ever, we'll see as we're seen,
And learn the deep meaning of things that have been;
Then droop not in sorrow, despond not in fear—
A glorious to-morrow is bright'ning and near;
When—blessed reward of each faithful endeavour!
True Christians with Christ shall be—soon and for ever.

M'FARLAND. 5s & 11s.

C. C. CONVERSE, 1874.

1. All ye who pass by, To Je-sus draw nigh; To you is it no-thing that Je-sus should die?
Our ran-som and peace, Our sure-ty He is; Come, see if there ev-er was sor-row like His.

Lesta Vese, 1874.

1. What sound is this? A song thro' heav'n re-sound-ing, God is love! God is love! And now from
earth, I hear the sound re-bound-ing, God is love! God is love! {Yes, while a-dor-ing hosts pro-
{Love is His na-ture, Love His
claim,}
name,}
My soul in rap-ture cries the same, God is love! God is love!

H. 13 *God is Love.*

2 This song repeat,
Repeat, ye saints in glory,
God is love! God is love!
And saints on earth,
Shout back the pleasing story,
God is love! God is love!
In this let earth and heaven agree,
To sound His love, so full and free;
And let the theme for ever be,
God is love! God is love!

H. 64 *Christ our Substitute.*
["Tune, McFarland."]

1 All ye who pass by,
To Jesus draw nigh;
To you is it nothing that Jesus should die?
Our ransom and peace,
Our surety He is:
Come, see if there ever was sorrow like His.

2 The Lord in the day
Of His anger did lay [away;
Our sins on the Lamb, and He bore them
He died to atone
For guilt not His own;
The Father afflicted for you His dear Son.

3 For sinners like me
He died on the tree;
His death is accepted; the sinner goes
My pardon I claim; [free;
A sinner I am,
A sinner believing in Jesus' dear name.

4 He purchased the grace
That now I embrace;
O Father! Thou knowest He died in my
His death is my plea, [place;
My advocate see, [swered for me.
And hear the blood speak that has an-

5 With joy we approve
The plan of His love,
A wonder to all, both below and above;
When time is no more,
We still shall adore [shore.
That ocean of love without bottom or

THE DYING CHRISTIAN. P. M.

EDWARD HARWOOD, 1707–1787.

1. Vi - tal spark of heav'n-ly flame, Quit, O quit this mor - tal frame. Tremb-ling, ho - ping,
ling'r - ing, fly - ing, O the pain, the bliss of dy - ing!
Cease, fond na - ture, cease thy strife, And let me lan - guish in - to life.
2. Hark! they whis - per! an - gels say — they whis - per: an - gels say,
Hark! they whis - per, etc., Hark! they whis - per:
Hark! hark! they whis - per: an - gels say, "Sis - ter spi - rit, come a - way!—
an - gels say,
Sis - ter spi - rit, come a - way! What is this ab - sorbs me quite,— Steals my sen - ses, shuts my

sight,—Drowns my spi - rit, draws my breath? Tell me, my soul, can this be death?—
Tell me, my soul, can this be death? 3. The world re - cedes; it dis - ap - pears;
Heav'n o - pens on my eyes; my ears With sounds se - raph - ic ring.
CHORUS.
Lend, lend your wings! I mount, I fly! O grave, where is thy vic - to - ry? O grave, where is thy vic - to - ry?
O death, where is thy sting? O grave, where is thy vic - to - ry? O death, where is thy sting?
Lend, lend your wings! I mount! I fly! O grave, where is thy vic to - ry, thy vic - to ry?

O grave, where is thy vic - to - ry, thy vic - to - ry? O death, where is thy sting?
O death, where is thy sting? Lend, lend your wings! I mount! I fly!
O grave, where is thy vic - to - ry, thy vic - to - ry? O death, O death, where is thy sting?
H. 640
RAMSEY. P. M.
Karl Reden, 1863.
1. Vi - tal spark of heav'n-ly flame, Quit, oh quit this mor - tal frame.
2. Hark! they whisper! an - gels say, Sis - ter spir - it, come a - way!
3. The world re - cedes; it dis - ap - pears; Hea - ven o - pens on my eyes; my
Trembling, ho - ping, ling'r - ing, fly - ing, Oh, the pain, the bliss, of dy - ing!
What is this ab - sorbs me quite, Steals my sen - ses, shuts my sight,
ears With sounds ser - a - phic ring. Lend, lend your wings! I mount, I fly! Oh
Cease, fond na - ture, cease thy strife, And let me lan-guish in - to life.
Drowns my spir - it, draws my breath? Tell me, my soul, can this be death?
grave, where is thy vic - to - ry? Oh death, where is thy sting?

ANTICIPATION. 8s 7s & 5s.

Rev. J. W. Dadmun, 1860.

1. In the Chris-tian's home in glo - ry, There re - mains a land of rest;
There my Sa-viour's gone be - fore me, To ful - fil my soul's re - quest,
There is rest for the wea - ry. There is rest for the wea - ry,
D. S. On the oth - er side of Jor - dan, In the sweet fields of E - den,
There is rest for the wea - ry, There is rest for you.
Where the tree of life is bloom - ing, There is rest for you.
D. S.

H. 255 *Rest for the Weary.*

1 In the Christian's home in glory,
There remains a land of rest,
There my Saviour's gone before me,
To fulfil my soul's request.
There is rest for the weary,
There is rest for the weary;
On the other side of Jordan,
In the sweet fields of Eden,
Where the tree of life is blooming,
There is rest for you.

2 This is not my place of resting,
Mine's a city yet to come;
Onward to it I am hasting,
On to my eternal home;
There is rest, etc.

3 In it all is light and glory,
O'er it shines a nightless day;
Ev'ry trace of sin's sad story,
All the curse hath passed away;
There is rest, etc.

4 There the Lamb our Shepherd leads us
By the streams of life along,
On the freshest pastures feeds us,
Turns our sighing into song;
There is rest, etc.

DR. JOHN CLARKE, 1800.
1. The voice of free grace cries, es - cape to the moun-tain, For Ad-am's lost
race Christ hath o - pened a fountain; {For sin and trans-gression, and
{Halle - lu - jah to the Lamb! who has
ev' - ry pol - lu - tion, His blood flows most freely in streams of sal - vation,
pur-chased our par - don, We'll praise Him a - gain when we pass o - ver Jordan,
His blood flows most freely in streams of sal - va - tion.}
We'll praise Him a - gain when we pass o - ver Jor - dan.}
D. S.

H. 605 *The Voice of Free Grace.*

2 Now glory to God in the highest is given,
Now glory to God is re-echoed in heaven;
Around the whole earth let us tell the glad story,
And sing of His love, His salvation and glory.
Hallelujah to the Lamb, etc.

3 O Jesus, ride on, Thy kingdom is glorious,
O'er sin, death and hell, Thou wilt make us victorious;
Thy name shall be praised in the great congregation,
And saints shall delight in ascribing salvation.
Hallelujah to the Lamb, etc.

4 When on Zion we stand, having gained the blest shore,
With our harps in our hands, we will praise evermore;
We'll range the blest fields on the banks of the river,
And sing hallelujah for ever and ever.
Hallelujah to the Lamb, etc.

DR. THOS. HASTINGS, 1831.

1. Thou art gone to the grave, but we will not de - plore thee;
Though sor - rows and dark - ness en - com - pass the tomb, The Sa-viour has
passed thro' its por - tals be - fore thee, And the lamp of His love is thy
guide thro' the gloom—And the lamp of His love is thy guide thro' the gloom.

H. 641 *Funeral Hymn.*

1 THOU art gone to the grave, but we will not deplore thee;
Though sorrows and darkness encompass the tomb;
The Saviour has passed through its portals before thee,
And the lamp of his love is thy guide through the gloom.

2 Thou art gone to the grave, we no longer behold thee,
Nor tread the rough path of the world by thy side; [to enfold thee,
But the wide arms of mercy are spread
And sinners may hope, since the Sinless hath died.

3 Thou art gone to the grave, and its mansions forsaking,
Perhaps thy tired spirit in doubt lingered long;
But the sunshine of heaven beamed bright on thy waking,
And the song that thou heardst was the Seraphim's song.

4 Thou art gone to the grave, but 'twere wrong to deplore thee,
When God was thy ransom, thy guardian and guide;
He gave thee, and took thee, and soon will restore thee,
Where death has no sting, since the Saviour has died.

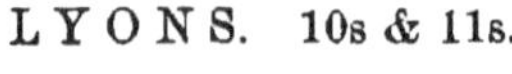
LYONS. 10s & 11s.

F. J. Hayden, 1770.

1. Tho' trou-bles as-sail, and dan-gers af-fright, Tho' friends should all fail, and foes all u-nite,

Yet one thing se-cures us, what-ev-er be-tide; The Scrip-ture as-sures us, the Lord will pro-vide.

H. 23 *The Lord will Provide.*

1 Though troubles assail, and dangers affright;
Though friends should all fail, and foes all unite,
Yet one thing secures us, whatever betide,
The Scripture assures us, the Lord will provide.

2 The birds without barn or store-house, are fed;
From them let us learn to trust for our bread;
His saints what is fitting shall ne'er be denied,
So long as 'tis written, the Lord will provide.

3 We may, like the ships, by tempest be tossed
On perilous deeps, but cannot be lost;
Though Satan enrages the wind and the tide,
The promise engages, the Lord will provide.

4 His call we obey, like Abram of old,
Not knowing our way, but faith makes us bold;
For though we are strangers, we have a good guide,
And trust in all dangers, the Lord will provide.

5 When Satan appears to stop up our path,
And fills us with fears, we triumph by faith;
He cannot take from us, though oft he has tried,
This heart-cheering promise, the Lord will provide.

6 He tells us we're weak, our hope is in vain;
The good that we seek, we ne'er shall obtain;
But when such suggestions our spirits have plied,
This answers all questions, the Lord will provide.

7 No strength of our own, or goodness we claim,
Yet since we have known the Saviour's great name,
In this our strong tower for safety we hide,
The Lord is our power, the Lord will provide.

8 When life sinks apace, and death is in view,
This word of His grace shall comfort us through,
No fearing or doubting, with Christ on our side,
We hope to die shouting, the Lord will provide.

H. 270 *The Triumph of Faith.*

1 Begone, unbelief, my Saviour is near,
And for my relief will surely appear;
By prayer let me wrestle, and He will perform;
With Christ in the vessel, I smile at the storm.

2 Though dark be my way, since He is my guide,
'Tis mine to obey, 'tis His to provide;
Though cisterns be broken, and creatures all fail,
The word He has spoken shall surely prevail.

3 His love, in times past, forbids me to think
He'll leave me at last, in trouble to sink;
Each sweet Ebenezer I have in review,
Confirms His good pleasure to help me quite through.

4 Why should I complain of want and distress,
Temptation or pain? He told me no less;
The heirs of salvation, I know from His word,
Through much tribulation must follow their Lord.

5 Since all that I meet shall work for my good,
The bitter is sweet, the medicine food;
Though painful at present, 'twill cease before long,
And then, O how pleasant the Conqueror's son.

GERMAN.

1. De - lay not, de - lay not, O sin - ner, draw near; The wa - ters of
life are now flow - ing for thee; No price is de - mand - ed, the
Sa - viour is here, Re - demp - tion is pur - chased, sal - va - tion is free.

H. 192 *Dangers of Delay.*

2 Delay not, delay not, why longer abuse
The love and compassion of Jesus thy God?
A fountain is opened, how canst thou refuse
To wash and be cleansed in His pardoning blood?

3 Delay not, delay not, O sinner, to come,
For mercy still lingers, and calls thee to-day;
Her voice is not heard in the vale of the tomb;
Her message unheeded will soon pass away.

4 Delay not, delay not, the Spirit of Grace,
Long grieved and resisted, may take its sad flight;
And leave thee in darkness to finish thy race,
To sink in the gloom of eternity's night.

5 Delay not, delay not, the hour is at hand;
The earth shall dissolve, and the heavens shall fade;
The dead, small and great, in the judgment shall stand;
What power then, O sinner, shall lend thee its aid?

H. 178 *The Harvest Past.*

1 Lo! Jesus, the Saviour, in mercy draws near,
Salvation He brings unto all who believe;
Ye mourners, dimiss all your doubting and fear,
The gracious Redeemer with gladness receive.

2 The day-star of promise illumines the sky,
And souls long benighted now welcome the dawn;
Embrace the glad season, or soon you may cry,
"The harvest is past, and the summer is gone."

3 The Spirit is striving with sinners to-day,
He graciously knocks at the door of your heart;
He comes the compassion of God to display,
Your sins to remove, and His love to impart.

4 Oh! welcome the Spirit, and grieve Him no more,
Nor wait till His offers of life are withdrawn,
Lest then you may cry, as your doom you deplore,
"The harvest is past, and the summer is gone."

HOME. 11s.

ENGLISH.

1. { 'Mid scenes of con - fu - sion and crea - ture com-plaints,
How sweet to my soul is com - mun-ion with [OMIT] saints; } To find at the ban-quet of
mer - cy there's room, And feel in the pre - sence of Je - sus at home;
Home, home, sweet, sweet home, Pre - pare me, dear Sa-viour, for hea - ven, my home.

H. 689 *Heaven the Christian's Home.*

1 'Mid scenes of confusion and creature complaints,
How sweet to my soul is communion with saints;
To find at the banquet of mercy there's room,
And feel in the presence of Jesus at home.

2 Sweet bonds, that unite all the children of peace;
And thrice blessed Jesus, whose love cannot cease;
Though oft from Thy presence in sadness I roam,
I long to behold Thee in glory at home.

3 I sigh from this body of sin to be free,
Which hinders my joy and communion with Thee;
Though now my temptations like billows may foam,
All, all will be peace, when I'm with Thee at home.

4 While here in the valley of conflict I stay,
O give me submission and strength as my day;
In all my afflictions, to Thee would I come,
Rejoicing in hope of my glorious home.

5 Whate'er Thou deniest, O give me Thy grace,
The Spirit's sure witness, and smiles of Thy face:
Inspire me with patience to wait at Thy throne,
And find even now a sweet foretaste of home.

6 I long, dearest Lord, in thy beauties to shine,
No more as an exile in sorrow to pine;
And in Thy dear image arise from the tomb,
With glorified millions, to praise Thee at home.

H. 421 *Faint yet pursuing.*

1 Though faint yet pursuing, we go on our way,
The Lord is our Leader, His word is our stay;
Though suff'ring, and sorrow, and trial be near,
The Lord is our Refuge, and whom can we fear?

2 And to His green pastures our footsteps He leads,
His flock in the desert how kindly He feeds;
The lambs in His bosom He tenderly bears,
And brings back the wand'rers all safe from the snares.

3 Though clouds may surround us, our God is our light;
Though storms rage around us, our God is our might;
So faint, yet pursuing, still onward we come:
The Lord is our Leader, and heaven our home.

George Kingsley, 1838.

1. I would not live al-way! I ask not to stay Where storm af-ter storm ris-es dark o'er the way;
The few lu-rid morn-ings that dawn on us here, Are e-nough for life's woes, full e-nough for its cheer.

H. 635 *Death Welcome to the Believer.*

2 I would not live alway, thus fettered by sin,
Temptation without and corruption within;
E'en the raptures of pardon is mingled with fears,
And the cup of thanksgiving with penitent tears.

3 I would not live alway; no, welcome the tomb;
Since Jesus hath lain there, I dread not its gloom;
There, sweet be my rest, till He bid me arise,
To hail Him in triumph descending the skies.

4 Who, who would live alway, away from his God,
Away from yon heaven, that blissful abode,
Where the rivers of pleasure flow o'er the bright plains,
And the noontide of glory eternally reigns;

5 Where the saints of all ages in harmony meet,
Their Saviour and brethren, transported to greet;
While the anthems of rapture unceasingly roll,
And the smile of the Lord is the feast of the soul.

H. 304 *Looking to Jesus.*

1 O eyes that are weary, and hearts that are sore,
Look off unto Jesus, and sorrow no more;
The light of His countenance shineth so bright,
That here, as in heaven, there need be no night.

2 When looking to Jesus, I go not astray,
My eyes are upon Him, He shows me the way:
The path may seem dark as He leads me along,
But, following Jesus, I cannot go wrong.

3 Still looking to Jesus, oh! may I be found,
When Jordan's dark waters encompass me round;
They'll bear me away in His presence to be,
And see Him still nearer whom always I see.

4 Then, then I shall know the full beauty and grace
Of Jesus my Lord, when I stand face to face—
Shall know how His love went before me each day,
And wonder that ever my eyes turned away.

H. 518 *Christ Precious.*

1 How loving is Jesus, who came from the sky,
In tenderest pity, for sinners to die;
His hands and His feet were nailed to the tree,
And all this He suffered for you and for me.

2 How precious is Jesus to all who believe!
And out of His fulness what grace they receive!
When weak, He supports them, when erring He guides:
And every thing needful He kindly provides.

3 Oh! give then to Jesus your earliest days;
They only are blessed who walk in His ways;
In life and in death He will still be your friend,
For whom Jesus loveth He loves to the end.

JOHN READING, 1760.
1. Ye ser-vants of God, your Mas - ter pro-claim, And pub - lish a - broad His
won - der - ful name; The name all-vic - to - rious of Je - sus ex - tol; His king-dom is
glo-rious, He rules o - ver all — His king-dom is glo-rious, He rules o - ver all.

H. 116 *Praise to the Most High.*

1 Ye servants of God, your Master proclaim,
And publish abroad His wonderful name;
The name all-victorious of Jesus extol;
His kingdom is glorious, He rules over all.

2 God ruleth on high, almighty to save;
And still He is nigh—His presence we have:
The great congregation His triumph shall sing,
Ascribing salvation to Jesus our King.

3 Salvation to God, who sits on the throne,
Let all cry aloud, and honour the Son;
The praises of Jesus the angels proclaim,
Fall down on their faces, and worship the Lamb.

4 Then let us adore, and give Him His right,
All glory and power, and wisdom and might,
All honour and blessing, with angels above,
And thanks never ceasing, for infinite love.

H. 430 *The Glorious King.*

1 Oh! worship the King all-glorious above;
Oh! gratefully sing His power and His love;
Our Shield and Defender, the Ancient of Days,
Pavilioned in splendour and girded with praise.

2 We sing of Thy might, we sing of Thy grace,
Whose robe is the light, whose canopy space;
Thy chariots of wrath the thunder-clouds form,
And dark is Thy path on the wings of the storm.

3 Frail children of dust, and feeble as frail,
In Thee do we trust, nor find Thee to fail;
Thy mercies how tender, how firm to the end,
Our Maker, Defender, Redeemer and Friend!

4 O measureless Might, ineffable Love,
While angels delight to hymn Thee above,
Thy ransomed creation, though feeble their lays,
With true adoration shall sing to Thy praise.

1. How firm a foun - da - tion, ye saints of the Lord, Is
laid for your faith in His ex - cel - lent word! What more can He say than to
you He hath said, You who un - to Je - sus for re - fuge have fled?

H. 235. *The Promises Precious.*

1 How firm a foundation, ye saints of the Lord,
Is laid for your faith in His excellent word!
What more can He say than to you He hath said,
You who unto Jesus for refuge have fled.

2 In every condition, in sickness, in health,
In poverty's vale, or abounding in wealth,
At home and abroad, on the land, on the sea,
"As thy days may demand, shall thy strength ever be.

3 "Fear not, I am with thee, O! be not dismayed,
I, I am thy God, and will still give thee aid:
I'll strengthen thee, help thee, and cause thee to stand,
Upheld by My righteous, omnipotent hand.

4 "When through the deep waters I call thee to go,
The rivers of woe shall not thee overflow;
For I will be with thee, thy troubles to bless,
And sanctify to thee thy deepest distress.

5 "When through fiery trials thy pathway shall lie,
My grace all-sufficient shall be thy supply;
The flame shall not hurt thee; I only design
Thy dross to consume, and thy gold to refine.

6 "E'en down to old age, all My people shall prove
My sovereign, eternal, unchangeable love;
And when hoary hairs shall their temples adorn,
Like lambs they shall still in My bosom be borne.

7 "The soul that on Jesus hath leaned for repose,
I will not, I will not desert to His foes;
That soul, though all hell should endeavour to shake,
I'll never, no never, no never forsake."

1. Joy-ful-ly, joy-ful-ly on-ward we move, Bound to the land of bright spi-rits a-bove.
An-gel-ic chor-is-ters sing as we come, "Joy-ful-ly, joy-ful-ly haste to your home;"
Soon with our pil-grim-age end-ed be-low,
Home to the land of bright spi-rits we go;
Pil-grims and stran-gers no more shall we roam, Joy-ful-ly, joy-ful-ly rest-ing at home.

H. 535 *Joyfully, Joyfully.*

1 Joyfully, joyfully onward we move,
Bound to the land of bright spirits above;
Angelic choristers sing as we come,
"Joyfully, joyfully haste to your home."
Soon with our pilgrimage ended below,
Home to the land of bright spirits we go;
Pilgrims and strangers no more shall we
Joyfully, joyfully resting at home. [roam,

2 Friends, fondly cherished, have passed on before, [shore;
Waiting, they watch us approaching the
Singing to cheer us thro' death's chilling gloom,
"Joyfully, joyfully haste to your home."
Sounds of sweet melody fall on the ear,
Harps of the blessed, your voices we hear;
Rings with the harmony heaven's high dome,—
"Joyfully joyfully haste to your home."

3 Death with his weapon may soon lay us low,
Safe in our Saviour, we fear not the blow;
Jesus hath broken the bars of the tomb,
Joyfully, joyfully will we go home;
Bright will the morn of eternity dawn,
Death shall be conquered, his sceptre be gone; [roam,
Over the plains of blest Canaan we'll
Joyfully, joyfully, with Christ at home.

H. 253 *The Disconsolate Comforted.*

[Tune, "Come Ye Disconsolate."]

1 Come, ye disconsolate, where'er ye languish, [kneel;
Come to the mercy-seat, fervently
Here bring your wounded hearts, here tell your anguish; [not heal.
Earth has no sorrows that heaven can-

2 Joy of the desolate, Light of the straying,
Hope of the penitent, fadeless and pure,
Here speaks the Comforter, in mercy saying, [not cure.
Earth has no sorrows that heaven can-

3 Here see the bread of life; see waters flowing [less in love;
Forth from the throne of God, bound-
Come to the feast prepared; come, ever knowing [remove.
Earth has no sorrows but heaven can

FOLSOM. 11s & 10s.

MOZART.

1. Hail the blest morn! see the great Me-di-a-tor Down from the re-gions of glo - ry de - scend;
Shep-herds, go wor-ship the Babe in the man-ger, Lo! for His guard, the bright an-gels at-tend.

H. 69 *Birth of Christ.*

2 Bright in the East, lo! the sun of the morning
Dawns on our darkness, and lends us [his aid,
While his pure light, the horizon adorning,
Guides where our infant Redeemer is laid.

3 Cold on His cradle the dew drops are shining,
Low lies His head with the beasts of [the stall,
Angels adore Him in slumber reclining,
Maker, and Monarch, and Saviour of all.

4 Say, shall we yield Him, in costly devotion,
Odours of Edom, and offerings divine?
Gems of the mountain, and pearls of the ocean,
Myrrh from the forest, or gold from [the mine?

4 Vainly we offer each ample oblation;
Vainly with gifts would His favour secure:
Richer by far is the heart's adoration;
Dearer to God are the prayers of the poor.

COMFORTER. 11s & 10s.

1. Come, ye dis - con-so-late, wher-e'er ye lan -guish, Come to the mer-cy-seat, fer-vent-ly kneel;
Here bring your wounded hearts, here tell your anguish; Earth has no sor-rows that heav'n cannot heal.

OLD TUNE.

1. Daugh-ter of Zi - on, a-wake from thy sad-ness; A-wake, for thy foes shall op-press thee no more;
Bright o'er the hills dawns the day-star of glad-ness; A-rise, for the night of thy sor-row is o'er.
Bright o'er thy hills dawns the day-star of glad-ness; A-rise, for the night of thy sor-row is o'er.

H. 565 *The Church Victorious.*

1 DAUGHTER of Zion, awake from thy sadness;
Awake, for thy foes shall oppress thee no more;
Bright o'er thy hills dawns the day-star of gladness;
Arise, for the night of thy sorrow is o'er.

2 Strong were thy foes, but the arm that subdued them,
And scattered their legions, was mightier far;
They fled, like the chaff, from the scourge that pursued them;
Vain were their steeds and their chariots of war.

3 Daughter of Zion, the Power that hath saved thee
Extolled with the harp and the timbrel should be;
Shout, for the foe is destroyed that enslaved thee,
The oppressor is vanquished, and Zion is free.

H. 265 *Peace in Believing.*
[TUNE, "NEW CONCORD."]

1 OH! how happy are they
Who the Saviour obey,
And have laid up their treasures above!
Oh! what tongue can express
The sweet comfort and peace
Of a soul in its earliest love?

2 It was heaven below
My Redeemer to know,
And the angels could do nothing more,
Than to fall at his feet,
And the story repeat,
And the Lover of sinners adore.

3 Oh! the rapturous height
Of that holy delight
Which I felt in the life-giving blood!
Of my Saviour possessed,
I was perfectly blest,
As if filled with the fulness of God.

4 Then, all the day long,
Was my Jesus my song,
And redemption through faith in His name;
Oh! that all might believe,
And salvation receive,
And their song and their joy be the same.

1. The God of Abram praise, Whose all suf-fi-cient grace Shall guide me all my hap-py days In all His ways;
He calls a worm His friend; He calls Him-self my God: And He shall save me to the end, Thro' Je-sus' blood.

H. 432 *The God of Abraham.*

1 The God of Abram praise,
  Whose all sufficient grace
 Shall guide me all my happy days
  In all His ways:
 He calls a worm His friend;
  He calls Himself my God:
 And He shall save me to the end,
  Through Jesus' blood.

2 Though nature's strength decay,
  And earth and hell withstand,
 To Canaan's bounds I urge my way
  At His command:
 The watery deep I pass
  With Jesus in my view;
 And through the howling wilderness,
  My way pursue.

3 He keeps His own secure,
  He guards them by His side;
 Arrays in garments white and pure
  His spotless bride:
 With streams of sacred bliss,
  With groves of living joys,
 With all the fruits of paradise
  He still supplies.

4 He by Himself hath sworn,
  I on His oath depend;
 I shall on eagles' wings be borne,
  To heaven ascend:
 I shall behold His face,
  I shall His power adore,
 And sing the wonders of His grace
  For evermore.

NEW CONCORD. 6s & 9s. POPULAR MELODY.

1. O how hap-py are they Who the Sa-viour o-bey, And have laid up their trea-sures a-bove!
O what tongue can ex-press The sweet com-fort and peace Of a soul in its ear-li-est love?

GOULD. 8s, 8s & 4s.

J. E. Gould, 1871.

1. My God, is an - y hour so sweet, From blush of morn to eve-ning star,

As - that which calls me to Thy feet — The hour of prayer.

H. 381 *The Hour of Prayer.*

1 My God, is any hour so sweet,
From blush of morn to evening star,
As that which calls me to Thy feet,
The hour of prayer?

2 Blest is that tranquil hour of morn,
And blest that hour of solemn eve,
When, on the wings of prayer up-borne,
The world I leave.

3 Then is my strength by Thee renewed;
Then are my sins by Thee forgiven;
Then dost Thou cheer my longing soul
With hopes of heaven.

4 No words can tell what sweet relief
There for my every want I find;
What strength for warfare, balm for grief,
What peace of mind.

5 Hushed is each doubt, gone every fear;
My spirit seems in heaven to stay;
And e'en the penitential tear
Is wiped away.

6 Lord, till I reach that blissful shore,
No privilege so dear shall be,
As this, my inmost soul to pour
In prayer to Thee.

H. 339 *Thy Will be Done.*

1 My God and Father, while I stray
Far from my home, on life's rough way,
Oh! teach me from my heart to say,
Thy will be done!

2 Let but my fainting heart be blest
With Thy sweet Spirit for its guest,
My God, to Thee I leave the rest;
Thy will be done!

3 Renew my will from day to day;
Blend it with Thine; and take away
All that now makes it hard to say,
Thy will be done!

4 Then, when on earth I breathe no more,
The prayer, oft mixed with tears before,
I'll sing upon a happier shore,
Thy will be done!

H. 288 *Seeking Christ's Presence.*

[Tune, "Zion's Pilgrim."]

1 O Thou in whose presence my soul takes delight,
On whom in affliction I call,
My comfort by day, and my song in the night,
My hope, my salvation, my all:

2 Where dost Thou at noontide resort with Thy sheep,
To feed on the pastures of love?
Say, why in the valley of death should I weep,
Or alone in the wilderness rove?

3 Oh! why should I wander an alien from Thee,
Or cry in the desert for bread?
Thy foes will rejoice when my sorrows they see,
And smile at the tears I have shed.

4 Restore, my dear Saviour, the light of Thy face,
Thy soul-cheering favour impart;
And let Thy sweet tokens of pardoning grace
Bring joy to my desolate heart.

Anon.

1. I think when I read that sweet sto-ry of old, When Je-sus was here a-mong men,
How He called lit-tle chil-dren as lambs to His fold, I should like to have been with them then.

H. 534 *The Good Shepherd.*

2 I wish that His hands had been placed on my head,
That His arms had been thrown around me,
And that I might have seen His kind look when He said,
"Let the little ones come unto Me."

3 Yet still to His footstool in prayer I may go,
And ask for a share in His love;
And if I thus earnestly seek Him below,
I shall see Him and hear Him above,—

4 In that beautiful place he has gone to prepare,
For all who are washed and forgiven;
And many dear children are gathering there,
"For of such is the kingdom of heaven."

5 I long for the joys of that glorious time,
The sweetest, and brightest, and best,
When the dear little children of every clime
Shall crowd to His arms, and be blest.

ZION'S PILGRIM. 11s & 8s.

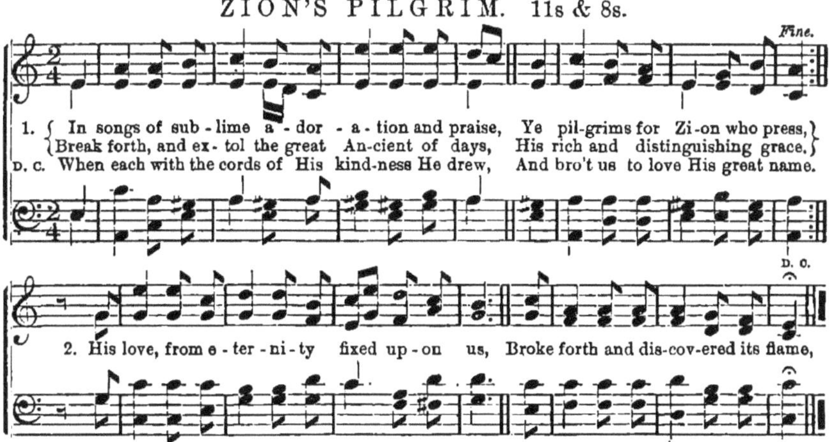
Fine.
1. { In songs of sub-lime a-dor-a-tion and praise, Ye pil-grims for Zi-on who press,
Break forth, and ex-tol the great An-cient of days, His rich and distinguishing grace. }
D. C. When each with the cords of His kind-ness He drew, And bro't us to love His great name.
D. C.
2. His love, from e-ter-ni-ty fixed up-on us, Broke forth and dis-cov-ered its flame,

H. 17 *Distinguishing Grace.*

3 Oh! had He not pitied the state we were in,
Our bosom His love had ne'er felt; [in sin,
We all would have lived, would have died, too,
And sunk with the load of our guilt,

4 What was there in us that could merit esteem,
Or give the Creator delight?
'Twas "even so, Father," we ever must sing,
"Because it seemed good in Thy sight."

5 'Twas all of Thy grace we were brought to obey,
While others were suffered to go
The road which by nature we chose as our way,
That leads to the regions of woe.

6 Then give all the glory to His holy name,
To Him all the glory belongs;
Be ours the high joy still to sound forth His fame,
And crown Him in each of our songs.

Dr. T. Hastings, 1832.

1. How calm and beau-ti - ful the morn That gilds the sa - cred tomb,
Where once the Cru-ci - fied was borne,
And veiled in mid-night gloom!
O! weep no more the Sa - viour slain; The Lord is ris'n—He lives a - gain.

H. 96 *Resurrection of Christ.*

1 How calm and beautiful the morn
That gilds the sacred tomb,
Where once the Crucified was borne,
And veiled in midnight gloom!
O! weep no more the Saviour slain;
The Lord is risen—He lives again.

2 Ye mourning saints, dry every tear
For your departed Lord.
"Behold the place—He is not here,"
The tomb is all unbarred;
The gates of death were closed in vain;
The Lord is risen—He lives again.

3 Now cheerful to the house of prayer
Your early footsteps bend;
The Saviour will Himself be there,
Your Advocate and Friend.
Once by the law your hopes were slain,
But now in Christ ye live again.

4 How tranquil now the rising day!
'Tis Jesus still appears,
A risen Lord, to chase away
Your unbelieving fears.
O! weep no more your comforts slain;
The Lord is risen—He lives again.

5 And when the shades of evening fall,
When life's last hour draws nigh,
If Jesus shines upon the soul;
How blissful then to die!
Since He has risen who once was slain,
Ye die in Christ to live again.

H. 530 *Children in Heaven.*

[Tune, "Canaan."]

1 Around the throne of God in heav'n
Thousands of children stand,
Children whose sins are all forgiven,
A holy, happy band;
Singing, glory, glory, glory be to
God on high.

2 In flowing robes of spotless white
See every one arrayed;
Dwelling in everlasting light,
And joys that never fade;
Singing, glory, glory, glory be to
God on high.

3 What brought them to that world above,
That heav'n so bright and fair,
Where all is peace, and joy, and love,—
How came those children there?
Singing, glory, glory, glory be to
God on high.

4 Because the Saviour shed His blood,
To wash away their sin;
Bathed in that pure and precious flood,
Behold them white and clean!
Singing, glory, glory, glory be to
God on high.

5 On earth they sought the Saviour's grace,
On earth they loved His name;
So now they see His blessed face,
And stand before the Lamb;
Singing, glory, glory, glory be to
God on high.

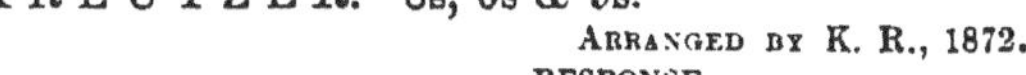

ARRANGED BY K. R., 1872.

RESPONSE.
1. { Ye err-ing souls, that wild-ly roam From heav'n and bliss a - stray,
Your Fa-ther's voice in-vites you home, He makes a feast to - day. }
Oh! I'll not die here, with want se-
vere, And starve in for - eign lands; In my Fa-ther's house are rich sup-plies, And bount-eous are His hands.

H. 172 *The Prodigal.*

1 Ye erring souls, that wildly roam
From heaven and bliss astray,
Your Father's voice invites you home,
He makes a feast to-day.

Res.—Oh! I'll not die here, with want severe,
And starve in foreign lands;
In my Father's house are rich supplies,
And bounteous are His hands.

2 And thou art bidden, weary one,
With wants and woes oppressed;
And every far-off wandering son
May be a welcome guest.
Res.—Oh! I'll not die here, &c.

3 Return, thou prodigal, return,
Thy Father bids thee come;
He doth thy needless absence mourn;
Thou erring child, come home.
Res.—Oh! I'll not die here, &c.

4 Come, for the feast already waits,
The fatlings all are slain;
Go, seek with haste His palace gates;
Nor shalt thou seek in vain.
Res.—Oh! I'll not die here, &c.

5 The Father stands and waits to greet
His late returning son;
Go, haste thee, child, He runs to meet
And clasp Thee as His own.
Res.—Oh! I'll not die here, &c.

CANAAN. 8s, 6s & 5s.

1. A-round the throne of God in heav'n, Thou-sands of chil-dren stand; Chil-dren whose sins are all for-giv'n, A
ho - ly hap - py band; Sing-ing, Glo - ry, glo-ry, glo-ry be to God on high.

ARIEL. C. P. M.

Dr. L. Mason, 1836.

1. O could I speak the match - less worth, O could I sound the glo-ries forth,
Which in my Sa - viour shine. I'd soar and touch the heav'n -ly strings,
And vie with Ga - briel while he sings,
In notes al - most di - vine — In notes al - most di - vine.

H. 40 *Character of the Redeemer.*

2 I'd sing the precious blood He spilt,
My ransom from the dreadful guilt,
Of sin and wrath divine;
I'd sing His glorious righteousness,
In which all-perfect, heavenly dress,
My soul shall ever shine.

3 I'd sing the characters He bears,
And all the forms of love He wears,
Exalted on His throne;
In loftiest songs of sweetest praise,
I would to everlasting days
Make all His glories known.

4 Soon the delightful day will come,
When my dear Lord will call me home,
And I shall see his face;
Then, with my Saviour, Brother, Friend,
A blest eternity I'll spend,
Triumphant in His grace.

H. 266 *Fleeing to Christ as a Refuge.*

[Tune, "Rapture."]

1 O Thou that hearest the prayer of faith,
Wilt Thou not save a soul from death,
That casts itself on Thee?
I have no refuge of my own,
But fly to what my Lord has done,
And suffered, once for me.

2 Slain in the guilty sinner's stead,
His spotless righteousness I plead,
And His atoning blood;
Thy righteousness my robe shall be,
Thy merit shall avail for me,
And bring me near to God.

3 Then snatch me from eternal death,
The spirit of adoption breathe,
His consolation send:
By Him some word of life impart,
And sweetly whisper to my heart,
"Thy Maker is thy Friend."

4 The king of terrors then would be
A welcome messenger to me,
To bid me come away:
Unclogged by earth, or earthly things,
I'd mount, I'd fly with eager wings,
To everlasting day.

GANGES. C. P. M.

CHANDLER.

1. A-waked by Si-nai's aw-ful sound, My soul in bonds of guilt I found, And knew not where to go;
E-ter-nal truth did loud pro-claim, "The sin-ner must be born a-gain," Or sink to end-less woe.

H. 199 *Necessity of Regeneration.*

2 When to the law I trembling fled,
It poured its curses on my head,
I no relief could find;
This fearful truth increased my pain,
"The sinner must be born again,"
And whelmed my tortured mind.

3 Again did Sinai's thunders roll,
And guilt lay heavy on my soul,
A vast oppressive load;
Alas! I read, and saw it plain,
"The sinner must be born again,"
Or drink the wrath of God.

4 The saints I heard with rapture tell,
How Jesus conquered death and hell,
And broke the fowler's snare;
Yet, when I found this truth remain,
"The sinner must be born again,"
I sunk in deep despair.

5 But while I thus in anguish lay,
The gracious Saviour passed this way,
And felt His pity move;
The sinner, by His justice slain,
Now by His grace is born again,
And sings redeeming love,

RAPTURE. C. P. M.

EDWARD HARWOOD, 1707-1787.

1. O Thou that hearest the prayer of faith, Wilt Thou not save a soul from death,
That casts it-self on Thee? I have no re-fuge of my own;
But fly to what my Lord has done, And suf-fered, once for me.

Dr. L. Mason, 1839.

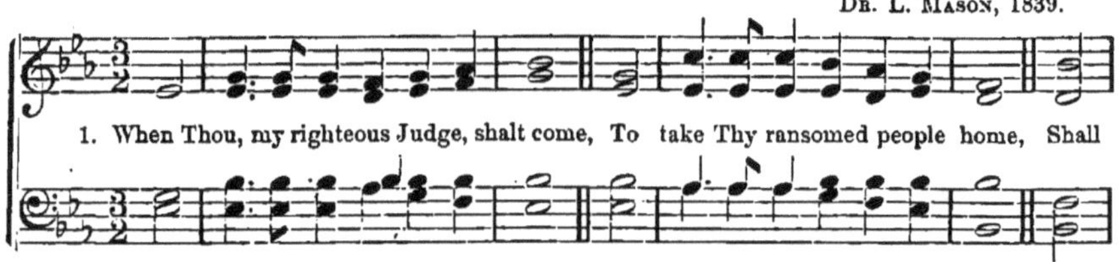
1. When Thou, my righteous Judge, shalt come, To take Thy ransomed people home, Shall

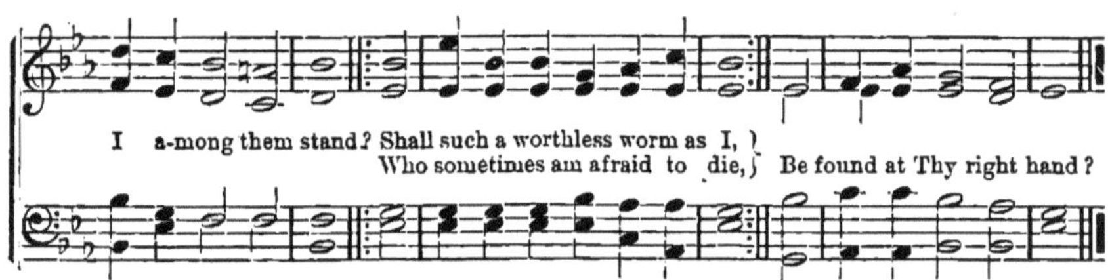
I a-mong them stand? Shall such a worthless worm as I,
Who sometimes am afraid to die,
Be found at Thy right hand?

H. 658 *Apprehension of Judgment.*

1 When Thou, my righteous Judge, shalt come,
To take Thy ransomed people home,
Shall I among them stand?
Shall such a worthless worm as I,
Who sometimes am afraid to die,
Be found at Thy right hand?

2 I love to meet among them now,
Before Thy gracious feet to bow,
Though vilest of them all;
But can I bear the piercing thought,
What if my name should be left out,
When Thou for them shalt call?

3 Prevent, prevent it by Thy grace;
Be Thou, dear Lord, my hiding-place,
In this the accepted day;
Thy pardoning voice, O let me hear,
To still my unbelieving fear,
Nor let me fall, I pray.

4 Let me among Thy saints be found,
Whene'er the archangel's trump shall sound
To see Thy smiling face;
Then loudest of the crowd I'll sing,
While heaven's resounding mansions ring
With shouts of sovereign grace.

H. 622 *The swiftness of Time.*

1 My days, my weeks, my months, my years,
Fly rapid as the whirling spheres
Around the steady pole:
Time, like the tide, its motion keeps,
Till I must launch through boundless deeps,
Where endless ages roll.

2 The grave is near the cradle seen;
The moments swiftly pass between,
And whisper as they fly,
Unthinking man, remember this,
Though fond of sublunary bliss,
Thou soon must gasp and die.

3 My soul, attend the solemn call;
Thine earthly tent must quickly fall,
And thou must take thy flight,
Beyond the vast expansive blue,
To sing and love as angels do,
Or sink in endless night.

H. 526 *Far at Sea.* Tune, "Adger,"

1 Star of peace to wanderers weary,
Bright the beams that smile on me;
Cheer the pilot's vision dreary,
Far, far at sea.

2 Star of hope, gleam o'er the billow,
Bless the soul that sighs for Thee,
Bless the sailor's lonely pillow,
Far, far at sea.

3 Star of faith, when winds are mocking
All his toil, he flies to Thee;
Save him, on the billows rocking,
Far, far at sea.

4 Star divine, Oh! safely guide him,
Bring the wanderer home to Thee;
Sore temptations long have tried him,
Far, far at sea.

KINGWOOD. C. P. M.

Lo! on a nar - row neck of land, 'Twixt two un-bound-ed seas I stand, 'Twixt two un-bound-ed
D. S. Re - moves me to you heavenly place, Re - moves me to you
Fine.
D. S.
seas I stand, Yet how in - sen - si - ble! A point of time, a mo-ment's space,
heavenly place, Or shuts me up in hell.

H. 621 *Time and Eternity.*

2 O God, my inmost soul convert,
And deeply on my thoughtless heart,
Eternal things impress;
Give me to feel their solemn weight,
And save me ere it be too late;
Wake me to righteousness.

3 Before me place in bright array
The pomp of that tremendous day,
When Thou with clouds shalt come
To judge the nations at Thy bar:
And tell me, Lord, shall I be there,
To meet a joyful doom?

4 Be this my one great business here,
With holy trembling, holy fear,
To make my calling sure;
Thine utmost counsel to fulfil,
And suffer all Thy righteous will,
And to the end endure.

5 Then, Saviour, then my soul receive,
Transported from this vale, to live
And reign with Thee above;
Where faith is sweetly lost in sight,
And hope, in full, supreme delight,
And everlasting love.

ADGER. 8, 7, 8, 4.

From the German.

1. Star of peace to wand'r-ers wea - ry. Bright the beams that smile on me;
Cheer the pi - lot's vi - sion drea - ry, Far, far at sea.

PILGRIM. 9s, 11s & 10s.

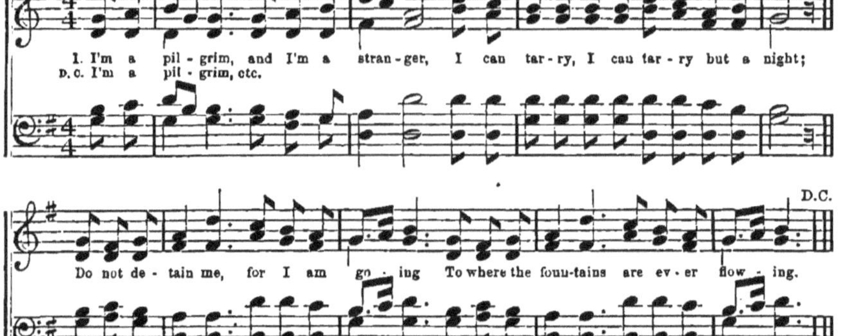
FINE.
1. I'm a pil - grim, and I'm a stran - ger, I can tar - ry, I can tar - ry but a night;
D. C. I'm a pil - grim, etc.
D.C.
Do not de - tain me, for I am go - ing To where the foun-tains are ev - er flow - ing.

2 There the sunbeams are ever shining,
I am longing, I am longing for the sight.
Within a country, unknown and dreary,
I have been wandering forlorn and weary
Cho.—I'm a pilgrim, etc.

3 Of that country, to which I'm going,
My Redeemer, my Redeemer is the light;
There are no sorrows, nor any sighing,
Nor any sin there, nor any dying.
Cho.—I'm a pilgrim, etc.

GLORIA IN EXCELSIS.

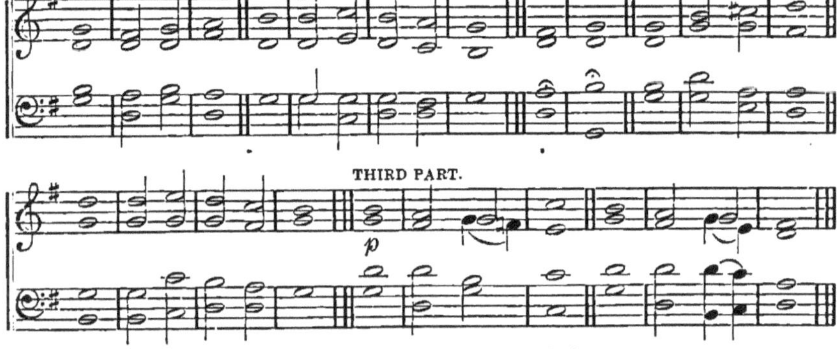
FIRST PART.
SECOND PART.
THIRD PART.
p

TO THE FIRST PART OF THE CHANT.

1. Glory be to | God on | high, || and on earth | peace, good | will towards | men.
2. We praise Thee, we bless Thee, we | worship | Thee, || we glorify Thee, we give thanks to Thee | for thy | great— | glory.

TO THE SECOND PART.

3. O Lord God, | Heavenly | King, || God the | Father Al— | mighty!
4. O Lord, the only-begotten Son, | Jesus | Christ, || O Lord God, Lamb of God, | Son . . of the | Fa— | ther!

TO THE THIRD PART.

5. That takest away the | sins . . of the | world, || have mercy up- | on— | us.
6. Thou that takest away the | sins . . of the | world, || have mercy up- | on—us.
7. Thou that takest away the | sins . . of the | world, || Re- | ceive our | prayer.
8. Thou that sittest at the right hand of | God the | Father, || have mercy up- | on— | us.

TO THE FIRST PART.

9. For Thou only | art— | holy, || Thou | only | art the | Lord.
10. Thou only, O Christ, with the | Holy | Ghost, || art most high in the | glory . of | God the | Father. || A- | men.

APPENDIX.

---

698 *The King of Glory.* 8s, 7s & 4s.

1 Glory be to God, the Father!
Glory be to God, the Son!
Glory be to God, the Spirit!
Great Jehovah, three in one!
Glory, glory,
While eternal ages run!

2 Glory be to Him who loved us,
Washed us from each spot and stain;
Glory be to Him who bought us,
Made us kings with Him to reign!
Glory, glory,
To the Lamb that once was slain!

3 Glory to the King of angels!
Glory to the church's King!
Glory to the King of nations!
Heaven and earth your praises bring;
Glory, glory,
To the King of glory bring!

4 Glory, blessing, praise eternal!
Thus the choir of angels sings!
Honour, riches, power, dominion!
Thus its praise creation brings:
Glory, glory,
Glory to the King of kings.

699 *Praise to the Trinity.* L. M.

1 Great One in Three, great Three in One!
Thy wondrous name we sound abroad;
Prostrate we fall before Thy throne,
O holy, holy, holy, Lord!

2 Thee, Holy Father, we confess;
Thee, Holy Saviour, we adore;
And thee, O Holy Ghost, we bless
And praise and worship evermore.

3 Thou art by heaven and earth adored:
Thy universe is full of Thee,
O holy, holy, holy Lord!
Great Three in One, great One in Three!

700 *Psalm* 145. L. M.

1 My God! my King! Thy various praise
Shall fill the remnant of my days:
Thy grace employ my humble tongue,
Till death and glory raise the song.

2 The wings of every hour shall bear
Some thankful tribute to Thine ear;
And every setting sun shall see
New works of duty done for Thee.

3 Thy truth and justice I'll proclaim:
Thy bounty flows an endless stream,
Thy mercy swift, Thine anger slow,
But dreadful to the stubborn foe.

4 But who can speak Thy wondrous deeds?
Thy greatness all our thoughts exceeds:
Vast and unsearchable Thy ways,—
Vast and immortal be Thy praise.

701 *"The Lord is King."* C. M.

1 Hail, holy, holy, holy Lord!
Let powers immortal sing;
Adore the co-eternal Word;
Rejoice, the Lord is King.

2 To Thee all angels cry aloud,
Thy name hosannas ring;
Around Thy throne their myriads crowd,
And shout, The Lord is King!

3 Hail Him, they cry, ye sons of light:
Of joy th' eternal Spring;
Praise Him, who formed you by His might;
Rejoice, the Lord is King!

4 Hail Him, ye saints! whose love for you
Has drawn the monster's sting:
Oh! render to the Lord His due:
Rejoice, the Lord is King!

5 Let worlds above and worlds below,
In songs united sing!
And, while eternal ages flow,
Rejoice, the Lord is King!

702 *God's Eternity and Majesty.* L. M.

1 Thee, Thee we praise, O God! and own
That Thou, the Lord, art God alone;
Thy praise supreme all nature sings,
Eternal Father! King of kings!

2 All angels and the cherubim—
The heavenly host, the seraphim—
Cease not to cry, "Be Thou adored,
O holy, holy, holy Lord!"

3 The heavens and earth are full of Thee—
Thy glory, power and majesty;
Th' apostles, prophets, martyrs, raise
To Thee their loudest songs of praise.

4 Thy holy church, in every land,
Exulting owns Thy ruling hand;
Infinite majesty is Thine,
Father eternal! power divine!

5 Thee, too, O Christ, they all confess—
Thee, King of glory! Thee they bless!
The Father's Son Thou art alone—
Partaker of th' eternal throne.

6 Thee, Father, Son, and Holy Ghost!
Thy saints, with all the heavenly host,
Confess, proclaim, extol, adore,
From day to day, for evermore.

703 *God's Sovereignty.* 7s.

1 Sovereign Ruler of the skies,
Ever gracious, ever wise,
All my times are in thy hand,
All events at Thy command.

2 Times of sickness, times of health;
Times of penury and wealth;
Times of trial and of grief;
Times of triumph and relief;

3 Times the tempter's power to prove;
Times to taste a Saviour's love;
All must come and last and end,
As shall please my heavenly Friend.

4 Thee at all times will I bless;
Having Thee, I all possess;
How can I bereaved be,
Since I cannot part with Thee?

704 *Creation and Redemption.* C. M.

1 We raise our songs, O God, to Thee,
And send them to Thy throne;
All glory to th' united Three—
The undivided One.

2 'Twas He—and we'll adore His name—
That formed us by a word;
'Tis He restores our ruined frame;
Salvation to the Lord!

3 Hosanna! let the earth and skies
Repeat the joyful sound;
Rocks, hills, and vales reflect the voice,
In one eternal round.

705 *The Holiness of God.* C. M.

1 Holy and reverened is the name
Of our eternal King;
"Thrice holy Lord!" the angels cry;
"Thrice holy!" let us sing.

2 The deepest reverence of the mind,
My soul! pay to thy God;
Lift, with thy hands, a holy heart,
To His sublime abode.

3 With sacred awe pronounce His name,
Whom words nor thoughts can reach;
A broken heart shall please Him more
Than the best forms of speech.

4 Thou holy God! preserve my soul
From all pollution free;
The pure in heart are Thy delight,
And they Thy face shall see.

706 *Psalm 89.* C. M.

1 The mercies of my God and King
My tongue shall still pursue:
Oh! happy they who, while they sing
Those mercies, share them too!

2 As bright and lasting as the sun,
As lofty as the sky,
From age to age, Thy word shall run,
And chance and change defy.

3 The covenant of the King of kings
Shall stand for ever sure;
Beneath the shadow of Thy wings
Thy saints repose secure.

L. O. Emerson.

1. Bless, O my soul! the living God; Call home thy thoughts that rove abroad;

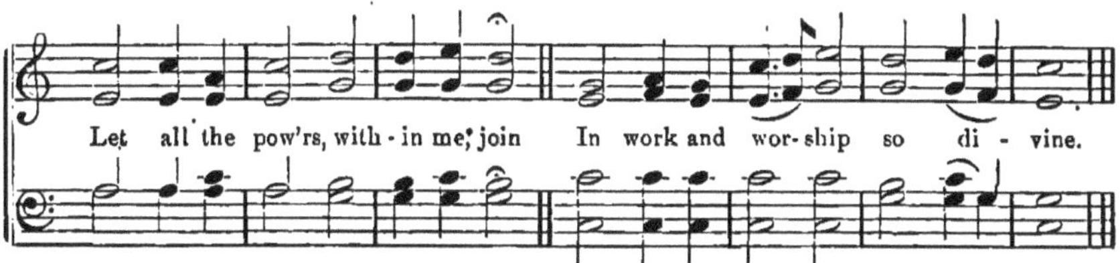
Let all the pow'rs, with - in me, join In work and wor-ship so di - vine.

4 Thine is the earth, and Thine the skies,
 Created at Thy will;
The waves at Thy command arise,
 At Thy command are still.

5 In earth below, in heaven above,
 Who, who is Lord like Thee?
Oh! spread the gospel of Thy love,
 Till all Thy glories see!

707 *Psalm* 103. L. M.

1 Bless, O my soul! the living God;
Call home thy thoughts that rove abroad;
Let all the powers within me join
In work and worship so divine.

2 Bless, O my soul! the God of grace;
His favours claim thy highest praise:
Why should the wonders He hath [wrought
Be lost in silence, and forgot?

3 'Tis He, my soul! that sent His Son
To die for crimes which thou hast done;
He owns the ransom, and forgives
The hourly follies of our lives.

4 Let the whole earth His power confess,
Let the whole earth adore His grace:
The Gentile with the Jew shall join
In work and worship so divine.

708 *God is Love.* C. M.

1 Come, ye that know and fear the Lord!
 And lift your souls above;
Let every heart and voice accord
 To sing that God is love.

2 This precious truth His word declares,
 And all His mercies prove;
Jesus, the Gift of gifts, appears,
 To show that God is love.

3 Behold His patience lengthened out,
 To those who from Him rove,
And calls effectual reach their hearts,
 To teach them, God is love.

4 The work begun is carried on,
 By power from heaven above;
And every step, from first to last,
 Declares that God is love.

5 Oh! may we all, while here below,
 This best of blessings prove:
Till warmer hearts, in brighter worlds,
 Shall shout that God is love.

709 *The Wisdom and Love of God.* 8s & 7s.

1 God is love: His mercy brightens
 All the path in which we rove;
Bliss He wakes and woe He lightens;
 God is wisdom, God is love.

2 Chance and change are busy ever;
 Man decays, and ages move;
But His mercy waneth never;
 God is wisdom, God is love.

3 Ee'n the hour that darkest seemeth,
 Will His changeless goodness prove;
From the gloom His brightness [streameth,
 God is wisdom, God is love.

4 He with earthly cares entwineth
Hope and comfort from above;
Every where His glory shineth;
God is wisdom, God is love.

710 *God's Faithfulness.* 7s.

1 Cast thy burden on the Lord,
Only lean upon His word;
Thou wilt soon have cause to bless
His eternal faithfulness.

2 He sustains thee by His hand,
He enables thee to stand;
Those, whom Jesus once hath loved,
From His grace are never moved.

3 Heaven and earth may pass away,
God's free grace shall not decay;
He hath promised to fulfil
All the pleasure of His will.

4 Jesus! Guardian of Thy flock,
Be Thyself our constant Rock;
Make us, by Thy powerful hand,
Strong as Zion's mountain stand.

711 *The Chorus of Angels.* C. M.

1 Calm on the listening ear of night
Come heaven's melodious strains,
Where wild Judea stretches far
Her silver-mantled plains.

2 Celestial choirs, from courts above,
Shed sacred glories there;
And angels, with their sparkling lyres,
Make music on the air.

3 The answering hills of Palestine
Send back the glad reply;
And greet, from all their holy heights,
The day-spring from on high.

5 O'er the blue depths of Galilee
There comes a holier calm,
And Sharon waves, in solemn praise,
Her silent groves of palm.

5 "Glory to God!" the sounding skies
Loud with their anthems ring—
"Peace to the earth, good-will to men,
From heaven's eternal King!"

712 *The Star of Bethlehem.* 7s.

1 As with gladness men of old
Did the guiding star behold:
As with joy they hailed its light,
Leading onward, beaming bright;
So, most gracious Lord, may we
Evermore be led to Thee.

2 Holy Jesus! every day
Keep us in the narrow way;
And, when earthly things are past,
Bring our ransomed souls at last
Where they need no star to guide,
Where no clouds Thy glory hide.

713 *Christ, the New-Born King.* 8s, 7s & 4s

1 Angels, from the realms of glory,
Wing your flight o'er all the earth:
Ye who sang creation's story,
Now proclaim Messiah's birth:
Come and worship,
Worship Christ, the new-born King.

2 Shepherds in the field abiding,
Watching o'er your flocks by night;
God with man is now residing,
Yonder shines the infant-light:
Come and worship,
Worship Christ, the new-born King.

3 Sages, leave your contemplations;
Brighter visions beam afar:
Seek the great Desire of nations,
Ye have seen His natal star:
Come and worship,
Worship Christ, the new-born King.

4 Saints in humble prayer are bending,
Watching long in hope and fear;
Suddenly the Lord, descending,
In His temple shall appear;
Come and worship,
Worship Christ, the new-born King.

714 *The Depths of Woe.* S. M.

1 O'erwhelmed in depths of woe,
Upon the tree of scorn
Hangs the Redeemer of mankind,
With deepest anguish torn.

2 The sun withdraws his light;
The mid-day heavens grow pale;
The moon, the stars, the universe,
Their Maker's death bewail.

3 Shall man alone be mute?
Come, youth and hoary hairs!
Come, rich and poor! come, all mankind!
And bathe those feet in tears.

GERMAN CHORAL

1. Be-yond where Kedron's waters flow Be - hold the suff'ring Sa-viour go To sad Geth-sem-a - ne!
His coun - te - nance is all di - vine, Yet grief ap - pears in ev' - ry line.

4 Come, fall before His cross,
Who shed for us His blood;
Who died a sacrifice of love,
To make us sons of God.

5 Jesus! all praise to Thee,
Our Joy and endless Rest!
Be Thou our Guide while pilgrims here,
Our Crown amid the blest!

715 *The Prayer of Agony.* 8s, 6s & 8s.

1 BEYOND where Kedron's waters flow,
Behold the suffering Saviour go
To sad Gethsemane!
His countenance is all divine,
Yet grief appears in every line.

2 He bows beneath the sins of men;
He cries to God, and cries again,
In sad Gethsemane;
He lifts His mournful eyes above—
"My Father, can this cup remove?"

3 With gentle resignation still,
He yielded to His Father's will,
In sad Gethsemane;
"Behold Me here, Thine only Son;
And Father! let Thy will be done."

4 The Father heard; and angels, there,
Sustained the Son of God in prayer,
In sad Gethsemane;
He drank the dreadful cup of pain;
Then rose to life and joy again.

5 When storms of sorrow round us sweep,
And scenes of anguish make us weep,
To sad Gethsemane
We'll look, and see the Saviour there,
And humbly bow, like Him, in prayer.

716 *Angels! Lament.* C. M.

1 ANGELS! lament; behold! your God
Man's sinful likeness wears;
Behold! upon th' accursed tree
Man's sins the Saviour bears.

2 O Christ! with wondering minds we see
What mighty love was Thine;
Did God consent to suffer thus?
And, oh! shall man repine?

3 No, Saviour! no; the power of death
Thy cross hath overcome,
To save us, not from earthly woe,
But from th' eternal doom.

717 *Christ Risen.* 7s.

1 ANGELS, roll the rock away!
Death yield up the mighty prey!
See, the Saviour quits the tomb,
Glowing with immortal bloom.
Alleluia! swell the lay!
Christ the Lord is risen to-day.

2 Shout, ye seraphs; angels, raise
Your eternal song of praise;
Let the earth's remotest bound
Echo to the blissful sound.
Alleluia! swell the lay!
Christ the Lord is risen to-day.

718 *The First-Begotten of the Dead.* C. P. M.

1 Come, see the place where Jesus lay,
And hear angelic watchers say,
"He lives, who once was slain:
Why seek the living midst the dead?
Remember how the Saviour said
That He would rise again."

2 O joyful sound! O glorious hour,
When by His own almighty power
He rose, and left the grave!
Now let our songs His triumph tell,
Who burst the bands of death and hell,
And ever lives to save.

3 The First-Begotten of the dead,
For us He rose, our glorious Head,
Immortal life to bring; [die?
What, though the saints like Him shall
They share their Leader's victory,
And triumph with their King.

4 No more they tremble at the grave,
For Jesus will their spirits save,
And raise their slumbering dust;
O risen Lord! in Thee we live,
To Thee our ransomed souls we give,
To Thee our bodies trust.

719 *The Resurrection of Christ.* C. M.

1 On this blest day, a brighter scene
Of glory was displayed,
By God, th' eternal Word, than when
This universe was made.

2 He rises, who our souls hath bought
With blood, and pains extreme;
'Twas great—to speak the world from
'Twas greater—to redeem. [naught—

720 *The Ascension.* 7s.

1 Hail the day that saw Him rise
To His throne above the skies;
Christ, the Lamb for sinners given,
Enters now the highest heaven.

2 There for Him high triumph waits;
Lift your heads, eternal gates;
He hath conquered death and sin;
Take the King of Glory in.

3 Lo, the heaven its Lord receives,
Yet He loves the earth He leaves;
Though returning to His throne,
Still He calls mankind His own.

4 See, He lifts His hands above;
See, He shows the prints of love;
Hark, His gracious lips bestow
Blessings on His Church below.

5 Still for us He intercedes,
His prevailing death He pleads;
Near Himself prepares our place,
He the first fruits of our race.

6 Lord, though parted from our sight,
Far above the starry height,
Grant our hearts may thither rise,
Seeking Thee above the skies.

721 *Christ's Exaltation.* L. M.

1 O Saviour, who for man hast trod
The winepress of the wrath of God,
Ascend and claim again on high
Thy glory left for us to die.

2 A radiant cloud is now Thy seat,
And earth lies stretched beneath Thy feet;
Ten thousand thousands round Thee sing,
And share the triumph of their King.

3 The angel-host enraptured waits;
"Lift up your heads, eternal gates!"
O God and Man! the Father's Throne
Is now for evermore Thine own.

4 Our great High Priest and Shepherd
Within the veil art entered now, [Thou
To offer there Thy precious blood
Once poured on earth a cleansing flood.

5 And thence the Church, Thy chosen bride,
With countless gifts of grace supplied,
Through all her members draws from
Her hidden life of sanctity. [Thee

6 O Christ, our Lord, of Thy dear care
Thy lowly members heavenward bear;
Be ours with Thee to suffer pain,
With Thee for evermore to reign.

722 *Crown the Saviour.* 8s, 7s & 4s.

1 Look, ye saints; the sight is glorious;
See the "Man of sorrows" now;
From the fight returned victorious,
Every knee to Him shall bow;
Crown Him! Crown Him!
Crowns become the Victor's brow.

2 Crown the Saviour, angels crown Him;
Rich the trophies Jesus brings;

On the seat of power enthrone Him,
While the vault of heaven rings;
Crown Him! Crown Him!
Crown the Saviour King of kings.

3 Sinners in derision crowned Him,
Mocking thus the Saviour's claim;
Saints and angels crowd around Him,
Own His title, praise His name;
Crown Him! Crown Him!
Spread abroad the Victor's fame!

4 Hark! those bursts of acclamation!
Hark! those loud triumphant chords!
Jesus takes the highest station;
O what joy the sight affords!
Crown Him! Crown Him!
King of kings, and Lord of lords.

723 *Christ Triumphant.* 8, 7s & 7s.

1 Who is this that comes from Edom,
All His raiment stained with blood,
To the captive bringing freedom,
Ransomed by the grace of God;
Glorious in the garb He wears,
Glorious in the spoil He bears?

2 'Tis the Saviour, now victorious,
Travelling onward in His might;
'Tis the Saviour; O how glorious
To His people, is the sight!
Satan conquered, and the grave,
Jesus now is strong to save.

3 Why that blood His raiment staining?
'Tis the blood of many slain;
Of His foes there's none remaining,
None, the contest to maintain;
They are fallen no more to rise;
All their glory prostrate lies.

4 Mighty Victor, reign for ever;
Wear the crown so dearly won;
Never shall Thy people, never,
Cease to sing what Thou hast done;
Thou hast fought Thy people's foes;
Thou hast healed Thy people's woes.

724 *The Manifestation of Christ.* 7s.

1 Son of God! to Thee I cry;
By the holy mystery
Of Thy dwelling here on earth,
By Thy pure and holy birth,—
Lord! Thy presence let me see;
Manifest Thyself to me!

2 Lamb of God! to Thee I cry;
By Thy bitter agony,
By Thy pangs, to us unknown,
By Thy Spirit's parting groan,
Lord! Thy presence let me see;
Manifest Thyself to me!

3 Prince of life! to Thee I cry;
By Thy glorious majesty,
By Thy triumph o'er the grave,
Meek to suffer, strong to save,
Lord! Thy presence let me see;
Manifest Thyself to me!

4 Lord of glory, God most high,
Man exalted to the sky!
With Thy love my bosom fill;
Prompt me to perform Thy will;
Then Thy glory I shall see;
Thou wilt bring me home to Thee.

725 *Jesus, the Great Deliverer.* 8s, 7s & 4s.

1 Jesus, Lord of life and glory!
Bend from heaven Thy gracious ear;
While our waiting souls adore Thee,
Friend of helpless sinners! hear;
By Thy mercy,
Oh! deliver us, good Lord!

2 Taught by Thine unerring Spirit,
Boldly we draw nigh to God,
Only in Thy spotless merit,
Only through Thy precious blood:
By Thy mercy,
Oh! deliver us, good Lord!

3 From the depth of nature's blindness,
From the hardening power of sin,
From all malice and unkindness,
From the pride that lurks within,
By Thy mercy,
Oh! deliver us, good Lord!

4 When temptation sorely presses,
In the day of Satan's power,
In our times of deep distresses,
In each dark and trying hour,
By Thy mercy,
Oh! deliver us, good Lord!

5 When the world around is smiling;
In the time of wealth and ease,
Earthly joys our hearts beguiling;
In the day of health and peace,
By Thy mercy,
Oh! deliver us, good Lord!

6 In the weary hours of sickness,
In the times of grief and pain,
When we feel our mortal weakness,
When the creature's help is vain;
By Thy mercy,
Oh! deliver us, good Lord!

7 In the solemn hour of dying,
In the awful judgment day,
May our souls on Thee relying,
Find Thee still our hope and stay:
By Thy mercy,
Oh! deliver us, good Lord!

726 *The all-sufficient Sacrifice.* C. M.

1 When, wounded sore, the stricken soul
Lies bleeding and unbound,
One only hand, a piercèd hand,
Can heal the sinner's wound.

2 When sorrow swells the laden breast,
And tears of anguish flow,
One only heart, a broken heart,
Can feel the sinner's woe.

3 When penitence has wept in vain
Over some foul, dark spot,
One only stream, a stream of blood,
Can wash away the blot.

4 'Tis Jesus' blood, that washes white,
His hand, that brings relief; [joys,
His heart, that's touched with all our
And feeleth for our grief.

5 Lift up Thy bleeding hand, O Lord!
Unseal that cleansing tide;
We have no shelter from our sin,
But in Thy wounded side.

727 *The Man of Sorrows.* C. M.

1 A pilgrim through this lonely world,
The blessèd Saviour passed;
A mourner all His life was He,
A dying lamb at last.

2 That tender heart that felt for all,
For all its life blood gave;
It found on earth no resting place,
Save only in the grave.

3 Such was our Lord: and shall we fear
The cross, with all its scorn?
Or love a faithless evil world,
That wreathed His brow with thorn?

4 No! facing all its frowns or smiles,
Like Him, obedient still,
We homeward press thro' storm or calm,
To Zion's blessèd hill.

728 *Jesus! our Redemption.* C. M.

1 O Christ! our Hope, our heart's Desire,
Redemption's only Spring!
Creator of the world art Thou,
Its Saviour and its King.

2 How vast the mercy and the love,
Which laid our sins on Thee,
And led Thee to a cruel death,
To set Thy people free!

3 But now the pains of death are past,
The ransom has been paid;
And Thou art on Thy Father's throne
In glorious robes arrayed.

4 O Christ! be Thou our present joy,
Our future great reward!
Our only glory may it be
To glory in the Lord!

729 *Hosanna to the Saviour.* L. M. 6 lines.

1 Hosanna to the living Lord!
Hosanna to th' Incarnate Word,
To Christ, Creator, Saviour, King,
Let earth, let heaven hosanna sing,
"Hosanna, Lord! Hosanna, Lord!
"Hosanna, in the highest!" sing.

2 "Hosanna! Lord!" Thine angels cry;
"Hosanna! Lord!" Thy saints reply;
Above, beneath us, and around,
The dead and living swell the sound,
Hosanna, Lord! etc.

3 O Saviour, with protecting care
Abide in this Thy house of prayer,
Where we Thy parting promise claim,
Assembled in Thy sacred name.—*Ch.*

4 But chiefest, in our cleansèd breast
Bid Thine eternal Spirit rest;
And make our secret soul to be
A temple pure and worthy Thee.—*Ch.*

5 So in the last and dreadful day,
When earth and heaven shall melt away,
Thy flock, redeemed from sinful stain,
Shall swell the sound of praise again.—*Ch.*

730 *Jesus adored.* L. M.

1 Jesus, my Lord, my God, my All!
Hear me, blest Saviour! when I call;
Hear me, and from Thy dwelling place,
Pour down the riches of Thy grace:
Jesus, my Lord! I Thee adore;
Oh! make me love Thee more and more.

2 Jesus! too late I Thee have sought;
How can I love Thee as I ought?
And how extol Thy matchless fame,
The glorious beauty of Thy name?
Jesus, my Lord! I Thee adore;
Oh! make me love Thee more and more.

3 Jesus! what didst Thou find in me,
That Thou hast dealt so lovingly?
How great the joy that Thou hast brought,
So far exceeding hope or thought!
Jesus! my Lord! I Thee adore;
Oh! make me love Thee more and more.

4 Jesus! of Thee shall be my song;
To Thee my heart and soul belong;
All that I have or am is Thine,
And Thou, blest Saviour! Thou art mine!
Jesus, my Lord! I Thee adore;
Oh! make me love Thee more and more.

731 *Christ, the supreme God and King.* L. M.

1 Around the Saviour's lofty throne,
Ten thousand times ten thousand sing;
They worship Him as God alone,
And crown Him—everlasting King.

2 Approach, ye saints! this God is yours;
'Tis Jesus fills the throne above:
Ye cannot fail, while God endures;
Ye cannot want, while God is love.

3 Jesus, thou everlasting King!
To Thee the praise of heaven belongs;
Yet, smile on us who fain would bring
The tribute of our humbler songs.

4 Though sin defile our worship here,
We hope ere long Thy face to view,
In heaven with angels to appear,
And praise Thy name as angels do.

732 *The Eternal Word.* C. M.

1 Awake, awake the sacred song
To our incarnate Lord!
Let every heart and every tongue
Adore th' eternal Word.

2 That glorious Word, that sovereign Power
By whom the worlds were made—
Oh, happy morn! illustrious hour!—
Was once in flesh arrayed!

3 Then shone almighty power and love,
In all their wondrous forms,
When Jesus left His throne above
To dwell with sinful worms.

4 Adoring angels tuned their songs
To hail the joyful day;
With rapture then let mortal tongues
Their grateful worship pay.

5 What glory, Lord, to Thee is due!
With wonder we adore;
But could we sing as angels do,
Our highest praise were poor.

733 *The forgiving One.* C. M.

1 What grace, O Lord! and beauty shone
Around Thy steps below!
What patient love was seen in all
Thy life and death of woe!

2 For, ever on Thy burdened heart
A weight of sorrow hung;
Yet no ungentle, murmuring word
Escaped Thy silent tongue.

3 Thy foes might hate, despise, revile,
Thy friends unfaithful prove;
Unwearied in forgiveness still,
Thy heart could only love.

4 Oh! give us hearts to love like Thee;
Like Thee, O Lord! to grieve
Far more for others' sins, than all
The wrongs that we receive.

5 One with Thyself, may every eye,
In us, Thy brethren, see
That gentleness and grace that springs
From union, Lord! with Thee.

734 *The Name of Jesus.* C. M.

1 Thou dear Redeemer, dying Lamb!
We love to hear of Thee;
No music like Thy charming name,
Nor half so sweet can be.

2 Oh, may we ever hear Thy voice
In mercy to us speak!
In Thee, O Lord, let us rejoice,
And Thy salvation seek.

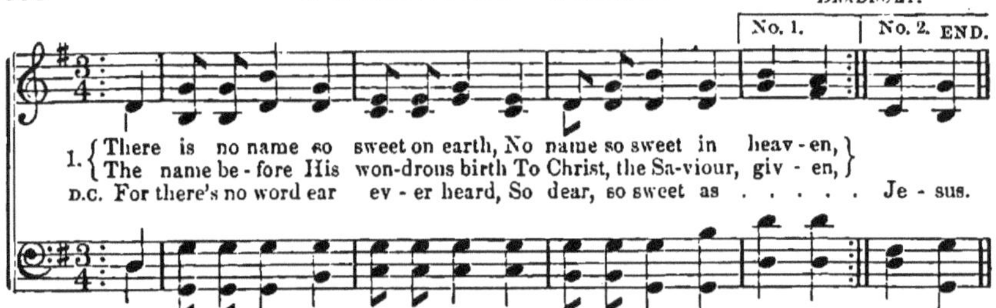
No. 1.
No. 2. END.
1. There is no name so sweet on earth, No name so sweet in heav - en,
The name be - fore His won-drous birth To Christ, the Sa-viour, giv - en,
D.C. For there's no word ear ev - er heard, So dear, so sweet as . . . . . Je - sus.

REFRAIN.
D.C.
We love to sing a - round our King, And hail Him bless - ed Je - sus;

3 Jesus shall ever be our theme,
While in this world we stay;
We'll sing of Jesus' lovely name,
When all things else decay.

4 When we appear in yonder cloud,
With all its favored throng,
Then we will sing, more sweet, more loud,
And Christ shall be our song.

735 *The Sweetest Name.* 8s & 7s, Iambic.

1 There is no name so sweet on earth,
No name so sweet in heaven—
The name before His wondrous birth,
To Christ the Saviour given.
We love to sing around our King,
And hail Him blessed Jesus;
For there's no word ear ever heard,
So dear, so sweet as Jesus.

2 His human name they did proclaim
When Abra'm's son they sealed Him—
The name that still, by God's good-will,
Deliverer revealed Him.—*Ch.*

3 And when He hung upon the tree,
They wrote His name above Him,
That all might see the reason we
For evermore must love Him.—*Ch.*

4 So now, upon His Father's throne,
Almighty to release us
From sin and pains, He gladly reigns,
The Prince and Saviour, Jesus.—*Ch.*

5 To Jesus every knee shall bow,
And every tongue confess Him,
And we unite with saints in light,
Our only Lord, to bless Him.—*Ch.*

6 O Jesus, by that matchless name,
Thy grace shall fail us never;
To-day as yesterday the same,
Thou art the same forever.—*Ch.*

736 *The Dearest Name.* C. M.

1 There is a name I love to hear,
I love to sing its worth;
It sounds like music in mine ear,
The sweetest name on earth.

2 It tells me of a Saviour's love,
Who died to set me free;
It tells me of His precious blood,
The sinner's perfect plea.

3 It tells me what my Father hath
In store for every day;
And, though I tread a darksome path,
Yields sunshine all the way.

4 It tells of One, whose loving heart
Can feel my deepest woe;
Who in each sorrow bears a part,
That none can bear below.

737 *The Wondrous Name.* C. M.

1 Jesus! the name high over all,
In hell, or earth, or sky;
Angels and men before it fall,
And devils fear and fly.

2 Jesus! the name to sinners dear,
The name to sinners given;
It scatters all their guilty fear;
It turns their hell to heaven.

3 Oh! that the world might taste and see
The riches of His grace;
The arms of love that compass me,
Would all mankind embrace.

4 His only righteousness I show,
His saving truth proclaim;
'Tis all my business here below,
To cry, "Behold the Lamb!"

738 *Christ our Hiding Place.* L. M.

1 Hail, sovereign Love, who first began
The scheme to rescue fallen man!
Hail, matchless, free, eternal grace,
That gave my soul a hiding-place!

2 Against the God that rules the sky
I fought with hands uplifted high;
Despised the offers of His grace,
Too proud to seek a hiding-place.

3 But thus the eternal counsel ran:
"Almighty love! arrest the man!"
I felt the sorrows of distress,
And found I had no hiding-place.

4 Eternal justice stood in view;
To Sinai's fiery mount I flew;
But justice cried, with frowning face,
"This mountain is no hiding-place."

5 But lo! a heavenly voice I heard,
And mercy's angel soon appeared,
Who led me on, a pleasing pace,
To Jesus Christ, my hiding-place.

6 On Him almighty vengeance fell,
Which must have sunk a world to hell;
He bore it for His chosen race,
And now He is my hiding-place.

739 *Christ All in All.* L. M.

1 Jesus, thou Joy of loving hearts!
Thou Fount of life! thou Light of men!
From the best bliss that earth imparts,
We turn unfilled to Thee again.

2 Thy truth unchanged hath ever stood;
Thou savest those that on Thee call;
To them that seek Thee, Thou art good,
To them that find Thee,—All in all!

3 We taste Thee, O Thou living Bread!
And long to feast upon Thee still:
We drink of Thee, the Fountain Head,
And thirst, our souls from Thee to fill.

4 Our restless spirits yearn for Thee,
Where'er our changeful lot is cast;
Glad when Thy gracious smile we see;
Blest when our faith can hold Thee fast.

5 O Jesus! ever with us stay;
Make all our moments calm and bright;
Chase the dark night of sin away;
Shed o'er the world Thy holy light.

740 *Christ our Light.* C. M.

1 Eternal Sun of righteousness,
Display Thy beams divine,
And cause the glory of Thy face
Upon my heart to shine.

2 Light, in Thy light, oh, may I see,
Thy grace and mercy prove;
Revived, and cheered, and blest by Thee,
The God of pardoning love.

3 Lift up Thy countenance serene,
And let Thy happy child
Behold, without a cloud between,
The Father reconciled.

4 On me Thy promised peace bestow,
The peace by Jesus given;
The joys of holiness below,
And then the joys of heaven.

741 *Access through Christ.* C. M.

1 The vail is rent—our souls draw near
Unto a throne of grace;
The merits of the Lord appear,
They fill the holy place.

2 His precious blood has spoken there,
Before and on the throne;
And His own wounds in heaven declare,
Th' atoning work is done.

3 "'Tis finish'd!" on the cross He said,
In agonies and blood;
'Tis finish'd! now He lives to plead
Before the face of God.

4 'Tis finished! here our souls have rest,
His work can never fail:
By Him, our Sacrifice and Priest,
We pass within the vail.

5 Within the holiest of all,
Cleansed by His precious blood,
Before the throne we prostrate fall,
And worship Thee, O God!

742 *Jesus our High Priest.* L. M.

1 Before the throne of God above
I have a strong, a perfect plea;
A great High Priest, whose name is Love,
Who ever lives and pleads for me.

2 My name is graven on His hands,
My name is written on His heart;
I know that, while in heaven He stands,
No tongue can bid me thence depart.

3 When Satan tempts me to despair,
And tells me of the guilt within,
Upward I look and see Him there,
Who made an end of all my sin.

4 Because the sinless Saviour died,
My sinful soul is counted free;
For God, the Just, is satisfied
To look on Him and pardon me.

5 Behold Him there! the bleeding Lamb!
My perfect, spotless Righteousness,
The great unchangeable, "I Am,"
The King of glory and of grace.

6 One with Himself, I cannot die,
My soul is purchased by His blood;
My life is hid with Christ on high,
With Christ, my Saviour and my God.

743 *Christ coming in triumph.* 8s, 7s & 4s.

1 Christ is coming! Let creation
Bid her groans and travail cease;
Let the glorious proclamation
Hope restore, and faith increase.
Come, Lord Jesus!
Come, thou blessed Prince of Peace!

2 Though once cradled in a manger,
Oft no pillow but the sod;
Here an alien and a stranger,
Mock'd of men, though Son of God,
All creation
Yet shall own Thy kingly rod.

3 Long Thine exiles have been pining,
Far from rest, and home, and Thee;
But, in heavenly vestures shining,
They shall soon Thy glory see.
Come, Lord Jesus!
Haste the joyous Jubilee!

4 With that "blessed hope" before us,
Let no harp remain unstrung;
Let the mighty Advent-chorus
Onward roll from tongue to tongue—
Hallelujah!
Come, Lord Jesus, quickly come.

744 *Effusion of the Spirit.* C. M.

1 Let songs of praises fill the sky!
Christ, our ascended Lord,
Sends down His Spirit from on high,
According to His word.

2 The Spirit, by His heavenly breath,
New life creates within;
He quickens sinners from the death
Of trespasses and sin.

3 The things of Christ the Spirit takes,
And to our hearts reveals;
Our bodies He His temple makes,
And our redemption seals.

4 Come, Holy Spirit, from above,
With Thy celestial fire;
Come, and, with flames of zeal and love,
Our hearts and tongues inspire.

745 *The Spirit Invoked.* L. M.

1 Come, O Creator Spirit blest!
And in our souls take up Thy rest;
Come, with Thy grace and heavenly aid,
To fill the hearts which Thou hast made.

2 Great Comforter! to Thee we cry;
O highest Gift of God most high!
O Fount of life! O Fire of love!
And sweet Anointing from above!

3 Kindle our senses from above,
And make our hearts o'erflow with love;
With patience firm, and virtue high,
The weakness of our flesh supply.

4 Far from us drive the foe we dread,
And grant us Thy true peace instead;
So shall we not, with Thee for guide,
Turn from the path of life aside.

746 *Prayer for the Spirit.* S. M. D.

1 Lord God, the Holy Ghost,
In this accepted hour,
As on the day of Pentecost,
Descend in all Thy power;
We meet with one accord
In our appointed place,
And wait the promise of our Lord,
The Spirit of all grace.

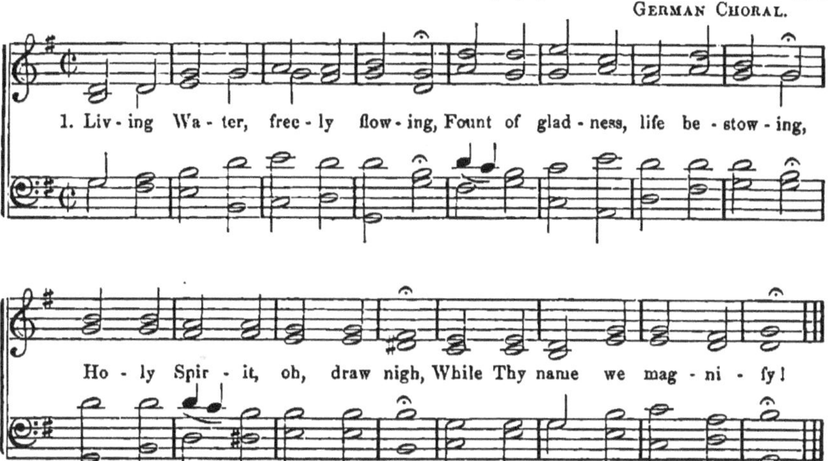
GERMAN CHORAL.
1. Liv - ing Wa - ter, free - ly flow - ing, Fount of glad - ness, life be - stow - ing,
Ho - ly Spir - it, oh, draw nigh, While Thy name we mag - ni - fy!

2 Like mighty rushing wind
Upon the waves beneath,
Move with one impulse every mind,
One soul, one feeling breathe:
The young, the old, inspire
With wisdom from above;
And give us hearts and tongues of fire
To pray, and praise, and love.

3 Spirit of light, explore
And chase our gloom away,
With lustre shining more and more
Unto the perfect day:
Spirit of truth, be Thou
In life and death our Guide;
O Spirit of adoption, now
May we be sanctified.

747 *Mission of the Spirit.* 8, 8, 7, 7.

1 Living Water, freely flowing,
Fount of gladness, life bestowing,
Holy Spirit, oh! draw nigh,
While Thy name we magnify!

2 Full of grace, from heaven Thou bendest,
And to lowest depths descendest;
Seeking, through a world of sin,
Souls whom Jesus died to win.

3 Where the contrite tear gives token
Of a heart by sorrow broken,
Breathing forth the breath of prayer—
O blest Spirit! Thou art there.

4 When the Word of revelation
Glows with tidings of salvation,
Through the cross of Christ made known,
There Thy saving power is shown.

5 O Eternal Spirit! hear us;
Let Thy power and presence cheer us;
With Thy life our souls inspire;
With Thy love our bosoms fire.

6 By the Father sent from heaven,
By the Saviour's promise given,
Thee we claim, O Power Divine!
Come, and make our hearts Thy shrine.

748 *Prayer for the promised Spirit.* C. M.

1 Enthroned on high, almighty Lord!
Thy Holy Ghost send down;
Fulfill in us Thy faithful word,
And all Thy mercies crown.

2 Though, on our heads, no tongues of fire
Their wondrous powers impart,
Grant, Saviour! what we more desire,
Thy Spirit in our heart.

3 Spirit of life, and light, and love!
Thy heavenly influence give;
Quicken our souls—born from above—
In Christ, that we may live.

4 To our benighted minds reveal
The glories of His grace,
And bring us, where no clouds conceal
The brightness of His face.

shed abroad—
;ing well,—
we in God,
well.

he Saviour. 8, 7s & 4s.

sin afflicted!
tless sorrow down,
convicted,
ss behold the crown;
esus;
ough Him alone.

e and wear it;
bedience sweet;
u strength to bear it,
m guides your feet
lory,
med captives meet.

pilgrims weary,
pened eyes,
deserts dreary,
ross supplies;
aste it
nortal rise.

rs of Life. L. M.

at thirsts draw nigh;"
the fallen race;
alvation buy,
ilk, and gospel grace.

change shall give,—
ve and are behind;
God receive,—
ce in Jesus find.

ig waters, come;
our Maker's call;
wanderers! home,
ace is free for all."

at the Door. C. M.

e Saviour stands,
very door;
sings in His hands,
oor.

h, "I bleed and die
My rest;
ile I'm passing by,
blessed.

My bleeding love,
way to hell?
realms above,
er dwell?

4 "Say, will you hear My gracious voice,
And have your sins forgiven?
Or will you make that wretched choice,
And bar yourselves from heaven?"

752 *Just as Thou Art.* 8s, 8s & 6s.

1 Just as thou art, without one trace
Of love, or joy, or inward grace,
Or meetness for the heavenly place,
O guilty sinner, come.
"The Spirit and the bride say, Come;"
Rejoicing saints re-echo, Come, [come,
Who faints, who thirsts, who will may
Thy Saviour bids thee come.

2 Thy sins I bore on Calvary's tree;
The stripes thy due were laid on Me,
That peace and pardon might be free;
O wretched sinner, come.—*Ch.*

3 Burdened with guilt, wouldst thou be blest?
Trust not the world, it gives no rest;
I bring relief to hearts oppressed:
O weary sinner, come.—*Ch.*

4 Come, leave thy burden at the cross,
Count all thy gains but empty dross;
My grace repays all earthly loss:
O needy sinner, come.—*Ch.*

5 Come, hither bring thy boding fears,
Thy aching heart, thy bursting tears;
'Tis mercy's voice salutes thine ears:
O trembling sinner, come.—*Ch.*

753 *The Accepted Time.* S. M.

1 Now is th' accepted time,
Now is the day of grace;
Now, sinners! come, without delay,
And seek the Saviour's face.

2 Now is th' accepted time,
The Saviour calls to-day;
Pardon and peace He freely gives:
Then why should you delay?

3 Now is th' accepted time,
The gospel bids you come;
And every promise, in His word,
Declares there yet is room.

754 *To-Day.* S. M.

1 Ye sinners! fear the Lord,
While yet 'tis called to-day;
Soon will the awful voice of death
Command your souls away.

2 Soon will the harvest close,
The summer soon be o'er;
And soon your injured angry God
Will hear your prayers no more.

3 Then, while 'tis called to-day,
Oh! hear the gospel's sound;
Come, sinners! haste, oh! haste away,
While pardon may be found.

755 *Psalm* 51. L. M.

1 Lord, I am vile, conceived in sin,
And born unholy and unclean;
Sprung from the man, whose guilty fall
Corrupts the race, and taints us all.

2 Soon as we draw our infant breath
The seeds of sin grow up for death:
Thy law demands a perfect heart—
But we're defiled in every part.

3 Great God! create my heart anew,
And form my spirit pure and true;
No outward rites can make me clean,—
The leprosy lies deep within.

4 No bleeding bird, nor bleeding beast,
Nor hyssop branch, nor sprinkling priest,
Nor running brook, nor flood nor sea,
Can wash the dismal stain away.

5 Jesus, my God, Thy blood alone
Hath power sufficient to atone:
Thy blood can make me white as snow,
No Jewish types could cleanse me so.

756 *Psalm* 51. L. M.

1 O Thou that hear'st when sinners cry,
Though all my crimes before Thee lie,
Behold me not with angry look,
But blot their memory from Thy book.

2 Create my nature pure within,
And form my soul averse to sin;
Let Thy good Spirit ne'er depart,
Nor hide Thy presence from my heart.

3 I cannot live without Thy light,
Cast out and banished from Thy sight;
Thy holy joys, my God, restore,
And guard me, that I fall no more.

4 Though I have grieved Thy Spirit, Lord,
His help and comfort still afford;
And let a sinner seek Thy throne,
To plead the merits of Thy Son.

757 *Psalm* 51. L. M.

1 A broken heart, my God, my King,
Is all the sacrifice I bring;
The God of grace will ne'er despise
A broken heart for sacrifice.

2 My soul lies humbled in the dust,
And owns Thy dreadful sentence just;
Look down, O Lord, with pitying eye,
And save the soul condemned to die.

3 Then will I teach the world Thy ways,
Sinners shall learn Thy sovereign grace;
I'll lead them to my Saviour's blood,
And then shall praise a pard'ning God.

4 Oh may Thy love inspire my tongue,
Salvation shall be all my song;
And all my powers shall join to bless
The Lord, my Strength and Righteousness.

758 *Pleading for Mercy.* L. M.

1 When at Thy footstool, Lord! I bend,
And plead with Thee for mercy there,
Oh! think Thou of the sinner's Friend,
And for His sake receive my prayer.

2 Oh! think not, of my shame and guilt,
My thousand stains of deepest dye;
Think of the blood which Jesus spilt,
And let that blood my pardon buy.

3 Think, Lord! how I am still Thine own.
The trembling creature of Thy hand!
Think how my heart to sin is prone,
And what temptations round me stand.

4 Oh! think upon Thy holy word,
And every plighted promise there;
How prayer should evermore be heard,
And how Thy glory is—to spare.

5 Oh! think not of my doubts and fears,
My strivings with Thy grace divine;
Think upon Jesus' woes and tears,
And let His merits stand for mine.

6 Thine eye, Thine ear, they are not dull;
Thine arm can never shortened be;
Behold me here! my heart is full;
Behold, and spare, and succour me!

759 *Redemption through Christ.* 10s

1 Weary of earth, and laden with my sin,
I look at heaven and long to enter in;
But there no evil thing may find a home:
And yet I hear a voice that bids me "Come."

2 So vile I am, how dare I hope to stand
In the pure glory of that holy land?
Before the whiteness of that throne appear?
Yet there are hands strech'd out to draw me near.

3 The while I fain would tread the heavenly
Evil is ever with me, day by day; [way,
Yet on mine ears the gracious tidings fall,
"Repent, confess; thou shalt be loosed from all."

4 It is the voice of Jesus that I hear,
His are the hands stretched out to draw me near,
And His the blood that can for all atone,
And set me faultless there before the throne.

5 'Twas He who found me on the deathly wild,
And made me heir of heaven the Father's child,
And day by day, whereby my soul may live,
Gives me His grace of pardon, and will give.

6 Yes, Thou wilt answer for me, righteous Lord:
Thine all the merits, mine the great reward;
Thine the sharp thorns, and mine the golden crown,
Mine the life won, and Thine the life laid down.

760 *Pleading for Mercy.* 7s.

1 God, my Father, hear me pray,
Wash my crimson guilt away;
Wretched, helpless, lost undone,
Hear me for Thy blessed Son,
Lord, unnumbered sins are mine,
But eternal love is Thine.

2 God, my Saviour, look on me,
All my guilt I cast on Thee!
Give my troubled spirit peace,
Bid my fears and sorrows cease.

3 God, my Comforter and Light!
Strengthen me with holy might,
Make Thy dwelling in my heart;
Faith, and joy, and hope impart!—

4 Blessed, glorious Trinity!
Holy, everlasting Three!
Hear, oh hear, my earnest prayer,
And my soul for heaven prepare.

761 *Flying to Christ.* L. M.

1 Jesus, the sinner's Friend, to Thee,
Lost and undone, for aid I flee;
Weary of earth, myself, and sin,
Open Thine arms and take me in.

2 What can I say Thy grace to move?
Lord, I am sin,—but Thou art love:
I give up every plea beside,
Lord, I am lost,—but Thou hast died!

762 *Taking Christ as a hiding-place.* C. M.

1 O Jesus, Saviour of the lost,
My rock and hiding-place,
By storms of sin and sorrow toss'd,
I seek Thy sheltering grace.

2 Guilty, forgive me, Lord, I cry;
Pursued by foes, I come;
A sinner, save me, or I die;
An outcast, take me home.

3 Once safe in Thine almighty arms,
Let storms come on amain;
There danger never, never harms;
There death itself is gain.

4 And when I stand before Thy throne,
And all Thy glory see,
Still be my righteouness alone
To hide myself in Thee.

763 *Going to Christ.* 8s & 7s.

1 Take me, O my Father, take me!
Take me, save me, through Thy Son;
That which Thou wouldst have me,
Let Thy will in me be done. [make me,
Long from Thee my footsteps straying,
Thorny proved the way I trod;
Weary come I now, and praying—
Take me to Thy love, my God!

2 Fruitless years with grief recalling,
Humbly I confess my sin;
At Thy feet, O Father, falling,
To Thy houshold take me in.
Freely now to Thee I proffer
This relenting heart of mine;
Freely life and soul I offer—
Gift unworthy love like Thine.

3 Once the world's Redeemer dying,
Bare our sins upon the tree;
On that sacrifice relying,
Now I look in hope to Thee:

Father, take me! all forgiving,
Fold me to Thy loving breast;
In Thy love forever living,
I must be forever best!

764 *Christ's Forever.* 7s.

1 Thine forever! God of love,
Hear us from Thy throne above!
Thine forever may we be,
Here, and in eternity!

2 Thine forever! oh, how blest
They who find in Thee their rest!
Saviour, Guardian, heavenly Friend,
Oh, defend us to the end!

3 Thine forever! Saviour keep
These Thy frail and trembling sheep.
Safe alone beneath Thy care,
Let us all Thy goodness share.

4 Thine forever! Thou our Guide,—
All our wants by Thee supplied,—
All our sins by Thee forgiven,—
Lead us, Lord, from earth to heaven!

765 *At the Cross.* C. M.

1 My heart dissolved to see Thee bleed,
This heart so hard before;
I hear Thee for the guilty plead,
And grief o'erflows the more.

2 'Twas for the sinful Thou didst die,
And I a sinner stand:
What love speaks from Thy dying eye,
And from each piercèd hand!

3 I know this cleansing blood of Thine
Was shed, dear Lord! for me!
For me, for all,—oh! grace divine!—
Who look by faith on Thee.

4 O Christ of God! O spotless Lamb!
By love my soul is drawn;
Henceforth, for ever, Thine I am;
Here life and peace are born.

5 In patient hope, the cross I'll bear;
Thine arm shall be my stay;
And Thou, enthroned, my soul shalt spare,
On Thy great judgment-day.

766 *Self-Consecration.* C. M.

1 My God! accept my heart this day,
And make it always Thine,
That I from Thee no more may stray,
No more from Thee decline.

2 Before the cross of Him who died,
Behold I prostratè fall;
Let every sin be crucified;
Let Christ be all in all.

3 May the dear blood, once shed for me,
My blest atonement prove,
That I, from first to last, may be
The purchase of Thy love.

4 Let every thought, and work, and word,
To Thee be ever given;
Then life shall be Thy service, Lord;
And death the gate of heaven.

767 *Faith in Christ.* S. M.

1 O Saviour, who didst come
By water and by blood;
Confessed on earth, adored in heaven,
Eternal Son of God!

2 Jesus, our life and hope,
To endless years the same;
We plead Thy gracious promises,
And rest upon Thy name.

3 By faith in Thee we live,
By faith in Thee we stand,
By Thee we vanquish sin and and death,
And gain the heavenly land.

4 O Lord, increase our faith;
Our fearful spirits calm;
Sustain us through this mortal strife,
Then give the victor's palm!

768 *All-sufficient Grace.* 7s.

1 Wait, my soul! upon the Lord,
To His gracious promise flee,
Laying hold upon His word:—
"As thy days, thy strength shall be."

2 If the sorrows of thy case
Seem peculiar still to thee,
God has promised needful grace;
"As thy days, thy strength shall be."

3 Days of trials, days of grief:
In succession thou may'st see;
This is still thy sweet relief:—
"As thy days thy strength shall be."

4 Rock of ages! I'm secure,
With Thy promise, full and free,
Faithful, in Thy covenant sure,
"As thy days thy strength shall be."

BAIRD. 6s.

KARL REDEN, 1874.

1. My Sa-viour, as thou wilt! Oh, may Thy will be mine! In - to Thy hand of love I
would my all re - sign; Through sor - row or through joy, . . . Con - duct me as Thy
sor - - row or thro' joy, Con - duct me
own, ... And help me still to say, My Lord, Thy will be done.
as thine own.

769 *Thy will be done.* 6s.

1 My Saviour, as Thou wilt!
Oh, may Thy will be mine!
Into Thy hand of love
I would my all resign;
Through sorrow or through joy,
Conduct me as Thine own,
And help me still to say,
My Lord, Thy will be done.

2 My Saviour, as Thou wilt!
If needy here and poor,
Give me Thy people's bread,
Their portion, rich and sure;
The manna of Thy word
Let my soul feed upon;
And if all else should fail,
My Lord, Thy will be done!

3 My Saviour, as Thou wilt!
Though seen through many a tear,
Let not my star of hope
Grow dim and disappear;
Since Thou on earth hast wept,
And sorrowed oft alone,
If I must weep with Thee,
My Lord, Thy will be done!

4 My Saviour, as Thou wilt!
All shall be well for me;
Each changing future scene
I gladly trust with Thee:
Straight to my home above
I travel calmly on,
And sing in life or death,
My God, Thy will be done!

770 *Thy will be done.* C. M.

1 LORD, as to Thy dear cross we flee,
And pray to be forgiven,
So let Thy life our pattern be,
And form our souls for heaven.

2 Help us, through good report and ill,
Our daily cross to bear;
Like Thee, to do our Father's will,
Our brother's griefs to share.

3 Let grace our selfishness expel,
Our earthliness refine;
And kindness in our bosoms dwell
As free and true as Thine.

4 If joy shall at Thy bidding fly,
And grief's dark day come on,
We, in our turn, would meekly cry,
"Father, Thy will be done!"

5 Kept peaceful in the midst of strife,
Forgiving and forgiven,
Oh! may we lead the pilgrim's life,
And follow Thee to heaven!

771 *Casting all Care on God.* C. P. M.

1 O Lord! how happy should we be,
If we could cast our care on Thee,
If we from self could rest;
And feel, at heart, that One above,
In perfect wisdom, perfect love,
Is working for the best!

2 How far from this our daily life,
Ever disturbed by anxious strife,
By sudden, wild alarms!
Oh! could we but relinquish all
Our earthly props, and simply fall
On Thine almighty arms!

3 Could we but kneel, and cast our load,
E'en while we pray, upon our God,
Then rise, with lightened cheer,
Sure that the Father, who is nigh
To still the famished raven's cry,
Will hear, in that we fear!

4 Lord! make these faithless hearts of ours
Such lessons learn from birds and flowers;
Make them from self to cease.
Leave all things to a Father's will,
And taste, before Him lying still,
E'en in affliction, peace.

772 *Submission in Affliction.* C. M.

1 Affliction is a stormy deep,
Where wave resounds to wave;
Though o'er my head the billows roll,
I know the Lord can save.

2 The hand that now withholds my joys
Can soon restore my peace;
And He who bade the tempest rise
Can bid that tempest cease.

3 Here will I rest, and build my hope,
Nor murmur at His rod;
He's more than all the world to me—
My Health, my Life, my God!

773 *Clinging to the Saviour.* 8s, 8s & 6s.

1 O Holy Saviour, Friend unseen;
Since on Thine arm Thou bid'st me lean,
Help me, throughout life's varying scene,
By faith to cling to Thee.

2 Blest with this fellowship divine,
Take what Thou wilt, I'll ne'er repine;
E'en as the branches to the vine,
My soul would cling to Thee.

3 Far from my home, fatigued, oppressed,
Here have I found a place of rest;
An exile still, yet not unblest,
While I can cling to Thee.

4 What, though the world deceitful prove,
And earthly friends and hopes remove?
With patient uncomplaining love
Still would I cling to Thee.

5 Oft, when I seem to tread alone [grown,
Some barren waste, with thorns o'er
Thy voice of love in gentlest tone,
Whispers, "Still cling to Me.

6 Though faith and hope may long be
I ask not, need not, aught beside; [tried,
How safe, how calm, how satisfied,
The souls that cling to Thee.

774 *One with Christ.* C. M.

1 Lord Jesus! are we one with Thee?
Oh! height, oh! depth of love!
With Thee we died upon the tree,
In Thee we live above.

2 Such was Thy grace, that, for our sake,
Thou didst from heaven come down;
Thou didst of flesh and blood partake,
In all our sorrows one.

3 Our sins, our guilt, in love divine,
Confessed and borne by Thee,
The gall, the curse, the wrath were Thine,
To set Thy members free.

4 Ascended now in glory bright,
Still one with us Thou art;
Nor life, nor death, nor depth, nor height,
Thy saints and Thee can part.

5 Soon, soon shall come that glorious day
When, seated on Thy throne,
Thou shalt to wondering worlds display
That Thou with us art one.

775 *Planted in Christ.* C. M.

1 Planted in Christ, the living Vine,
This day, with one accord,
Ourselves, with humble faith and joy,
We yield to Thee, O Lord!

2 Joined in one body may we be:
One inward life partake;
One be our heart, one heavenly hope
In every bosom wake.

3 In prayer, in effort, tears, and toils,
One wisdom be our guide;
Taught by one Spirit from above,
In Thee may we abide.

4 Then, when among the saints in light
Our joyful spirits shine,
Shall anthems of immortal praise,
O Lamb of God, be Thine!

776 *Christ's Kingdom.* S. M.

1 Oh, what, if we are Christ's,
Is earthly shame or loss?
Bright shall the crown of glory be,
When we have borne the cross.

2 Keen was the trial once,
Bitter the cup of woe,
When martyred saints, baptized in blood,
Christ's sufferings shared below.

3 Bright is their glory now,
Boundless their joy above,
Where, on the bosom of their God,
They rest in perfect love.

4 Lord, may that grace be ours!
Like them in faith to bear
All that of sorrow, grief, or pain,
May be our portion here!

5 Enough, if Thou at last
The word of blessing give,
And let us rest beneath Thy feet,
Where saints and angels live!

777 *Christ my all.* 8s, 8s & 4s.

1 Jesus, my Saviour! look on me,
For I am weary and opprest;
I come to cast myself on Thee:
Thou art my Rest.

2 Look down on me, for I am weak,
I feel the toilsome journey's length;
From Thee almighty aid I seek:
Thou art my Strength.

3 I am bewilder'd on my way,
Dark and tempestuous is the night;
O send Thou forth some cheering ray;
Thou art my Light.

4 When Satan flings his fiery darts,
I look to Thee; my terrors cease;
Thy cross a hiding-place imparts:
Thou art my Peace.

5 Standing alone on Jordan's brink,
In that tremendous latest strife,
Thou wilt not suffer me to sink:
Thou art my Life.

6 Thou wilt my every want supply,
E'en to the end, whate'er befall;
Through life, in death, eternally,
Thou art my All.

778 *Burden cast on God.* S. M.

1 How gentle God's commands!
How kind His precepts are!—
"Come, cast your burdens on the Lord,
And trust His constant care."

2 While Providence supports,
Let saints securely dwell;
That hand, which bears all nature up,
Shall guide His children well.

3 Why should this anxious load
Press down your weary mind?
Haste to your heavenly Father's throne,
And sweet refreshment find.

4 His goodness stands approved,
Down to the present day:
I'll drop my burden at His feet,
And bear His song away.

779 *Triune Guidance.* 8s, 7s.

1 Lead us, heavenly Father! lead us
O'er the world's tempestuous sea;
Guard us, guide us, keep us, feed us,
For we have no help but Thee;
Yet possessing every blessing,
If our God our Father be.

2 Saviour! breathe forgiveness o'er us;
All our weakness Thou dost know;
Thou didst tread this earth before us;
Thou didst feel its keenest woe;
Lone and dreary, faint and weary,
Through the desert Thou didst go.

3 Spirit of our God! descending,
Fill our hearts with heavenly joy;

C. C. Converse, 1871.

No. 1.
No. 2.
END.
1. { What a friend we have in Je - sus, All our sins and griefs to bear; }
{ What a priv - i-lege to car - ry
D.C. All be-cause we do not car - ry
Ev - ery thing to God in prayer.
Ev - ery thing to God in prayer.
D.C.
Oh, what peace we oft - en for - feit, Oh, what need-less pain we bear—

Love with every passion blending,
Pleasure that can never cloy;
Thus provided, pardoned, guided,
Nothing can our peace destroy.

780 *Going to Jesus in Prayer.* 8s & 7s.

1 What a Friend we have in Jesus,
All our sins and griefs to bear;
What a privilege to carry
Everything to God in prayer.
Oh, what peace we often forfeit,
Oh, what needless pain we bear—
All because we do not carry
Everything to God in prayer.

2 Have we trials and temptations?
Is there trouble anywhere?
We should never be discouraged,
Take it to the Lord in prayer.
Can we find a friend so faithful,
Who will all our sorrows share?
Jesus knows our every weakness,
Take it to the Lord in prayer.

3 Are we weak and heavy-laden,
'Cumbered with a load of care?
Precious Saviour, still our refuge,
Take it to the Lord in prayer.
Do thy friends despise, forsake thee?
Take it to the Lord in prayer;
In His arms He'll take and shield thee;
Thou wilt find a solace there.

781 *Psalm* 23: 2 8s & 7s.

1 Heavenly Shepherd, guide us, feed us,
Through our pilgrimage below;
And beside the waters lead us,
Where Thy flock rejoicing go.

2 Lord, Thy guardian presence ever,
Meekly bending, we implore;
We have found Thee, and would never,
Never wander from Thee more.

782 *"Lord, help me."* C. M.

1 Oh, help us, Lord; each hour of need
Thy heavenly succour give;
Help us in thought, and word, and deed,
Each hour on earth we live.

2 Oh, help us when our spirits bleed
With contrite anguish sore;
And when our hearts are cold and dead,
Oh, help us, Lord, the more.

3 Oh, help us through the prayer of faith
More firmly to believe;
For still the more the servant hath,
The more shall He receive.

4 Oh, help us, Jesus, from on high;
We know no help but Thee;
Oh, help us so to live and die
As Thine in heaven to be.

783 *Perfect Freedom.* C. M.

1 If Thou impart Thyself to me,
No other good I need:
If Thou, the Son, shalt make me free,
I shall be free indeed.

2 I cannot rest till in Thy blood
I full redemption have;
But Thou, through whom I come to God,
Canst to the utmost save.

3 From sin,—the guilt, the power, the pain,—
Thou wilt redeem my soul;
Lord, I believe—and not in vain;
My faith shall make me whole.

4 I, too, with Thee, shall walk in white;
With all Thy saints shall prove
The length, and depth, and breadth, and height,
Of everlasting love.

784 *Hope in Christ's Coming.* C. M.

1 The Prince of Life once slain for us
Ascended up on high;
Captivity was captive led,
And Christ no more can die.

2 With Jesus we are crucified,
With Christ our Head we live;
The glory, first by Him obtain'd,
To us the Lord shall give.

3 His word is faithfulness and truth—
"Behold, I quickly come;"
And faith, still counts the promise sure,
Amidst the deepest gloom.

4 Jesus at His appointed hour
In glory shall appear;
Then, fashion'd by His mighty hand,
We shall His image bear.

5 Thou Son of God! the heavenly Man!
Head of Thy ransom'd seed!
We treasure up the precious word—
"The Lord is risen indeed."

785 *Support in Trial.* 7s.

1 Oft in danger, oft in woe,
Onward, Christians, onward go;
Bear the toil, maintain the strife,
Strengthened with the Bread of Life.

2 Let not sorrow dim your eye,
Soon shall every tear be dry;
Let not fear your course impede,
Great your strength, if great your need.

3 Let your drooping hearts be glad;
March in heavenly armour clad;
Fight, nor think the battle long,
Soon shall victory wake your song.

4 Onward then to glory move;
More than conquerors ye shall prove;
Though opposed by many a foe,
Christian soldiers, onward go!

786 *Walking in Light.* C. M.

1 Walk in the light! so shalt Thou know
That fellowship of love,
His Spirit only can bestow,
Who reigns in light above.

2 Walk in the light! and Thou shalt find
Thy heart made truly His,
Who dwells in cloudless light enshrined,
In whom no darkness is.

3 Walk in the light! and e'en the tomb
No fearful shade shall wear;
Glory shall chase away its gloom,
For Christ hath conquered there.

4 Walk in the light! and Thou shalt see
Thy path, though thorny, bright;
For God by grace shall dwell in thee,
And God Himself is light.

787 *The Fellowship of Saints.* C. M.

1 In one fraternal band of love,
One fellowship of mind,
The saints below and saints above
Their bliss and glory find.

2 Here, in their house of pilgrimage,
Thy statutes are their song;
There, through one bright, eternal age,
Thy praises they prolong.

3 Lord, may our union form a part
Of that thrice happy whole;
Derive its pulse from Thee, the heart;
Its life from Thee, the soul.

788 *The Law of Love.* S. M.

1 Oh! happiest work below,
Earnest of joy above,
To sweeten many a cup of woe,
By deeds of holy love!

2 Lord! may it be our choice
This blessèd rule to keep,
"Rejoice with them that do rejoice,
And weep with them that weep."

3 God of the widow! hear;
Our work of mercy bless;
God of the fatherless! be near,
And grant us good success.

789 *Christ relieved in His Saints.* C. M.

1 Jesus, my Lord! how rich Thy grace!
Thy bounties—how complete!
How shall I count the matchless sum?
How pay the mighty debt?

2 High on a throne of radiant light,
Dost Thou exalted shine;
What can my poverty bestow,
When all the worlds are Thine.

3 But Thou hast brethren here below,
The partners of Thy grace;
And wilt confess their humble names
Before Thy Father's face.

4 In them may'st Thou be clothed, and fed,
And visited, and cheered;
And, in their accents of distress,
My Saviour's voice be heard.

790 *Psalm* 95. L. M.

1 Oh! come, loud anthems let us sing,
Loud thanks to our almighty King!
For we our voices high should raise,
When our salvation's Rock we praise

2 Into His presence let us haste,
To thank Him for His favours past;
To Him address, in joyful songs,
The praise that to His name belongs.

791 *Morning and Evening Hymn.* L. M.

1 O Jesus, Lord of heavenly grace,
Thou Brightness of Thy Father's face,
Thou Fountain of eternal light, [night!
Whose beams disperse the shades of

2 Come, holy Sun of heavenly love!
Send down Thy radiance from above,
And to our inmost hearts convey
The Holy Spirit's cloudless ray.

3 Oh! hallowed thus be every day!
Let meekness be our morning ray,
And faithful love our noon-day light,
And hope our sunset, calm and bright.

4 O Christ! with each returning morn,
Thine image to our hearts is borne;
Oh! may we ever clearly see
Our Saviour and our God in Thee!

792 *Evening Devotion.* 8s & 7s.

1 Hear my prayer, O Heavenly Father,
Ere I lay me down to sleep;
Bid Thine angels, pure and holy,
Round my bed their vigil keep.

2 Great my sins are, but Thy mercy
Far outweighs them every one;
Down before the cross I cast them,
Trusting in Thy help alone.

3 Keep me through this night of peril,
Underneath its boundless shade;
Take me to Thy rest, I pray Thee,
When my pilgrimage is made.

4 Pardon all my past transgressions,
Give me strength for days to come;
Guide and guard me with Thy blessing,
Till Thine angels bid me home.

793 *Evening Twilight.* C. M.

1 Hail, tranquil hour of closing day!
Begone, disturbing care!
And look, my soul! from earth, away
To Him who heareth prayer.

2 How sweet the tear of penitence
Before His throne of grace,
While, to the contrite spirit's sense,
He shows His smiling face.

3 How sweet, through long-remembered
His mercies to recall, [years,
And, pressed with wants, and griefs, and
To trust His love for all. [fears,

4 How sweet to look, in thoughtful hope,
Beyond this fading sky,
And hear Him call His children up
To His fair home on high.

5 Calmly the day forsakes our heaven,
To dawn beyond the west;
So let my soul, in life's last even,
Retire to glorious rest.

794 *Lying down to Rest.* 8s, 7s & 7s.

1 Through the day Thy love has spared us;
Now we lay us down to rest,
Through the silent watches guard us;
Let no foe our peace molest;
Jesus, Thou our guardian be;
Sweet it is to trust in Thee.

2 Pilgrims here on earth, and strangers,
Dwelling in the midst of foes;

EVENTIDE. 10s.

WILLIAM HENRY MONK, 1861.

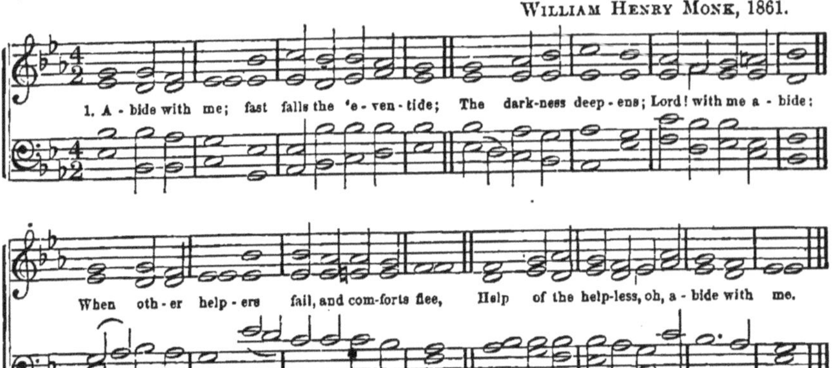
1. A - bide with me; fast falls the e - ven - tide; The dark-ness deep - ens; Lord! with me a - bide;
When oth - er help - ers fail, and com-forts flee, Help of the help-less, oh, a - bide with me.

Us and ours preserve from dangers;
In Thine arms may we repose;
And, when life's short day is past,
Rest with Thee in heaven at last.

795 *At Eventide.* 10s.

1 ABIDE with me; fast falls the eventide;
The darkness deepens; Lord, with me abide;
When other helpers fail, and comforts flee,
Help of the helpless, oh! abide with me.

2 Swift to its close ebbs out life's little day;
Earth's joys grow dim, its glories pass away;
Change and decay in all around I see;
O Thou who changest not, abide with me.

3 I need Thy presence every passing hour;
What but Thy grace can foil the tempter's power?
Who like Thyself my guide and stay can be?
Through cloud and sunshine, Lord, abide with me.

4 I fear no foe with Thee at hand to bless;
Ills have no weight, and tears no bitterness;
Where is death's sting, where, grave, thy victory?
I triumph still, if Thou abide with me.

5 Hold Thou Thy cross before my closing eyes;
Shine through the gloom, and point me to the skies;
Heaven's morning breaks, and earth's vain shadows flee;
In life, in death, O Lord, abide with me.

796 *The Sabbath.* H. M.

1 AWAKE, ye saints, awake,
And hail this sacred day;
In loftiest songs of praise
Your joyful homage pay:
Welcome the day that God hath blest,
The type of heaven's eternal rest.

2 On this auspicious morn
The Lord of life arose;
He burst the bars of death,
And vanquish'd all our foes:
And now He pleads our cause above,
And reaps the fruits of all His love.

3 All hail, triumphant Lord!
Heaven with hosannas rings;
And earth, in humbler strains,
Thy praise responsive sings:
Worthy the Lamb that once was slain,
Through endless years to live and reign.

4 Great King, gird on Thy sword,
Ascend Thy conquering car;
While justice, truth and love
Maintain Thy glorious war:
This day let sinners own Thy sway,
And rebels cast their arms away.

797 *Opening or Closing Hymn.* L. M.

1 Preserved by Thine almighty power,
O Lord, our Maker, Saviour King!
And brought to see this happy hour,
We come Thy praises here to sing.

2 We praise Thee for Thy constant care,
For life preserved, for mercies given;
Oh! may we still those mercies share,
And taste the joys of sins forgiven!

3 And when on earth our days are done,
Grant, Lord, that we at length may join,
Pastors and people round Thy throne,
The song of Moses and the Lamb.

798 *Psalm 100.* L. M.

1 Ye nations round the earth! rejoice
Before the Lord, your sovereign King;
Serve Him with cheerful heart and voice;
With all your tongues His glory sing.

2 The Lord is God; 'tis He alone
Doth life and breath and being give;
We are His work, and not our own;
The sheep that on His pastures live.

3 Enter His gates with songs of joy;
With praises to His courts repair;
And make it your divine employ
To pay your thanks and honours there.

4 The Lord is good, the Lord is kind;
Great is His grace, His mercy sure;
And the whole race of man shall find
His truth from age to age endure.

799 *Homage and Devotion.* S. M.

1 With joy, we lift our eyes
To those bright realms above,
That glorious temple in the skies
Where dwells eternal love.

2 Before Thy throne we bow,
O Thou almighty King!
Here we present the solemn vow,
And hymns of praise we sing.

3 While in Thy house we kneel,
With trust and holy fear,
Thy mercy and Thy truth reveal,
And lend a gracious ear.

800 *Delight in God's Worship.* S. M.

1 We love the place, O God!
Wherein Thine honour dwells;
The holy joy of Thine abode
All earthly joy excels.

2 It is the house of prayer,
Wherein Thy servants meet;
And Thou, O Lord, art ever there
Thy chosen flock to greet.

3 We love the Word of life,
The Word that tells of peace,
Of comfort in the Christian strife,
And joys that never cease.

4 We love to sing Thy praise
For mercies freely given;
But oh! we wait, we long to raise
Triumphant songs in heaven.

5 Lord Jesus! give us grace
On earth to love Thee more,
In heaven to see Thy glorious face,
And with Thy saints adore.

801 *The Presence of Christ.* L. M.

1 How sweet to leave the world awhile,
And seek the presence of our Lord!
Dear Saviour! on Thy people smile,
And come, according to Thy word.

2 From busy scenes we now retreat,
That we may here converse with Thee:
Ah! Lord! behold us at Thy feet;—
Let this the gate of heaven be.

3 Chief of ten thousand! now appear,
That we by faith may see Thy face.
Oh! speak, that we Thy voice may hear,
And let Thy presence fill this place.

802 *Close of Worship.* S. M.

1 Once more, before we part,
Oh! bless the Saviour's name;
Let every tongue and every heart
Adore and praise the same.

2 Lord! in Thy grace we came;
That blessing still impart;
We met in Jesus' sacred name,
In Jesus' name we part.

3 Still on Thy holy word
Help us to feed and grow;
Still to go on to know the Lord,
And practise what we know.

4 Now, Lord! before we part,
Help us to bless Thy name:
Let every tongue and every heart
Adore and bless the same.

803 *Benediction.* C. M

1 The God of peace, who from the dead,
Hath raised our dying Lord,
And, through the covenant in His blood,
Our souls to peace restored:—

2 Confirm our hearts, in each good work,
To do His perfect will;
That, made well-pleasing in His sight,
Our course with joy we fill.

3 So shall we, in His heavenly courts,
Hereafter, ever live;
And to His name, through Jesus Christ,
Eternal glory give.

804 *Support in God's Covenant.* C. M.

1 My God! the covenant of Thy love
Abides for ever sure;
And, in its matchless grace, I feel
My happiness secure.

2 What though my house be not with Thee,
As nature could desire!
To nobler joys than nature gives
Thy servants all aspire.

3 Since Thou, the everlasting God,
My Father art become,
Jesus, my Guardian and my Friend,
And heaven my final home;—

4 I welcome all Thy sovereign will,
For all that will is love;
And when I know not what Thou dost,
I wait the light above.

5 Thy covenant in the darkest gloom
Shall heavenly rays impart,
And when my eyelids close in death,
Sustain my fainting heart.

805 *Baptism.* L. M.

1 'Twas the commission of our Lord
"Go teach the nations, and baptize;"
The nations have received the word,
Since He ascended to the skies.

2 He sits upon the eternal hills,
With grace and pardon in His hands,
And sends His covenant with the seals
To bless the distant Gentile lands.

3 "Repent, and be baptized," He saith,
"For the remission of your sins;"
And thus our sense assists our faith,
And shows us what the gospel means.

4 Our souls He washes in His blood,
As water makes the body clean;
And the good Spirit from our God
Descends like purifying rain.

5 Thus we engage ourselves to Thee,
And seal our covenant with the Lord;
Oh! may the great eternal Three
In heaven our solemn vows record.

806 *The Covenant of Baptism.* C. M.

1 The promise of my Father's love
Shall stand forever good:—
He said, and gave His soul to death,
And sealed the grace with blood.

2 To this dear covenant of Thy word,
I set my worthless name;
I seal the engagement of my Lord,
And make my humble claim.

3 I call that legacy my own,
Which Jesus did bequeath;
'Twas purchased with a dying groan,
And ratified in death.

4 Sweet is the memory of His name,
Who blessed us in His will,
And to His testament of love,
Made His own life the seal.

807 *Children brought to Jesus.* L. M.

1 A little child the Saviour came,
The mighty God was still His name,
And angels worship, as He lay,
The seeming infant of a day.

2 He who, a little child, began
The life divine to show to man,
Proclaims from heaven the message free,
Let little children come to Me.

3 We bring them, Lord! and with the sign
Which Thou hast given, we name them Thine;
Their souls with saving grace endow,
Baptize them with Thy Spirit now.

808 *The Lambs of the Flock.* L. M.

1 With thankful hearts our songs we raise,
To celebrate the Saviour's praise;
Yet who, but saints in heaven above,
Can tell the riches of His love?

2 He, the good Shepherd, kindly leads
The wanderer, and the hungry feeds;
Deigns in His arms the lambs to bear,
And makes them His peculiar care.

3 Jesus! to Thy protecting wing,
Our helpless little ones we bring; [they
Oh! grant them grace and strength, that
May find and keep the heavenward way.

809 *"This do in remembrance of Me."* 7s.

1 Bread of heaven, on Thee we feed,
For Thy Flesh is meat indeed;
Ever may our souls be fed
With this true and living Bread;
Day by day with strength supplied
Through the life of Him who died.

2 Wine of heaven, Thy Blood supplies
This blest cup of sacrifice;
Lord, Thy wounds our healing give,
To Thy cross we look and live:
Jesus, may we ever be
Grafted, rooted, built in Thee.

810 *Christ the living Bread.* L. M.

1 Away from earth my spirit turns,
Away from every transient good;
With strong desire my bosom burns,
To feast on heaven's diviner food.

2 Thou, Saviour! art the living bread;
Thou wilt my every want supply;
By Thee sustained, and cheered, and led,
I'll press through dangers to the sky.

3 What though temptations oft distress,
And sin assails and breaks my peace;
Thou wilt uphold, and save, and bless,
And bid the storms of passion cease.

4 Then let me take Thy gracious hand,
And walk beside Thee onward still;
Till my glad feet shall safely stand,
Forever firm on Zion's hill.

811 *Christ the Corner-stone.* H. M.

1 Christ is our Corner-stone;
On Him alone we build;
With His true saints alone
The courts of heaven are filled:
On His great love our hopes we place,
Of present grace and joys above.

2 Oh! then, with hymns of praise
These hallowed courts shall ring!
Our voices we will raise,
The Three in One to sing;
And thus proclaim in joyful song,
Both loud and long, that glorious Name.

3 Here, gracious God! do Thou
Forevermore draw nigh;
Accept each faithful vow,
And mark each suppliant sigh:
In copious shower, on all who pray,
Each holy day, Thy blessings pour.

4 Here may we gain from heaven
The grace which we implore,
And may that grace, once given,
Be with us evermore,—
Until that day when all the blest
To endless rest are called away.

812 *The Kingdom of Grace and Glory One.* C. M.

1 Happy the souls to Jesus join'd,
And saved by grace alone;
Walking in all His ways, they find
Their heaven on earth begun.

2 The Church triumphant in Thy love,
Their mighty joys we know:
They sing the Lamb in hymns above,
And we in hymns below.

3 Thee in Thy glorious realm they praise,
And bow before Thy throne;
We, in the kingdom of Thy grace:
The kingdoms are but one.

4 The holy to the holiest leads;
From thence our spirits rise;
And He that in Thy statutes treads
Shall meet Thee in the skies.

813 *Honouring Christ's Cause.* 8s & 7s.

1 Praise the Saviour, all ye nations!
Praise Him, all ye hosts above!
Shout, with joyful acclamations,
His divine victorious love;
Be His kingdom now promoted,
Let the earth her monarch know;
Be my all to Him devoted,
To my Lord my all I owe.

2 With my substance, I will honour
My Redeemer and my Lord;
Were ten thousand worlds my manor,
All were nothing to His word;
While the heralds of salvation
His abounding grace proclaim,
Let His friends of every station
Gladly join to spread His fame.

814 *Contributions for Christ's Cause.* S. M.

1 Thy bounties, gracious Lord!
With gratitude we own;
We bless Thy providential grace
Which showers its blessings down.

2 With joy the people bring
Their offerings round Thy throne;
With thankful souls, behold! we pay
A tribute of Thine own.

3 Let the Redeemer's blood
Diffuse its virtues wide;
Hallow and cleanse our every gift,
And all our follies hide.

4 Oh! may this sacrifice
To Thee, the Lord, ascend—
An odor of a sweet perfume,
Presented by His hand.

5 Well pleased our God shall view
The products of His grace;
And, in a plentiful reward,
Fulfill His promises.

815 *The Labourers Few.* S. M.

1 Lord of the harvest! hear
Thy needy servants' cry;
Answer our faith's effectual prayer,
And all our wants supply.

2 On Thee we humbly wait;
Our wants are in Thy view;
The harvest, truly, Lord! is great,
The labourers are few.

3 Convert and send forth more
Into Thy church abroad;
And let them speak Thy word of power,
As workers with their God.

4 Oh! let them spread Thy name,
Their mission fully prove;
Thy universal grace proclaim,—
Thine all redeeming love.

816 *Longing for a Revival.* S. M.

1 Oh! for the happy hour
When God will hear our cry;
And send, with a reviving power,
His Spirit from on high!

2 We meet, we sing, we pray,
We listen to the word,
In vain; we see no cheering ray,
No cheering voice is heard.

3 Our prayers are faint and dull,
And languid all our songs;
Where once with joy our hearts were full,
And rapture tuned our tongues.

4 While many seek Thy house,
How few, around Thy board,
Meet to recount their solemn vows,
And bless Thee as their Lord!

5 Thou, Thou alone canst give
Thy gospel sure success;
Canst bid the dying sinner live
Anew in holiness.

6 Come, then, with power divine,
Spirit of life and love!
Then shall our people all be Thine,
Our church, like that above.

817 *A Revival Sought.* S. M.

1 Revive Thy work, O Lord!
Thy mighty arm make bare;
Speak, with the voice that wakes the dead,
And make Thy people hear.

2 Revive Thy work, O Lord!
Disturb this sleep of death;
Quicken the smouldering embers now,
By Thine almighty breath.

3 Revive Thy work, O Lord!
Exalt Thy precious name;
And, by the Holy Ghost, our love
For Thee and Thine inflame.

4 Revive Thy work, O Lord!
And give refreshing showers;
The glory shall be all Thine own,
The blessing, Lord! be ours.

818 *Fountain of Life.* 8s, 7s & 4s.

1 See, from Zion's sacred mountain,
Streams of living water flow!
God has opened there a fountain,
That supplies the world below:
They are blessèd,
Who its sovereign virtues know.

2 Through ten thousand channels flowing,
Streams of mercy find their way;
Life, and health, and joy bestowing;
Hear this king of glory say—
Oh! ye nations!
Hail the long-expected day.

LEXINGTON. 7s & 6s.

WESTERN MELODY.

No. 1.
No. 2.
END.
1. The morning light is break-ing; The darkness dis - ap - pears;
The sons of earth are wak - ing
To pen - i - ten - tial tears;
D.S. Prepared for Zi - on's war.
Each breeze, that sweeps the ocean, Brings tid-ings, from a - far, Of na-tions in com-mo-tion,
D.S.

819 *Morning Light.* 7s & 6s.

1 THE morning light is breaking,
The darkness disappears,
The sons of earth are waking
To penitential tears:
Each breeze that sweeps the ocean
Brings tidings from afar
Of nations in commotion,
Prepared for Zion's war.

2 Rich dews of grace come o'er us
In many a gentle shower,
And brighter scenes before us
Are opening every hour;
Each cry to heaven going
Abundant answers brings,
And heavenly gales are blowing
With peace upon their wings.

3 See heathen nations bending
Before the God we love,
And thousand hearts ascending
In gratitude above;
While sinners now confessing,
The gospel call obey,
And seek the Saviour's blessing—
A nation in a day.

4 Blest river of salvation,
Pursue thy onward way,
Flow thou to every nation,
Nor in thy richness stay;
Stay not, till all the lowly
Triumphant reach their home;
Stay not, till all the holy
Proclaim, "The Lord has come."

820 *The latter day Glory.* 7s & 6s.

1 AND is the time approaching,
By prophets long foretold,
When all shall dwell together,
One Shepherd and one fold?
Shall every idol perish,
To moles and bats be thrown,
And every prayer be offer'd
To God in Christ alone?

2 Shall Jew and Gentile, meeting
From many a distant shore,
Around one altar kneeling,
One common Lord adore?
Shall all that now divides us
Remove and pass away,
Like shadows of the morning
Before the blaze of day?

3 Shall all that now unites us
More sweet and lasting prove,
A closer bond of union,
In a blest land of love?
Shall war be learn'd no longer,
Shall strife and tumult cease,
All earth His blessed kingdom,
The Lord and Prince of Peace?

4 Oh, long-expected dawning,
Come with thy cheering ray!
When shall the morning brighten,
The shadows flee away?
Oh, sweet anticipation!
It cheers the watchers on
To pray, and hope, and labour,
Till the dark night be gone.

821 *Zion Triumphant.* L. M.

1 Triumphant Zion! lift Thy head
From dust, and darkness, and the dead;
Though humbled long, awake at length,
And gird thee with thy Saviour's strength.

2 Put all thy beauteous garments on,
And let thine excellence be known:
Deck'd in the robes of righteousness,
The world thy glories shall confess.

3 No more shall foes unclean invade,
And fill thy hallow'd walls with dread;
No more shall hell's insulting host
Their victory and thy sorrows boast.

4 God from on high has heard thy prayer,
His hand thy ruins shall repair:
Nor will thy watchful Monarch cease
To guard thee in eternal peace.

822 *Triumphs of the Gospel.* 7s.

1 Who are these, that come from far,
Led by Jacob's rising star?
Strangers now to Zion come,
There to seek a peaceful home.

2 Lo! they gather like a cloud,
Or as doves their windows crowd;
Zion wonders at the sight,—
Zion feels a strange delight.

3 Zion now no more shall sigh,
God will raise her glory high;
He will send a large increase,—
He will give His people peace.

823 *The Sending Forth of Missionaries.* L. M.

1 Ye Christian hearlds, go, proclaim
Salvation in Emmanuel's name:
To distant climes the tidings bear,
And plant the rose of Sharon there.

2 God shield you with a wall of fire,
With holy zeal your hearts inspire,
Bid raging winds their fury cease,
And calm the savage breast to peace.

3 And when your labours all are o'er,
Then may we meet to part no more;
Meet with the ransomed throng to fall,
And crown the Saviour Lord of all.

824 *Light for the Gentiles.* 8s, 7s & 4s.

1 Light of them that sit in darkness!
Rise and shine, Thy blessings bring;
Light, to lighten all the Gentiles!
Rise with healing in Thy wing:
To Thy brightness,
Let all kings and nations come.

2 May the heathen, now adoring
Idol-gods of wood and stone,
Come, and, worshiping before Him,
Serve the living God alone:
Let Thy glory
Fill the earth, as floods the sea.

825 *The Heathen calling for the Gospel.* 8s. 7s & 4s.

1 Souls in heathen darkness lying,
Where no light has broken through,
Souls that Jesus bought by dying,
Whom His soul in travail knew—
Thousand voices
Call us, o'er the waters blue.

2 Christians, hearken! None has taught them
Of His love so deep and dear;
Of the precious price that bought them;
Of the nail, the thorn, the spear;
Ye who know Him,
Guide them from their darkness drear.

3 Haste, oh haste, and spread the tidings
Wide to earth's remotest strand;
Let no brother's bitter chidings
Rise against us when we stand
In the judgment,
From some far, forgotten land.

4 Lo! the hills for harvest whiten,
All along each distant shore;
Seaward far the islands brighten;
Light of nations! lead us o'er:
When we seek them,
Let Thy Spirit go before.

826 *The Triumphant Reign of Christ.* 7s.

1 See the ransomed millions stand,
Palms of conquest in their hand!
This, before the throne, their strain:—
"Hell is vanquished; death is slain!

2 Blessing, honour, glory, might,
Are the Conqueror's native right;
Thrones and powers before Him fall,—
Lamb of God, and Lord of all!"

3 Hasten, Lord! the promised hour;
Come in glory, and in power;
Still Thy foes are unsubdued;
Nature sighs to be renewed.

4 Time has nearly reached its sum;
All things, with Thy bride, say, "Come!"
Jesus! whom all worlds adore,
Come,—and reign for evermore.

827 *The Church Glorified in Christ.* C. M.

1 Bride of the Lamb, awake! awake!
Why sleep for sorrow now?
The hope of glory, Christ, is thine,
An heir of glory thou.

2 Thy spirit, through the lonely night,
From earthly joy apart,
Hath sigh'd for one that's far away—
The Bridegroom of thy heart.

3 But see, the night is waning fast,
The breaking morn is near;
And Jesus comes, with voice of love,
Thy drooping heart to cheer.

4 He comes—for, oh! His yearning heart
No more can bear delay—
To scenes of full unmingled joy
To call His Bride away.

5 Thou, too, shalt reign—He will not wear
His crown of joy alone!
And earth His royal Bride shall see
Beside Him on the throne.

6 Then weep no more—'tis all thine own—
His crown, His joy divine,
And, sweeter far than all beside,
He, He Himself is thine.

828 *The Final Anthem of Triumph.* L. M.

1 Soon may the last glad song arise
Through all the millions of the skies,—
That song of triumph, which records,
That all the earth is now the Lord's.

2 Let thrones, and powers, and kingdoms be
Obedient, mighty God! to Thee;
And, over land, and stream, and main,
Wave Thou the sceptre of Thy reign.

3 Oh! that the anthem now might swell,
And host to host the triumph tell,—
That not one rebel heart remains,
But over all the Saviour reigns.

829 *Death and Eternity.* C. M.

1 Stoop down, my thoughts, that use to rise!
Converse awhile with death;
Think how a gasping mortal lies,
And pants away his breath!

2 But, oh! the soul, that never dies!
At once it leaves the clay;
Ye thoughts! pursue it where it flies,
And track its wondrous way.

3 And must my body faint and die?
And must this soul remove?
Oh! for some guardian angel nigh,
To bear it safe above!

4 Jesus! to Thy dear, faithful hand,
My naked soul I trust;
And my flesh waits for Thy command
To drop into my dust.

830 *The Hour of Departure.* L. M.

1 I come, I come, at Thy command;
I give my spirit to Thy hand;
Stretch forth Thine everlasting arms,
And shield me in the last alarms.

2 Not in mine innocence I trust;
I bow before Thee in the dust;
And, through my Saviour's blood alone,
I look for mercy at Thy throne.

3 I leave the world without a tear,
Save for the friends I held so dear;
To heal their sorrows, Lord! descend,
And to the friendless prove a Friend.

831 *The Final Struggle.* 8s & 7s.

1 Tarry with me, oh my Saviour!
For the day is passing by;
See! the shades of evening gather,
And the night is drawing nigh;
Deeper, deeper grow the shadows,
Paler now the glowing west;
Swift the night of death advances;
Shall it be the night of rest?

2 Lonely seems the vale of shadow;
Sinks my heart with troubled fear;
Give me faith for clearer vision,
Speak Thou, Lord! in words of cheer;

Let me hear Thy voice of mercy,
Calming all these wild alarms;
Let me, underneath my weakness,
Feel the everlasting arms.

3 Feeble, trembling, fainting, dying,
Lord! I cast myself on Thee;
Tarry with me through the darkness;
While I sleep, still watch by me.
Tarry with me, oh my Saviour!
Lay my head upon Thy breast
Till the morning; then awake me—.
Morning of eternal rest!

832 *Death Dreadful, or Delightful.* C. M.

1 Death! 'tis a melancholy day
To those that have no God,
When the poor soul is forced away
To seek her last abode.

2 In vain to heaven she lifts her eyes,
But guilt, a heavy chain,
Still drags her downward from the skies
To darkness, fire, and pain.

3 He is a God of sovereign love
That promised heaven to me,
And taught my thoughts to soar above,
Where happy spirits be.

4 Prepare me, Lord! for Thy right hand;
Then come the joyful day!
Come, death! and some celestial band!
To bear my soul away.

833 *Dying, not Death.* S. M.

1 It is not death to die,—
To leave this weary road,
And, midst the brotherhood on high,
To be at home with God.

2 It is not death to close
The eye long dimmed by tears,
And wake, in glorious repose
To spend eternal years.

3 It is not death to fling
Aside this sinful dust,
And rise, on strong exulting wing,
To live among the just.

4 Jesus, Thou Prince of life!
Thy chosen cannot die;
Like Thee, they conquer in the strife,
To reign with Thee on high.

834 *The Dying Christian.* L. M.

1 Gently, my Saviour! let me down,
To slumber in the arms of death;
I rest my soul on Thee alone,
E'en till my last, expiring breath.

2 Soon will the storm of life be o'er,
And I shall enter endless rest;
There I shall live to sin no more,
And bless Thy name, for ever blest.

3 Bid me possess sweet peace within;
Let childlike patience keep my heart;
Then shall I feel my heaven begin,
Before my spirit hence depart.

4 Oh! speed Thy chariot, God of love!
And take me from this world of woe;
I long to reach those joys above,
And bid farewell to all below.

5 There shall my raptured spirit raise
Still louder notes than angels sing,—
High glories to Immanuel's grace,
My God, my Saviour, and my King!

835 *A Pastor's Death.* S. M.

1 Rest from thy labour, rest,
Soul of the just, set free!
Blest be thy memory, and blest
Thy bright example be!

2 Now,—toil and conflict o'er,—
Go, take with saints thy place;
But go, as each hath gone before,
A sinner saved by grace.

3 Lord Jesus! to Thy hands
Our pastor we resign;
And now we wait Thine own commands:
We were not his, but Thine.

4 Thou art Thy church's Head;
And, when the members die,
Thou raisest others in their stead:
To Thee we lift our eye.

5 On Thee our hopes depend;
We gather round our Rock;
Send whom Thou wilt; but condescend
Thyself to feed Thy flock.

836 *The Fathers Gone.* S. M.

1 How swift the torrent rolls,
That bears us to the sea!—
The tide that bears our thoughtless souls
To vast eternity!

THOMAS HASTINGS.

1. What is life? 'tis but a va-por, Soon it van-ish - es a - way: Life is but a dy - ing ta - per, O my soul, why
wish to stay? Why not spread thy wings and fly Straight to yonder world of joy, Straight to yonder world of joy.

2 Our fathers,—where are they,
With all they called their own?
Their joys and griefs, and hopes and cares,
And wealth and honour gone?

3 God of our fathers! hear,
Thou everlasting Friend!
While we, as on life's utmost verge,
Our souls to Thee commend.

4 Of all the pious dead
May we the footsteps trace,
Till with them, in the land of light,
We dwell before Thy face.

837 *Life a Vapour.* 8s, 7s & 7s.

1 WHAT is life? 'tis but a vapour;
Soon it vanishes away;
Life is like a dying taper;
Oh, my soul! why wish to stay?
Why not spread thy wings, and fly
Straight to yonder world of joy?

2 See that glory—how resplendent!
Brighter far than fancy paints;
There, in majesty transcendent,
Jesus reigns—the King of saints:—
Spread thy wings, my soul! and fly
Straight to yonder world of joy.

3 Joyful crowds, His throne surrounding,
Sing with rapture of His love;
Through the heavens His praises sounding,
Filling all the courts above:
Spread thy wings, my soul! and fly
Straight to yonder world of joy.

4 Go, and share His people's glory,
Midst the ransomed crowd appear;—
Thine a joyful, wondrous story,
One that angels love to hear:
Spread thy wings, my soul! and fly
Straight to yonder world of joy.

838 *The Prospect of Heaven.* C. P. M.

1 WITH joy shall I behold the day
That calls my willing soul away,
To dwell among the blest:
For, lo! my great Redeemer's power
Unfolds the everlasting door,
And points me to His rest.

2 E'en now, to my expecting eyes
The heaven-built towers of Salem rise;
Their glory I survey;
I view her mansions that contain
Th' angelic host, a glorious train,
And shine with cloudless day.

3 Thither, from earth's remotest end,
Lo! the redeem'd of God ascend,
Borne on immortal wing;
There, crown'd with everlasting joy,
In ceaseless hymns their tongues employ,
Before th' Almighty King.

4 Mother of cities! o'er thy head
Bright peace, with healing wings outspread,
For evermore shall dwell:
Let me, blest seat! my name behold
Among thy citizens enroll'd,
And bid the world farewell.

German Melody. AD. LOWELL MASON.

1. { For thee, oh dear, dear coun-try, Mine eyes their vig-ils keep; / For ver-y love, be-hold-ing Thy hap-py name they weep. } The men-tion of thy glo-ry
Is unc-tion to the breast, And med-i-cine in sick-ness, And love, and life, and rest.

839 *Paradise of Joy.* 7s & 6s.

1 FOR thee, oh dear, dear country!
Mine eyes their vigils keep;
For very love, beholding
Thy happy name they weep;
The mention of Thy glory
Is unction to the breast,
And medicine in sickness,
And love, and life, and rest.

2 Oh! one, oh only mansion!
Oh! Paradise of joy!
Where tears are ever banished,
And smiles have no alloy;
The Lamb is all thy splendor,
The Crucified thy praise;
His laud and benediction
Thy ransomed people raise.

3 Thou hast no shore, fair ocean!
Thou hast no time, bright day!
Dear fountain of refreshment
To pilgrims far away!
Upon the Rock of ages,
They raise Thy holy tower;
Thine is the victor's laurel,
And Thine the golden dower.

840 *The Golden City.* 7s & 6s.

1 JERUSALEM, the golden,
With milk and honey blest!
Beneath thy contemplation
Sink heart and voice oppressed:
I know not, oh! I know not
What social joys are there,
What radiancy of glory,
What light beyond compare.

2 They stand, those halls of Zion,
All jubilant with song,
And bright with many an angel,
And all the martyr throng;
The Prince is ever in them,
The daylight is serene;
The pastures of the blessèd
Are deckèd in glorious sheen.

3 There is the throne of David;
And there, from care released,
The song of them that triumph,
The shout of them that feast:
And they who, with their Leader,
Have conquered in the fight,
For ever and for ever
Are clad in robes of white.

4 Oh! sweet and blessèd country!
The home of God's elect;
Oh! sweet and blessed country,
That eager hearts expect!
Exult, oh dust and ashes!
The Lord shall be thy part;
His only, His for ever,
Thou shalt be, and thou art!

841 *Present and Eternal Life.* 7s & 6s.

1 Brief life is here our portion;
Brief sorrow, short-lived care;
The life that knows no ending,
The tearless life, is there:
O happy retribution!
Short toil, eternal rest;
For mortals, and for sinners,
A mansion with the blest!

2 There Jesus shall embrace us,
There Jesus be embraced—
The spirit's food and sunshine—
Whence earthly love is chased:
Yes! God, my King and Portion,
In fullness of His grace,
We then shall see forever,
And worship face to face.

842 *Psalm* 137. S. M.

1 Far from my heavenly home,
Far from my Father's breast,
Fainting, I cry:—"Blest Spirit! come,
And speed me to my rest.

2 "Upon the willows long
My harp has silent hung;
How should I sing a cheerful song,
Till Thou inspire my tongue?"

3 My spirit homeward turns,
And fain would thither flee;
My heart, O Zion! droops and yearns,
When I remember thee.

4 To thee, to thee I press—
A dark and toilsome road;
When shall I pass the wilderness,
And reach the saints' abode?

5 God of my life! be near!
On Thee my hopes I cast;
Oh! guide me through the desert here
And bring me home at last.

843 *The Peaceful Fold.* C. M.

1 There is a fold, whence none can stray,
And pastures ever green,
Where sultry sun, or stormy day,
Or night is never seen.

2 Far up the everlasting hills,
In God's own light it lies;
His smile its vast dimension fills
With joy that never dies.

3 Soon at His feet my soul will lie
In life's last struggling breath;
But I shall only seem to die,
I shall not taste of death.

4 Far from this guilty world to be
Exempt from toil and strife;
To spend eternity with Thee—
My Saviour! this is life.

844 *The Hope of Heaven.* C. M.

1 My thoughts surmount these lower skies,
And look within the veil;
There springs of endless pleasure rise,
The waters never fail.

2 There I behold, with sweet delight,
The blessèd Three in One;
And strong affections fix my sight
On God's incarnate Son.

3 His promise stands for ever firm,
His grace shall ne'er depart,
He binds my name upon His arm,
And seals it on His heart.

4 I would not be a stranger still
To that celestial place,
Where I for ever hope to dwell
Near my Redeemer's face.

845 *A Home Above.* S. M.

1 I have a home above,
From sin and sorrow free;
A mansion, which eternal Love
Designed and formed for me.

2 My Father's gracious hand
Has built this sweet abode;
From everlasting it was planned,—
My dwelling-place with God.

3 My Saviour's precious blood
Has made my title sure;
He passed thro' death's dark raging flood,
To make my rest secure.

4 The Comforter has come,
The earnest has been given;
He leads me onward to the home
Reserved for me in haven.

846 *Rest in Heaven.* S. M.

1 And is there, Lord! a rest,
For weary souls designed,
Where not a care shall stir the breast,
Or sorrow entrance find?

2 Is there a blissful home,
Where kindred minds shall meet,
And live, and love, nor ever roam
From that serene retreat?

3 Are there bright, happy fields,
Where naught that blooms shall die;
Where each new scene fresh pleasure yields,
And healthful breezes sigh?

4 Are there celestial streams,
Where living waters glide,
With murmurs sweet as angel dreams,
And flowery banks beside?

5 For ever blessèd they,
Whose joyful feet shall stand,
While endless ages waste away,
Amid that glorious land!

6 My soul would thither tend,
While toilsome years are given;
Then let me, gracious God! ascend
To sweet repose in heaven.

847 *The Heavenly Home.* Tune, Zerah.

1 Sweet land of rest! for thee I sigh;
When will the moment come,
When I shall lay my armour by,
And dwell with Christ at home?
My heavenly home, my sweet, sweet home!
And dwell with Christ at home.

2 On earth no tranquil joys I know,
No peaceful sheltering dome;
This world's a wilderness of woe,
This world is not my home.

3 To Jesus Christ I sought for rest,
He bade me cease to roam,
And fly for succour to His breast,
And He'd conduct me home.

4 Weary of wandering round and round
This vale of sin and gloom,
I long to quit th' unhallowed ground,
And dwell with Christ at home.

5 How long, dear Lord! wilt Thou delay,
When will Thy chariot come,
And fetch my waiting soul away
To heaven, my destined home?

848 *Phil.* 3: 20. C. M.

1 While thro' this changing world we roam
From infancy to age,
Heaven is the Christian pilgrim's home,
His rest at every stage.

2 From earth his freed affections rise,
To fix on things above,
Where all his hope of glory lies,
Where all is perfect love.

3 There, too, may we our treasure place—
There let our hearts be found;
That still, where sin abounded, grace
May more and more abound.

4 Henceforth, our conversation be
With Christ before the throne;
Ere long we, eye to eye, shall see,
And know as we are known.

849 *The Saints in Glory.* 8s & 7s.

1 Hark! the sound of holy voices,
Chanting at the crystal sea,—
Alleluia! alleluia!
Alleluia! Lord! to Thee.

2 Multitudes, which none can number,
Like the stars in glory stand,
Clothed in white apparel, holding
Palms of victory in their hands.

3 They have come from tribulation,
And have washed their robes in blood,
Washed them in the blood of Jesus;
Tried they were, and firm they stood.

4 Gladly, Lord! with Thee they suffered;
Gladly, Lord! with Thee they died;
And, by death, to life immortal
They were born and glorified.

5 Now they reign in heavenly glory,
Now they walk in golden light,
Now they drink, as from a river,
Holy bliss and infinite.

6 Love and peace they taste for ever,
And all truth and knowledge see
In the beatific vision
Of the blessèd Trinity.

850 *Pestilence.* C. M.

1 In grief and fear, to Thee, O Lord,
We now for succour fly,
Thine awful judgments are abroad,
Oh! shield us lest we die.

2 The fell disease on every side
Walks forth with tainted breath;
And pestilence, with rapid stride,
Bestrews the land with death.

3 Oh! look with pity on the scene
Of sadness and of dread,
And let Thine angel stand between
The living and the dead.

4 With contrite hearts to Thee, our King,
We turn who oft have strayed;
Accept the sacrifice we bring,
And let the plague be stayed.

851 *Harvest.* C. M.

1 Lord in Thy name Thy servants plead,
And Thou hast sworn to hear;
Thine is the harvest, Thine the seed,
The fresh and fading year.

2 Grant us, with precious things brought [forth
By sun and moon below,
A place in Thy new heavens and earth,
Where richer harvests grow.

852 *New Year.* C. M.

1 When brighter suns and milder skies
Proclaim the op'ning year,
What various sounds of joy arise!
What prospects bright appear!

2 Earth and her thousand voices give
Their thousand notes of praise;
And all that by His mercy live,
To God their offering raise.

3 Thus, like the morning, calm and clear,
That saw the Saviour rise,
The spring of heaven's eternal year
Shall dawn on earth and skies.

4 No winter there, no shades of night,
Obscure those mansions blest,
Where in Thy happy fields of light,
The weary are at rest.

DOXOLOGIES.

C. M.

To Father, Son, and Holy Ghost,
The God whom we adore,
Be glory as it was, is now,
And shall be evermore.

C. M.

Let God the Father, and the Son,
And Spirit be adored,
Where there are works to make Him [known,
Or saints to love the Lord.

C. M. D.

The God of mercy be adored,
Who calls our souls from death:
Who saves by His redeeming Word,
And new creating breath.
To praise the Father, and the Son,
And Spirit, all divine,
The One in Three, and Three in One,
Let saints and angels join.

L. M.

Praise God, from whom all blessings flow;
Praise Him, all creatures here below;
Praise Him above, ye heavenly host;
Praise Father, Son, and Holy Ghost.

L. M.

To God the Father, God the Son,
And God the Spirit, Three in One,
Be honour, praise, and glory given,
By all on earth, and all in heaven.

L. M. D.

Glory to God the Trinity,
Whose name has mysteries unknown;
In essence One, in persons Three;
A social nature, yet alone.
When all our noblest powers are joined
The honours of Thy name to raise:
Thy glories overmatch our mind,
And angels faint beneath the praise.

S. M.

Ye angels round the throne,
And saints that dwell below,
Worship the Father, love the Son,
And bless the Spirit too.

S. M.

Give to the Father praise,
Give glory to the Son,
And to the Spirit of His grace
Be equal honours done.

S. M. D.

We bless the Father's name,
Who chose us in His love;
To God the Son, we give the same,
Our Advocate above.
The Spirit, too, we bless,
And raise His honours high;
Who conquers by His sovereign grace,
And brings us strangers nigh.

H. M.

To God the Father's throne
  Perpetual honours raise;
Glory to God the Son;
  To God the Spirit praise:
With all our powers, eternal King,
Thy name we sing, while faith adores.

C. P. M.

To Father, Son, and Holy Ghost,
Be praise amid the heavenly host,
  And in the church below; [breath,
From whom all creatures draw their
By whom redemption blessed the earth,
  From whom all comforts flow.

L. P. M.

Now to the great, and sacred Three,
The Father, Son, and Spirit, be
  Eternal power and glory given,
Through all the worlds where God is
By all the angels near the throne, [known,
  And all the saints in earth and heaven.

10s & 11s.

By angels in heaven of every degree,
And saints upon earth, all praise be addressed
To God in three Persons, one God ever blest,
As it has been, now is, and always shall be.

7s.

Sing we to our God above,
Praise eternal as His love;
Praise Him, all ye heavenly host,
Father, Son, and Holy Ghost.

7s.

Holy Father, holy Son,
Holy Spirit, Three in One!
Glory as of old to Thee
Now and evermore shall be.

7s.

Praise the name of God most high,
Praise Him, all below the sky,
Praise Him, all ye heavenly host,
Father, Son, and Holy Ghost:
As through countless ages past
Evermore His praise shall last.

8s.

All praise to the Father, the Son,
  And Spirit, thrice holy and bless'd,
Th' eternal, supreme Three in One,
  Was, is, and shall still be address'd.

7s, 6s & 7s.

To the Father, to the Son,
  And Spirit ever bless'd,
Everlasting Three in One,
  All worship be address'd:
Praise from all above, below,
  As throughout the ages past,
Now is given, and shall be so,
  While endless ages last.

8s & 7s.

Praise the Father, earth, and heaven;
  Praise the Son, the Spirit praise;
As it was, and is, be given
  Glory through eternal days.

8s & 7s.

May the grace of Christ our Saviour,
  And the Father's boundless love,
With the Holy Spirit's favour,
  Rest upon us from above.
Thus may we abide in union
  With each other and the Lord,
And possess, in sweet communion,
  Joys which earth cannot afford.

8s, 7s & 4s, or 8s & 7s, 6 lines.

Glory be to God the Father,
  Glory to th' eternal Son;
Sound aloud the Spirit's praises;
  Join the elders round the throne;
    Hallelujah, [Hallelujah,]
  Hail the glorious Three in One.

11s.

O Father Almighty, to Thee be addressed,
With Christ and the Spirit, one God ever blest,
All glory and worship from earth, and from heaven,
As was, and is now, and shall ever be given.

11s & 8s.

All praise to the Father, all praise to the Son,
  All praise to the Spirit, thrice blest.
The Holy, Eternal, Supreme Three in One,
  Was, is, and shall still be addressed.

Chorus.

Glory, honour, praise and power,
  Be unto the Lamb for ever;
Jesus Christ is our Redeemer;
  Hallelujah! Hallelujah!

INDEX OF FIRST LINES.

THE FIGURES DESIGNATE THE PAGES OF THE BOOK.

PAGE.
165 According to Thy gracious word,
239 A charge to keep I have,
140 Adored for ever be the Lord,
261 A few more years shall roll,
34 Afflicted saint, to Christ draw near,
215 After Thy loving-kindness, Lord,
249 Ah! how shall fallen man,
59 Ah! wretched souls, who strive in vain,
222 Alas! and did my Saviour bleed?
192 Alas! how changed that lovely flower!
114 Alas! what hourly dangers rise,
134 All hail, the power of Jesus' name,
146 All lands to God in joyful sounds,
31 All people that on earth do dwell,
135 All ye that love the Lord, rejoice,
323 All ye who pass by,
147 Almighty Father, gracious Lord,
104 Almighty God, eternal Lord,
213 Almighty God, Thy word is cast,
137 Amazing grace, how sweet the sound,
136 Am I a soldier of the cross?
208 Amidst the cheerful bloom of youth,
35 Among the assemblies of the great,
233 And am I born to die?
233 And canst thou, sinner, slight,
293 And is it so? a little while,
45 And is the gospel peace and love?
202 And let this feeble body fail,
255 And must this body die?
235 And will the God of grace?
258 And will the Judge descend?
73 Another six days' work is done,
175 Approach, my soul, the mercy-seat,
117 Are all the foes of Zion fools?
265 Arise, my soul, arise,
123 Arise, O King of grace, arise,
60 Arm of the Lord, awake, awake,
342 Around the throne of God in heaven,
62 Ascend Thy throne, almighty King,

PAGE.
73 Asleep in Jesus, blessed sleep,
178 As on the cross the Saviour hung,
180 As pants the hart for cooling streams,
63 As when the weary traveller gains,
68 At Thy command, our dearest Lord,
196 Author of good, to Thee we turn,
245 Awake, and sing the song,
345 Awaked by Sinai's awful sound,
199 Awake, my heart, arise, my tongue,
49 Awake, my soul, and with the sun,
102 Awake, my soul, in joyful lays,
167 Awake, my soul, stretch every nerve,
135 Awake, my soul, to sound His praise,
74 Awake our souls, away our fears,
205 Awake, sweet gratitude, and sing,
228 Awake, ye saints, to praise your King,
31 Before Jehovah's awful throne,
112 Begin, my tongue, some heavenly theme,
330 Begone, unbelief, my Saviour is near,
99 Behold a stranger at the door,
145 Behold how good a thing it is,
46 Behold, O God, what cruel foes,
62 Behold the expected time draw near,
112 Behold the glories of the Lamb,
37 Behold the man, how glorious he,
236 Behold the morning sun,
216 Behold, the mountain of the Lord,
107 Behold the Saviour of mankind,
52 Behold the sin-atoning Lamb,
165 Behold Thy waiting servant, Lord,
114 Behold us, Lord, and let our cry,
229 Behold what condescending love,
234 Behold what wondrous grace,
211 Be merciful to me, O God,
192 Beneath our feet, and o'er our head,
115 Bestow, dear Lord, upon our youth,
232 Blest are the sons of peace,
200 Blest are the souls who hear and know,
178 Blest are the undefiled in heart,

INDEX TO APPENDIX.

ALPHABETICAL INDEX OF TUNES.

METRICAL INDEX OF TUNES.

C. M. D.

C. P. M.

C. H. M.

PAGE.

S. M.

S. M. D.

S. H. M.

S. P. M.

H. M.

7s. 4 Lines.

PAGE.

7s. 6 Lines.

7s. 8 Lines.

7s & 6s.

7s, 6s & 7s.

8s & 7s. 4 Lines.

8s &7s. 6 Lines.

8s & 7. 8 Lines.

☞ The tunes of the late Dr. Lowell Mason have been inserted by permission of Oliver Ditson & Co., Boston, Mass.; those of Dr. Thomas Hastings by his own permission; and those of Prof. Wm. B. Bradbury by permission of Biglow & Main. Many other tunes have also been inserted by special permission.

INDEX OF SUBJECTS.

The figures refer to the numbers of the Psalms and Hymns, for which see the Numerical Index, pp. 3–30.

PSALMS.

HYMNS.

APPENDIX.

RULES OF PARLIAMENTARY ORDER.*

Of Opening the Sessions.

1. The Moderator shall take the chair precisely at the hour to which the court stands adjourned; shall immediately call the members to order; and on the appearance of a quorum, the session shall be opened with prayer.

2. If a quorum be assembled at the hour appointed, and the Moderator be absent, the last Moderator or oldest minister present, shall take the chair without delay.

3. If a quorum be not assembled at the hour appointed, any two members shall be competent to adjourn from time to time, that an opportunity may be given for a quorum to assemble.

4. After calling the roll, and marking the absentees, the minutes of the last sitting shall be read, and if requisite, corrected.

Of the Moderator.

5. It shall be the duty of the Moderator to preserve order, and to conduct all business before the court to a speedy and proper result.

6. He is to propose to the court every subject of deliberation that comes before it.

7. He may propose what appears to him the most regular and direct way of bringing any business to issue.

8. He shall always announce the names of members rising to speak, prevent them from interrupting each other, and require them in speaking always to address the Chair.

9. He shall prevent a speaker from deviating from the subject, and from using personal reflections.

10. He shall silence those who refuse to observe order.

11. He shall prevent members leaving the court without his permission.

12. He shall, when the deliberations are ended, put the question, and call the vote.

13. In all questions he shall give a clear and concise statement of the object of the vote, and the vote being taken, he shall declare how the question is decided.

14. He shall carefully keep notes of the orders of the day, and call them up at the times appointed.

15. He may speak to points of order in preference to other members, rising from his seat for that purpose, and shall decide questions of order subject to an appeal to the court, without debate, by any two members.

16. If any member consider himself aggrieved by a decision of the Moderator, it shall be his privilege to appeal to the court, and the question on such appeal shall be taken without debate.

17. It is his duty to appoint all committees except in those cases in which the court shall decide otherwise.

18. When a vote is taken by ballot, or by yeas and nays, he shall vote with the other members; in other cases, when the court is equally divided, he shall possess the casting vote. If he be not willing to decide, he shall put the question a second time, and if the court be again equally divided, and he decline to give his vote, the question shall be lost.

19. He may call any member to the chair, to preside temporarily.

Of the Clerk.

20. As soon as possible after the commencement of the first session of every court, the clerk shall form a complete roll of the members present, and put the same into the hands of the Moderator; and whenever any additional members take their seats, he shall add their names in their proper places to the said roll.

21. He shall immediately file all papers in the order in which they have been read, with proper endorsements, and keep them in perfect order.

Of the Order of Business.

22. After the reading of the minutes of the preceding day, the following order of business shall be observed:

First, The receiving of

(*a*) Communications addressed to the body.

(*b*) Reports of standing committees.

* These rules were adopted by the General Assembly of 1866, and have been observed by each subsequent Assembly. As several of the lower courts have also adopted them, and as it is important for our judicatories and officers to have some manual on this subject of convenient access, these rules are here published, but, of course, form no part of the Constitution of the Church.

(c) Reports of select committees.

(d) Resolutions; each of which papers may, by unanimous consent, be taken up immediately on presentation, but if objection be made it shall be docketed.

Secondly, The unfinished business in which the court was engaged at the last preceding adjournment, in preference to orders of the day; but such unfinished business may, on motion without debate, be laid on the table, to proceed with the special order.

Thirdly, As soon as the special order and the unfinished business are disposed of, the business on the docket will be called; but motions to elect officers, to appoint committees, and to enrol members, shall always be in order, unless a member is speaking, or the court is voting.

Of Motions.

23. A motion must be seconded, and afterward repeated by the Moderator, or read aloud, before it is debated: but this shall be no bar to explanation of the object of any motion by the mover, provided he does not exceed five minutes; and every motion shall be reduced to writing, if the Moderator or any member require it.

24. The mover of a resolution is entitled to the floor if he so desire, after the Moderator has stated the question.

Of Withdrawal of Motions.

25. Any member who shall have made a motion shall have liberty to withdraw it with the consent of his second, before any debate has taken place thereon, but not afterward without the leave of the court.

Of Limitations of Debate.

26. Motions to lay on the table, to docket, to take up business, and to adjourn, and the call for the question, shall be put without debate. On questions of order, postponement, or commitment, no member shall speak more than once. On all other questions, each member may speak twice, but not oftener, without express leave of the court.

Of Privileged Questions.

27. When a question is under debate, no motion shall be received unless to adjourn, to docket, to lay on the table, to amend, to postpone indefinitely, to postpone to a day certain, or to commit; which several motions shall have precedence in the order in which they are herein arranged; and the motion for adjournment shall always be in order.

Of "the Question."

28. When any member shall call for "*the question*," the Moderator shall, without debate, put the vote, "Is the court ready for the question?" If the call be seconded by a majority of members present, the vote shall immediately be taken on the pending question, whatever it may be, without further debate.

Of Division of the Question.

29. If a motion under debate contains several parts, any two members may have it divided, and a question taken on each part.

Of Amendments.

30. An amendment may be moved on any question, as also an amendment to the amendment, which shall be decided before the original proposition; but two distinct amendments to the pending question shall not be entertained at the same time, whether moved as substitutes for the whole matter, or as changing any part thereof.

31. One proposition may be substituted for another, when the substitute covers the whole matter of the original, and this shall be done by moving to strike out the original, and to insert the substitute.

Of Reconsideration.

32. A question shall not be reconsidered at the same sessions of the court at which it has been decided, unless by the consent of a majority of the members who were present at the decision, and unless the motion to reconsider be made by a person who voted with the majority.

33. A subject which has been indefinitely postponed shall not be again called up during the same sessions of the court, unless by the consent of three-fourths of the members who were present at the decision.

Of Speakers.

34. If more than one member rise to speak at the same time, the member who is most distant from the Moderator's chair shall speak first.

35. Every member, when speaking, shall address himself to the Moderator, and shall treat his fellow-members, and especially the Moderator, with decorum and respect.

Of Interruptions.

36. No speaker shall be interrupted unless he be out of order, or for the purpose of correcting mistakes or misrepresentations.

Of Voting.

37. Members shall not decline voting, unless excused by the court.

38. When various motions are made with respect to the filling of blanks with particular numbers or times, the question shall always be first taken on the highest number and the longest time.

39. When the Moderator has commenced taking the vote, no further debate or remark shall be admitted, unless there has evidently been a mistake; in which case the mistake shall be rectified, and the Moderator shall recommence taking the vote.

40. The yeas and nays on any question shall not be recorded, unless it be required by one-third of the members present; and every member shall vote "yea" or "nay," unless excused by the court. In a judicial case, members thus excused shall not be allowed a vote in any of the subsequent proceedings relating thereto.

41. In all elections it shall require a majority of the votes cast to elect.

Of Committees.

42. The person first named on any committee shall be considered as the chairman thereof, whose duty it shall be to convene the committee and preside therein; and in case of his absence, or inability to act, the second named member shall take his place and perform his duties.

Of Private Sessions.

43. All courts have a right to sit in private on business which, in their judgment, ought not to be matter of public speculation.

Of the Committee of the Whole.

44. Every court has a right to resolve itself into a committee of the whole, or to hold what are commonly called *interlocutory meetings*, in which members may freely converse together without the formalities necessary in their ordinary proceedings. In all such cases the Moderator shall name the member who is to preside as chairman. If the committee be unable to agree, a motion may be made that the committee rise, and upon the adoption of such motion the Moderator shall resume the chair, and the chairman of the committee shall report what has been done, and ask that the committee be discharged, which being allowed, the matter shall be dropped. If the committee shall agree upon the report to be made, or have made progress in the same without coming to a conclusion, the committee may rise, report what has been done, and, if the case require, may ask leave to sit again; or the committee of the whole may be dissolved, and the question considered by the court in the usual order of business.

Of Decorum.

45. Without express permission, no member of a court, while business is going on, shall engage in private conversation; nor shall members address one another, nor any person present, but through the Moderator.

46. When more than three members of the court shall be standing at the same time, the Moderator shall require all to take their seats, the person only excepted who may be speaking.

47. If any member act in any respect in a disorderly manner, it shall be the privilege of any member, and the duty of the Moderator, to call him to order.

48. No member shall retire from any court without the leave of the Moderator, nor withdraw from it to return home without the consent of the court.

Of Cases unprovided for.

49. All cases that may arise, not provided for in the foregoing rules, shall be governed by the general principles of parliamentary law.

Of Closing the Sessions.

50. The Moderator of every court, above the church sessions, in finally closing its sessions, in addition to prayer, may cause to be sung an appropriate psalm or hymn, and shall pronounce the apostolical benediction.

Of Applause.

51. All expressions of approbation or disapprobation, by clapping of hands, or stamping, or any audible applause, shall be considered disorderly.

www.ingramcontent.com/pod-product-compliance
Lightning Source LLC
Chambersburg PA
CBHW032316280326
41932CB00009B/835

* 9 7 8 3 3 3 7 0 2 0 7 9 8 *